FAMILY PRACTICE IN THE EASTERN MEDITERRANEAN REGION

UNIVERSAL HEALTH COVERAGE AND QUALITY PRIMARY CARE

T0384042

ABOUT THE SERIES

The WONCA Family Medicine series is a collection of books written by world-wide experts and practitioners of family medicine, in collaboration with The World Organization of Family Doctors (WONCA).

WONCA is a not-for-profit organization and was founded in 1972 by member organizations in 18 countries. It now has 118 Member Organizations in 131 countries and territories with membership of about 500,000 family doctors and more than 90 per cent of the world's population.

Family practice is the best way to provide integrated health services at the primary health care level. With an emphasis on health promotion and disease prevention, family practice helps keep people out of hospitals, where costs are higher and outcomes are often worse. Strong political commitment is essential to improve access, coverage, acceptability and quality of health services, and to ensure continuity of care.

Dr Tedros Adhanom Ghebreyesus
Director-General, World Health Organization

FAMILY PRACTICE IN THE EASTERN MEDITERRANEAN REGION

UNIVERSAL HEALTH COVERAGE AND QUALITY PRIMARY CARE

EDITED BY

Hassan Salah • Michael Kidd

CRC Press
Taylor & Francis Group
Boca Raton London New York

CRC Press is an imprint of the
Taylor & Francis Group, an **informa** business

The authors alone are responsible for the views expressed in their contributions to this book and they do not necessarily represent the views, decisions or policies of the institutions with which they are affiliated, including the World Health Organisation and the World Organisation of Family Doctors (WONCA). Where authors are staff members of the World Health Organization, their contributions do not necessarily represent the decisions or policies of the World Health Organization.

CRC Press
Taylor & Francis Group
6000 Broken Sound Parkway NW, Suite 300
Boca Raton, FL 33487-2742

© 2019 by Taylor and Francis Group, LLC excepting chapters authored by staff of the World Health Organization, copyright of which shall remain exclusively vested in the World Health Organization (WHO)

CRC Press is an imprint of Taylor & Francis Group, an Informa business

No claim to original U.S. Government works

Printed on acid-free paper

International Standard Book Number-13: 978-1-138-49864-8 (Hardback)
International Standard Book Number-13: 978-1-138-49858-7 (Paperback)

This book contains information obtained from authentic and highly regarded sources. Reasonable efforts have been made to publish reliable data and information, but the author and publisher cannot assume responsibility for the validity of all materials or the consequences of their use. The authors and publishers have attempted to trace the copyright holders of all material reproduced in this publication and apologize to copyright holders if permission to publish in this form has not been obtained. If any copyright material has not been acknowledged please write and let us know so we may rectify in any future reprint.

Except as permitted under U.S. Copyright Law, no part of this book may be reprinted, reproduced, transmitted, or utilized in any form by any electronic, mechanical, or other means, now known or hereafter invented, including photocopying, microfilming, and recording, or in any information storage or retrieval system, without written permission from the publishers.

For permission to photocopy or use material electronically from this work, please access www.copyright.com (http://www.copyright.com/) or contact the Copyright Clearance Center, Inc. (CCC), 222 Rosewood Drive, Danvers, MA 01923, 978-750-8400. CCC is a not-for-profit organization that provides licenses and registration for a variety of users. For organizations that have been granted a photocopy license by the CCC, a separate system of payment has been arranged.

Trademark Notice: Product or corporate names may be trademarks or registered trademarks, and are used only for identification and explanation without intent to infringe.

**Visit the Taylor & Francis Web site at
http://www.taylorandfrancis.com**

**and the CRC Press Web site at
http://www.crcpress.com**

We dedicate this publication to the people of the Member States of the Eastern Mediterranean Region, and to the Region's health care workforce, the women and men who have committed their lives to providing high quality primary health care to the people and communities that they serve.

Contents

Foreword

We are delighted to see this book come into print, as it celebrates a long journey for family practice in the region. It is also wonderful in its timing, as it coincides with the 40th anniversary of the Alma-Ata Declaration – when the need to strengthen primary health care to fulfil universal health coverage is in the world's gaze. The chapters address both country-level experiences and the key dimensions which affect universal health coverage and must include – whole systems' capacity, financing models, workforce and training, and integrated needs-based care. There is emphasis on both subjective and objective domains – what patients want, how their lives and opportunities can be maximized by health interventions and accessible effective health care, and how to address population needs. There is also reflection on the modern health workforce, with appropriate use of multidisciplinary teams and modern information technologies.

The most novel thing about the book is its focus on family medicine and family practice – a new speciality to many, and an approach that is still being implemented in many parts of the region. Globally, the last 50 years have seen a move for all doctors to have a speciality training. For primary health care, this means training generalist physicians who can integrate diagnosis, health education, treatment, and ongoing care for patients across the life course and different health problems. The Eastern Mediterranean Region has been innovative in trying to upskill and upscale its "GP" workforce to meet the needs and opportunities of the 21st century citizen, and has taken on board the increasing evidence that family doctors with a postgraduate speciality training are highly cost-effective for any health system – because they use their skills to diagnose early, deal with multiple problems at the same time, and support both their teams and patients to work together to maximize health gains. Medical expertise is expensive, and its best use is a key aspect of affordable high-quality health coverage. For those unfamiliar with family practice, this book allows major insights into how countries have built this new workforce into their health systems, and how it can add value.

Of course, no one achieves anything alone. Effective universal health coverage needs appropriate financing, infrastructure, and action on the causes of ill-health as well as a strong workforce. The impact of family doctors depends on the system they work in, the conditions they work under, and the team they have around them. The World Health Organization and the World Organization of Family Doctors are delighted to see this book celebrate the work of so many in the Eastern Mediterranean Region, and hope that it will contribute to the future health care and wellbeing in the people of the region. Thanks to all those involved.

Dr Ahmed Al Mandhari
Regional Director
World Health Organization
Eastern Mediterranean Region

Professor Amanda Howe
President
World Organization of Family Doctors

Preface

We are celebrating the 40th anniversary of the Declaration of Alma-Ata by the publication of this book for the Eastern Mediterranean Region (EMR). On 25–26 October 2018, world leaders unite to renew commitment to strengthening primary health care to achieve universal health coverage and the Sustainable Development Goals. That commitment is expressed in a new Declaration which emphasizes the need to modernize primary health care and addresses current and future challenges in health systems while maintaining the core values and principles represented in the original Alma-Ata Declaration in 1978.

Universal Health Coverage (UHC) means that all people and communities can access the promotive, preventive, curative, rehabilitative, and palliative health services they need, of sufficient quality to be effective, while also ensuring that the use of these services does not expose the user to financial hardship. The journey towards UHC requires strengthening of health systems including effectively addressing social and environmental determinants of health through intersectoral action. Social health protection and equity are key considerations in UHC.

Half of the world population lacks access to essential health services, and this certainly applies to a major part of the population in the Eastern Mediterranean Region. As stated by Dr Tedros, the Director General of the World Health Organization (WHO), "implementing UHC is a political more than an economic challenge". With the 2030 Agenda for Sustainable Development, the world has signed up for UHC by 2030, meaning that a global commitment has already been made. Now is the time to transform this global commitment into national action. The World Bank estimates that 90% of all health needs can be met at the primary health care level.[1] Investing to build quality, accessible, and equitable primary health-care services is the most practical, efficient, and effective first step for countries working to deliver UHC.

In May 2016, the 69th World Health Assembly adopted a framework on strengthening integrated, people-centred health services in Resolution WHA69.24. The resolution urged Member States to implement the framework, as appropriate, and make health-care systems more responsive to people's needs. This was followed at the 63rd session of the Regional Committee for the Eastern Mediterranean in October 2016 by the adoption of Resolution EM/RC63/R.2 on scaling up family practice: progressing towards universal health coverage. In this resolution, the Regional Committee urged Member States to incorporate the family practice approach into primary health-care services as an overarching strategy to advance towards universal health coverage.

Family practice can be defined as the health-care services provided by a family physician and his/her team, characterized by comprehensive, community-oriented, continuous, coordinated,

---

[1] Doherty G and Govender R, 'The cost effectiveness of primary care services in developing countries: A review of international literature', Working Paper No. 37, Disease Control Priorities Project, World Bank, WHO and Fogarty International Centre of the U.S. National Institutes of Health, 2004, https://www.researchgate.net/ publication/242783643_The_Cost-Effectiveness_of_Primary_Care_Services_in_Developing_Countries_A_Review_of_the_International_Literature Henceforth 'World Bank Report'.

collaborative, personal, and family services according to the needs of the individual and their family throughout the life course.

There is growing political commitment among countries of the Eastern Mediterranean Region to adopt the family practice approach to improving service provision. Despite that commitment, family practice faces major challenges in most of the Region's Member States including inadequate health facilities infrastructure, low community awareness, and insufficient technical capacity for expansion. A shortage of qualified family physicians means that 93% of health facilities are managed by physicians with no postgraduate training. The poor image of many public sector health services contributes to their underutilization. The quality and efficiency of services are further impaired by the lack of functioning referral systems and hospital networks.

There are significant challenges to ensuring effective participation and contribution of the private sector towards the achievement of public health goals. The private health sector is very active in delivering ambulatory care services in the Eastern Mediterranean Region. Up to 70% of out-patient services are provided by members of the private health sector in the Region. This needs to be taken into account in the development of strategies to strengthen primary health care and introduce family practice. The private health sector has grown with minimal policy direction and support and is rarely addressed in governments' health sector planning processes. In many countries, the private sector has emerged as a consequence of inadequate and underperforming public sector health services. Effective engagement with the private health sector for service delivery through the family practice approach is key to achieving universal health coverage.

The book is a collaborative effort between the World Health Organization (WHO) and the World Organization of Family Doctors (WONCA). It is the first such endeavour for the EMR. The book has 34 chapters, including Region-specific chapters, which highlight several EMR-relevant policy topics and how these are being addressed across the Region, and chapters outlining the current status of family practice in each of the 22 EMR countries. The authors represent a wide spectrum of global, regional, and national experts in family practice. Country-specific chapters cover primary health care and family practice development in each country with a focus on challenges, successes, and lessons learned.

This book is directed at policy makers, health professionals, health educators, and health students. It examines ways primary health care is being developed and improved in high-, middle-, and low-income countries, and in countries experiencing emergencies.

Hassan Salah (editor), Michael Kidd (editor), and Zafar Mirza
(Director of Health System Development,
Eastern Mediterranean Regional Office of the World Health Organization)
August 2018

Acknowledgements

The idea of this book was initiated in discussions between the World Health Organization (WHO) and the World Organization of Family Doctors (WONCA) during the Fourth WONCA East Mediterranean Region Family Medicine Congress held in March 2017 in Abu Dhabi in the United Arab Emirates. This is the first major collaborative effort between the two organizations in this region.

We acknowledge the outstanding and mammoth work of the 90 authors and co-authors who contributed 34 chapters to this book. They represent a renowned group of national, regional, and global primary health-care experts who volunteered their time and talents to this work. We enjoyed working with them and look forward to starting the next phase in developing the second edition of the book, due to be released in October 2020.

We thank the Health System Development Department staff of WHO EMRO who participated in reviewing the 22 country chapters, Dr Adi Al-Nuseirat, Dr Ilker Dastan, Dr Karim Ismail, Dr Mondher Letaief, Dr Arwa Oweis, Dr Hamid Ravaghi and Dr Gohar Wajid.

We thank Mr Guy Penet, and Mr Driss Aboulhoucine, the Publishing and Web Support Team of WHO EMRO, for having reviewed the Arabic and French chapters of the book, and our professional editors, Mrs Alice Grainger Gasser, Mrs Suzi Balaban, and Mrs Lesley Whiting.

Special thanks to Mr Hatem Adel el Khodary, Director of the Department of Administration and Finance at WHO EMRO, and to Mr Kenneth Charles Piercy of the Legal Department of WHO Headquarters, for finalizing the intricate contractual formalities between Taylor & Francis/CRC Press, the World Health Organization, and the World Organization of Family Doctors.

We thank Dr Garth Manning, WONCA Chief Executive Officer, for his continued support for this and the many other WONCA collaborations with WHO.

We thank the Japanese government for its financial support to WHO for Universal Health Coverage, and we express our deep appreciation to the EU–Luxembourg–WHO Universal Health Coverage Partnership for its generous funding to partially support this publication for the WHO Eastern Mediterranean Region Office.

Finally, we thank the team at Taylor & Francis/CRC Press for their great support throughout the preparation and publication of this book, especially Ms Joanna Koster, Ms Julia Molloy, Ms Linda Leggio, and Ms Lara Silva McDonnell.

Editors

Hassan Salah is Primary Health Care Regional Advisor, and Integrated Service Delivery Team Lead, Eastern Mediterranean Regional Office, World Health Organization. Salah is a medical doctor, with a Master's Degree from Harvard School of Public Health.

Michael Kidd is an Australian family doctor and medical researcher. He served as WONCA President from 2013–2016. He is Director of the WHO Collaborating Centre on Family Medicine and Primary Care, and Professor and Chair of the Department of Family and Community Medicine at the University of Toronto in Canada. He also has academic appointments with the Murdoch Children's Research Institute in Melbourne, and as Honorary Professor of Global Primary Care at Flinders University in Australia.

Contributors

Mohsen A'arabi is Vice-Chancellor for Public Health in Mazandaran University of Medical Sciences, Iran. He has served as Head of the Department of Family Medicine in the Medical School, which is one of the leading departments in the training of family medicine, Islamic Republic of Iran. He earned his PhD in epidemiology in the United Kingdom.

Lubna Al-Ansary is Assistant Director General for Metrics and Measurement, WHO, Geneva, Switzerland. She was professor of Family Medicine at the College of Medicine and holder of the Bahamdan Research Chair for Evidence-Based Health Care and Knowledge Translation at King Saud University (KSU). She was a member of the Shura (Consultative) Council in KSA from 2013 to 2016.

Haifa Hamad Fares Al Ali is Consultant Family Physician and Head of Health Program section in the Primary Care Department, United Arab Emirates Ministry of Health and Prevention. She is Director of the MOHAP Family Medicine Residency Program and General Coordinator of the National Periodic Health Screening Initiative. She trained in Strategic Innovation for Community Health and Leadership.

Abdul Munem Al Dabbagh is Professor of Family Medicine and Chairman of the Scientific Council of Family Medicine in the Iraqi Board for Medical Specializations. He is the principal founder and scientific adviser of the Iraqi Family Physician Society and the Managing Editor of the *Iraqi Postgraduate Medical Journal*, as well as author and coauthor of more than 25 articles in the field of family and community medicine. He is WONCA East Mediterranean Region Honorary Secretary General and has worked as a WHO temporary adviser.

Huda Al-Duwaisan is the Director of the Yarmouk Primary Health Care Clinic and Head of the Primary Health Care Faculty at the Kuwait Institute for Medical Specialization, Kuwait. She is a trainer and examiner in the Family Medicine Board in Kuwait. She received her fellowship in Family Medicine from the United Kingdom's Royal College of General Practitioners.

Naeema Al Gasseer is WHO Representative in Sudan and served as representative in Egypt and Iraq. She is a nurse midwife by background and has been involved in setting strategies for various health priorities aligned with global goals. She received an Honorary Doctorate of Science (DSci) from Glasgow Caledonian University, Scotland in 2005.

May Hani Al Hadidi has 30 years of experience in PHC and Family Medicine. She is currently Head of Family Medicine Specialty at the Ministry of Health, Director of Maternal and Child Health Directorate and Manager of the Comprehensive Postpartum Project Centre at Al-Basheer Hospital, Jordan. She is an examiner with the Family Medicine Board, Jordan Medical Council, and a member of Teaching Family Medicine in Mutah University.

Thamer Al Hilfi is a Senior WHO National Professional Officer, Category 02 leader of Noncommunicable Disease (NCD), and Consultant at the Ministry of Health for Public Health Programmes, Iraq. He worked as the Director of the Accreditation and Quality Assurance Unit at Al Kindy College of Medicine. He is former acting chief of party for the USAID Primary Health Care Project.

Said Al Lamki is the Director General of Primary Health Care in the Ministry of Health, Oman. He has a bachelor's degree in medicine with a master's in public health from the University of Bath and master's in total quality management from the University of Birmingham. He is a Fellow at the Faculty of Public Health at the Royal College, United Kingdom.

Ahmed Salim Saif Al-Mandhari is the Director General at the Oman Ministry of Health Quality Assurance Centre. He graduated from the College of Medicine and Health Sciences at Sultan Qaboos University and has a diploma in tropical medicine and hygiene and a PhD in health-care quality management from the University of Liverpool. He is an international member of the Royal College of General Practitioners.

Ali Al-Mudhwahi is Public Health Advisor and Board Member of the Yemen Family Care Association (YFCA). He supports health emergency activities for Global Health Development (GHD) in Yemen. He is an MD with a master's in public health and is a candidate for a PhD in health systems.

Wadeia Mohammed Al Sharief is a Consultant Family Physician and Assistant Professor in University of Sharjah and Dubai Medical College, United Arab Emirates. She is Director of the Family Medicine Dubai Residency Program and President of the Emirates Family Medicine Society, Emirates Medical Association. She is the UAE Representative Member in the Council of Arab Health Ministers, Arab Board of Health Specializations.

Zelaikha Mohsin Al-Wahedi is the Executive Director of Workforce Development and Training at the Primary Health Care Corporation in Qatar. She is Assistant Professor of Family Medicine in Clinical Medicine, Weill Cornell Medical College, and is a highly committed senior consultant and strong advocate of Family Medicine. She has been leading the family medicine residency programme, services, and practice in the State of Qatar since 1999.

Mariam Ali Abdulmalik is the Managing Director of the Primary Health Care Corporation (PHCC), running over 23 health centres across the state, serving more than 85% of Qatar's population. As PHCC leader, She holds overall responsibility and authority to deliver strategic change and implement Qatar's National Primary Health Care Strategy.

Faisal Abdullatif Alnasir is Professor of Family Medicine and honorary faculty of Imperial College, London; Fellow of the Royal College of General Practitioners and College of Public Health; and a member of Irish College of General Practitioners. He was the Vice-President and Chairman of Family Department at Arabian Gulf University, Bahrain.

Eman Abdelkreem Hassan Aly has 20 years of experience in public health services, field epidemiology (FETPs), and statistics at the national and the regional level. She has extensive experience in designing, implementing, coordinating, and supervising disease surveillance systems. She has worked in epidemiological studies, outbreak investigation, and surveys, including programme monitoring and evaluation as well as developing electronic routine health information management systems.

Mohammad Assai Ardakani is the WHO Representative in Pakistan. He worked as EMRO Regional Adviser for Community Based Initiatives from 2004 to 2012. He was the Coordinator of Integrated Service Delivery with a focus on primary health care, hospital management, quality, and safety and emergency care services between 2013–2016. He has a doctorate in medicine and surgery from Dow Medical College, Karachi as well as master of public health from Dundee University of Scotland.

Adel Al-Sayyad is a certified family physician and a holder of a master's degree in Epidemiology from London School of Hygiene and Tropical Medicine. He is a Consultant in Family Medicine, Public Health and Epidemiology, and Chief of the Disease Control Section in the Ministry of Health, Bahrain.

Mona Ahmed Almudhwahi is a medical doctor, holding a master's in public health from Johns Hopkins University, United States of America. She joined the WHO in 2001 serving two country offices, Yemen and Somalia, in the areas of health system strengthening, maternal and child health, non-communicable diseases, and, more recently, emergency preparedness and response.

Oraib Alsmadi is an expert in health-care management and quality improvement. She is a Family Medicine Consultant with 25 years of experience in the primary health care field in Jordan. Currently, she is the Service Delivery Improvement Team Leader in Abt Associates Incorporation, Jordan.

Walid Ammar, MD, PhD, is Director General of the Lebanese Ministry of Public Health. He served as a member of the Executive Board (EB) at the World Health Organization (2012–2015) and is currently a member of the WHO Emergencies Oversight and Advisory Committee. He is a professor at the Lebanese University and Senior Lecturer at the American University of Beirut.

Marie Andrades is Associate Professor of Family Medicine at Aga Khan University in Pakistan. She is Dean of Family Medicine Faculty, College of Physicians and Surgeons, Pakistan and has been examination convenor for the MRCGP[INT] South Asia examination. She is a trainer and examiner in Family Medicine nationally and internationally.

Mohsen Asadi-Lari is Professor of Epidemiology, Iran University of Medical Sciences (IUMS), Tehran, and Acting Minister for International Affairs, Ministry of Health and Medical Education, IR Iran. He has more than 25 years of experience in public health at national and international levels, specializing in communicable diseases, public health emergencies, non-communicable diseases, and health diplomacy. He has contributed to national and international research projects and played an important role in WHO at regional and global levels.

Muna Taher Aseel is a Senior Family Medicine Consultant and the Programme Director of the ACGME-I accredited Family Medicine Residency Programme, PHCC-HMC, Qatar. She earned her MD from King Faisal University, Kingdom of Saudi Arabia (1999) and the Arab Board (2005). Her interests include paediatrics, diabetes, bronchial asthma, mental health, medical education, health-care leadership, and management.

Magdy Bakr, MD, graduated from Cairo University. He started in hospital management in 1988 then progressed into the national health system in 2000. From 2000 to 2007, he served as a member of the European Commission Technical Assistance Team, providing support to Egypt's Government Health Sector Reform Program, then joined the WHO from 2008 to 2018, working as a WHO focal person for health system strengthening.

Azza Mohamed Badr is a biostatistician, health information expert, biochemist, and medical environmental scientist. She is Civil Registration and Vital Statistic (CRVS) Regional Expert in the WHO EMRO. Prior to 2013, she served as planning, monitoring, and evaluation officer and health situation and trend assessment officer, WHO EMRO. She worked with the American Navy (NAMRU-3) as a research assistant from 1980 to 1986.

Shannon Barkley is a Technical Officer for Primary Health Care Services at the World Health Organization (WHO). She has an MD and MPH, with specialties in family medicine and advanced hospital medicine. She has supported effective primary health care among underserved communities through direct service provision, health workforce education, service delivery policy, and monitoring and evaluation.

Fatemah Ahmed Bendhafari is a senior specialist family physician at Yarmouk Health Centre and a Certified Trainer for General Practitioners (RCGP/INT), Kuwait. She has worked with WHO-EMRO in on-site training of regional master trainers in family practice. She is the Head of Primary Care Domain, Canadian accreditation at Yarmouk Health Centre and a member of the Royal College of General Practitioners, United Kingdom.

Majid Bitar is the Director of the Family Medicine Program in the Primary Healthcare Directorate, Ministry of Health, Syria. He has Syrian Board in Family Medicine and Masters of Health System Management, University of Liverpool, Faculty of Health and Life Sciences School. He is a certified trainer on the Early Warning Alert and Response System (EWARS) for Communicable Diseases.

Noha Dashash is a Consultant Family Physician and Assistant Director of Health Affairs, MoH, Jeddah, Kingdom of Saudi Arabia. She is a member of the teaching staff and family medicine research coordinator of the Postgraduate Joint Programme of Family and Community Medicine. She is the President of the Saudi Scientific Society of Evidence-Based Health Care.

Henry Victor Doctor is a demographer and public health researcher. He serves as a Technical Officer (Health Information and Statistics) in the WHO EMRO. He held previous technical, academic, and research appointments within the United Nations Office on Drugs and Crime, Columbia University, Swiss Tropical and Public Health Institute, University of the Western Cape, and Statistics South Africa.

Omaima El-Gibaly is Professor and Head of the Department of Public Health, Assiut University, Egypt. She established and led the Primary Health and Social Care Services Centre at Assiut University to serve as an outlet for training family physicians from 1996 to 2000, and has coordinated training of the Ministry of Health and Population physicians in Family Medicine, at Assiut University.

Arwa Eissa is the Head of the Primary Health Care Centers Department, Ministry of Health, Syria. She is a trainer for primary health care facilities staff on family practice implementation, and a certified Quality Accreditor and trainer on the Early Warning Alert and Response System (EWARS) for Communicable Diseases.

Mona Hafez Mahmoud El Naka is the First Undersecretary and Head of Primary Health Care Sector, Ministry of Health and Population, Egypt. Holding a master's degree in paediatrics, She has worked in teaching hospitals and the Healthy Mother/ Healthy Child Project, responsible for the training programs of nurses and doctors.

Heba Fouad is Technical Officer in charge of the Noncommunicable Disease (NCD) Surveillance Unit, in the NCD and Mental Health (NMH) Department at the WHO Regional Office for the Eastern Mediterranean. She is a medical doctor with master and doctoral degrees from Alexandria University, Faculty of Medicine. Her work as an epidemiologist has focused on NCDs and NCD risk factor surveillance and capacity building in the Eastern Mediterranean Region.

Ali Mtiraoui is President of the University of Sousse, Tunisia; former Dean of the Faculty of Medicine of Sousse; and former Director of the Department of Family and Community Health. She served as a public medical educator, health physician, and general practitioner at several levels of the health-care system in Tunisia, including as Regional Director in Primary Health Care.

Ibrahim El-Ziq is WHO Representative, Kingdom of Saudi Arabia, Kuwait, and Bahrain. Prior to this, he worked as UNICEF Regional Representative in the Gulf countries, UNICEF Chief of Immunization in Denmark, Chief of Health and Nutrition at UNICEF Pakistan, senior health advisor to the European Union, Deputy Director at Harvard Institute for International Development, Harvard University, and Senior Health Advisor to Department for International Development (DFID).

Taghreed Mohamed Farahat is a Professor of Community and Family Health, Family Medicine Department, Faculty of Medicine, Menoufia University, Egypt. A Member of the Egyptian University Promotion Committee (EUPC) and Chairperson of the Egyptian Family Medicine Association (EFMA), she is the Head of the Research Committee and Executive Board Member of WONCA East Mediterranean Region.

Fethiye Gülin Gedik is Coordinator, Health Workforce Development at the WHO Regional Office for the Eastern Mediterranean. She is a physician with postgraduate training in public health and health economics. She has over 25 years of experience in health policies, systems, and human resources at national and international levels. She has worked at WHO HQ and Regional Offices for Europe (Bishkek and Copenhagen) and Western Pacific.

Ann-Lise Guisset is a Technical Officer at the WHO, where she supports hospital sector transformation to implement integrated people-centred health systems. She worked in various capacities at WHO Regional (Europe) and country (Tunisia) offices on hospital quality, health system performance assessment, and national policy development. She has a master's in business administration and a PhD in public health.

Hachri Hafid has been Health Systems Officer at the WHO Morocco Office since 2014. He has 17 years of experience in the Ministry of Health as a general practitioner, responsible for the management of sectoral projects. He is a teacher and researcher at the National School of Public Health and Director of Primary Health Care.

Eiman Hag is a public health professional with seven years of experience in health systems and public health research, policy, and teaching. She is the Head of the Evidence Generation Department at the Public Health Institute, Sudan. She trained as a dentist before pursuing a public health career.

Ghassan Hamadeh is currently Chair of Family Medicine and Chief Medical Information Officer (CMIO) at the American University of Beirut Medical Center. He is the President of the Arab Board of Family Medicine and is American board certified in both Family Medicine and Clinical Informatics.

Hossein Hamam is an educational project manager with extensive experience designing and implementing e-learning projects at the post-secondary level. His research interests include instructional systems that support adult education and lifelong learning.

Asmus Hammerich is Director for Noncommunicable Diseases and Mental Health (NMH) at the WHO EMRO. He has served as WHO Representative in Uzbekistan and as Deputy WHO Representative in Laos. Prior to joining WHO, he led bilateral GIZ- and DFID-supported public health programs in Indonesia, India, and Rwanda. He has also practiced as a family physician in Britain and Germany.

Lisa Hirschhorn is Professor of Medical Social Sciences at Northwestern University Feinberg School of Medicine, United States of America. Trained in infectious diseases, primary care, and public health, she is a leader in implementation science focused on evaluating and spreading effective approaches to improve quality and equity of care delivery globally.

Syed Jaffar Hussain is the WHO Representative in Libya. He earlier served as Regional Adviser for Healthy Lifestyle Promotion at the WHO Eastern Mediterranean Regional Office. He has a doctorate in public health from Atlantic International University, Hawaii, and a master's in hospital and health services management from the University of Leeds, United Kingdom.

Nagwa Nashat Hegazy is Assistant Professor in Family Medicine, Family Medicine Department, Faculty of Medicine, Menoufia University, Egypt, as well as an Executive Board Member of the Egyptian Family Medicine Association (EFMA), Scientific Board Member of the Egyptian Fellowship of Family Medicine, and Chair of the Al-Razi Young Doctor Movement for the East Mediterranean Region.

Shafiqullah Hemat, MD, PhD, is a public health expert currently working as Director of Health Promotion at the Ministry of Public Health, Afghanistan. He has around 20 years of working experience with government, UNICEF, WHO, and non-governmental organisations (NGOs). He is a public health lecturer with several publications in international journals.

Amanda Howe is a practicing family doctor. Part of the founding team for a new medical programme at the University of East Anglia, she is currently Professor of Primary Care there. She has served as an Officer of the Royal College of General Practitioners and is President of the World Organization of Family Doctors (2016–2018).

Abdihamid Ibrahim is a medical doctor and health systems management specialist. He is a WHO Technical Officer in Somalia with over eight years of experience working with public, non-governmental, and international organizations, including the United Nations. He has held the positions of clinician, health programme manager, and senior government official.

Ghasem Janbabaei is the Deputy for Curative Affairs, Ministry of Health and Medical Education, Islamic Republic of Iran. He was Chancellor of Mazandaran University during the first four years of the Health Transformation Plan. He was the Head of the Mazandaran Provincial Executive Board of Family Physician Programme for four years.

Edward Kelley is Director of the Department of Service Delivery and Safety at the WHO HQ and is the lead for WHO's work on strengthening health systems and security. Before joining WHO, he served as Director of the National Healthcare Reports for the United States Department of Health and Human Services in the Agency for Healthcare Research and Quality.

Abdoulaye Konate is a medical doctor who graduated in 2005 from the University of Cocody, Abidjan, Côte d'Ivoire. He obtained a master's in health economics from the High Institute of Health Management, CESAG, Dakar, Senegal, in 2008. In 2014, after working several years with UNICEF as a Health Specialist, he joined the WHO as a Technical Officer based in Djibouti, in charge of health system strengthening.

Merette Khalil graduated from Saint Louis University with studies in public health, business administration, and international social justice. She served in a primary care community clinic in Washington, DC, focusing on patient advocacy, team-based care coordination, and women's empowerment. Currently, she is a member of the Health Workforce Development team volunteering in the Health Systems Department at WHO EMRO.

Mondher Letaief is a Regional Adviser in the Health System Development Department responsible for Healthcare Quality and Safety programme in WHO EMRO. He worked as Professor of Preventive Medicine and has published more than 60 papers in peer-reviewed journals.

Gemma Lyons is a Technical Officer on Non-Communicable Diseases (NCDs) at WHO Country Office in Saudi Arabia. She has a bachelor's degree in sciences from the University of Cambridge and an MPH with distinction from The University of Sheffield in the United Kingdom. She worked as a Public Health Strategist and Programme Manager on NCDs in the United Kingdom before joining WHO EMRO.

Hind Amin Merghani has been the Head of the Policy and Development Department at the Public Health Institute, Sudan, since October 2015. She is a dentist and was awarded an MPH degree in 2010, followed by a degree in Dental Public Health in 2015. She has extensive experience in the area of policy development and health systems research.

Zafar Mirza is Director of Health System Development at the Eastern Mediterranean Regional Office of WHO, covering 22 countries. He is a medical doctor from Pakistan with a postgraduate degree in public health. Before joining WHO in 2004, he served as a founding Executive Director of the Network for Consumer Protection in Pakistan.

Xavier Mòdol is a medical doctor specializing in Family Medicine and has an MSc in health policy planning and financing. His experience of almost 30 years covers over 15 conflict countries. His expertise and experience in health systems include health system recovery, essential health service packages, and health financing.

Ghaith Sabri Mohammed is a Fellow of the Iraqi Board for Medical Specializations and a consultant family physician in the Iraqi Ministry of Health in Bab Al Muadham Family Health Care Centre. He is also a member of the executive board of the Al-Razi Group for young family doctors, WONCA EMR. He is supervisor and field trainer in the Iraqi and Arab Family Medicine residency programmes.

Hernan Montenegro is currently Coordinator of the Services Organization and Clinical Interventions Unit, Service Delivery and Safety Department, at the WHO HQ. He has an MD from the University of Chile, a specialist in public health degree from the University of Chile, and a master's in public health from Johns Hopkins University, United States of America.

Kashmira Nanji is a Lecturer in the Department of Family Medicine at Aga Khan University, Pakistan. She is a trained epidemiologist and biostatistician with numerous publications in various national and international journals. Her research interests are Primary Care and Noncommunicable Diseases (NCD).

Stephanie Ngo is a Consultant at the WHO Regional Office for the Western Pacific, where she supports health service delivery reform for universal health coverage. Her areas of expertise include health systems, health policy, patient experience, quality improvement, and integrated care. She holds bachelor's degrees in both nursing and behavioural neuroscience and is currently pursuing a master's in public health.

Bashir Noormal is the Director General of the Afghanistan National Public Health Institute. He worked as Associate Professor of Kabul Medical Institute and training coordinator/HRD program manager for WHO Afghanistan from 1997–2004. He is the Chair of IRB Afghanistan, a member of IANPHI, EMPHNET, CBRN, and a member of the Advisory Board of TEPHINET.

Abdalla Sid Ahmed Osman is a public health professional with extensive national, regional, and international health development experience. He served as a Senior National Advisor to the government in the capacity of Minister, Undersecretary, and Director of Planning, Sudan. As chairman of the Country Coordinating Mechanism and Gavi Committee, he had a leading role in the planning and implementation of the national health policy.

Mona Osman is an instructor of Clinical Family Medicine, the Medical Director of the Family Medicine Clinics, and the coordinator of community and outreach activities in the Department of Family Medicine at the American University of Beirut Medical Center (AUBMC). She is the co-director of the Refugee Health Program at the American University of Beirut (AUB).

Arwa Oweis is the Regional Adviser for Nursing and Midwifery and Allied Health Personnel at WHO Regional Office for the Eastern Mediterranean. She has served as Dean of Nursing at Jordan University of Science and Technology, and at the University of Philadelphia in Amman, Jordan. She has published more than 25 journal articles and book chapters and served on editorial boards of international nursing journals.

Nuria Toro Polanco is a Technical Officer on Health Care Service at the WHO, where she supports the implementation of the framework on integrated people-centred health services. She has a master's in business analysis and a diploma in health management. Her areas of expertise include health services delivery reform, integrated care and management, and evaluation.

Waris Qidwai is Professor of Family Medicine at Aga Khan University, Pakistan. He has over 180 published papers and has served as Chair of the International Federation of Primary Care Research and as Chair of the WONCA Working Party on Research. He is a Trainer and Examiner in Family Medicine and provides editorial support to more than two dozen medical journals.

Alissar Rady is National Professional Officer at WHO Lebanon. She began her career as a Family Physician then shifted to public health, working with the WHO and other international organizations including the World Bank, ILO, UNFPA, and UNICEF. She supervises master's students in public health in three universities.

Arash Rashidian is the Director of Information, Evidence, and Research in the WHO Eastern Mediterranean Region. He is also the Executive Editor of the *Eastern Mediterranean Health Journal*. Previously, he was Professor of Health Policy and Deputy Chancellor (Tehran University of Medical Sciences), and prior to that has held senior academic, managerial, and honorary positions in the United Kingdom, Iran, and Pakistan.

Mohammadreza Rahbar MD, MPH, is a PhD candidate, with the Skin and Stem Cell Research Centre, Tehran University of Medical Sciences (TUMS), IR Iran. He has served as Head of Human Resource Management Group, Centre for Health Networks Management and as Deputy for Health, Ministry of Health and Medical Education. With 20 years of scientific and executive experience in different fields, positions, and tasks he has held roles in human resource development, health programme planning, health sector reforms, primary health care, and family practice development.

Mays Raheem is a Teaching Fellow at the WHO Collaborating Centre for Public Health Education and Training at the Department of Primary Care and Public Health, Imperial College London, United Kingdom. She is actively involved in health system–strengthening research, assessing and building health leadership capacity with a particular focus on low- and middle-income countries, health systems in transition, and post-conflict countries.

Asa'd Ramlawi is the Deputy Minister of Health and the former Director General of Primary Health Care and Public Health, Ministry of Health, Palestine. He is a medical doctor with a specialty in tropical medicine. He has taken a leading role in implementing several national initiatives in the Palestinian health-care system at the primary and secondary levels.

David Rawaf is an MBBS (MD–Merit) and BSc (Hons) graduate and anatomy demonstrator from St. George's, University of London, United Kingdom. He is a Clinical and Education Fellow in Trauma and Orthopaedics at University College London Hospital and undertakes research and design for the Imperial College WHO Collaborating Centre for Public Health Education and Training.

Salman Rawaf is Professor of Public Health and Director of the WHO Collaborating Centre for Public Health Education and Training at Imperial College London in the United Kingdom. He served for 23 years as Director of Public Health in South West London, leading on major innovative approaches to health improvement and service delivery. His contributions to global health through health systems development are well known in over 50 countries.

Gerald Rockenschaub is the Head of the WHO Office for the occupied Palestinian territory. He joined the World Health Organization in 2004 as Regional Adviser for the WHO European Region. He is a medical doctor and surgeon with a degree in public health. He has managed various international health programs, working with the Red Cross and non-governmental organization (NGOs)..

Belgacem Sabri is the Head of the Tunisian Association for Defending the Right to Health and former State Minister for Migration and Social Inclusion. He is the Director of Health System Development at WHO EMRO. He has served as a public health physician, general practitioner, and medical inspector in the Tunisian health-care system.

Rand Salman is the Director of the Palestinian National Institute of Public Health, one of the WHO projects in Palestine. She is a medical doctor with a specialty in Community Medicine and a sub-specialty in epidemiology. She has carried out substantial role in designing and implementing several projects funded by USAID, United Nations agencies, and international non-governmental organization (NGOs).

Aziz Sheikh is Professor of Primary Care Research and Development and Director of the Usher Institute of Population Health Sciences at The University of Edinburgh in Scotland. He is Director of the National Institute for Health Research (NIHR) Global Respiratory Health Unit (RESPIRE), Co-Director of the National Health Service (NHS) Digital Academy, and an adviser to the World Health Organization.

Sameen Siddiqi is currently the Chair of the Department of Community Health Sciences at the Aga Khan University Karachi, Pakistan. Previously, he worked as a Director of Health Systems for the World Health Organization's Regional Office for the Eastern Mediterranean. His areas of interest include health governance and financing, private health sector, and quality and safety of care.

Slim Slama is Regional Adviser in charge of Noncommunicable Diseases Prevention (NCP) and Management units (NCM) in the Department of Non-Communicable Diseases and Mental Health (NMH) at the WHO Regional Office for the Eastern Mediterranean in Cairo, Egypt. He is a specialist in internal medicine and has an MPH from the London School of Hygiene and Tropical Medicine.

Najibullah Safi has worked in the Afghan health system since 1998 in various capacities: in the public sector, non-governmental organisations (NGOs), and WHO. He is currently working with the Afghanistan WHO Country Office as Program Manager for Health System Development. His areas of expertise are health systems management, health financing, research, quality improvement, surveillance, and infectious disease control.

Amina Sahel is the Director of Primary Health Care Department and a strong advocate for the introduction and establishment of a family practice programme in Morocco. She is a general practitioner and holds a master's degree in community health and health promotion.

Hasti Sanaei-Shoar is a medical doctor, Community Medicine Specialist, and Senior Expert of HRM group, Centre for Health Networks Management, Ministry of Health and Medical Education, IR Iran. She has over 10 years of experience in health networks and different fields. She has held roles in human resources development, programme planning, primary health care, and family practice programme development. She has contributed to designing training packages for community health workers and family physicians.

Mohammed Rasoul Tarawneh is the President of the Jordan Society of Family Medicine, and the Secretary General of the High Health Council. He is a former Director of Noncommunicable Diseases (NCD) at the Ministry of Health. He is the Head of the Family Medicine specialty, Jordan Medical Board in Family Medicine.

Zia UlHaq is the Director at Institute of Public Health & Social Sciences, Khyber Medical University, Pakistan. He earned his PhD from the University of Glasgow in Scotland, and is Principle Investigator of several large ongoing studies. He played an important role in implementing the Family Medicine approach and is a technical member of many health committees. He has been honoured with the National Best University Teacher and lifetime achievement awards in Pakistan.

Gohar Wajid is a medical doctor and health professions educationist, currently working as Technical Officer for Health Professionals' Education in the WHO EMRO. He is responsible for contributing to universal health coverage through promoting health professionals' education in the Eastern Mediterranean Region, strengthening the family practice-based approach, and advising Member States to address the issue of shortage of health workers through promoting high-quality education.

CHAPTER 1

The global movement towards integrated people-centred health services: The role of family practice*

Shannon Barkley, Nuria Toro Polanco, Hernan Montenegro, Ann-Lise Guisset, Stephanie Ngo, and Edward Kelley

INTRODUCTION: GLOBAL HEALTH LANDSCAPE – CHALLENGES AND OPPORTUNITIES

The era of the Millennium Development Goals (1990–2015) saw unprecedented progress in targeted areas of health: the global under-five mortality rate declined by more than half, dropping from 90 to 43 deaths per 1000 live births; the maternal mortality ratio declined by 45% worldwide; new human immunodeficiency virus (HIV) infections fell by approximately 40% between 2000 and 2013, from an estimated 3.5 million cases to 2.1 million; and tuberculosis prevention, diagnosis, and treatment interventions saved an estimated 37 million lives.[1] Indeed, the past decades offer much to celebrate.

Yet, despite significant advances in people's health and life expectancy in recent years, improvements have been unequal across and within the populations of countries. In addition, as maternal–child health improves, new health challenges are emerging related to demographic

---

* This chapter will refer to both family practice and family medicine/general practice and differentiates these terms as follows: *family practice* refers to health-care services provided by teams of providers trained to provide health-care services for all individuals regardless of age, sex, or type of health problem; provides primary and continuing care for entire families within their communities; addresses physical, psychological, and social problems; coordinates comprehensive health-care services with other specialists as needed. Family practice can also be equated to "people-centred" primary health care as defined by the World Health Report 2008. *Family medicine/general practice* refers to physician specialists who have received specialty training to provide medical care within the family practice setting.

and epidemiologic shifts. The world's population is facing urbanization, migration, ageing, the global tendency towards unhealthy lifestyles, the dual disease burden of communicable and non-communicable diseases, multi-morbidities, increasing disease outbreaks, and complex emergencies, while social participation and expectations are on the rise.

Designed to address health problems of the past, most countries' health systems are not fit-for-purpose to address the challenges of the 21st century. This chapter will discuss how transforming health systems to become more integrated and people-centred, including a renewed emphasis on primary health care (PHC), can address current demographic, epidemiologic, and health system challenges. In particular, it will pay attention to how family practice enables high-performing PHC.

CONTEXT: HEALTH SYSTEM CHALLENGES

Today's health systems are not as accessible as they should be. Currently, it is estimated that at least half of the world's population still lacks access to essential health services.[2] In addition to an inadequate response to financial and geographical barriers, access is further challenged in countries that continue to face problems ensuring basic inputs to the health system, including an adequate health work force and the availability of essential medicines. Even for high priority conditions, such as maternal and child health, coverage of basic services (for example, antenatal care and the presence of a skilled birth attendant at delivery) remains low in many countries.[3]

Where care is accessible, it is too often fragmented or of poor quality. Continuity of care, particularly important in the setting of chronic disease, is poor for many health conditions. Care fragmentation and disorganization, owing to weak referral systems, results in poorer outcomes and increased cost. The focus on hospital-based, disease-based, and self-contained "silo" curative care models, rather than appropriately emphasizing PHC, further undermines the ability of health systems to provide universal, equitable, high-quality, and financially sustainable care. Parallel service delivery platforms, with people seeking care in both public and private sectors, can further contribute to fragmentation.

Service providers are often unaccountable to the populations they serve and, therefore, have limited incentive to provide responsive care that matches the needs of their users. People are at times not empowered to make appropriate decisions about their own health and health care, or exercise control over decisions about their health and that of their communities. Consequently, the responsiveness of the health system and satisfaction with health services remain low in many countries (Table 1.1).[4]

Health system challenges are made even more visible in the context of complex emergencies which reduce access to essential PHC services. The number of persons affected by humanitarian emergencies worldwide is unprecedented; in 2017, the United Nations Office for the Coordination

TABLE 1.1 Key facts: Global service delivery challenges

- At least half of the world's population lacks access to essential health services that could be delivered through primary care[2]
- The world is facing a projected shortfall of 18 million health workers
- Globally, up to 40% of all health-care spending is wasted through inefficiency
- In the Americas, only 22% of primary care providers rate their referral systems with specialized services as good or very good
- In Africa, 45% of people rate their level of involvement in decision-making about health services as "poor"
- Of 421 million hospitalizations globally each year, about 1 in 10 results in harm to the patient
- In 2009, non-communicable diseases accounted for 45% of the burden of disease, but only 1% of donor funding for health

of Humanitarian Affairs estimated that 128 million people needed humanitarian assistance.[5] More than half of these, 65.6 million, have been forcibly displaced as a result of armed conflict, civil strife, or human rights violations. Among these are 22.5 million refugees and 40.3 million internally displaced people.[6]

While the underlying causes of complex emergencies vary, the resultant population displacement and health systems destabilization have predictable health consequences. These include increased mortality rates (in some situations greater than ten times above baseline rates). Historically, the causes of the high morbidity and mortality rates have been infectious disease outbreaks, exacerbation of endemic infectious diseases, and acute malnutrition. However, increased availability of interventions for these conditions and the rise in conflicts in higher-income countries have led to an increasing burden of disease in complex emergencies from chronic conditions such as tuberculosis, cardiovascular disease, and diabetes, as well as mental health.[7] Ensuring that PHC services continue to be available in regions experiencing complex emergencies is, therefore, essential.

INTEGRATED PEOPLE-CENTRED HEALTH SERVICES SUPPORT ACHIEVEMENT OF UNIVERSAL HEALTH COVERAGE

In 2015, countries adopted the Sustainable Development Goals (SDGs), including Goal 3 for health: Ensure healthy lives and promote wellbeing for all at all ages.[8] Target 3.8 of SDG 3 – achieving universal health coverage (UHC), including access to quality essential health-care services – is fundamental to obtaining the goal of health for all. UHC means that all individuals and communities receive the health services they need without experiencing financial hardship. It includes the full spectrum of essential, quality health services, from health promotion to prevention, treatment, rehabilitation, and palliative care.[9] Historically, discussions of UHC prioritized three dimensions of coverage: population coverage, service coverage, and financial coverage or financial protection.[10] Importantly, however, the description of UHC is evolving to emphasize not only what services are covered, but also how they are delivered, funded, and managed.[14]

For UHC services to be effective and for financing of services to be sustainable, a fundamental shift in the way services are organized and delivered is needed. This includes reorienting health services to ensure that care is provided in the most appropriate and cost-effective setting, with the right balance between out-patient and in-patient care while strengthening the coordination of care across settings. Health services should be organized around the comprehensive needs and expectations of people and communities, empowering them to take a more active role in their health and health system.

PHC-orientation within health systems is associated with better outcomes that are accessible, equitable, effective, safe, people-centred care – and is therefore essential to achieving the goals for effective coverage. PHC-orientation is also cost-effective, promoting sustainability of health system financing and enabling progressive realization of UHC. PHC, with its emphasis on whole-person care, coordination, and continuity is also associated with higher levels of responsiveness.[11]

THE GLOBAL MOVEMENT TOWARDS INTEGRATED, PEOPLE-CENTRED HEALTH SERVICES

Recognizing the need to transform health systems to reach Sustainable Development Goal 3: "ensure healthy lives and promote well-being for all at all ages", the 69th World Health Assembly adopted the Framework on integrated, people-centred health services and urged countries to implement this framework at regional and country levels, in accordance with national contexts and priorities. By adopting this resolution, delegations from Member States acknowledged the importance of integrated people-centred health services (IPCHS), including strengthening PHC, for achieving UHC and the health-related sustainable development goals, and requested that the World Health Organization (WHO) take specific actions to support Member States.[12]

This Framework puts the comprehensive needs of people and communities, not only treatment of specific diseases, at the centre of health systems, and empowers people to have a more active role in their own health. It casts a vision for a world in which "all people have equal access to quality health services that are co-produced in a way that meets their life course needs, are coordinated across the continuum of care, and are comprehensive, safe, effective, timely, efficient, and acceptable; and all carers are motivated and skilled and operate in a supportive environment".[13]

The Framework on IPCHS proposes five interdependent strategies for health services to become more integrated and people-centred. It calls for reforms to reorient health services, putting individuals, families, carers, and communities at their centre, supported by responsive services that better meet their needs, and that are coordinated both within and beyond the health sector, irrespective of country setting or development status. These reforms also incorporate a human rights approach, enshrining access to health care as a basic right, without distinction of ethnicity, religion, gender, age, disability, political belief, and economic or social condition. The strategies of the framework are further described through approaches, policy options, and interventions (Table 1.2). Attainment of these five strategies cumulatively will help to build more effective health services; lack of progress in one area will potentially undermine progress in other areas. The five interdependent strategies are:

1. *Empowering and engaging people and communities*: Empowering and engaging people is about providing the opportunity, skills, and resources that people need to be articulate and empowered users of health services and advocates for a reformed health system.
2. *Strengthening governance and accountability:* Good governance is transparent, inclusive, and makes the best use of available resources and information to ensure the best possible results. It is reinforced by a robust system for mutual accountability among policy-makers, managers, providers, and users. Strengthening governance requires a participatory approach to policy formulation, decision-making and performance evaluation at all levels of the health system, from policy-making to the clinical intervention level.
3. *Reorienting the model of care*: Reorienting the model of care means ensuring that efficient and effective health-care services are designed, purchased, and provided through innovative models of care that prioritize primary and community-care services, and the co-production of health. This encompasses the shift from in-patient to out-patient, and ambulatory care and from curative to preventive, such that an appropriate balance is found between primary care, specialized out-patient care, and hospital in-patient care.
4. *Coordinating services within and across sectors*: This requires integration of health-care providers within and across health-care settings, development of referral systems and networks among levels of care, and the creation of linkages between health and other sectors. It encompasses intersectoral action at the community level to address the social determinants of health and optimize use of scarce resources, including, at times, through partnerships with the private sector. Coordination does not necessarily require the merging of the different structures, services or workflows,

TABLE 1.2 Framework on integrated people-centred health services: Strategies, strategic approaches, policy options, and interventions[4]

Strategic approaches	Policy options and interventions
Strategy 1: Empowering and engaging people and communities	
Empowering and engaging individuals and families for co-production of care and self-management, particularly for chronic diseases. Building reciprocal relationships between providers and users of health services to improve the quality and experience of care.	• Health education[†] • Informed consent[†] • Shared clinical decision-making[†] • Self-management including personal care assessment & treatment plans[†] • Knowledge of health system navigation[†]
Empowering and engaging communities to generate changes in their living environments as well as to influence the way in which care is funded, planned and provided.	• Community delivered care[‡] • Community health workers[‡] • Development of civil society • Strengthened social participation in health
Empowering and engaging informal carers to provide high-quality interventions, and to serve as advocates for the recipients of care, both within the health system and at the policy level.	• Training for informal carers[†] • Informal carer networks • Peer support and expert patient groups[‡] • Caring for the carers • Respite care
Reaching the underserved and marginalized to address the social determinants of health and ensure universal access to quality health services. This is essential for fulfilling broader societal goals such as equity, social justice and solidarity, and helps to create social cohesion.	• Integration of health equity goals into health sector objectives • Provision of outreach services for the underserved including mobile units • Transport systems and telemedicine[‡] • Outreach programmes for disadvantaged/marginalized populations[‡] • Expansion of primary care-based systems[†]
Strategy 2: Strengthening governance and accountability	
Bolstering participatory governance. The stewardship role of the health ministry is essential for good governance in health, and involves the identification and participation of community stakeholders so that voices are heard and consensus is achieved. It is also needed to ensure that the different goals of donor agencies and vertical programmes tackling specific diseases do not hinder the ability of health systems to focus on community health and wellbeing.	• National health policies, strategies and plans promoting integrated people-centred health services • Community participation in policy formulation and evaluation • Community representation at health care facilities' boards[†] • Strengthened health services governance and management at subnational, district and local levels[‡] • Harmonization and alignment of donor programmes with national policies, strategies and plans • Decentralization, where appropriate, to local levels • Comprehensive planning across the public/private sector
Enhancing mutual accountability. Strengthening accountability of health systems requires joint action at all levels to improve service organization and delivery, health policy in health and non-health sectors, public and private sectors, and people, towards a common goal.	• Health rights and entitlements • Performance based financing and contracting[‡] • Population registration with accountable care provider(s)[†] • Provider report cards and balanced scorecard[‡] • Patient satisfaction surveys[‡] • Patient-reported outcomes[‡]

(Continued)

TABLE 1.2 (CONTINUED) Framework on integrated people-centred health services: Strategies, strategic approaches, policy options, and interventions[4]

Strategic approaches	Policy options and interventions
Strategy 3: Reorienting the model of care	
Defining service priorities based on life course needs means appraising the package of health services offered at different levels of the care delivery system based on the best available evidence, covering the entire life course.	• Local health needs assessment based on existing patterns of communicable and non-communicable diseases[‡] • Comprehensive packaging of services for all population groups defined by means of a participatory and transparent process • Gender, cultural and age-sensitive services[†]
Revaluing promotion, prevention and public health means placing increased emphasis and resources on promotive, preventive and public health services.	• Monitoring population health status[†] • Population risk stratification[‡] • Surveillance, research and control of risks and threats to public health • Improved financial and human resources allocated to health promotion and disease prevention[†]
Building strong primary care-based systems promotes coordination and continuous care over time for people with complex health problems, facilitating intersectoral action in health. It calls for interprofessional teams to ensure the provision of comprehensive services for all. It prioritizes community and family-oriented models of care as a mainstay of practice with a focus on disease prevention and health promotion.	Primary care services with a family and community-based approach[†] Multidisciplinary primary care teams[†] Ensuring adequate financing directed to primary care[‡] Ensuring adequate human resources in primary care[†] Family medicine[†] Gatekeeping to access other specialized services[‡] Greater proportion of health expenditure allocated to primary care[‡]
Shifting towards more out-patient and ambulatory care. Service substitution is the process of replacing some forms of care with those that are more efficient for the health system; finding the right balance between primary care, specialized out-patient care and hospital in-patient care, recognizing that each has an important role.	• Home care, nursing homes and hospices[‡] • Repurposing secondary and tertiary hospitals for acute complex care only • Out-patient surgery • Progressive patient care
Innovating and incorporating new technologies. New information and communication technologies allow new types of information integration. When used appropriately, they can assure continuity of information, track quality, facilitate patients' empowerment and reach geographically isolated communities.	• Shared electronic medical record[‡] • Telemedicine[‡] • Health[‡]
Strategy 4: Coordinating services within and across sectors	
Coordinating care for individuals – a range of strategies that can help to achieve better continuity of care and enhance the patient's experience with services, particularly during care transitions. This approach also covers improved information flows and maintenance of trustworthy relationships with providers over time.	• Care pathways[‡] • Referral and counter-referral systems[‡] • Health navigators[‡] • Case management[‡] • Improved care transition[†] • Team-based care[†]
Coordinating health programmes and providers includes bridging the administrative, informational and funding gaps between levels of care and providers.	• Regional or district-based health service delivery networks[‡] • Purchasing integrated services • Integrating vertical programmes into national health systems • Incentives for care coordination[‡]

(Continued)

TABLE 1.2 (CONTINUED)   Framework on integrated people-centred health services: Strategies, strategic approaches, policy options, and interventions[4]

Strategic approaches	Policy options and interventions
Coordinating across sectors encompasses sectors such as social services, finance, education, labour, housing, the private sector and law enforcement, among others. It necessitates strong leadership from the health ministry to coordinate intersectoral action, including coordination for early detection and rapid response to health crises.	• Health in all policies • Intersectoral partnerships • Merging of health sector with social services • Working with education sector to align professional curriculum towards new skills needed[†] • Integrating traditional and complementary medicine with modern health systems • Coordinating preparedness and response to health crises
Strategy 5: Creating an enabling environment	
Strengthening leadership and management for change. All health-care professionals, and especially clinicians, need to be engaged in management and leadership for change in continuous partnership with local communities. Achieving people-centred and integrated care requires the application of complex processes that warrant an underlying change in management strategy.	• Transformational and distributed leadership • Change management strategies
Strengthening information systems and knowledge management. Development of information systems and an organizational culture that supports monitoring and evaluation, knowledge sharing and using data in decision-making is also a prerequisite for transformational change.	• Development of information systems[‡] • Systems research • Knowledge management
Striving for quality improvement and safety. These efforts include technical experiential and perceived quality.	• Quality assurance[†] • Creating a culture of safety[†] • Continuous quality improvement[†]
Reorienting the health workforce to ensure an appropriate skills mix in order to meet population health needs equitably and sustainably. Health workers must be organized around teams and supported with adequate processes of work, clear roles and expectations, guidelines, opportunities to correct competency gaps, supportive feedback, fair wages, and a suitable work environment and incentives.	Tackling health workforce shortages and maldistribution[†] Health workforce training[†] Multi-professional teams working across organizational boundaries[†] Improving working conditions and compensation mechanisms Provider support groups Strengthening professional associations[‡]
Aligning regulatory frameworks. Regulation plays a key role in establishing the rules within which professionals and organizations must operate – for example, in terms of setting new quality standards or paying for performance targets.	Aligning regulatory framework
Improving funding and reforming payment systems to promote adequate levels of funding and the right mix of financial incentives in a system that supports the integration of care between providers and settings and protection of patients against undue out-of-pocket expenditures on health.	• Assuring sufficient health system financing and aligning resource allocation with reform priorities • Mixed payment models based on capitation[‡] • Bundled payments[‡]

but rather focuses on improving the delivery of care through the alignment and harmonizing of the processes and information among the different services.
5. *Creating an enabling environment*: This process brings together all stakeholders to
undertake transformational change. This complex task will involve a diverse set
of processes to bring about the necessary changes in leadership and management,
information systems, methods to improve quality, reorientation of the workforce,
legislative frameworks, financial arrangements, and incentives.

Action towards each strategy is necessary at different levels of the health system and by different actors – from policy makers implementing strategic changes, to health managers organizing
and operating services differently, to health providers working differently across settings and
with patients and families, and to individuals, families and communities taking a more active
role in their own health and advocating for changes in the health system.

While Strategy 3 explicitly mentions reorienting health services to prioritize primary and
community-care services, PHC approaches, policies, and interventions underpin the successful implementation of all five strategies. The policy options and interventions most relevant to
family practice by nature of the discipline are indicated with † in Table 1.2. In addition, there
are a set of policy options and interventions that improve quality and people-centredness of primary care but may not be explicitly included in the implementation of family practice in many
settings. These actions, which would further enhance the performance of family practice, but
are seen in health systems with more robust support to primary care, are indicated with a ‡ in
Table 1.2.

Action to move towards more IPCHS can be taken by health system actors in all countries,
regardless of development context. However, the precise policy options and interventions, as
well as their prioritization, must be chosen in response to local needs and the level of health
system development, as well as values and preferences. Changes will be needed in governance
structures and financing schemes, in supply and type of health system inputs (including medicines, health information systems, health workforce), as well as service organization. Realization
of integrated people-centred health services relies on adequate health system inputs, including the availability, accessibility, and quality of health workers and the services they provide.
Integrated, people-centred health services require particular health workers with relevant skills,
including teams of health workers trained in family and community models of care.

Developing more integrated people-centred care systems has the potential to generate significant benefits to the health of all people and communities, to providers, and to health systems
(Table 1.3). These improvements include improved access to care, improved health and clinical
outcomes, better health literacy and self-care, increased satisfaction with care, improved job
satisfaction for health workers, improved efficiency of services, and reduced overall costs.[4,14]

THE ROLE OF FAMILY PRACTICE IN DELIVERING
INTEGRATED PEOPLE-CENTRED HEALTH SERVICES

A reorientation of health services towards primary care is foundational to the success of integrated people-centred health services and UHC. Decades of research comparing health system
performance confirm that health systems built on high-quality primary care result in better
health outcomes, better quality of life, more equitably, and at a lower relative cost compared
to those that overemphasize specialty or in-patient care. Research has also identified the characteristics that are shared by high-performing primary care systems, those qualities that most
ensure primary care serves its crucial function. These characteristics influence access, equity,
cost-effectiveness, safety, and effectiveness of primary care: first-contact, person-centred,

TABLE 1.3 The benefits of integrated people-centred health services[14]

For individuals and their families
- Increased satisfaction with care and better relationships with care providers
- Improved access and timeliness of care
- Improved health literacy
- Shared decision-making with professionals
- Increased involvement in care planning
- Increased ability to self-manage and control long-term health conditions
- Better coordination of care across different care settings

For communities
- Improved access to care, particularly for marginalized groups
- Improved health outcomes and healthier communities, including greater levels of health seeking behaviour
- Greater influence on, and better relationships with, care providers
- Increased trust in care services
- Participatory representation in decision making about health resources
- Care more responsive to community needs
- Improved response to outbreaks and health crises

For health professionals and community health workers
- Improved job satisfaction
- Improved workloads and reduced burnout
- Role enhancement including expanded skills with a wider range of responsibilities
- Education and training opportunities to learn new skills (such as team-based care)
- Appropriate incentives
- Opportunities for career advancement

For health systems
- Reduced adverse events
- Improved diagnostic accuracy
- Improved timeliness and appropriateness of referrals
- Reduced hospitalizations and reduced length of stay (owing to stronger primary and community care services and better management and coordination of care)
- Reduced duplication of health investments and services
- Resource utilization responsive to needs

continuous, comprehensive, coordinated, family and community oriented.[19] For primary care to deliver on the promises of being cost-effective and high-quality, these aspects of primary care must be fostered through health system policy and planning, and their performance continuously monitored and managed.

Given its foundational importance to health systems, primary care has never left the policy agenda; however, in many countries, primary care still does not receive the attention, resources or support necessary to fulfil its fundamental role. As a result, too often primary care falls short of its potential. For primary care to fulfil its critical role for future health needs, reforms must provide structural and financial support and reorient the models of health care to meet today's health demands.

Essential to the delivery of high-performing PHC is an available, accessible, and quality health workforce with an appropriate skill mix. The world is facing a shortage of 18 million health workers to achieve the SDGs.[5] Overcoming the deficit in health workers and the geographical imbalances in supply depends, in part, on maximizing efficiencies of a service delivery model that encourages team-based care at the primary level. Team-based care relies on various professional and non-professional cadres of health worker operating in closer collaboration and with a context-appropriate scope of practice. This approach responds to the health worker deficit by taking maximal advantage of the contribution of each member of the team, utilizing the particular capacities of different typologies of health worker, and allowing health workers to operate within the full scope of their profession while avoiding under-utilization of skills.[15]

Recognizing that the ideal composition of PHC teams will vary according to demographic, epidemiologic, health system, and country contextual needs, there is increasing recognition that mature, high-performing models of primary health care with family practice teams, including family medicine/general practice are important. Numerous country reviews demonstrate an improvement in quality of care and responsiveness through the introduction of family practice. Strong examples of this are illustrated in the case of Brazil (Box 1.2), China, Thailand (Box 1.3), and several countries in the Eastern Mediterranean region; even if the specific modalities of family medicine and family-oriented models of care differ by country.[16]

BOX 1.1   CASE STUDY: ESTABLISHING FAMILY MEDICINE AS A SPECIALTY TO STRENGTHEN PHC IN ESTONIA[18]

In 1993 Estonia established family medicine as a medical specialty with the goal of training a cadre of recognized PHC providers to serve as the point of first contact and gatekeepers to other health services. This focus on ensuring effective and quality PHC delivery was reinforced by national leadership through the Health Services Organization Act of 2002, which stated that the PHC provider must act as the first point of contact for care and that family doctors were to be the main providers of PHC. Patients are encouraged to have their first visit with a family doctor or they must pay the full cost of any subsequent specialist visit. Through geographical empanelment, practice-based patient registers are created and all Estonians must register with a family doctor. Patients with acute conditions must be able to have an appointment on the same day that it is requested and patients with chronic diseases must be able to see the physician within three days. To further decrease the reliance on specialists, the role of family doctors in the care of individuals with chronic illnesses has also been strengthened. Family doctors receive specialist training and, starting in the 1990s, evidence-based guidelines for the management of acute and chronic conditions were introduced to further standardize the provision of high-quality care. These guidelines provided family doctors with the knowledge to effectively manage these patients in the PHC setting and reduce complications and referrals to specialists. Most recently, telemedicine and EHealth have contributed to strengthening the PHC system.

As a result, Estonia has nearly achieved UHC through the Estonian Health Insurance Fund (EHIF) and Statutory Health Insurance (SHI) and 95% of its population is now covered for both curative and preventive services. More than 90% of the population reports knowing their primary care physician well and more than 85% of the population reports high levels of satisfaction with care. The country has been able to reduce the number of hospitals. With this shift in focus, patient access to and use of PHC has increased dramatically, as have health outcomes and service delivery measures.

BOX 1.2   A COMMUNITY-BASED APPROACH TO COMPREHENSIVE PRIMARY HEALTH CARE IN BRAZIL[20]

Since the mid-1980s, Brazil has converted the structure of its PHC workforce to a team-based model in which Family Health Teams composed of one physician, one nurse, and four to six Community Health Agents (CHAs) care for patient populations. The CHAs provide health promotion, prevention, education, screening, and data collection, often in the communities in which they live, allowing for the formation of strong relationships with community members. CHAs identify and then refer high-risk patients to the clinical team for treatment and then coordinate with clinicians to ensure that patients adhere to the treatment, attend follow-up appointments, and complete rehabilitation. The model utilizes "empanelment", a process of assigning patients to a primary health care team, as a core strategy for delivering quality care. Every individual is assigned to a Family Health Team (FHT); each FHT is responsible for providing services for up to 1000 families (approximately 4000 individuals) located in a specific geographical area. In coordination with the basic clinical staff in the FHT, separate primary health-care support teams provide additional care to empaneled populations. These support teams can include nutritionists, social workers, psychologists, obstetricians and gynaecologists, and public health workers.

The Family Health Program, with FHTs at its core, has proven successful and cost-effective, improving accessibility, comprehensiveness, continuity of care, and health outcomes for patients. The model has been effective in addressing health disparities, with the most dramatic improvements seen in the poorest municipalities.

BOX 1.3   SCALING UP FAMILY MEDICINE IN THAILAND AS PART OF UHC[11]

Hospital medicine was introduced in Thailand in 1988 and became the norm, conferring high social status and prestige on its practitioners, whereas ambulatory family practice was almost absent. When the Thai universal coverage scheme, known as the "30 Baht" scheme, was established in 2002, insured persons had to register with a contracted primary care unit. Thailand had limited experience with family medicine doctors, and the experience that did exist was primarily through demonstration sites in specific provinces.

In an effort to quickly obtain a large number of family medicine physicians at the early stage of the universal coverage policy, doctors who showed interest and had more than five years of experience in any branch of medicine, were offered conversion courses to familiarize them with the concepts of family medicine. These courses were planned on a twice yearly basis from 2001 to 2003. Altogether, 6127 doctors participated in this programme. Progress slowed from 2004–2011 when the fast track training ceased and only 106 family doctors were trained. In 2012, a new "family practice learning" programme was launched to provide postgraduate training in family medicine.

Scaling-up family medicine in Thailand has been a challenge. Perhaps most significant is the fact that almost all health professionals in Thailand come from a hospital-centred culture. Even if policy-makers are familiar with the concepts of primary care and family medicine, they are unlikely to have practical experience of it. Continuously clarifying the aims and strategies of family medicine has been important to sustain support for the reforms.

While the size and composition of a family practice team will vary with local disease burden and service delivery needs, family practice training shares characteristics, knowledge, and skills throughout the world. Family practice, by its nature, aligns with the characteristics of high-performing, people-centred PHC and, therefore, IPCHS. Family practice takes care of individuals in the context of family and community irrespective of race, culture, or social class. Due to their comprehensive training, family practice teams are enabled to care for most of life-course health needs (whole-person care), considering an individual's cultural, socioeconomic, and psychological background. This broad training also enables them to diagnose, manage, and treat undifferentiated problems effectively. Family practice teams provide ongoing continuity of care and are trained to coordinate and integrate care across the health system when needed. Family practice contributes to health systems, not only through direct service delivery and coordination, but also through management of health systems, policy advocacy, and leadership.[11]

As with any specialty, ensuring adequate competency within the family practice workforce requires providers have the information (knowledge), skills (knowing how to do), attitudes (knowing how to be), and experience to practice. This is true not only for clinical and medical-technical skills, but also for "soft skills" like communication, collaboration, and working in teams.

TABLE 1.4 Characteristics of high-performing primary care[19]

Characteristic	Description	Promoting factors (policy, management, facility level)
General	Addresses unselected health problems of the whole population; takes care of a defined practice population	• Broad expertise in prevention, promotion, diagnosis, treatment, rehabilitation and palliation for the life-course health needs • Population registration and rostering
First contact	Care is first sought from the primary care provider for most new health needs throughout life	• Strengthened gatekeeping function • Financial incentives for care seeking at PHC • Outreach services for the underserved including mobile units, transport systems and telemedicine
Person-centred	Care is respectful of and responsive to individual preferences, needs, goals and values, and sees the individual as a whole, in the context of their biological, psychological, and social context rather than a disease-oriented approach	• Health education • Informed consent • Shared decision making between individuals, families, carers and providers • Self-management including personal treatment plans • Cultural competency training • Goal-oriented care • Assessment of patient and provider experience
Continuous	People continue to seek care with their PHC team for ongoing health needs, enabling enduring and empowering relationships between people and their care team	• Population registration and rostering • Proactive population management for prevention and chronic disease • Promoting continuity with a care team as a goal • Skill mix of care team to provide comprehensive services and reduce referrals • Longitudinal patient records
Comprehensive	PHC is able to meet the vast majority of health needs people encounter throughout their lives; provides integrated health promotion, disease prevention, treatment, rehabilitation, and palliation for physical, psychological, and social needs	• Comprehensive package of services available and financed at primary care level • Transform education focusing on competency gaps • Multi-professional team-based care with a context-appropriate skill mix • Adequate infrastructure, medical technology, diagnostics, and medications available at PHC level to enable full scope of practice
Coordinated	When additional services are needed, primary care teams ensure coordination with other providers and settings, sharing both information and treatment plans	• Functional systems for referral and counter-referral with specialty care, hospital care, long-term care, home care and social care • Care pathways • Health navigators/case management • Improved care transitions • Team-based care • Incentives for care coordination • Electronic health records
Family & community-oriented	Addresses the health problems of individuals in the context of their family circumstances, their social and cultural networks, and life in the local community; takes care of a defined practice population	• Family practice • Training for informal carers • Informal carer networks • Peer support and expert patient groups • Community delivered care • Community representation on facilities' boards • Monitoring population health/disease burden • Population risk stratification

These competencies should be introduced, reinforced, and consolidated through pre-service education, continuing professional development, performance improvement, and leadership.[17]

The introduction and reinforcement of family practice approaches are integral to achieving more integrated and people-centred health systems. In turn, the attributes of family practice can be further enhanced through broader system transformations, such as:

- *Financing*: UHC to ensure affordability and access, adequate payment for family practice providers relative to providers in other settings and specialties to appropriately recruit providers, financial and professional incentives to promote PHC workforce retention.[18]
- *Quality of care infrastructure*: Performance management infrastructure, continuous quality improvement strategies, monitoring quality including both technical (health outputs and outcomes) and experiential aspects (such as communication, respect, dignity, self-management, relationship, facility infrastructure, and satisfaction), and accreditation mechanisms.

Table 1.4 describes additional policy options and interventions to support the key functions of family practice and PHC in the health system. How well PHC and family practice are supported by the broader health system will have implications for their ability to deliver on the promise of delivering high-quality care more equitably and in a cost-effective manner.[20]

CONCLUSION

Global health and health systems are facing novel challenges in the 21st century. To meet these challenges and achieve our collective goals requires a reorientation of health systems to be more integrated, and people-centred, built on a foundation of high-performing PHC. A family practice approach is a key method to achieving high-performing PHC, thereby promoting more integration and people-centredness, but also is reinforced by the broader system changes that are promoted through the WHO Framework on integrated people-centred health services. Only through context-appropriate application of these principles will the world be able to deliver on the promise of UHC.

REFERENCES

1. United Nations. *The Millennium Development Goals Report 2015*. New York: United Nations, 2015. Available from: http://www.un.org/millenniumgoals/2015_MDG_Report/pdf/MDG%202015%20rev%20%28July%201%29.pdf [Accessed 23 April 2018].
2. World Health Organization and the International Bank for Reconstruction and Development/The World Bank. *Tracking Universal Health Coverage: 2017 Global Monitoring Report*. Geneva: World Health Organization, 2017. Available from: http://documents.worldbank.org/curated/en/640121513095868125/pdf/122029-WP-REVISED-PUBLIC.pdf [Accessed 23 April 2018].
3. Countdown to 2015: maternal, newborn and child survival. Country profiles. Available from: http://www.countdown2015mnchcountdown2015mnch.org/country-profiles [Accessed 22 January 2018].
4. World Health Organization (WHO). Framework on integrated, people-centered health services: Report by the Secretariat. Geneva: World Health Organization, 2016. Available from: http://www.who.int/global-coordination-mechanism/working-groups/Policy_Brief_People-centerd_HC_EB138_37-en.pdf [Accessed 23 April 2018].
5. United Nations Office for Coordination of Human Affairs (OCHA). *Plan and Budget 2017*. March 2017. Available from: https://www.unocha.org/sites/unocha/files/OCHA_P_B_2017.pdf [Accessed 6 February 2018].
6. UNHCR. *Global Trends: Forced displacement in 2016*. Available from: www.unhcr.org/globaltrends2016 [Accessed 6 February 2018].

7. Centers for Disease Control and Prevention. Public Health Response to Humanitarian Emergencies, 2007–2016. Boyd AT, et al. *Supplement issue: Global Health Security Supplement,* s.l.: CDC, December 2017, Volume 23, Supplement.

8. United Nations. *Sustainable Development Goals: 17 Goals to Transform our World.* Available from: http://www.un.org/sustainabledevelopment/health/ [Accessed 22 nd January 2018].

9. WHO. *Universal health coverage (UHC).* Fact Sheet. Available from: http://www.who.int/mediacentre/factsheets/fs395/en/ [Accessed 22 January 2018].

10. WHO. World Health Report: *Health systems financing: the path to universal coverage.* Geneva: World Health Organization, 2010.

11. WHO. *People-Centred and Integrated Health Services: A Review of the Evidence.* Geneva: World Health Organization Press, 2015. WHO/HIS/SDS/2015.7.

12. WHO. World Health Assembly resolution 69.24, Strengthening integrated, people-centred health services, 2016.

13. WHO. Framework on integrated, people-centred health services: Report by the Secretariat, 2016. A69/39.

14. Starfield B, Shi L, Macinko J. Contribution of primary care to health systems and health. *Millbank Quarterly,* 2005; 83: 457–502.

15. WHO. *Global Strategy on Human Resources for Health: Workforce* 2030. Geneva: WHO Press, 2016. ISBN 978-92-4-151113-1.

16. Montenegro H, et al. Family medicine in lower- and upper-middle income countries. In: Kidd M. *The Contribution of Family Medicine to Improving Health Systems,* 2nd Edition. London: Radcliffe Publishing, 2013.

17. Pan American Health Organization (PAHO). *Core Competencies for Public Health: A Regional Framework for the Americas.* Washington, D.C.: PAHO, 2013. ISBN 978-92-75-11815-3.

18. Primary Health Care Performance Initiative (PHCPI). *Promising Practices Estonia: Establishing Family Medicine as a Specialty to Strengthen Primary Health Care.* 2015. Available from: https://phcperformanceinitiative.org/promising-practices/estonia [Accessed 3 February 2018].

19. Kidd M. *The Contribution of Family Medicine to Improving Health Systems: A Guidebook from the World Organization of Family Doctors,* 2nd Edition. London: Radcliffe Publishing, 2013. ISBN978-184619-954-7.

20. PHCPI: Promising Practices. *Brazil: A Community-Based Approach to Comprehensive Primary Care.* 2015. Available from: http://www.phcperformanceinitiative.org/tools/promising-practices/brazil [Accessed 3 February 2018].

CHAPTER 2

Scaling up family practice: Progressing towards universal health coverage in the Eastern Mediterranean Region

Zafar Mirza, Mohammad Assai Ardakani, and Hassan Salah

INTRODUCTION

Resolution World Health Assembly (WHA) Resolution 69.24 "Strengthening Integrated, People-Centred Health Services [IPCHS]" was endorsed by the 69th session of the WHA held in May 2016. The IPCHS resolution urged Member States to implement, as appropriate, the framework of action and make health-care systems more responsive to people's needs. In the Eastern Mediterranean Region Office this strategy is operationalized on the level of primary care service through the Family Practice (FP) programme. The Eastern Mediterranean Regional Committee, at its 63rd session in October 2016, adopted the resolution for Agenda item 4(a) "Scaling up family practice: progressing towards universal health coverage". The resolution urged Member States to incorporate the FP approach into primary health-care services as an overarching strategy to advance towards universal health coverage. (See Annex 1 for copy of the resolutions.)

Family practice can be defined as the health-care services provided by a family physician and his/her team, characterized by comprehensive, community-oriented, continuous, coordinated, collaborative, personal, and family services according to the needs of the individual and their family throughout the life course. Family practice, as a first point of contact with the health service, is key to delivering effective health services and improving health through holistic approaches that ensure continuity of care. Family practice can deal with the majority of the health and health-care needs of individuals, their families, and their communities.[1]

The terms "family practice" and "family medicine" are often used interchangeably in the literature. The latter is defined as the specialty of medicine concerned with providing comprehensive care to individuals and families, and integrating biomedical, behavioural, and social sciences. As an academic medical discipline, it includes comprehensive health-care services, education, and research.[1]

The scope of services delivered by family practice requires a multidisciplinary team and the spirit of family practice emphasizes a team approach to service delivery. The composition of the team may vary among countries depending on the service package, structures, resources, and availability of human resources, but should include at least a family physician and a nurse.

The evidence supports the contribution of a well-trained family practice team to improving access to quality care. The family physician and nurse are the backbone of family practice. However, there is a worldwide shortage of family physicians, with an acute situation in the Eastern Mediterranean Region.

As well as improving training capacities, labour market dynamics should be considered in attracting and retaining health workers to work in family practice settings. Most countries in the Region face workforce challenges in primary care settings, especially in rural and remote areas. Thus, adequate incentives should be introduced to attract physicians to specialization in family medicine, as well as for the other professionals that are included in the family practice team. These incentives, which may be both financial and non-financial, as well as professional and personal, need to be designed to meet both the needs of communities and the preferences of health professionals.

Almost half the countries in the Region have already adopted models of family practice and are at different stages of implementation. Several countries have yet to evolve workable family practice models due to challenges such as the lack of trained family physicians, lack of integration of prevention and care of non-communicable diseases and mental health, and weak information and surveillance systems.

ASSESSMENT OF FAMILY PRACTICE IN THE REGION

A survey of family practice in the Eastern Mediterranean Region was conducted by the World Health Organization (WHO) in 2014, and the results were updated in 2015–2016. The assessment covered 13 core elements of family practice in all 22 countries of the Region, covering the status of the service delivery infrastructure, challenges, opportunities, and key action-oriented interventions needed to improve service delivery through the family practice approach. The information was verified by the family practice focal points at national Ministries of Health.

Elements related to awareness of the community in the catchment area:

1. Registration of catchment population and development of family/individual folder
2. Development family physician roster
3. Community engagement

Elements related to the family health centre:

4. Essential health services package
5. Essential medicine list
6. Staff pattern based on family practice with updated job descriptions
7. Family health centre facility with standard sets of medical equipment and furniture

Elements related to management:

8. Training programmes based on the new job descriptions
9. Short-term on-the-job training for general practitioners

10. Treatment protocols
11. Referral system
12. Primary health-care information system for family practice
13. Quality and accreditation programme

The results of the assessment are summarized below into two major areas, service delivery and production of family physicians.

For the analysis of challenges, identification of priorities, and delineating options and strategies, the countries of the Region have been categorized in three broad groups based on population health outcomes, health system performance, and level of health expenditure: Group 1 countries in which socioeconomic development has progressed considerably over the last four decades, supported by high income; Group 2 countries, largely middle-income, which have developed an extensive public health service delivery infrastructure but which face resource constraints; Group 3 countries which face major constraints in improving population health outcomes as a result of lack of resources for health, political instability, conflicts, and other complex development challenges. Group 1 countries are Bahrain, Kuwait, Qatar, Saudi Arabia, Oman, and the United Arab Emirates. Group 2 countries are Egypt, the Islamic Republic of Iran, Iraq, Jordan, Lebanon, Libya, Morocco, Palestine, Syria, and Tunisia. Group 3 countries are Afghanistan, Djibouti, Pakistan, Somalia, Sudan, and Yemen (Tables 2.1 through 2.3).

SERVICE DELIVERY

The assessment found that 16 countries (72%) have included family practice in their national health policy and plans and have established a unit or appointed a focal point responsible for the programme, with 13 of these 16 countries having expansion plans for a family practice programme. The proportion of primary health-care facilities fully implementing a family practice programme and the number of family physicians varies tremendously between the three identified groups of countries and even between countries within each group.

In Group 1 countries, service delivery based on the family practice approach ranges from 14% to 100% of primary health-care facilities, with a range of 0% to 63% in Group 2 countries, and 0% to 14% in Group 3 countries. The density of family physicians to the general population varies from none to 1.84 per 10,000. Despite reasonably good political support for family practice programmes in Group 1 countries, the density of family physicians was less than 0.31 per 10,000 population in 2015.

Population registration of over 80% of the catchment population exists in six of the 22 countries, while in Bahrain, Kuwait, and the United Arab Emirates, physicians are assigned for a specific number of families. In the other countries, families may see a different physician or different facility on each visit, except in the Islamic Republic of Iran, Jordan, and Pakistan, but only in primary health-care facilities where the programme is being implemented.

All countries in the Region have developed an essential health services package, although full implementation exists in only 14 countries; in the other eight countries implementation is partial or non-existent. In addition, all have developed an essential medicines list. Although 17 countries reported the availability of medicines in primary health-care facilities, the extent of full availability at all times in all primary health-care facilities needs to be further assessed.

Referral guidelines are available in 15 countries but are functioning only in five countries. Non-emergency patients can approach hospitals directly in 14 countries. The assessment found that 17 countries do not have a functioning referral system despite the availability of guidelines.

Family or individual health folders/records are available in 14 countries, but huge variations between and within countries exist. Primary health-care facilities in 18 countries have

TABLE 2.1 Projection of family physician production to 2030 in Group 1 countries

Country	Annual family physician output (2015)	Family physician working at Ministry of Health primary health-care facilities (2015)	Family physician/ 10,000 (2015)	With current annual increase by 2030			With recommended annual increase by 2030			
				Cumulative trained family physicians with current annual increase	Family physicians working at Ministry of Health primary health-care facilities	Family physicians/ 10,000	Recommended increase/year to reach 3 family physicians/10,000 (%)	Cumulative trained family physicians with recommended increase (%)	Family physicians working at Ministry of Health primary health-care facilities	Family physicians/ 10,000
Bahrain	22	228	1.84	330	558	3.40	0	330	558	3.40
Kuwait	35	194	0.64	525	719	1.49	10	1223	1417	2.93
Oman	20	143	0.4	300	443	0.90	17	1313	1456	2.96
Qatar	12	139	0.64	180	319	1.16	15	657	796	2.88
Saudi Arabia	140	600	0.25	2100	2700	0.76	20	12,102	12,102	3.56
United Arab Emirates	10	36	0.05	150	186	0.15	36	3767	3803	3.08
Subtotal	239	1340	0.31	3585	4925	0.79	19	19,392	20,732	3.34

TABLE 2.2 Projection of family physician production to 2030 in Group 2 countries

Country	Annual family physician output (2015)	Family physicians working at Ministry of Health primary health-care facilities (2015)	Family physicians/ 10,000 (2015)	With current annual increase by 2030			With recommended annual increase by 2030			
				Cumulative family physicians trained with current annual increase	Family physicians working at Ministry of Health primary health-care facilities	Family physicians/ 10,000	Recommended increase/year to reach 3 family physicians/10,000 (%)	Cumulative family physicians trained with recommended increase (%)	Family physicians working at Ministry of Health primary health-care facilities	Family physicians/ 10,000
Egypt	180	256	0.05	2700	2956	0.29	29	35,701	35,957	3.51
Iran (Islamic Republic of)	810	0	0.10	12,150	12,150	1.33	10	28,309	28,309	3.10
Iraq	120	833	0.27	1800	2633	0.52	25	16,453	17,286	3.39
Jordan	35	221	0.33	525	746	0.80	19	2760	2981	3.19
Lebanon	27	19	0.09	405	424	0.82	16	1618	1637	3.17
Libya	10	100	0.17	150	250	0.34	30	2175	2275	3.05
Morocco	50	0	0.01	750	750	0.19	31	11,921	11,921	3.04
Palestine	4	18	0.05	60	78	0.12	39	1977	1995	3.11
Syrian Arab Republic	20	201	0.10	300	501	0.17	38	9033	9234	3.08
Tunisia	80	150	0.20	1200	1350	1.07	13	3654	3804	3.03
Subtotal	1336	1798	0.11	20,040	21,838	0.62	30	113,601	115,399	3.25

TABLE 2.3 Projection of family physician production to 2030 in Group 3 countries

Country	Annual family physician output (2015)	Family physician working at Ministry of Health primary health-care facilities (2015)	Family physicians/ 10,000 (2015)	With current annual increase by 2030			With recommended annual increase by 2030			
				Cumulative family physicians trained with current annual increase	Family physicians working at Ministry of Health primary health-care facilities	Family physicians/ 10,000	Recommended increase/year to reach 3 family physicians/10,000 (%)	Cumulative family physicians trained with recommended increase (%)	Family physicians working at Ministry of Health primary health-care facilities	Family physicians/ 10,000
Afghanistan	6	20	0.01	90	110	0.03	55	12,092	12,112	2.78
Djibouti	0	0	0.00	0	0	0.00	0	0	0	0.00
Pakistan	4	18	0.00	60	78	0.00	82	70,686	70,704	3.05
Somalia	0	0	0.00	0	0	0.00	0	0	0	0.00
Sudan	435	46	0.13	6525	6571	1.19	10	15,203	15,249	2.77
Yemen	0	3	0.00	0	3	0.00	0	0	3	0.00
Subtotal	445	87	0.02	6675	6762	0.18	50	97,981	98,068	2.57

information on morbidity and mortality, which is used for planning in 14 countries. Feedback to the primary care level from a higher level occurs in 12 countries. An electronic information system in primary health-care facilities is fully implemented in three countries, and partially in eight. Disaggregated data at the primary health-care level is available in 13 countries.

PRODUCTION OF FAMILY PHYSICIANS

Although there is a worldwide shortage of family physicians, the situation in the Region is acute and requires urgent action. To assess the situation, the WHO, in collaboration with Aga Khan University and the World Organization of Family Doctors (WONCA), conducted a literature review and key informant survey in 2014 on family medicine education and training programmes in the Region.

There are at least eight countries, including Afghanistan, Egypt, Iraq, Lebanon, Morocco, Pakistan, Saudi Arabia, and Sudan, that provide a postgraduate diploma in family medicine. The length of the course varies between six months, as in Sudan, to three years, as in Afghanistan.

Egypt runs a two-year diploma in family medicine, with an annual intake of 180 doctors, and recently introduced both the Egyptian and the Arab board training programmes. Jordan has a four-year residency programme with an annual intake of 35 doctors.

The Islamic Republic of Iran has recognized the need for cost-effective and preventive health care and has embarked on implementing the family medicine model. A two-year Master of Public Health (MPH) programme in family medicine through distant training was started in the Islamic Republic of Iran in 2015; the duration of the course was recently reduced to one year for general practitioners with work experience at the primary health-care level. This programme has an annual intake of 500. Currently, eight universities in the Islamic Republic of Iran have graduated 60 postgraduate students with a family medicine MPH or diploma degree. The duration of training for diploma holders is two years and three years for MPH holders.

Recently, Morocco developed a bridging programme, where general practitioners with four years' work experience can participate in a two-year training course managed by the Public Health Institute in Rabat, leading to a diploma in family health. The two-year training course is divided into different theory and practical phases, with the practical sessions held inside the participants' own health-care facilities. Thus far, 25 physicians with four years' work experience at the primary health-care level have enrolled in the programme. A similar course is planned in eight other universities in Morocco. Graduates who are government employees receive a monthly financial incentive to undertake this training.

Saudi Arabia started a 14-month diploma in family medicine in 2008; currently, it runs for 24 months with an annual intake of 70–75 students. A diploma in family medicine exists in Sudan, lasting six months, and offering career opportunities in Saudi Arabia after completion. This is in addition to a two-year master's programme in Sudan that allows physicians to get training on-the-job and postgraduate certification in family medicine.

CHALLENGES IN SCALING UP FAMILY PRACTICE IN THE REGION

Analysis of the information gathered highlighted several challenges in scaling up family practice in the Region. These challenges are outlined below, grouped into the four categories of governance, service delivery, production of family physicians, and partnership with private providers.

GOVERNANCE

Family practice has strong political support in Group 1 countries, limited support in Group 2 countries, and support that is limited or absent in Group 3 countries.

The health system infrastructure in several Group 2 and Group 3 countries is not consistent with family practice requirements. Family practice is still a new concept to many of the health ministries in the Region and there is often insufficient political support to strengthen the necessary interventions.

There is a lack of technical skills for family practice implementation among many Ministry of Health professional staff and managers. In addition, almost half of Group 2 countries have experienced political changes in recent years, including Egypt, Iraq, Libya, the Syrian Arab Republic, and Tunisia. As a result, family practice has not been recognized as a long-term priority in several countries.

The absence of a well-functioning district health system, inadequate capacity among district health authorities, lack of planning, monitoring and supervision capacities, and limited involvement of communities, have all led to very limited success in decentralization efforts.

Although some countries of the Region are implementing family practice, there is a need for a regional roadmap/strategy in line with the requirements of each group of countries. This would assist Member States in developing their own national work plan to support strengthening primary health care through the family practice approach.

SERVICE DELIVERY

All Group 1 countries, and a few Group 2 countries, have a policy of adopting the family practice approach. While some progress has been made, implementation has been fragmented and patchy. For instance, while all countries provide an essential health services package, quality of care remains a major challenge in most primary health-care facilities.

Due to the limited quality of services at public primary health-care facilities, there has been a proliferation of the unregulated private health sector in all countries of the Region. For example, 62% of so-called primary health-care services and ambulatory care services in Egypt, and 83% in Pakistan, are provided by the private health sector, which is associated with high out-of-pocket spending in most countries.

Patient safety, quality, and accreditation of health services are serious challenges in all countries. Regional studies in Egypt, the Islamic Republic of Iran, Iraq, Jordan, Morocco, and Sudan have found a prevalence of adverse events of 18% among in-patients. Many countries have developed national accreditation programmes, while others rely on external accreditation programmes.

Weak referral systems are leading to high utilization of hospitals, accounting for 60–80% of Ministry of Health budgets, while budget allocation to primary health-care services in most countries of the Region remains very limited.

Integration of care for non-communicable diseases and mental health in the essential health services package continues to be a challenge. A WHO assessment in 2014 found that only 50% of primary health-care services in five countries conducted screening for diabetes and hypertension.[2]

Because of demographic transition and population ageing, Group 1 countries have moved towards limited scale home health-care for the elderly and people with a disability. Countries in all three groups need initiatives to increase provision of home health care.

Although community-based initiatives have been piloted in the Region for over two decades, through community health worker programmes in Afghanistan, Egypt, the Islamic Republic of Iran, Pakistan, Somalia, and Sudan, community engagement needs to be scaled up in countries as an integral part of primary health care and the delivery of family practice services.

PRODUCTION OF FAMILY PHYSICIANS

Lack of central workforce planning is a key challenge in many countries, along with a lack of coordination between Ministries of Health, Ministries of Higher Education, and academic institutions.

The shortage of family physicians is a major challenge caused by several factors, including the absence of a vision for family practice, limited community awareness, reflected in the absence of community demand for family physicians, and often undefined professional career paths for family physicians in both the public and private sectors.

PARTNERSHIP WITH PRIVATE PROVIDERS

Ministry of Health efforts mainly have been directed towards implementing family practice in the public sector, which in many countries provides less than 30% of out-patient services, private clinics being the major providers in these countries.[3] International experience shows that the private sector can play an important role in delivering family practice services.

Weak regulation mechanisms for public–private partnerships, lack of a clear mechanism for contracting the private sector for the provision of primary health-care services, and lack of performance criteria are all major challenges in the implementation of family practice.

PRODUCTION OF FAMILY PHYSICIANS AND RECOMMENDED ACTIONS

Given the huge gaps that exist in the production of family physicians in the Region, this section examines the current availability of family physicians and provides options for overcoming the shortage.

The annual output of trained family physicians in 2015 was around 2020 for the 22 countries in the Region, representing 0.08 family physicians/10,000 population. Taking the current annual production of family physicians and population projections to the year 2030 into account, the expected ratio (without considering those who may leave family practice and those who retire) will increase to 0.42 family physicians/10,000 population if countries follow with the same trend of inputs for family medicine postgraduate training, including all postgraduate family medicine certified degrees.

WONCA recommends three to six family physicians per 10,000 population, as exists in most European countries. To reach an optimal number of three family physicians/10,000 population by the year 2030, countries in the Region need to increase their annual production of family physicians by different rates, varying from 0% to 36% in Group 1 countries, 10% to 39% in Group 2 countries, and 10% to 82% in Group 3 countries. Delivering family practice services cannot be done through public sector providers alone and the implementation of family practice must extend to private sector health-care providers.

Working towards the Sustainable Development Goals target for achievement of universal health coverage by the year 2030 and focusing on the acute shortage of qualified family physicians in the Region, two scenarios have been devised. In the first scenario, if the existing rate of production of family physicians continues, then only Bahrain will reach, and be able to maintain, the ratio of three family physicians/10,000 population by 2030. In the second scenario, the required rate of increase in the production of family physicians needed to achieve 100% coverage with three family physicians/10,000 population by 2030 has been calculated. The recommended annual increase in this scenario ranges from 3.56% for Saudi Arabia to 2.77% for Sudan.

A complementary strategy is to implement a national bridging programme to upgrade general practitioners as family physicians. In this chapter a general practitioner refers to a physician who has completed a basic undergraduate medical degree but has not received specialized training focused on the core principles of primary care/family practice, or training in another specialty. A six-month online course has been developed by WHO and the American University of Beirut to orient and train general practitioners to become family physicians. This course can be part of a national bridging programme and is not a replacement for the full training of family physicians but serves as an interim arrangement to upskill existing general practitioners. Once the existing generation of general practitioners has been transformed into family physicians, it is expected that all new medical graduates will have to undertake full training to become qualified family physicians. Different models of bridging programmes of varying lengths are available.

Assessment of primary health care in the 22 countries of the Region has found that 90% to 97% of primary health-care facilities are currently managed by general practitioners, who work without further specialized training after graduating from medical school. The number of general practitioners working at public primary health-care facilities varies, including 15,000 in Egypt, 9,000 in the Islamic Republic of Iran, and 6,000 in Saudi Arabia.

A WHO assessment of the status of family medicine education and training in 2014 found that almost 80% of medical schools in the countries of the Region did not have academic departments of family medicine, and the situation was worse among the newly emerging private medical schools. Family medicine, as a specialty, is less attractive to medical graduates compared with other specialties; the specialty is not well recognized by the public and other health professionals in many countries, and currently offers lesser pay and incentives in some countries, especially in Group 2 and 3 countries.[4]

In addition, the lack of role models for medical students, the nature of undergraduate medical education experience in family medicine, with much training being hospital-based, and the lack of exposure to family medicine at undergraduate level, do not augur well for the scaling up of family medicine departments in medical schools. Challenges include medical school curricula that are vertical, non-integrated, and hospital-orientated, often based in university hospitals, and health systems that are mainly curative with a lack of the continuity of care needed given the increasing burden of non-communicable diseases and other chronic health problems.

Successful transitional retraining programmes for general practitioners have been developed in other regions of the world in countries as diverse as Bulgaria, Croatia, the Czech Republic, Estonia, Hungary, Kyrgyzstan, Lao People's Democratic Republic, Latvia, Lithuania, Poland, Portugal, the Republic of Korea, Romania, the Russian Federation, Sri Lanka, Turkey, and Vietnam. Some countries also retrain specialists, including those who had specialized in paediatrics and internal medicine, to become family doctors.[5]

A national bridging programme for upskilling general practitioners in family medicine in each country in the Region is proposed. This will have the following outlines:

1. The objective will be to improve the technical skills of general practitioners and to overcome the shortage of family physicians.
2. The training will be compulsory and cover all general practitioners working in public facilities with more than five years' work experience and no postgraduate specialty training or qualifications.
3. To bridge the gap, it is recommended that there is a maximum of 12 months of training for general practitioners. The first six months will be through the WHO online course on building capacities of general practitioners in family medicine; WHO is providing training on the online course to trainers in all countries of the

Region. Each country will decide on the duration of the practical training element and the degree acquired.
4. To cover 100% of general practitioners with the training, each country will require a certain rate to go through training annually.

PROJECTION OF FAMILY PHYSICIAN PRODUCTION TO 2030 IN COUNTRIES BY GROUP ACCORDING TO THE DIFFERENT SCENARIOS

Group 1 countries

In Group 1 countries, annual production of family physicians has been increased over the last few years reaching 239 in 2015, with a ratio of 0.31 family physicians per 10,000 population (Table 2.1).

Taking into consideration the current production of family physicians and population projections, the ratio will be tripled by 2030 to reach 0.79 family physicians per 10,000 population.

To reach the optimal ratio of one family physician per 3300 population, taking into consideration population projections by 2030, each country needs to increase its annual production of family physicians. The increases required vary from 10% for Kuwait to 36% for the United Arab Emirates. Bahrain will be the only country to reach the optimal number of family physicians by 2030 given the current annual production of 22 family physicians per year.

Country training capacity varies from 30 family medicine departments in medical schools in Saudi Arabia to one department in most of the other five Group 1 countries.

Meanwhile, to improve the quality of service provision at the primary health-care level, it is recommended to enrol general practitioners in a compulsory transitional training programme that should cover 100% of the current general practitioners in the Group 1 countries (a total of 10,969 doctors).

Group 2 countries

In Group 2 countries, annual production of family physicians has increased over the last few years reaching 1336 in 2015, with a ratio of 0.11 family physicians per 10,000 population (see Table 2.2).

Taking into consideration the current production of family physicians and population projections, the ratio will be 3.5 times more by 2030, reaching 0.62 family physicians per 10,000 population. The expected ratio varies among countries from 0.12 in Palestine to 1.33 in the Islamic Republic of Iran, which has initiated major family medicine programmes in several universities.

To reach the optimal ratio of one family physician/3300 population, taking into consideration population projections by 2030, each country needs to increase its annual production of family physicians. The increases required vary from 10% for the Islamic Republic of Iran to 39% for Palestine.

Similar to Group 1 countries, it is recommended that Group 2 countries enrol general practitioners in a compulsory transitional training programme on family medicine, preferably of less than 12 months' duration. The training should cover 100% of current general practitioners (a total of 45,988 doctors).

Group 3 countries

Group 3 countries generally have a very limited annual production of family physicians. Sudan is the only country with a reasonable annual production, of 435 family physicians. It is

TABLE 2.4 Framework for action on advancing family practice towards achieving universal health coverage in the countries of the Eastern Mediterranean Region

Major areas	Actions for countries Short term (24 months)	WHO support
Governance and regulation	Incorporate family practice programme as an overarching strategy for service provision within the framework of universal health coverage and national health policies and plans. Assign and provide resources to the primary health-care unit in the Ministry of Health to coordinate family practice activities. Update regulations for supporting implementation and expansion of a family practice programme. Establish national training programme for general practitioners on family medicine. Develop a health information and reporting system to monitor primary health-care performance. Introduce professional/financial incentives for physicians to enrol in postgraduate family medicine programmes. Strengthen public–private partnerships in service delivery through the family practice approach.	Assist Member States to publish and disseminate good practices and short policy briefs on the family practice programme. Assist in making rational projections for production of family physicians and family practice team members. Develop and present evidence case, essential standards for family practice elements and operational guide for adaptation by countries.
Scaling up of family medicine training programme	Advocate with deans of faculties of medicine to establish, strengthen, and expand family medicine departments. Follow WHO recommended annual increase of family physicians up to 2030. Implement WHO online short training programme of general practitioners in family medicine. Develop continuous professional development programmes for recertification in family medicine. Harmonize curriculum, evaluation, and standards of family medicine board certified programmes. Integrate a modified family medicine teaching programme in medical schools.	Prepare policy briefs and present to deans and chancellors of medical institutions on the need to strengthen family medicine departments. Scale up online six-month training courses for orientation of general practitioners on family medicine. Establish a group of regional experts to review and harmonize family medicine training programmes across the Region.
Financing	Introduce family practice financing as an integral part of the national health financing strategy, ensuring availability of sustainable funding for implementing/expanding family practice. Engage in strategic purchasing for family practice from public and private providers. Design and cost essential health services packages to be implemented through family practice and identify target population to be covered. Agree on implementation modalities of essential health services packages delivered by public/nongovernmental/private health sector providers. Build capacity to undertake contracting for family practice including outsourcing of services provision. Decide on and pilot "provider payment modalities", for example, capitation, case payment, and necessary performance-based payment or their combinations.	Update tools and guidelines for design and costing of essential health services packages and provide training in their use and implementation. Synthesize and disseminate country experiences in financing family practice under different health financing systems and provide related technical support to Member States. Disseminate WHO guidelines and provide technical support to Member States on strategic purchasing and provider (public/private) payment methods.

(*Continued*)

TABLE 2.4 (CONTINUED) Framework for Action on Advancing Family Practice towards Achieving Universal Health Coverage in the Countries of the Eastern Mediterranean Region

Major areas	Actions for countries Short-term (24 months)	WHO support
Integration and quality assurance of services	Use 13 core family practice elements as a guide to improve quality of primary care services. Assess service delivery to review integration of priority programmes in primary health-care services. Introduce functional integration of health services through multitasking and staff training. Implement integration in all programmes in specific areas: training, supervision, health promotion, health information system, drug supply, and laboratory services. Develop training and continuous professional development programmes for primary health-care workers on improving quality of service delivery. Strengthen supervision and monitoring functions addressing quality of care. Introduce/institutionalize accreditation programmes to support primary health-care performance. Enforce accreditation of primary health-care facilities.	Continue to share best practices and exchange experiences. Develop an integrated district health system based on the family practice approach assessment tool. Expand the regional framework on quality indicators at primary care level.
Community empowerment	Launch community-wide campaign to encourage population to register with reformed health facilities in the catchment population (including civil registration and vital statistics). Strengthen, initiate, and support training of community health workers/outreach teams and scaling up of home health care as an integral part of the family practice approach. Encourage the health volunteers approach to bridge households with health-care facilities and train volunteers in the use of WHO manuals. Organize orientation training for staff of health facilities on communication skills. Develop multimedia educational campaigns.	Update tools and guides for community engagement in family practice. Provide technical support in developing a communication strategy for family practice programmes. Exchange successful experiences of community volunteer programmes in support of family practice. Provide technical support to increase access to primary health-care services through community health workers, outreach teams and home health-care strategies.

recommended that Sudan should increase its annual ratio by 10% to reach three family physicians per 10,000 population by 2030 (Table 2.3).

Countries in Group 3 need to enrol general practitioners in a transitional compulsory training programme on family medicine, preferably of less than 12 months' duration. The training should cover 100% of current general practitioners (total of 178,551 doctors). Based on the total number of general practitioners per country, there is a need to enrol a certain percentage of general practitioners every year until 2030, taking into consideration that the actual number of trained general practitioners every year will be less than the year before.

FRAMEWORK FOR ACTION ON ADVANCING FAMILY PRACTICE TOWARDS UNIVERSAL HEALTH COVERAGE IN THE REGION

This chapter proposes a framework for action on advancing family practice towards universal health coverage that consists of the following five major areas with actions outlined for countries and WHO (Table 2.4).

1. *Governance*: Health systems need to be reoriented and their capacity needs to be developed to support family practice. Governments need to ensure political commitment and develop appropriate polices, regulations, and prepayment schemes for the provision of an essential health services package through the family practice approach.
2. *Scaling up of family medicine training programmes*: To increase the number of licensed family physicians, the discipline of family medicine needs to be established and strengthened. As a transitional arrangement, suitable bridging programmes are needed to upgrade general practitioners to family physicians.
3. *Financing*: Countries need to enhance financing, undertake costing of essential health services packages, and practice strategic purchasing.
4. *Integration and quality assurance of services*: A range of well-selected, quality assured health services should be provided in an integrated manner through family practice backed up by a robust referral system. Health facilities must be accredited.
5. *Community empowerment*: Community leaders and volunteers can bridge households to health-care facilities. Community participation in health care needs to be strengthened by building on local systems of engagement and by respecting local cultures and belief systems.

CONCLUSION

The family practice approach is considered to be the best way to provide integrated health services at the primary health-care level. With few exceptions, the countries of the Region are at a low level of family practice development. Strong political commitment is needed to improve access, coverage, acceptability, and quality of health services, and to ensure continuity of care, through the family practice approach.

Taking into consideration the difference between the three groups of countries in the Region in terms of annual production of family physicians, current number of general practitioners, and family medicine training capacity, there is no one solution to suit all. Countries need to be committed to increase the production of family physicians by the year 2030 to have one family physician per 3300 population. Meanwhile, countries need to implement a national training programme to upskill existing general practitioners about family practice.

Despite the daunting multiple challenges, a framework for action to advance family practice to support universal health coverage in the Region can help improve the situation by employing transitional and long-term strategies to overcome the acute shortage of family physicians in many countries and strengthen health systems to support family practice. WHO can assist country efforts in establishing robust family practice in the Region. Countries are urged to support family practice programmes as a national health goal and to incorporate them in their national health policies and plans.

Annex 1:
REGIONAL COMMITTEE FOR THE
EASTERN MEDITERRANEAN

EM/RC63/R.2
October 2016

Sixty-Third Session
Agenda item 4 (a)

Scaling up family practice: Progressing towards universal health coverage

The Regional Committee,

Having discussed the technical discussion paper on scaling up family practice: progressing towards universal health coverage;

Recalling resolutions WHA69.24 on strengthening integrated people-centred health services and

EM/RC60/R.2 on universal health coverage and;

Recalling also the World Health Report 2008 on primary health care and the World Health Report 2010 on health systems financing;

Recognizing the key elements of WHO's comprehensive approach to universal health coverage, which embraces the values and principles of primary health care including community engagement;

1. **CALLS ON** Member States to:
    1.1 Incorporate the family practice approach into primary health-care services as an overarching strategy to advance towards universal health coverage;
    1.2 Strengthen the capacity of family medicine departments in the public health institutes and medical education institutions in order to increase the number of family physicians to reach 3 per 10,000 population by 2030 and also establish bridging programmes for general physicians;
    1.3 Strengthen public–private partnerships in service delivery through the family practice approach;
    1.4 Ensure availability of sustainable funding for implementing/expanding family practice as an integral part of the national health financing strategy;
    1.5 Strengthen and cost essential health services packages in order to deliver these through health-care facilities providing health services based on family practice for the catchment population;
    1.6 Put in to place a system for monitoring and evaluation of training in family practice;
    1.7 Adopt WHO quality indicators for improving services at primary health-care facilities.

2. **REQUESTS** the Regional Director to:
    2.1 Provide technical support to Member States to establish and strengthen provision of integrated health services based on a family practice approach;
    2.2 Establish a group of experts to review and harmonize family medicine training programmes across the Region, and expand the use of the online bridging training programme for general physicians;
    2.3 Report on progress in implementation of this resolution to the 65th and 67th sessions of the Regional Committee.

REFERENCES

1. Boelen C, World Organization of National Colleges, Academies, and Academic Associations of General Practitioners/Family Physicians. *World Health Organization. Improving Health Systems: the Contribution of Family Medicine: A Guidebook*. Singapore: World Organization of Family Doctors; 2002.
2. World Health Organization, Quality assessment of service provision at primary health care level. Unpublished WHO 2014.
3. World Health Organization. *Role and Contribution of the Private Sector in Moving Towards Universal Health Coverage*. Cairo: WHO Regional Office for the Eastern Mediterranean, 2016 Available from: http://applications.emro.who.int/dsaf/EMROPUB_2016_EN_18890.pdf?ua=1 [Accessed 22 August 2016].
4. World Health Organization. Current Status of Family Medicine Education and Training in Eastern Mediterranean Region. WHO; 2014.
5. Kidd M (ed). *The Contribution of Family Medicine to Improving Health Systems: A Guidebook from the World Organization of Family Doctors*, 2nd edition. London: Radcliffe Health; 2013.

CHAPTER 3

Universal health coverage: Challenges and opportunities for the education of the health workforce

Amanda Howe

Note: In this chapter "student" or "learner" is frequently used without specific reference to undergraduate/basic or postgraduate setting, and may also refer to different health professional groups, as the educational principles are similar. If a specific discipline for the primary care setting is referenced, this will usually be indicated in the text.

INTRODUCTION

The stated intention of universal health coverage (UHC) is to allow all people to access affordable good quality health services when needed. This requires both availability of a health workforce with appropriate knowledge and skills at all points of care, and a health system that supports delivery of appropriate care for different individuals across the lifecycle. Any country with a genuine wish to implement UHC will need to consider the implications for training and retaining of the necessary workforce, and encourage those responsible (usually universities, ministries, professional societies, and accrediting bodies) to align their programmes to this overall strategic goal. As current models of care and speciality workforce supply patterns may not be adequate for the achievement of UHC, this implies a review and reform of both workforce distribution and training capacity and curricula. This chapter therefore considers the principles of appropriate training, some of the challenges that may occur, and the scope of considerations that can achieve meaningful UHC. It also gives some examples of good practice from the Eastern Mediterranean Region.

CURRICULUM CONTENT FOR UHC

Whether training doctors, nurses, or other health workers, there are some core professional principles which underpin UHC – the first is the principle of *equity*, defined as *"the principle and practice of ensuring the fair and just allocation of resources, programmes, opportunities and decision-making to all groups, while reflecting different needs and requirements".** Learning to put the needs of others above one's own, and to treat people who are very different from oneself with respect and compassion, requires very different educational approaches from the learning of technical skills or bioscientific facts.

Another is the principle of "generalism"– if health workers are to address promotive, preventive, curative, rehabilitative, and palliative aspects of care, they will need to gain and be willing to utilize a broad range of knowledge, even within their own subject or scope of practice.[1] For example, a cancer specialist team not only should be able to diagnose and treat a patient with cancer, but also assist them and their families with the major psychological impacts of having a serious illness and life-changing therapies (e.g. disfiguring surgery or chemotherapy causing sub-fertility); and work with them until the end if cancer recurs. Similarly, primary health-care workers need to be able to intervene and care for patients with more than one type of problem. The young man who is noted to smoke heavily, has a family history of diabetes, and who has a low paid job in a local factory can potentially start a very important discussion about preventive self-care while he is attending because of a dog bite. The elderly lady who has hypertension and type 2 diabetes, whose daughter mentions she is "getting very muddled" while she is attending for a routine review, may need a "switch" to a general medical assessment to avoid preventable risks and deteriorations, and the daughter also needs follow-up.

A third principle is "integration" – the World Health Organization (WHO) recommends care which is integrated and person-centred, by which is meant a genuine intention and ability to engage with people and communities in their many unique and diverse aspects, and to work with as many different aspects of care at the same time as is feasible and effective.[2] Learning to be person-centred rather than disease-centred is a key aspect of a modern curriculum, and again may need different methods of both learning and assessment to become embedded in the professional's practice.

And finally, the principle of "academic analysis", whereby the health worker routinely asks themselves why something is occurring, considers the evidence base that can be applied to the problem, and looks for ways to improve and learn from each problem in practice.[3]

Working with these four principles of equity, generalism, integration, and academic analysis, we can begin to see why modern health professional training needs to be different to deliver UHC. An example from the author's own professional lifecycle shows a stark contrast between medical training in the United Kingdom in the 1970s and 40 years later (Table 3.1).

METHODS FOR TRAINING THE MODERN HEALTH WORKFORCE

A simple way to approach curriculum reform is to ensure that curriculum headings, skills, and learning outcomes include major domains such as "personal and professional", "communication", and "academic", as well as "scientific" and "clinical".[4] In addition, at postgraduate level service, management competencies such as "clinical governance" or "patient safety" may also be useful to ensure that a patient and systems overview becomes the norm for practice. The way in which the desired learning outcomes are attained can then be planned, and the best mix

---

* As used in the World Organization of Family Doctors policies on equity.

TABLE 3.1 Modernizing medical education: Changes in the last 40 years in the United Kingdom

1976

Preclinical – clinical split – with no patient contact in first three years

Lectures/labs/dissection room are the main locations of learning in early years of course

Ward based apprenticeship in Years 4 to 6 mainly attached to in-patient wards of hospitals

Disease-based learning focused on bioscience and body systems – e.g. Anatomy, Pharmacology

Only one week of family medicine in six years of medical student training. Few family medicine academic units, usually with very weak, if any, presence in the medical school at any level

No required postgraduate training prior to entering general practice/family medicine as an unsupervised independent medical practitioner

2016

Family medicine academic presence in all medical schools

Community placements throughout medical student training with patient contact through family doctors from Year 1

Integrated theory and practice – lectures, seminars, skill sessions, clinical, and patient cases all aligned

Applied learning methods, including problem-based learning and simulations of clinical and consultation skills

Principle of "learning from people about people" applied to medical training

General practitioner/family medicine-led teaching is a minimum of around 25% of undergraduate clinical time

Postgraduate family medicine speciality training is mandatory for becoming a family doctor (and 40% of medical graduates train to become family doctors)

Other speciality training often also includes postgraduate placements in family medicine

Training input provided by family medicine to other disciplines – e.g. family medicine tutors involved in nursing and pharmacist student placements to increase awareness of population needs, social diversity, and dealing with people with multiple care needs

Increased emphasis on medicine and nursing as university academic qualifications, including identification of relevant literature and projects, writing essays, and presentations

---

of educational methods will depend on who the learners are, their prior background, and the resources available.

Lectures are suitable for key factual overviews, but adult learning methods need to be developed in training, where health professionals learn to identify their learning needs and how to meet these. Self-directed learning leading to case presentations, student-led seminars, and responsibility for specific projects, will all enable the move towards educational autonomy. Peer and tutor feedback and formal assessment of the learners' "products" ensures that we learn to produce good work, and meet our team's needs as well as our own. Simulations, both of technical tasks and of consultation skills, are a crucial part of rehearsing new skills in a safe way before live-patient contact is needed, and many good resources exist to show how to do this in an increasingly challenging way over a training period. The precise tasks and scenarios will, of course, vary according to the professional group, their prior experience, and the desired outcomes.

Repeated patient contact is crucial to learning to apply the needed skills in the clinical and personal environment, and an appropriate case mix will need to be assured for the specific course. For example, Year 1 residents can start with stable patients with good cognition and known diagnoses coming for review, then progress through patients with known cardiac, respiratory, endocrine, and neurological conditions, coming later in their training to patients with undiagnosed problems and multiple complex conditions, including mental illness and dementia. Even in working environments, patients can be selected by supervisors for the needs of the learner and keeping a list of patients seen allows identification of gaps in experience. Attention to social demography is also needed: has the learner had a chance to work with patients across the range of age, gender, ethnicity, educational background, and life experiences so that they develop the skills of flexible communication with consistent empathic and clinical attention?

Specific projects may be appropriate to enable learners to develop an awareness of population health needs and the duty of health workers to attend to overall needs as well as individual demands. Community-oriented primary care is a method that has frequently been used in this context and can be a "win win" if designed to assist communities to identify and better meet their own health needs. Students will be proud to have contributed something to the system and will be more motivated than they would be by a purely theoretical project. Similarly, doing a quality improvement or audit project for a clinical team will develop useful skills while delivering something of value to the local setting, and will build on their professional commitment to equity – *"do we know who is not attending for their well women checks and what are the barriers to this?"*; generalism and integration – *"how many patients are attending our clinic for routine chronic disease reviews, and how feasible would it be to bring them to one appointment rather than organize these by disease based clinics?"*; and person-centredness – *"let's find a validated survey that measures this, adapt it for our setting if needed, and see how we are doing!"* Educational leads for the training can agree suitable projects for the learning outcomes and assessment criteria, while giving local clinicians and communities a choice of topic and design.

Finally, much modern education benefits from the Internet, with its opportunities for online courses, group tutorials with learners in different sites, access to relevant resources (YouTube videos of how to perform technical examinations and tasks, access to academic literature, online lectures, etc.), and self-directed learning. This can avoid the need for students to be in the same place to be taught, and support consistent supervision and mentorship even while learners are at locations remote from the university or main training centre. It also makes tutor feedback/liaison easier and quicker. These are just a few of the educational approaches that enable a modern integrated curriculum to continuously link new learning with the context of the patient and the engagement of the student as an active learner and developing health professional.

CHANGING THE LEARNING ENVIRONMENT

The implications of such approaches include a need for exposure to communities outside the hospital setting, and to a variety of settings where services are needed but which may fall outside the immediate geographical environment of the university or teaching hospital. The "usual" principles of creating an effective learning environment apply – clinical opportunities that are consistent with the needs of the learner, well supervised, with timely opportunities for observation and feedback, also consistently drawing on the relevant evidence to make informed and "evidence-based" decisions.[5]

It is also important to note that many students, especially those entering medical training, will themselves come from privileged backgrounds where they may have had little contact with those from less economically advantaged backgrounds. Even in a diverse world, people tend to have family and social networks within specific ethnic or faith groups, and so assisting health workers in training to have a positive experience of those who are different from themselves is an important step in the ability to undertake person-centred and inclusive care. Barriers of gender, age, and race can be overcome, as can fear of dealing with frailty, pain, psychological disturbance, and addictions, by supervised exposure to selected patients in a "safe" setting where learners gain competence and confidence. Role models are important, so that those in positions of respect and power as clinical tutors manifest person-centredness, and prioritize care of the more needy during their teaching and clinical practice. Indeed, it is sometimes by the learners' experience of being treated themselves in a person-centred way that they themselves are motivated to practise in a similar way.[6]

Similarly, it is important that the different specialities and settings for training have the same ethos and principles, and do not undermine each other. For example, denigrating people who choose to work in settings of urban or rural disadvantage, or in community rather than hospital settings, may undermine future career choices and weaken intersectoral collaborations.[7] In addition, having tutors from multiple backgrounds working together to support new professionals, plus structuring ways for students to work together in different teams, makes the point that the modern health worker needs to learn to be effective as part of a team.[8] Consistent expectations that those in training should, where possible, reference their decisions and opinions to the literature, will help health workers to identify suitable sources, and encourage evidence-based practice in the longer term. Finally, consistent opportunities to simulate human dilemmas as well as technical tasks – for example, learning how to explain the outcome of a cardiopulmonary resuscitation exercise to distressed relatives, as well as being able to perform the technical task competently, will retain person-centredness and help build ethical and communicative competencies.

PRIORITISING SPECIFIC WORKFORCE NEEDS

UHC needs more practitioners to work in primary care settings. This means more community health workers, more community-based nurses with generalist skills, and more family doctors – whose skill set is defined as "A doctor who is trained to deal with people across all life stages: a generalist who can deal with all types of health problem at point of first contact in a community, and offering a service that is *comprehensive, accessible, focuses on a specific community, allows continuity over time, and is centred on the care of people not specific parts of their body or diseases*".[9]

Even with excellent values and educational design, increased workforce capacity for PHC is unlikely to be realized unless there is a specific strategic impetus towards training health professionals who expect to work in primary health-care settings. This means that those in leadership positions need to consciously champion the goal to deliver around 50% of the trained workforce into community and district settings (including prehospital or first level district hospitals). Without such targets, situations such as in Africa, which "bears 24% of the global disease burden, has only 3% of the world's health workforce, and less than 1% of the world's financial resources for health", show how a free market will not lead to the right balance of workforce for the people, even if many training providers claim to be aiming to deliver new workforce needs.[10] Holding leaders to account for delivery on workforce planning is difficult, given the flux of political processes, but targets need to be set for the educational system, and rewarded according to outputs. The Eastern Mediterranean Region has already made significant efforts in this regard – detailed analyses of the workforce profiles of all the countries are conducted by the World Health Organization, some countries such as Bahrain, Iran, and Egypt have robust models of family medicine and systematic primary health care, and there is a regionwide target to upskill existing general practitioners (GPs: doctors working in first-line care with no postgraduate qualification or required Continuing Professional Development) through online educational opportunities and mentorship.[11] This has the potential to bring the 235,000 unqualified GPs in the region towards competencies of modern practice. The numbers of fully specialized family doctors also need to increase.[12]

CHALLENGES AND BARRIERS

Readers may already be considering the following questions:

- How can we offer effective community placements when we do not yet have a working family medicine system in primary care?
- How can we ensure learners can be taught in areas of urban or rural poverty in a way that will encourage rather than discourage them?
- How am I going to change the minds of the existing hospital specialists who do not want to yield curriculum time or space?
- How can we ensure that enough medical graduates (a) choose to be generalists, (b) choose to be family doctors, and (c) stay in the country once qualified?
- How can we keep our teams up to date and performing at a high level?
- How many nurses/community health workers/doctors/pharmacists should we train, how can we afford them, and what shall we do with the existing workforce, which may need updating and upskilling?
- The values you describe are really different from those I see in action around me which are much more competitive and market driven – how can we change the culture?

These and the many other questions about workforce design are important for clinical educators and academic training units as well as for professional and political leaders, and some strategies are offered in the next section to assist.

STRATEGIES FOR EFFECTIVE CHANGE (BOX 3.1)

1. Use early innovators and pilot sites in centres of excellence.

   Many countries will have primary health-care centres which vary across settings – some may be more developed than others, and of varying quality and training capacity. Some may also have centres where family medicine already exists – perhaps only a single medical school where the family medicine academic team are running an integrated chronic care clinic for adults with multiple non-communicable diseases; or a scheme where the first generation of family medicine specialists are adding to the scope of

---

BOX 3.1   SUMMARY OF STRATEGIES FOR CHANGE

1. Show how new ways of working can have an impact by creating excellent "pilots" in high profile areas.
2. Upskill and use the existing workforce for training – this uses their experience, but also provides them with CPD.
3. Manage curriculum change effectively – have a systematic overview but plan change over time.
4. Keep practice generalist – health professionals need to address individual and population health needs.
5. Use multilevel advocacy – work at the individual, local, and national levels to effect change.
6. Use professional networks – to lead, add impact, test ideas, and get evidence from new research.
7. Consider appropriate financial and professional incentives – these can be important to ensure systems change.
8. Be aware of the societal context of health workforce training – many factors affect the outcome.
9. Do the best you can where you can – we can all make a difference in our own place.
10. Appeal to principle – clarity about the key principles and evidence can be persuasive.

existing services, with good effect. Placements in these clinics for students and post-graduate doctors should be a priority, so that learners will carry the news forward, and professional bodies and accreditors will seek to encourage other providers to develop the same models and opportunities. Professional leads should also ensure that they get "before and after" data on recognized primary care indicators to demonstrate the impacts of new models of care, and use this in teaching, through academic publication, and even for ministerial communications to show what is being achieved through these reforms. Learners in these settings can help to gather and analyse data as part of their own professional development.

2. Upskill and use the existing workforce for training.

Many countries may have doctors and nurses working in the community or private sector, who have many years of experience, but have not received any modern training or even engaged in continuing professional development (CPD). Approaches which include this workforce by giving them both updated clinical training, and the opportunity to support new placement opportunities, can be "win win": becoming part of an educational programme can raise morale and status, and affect clinical care through updated knowledge. Such an initiative will, however, need to ensure that there is a "return on investment" – the programme must result in good quality placements, and also avoid the learning of poor practice or a negative image of community/rural practice as "old fashioned" – learners must understand the history of the system and why this is being changed.

3. Manage curriculum change effectively.

Many reforms such as bringing patient contact into the earlier years of medical student training, or developing a "problem-based learning" approach to integrated and applied knowledge, will need well-planned reform. Deans and other key academic and professional leads will need to believe that workforce changes are needed for UHC, and to agree that the production of yet more super-specialists for hospital nursing and medicine may not best meet the needs of their people. Appointment of academics with health educationalist expertise is an important approach to ensure that curriculum and assessment reforms are founded on robust principles, and champions from other specialities – sometimes people who have already worked in systems with strong primary health care – may be valuable in helping to design and deliver reforms. The cycle of "Plan-Do-Study-Act", with different components being implemented in a stepwise fashion, can help to allow both learners and tutors to experience change and be part of its further implementation. Having the right arguments does not necessarily win over hearts and minds; just as with person-centred care, understanding the views and priorities of others may be important; the change management literature shows that an appreciation that most changes require stages of explanation and discussion, planning, implementation, and reflection to maximize collective ownership of the changes, and attention to group dynamics and existing professional power structures will assist those aiming for reform both to tolerate and utilize these human aspects to an effective end.

4. Keep practice generalist.

The modern workforce will need to be flexible and learn on the job. A service for patients with multiple health needs, as defined in the UHC initiative, will need workers at all levels who can educate, make preliminary assessments of new symptoms and presentations, offer self-care advice, and not automatically refer on for all requests that do not immediately fit their specific expertise. Particularly, those working in primary health care and at first point of assessment will need to have generalist skills so that, for example, clues to the cause of a local disease outbreak, or a new drug reaction, or a family affected by domestic partner abuse, may be picked up and followed up by any worker in the team. Good working relationships, access to another professional locally with additional skills to advise, and an attitude that says "I am not sure what this means, but it is my/our responsibility to help find out" is the essence of a generalist. This will avoid excessive referral and fragmented care, and the system needs to train and support this type of work rather than incentivizing onward referral or repeated appointments.

5. Undertake multilevel advocacy.[13]

The classic triad of action at the "micro, meso, and macro" levels can be useful as a framework for action, as most systems do not change because of action at just one level. Learners who have experienced a new learning opportunity, together with the clinicians and perhaps also the patients involved, can be strong voices for change in the system, while at the other end of the social hierarchy change can be driven by the demands of professional and political leaders, including the WHO. If modernized courses begin to attract increased funding and more learners, educational providers will shift from reluctant to keen, and will support new courses. And within the academic community publishing will always have an impact on the perception of both peers and learners.

6. Use professional networks.

Many groups like the World Organization of Family Doctors (WONCA) use their professional networks to share these kinds of experiences and knowledge, disseminating evidence and mentoring others who are earlier in the path of change. Networks between countries can allow regional exchanges and mutual learning, while specific networks, such as the European Union of General Practitioners (UEMO), the Association for Medical Education in Europe (AMEE), the WONCA Working Party on Education, and The Network: Towards Unity for Health, can add strong value to educational initiatives. Exchanges and electives for learners during their early careers may also enable them to realize possibilities they have not seen in their own system. External examiners are needed for most accredited health professional training, and these colleagues can be useful for adding new ideas and guiding peers in academic settings while they fulfil their formal duties.

7. Consider appropriate financial and professional incentives.

Many countries that wish to change the balance of their workforce will need to consider how they design the workforce pipeline to attract people into new courses and disciplines. Options can include dedicated courses for new workforce members; course fee reductions; enhanced salaries; supported living and working allowances; promotion of status and reputation through the media, local communities, and national recognition; and also, ongoing CPD to ensure further professional support and development.

8. Be aware of the societal context of health workforce training.

Family doctors often meet patients whose healthy life opportunities have been damaged by poverty, adverse life events such as forced migration, poor access to education, and consequent problems with adult life and employment. Similarly, educators are aware of the very different patterns of access into health professional training, particularly for medicine, which requires a high standard of school education to achieve the highly competitive academic entry scores. Many potential candidates are also excluded by a lack of cultural aspiration – they do not believe they could be good enough to become a health professional – or by lack of family support for the direct costs of their training fees. Furthermore, market forces such as the opening of private medical schools where only those able to pay high fees, or have the chance to buy additional tutoring, may make a major difference to who qualifies. But there is also great advantage to becoming employed in health and social care, as the recent World Health Organization Statement points out – training more health workers adds to the system's capacity, educates a new worker to a higher level, and brings an additional income into a family and community.[14]

There are significant societal and political choices which are made "upstream" of education and training that may – or may not – increase health workers' motivation to enter a system that supports UHC. A system where only the children of the rich can access professional education, and where they then expect high earnings to compensate for their investment, or where society does not respect the value of being, for example, a community health worker, may not attract and deliver the new types of health workers that are needed. A society that plans a strong health workforce at all levels needed by the community, schools which prepare students for these opportunities, outreach schemes that encourage students to be recruited from and return to their own communities in areas of need, and an explicit aim to support bright candidates from less advantaged backgrounds to receive additional tutoring or work opportunities so that they can achieve entry level criteria, are some important ways by which workforce capacity can be extended – and there is evidence that students recruited through these kinds of schemes are more likely to commit to working in the settings where they are most needed.

Similarly, it is only through explicit attempts to manage health-care markets that both internal and external brain drains can be minimized. One of the recurring concerns of publicly funded health worker training is that those newly qualified will then leave the country without any return on the investment. At the individual level, health professionals trained to be competent with needy patients, and who are clear about the important role they offer, are less likely to be tempted into a setting that narrows both their population and their scope of practice, but a very different salary in one sector to another may tempt any of us, so educators may also need to advocate for conditions which they feel will support the retention of the workforce where it is most needed. This may be a role for professional leaders, or for us as citizens.

9. Do the best you can where you can.

Many health professionals will have the opportunity to train others during their working lifetime, and this can refresh practice and give additional expertise. Most people will not be major players in a university or a national professional member organization, nor will they run a ministry of health – but offering excellent placements which develop others to be person-centred and socially just practitioners is a wonderful legacy of a lifetime's work in the demanding world of health care. Some innovations in health-care education have started with staff who work with the least well supported communities, because they have advocated and/or demanded the right for those communities to offer training and to get more capacity to ensure their future health-care coverage.

10. Appeal to principle.

Finally, many fights are hard to win, and those in the frontline sometimes wonder why they started or if the cause is just. Strengthening PHC for the delivery of UHC for all is hard to dispute. When the dean of any medical school is disputing the need to let some of the neurology training posts move into the family medicine department, she or he may be persuaded by being reminded of the international expectations that medical schools have *"the obligation to direct their education, research and service activities towards addressing the priority health concerns of the community, region, and/or nation they have a mandate to serve"* and the government and the people will thank the dean for doing so.[15]

CONCLUSION

Multiple factors influence education and training, but for universal health coverage to have a meaningful future there must be a health workforce that is trained to work across different needs at the first point of care, with health professionals who are committed to working in primary care settings, and to meeting the needs of all people. The educators in the Eastern Mediterranean Region, like those elsewhere, have a crucial role in shifting the balance of the learning environment away from the laboratory and super-speciality high cost tertiary care settings, towards the broader context of common problems played out in all parts of society, and equipping the future workforce to be competent and motivated to address the personal and population needs of the communities they will serve. This needs a change in curriculum, educational methods, and training culture – as well as change elsewhere in the system. The Eastern Mediterranean Region has many experienced clinicians and educators, with some mature examples of UHC, and this chapter hopefully will act both as a resource and as a reminder of what we can all achieve together.

REFERENCES

1. Howe A. *Why Expertise in Whole Person Medicine Matters.* London: RCGP, 2012. Available from: http://www.rcgp.org.uk/policy/rcgp-policy-areas/~/media/Files/Policy/A-Z-policy/Medical-Generalism-Why_expertise_in_whole_person_medicine_matters.ashx [Accessed 3 January 2018].
2. WHO. *Framework on Integrated Person-Centred Health Services.* 2016. Available from: http://apps.who.int/gb/ebwha/pdf_files/WHA69/A69_39-en.pdf?ua=1 [Accessed 14 January 2018].
3. Greenhalgh T, Douglas HR. Experiences of general practitioners and practice nurses of training courses in evidence-based health care: A qualitative study. *British Journal of General Practice,* 1999; 49: 536–540.
4. See for example The WONCA Global Standards for Postgraduate Family Medicine Education. WONCA: Working Party on Education, 2013. Available from: http://www.globalfamilydoctor.com/site/DefaultSite/filesystem/documents/Groups/Education/WONCA%20ME%20stds_edit%20for%20web_250714.pdf [Accessed 14 January 2018].
5. Kilminster S, Cottrell D, Grant J, Jolly B. AMEE Guide No. 27: Effective educational and clinical supervision. *Medical Teacher,* 2007; 29(1): 2–19. Available from: https://doi.org/10.1080/01421590701210907.
6. Howe, A. Patient-centred medicine through student-centred teaching – a student perspective on the key impacts of community-based learning in undergraduate medical education. *Medical Education,* 2001; 35: 666–672. Available from: https://onlinelibrary.wiley.com/doi/abs/10.1046/j.1365-2923.2001.00925.x.
7. Wass V. *By Choice not By Chance – Supporting Medical Students Towards Careers in General Practice.* London: Health Education England, 2017. Available from: https://www.hee.nhs.uk/printpdf/our-work/hospitals-primary-community-care/primary-community-care/supporting-medical-students-towards-careers-general-practice [Accessed 14 January 2018].
8. Howe A, Crofts D, Billingham K. Can nurses teach tomorrow's doctors? A nursing perspective on interdisciplinary community-based medical education. *Medical Teacher,* 2000; 22(6): 576–581. Available from: https://doi.org/10.1080/01421590050175569.
9. Allen J, Gay B, Crebolder H, Heyrman J, Svab I, Ram P. The European definition of family practice/general medicine, EURACT (Short version). 2005. Available from: http://www.woncaeurope.org/sites/default/files/documents/Definition%20EURACTshort%20version.pdf.
10. World Health Organization. Report on the WHO/PEPFAR Planning Meeting on Scaling Up Nursing and Medical Education. Geneva, 13 to 14 October 2009. Available from: www.who.int/hrh/resources/scaling-up/en/index.html.
11. See section p. 221 onwards in Kidd M, Ed. The WONCA Guidebook: *The Contribution of Family Medicine to Improving Health Systems: A Guidebook from the World Organization of Family Doctors,* 2nd Edition. 2013. ISBN: 9781846195549.
12. Regional Committee for the Eastern Mediterranean, Sixty-third session. *Scaling up family practice: Progressing towards universal health coverage* 4(a). 1 EM/RC63/Tech.Disc.1 Rev.1, September 2016.

13. Start D, Hovland I. *Tools for Policy Impact – A Handbook for Researchers.* London: Overseas Development Institute, 2004.
14. *Dublin Declaration on Human Resources for Health – Building the Workforce of the Future.* 2017. Fourth Global Forum on Human Resources for Health, 13–17 November, 2017. Available from: http://www.who.int/hrh/events/Dublin_Declaration-on-HumanResources-for-Health.pdf.
15. Boelen C, Heck J. *Defining and Measuring the Social Accountability of Medical Schools.* Geneva: WHO, 1995.

CHAPTER 4

Proactive primary care: Integrating public health into primary care

Salman Rawaf, Mays Raheem, and David Rawaf

INTRODUCTION

Access to health and health care is changing all over the world. Population growth, ageing populations, and technology are the triggers for such change. This is fuelled by increasing public expectations and demands on services at all levels and continuing beyond any illness episode. Worldwide, populations are rapidly ageing; each person aspires to live a long and healthy life. However, ageing populations will inevitably have an increased demand for health and social care services.

Older people account for a greater proportion of the global burden of disease and health-care needs than younger people. Recent evidence suggests that many of the challenges associated with population ageing can be addressed by changes in behaviour and policy, especially those that promote good health in older age.[1] A comprehensive public health approach to population ageing must be at the heart of any health system. Such an approach should reflect the needs, capacities, and aspirations of the population and changing contexts.[1,2] It should also address the inequities in health service provision.

With increasing health literacy, people are keen to promote and protect their health, rather than seeking help only when illnesses occur. Public awareness and understanding of technology in medicine and health is leading to increased real demand and proactivity in seeking services, whether this is by asking a clinician to provide a particular technology or to make a referral.[3] Furthermore, regular use of technology devices, such as mobile phone apps and the Internet, for managing or tracking health, has encouraged and helped many people to improve their health.[4] It is suggested that huge advancements in technology within a relatively short timeframe could have significant implications for delivery of health and social care services. Training of the health-care workforce is needed to deliver a more proactive and efficient service that is designed to meet both population and individual needs.[5]

SHIFTING SYSTEM FOCUS TOWARDS PREVENTION AND WELLBEING

"If general practice [primary care] isn't public health, then what is it? It's not just cure, it's prevention, it's diagnosis – it's the whole lot." A general practitioner (GP) from Northwest England expressed his experience about the integration of public health and primary care.[6]

Health system reforms today aim to achieve greater promotion of wellbeing and prevention of ill-health. This will certainly help in improving health and address a number of challenges by avoiding the development or deterioration of long-term conditions and expensive future treatments and care. This has the huge potential to decrease unnecessary demands and free up resources to strengthen health systems. Evidence shows that shifting towards, and spending resources on, wellbeing and prevention saves lives and improves quality of life. Edelman's study across 12 countries shows that the majority of people believe that health is "about more than being disease free".[4] These people also think that "personal and social behaviours have the biggest impact on their health".[4]

PRIMARY CARE

Primary care has been demonstrated worldwide to be associated with enhanced access to health services, better health outcomes, and a decrease in hospitalization and use of emergency departments.[7,8] Primary care can also help counteract the negative impact of poor economic conditions on health.[9] Traditional primary care focuses on personal health-care services and continuity of care. The "disease model" of the 1970s, which is still prevalent today in most countries of the world, is changing rapidly. The transformation of primary care is driven by population growth, ageing populations, disease burden and technological advances (Figure 4.1). Proactive and personalized primary care is what today's population needs.[10] Proactive primary care means radical change to the current model of service; it includes integrating key public health functions and interventions into primary care service.

"Comprehensive proactive" primary care means: a primary care-led health service, that is proactive, focusing on preventive and public health interventions, personalized and person-centred care, total care, and seamless integrated service.

Barbara Starfield simply defined primary care as "the first level of contact with the health system to promote health, prevent illness, care for common illnesses, and manage ongoing health problems".[12] Therefore, primary care is the backbone of any effective health system.

In developed countries, where primary care is given the priority it deserves, it has the following characteristics:[13]

1. It functions as a single portal entry to the health and health-care process.
2. It is available 24 hours a day.
3. It is the first and vital contact of care involving assessment, diagnosis, triage, and management or resolution of defined problems.

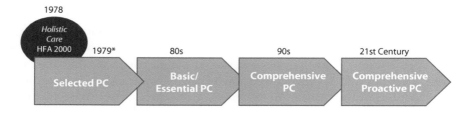

FIGURE 4.1 Transformation of primary care since the Alma-Ata Declaration in 1978.[11]

4. It serves a gate-keeping function into secondary care through selective referrals.
5. It works long term with a continuity of personal and family care.
6. It addresses clinical morbidity, as well as health, social problems, and local needs, occurring in small populations.
7. It is delivered proactively; preventive care provides early interventions to prevent escalation of health-care needs.
8. It functions as a stakeholder in local public health issues (the family physician has the opportunity to become the leader, provider, and initiator of good health in the local community).

The uniqueness of primary care is its delivery through multidisciplinary teams, with family physicians at the heart of these teams. Family physicians are specialists; they are trained medical practitioners who promote health, prevent disease, treat acute and chronic illnesses, and provide continuity of care for people of all ages and both sexes with the main aim to improve individual health (of those registered with the practice) and community health (in relation to the small population they serve). In addition, they have particular skills in dealing with people with complex health issues and co-morbidities.[10]

Data from the British National Health Service (NHS) clearly shows the substantial benefits of providing comprehensive primary care based on family practice to the whole population. Over 95% of the patient contacts with the NHS take place in primary care.[14] Furthermore, family physicians only refer to secondary care around 5% of patients from consultations.[15] Analysis of NHS daily activities clearly indicates the value and effectiveness of these primary care services, with more than 85% of health and health-care needs dealt with at this level, high patient satisfaction, and care delivered at a decidedly low cost to the health system.[9,16,17]

The evidence is very clear and explicit: a health system which is not primary care led is a weak and expensive system, and primary care without fully trained family physicians is consequently of poor quality. Indeed, countries more oriented to primary care have populations with better health and services that are delivered at a lower cost.[9,10,12]

Transforming primary care into a proactive programme of promoting health and preventing diseases, in addition to diagnosis, treatment, and care, is a logical step towards its development (Figure 4.1). Since the 1980s there has been a growing interest in the role of family physicians and their teams in public health activities. Primary care is always regarded as the basic building block of public health, and it is seen as a logical location for local public health interventions. The Alma-Ata Declaration in 1978 identified the role of GPs in public health as important, and 30 years later in a report on primary care, the World Health Organization (WHO) confirmed this special relationship.[18,19]

Primary care centres are located close to people's homes. Primary care, and specifically the family physician's service, remains the most-accessed part of the health system in many countries where primary care is fully developed.[20] In the United Kingdom (UK), a country with a long history of well-established and comprehensive primary care service, some initiatives have sought to provide alternate first points of contact, such as increased advice roles for pharmacists and the development of telephone advice lines and walk-in centres. However, their effectiveness has not been proven, and GPs remain the patient's most popular and frequent first point of contact with the NHS.[6,21] Family physicians in the United Kingdom, or GPs, are regarded as "key agents", having the best and most frequent opportunities to improve public health.[22]

In the last decade, the Royal College of General Practitioners (RCGP) in the United Kingdom has put huge professional and political pressure on the UK Government, which has had to change its emphasis towards a holistic approach to health.[23] The RCGP has stated that GPs play a crucial role in promoting health and preventing disease. Its curriculum statement on health promotion encourages GPs to be proactive in consultations to, for example, "discuss healthy living with patients and the early detection of illness" and to "provide appropriate diagnostic, therapeutic and preventative services to individuals, and to the registered population".[23] The introduction of the Quality and Outcome Framework and the NHS Health Check has moved the agenda even further by introducing systematic population-based approaches to public health in addition to opportunistic ones.[6,24]

WHAT IS PUBLIC HEALTH IN THE CONTEXT OF PRIMARY CARE? AND HOW CAN INTEGRATION BE ACHIEVED?

Public health, which is described in some countries as public health medicine, or community medicine, is a multidisciplinary specialty, which is defined as "the science and art of preventing disease, prolonging life and promoting health through the organized efforts and informed choices of society, organizations (public and private), communities and individuals".[25] In Acheson's 1988 report *Public Health in England*, the definition was retained but shortened to "the science and art of preventing disease, prolonging life and promoting health through the organised efforts of society".[26]

The ten essential public health functions are designed to provide the necessary tools to improve health through health promotion, protection, and disease prevention at population and individual levels (Figure 4.2). Not all public health functions however, can be delivered at primary care level.

Functions 5, 6, 7, and 8 can be integrated into primary care for both individual and population health.[27]

Understanding the health needs of the population is a very important process to shape public health service within primary care service delivery. Such needs assessment must be ongoing as the population's needs change.[28]

As Figure 4.3 indicates, in any given population at any given time, the burden of acute conditions affects approximately 10% of the population (with similar figures for disability). The remaining 80% are either healthy or living with one or more risks to their health (e.g. hypertension, smoking, obesity, dyslipidaemia, glucose intolerance).[29] Most health systems are based on

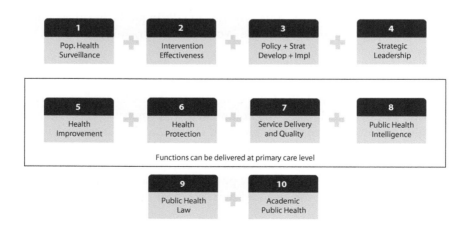

FIGURE 4.2 The ten essential public health functions.

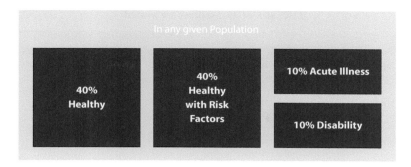

In any given Population

40%
Healthy

40%
Healthy
with Risk
Factors

10% Acute Illness

10% Disability

FIGURE 4.3 Rawaf's model for health and disease burden.[29]

a disease model with little or no expenditure on maintaining the health of the "healthy" population or identifying and addressing risks to health early on. Most of the expenditure remains focused on hospital (secondary) care and costly specialist services (tertiary). This is largely due to the focus of the medical school curriculum and the higher medical specialist training programmes that have been developed. Little or no exposure to public health and primary care is common in the developing world, despite those members of the population with higher disease burden needing more public health and primary care.[30] Prevention and public health interventions are usually long term and policy makers at all levels, with their often short-term perspective, find it difficult to relate to them.

However, most of the population-based functions of public health should be delivered to individuals and the population in a primary care setting. Integration of these two services is essential for both the health of the population and individual personal health. Thus, strengthening the relationship between public health and primary care should be the main focus of action in both arenas.

There is enormous potential for general practice/family medicine to take a more proactive role in prevention, public health, and ill-health. Public health guidance from the UK National Institute for Health and Clinical Excellence (NICE) advises primary care professionals, such as GPs, to opportunistically and proactively carry out activities such as brief interventions.[31] However, for example, in the case of smoking, GPs frequently respond to requests for help with giving up smoking rather than proactively engaging existing smokers. Such reactive approaches to health must be changed to more proactive ones.[6,32] The evidence base concerning the role of health promotion in general practice is a growing field; and general practice, public health, and academics are working together to improve the evidence base.

THE VALUE OF TWO NATURAL ALLIES

A health system is the product of a country's culture and the way people are willing to fund it, to ensure equity and fairness. There is no ideal health system. Each system has its strengths and weaknesses.[33] However, the best systems are those able to secure the health of the whole population.[34] Securing the health of the whole population cannot be achieved without universal coverage achieved through effective comprehensive primary care that focuses not only on disease but also on health and how to improve it. A strong proactive public health function is required within primary care to protect the health of the population and individuals, promote health, and prevent disease.

Proactive primary care saves lives, reduces the burden of disease, and improves the quality of life.[35] It is also a crucial source of productivity improvement and seamless service (Figure 4.4).

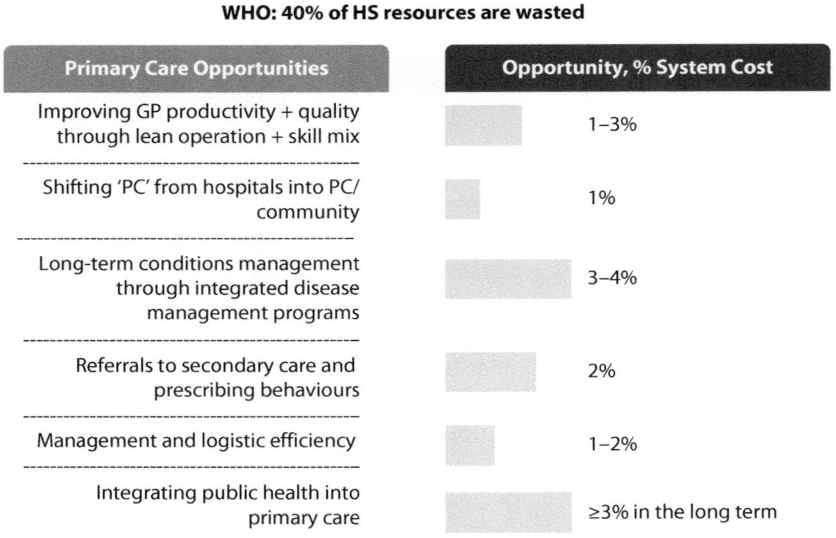

WHO: 40% of HS resources are wasted

Primary Care Opportunities	Opportunity, % System Cost
Improving GP productivity + quality through lean operation + skill mix	1–3%
Shifting 'PC' from hospitals into PC/ community	1%
Long-term conditions management through integrated disease management programs	3–4%
Referrals to secondary care and prescribing behaviours	2%
Management and logistic efficiency	1–2%
Integrating public health into primary care	≥3% in the long term

FIGURE 4.4 Proactive and integrated primary care is a crucial source of productivity improvement.[36]

Considerable overlap exists in the roles, responsibilities, and functions between the two specialties of public health and primary care, especially related to protection and promotion of health, and disease and injury prevention.[19] There are two possible scenarios of integration: the first is a full integration and the second is based on two separate organizational structures, each remaining independent but where professionals work together and share the same aim and objectives. In either scenario, some may strongly hold the view that the function of primary care is already very challenging without adding further responsibility for population-based public health activities. However, evidence shows clearly that both primary care and public health would gain if these functions were viewed as natural allies.[37]

The real challenge to any health system is how to strengthen the relationship between primary care and public health to synergistically enhance both functions. In the United Kingdom, the National Health Service provides an excellent example of strong collaboration between two separate specialties. Both aim to improve the health of the population they serve. Public health achieves this through health needs assessment, defining priorities, providing evidence of effectiveness, developing strategies for population-wide interventions in promoting health, protecting health, preventing disease and injury, and evaluation of health impacts.

General practice focuses on personal and family care interacting with the person in a holistic way.[38] Through such personal and continuous care the GP is able to implement public health strategies for a healthy lifestyle (e.g. smoking cessation, dietary advice, weight control, active living, stress control), early recognition of disease (e.g. systematic and opportunistic screening), early intervention to address risk factors (e.g. hypertension, hyperlipidaemia, smoking), and health protection (e.g. immunization including influenza vaccine, notifications of infectious disease). With the decline of infectious disease and increase in lifestyle-related diseases and conditions, such collaboration between public health and primary care is vital for reducing the burden of non-communicable diseases (NCDs) in communities, reducing the costs to the health system, and improving equity in health.[39]

MODELS AND EXPERIENCE OF INTEGRATING PUBLIC HEALTH INTO PRIMARY CARE

Primary care strategies and operational changes to integrate public health actions into primary care should include:[9,40,41]

- Targeting health improvement actions and resources to the most disadvantaged areas
- Building capacity in primary care to deliver proactive, preventive care, and
- Providing early interventions to prevent escalation of health-care needs

The literature and key informants provide several possible models to integrate public health into primary care within the three strategic directions mentioned above. Rawaf described five models of integration:[13]

1. Integrating public health professionals into primary care – representatives from both organizations working together in the same settings[6]
2. Incorporating public health functions within primary care settings (including well-being and preventive services as part and parcel of comprehensive and proactive benefit packages)[6,47]
3. Primary care services within public health settings
4. Building public health incentives into primary care
5. Training primary care staff (mainly doctors)[42] in public health (either through dual specialists training or a family physician trained with special interest in public health)[43,44]

These models are based on adaptability within health systems to achieve the best possible results through integration. More details of each model are outlined below.

INTEGRATING PUBLIC HEALTH PROFESSIONALS INTO PRIMARY CARE

In this model, there is no suggestion of full integration of public health and primary care, but rather the integration of some public health professionals into primary care teams. Iran has used such a model in rural primary health care (PHC) for the last 35 years, although this model has not been extended to the 70% of the nation's population living in urban areas.[45] One of the aims of the PHC network in Iran was to integrate public health activities, including malaria control, family planning, school health, and environmental health, into primary care services.[45] However, the system did not evolve according to the population's needs.[46]

Brazil too has integrated many public health functions into primary care through community health workers. These workers are involved directly with families in supporting chronic disease management, triaging conditions like anaemia or dehydration, managing disease-specific programmes, for example, for tuberculosis, providing sexual health advice, providing pre- and postnatal care (including breastfeeding assistance), child development assessment, cancer screening, supporting immunization programmes, infectious disease monitoring, and health promotion advice.[47]

Placing a public health physician in a practice may not be the optimal approach for transferring public health knowledge; however, topics important to the practice lend themselves to such an intervention with potential long-term benefit for public health and primary care.[48] Time constraints limit the ability of primary care physicians to comply with preventive service recommendations.[49]

COMPREHENSIVE AND PROACTIVE BENEFIT PACKAGES THAT INCLUDE PUBLIC HEALTH

Medicare in the United States has recognized that preventive interventions at personal care level within the primary care context will save money and provide an additional health benefit. Medicare provides a range of public health and preventive services with primary care.[50]

Burton and colleagues investigated whether adding preventive services to benefits for older Medicare beneficiaries would affect utilization and costs under Medicare. There appears to be a modest health benefit with no negative cost impact. This finding gives an early quantitative basis for the discussion of whether to extend Medicare benefits to include a general preventive visit from a primary care clinician, moving from essential to comprehensive services.[51] Cohen and colleagues suggest that substantial resources can be saved through prevention.[52] Although some preventive measures do save money, the vast majority reviewed in the health economics literature do not.

Another study has shown that the benefit of preventive services to older Medicare beneficiaries would appear to provide a modest health benefit with no negative cost impact. Medicare now provides a range of preventive public health services within their primary care programme (about 20 public health interventions).[53]

PRIMARY CARE SERVICES WITHIN PUBLIC HEALTH SETTINGS

In countries where primary care does not provide universal coverage and especially those operating largely under private control (for example in the United States), public health agencies have undertaken a role as a provider of last resort for the socially disadvantaged.[54] Such a model tends to develop through opportunity rather than by design and addresses only the specific needs of specific groups and not the entire population. Such a model should be the exception and not the rule. Strengthening public health with universal coverage and access to all, irrespective of people's ability to pay for it, should be the aim of all modern health systems (Table 4.1).

BUILDING PUBLIC HEALTH INCENTIVES INTO PRIMARY CARE

Across its 70 years of history, the NHS has introduced various changes and incentives to promote the health of the population through general practice/primary care (and indeed other services) in order to improve the quality of services and target certain conditions and populations.[55]

Before the NHS Quality and Outcome Framework (QOF) was introduced, there was modest experience in the use of incentives for general practice. These incentives led to an increase in immunization rates, cervical cytology rates, breast cancer screening, and many other public health interventions.[56] In 2004, QOF was introduced as part of a new General Medical Service Contract. The QOF is a voluntary incentive scheme for GP practices, rewarding them for how

TABLE 4.1 Some of the public health activities in primary care

Immunizations and vaccinations (including influenza and emergency)
National child and adult screening programmes
Early detection of risk to health (mainly the those related to NCDs – smoking, alcohol, hypertension, hyperlipidaemia, hyperglycaemia)
Health checks (e.g. NHS health check introduced in 2009)
NCD control and management (within the national policies and national service frameworks)
Health education programmes
Behaviour change programmes
Engaging the public (e.g. self-care, health clubs)

well they care for patients and provide quality preventive care measures. The QOF gives an indication of the overall achievement of a practice through a points system. Practices aim to deliver public health interventions and high-quality care across a range of areas, for which they score points. Put simply: the higher the score, the higher the financial reward for the practice. The final payment is adjusted to take account of the practice list size and the prevalence of the target conditions. Results are published annually.

The QOF has five main components, known as domains. Each domain consists of a set of measures of achievement, known as indicators, against which practices score points. More than 150 indicators exist including those addressing clinical factors (65 indicators), organization, additional services, patient experience, and holistic care. An example of diabetes indicators is given in Table 4.2.

Since the introduction of QOF, nearly all practices have been enrolled in the scheme, and indeed gain around 25% of their income through this new method of additional payments. Overall mean quality scores for aspects of care linked to incentives were higher than aspects of care not linked to incentives.[58] NICE is reviewing QOF indicators and the ways in which GPs are working to improve health and quality of care.[59] Assessment so far shows modest improvements in asthma and diabetes care, reduction in inequalities in managing NCDs, reduction in emergency admissions, and increased frequency of monitoring patients with severe mental illness.[60–62] However, some see the future is bright in shaping proactive primary care through incentives such as QOF.[58]

In the United States, the health reforms debate is ongoing about how payment systems can advance health as the fundamental priority. Three possible ways to improve the integration of public health and primary care have been proposed. Firstly, every American should have access to the clinical preventive services that are appropriate to him or her without co-payment. Secondly, grant support should be set aside for community-based initiatives that are necessary to improve the health and health care of the residents of each community. Finally, resources to address the overall health-care needs of a population should be shaped by a blend of the community's health needs and the community's efforts, as reflected by metrics that indicate trends in the determinants of population health.[63]

TABLE 4.2 England NHS: General practice QOF indicators for diabetes[57]

Quality domain	Indicator	Point	Threshold
Structural	The practice can produce a register of all patients aged 17 years and over with diabetes mellitus, which specifies whether the patient has type 1 or type 2 diabetes	6	NA
Process	The percentage of patients with diabetes who have a record of HbA1c or equivalent in the previous 15 months	3	40–90%
Process	The percentage of patients with diabetes whose notes record BMI in the previous 15 months	3	40–90%
Process	The percentage of patients with diabetes who have a record of the blood pressure in the previous 15 months	3	40–90%
Outcome	The percentage of patients with diabetes in whom the last HbA1c is 7 or less in the previous 15 months	17	40–50%
Outcome	The percentage of patients with diabetes whom the last blood pressure is 145/85 or less	18	40–60%
Outcome	The percentage of patients with diabetes whose last measured total cholesterol in the previous 15 months is 5 mmol/l or less	6	40–70%

Source: www.nhsemployers.org

TRAINING PRIMARY CARE STAFF IN PUBLIC HEALTH

With accumulating evidence on the value of public health interventions in primary care, the importance of providing (and evaluating) person-centred care,[41] and the importance of addressing the growing number of NCDs and encouraging positive and healthy lifestyles in individuals and communities, many primary care doctors and nurses are undertaking training in public health.[42]

For example, the UNRWA (the United Nations Relief and Works Agency for Palestine Refugees in the Near East) provides assistance, protection, and advocacy for some five million registered Palestinian refugees in Jordan, Lebanon, Syria, and the occupied Palestinian territory. Through the agency's network of primary health-care facilities and mobile clinics in four countries, services are offering preventive care, general medicine, and specialist care for each stage of life. In a population living in exceptional circumstances as refugees, mainly in adverse conditions, the public health needs are very high. Many doctors and nurses in the agency either studied a Master of Public Health programme or are planning to do so. The aim is to fully integrate primary care into public health. UNRWA primary care clinics are operating independently of the host country's health system and are funded almost entirely by voluntary contributions from United Nation Member States. However, there is increasing coordination between state primary care and UNRWA with the aim of coordinating policies, minimizing duplication, and enhancing advances in both services.

In the United Kingdom, some family physicians are developing a special interest in public health through formal training programmes described as "GPs with special interest" (GPwSI).[47] Such a model of integration of primary care and public health institutional supports, including incentives and a coordination framework, may be the best for effectively integrating these two services to improve the population's health.

TRAINING AND SKILLS NEEDED FOR INTEGRATION

Many family physicians shy away from delivering an effective public health service as they feel they lack the skills needed. New training curricula provide a wide range of skills related to ill-health prevention and public health. Additional training in public health would add great value to the skills of doctors and nurses working in family practice. With the growing evidence base, guidance from organizations like NICE, and changing responsibilities, the time is ripe for primary care and family physicians worldwide to become more proactive to improve their work in public health and ill-health prevention. Societies demanding such change and health systems, which are primary care led, are more amenable for such positive change, than those which are not.

CONCLUSION

Proactive primary care has a crucial role in promoting healthier lifestyles through each and every contact with members of the public. Primary care professionals should "make every contact count", with health deemed a priority. Primary care physicians and nurses will need to be trained in public health and have the skills to be proactive in promoting public health and wellbeing, which in turn will have implications for training both the members of existing primary care teams and new recruits. The shift towards prevention could alter the shape of the workforce, with more people delivering early intervention and public health services, rather than acute interventions. The five models described in this chapter provide great opportunity to radically change primary care services to provide a truly universal and comprehensive proactive health service for all and achieve the dream of the Alma-Ata Declaration as stated 40 years ago: health for all.

REFERENCES

1. Beard JR, Bloom DE. Towards a comprehensive public health response to population ageing. *Lancet*. 2015;385(9968): 658–661. Available from: https://www.thelancet.com/journals/lancet/article/PIIS0 140-6736(14)61461-6/abstract.
2. Lloyd-Sherlock P, McKee M, Ebrahim S. WHO washes its hands of older people. *Lancet*. 2018;391(10115): 25–26. Available from: doi: 10.1016/S0140-6736(17)33313-5.
3. Liddell A, Adshead S, Burgess E. *Technology in the NHS: Transforming the Patient's Experience of Care*. London: The King's Fund; 2008. Available from: https://www.kingsfund.org.uk/sites/default/files/Techno logy-in-the-NHS-Transforming-patients-experience-of-care-Liddell-Adshead-and-Burgess-Kings-Fund-October-2008_0.pdf.
4. Edelman. *Edelman Health Barometer*. 2011. Available from: http://healthbarometer.edelman.com/wp-co ntent/uploads/downloads/2011/10/Edelman-Health-barometer-2011-global-Deck-10.19.11.pdf.
5. Envisioning Technology. *Envisioning the Future of Health Technology*. 2013. Available from: http://env isioningtech.com/health/.
6. Boyce T, Peckham S, Hann A, Trenholm S. *A Pro-active Approach: Health Promotion and Ill-health Prevention*. London: The King's Fund; 2010.
7. Kane RL, Keckhafer G, Flood S, et al. The effect of evercare on hospital use. *Journal of the American Geriatrics Society*. 2003;51(10): 1427–1434. Available from: http://europepmc.org/abstract/med/14511163.
8. Cook EJ, Randhawa G, Guppy A, Large S. A study of urgent and emergency referrals from NHS Direct within England. *BMJ Open*. 5(5). Available from: https://bmjopen.bmj.com/content/5/5/e007533.
9. Shi L. The impact of primary care: A focused review. *Scientifica*. 2012. Available from: http://dx.doi. org/10.6064/2012/432892.
10. Department of Health. *Transforming Primary Care*. London. Available from: https://www.gov.uk/g overnment/uploads/system/uploads/attachment_data/file/304139/Transforming_primary_care.pdf.
11. Rawaf S. Primary Care Reforms: towards integrated and person-centred care. [Lecture] Copenhagen: WHO EURO, 2–4 May 2016.
12. Starfield B, Shi L, Macinko J. Contribution of primary care to health systems and health. *Milbank Quarterly*. 2005;83(3): 457–502.
13. Rawaf S. Medico de familia na saude publica (Family Physicians and Public Health). In Gusso G and Lopes JMC (Eds): *Tratado de Medicina de Familia e Communidade: principios, formaco et practica*. Sao Paulo. 2012. p.19–27. Available from: https://www.scribd.com/document/358930369/Tratado-de-Me dicina-de-Familia-e-Comunidade-Gusso-2012-Vol-1-pdf.
14. Royal College of General Practitioners. *Discover General Practice*. Available from: http://www.rcgp.org. uk/training-exams/discover-general-practice.aspx.
15. National Audit Office. 2005.
16. Foot C, Naylor C, Imison C. *The Quality of GP Diagnosis and Referral*. London: The King's Fund; 2010.
17. Roland M, Everington S. Tackling the crisis in general practice: If general practice fails, the whole NHS fails. *BMJ*. 2016;352: i942. Available from: https://www.bmj.com/content/352/bmj.i942.
18. World Health Organization. *Health for all 2000*. Alma-Ata Declaration. Geneva. 1978.
19. Rawaf S, De Maeseneer J, Starfield B. From Alma-Ata to Almaty: A new start for primary health care. *Lancet*. 2008;372(9647): 1365–1367. Available from: https://www.thelancet.com/journals/lancet/article/ PIIS0140-6736(08)61524-X/abstract.
20. World Health Organization. *Primary care: Now more than ever*. World Health Report 2008. Geneva.
21. Pope C, Turnbull J, Jones J, et al. Has the NHS 111 urgent care telephone service been a success? Case study and secondary data analysis in England. *BMJ Open*. 2017;7(5): e014815. Available from: doi:10.1136/ bmjopen-2016-014815.
22. Wirrmann EJ, Carlson CL. Public health leadership in primary care practice in England: Everybody's business? *Critical Public Health*. 2005;15(3): 205–217. Available from: https://www.tandfonline.com/doi/ abs/10.1080/09581590500371305.
23. Royal College of General Practitioners. *5 Healthy People: Promoting Health and-Preventing Disease*. London. 2007. Available from: https://www.gponline.com/rcgp-curriculum/healthy-people.
24. Peckham and Ham 2008.
25. Winslow CEA. The untilled fields of public health. *Science*. 1920;51(1306): 23–33. Available from: http:// science.sciencemag.org/content/51/1306/23.

26. Acheson D. *Public Health in England. Report of the Committee of Inquiry into the Future Development of the Public Health Function.* London: DHSS; 1988.

27. Rawaf S. *The Future of Public Health.* [Lecture] Imperial College London. January 2018.

28. Rawaf S, Marshall F. Drug misuse: The ten steps for needs assessment. *Public Health Medicine.* 1999;1: 21–26.

29. Rawaf S. Health in Wandsworth. *The Independent Annual Report of the Director of Public Health.* London: WPCT. 2004.

30. Heath I. A general practitioner for every person in the world. *BMJ.* 2008;336: 861. Available from: https ://doi.org/10.1136/bmj.39548.435023.59.

31. National Heart, Lung and Blood Institute. *Clinical Guidelines on the Identification, Evaluation and Treatment of Overweight and Obesity in Adults: The Evidence Report.* Bethesda, Maryland: NHLBI. 1998. Available from: www.nhlbi.nih.gov/guidelines/obesity/ob_home.htm.

32. National Institute for Health and Clinical Evidence. *Four Commonly Used Methods to Increase Physical Activity.* London. 2006. Available from: http://guidance.nice.org.uk/PH2

33. National Institute for Health and Clinical Evidence. *Obesity: The Prevention, Identification, Assessment and Management of Overweight and Obesity in Adults and Children.* London. 2006. Available from: http://guidance.nice.org.uk/CG43.

34. Wanless D. *Securing Good Health for the Whole Population: Final Report.* London: HMSO. 2004.

35. Baker R, Honeyford K, Levene LS, et al. Population characteristics, mechanisms of primary care and premature mortality in England: A cross-sectional study. *BMJ.* 2016;6: e009981. Available from: http:// dx.doi.org/10.1136/bmjopen-2015-009981.

36. Rawaf S. Primary Care & Family Practice: Western & Eastern Mediterranean Perspectives. [Lecture] Cairo. WHO EMRO. 27 November 2017.

37. Wang W, Shi L, Yin A, et al. Contribution of primary care to health: An individual level analysis from Tibet, China. *International Journal for Equity in Health.* 2015;14: 107. Available from: https://equityh ealthj.biomedcentral.com/articles/10.1186/s12939-015-0255-y.

38. Amati F, McDonald A, Majeed A, Dubois E, Rawaf S. Implementation and evaluation of patient-centred care in experimental studies from 2000-2010: Systematic review. *International Journal of Person Centered Medicine.* 2011;1(2). Available from: http://www.ijpcm.org/index.php/IJPCM/article/view/47.

39. Ruano A, Furler J, Shi L. Interventions in primary care and their contributions to improving equity in health. *International Journal for Equity in Health.* 2015;14: 153.

40. Watt G. *Supporting Health Improvement in Primary Care.* Glasgow. Available from: http://www.thpc .scot.nhs.uk/PDFs/P2010/GWatt_%20paper.pdf.

41. Bream E. *Prevention 2010: Engagement and Concordance: Evidence Overview.* Edinburgh. Available from: http://scotland.gov.uk/Resource/Doc/924/0031658.pdf.

42. Ciliska D. Educating for evidence based practice. *Journal of Professional Nursing.* 2005;21(6): 3 45–50.

43. Carter J. How can a GP participate in public health? *BMJ Career,* 2004. Available from: http://careers. bmj.com/careers/advice/viewarticle.html?id=360.

44. Bradley S, McKelvey SD. General practitioners with a special interest in public health; at last a way to deliver public health in primary care. *Journal of Epidemiology and Community Health.* 2005;59: 920–923.

45. Watt G. *Supporting Health Improvement in Primary Care.* Glasgow. 2006. Available from: http://www .thpc.scot.nhs.uk/PDFs/P2010/GWatt_%20paper.pdf.

46. Manenti A. Health situation in Iran. *Medical Journal of Islamic Republic of Iran.* 2011; 25(1): 1–7.

47. Wadge H, Bhatti Y, Carter A, et al. *Brazil's Family Health Strategy: Using Community Health Care Workers to Provide Primary Care.* The Commonwealth Fund. 13 Dec 2016.

48. Ayres PJ, Pollock CT, Wilson A, Fox P, et al. Practical public health in a primary care setting: Discrete projects confer discrete benefits but a long-term relationship is needed. *Journal of Management in Medicine.* 1996;10(4): 36–48.

49. Yarnall KSH, Pollak KI, Ostbye T, et al. Primary care: Is there enough time for prevention? *American Journal of Public Health.* 2003;93(4): 635–641.

50. Centres for Medicare and Medicaid Services. *Staying Healthy: Medicare's Preventive Services.* 2017. Available from: https://www.medicare.gov/Pubs/pdf/11100-Staying-Healthy.pdf.

51. Burton LC, Paglia MJ, German P, et al. The effect among older persons of a general preventive visit on three health behaviors: Smoking, excessive alcohol drinking, and sedentary lifestyle. *Preventive Medicine.* 1995;24(5): 492–497.

52. Cohen JT, Neumann PJ, Weinstein MC. Does preventive care save money? Health economics and the presidential candidates. *New England Journal of Medicine.* 2008; 14;358(7):661–663.
53. Burton LC, Paglia MJ, German P, et al. Preventive services for the elderly: Would coverage affect utilization and costs under Medicare? *American Journal of Public Health.* 1995;85(3): 387–391.
54. Starfield B. Public health and primary care: A framework for proposed linkages. *American Journal of Public Health.* 1996;86(10): 1365–1369.
55. Commonwealth Fund. *Mirror, Mirror: International Comparison Reflects Flaws and Opportunities for Better US Healthcare.* New York. 2017. Available from: http://www.commonwealthfund.org/interact ives/2017/july/mirror-mirror/.
56. Baker D, Middleton E. Cervical screening and health inequality in England in the 1990s. *Journal of Epidemiology and Community Health.* 2003;57(6): 417–423.
57. Langdown C, Peckham S. The use of financial incentives to help improve health outcomes: Is the quality and outcomes framework fit for purpose? A systematic review. *Journal of Public Health.* 2014;36(2): 251–258. Available from: https://doi.org/10.1093/pubmed/fdt077.
58. Campell SM, Reeves D, Kontopantelis E, et al. Effects of pay for performance on the quality of primary care in England. *New England Journal of Medicine.* 2009; 361:368–378.
59. National Institute for Health and Clinical Excellence. *About the Quality and Outcomes Framework (QOF).* Available from: http://www.nice.org.uk/aboutnice/qof/qof.jsp.
60. Roland M, Guthrie B. Quality and outcomes ramework: What have we learnt? *BMJ.* 2016;354: i4060.
61. Marshall M, Roland M. The future of the quality and outcomes framework in England. *BMJ.* 2017;359: j4681.
62. Kontopantelis E, Olier I, Planner C, et al. Primary care consultation rates among people with and without severe mental illness: A UK cohort study using the Clinical Practice Research Datalink. *BMJ Open.* 2015;5: e008650. https://bmjopen.bmj.com/content/5/12/e008650.
63. McGinnis JM. Observations on incentives to improve population health. *Preventing Chronic Disease.* 2010;7(5): A92. Available from: https://www.ncbi.nlm.nih.gov/pmc/articles/PMC2938408/.

CHAPTER 5

Health information in primary care and family practice: Concept, status, and a vision for the Eastern Mediterranean Region (EMR)

Arash Rashidian, Henry Victor Doctor, Eman Abdelkreem Hassan Aly, and Azza Mohamed Badr

BACKGROUND: IMPORTANCE OF ROUTINE HEALTH INFORMATION SYSTEMS

A health information system (HIS) is an "integrated effort to collect, process, report and use health information and knowledge to influence policy-making, programme action and research".[1] HIS is one of the essential building blocks of a health system, enabling decision-makers at all levels of the health system to identify health challenges and make optimal allocation of scarce resources to achieve health improvements.[2] A robust HIS that generates reliable, timely, and high-quality data is among several factors that enable policy makers to make evidence-based decisions. Since the 1990s, the role of HIS in improving health outcomes has gained prominence. In particular, countries are implementing interventions to strengthen HIS by addressing problems in HIS completeness, accuracy, and timeliness. These efforts have become inevitable within the context of the global agenda for sustainable development, calling for countries to generate better data from multiple sources to support improvements in health-care service delivery.[3]

Health data and information come from two main categories: population-based data sources (censuses, vital registration, and household surveys) and institution-based data sources (facility surveys, facility records, individual records).[4] Routine health information systems (RHIS) data, also called health facility and community information systems, are recognized as the backbone of facility-level, micro-planning, and higher-level (e.g. district, regional, national) decision making, resource allocation, and health strategy development.[2,5] Routine HIS consists of data collected at regular intervals in public, private, and community-level health facilities and institutions. The data provides an opportunity to study dynamics in health status, health services, and health resources.

At the individual and community level, health information supports effective clinical management and assessment of the extent to which services are responding to community needs. District level officials require information to make decisions regarding functioning of health facilities and the entire health system. National-level officials are interested in information for development of policy strategies.[6] In primary health care (PHC), the use of reliable HIS technology can lead to increased productivity, enhance quality of health care through sharing of health information across settings, and minimize medical errors. Reliable RHIS have the potential to decrease time spent on diagnosis and treatment and subsequently decrease time spent on patient visits.[7]

Despite the renewed interest and significant investments in RHIS data for country-led programmes and policy making, there are major obstacles that impede the quality and effective use of RHIS data. A common concern in many settings relates to delayed submission of reports including incomplete and inaccurate data from health facilities and districts. Such data quality issues undermine credibility and compromise use of RHIS-based indicators. However, there are effective, novel, and innovative approaches, often using information technology (IT) for improving routine HIS data particularly in low- and middle-income countries (LMICs). These methods have led to significant improvements in data quality by taking advantage of the available electronic data systems to enhance data collection, processing, analysis, and use of information.[8] Data quality assessments and ensuing improvement plans have also led to widespread use of routine HIS data for decision making.[9]

THE ROLE OF DATA AND INFORMATION IN PRIMARY HEALTH CARE AND FAMILY PRACTICE

Concept and role

An effective primary care programme is not limited to a point of personal health care or public health service; rather it has a role to ensure effective coordination with different layers of a health-care system, as well as other related sectors that affect the health of the population. This role has been strongly emphasized in the 1978 Alma-Ata Declaration and what has followed it. This coordinating role cannot be accomplished without timely and reliable sources of data and information that link the status and needs of the population with the risks and threats in the community. Information is also required on the delivery of services and resources devoted to them. In technical terms, a HIS is needed that collects data on individual demographic and risk characteristics, as well as health-care needs and service utilization. With appropriate safeguards, such data can be linked with other important sources of routine and administrative data, including civil registration systems. Ideally, all the data related to one person will be synchronized. However, in a world with many vertical care programmes, such simple expectations may not always materialize. The lack of such links and data sources are among the prime reasons most PHC systems fail to achieve their intended objectives.

In a more specific context related to the provision of care, primary care (and family practice) have important roles that include "integrated" (i.e. comprehensive, coordinated, continuous) and "accessible" provision of care.[10] Effective data and information flows are important for the coordination of care. Continuity of care refers to ensuring the patient is cared for over time; this is mainly achieved through clinician continuity (e.g. the patient's own family physician).

However, "data continuity" is a main requirement of achieving this key objective of a primary care system.[11] Data continuity is important across time (e.g. as the patient gets older and requires different types of care and services), and across service provision (e.g. when the patient receives services from different providers).

Additional to the above considerations, referral systems (from primary care to secondary care and back again) cannot effectively operate unless timely and reliable information is available between the levels of health care. All these considerations together provide a compelling picture why HIS is essential to any primary care system.[11]

General approach to routine health information system data

RHIS data is largely gathered by health-care providers during their routine work, or by supervisors; and through implementation of routine health facility surveys. Sources of RHIS data are generally individual patient health records, records of services delivered, and records of health resources. An effective and functional HIS requires deployment and application of standards across various components of processes related to data collection, processing, quality assurance, analysis, dissemination, sharing, and use. This approach is key, particularly during the implementation of facility-based information systems.[12]

Key approaches to collecting facility-based information entail the collection of routine data from health services in public and private sectors (including non-government organizations (NGOs), non-profit, for profit, and faith-based health facilities). The approach also includes collection of data within health facilities from service delivery records and patient-provider interactions including service provision at the community level. For example, community health workers (CHWs) and health visitors have been providing health service in communities in many LMICs for a considerable time.[13,14] Facility-based information systems can also include data collected from health-related service delivery sites such as schools, workplaces, and other community sites. Besides routine data collection, information can also be collected through periodic facility assessments and surveys to provide objective and independent information on health service distribution, capacities, and quality of care.

Implementation of facility-based information systems has created opportunities for collection of information related to the efficacy of interventions, treatment administration, and related outcomes. When such data are collected, they can be used for a wide range of purposes, including managing patient care, epidemiological surveillance, monitoring of intervention-specific programmes, and quality assessments. Further, these data can be useful in complementing other sources of data to detect and report epidemic outbreaks.[15]

Tools for collecting routine health information system data

Key sources of RHIS data include individual patient records, family record cards, admission and discharge registers, ward registers, community-level records, and records of health interventions delivered in non-health settings. These sources are simplified into three groups: individual record systems including electronic health records, facility records, and community-based records.[15]

Individual record systems constitute the majority of data collected at the health-facility level, where all individuals are assigned a card or file and details are recorded of their interactions with health service providers. An individual file contains key patient identification details, as well as diagnosis and treatment carried out during all visits. There are variations of individual files, with some health facilities providing a record for each patient, others using a paper-based record book to record patient information, and others using an electronic database to record data. Standard data records include name, address, and other identifying characteristics, clinical diagnosis, results of laboratory and diagnostic tests, list of drugs prescribed, money paid for services, health education and other information given to the patient, preventive activities (e.g. antenatal care or postnatal care), health promotion activities (e.g. healthy lifestyle advice), and rehabilitation services (e.g. physiotherapy).

Electronic health records (EHRs) are preferred to the paper-based systems mostly used in LMICs in the Eastern Mediterranean Region (EMR). The use of EHRs will become increasingly universal, consistent with ongoing technological advances supporting seamless collection of patient data using computers, mobile phones, and tablets. Common advantages of EHRs include timely collection of data, continuity of care with client reminders about follow-up procedures, potential to improve aspects of quality of care, seamless communication between different medical and administrative units, speedy reporting processes for facility and system management, and direct linkage of administrative functions such as billing and stock control.[15]

The evolution, increasing use, and advantages of EHR have been well acknowledged.[16] However, EHR implementation requires the availability of selected skills for HIS staff and appropriate resources. Availability of advanced technology, networking skills, infrastructure, and maintenance are not only critical, but often non-existent, in remote facilities in most LMICs. Availability of these resources and expertise is important but ensuring that health facility staff understand and use the data collected remains a challenge in many settings if proper capacity building has not been planned and implemented.

Facility-based registers include tools that collect data on patient admissions and discharges, patient conditions that need follow-up over extended periods (e.g. antenatal care, courses of immunization, family planning, or tuberculosis treatment). The facility-based register also supports the generation of indicators for periodic reporting of all patient records. In order to enhance continuity of quality of care, facility-based registers are expected to assist health providers in reviewing patients who have attended clinics as expected and those who need follow-up or tracing in the community.[17]

Other routine health service registry data can come from hospital discharge reports which can be used to monitor the quality of health services and for capturing treatment interventions. Hospital discharge reports includes individual records focusing on selected dimensions such as patient–provider interactions, demographic data (e.g. age and sex), treatment and interventions, and cause of admission and discharge.[15]

Community recording systems have evolved as one of the innovative approaches to improving data collection at all levels. Most governments have adopted a PHC strategy that recognizes the need to reorganize the traditional health services system and adapt to the needs and limitations identified at the community level. This can be done through community engagement in planning and management of local health services. Common approaches to community recording systems focus on monitoring health activities performed in the community, generating representative data on the health status and living environment of the communities served, including data on births and deaths in the community, and delivering health services that are more accessible to the members of the community.[15] Despite these novel approaches to PHC delivery, community reporting is challenged by the definition of who does the reporting. Reliance on CHWs is challenged by problems associated with the nature and engagement of their work. It has been reported that most CHWs would prefer to report events of births than deaths, thereby leading to bias in the information that is collected.[18]

The next section describes and contrasts approaches to collection and use of data for PHC and family practice in 11 countries, largely focusing on whether there is an information system, whether it is paper based or electronic, degree of functionality, inclusion of data from both private and public sectors, linkages with other levels of care, continuity within primary care, and national data aggregation and reporting mechanisms.

INFORMATION SYSTEMS IN PRIMARY HEALTH CARE: SELECTED CASE STUDIES

In this section, we describe the range of PHC information systems, their functionality, and reporting mechanisms used in selected countries in the Eastern Mediterranean Region.

Bahrain's primary health-care information system

Recognizing the importance of health information technology and the need to develop a national HIS, the Bahrain Health Information Centre was established within the Ministry of Health (MoH) in the early 1980s. Initially, the main role of the centre was to compile statistical information and publish it in the MoH's annual report. In 1997, the centre was upgraded to become the Health Information Directorate with an expanded role to take full responsibility in developing the HIS for the MoH. The overarching agenda of the Health Information Directorate is to provide high-quality information to the public and support improvements in health service delivery at a reasonable cost. This agenda is achieved through the Directorate's four main sections: application development, decision support unit, technical support units, and a projects office. In addition to conducting statistical analyses and annual reporting of health data in the country, the Health Information Directorate developed an automated system to manage various support functions and all patient socio-medical information.

In 2011, the MoH started implementation of the National HIS programme, called I-SEHA, to improve service delivery by linking citizens and residents of the kingdom with the providers and suppliers of health-care services, including payers and regulators. In brief, the main objectives of I-SEHA are to develop technical health service systems by applying the latest techniques on health services to improve services for patients and increase the efficiency (quality and speed) of delivery. The I-SEHA programme also includes the provision of electronic services for the implementation of the e-Government project through the provision of all electronic health services such as patient appointments, results of X-rays and laboratory tests, and requests for registration of births and deaths.[19] Through I-SEHA, the National Health Information Centre will be able to implement real-time online analytical decision support tools to assist in the improvement of daily operations and clinical practice. This will include data warehouse decision support tools for analysing retrospective information that will assist in prospectively planning improvements in quality and effectiveness of services, as well as efficient utilization of resources. I-SEHA also provides reliable information for evidence-based decision making to improve individual behaviour, patient care, administration, research, and education, and to monitor and measure health outcomes.

I-SEHA is implemented in the Salmaniya Medical Complex (SMC), King Hamad University Hospital, MoH peripheral hospitals, and all health centres. Through I-SEHA, all health facilities are equipped with a modern and integrated clinical and administrative system that supports daily operations and clinical practice. The I-SEHA programme implementation consisted of three phases: Phase 1 focused on implementation of the system in PHC centres; Phase 2 focused on implementation for SMC hospitalization services; and Phase 3 focused on updating deployed systems with additional services and modules in other hospitals and health centres.

While I-SEHA and related initiatives have led to regular generation of data that are published annually, there is a need for detailed analyses of the available data, and the analyses need to be complemented by health-system research to generate evidence to support decision making. While the annual report of the Health Information Directorate provides information related to health indicators, facilities, human resources, and activities within the MoH, as well as some private health organizations, there is a need to enhance the national HIS to provide necessary data on health-care spending, particularly on private services. This can be achieved through household expenditure and utilization surveys as well as analysis of national health accounts.

Egypt's primary health-care information system

Egypt's health information centre at the Ministry of Health and Population (MoHP) has been functional since the 1950s; it has maintained a database of all births and deaths in Egypt since then. The MoHP also maintains a national system for surveillance of 26 communicable and endemic diseases, across all areas of the country. A stepwise approach for surveillance of risk factors for non-communicable diseases (NCDs) has also been developed. The coordination of surveillance activities for communicable and NCDs, including traffic injuries, lies with the Epidemiological Surveillance Unit, which was established in MoHP in 1999.

Egypt has a management information system for primary health centres which cover 90% of the population. The system aggregates data from the PHC centres to the health directorate level and then up to the central MoHP level. The system is paper-based at the PHC level and electronic-based at the health directorate level. Information on the activities of the PHC centres is collected monthly. However, the MoHP does not publish an annual statistical report, and data produced are not used for decision making. Ensuring comprehensive coverage of reported data remains a challenge. Reporting of data from the private sector and facilities maintained by other organizations, such as the armed forces, is limited. Thus, building an integrated HIS covering all areas and levels, including the development of dashboards for decision makers at all levels, is essential for the new health insurance system being rolled out.

In 2007, USAID launched a project to help build health management information systems (HMIS) in Egypt with the following guiding principles: avoiding creation of a project-based information system; playing a coordinating role; defining and prioritizing objectives; building organizational capacity; making available consolidated information at MoHP headquarters; producing information at the governorate level for local decision-making; strengthening human resources; avoiding introduction of information technology faster than capacity is developed to use the technology; using the private sector for support; establishing official standard coding systems; and developing a workplan with well-defined stages and tasks.

Developing the national HIS and monitoring framework is a priority for the government. By positioning universal health coverage as a high priority in its political agenda and strategic vision for 2030, there is a need to reform the entire health sector, with the information system and monitoring framework at the centre of this endeavour. Efforts are in progress to institutionalize HIS by establishing a multisectoral HIS steering committee to provide sound health information governance, establish a data warehouse for the health sector, strengthen civil registration and vital statistics (CRVS) (particularly improving cause of death reporting), developing a national research strategy, and other strategies enhancing decision making at all levels.[20]

Iran's primary health-care information system

Under the theme "health for all", Iran developed its PHC system with full deployment in 1985. The PHC system is structured according to the geographical distribution of urban and rural areas. The village health house and larger rural health centres constitute the first level of population and family health services in rural areas and over 85% of the rural population are covered by these health facilities. Similarly, health posts and larger health centres are the first level of service provision in urban areas. The second level of management of this structure is district health centres that function under the supervision of provincial medical science universities.[21]

In rural areas, key data collection activities focus on the registration of vital events and family data including mortality by age group, sex, and cause of death, births by outcome, and basic service delivery for maternal, neonatal, and child health services. Household health records also provide another source of PHC data. At the peripheral level, data collection is paper-based and aggregated data are transferred to district health centres where they are entered into computers and sent to the capital for consolidation.[22,23] The country uses different tools, such as the Health Information Management Panel (HIMP), to monitor and disseminate health information. The HIMP is a tool developed and used at each level of primary care to provide access to key indicators about health service delivery for decision making. Indicators are defined based on the level of the health-care services, including at province, district, and health facility levels. The panels aim to display health information and indicators across the service delivery levels, provide a summary of health status by region, and monitor the trend of diseases and population health. Health indicators are displayed on the walls of health facilities throughout the year as well as at managerial levels at health district, provincial, and national levels. This system of data display was a feature of the PHC in Iran from early days, based on an approach widely known as the "vital horoscope". Indicators are updated on a monthly or annual basis and are accessible to all relevant staff.

The National Institute of Health Research (NIHR) established a national health observatory in 2009. In addition to its core mandate of monitoring population health status, burden of diseases, and programme activities, the NIHR provides planners and decision makers with standardized tools to measure the impact of service delivery, promote effective communication with policy makers, promote information sharing with all concerned entities, and support public health research. The health observatory produces annual health review reports, periodic health-system operation reports outlining the trends of national health indicators, and ad hoc reports as requested by decision making councils within the health system.[23,24] Despite some of the notable attributes of the Iran HIS, existing PHC information systems are beset with, among other problems, a deficiency of computerized facilities for recording data and web-based technologies to transfer information from one level to the other, and a shortage of information and communications technology infrastructures between the various stages of the information production process.[25]

Jordan's primary health-care health information system

Jordan's MoH service delivery is established at three levels: primary, secondary, and tertiary. PHC is the key mode to implement health-care programmes. The main public health-care providers are the MoH, the Royal Medical Services (RMS), and the university hospitals (Jordan University Hospital and King Abdullah University Hospital). In addition, there are several specialist health-care providers, including the King Hussein Cancer Centre. Services from the public health sector are complemented by the private sector, which includes both private for profit and not-for-profit, mostly working in peripheral areas. The United Nations Relief and Works Agency (UNRWA) also provides health-care services throughout Jordan.[26]

Routine HIS and surveillance systems for PHC include information emanating from public and private health services, those resulting from the notifiable diseases surveillance systems, including information on available human resources, drugs and supplies, blood banks, equipment, and infrastructure, as well as financial resources. RHIS data collection in most health directorates is largely paper-based with selected facilities implementing an electronic-based system. Both data collection systems are managed through the Directorate of Information and

Studies. As of October 2016, aggregated information from hospitals and PHC centres was collected using 30 different paper forms, 20 of which were computerized.[26]

RHIS data collection also focuses on notifiable diseases, NCDs, mental diseases, and service delivery (e.g. antenatal and postnatal care, family planning, child care services, and postpartum and post-abortion family planning services). Data are collected in health facilities and transferred to the central level at the MoH for electronic processing, and then compiled monthly and published through an "Annual Statistical Report" which is produced by the Information and Studies Directorate of the MoH.

The "Hakeem" programme is the first national initiative to computerize the public healthcare sector. Launched in October 2009, the programme aims to facilitate efficient, high-quality health care in Jordan through nationwide implementation of EHR. Using Hakeem, physicians, pharmacists, medical technologists, and other clinicians can access electronic medical records of patients within participating health facilities by entering the patient's national identity number. Records that can be accessed through Hakeem include comprehensive medical and surgical history, physical examinations, procedural and surgical reports, current medications, allergies, as well as in-patient and out-patient clinic visit notes. Hakeem also provides online access to laboratory results, digital radiological exams, electrocardiograms, endoscopic biopsies, eye exams, and videos of echocardiograms and angiograms.

In partnership with the World Health Organization (WHO), the MoH developed an Interactive Electronic Reporting System (IERS) in 2015 which uses mobile tools and an online framework to collect, analyse, and report surveillance data.[27] IERS is an integrated disease surveillance system to monitor the status and functioning of HIS, and for monitoring diseases of public health importance among refugees and host communities. IERS surveillance reports are available within one hour. With at least 70% coverage of PHC facilities since December 2017, the MoH is planning to scale-up IERS to provide real-time data and serve a wide range of surveillance programmes with flexibility to include other data collection modules. IERS provides real-time, case-based data using ICD-10 coding and automatically generates short message services (SMS) and email alerts for notification of disease outbreaks and alerts for public health thresholds of events that require immediate action. IERS also facilitates clinical decision and management approaches to investigations, medical treatment, and assessment of treatment outcomes for NCDs.[27]

Health-service delivery in Jordan includes recording of basic data about the client, the conditions observed, and the services delivered. These individual records form a foundation for providing ongoing integrated care, and for assessing the quality of care for individuals. In Jordan, institution-based data sources of the routine HIS exist in all the directorates of the MoH, private and university hospitals, MoH vertical surveillance programmes, RMS, UNRWA, and health professional associations. PHC data cover areas related to general consultations, dental, general practice, and medical services (e.g. laboratory and radiology). Hospital data cover areas related to morbidity, mortality, service delivery, blood bank services, renal dialysis services, births, and surgical operations. Surveillance system data sources are generally not comprehensive, while the private sector does not report to the directorates of communicable diseases, NCDs, maternal and child health, or the cancer registry. The private sector and UNRWA health facilities report only to communicable disease surveillance systems for diseases notifiable by law of an epidemic-prone nature and for diseases of global and regional concern such as polio.[26]

Kuwait's primary health-care health information system

There are 92 PHC centres in Kuwait providing services to people in the six health regions (i.e. Asimah, Hawali, Ahmadi, Jahra, Farwania, and Al Sabah). Each region is served by several PHC centres and one of the six general hospitals: Sabah 1, Amiri, Mubarak Al-Kabeer 1, Farwaniya, Adan and Jahra. The PHC centres provide general, maternal, and child health, diabetes, and dental clinics. The centres also offer preventive care and school health services. Mental health-care services have also been incorporated in health care offered at PHC level.

Strengthening HIS and applied research are some of the key activities planned by the health sector according to the 2015–2019 national health plan. Kuwait's HIS generates data of high quality on morbidity, mortality, vital health statistics, and utilization from all levels of health-care delivery. Detailed statistics are available for primary, secondary, and specialized care. However, there are separate systems of data collection for PHC facilities, and for secondary and tertiary health-care hospitals, and separate reporting systems for preventive and curative care. Other than regional offices, there are three central departments involved in data collection and management: the Department of Statistics and Medical Records which collects data from public and private hospitals; the Public Health Department which focuses on preventive services data; and the PHC Department which receives data from PHC centres. The records and data in centres are computerized and it is planned that they will be connected to the secondary and tertiary hospital network. One of the key priorities of the MoH is to leverage the existing technology and improve the referral and follow-up system between primary, secondary, and tertiary levels.

The MoH issues an Annual Statistical Report in addition to the Annual Vital Statistics Report. Various health programmes generate their own reports which are not part of the RHIS. The Department of Statistics and Medical Records is the main department responsible for management of data and information products within the MoH.[28] The Public Health Department receives data on preventive services directly from health centres and hospitals and issues detailed weekly reports that include epidemiological, disease surveillance, and other preventive activities. The information is also sent to the Department of Statistics and Medical Records.

A challenge of the current system, however, is that individual systems are not connected. Information collection is focused on hospital matters and therefore, public health-related information systems need strengthening. There is also a need to strengthen operation research and generation of evidence for policy and decision making. There is also a need to continuously assess the performance of the current information systems and to develop a strategic plan to connect various information systems in the health sector. Such a system should be flexible and all-encompassing to provide easy access for users at different levels.

Libya's primary health–care health information system

Health service delivery in Libya is provided at three levels: primary, secondary, and tertiary. The public health sector is the main health services provider. Delivery is implemented through a network of PHC units, centres, polyclinics, rehabilitation centres, general hospitals in urban and rural areas, and tertiary care specialized hospitals.[29] However, Libya's health system has been facing the worst humanitarian crisis in its recent history. The increased clashes and administrative disputes since mid-2014 led to freezing of the implementation and approval of new health policies. The health sector is highly dependent on a foreign health workforce and the protracted humanitarian crisis has led to the exodus of foreign workers. To a large extent, fragmented governance, limited financial resources, inadequate human resources, and acute shortage of basic life-saving medicines and equipment have characterized Libya's health system recently.[30]

Results from the 2016 Service Availability and Readiness Assessment (SARA) showed that 19% of the 97 hospitals and 20% of the 1355 PHCs (including polyclinics, health centres, and units) were closed. The availability and readiness of services in PHCs and hospitals was significantly low. Lack of readiness was influenced by an acute shortage of life-saving medicines, medical supplies, and equipment, including critical shortages of human resources, such as specialized physicians, nurses, midwives, and technicians. These shortages were acute at the primary care level. Provision of PHC services, especially for communicable diseases among migrants and refugees in detention centres, has been a major challenge.[31]

Routine health information emanates from two main sources: the statistical offices of each hospital and the statistics units of each directorate of health at the district level. In order to improve preventive health care, detection, and response to diseases, the National Centre for Disease Control (NCDC) was established in 2002 to guide different programmes on communicable diseases. In 2010 the NCDC was designated to guide the NCD preventive and control programmes. The NCDC has 51 adult vaccination centres and a network of 36 programme managers implementing the immunization programme at the district level. Reporting and communication within the network have improved recently and most sentinel sites are reporting regularly to the NCDC.[30]

A range of services are provided at the PHC level and information is collected for the following services: maternal and child health; early diagnosis of infectious diseases and implementation of local control measures; health promotion; registration and follow-up of chronic diseases; curative services; nutrition awareness; water quality monitoring; and monitoring environmental health at the community level. The MoH Health Information Centre is responsible for compiling all RHIS data. Health information is received directly from the statistical offices of all the hospitals and from the statistical units of the directorate of health at the district level. Before the conflict, 23 sub-centres of the MoH Health Information Centre were responsible for collecting, collating, and transmitting data to the central level at the MoH through electronic reporting. Despite major gaps in the information that was collected and reported, data on disease burden, service usage, and outcome were available for decision making and for compiling an annual report. Since 2013, however, the annual report has not been published due to fragmented data collection efforts. Out of all the 1559 health-care facilities, only a limited number were reporting this data. As documented in the 2016 SARA report, some of the reasons for non-reporting include closure of some health facilities, non-availability of human resources, limited Internet connectivity, and using older versions of data recording tools.[31]

To strengthen Libya's HIS and RHIS, WHO in collaboration with the MoH, conducted an assessment of the HIS in 2017 to commence the main activities of a two-year European Union (EU) funded project: Strengthening Health Information System and Medical Supply Chain Management (SHAMS). The assessment identified a set of priority actions to enhance the functionality of HIS. Since then, the MoH has started efforts to strengthen the national HIS, supported by WHO and with funding from the EU. One of the key interventions is to pilot a District Health Information System (DHIS-2) in selected facilities as part of efforts to enhance information gathering, analysis, and use for decision making at all levels of health service delivery. A national scale-up of DHIS-2 is envisioned to enhance reporting of core health indicators at the national, regional, and international level.

Oman's primary health-care health information system

The health-care system in the Sultanate of Oman consists of public and private sectors, and both have demonstrated tremendous improvement in the quality of health service delivery over a considerable time. The public health sector is considered the major provider of health care.[32,33] The public health-care system is three-tiered: primary care units (health centres and polyclinics) that provide basic health-care services; secondary care units at "wilayat" (province level) which provide multi-specialized services; and tertiary care units at reference hospitals which provide highly specialized services.[32,33]

The HIS comprises different modules for different specialties. However, the core module is called the Electronic Patient Record (EPR) which provides information on patient sociodemographic data, doctor notes, investigations made, and reports of outcomes. The development of a health information management system to support the health-care delivery system required tailored software, hardware, and skilled human resources to implement a fast, secure, and reliable system that generates data of high quality to improve service quality and reduce the cost of service delivery.[32,33]

Several initiatives have been made to shift towards an IT-based HIS management system since 1987. However, there was neither a clear vision nor a predefined strategy. In 1994, the MoH adopted its own tailored system for HIS management. By 2004, the HIS management system was fully implemented with a well-defined strategy. This system is called "Al-Shifa" and is a comprehensive health-care information management system developed as a complete solution for health-care facility management, covering electronic medical records, assets, inventory, and human resource management, among others. The Al-Shifa system aims at developing a national unified information management system for health services provided by public health facilities at all levels under supervision of the MoH.

In 2008, system mergers and improvements were made leading to a unified national system called Al-Shifa 3plus. This is a fully integrated system that supports data transfer between units at all service delivery levels. The system is managed by the Directorate General of Information Technology in the MoH. There are more than 200 public health-care institutes using the system, serving around 85% of health-care seekers in Oman.[32,33] Al-Shifa 3plus has modules that support data collection on clinical activities, national-level key performance indicators from 200+ health-care centres, e-referral and e-notification, more than 70 health-care facility referral mechanisms including appointments, ambulatory care, laboratory and other investigation support care, and a blood bank management system.[34]

The MoH health information management strategy for Oman is to enhance Al-Shifa 3plus and establish a unique patient identification system using the national identifier for each Omani patient and the residency number for expatriates; it also aims to build an e-health record repository. The strategic objective aims to have a secure, connected, consistent, and cohesive national health-care services management system working within a defined legal framework that regulates the confidentiality and privacy of e-health information. Al-Shifa 3plus saves 60% of medical personnel time by improving quality of care through better patient communication through use of SMS. Moreover, Al-Shifa 3plus reduces waiting time; improves records auditing; improves management of medical resources, stores, and pharmacies; enhances referral; and improves overall transparency of the health-care process. Not only does Al-Shifa 3plus provide automated statistical production for health planning and utilization of care, it is also considered a rich source of medical information for researchers. Despite these innovative developments, data quality issues (e.g. accuracy and completeness), weak ICT infrastructure, lack of skilled IT staff, security of the data, and legal issues constitute the main challenges to the current IT system. Securing sufficient funding for a sustainable e-health programme also remains a significant challenge.[32,33]

Pakistan's primary health–care health information system

With an estimated population of 213 million in 2017, Pakistan has a mixed health system that includes the public sector, private sector, parastatal health system, civil society, and philanthropic donors. Despite concerns about the quality of service delivery, a key strength of the government's health-care system is its PHC outreach, which is implemented at the community level through a cadre of 100,000 Lady Health Workers (LHWs), including an increasing number of community midwives and other CHWs.[35] Pakistan's health system is beset with vertical service delivery structures, low performance accountability within the government, and challenges with the quality of services. The private sector is largely unregulated for quality of care and pricing which impacts the quality of preventive and promotive health services. The public sector is inadequately staffed, and both job satisfaction and work environment are areas identified for improvement in the National Heath Vision 2016–2025.

Pakistan's HIS is fragmented, vertical, and largely oriented to serve vertical health programmes and provide district health information. RHIS data are collected at district and provincial levels through the District Health Information System (DHIS) and Management Information System (MIS). The government developed the health MIS in 1992, and subsequent reviews led to implementation of the DHIS platform across the country in a phased approach since 2005 in Khyber Pakhtunkhwa (KP), Punjab, Baluchistan, and Sindh provinces; in Federally Administered Tribal Areas (FATA) and in the Azad Jammu and Kashmir regions. Pakistan is also working towards integration of an HIV/AIDS, tuberculosis, and malaria specific MIS onto a single platform and linking it with the national HIS dashboard. The National Tuberculosis Control Programme at the federal level is implementing DHIS-2 as a reporting system in some districts. The Directorate of Malaria Control is developing a reporting mechanism using DHIS-2 for selected districts. The National AIDS Control Programme also collects data through an online reporting tool from antiretroviral therapy sites. Other initiatives include the Prime Minister's National Health Programme, which has an online case-based system that is operational and maintained at the federal level. The nutrition programme is collecting data through an online reporting tool from some districts of KP and FATA.[36]

The fragmented and vertical data collection systems have been recognized as a challenge by HIS national stakeholders. PHC services across the country are delivered from basic health units and rural health centres. Although most services are provided from the same premises, each service is managed independently of the other closely interrelated services. Individual programmes prepare statistical reports and send them directly to the district supervisor who forwards the same reports to the province. The reports on health promotion activities carried out in the communities by local health workers (LHWs) bypass the facilities. The head of the facility is neither fully responsible for all the services the facility collectively delivers, nor is there a mechanism for the head to know the overall health status of the catchment population or complete performance of the health unit. Thus, both the service delivery systems and data management systems are overly fragmented.[36]

A WHO-led review of the national HIS in 2017 identified several priority actions to address fragmentation challenges and enhance reporting of core health indicators at the national, regional, and international level.[36] One of the priority actions is to implement and consistently use DHIS-2 as the main system across all provincial departments of health. A gradual shift to DHIS-2 is being planned to build coherence across systems and to implement an Integrated Disease Surveillance and Response System across the country. These priority actions also are consistent with the 2016–2025 National Health Vision aiming at incorporating innovative technologies into the district HISs to facilitate evidence-based decision making and build coherence across HISs to monitor the Sustainable Development Goals and progress on national health targets.[35]

Palestine's primary health-care health information system

Health-care delivery for Palestinians is managed through the MoH, UNRWA, NGOs, and private non-profit providers. The public health sector provides primary and secondary level care through PHC centres and hospitals, the majority of which are owned by the MoH.[37,38]

The predominant function of the PHC centres is to control infectious diseases and improve maternal and child health. The success of PHC service delivery is demonstrated through high immunization coverage, improved maternal and child health outcomes, and the scaling up of services to contain the burden of non-communicable diseases that are gradually replacing the burden of infectious and perinatal conditions. Among the key priorities outlined in the National Health Strategy (2014–2016) is the development of infrastructure at both primary and secondary level for prevention and control of non-communicable diseases, including mental health.[37,39]

Data collection and storage at PHC centres is paper-based, covering the following services: maternal and child health (MCH), morbidity, dental health, vaccination, communicable diseases, and NCDs. Using standardized formats, data are aggregated monthly and transferred to the district level for electronic data entry, and then sent to the Palestinian Health Information Centre (PHIC) for consolidation. The PHIC generates quarterly reports focusing on primary care service performance indicators and morbidity data at the national level. Monthly and weekly epidemiological reports are shared with MoH technical programmes. A challenge, however, is that various departments at the MoH have their own databases, thereby leading to incompatibility of different databases and inadequate use of data.

Previous assessments and joint WHO–MoH missions have identified a number of weaknesses of the national HIS which include lack of allocated resources for health management information systems, use of inappropriate hardware and software, and lack of standard operating procedures at the regional and national levels.[38] To address some of these challenges, the National Institute of Public Health was established as a joint WHO–MoH initiative to support use of data and research evidence for decision making, enhance the national HIS, act as a hub for public health professionals and researchers, and enhance networks between public health institutions to maximize utilization of health information.[37]

Sudan's primary health-care health information system

The Sudan Federal Ministry of Health (FMoH) developed a PHC expansion plan (2014–2016) aiming to improve access to quality health-care services and expand the coverage of services from 86% to 100%. The health-care delivery system is implemented at three levels: federal, state, and local. Health-care facilities at local levels are primary health units (PHU), PHC centres, and rural hospitals. PHUs deliver integrated PHC services, whereas health centres are considered the referral facility at this level. The standard population for service coverage is 5000 for basic health units and 20,000 to 50,000 for health centres. However, there are no updated population data at PHU/PHC level to enable calculation of health-service coverage at the sub-national level.

Health services provided at all levels of care include maternal and child health, family planning, immunization, and communicable diseases control including bilharziasis, malaria, tuberculosis, HIV/AIDS, leishmaniasis, other neglected tropical diseases, and NCDs. NGOs provide PHC services in cooperation with the FMoH, in addition to private clinics and hospitals in urban areas which provide secondary and tertiary health-care services.[40,41,42]

The FMoH, with collaboration from WHO, is enhancing operations of the national HIS using modern technology to improve data management, and the development of national and sub-national health indicators in line with global health goals and targets. Strategic interventions to enhance HIS commenced in 2016 and largely focus on shifting from paper-based to electronic HIS. The interventions are being implemented in a phased approach focusing on three pillars of information management system development: establishment of electronic information management systems at local, state, and federal level; integration within the FMOH health-care and disease programme; and building national capacity in HIS management and information technology.

Information systems in PHC/PHUs and hospitals is paper-based using standardized registries which are revised and updated by technical programmes in the FMOH. Modules of data collection cover services related to vaccination, nutrition, maternal, neonatal, child, and out-patient visits, in addition to hospital admission and morbidities recorded on the hospital data system. Monthly aggregated data are transferred to local and state level for consolidation and electronic data entry. This is followed by transfer of data to the federal level to generate information products on service delivery performance and burden of disease monitoring indicators. Key national HIS challenges include limited system coverage due to resistance in some administrative areas to the adoption of the new electronic system, limited infrastructure, and lack of relevant skilled staff to generate reliable data and information products on health indicators and health-system performance.

Syria's primary health-care health information system

In 2014, an assessment of the national HIS conducted by the MoH identified four areas for improvement, namely: the need for an organizational, regulatory, and legislative framework; availability of information, both its quality and quantity, as well as its accessibility; usage and protection of information; and sources of widely used indicators. However, since the onset of the crisis and conflict situation the Syrian HIS has been largely dependent on the Health Resources and Services Availability Mapping System (HeRAMS).

HeRAMS is a standardized approach, supported by a software-based platform, that aims to strengthen the collection, collation, and analysis of information on the availability of health resources and services in humanitarian emergencies. The key information collected through HeRAMS includes functionality status, accessibility, health infrastructure, human resources, availability of health services, equipment, and medicines at primary and secondary levels of care. HeRAMS was implemented in Syria in early 2013 after consultative meetings with the Syrian MoH and health-sector partners to customize the tool according to the priority needs of the health sector. New data collection mechanisms (i.e. tele-reporting and tele-assessment) were introduced to address the shortage of timely and relevant information. Information flow and reporting channels have been streamlined at various levels of reporting from health-facility level to health directorate and central level. Through HeRAMS reports, decision makers can monitor the health situation at PHC and secondary health-care levels, measure gaps, improve planning of resources, implement evidence-based actions, and enhance coordination and accountability.

Reporting is monthly for hospitals and quarterly for health centres. Ninety percent of public health facilities have been assessed using HeRAMS. Analysis of HeRAMS data in 2014 showed that the overall performance of health centres in Syria was weak but had improved, scoring an average of 0.51 (out of a composite index of 1), that is, the average performance of health centres in Syria in 2014 was 51% of the optimal "best performance". The improvement is mainly correlated with accessibility, which improved notably during 2014. The readiness measures from HeRAMS 2014 data showed that health centres experienced chronic shortages of medicines, equipment, and services. Analysis of HeRAMS data from the second quarter of 2017 showed that, of the 1806 assessed public health centres, 46% (827) were reported as fully functioning, 22% (88) were partially functioning, and 32% (586) were non-functioning (completely out-of-service), while the functionality status of 0.3% (5) of health centres was unknown.[43] Additional analyses of HeRAMS from 2017 demonstrate the dismal situation with PHC service delivery associated with significant accessibility problems and infrastructural damage, among other challenges.

An Early Warning Alert and Response System (EWARS) is part and parcel of the HIS in Syria. Its primary objective is to rapidly detect and respond to signals that might indicate outbreaks and clusters of epidemic-prone diseases. EWARS was implemented in 2012 in Syria and the reporting format was agreed upon based on the epidemiological situation and risk assessment. EWARS has two main components: an immediate alert component, which signals the early stages of an outbreak; and a weekly reporting component, which reports weekly data aggregated by health facilities. These complementary components ensure timely detection and verification of outbreaks and effective monitoring of morbidity patterns. Initially, 104 sentinel sites for EWARS were selected nationwide covering the 14 governorates. This has been expanded to cover 1100 sites including the MoH, private physicians, and NGO health facilities. Data collection from the sentinel sites is conducted on a weekly basis and sent to the central level where the data are analysed to produce a weekly bulletin for dissemination to all health partners.[44]

In order to enhance data availability for decision making, the MoH, in collaboration with WHO, implemented SARA in 2018. It was implemented as a census covering 2500 public PHC centres and includes data collection about health facility visits with data collected based on key informant interviews and observation of key health-system delivery attributes. While current data collection initiatives in Syria provide information on PHC services, key challenges experienced during data collection and reporting include accessibility and security, continuous power cuts, and lack of network coverage in many governorates.

CONCLUSION

While HISs are essential for the effective conduct of primary care and family practice approaches, countries in the EMR vary substantially in their methods of collection, use, and oversight of HISs. Even in countries with similar PHC prototypes, based on WHO recommendations, the HISs vary to a large extent. This may be partly because, from the start, a systemic approach was not offered for HIS implementation alongside primary care; and the minimum characteristics of an effective HIS were not defined in detail.

Despite these variations, a brief overview of the HIS in different countries' primary care systems provides enough insight for action and some opportunities for learning. WHO in the EMR has a plan of action to improve HIS. This plan of action includes a regional framework for the collection and reporting of core indicators, a plan for improving national CRVS systems, with a focus on mortality registration and accurate certification of causes of death, and a model for the conduct of comprehensive HIS assessments.[45–47] The latter provides ample attention to the organization of national HISs, including in primary care, and we hope it will help the consolidation of actions to support continuous improvement of primary care systems.

REFERENCES

1. Lippeveld T. Routine health information systems: The glue of a unified health system. [Keynote address] *Workshop on Issues and Innovation in Routine Health Information in Developing Countries*. Potomac, Washington, DC. 14–16 March 2001.
2. Mutale W, Chintu N, Amoroso C, Awoonor-Williams K, Phillips J, Baynes C, et al. Improving health information systems for decision making across five sub-Saharan African countries: Implementation strategies from the African Health Initiative. *BMC Health Services Research*. 2013;13(Suppl 2): S9. Available from: http://www.biomedcentral.com/1472-6963/13/S2/S9 [Accessed 17 February 2018].
3. Lippeveld T. Routine health facility and community information systems: Creating an information use culture. *Global Health: Science and Practice*. 2017;5(3): 338–340.
4. Health Metrics Network. *Assessing the National Health Information System: An Assessment Tool Version 4.00*. Geneva: World Health Organization; 2008.
5. WHO. *Framework and Standards for Country Health Information Systems*. 2nd edition. Geneva: World Health Organization; 2008.
6. AbouZahr C, Boerma T. Health information systems: The foundations of public health. *Bulletin of the World Health Organization*. 2005;83: 578–583.

7. Sarma S, Hajizadeh M, Thind A, Chan R. The association between health information technology adoption and family physician's practice patterns in Canada: Evidence from 2007 and 2010 National Physician Surveys. *Healthcare Policy.* 2013;9(1): 97–117.

8. Wagenaar BH, Sherr K, Fernandes Q, Wagenaar AC. Using routine health information systems for well-designed health evaluations in low- and middle-income countries. *Health Policy and Planning.* 2016;31(1): 129–135.

9. WHO. *Data Quality Review: A Toolkit for Facility Data Quality Assessment. Module 1. Framework and Metrics.* Geneva: World Health Organization; 2017.

10. Institute of Medicine. *Defining Primary Care: An Interim Report.* Washington DC: The National Academies Press; 1994. Available from: https://www.nap.edu/catalog/9153/defining-primary-care-an-in terim-report.

11. WHO. *The World Health Report 2008: Primary Health Care Now More than Ever.* Geneva: World Health Organization; 2008.

12. Belay H, Lippeveld T. *Inventory of PRISM Framework and Tools: Application of PRISM Tools and Interventions for Strengthening RHIS Performance.* MEASURE Evaluation. Working Paper Series No. 13-138; 2013.

13. Schneider H, Okello D, Lehmann U. The global pendulum swing towards community health workers in low- and middle-income countries: A scoping review of trends, geographical distribution and programmatic orientations, 2005 to 2014. *Human Resources for Health.* 2016;14: 65. Available from: https://hu man-resources-health.biomedcentral.com/articles/10.1186/s12960-016-0163-2.

14. Javanparast S, Baum F, Labonte R, Sanders D, Rajabi Z, Heidari G. The experience of community health workers in Iran: A qualitative study. *BMC Health Services Research.* 2012;12: 291. Available from: https:// bmchealthservres.biomedcentral.com/articles/10.1186/1472-6963-12-291.

15. Heywood A, Boone D. *Guidelines for Data Management Standards in Routine Health Information Systems.* Chapel Hill: MEASURE Evaluation. Document MS-15-99; 2015.

16. Evans RS. Electronic health records: Then, now and in the future. *Yearbook of Medical Informatics.* 2016; Suppl 1: S48-61. Available from: https://doi.org/10.15265/IYS-2016-s006.

17. WHO. *Health Facility Information Resource Kit. Product of a Technical Consultation on Monitoring Results with Health Facility Information Systems.* Geneva: World Health Organization; 2014.

18. WHO. *Meeting Report: African Mortality Statistics Expert Workshop.* Cairo, Egypt, 28 September–1 October 2015. Cairo: WHO Regional Office for the Eastern Mediterranean.

19. WHO. *Bahrain Health Profile 2015.* Cairo: WHO Regional Office for the Eastern Mediterranean; 2017. Available from: https://extranet.who.int/iris/restricted/bitstream/10665/254905/1/EMROPUB_2017_E N_19616.pdf?ua=1 [Accessed 23 February 2018].

20. WHO. *Egypt Health Profile 2015.* Cairo: WHO Regional Office for the Eastern Mediterranean; 2016. Available from: http://applications.emro.who.int/dsaf/EMROPUB_2016_EN_19264.pdf?ua=1&ua=1 [Accessed 22 February 2018].

21. Moshiri E, Rashidian A, Arab M, Khosravi A. Using an analytical framework to explain the formation of primary health care in rural Iran in the 1980s. *Archives of Iranian Medicine.* 2016;19(1): 16–22.

22. Khosravi A, Motlagh ME, Emami Razavi SH. The Iranian vital horoscope; appropriate tool to collect health statistics in rural areas. *Iranian Journal of Public Health.* 2009;38(Suppl.1): 74–80.

23. WHO. *Islamic Republic of Iran health profile 2015.* Cairo: WHO Regional Office for the Eastern Mediterranean; 2016. Available from: http://applications.emro.who.int/dsaf/EMROPUB_2016_EN_1 9265.pdf?ua=1&ua=1 [Accessed 19 February 2018].

24. Rashidian A, Damari B, Larijani B, Vosoogh Moghadda A, Alikhani A, Shadpour K, et al. Health observatories in Iran. *Iranian Journal of Public Health.* 2013;42(Suppl 1): 84–87.

25. YazdiFeyzabadi V, Emam M, Mehrolhassani MH. Health information system in primary health care: The challenges and barriers from local providers' perspective of an area in Iran. *International Journal of Preventive Medicine.* 2015;6: 57. Available from: https://www.ncbi.nlm.nih.gov/pubmed/26236444.

26. WHO. *Assessment of the Jordanian health information system.* Cairo: WHO Regional Office for the Eastern Mediterranean; 2017.

27. Sheikhali SA, Abdallat M, Mandalla S, Al Qaseer B, Khorma R, Malik M, et al. Design and implementation of a national public health surveillance system in Jordan. *International Journal of Medical Informatics.* 2016;88: 58–61.

28. WHO. *Kuwait health profile 2015*. Cairo: WHO Regional Office for the Eastern Mediterranean; 2016. Available from: http://applications.emro.who.int/dsaf/EMROPUB_2016_EN_19271.pdf?ua=1&ua=1 [Accessed 24 February 2018].

29. WHO. *Libya health profile 2015*. Cairo: WHO Regional Office for the Eastern Mediterranean; 2017. Available from: http://applications.emro.who.int/dsaf/EMROPUB_2016_EN_19271.pdf?ua=1 [Accessed 24 February 2018].

30. WHO. *Libya: Country Cooperation Strategy at a Glance*. Cairo: WHO Regional Office for the Eastern Mediterranean; 2017.

31. WHO, Ministry of Health Libya. *Service Availability and Readiness Assessment of the Public Health Facilities in Libya*. Tripoli: World Health Organization and Ministry of Health; 2017.

32. Al-Gharbi KN, Gattoufi SM, Al-Badi AH, Al-Hashmi AA. Al-Shifa health care information system in Oman: A debatable implementation. *Electronic Journal of Information Systems in Developing Countries*. 2015;66(1): 1–17.

33. WHO. *Oman Health Profile 2015*. Cairo: WHO Regional Office for the Eastern Mediterranean; 2016. Available from: http://applications.emro.who.int/dsaf/EMROPUB_2016_EN_19273.pdf?ua=1&ua=1 [Accessed 23 February 2018].

34. Khan SF, Ismail MY. Al-Shifa: Case study on Sultanate of Oman's National Healthcare Information System. *Indian Journal of Science & Technology*. 2017;10: 17. Available from: doi: 10.17485/ijst/2017/v10i17/113060.

35. Government of Pakistan. *National Health Vision 2016-2025*. Islamabad: Ministry of National Health Services, Regulations and Coordination; 2016.

36. WHO. *Pakistan Health Information System: Assessment and Roadmap of Priority Actions*. Cairo: Regional Office for the Eastern Mediterranean; 2017.

37. WHO. *Palestine Health Profile 2015*. Cairo, Egypt: Regional Office for the Eastern Mediterranean; 2016. Available from: http://applications.emro.who.int/dsaf/EMROPUB_2016_EN_18926.pdf?ua=1&ua=1 [Accessed 24 February 2018].

38. Mimi Y. The Routine Health Information System in Palestine: Determinants and Performance. 2015; Unpublished Doctoral Thesis. London: City University, School of Informatics. Available from: http://openaccess.city.ac.uk/13430/ [Accessed 25 February 2018].

39. Palestine Ministry of Health. *Strengthening the Primary Health Care System in Palestine*. Fact Sheet. Available from: http://www.itcoop-jer.org/sites/default/files/booklet_POSIT_20_1_2015_FINAL.pdf [Accessed 22 February 2018].

40. WHO. *Sudan Health System Profile*. Cairo: WHO Regional Office for the Eastern Mediterranean. 2006; Available from: http://apps.who.int/medicinedocs/documents/s17310e/s17310e.pdf [Accessed 22 February 2018].

41. Ebrahim EMA, Ghebrehiwot L, Abdalgfar T, Juni MH. Health care system in Sudan: Review and analysis of strength, weakness, opportunity, and threats. *Sudan Journal of Medical Sciences*. 2017;12(3): 133–150.

42. WHO. *Sudan Health Profile 2015*. Cairo, Egypt: WHO Regional Office for the Eastern Mediterranean; 2017. Available from: https://extranet.who.int/iris/restricted/bitstream/10665/254895/1/EMROPUB_2017_EN_19610.pdf?ua [Accessed 24 February 2018].

43. WHO. *HeRAMS Syria: Second Quarter 2017. Snapshot for Public Health Centres*. 2017. Damascus: World Health Organization. Available from: http://applications.emro.who.int/docs/COPub_SYR_pub_health_centres_2nd_q_2017_EN_19220.pdf?ua=1 [Accessed 24 February 2018].

44. WHO. *EWARS: The Early Warning Alert and Response System. Syrian Arab Republic*. 2018. Damascus: World Health Organization. Available from: http://www.emro.who.int/syr/publications-other/ewars-weekly-bulletin.html [Accessed 25 February 2018].

45. Alwan A, Ali M, Aly E, Badr A, Doctor H, Mandil A, Rashidian A, Shideed O. Strengthening national health information systems: Challenges and response. *Eastern Mediterranean Health Journal*. 2016;22(11): 840–850.

46. WHO. *Regional Strategy for the Improvement of Civil Registration and Vital Statistics System 2014–2019*. Cairo: WHO Regional Office for the Eastern Mediterranean; 2014.

47. WHO. *Framework for Comprehensive Health Information System Assessments: Version 2*. Cairo: WHO Regional Office for the Eastern Mediterranean; 2016.

CHAPTER 6

Integration of non-communicable diseases in primary health care in the WHO Eastern Mediterranean Region

Slim Slama, Gemma Lyons, Heba Fouad,
Shannon Barkley, and Asmus Hammerich

INTRODUCTION

In 1978, the Alma-Ata Declaration stated, "Primary health care is essential health care based on practical, scientifically sound, and socially acceptable methods and technology made universally accessible to individuals and families in the community".[1] Since then, strides have been made increasing the availability and improving the quality of primary health care (PHC) around the globe. However, new health challenges have been emerging too, including the burden of non-communicable diseases (NCDs) – namely cardiovascular diseases, diabetes, cancer, and chronic respiratory diseases.

In an effort to combat the epidemic, the United Nations (UN) held a high-level meeting on NCDs in 2011 and developed international targets to guide and support national responses.[2]

PHC is vitally important for the prevention and control of these diseases. When appropriately resourced and organized to adhere to principles that ensure high performance (first access, comprehensive, continuous, coordinated, and people-centred), PHC becomes the most efficient and effective setting in which to manage common chronic conditions and multimorbidity. Indeed, patients with NCDs are commonly diagnosed, referred, and treated through PHC, and these services also provide an opportunity for both primary and secondary prevention of these diseases in an integrated manner. WHO has developed a set of 10 Progress Monitoring Indicators to report to the UN General Assembly, and two of these refer specifically to the role of PHC.[3] One is on the availability of evidence-based guidelines/protocols/standards for NCD management in PHC, and the other on the provision of drug therapy at the PHC level.

The Eastern Mediterranean Region (EMR) is one of the six WHO regions around the globe tasked with the prevention and control of NCDs. The region comprises 22 countries in the Middle East and North Africa, spanning various levels of health system development.[4] While the high-income countries in the region have well-established and well-funded health systems, others have very underdeveloped systems and access to them is limited. On top of this, a number of countries within the region are affected by conflict and humanitarian crises (Afghanistan, Syria, Somalia, Libya, Iraq, Yemen) and host a huge proportion of the world's refugees (Lebanon, Jordan).[5]

This chapter aims to review the current regional situation of NCD integration in PHC, describe the WHO regional initiative, provide examples from the region, and discuss the key challenges and policy options for progress in this field.

WHAT IS NCD INTEGRATION?

A standard definition for NCD integration within PHC does not yet exist. However, it can be described as the process of embedding NCDs into PHC across all health system domains. WHO has defined the health system building blocks as:[6]

- Leadership and governance
- Health financing
- Health workforce
- Medical products, vaccines, and technologies
- Health information
- Health service delivery

For example, integration at the governance level would include strategies such as a financed and operational national NCD plan that includes a monitoring and evaluation framework. At the human resources level, integration requires strategies such as the inclusion of NCD knowledge and competencies in the training, recruitment, and retention of the PHC workforce, an emphasis on interdisciplinary teamwork, and role allocation to ensure appropriate use of available resources based on population health needs. Importantly, some competencies and approaches might be shared across all four of the major NCDs, such as targeting their shared risk factors. However, other strategies, such as early diagnosis of cancer, are specific to only that disease (Table 6.1).

For the purposes of this chapter, the definition for NCD integration within PHC will be:

> The inclusion and operationalisation of suitable policies, strategies and programmes for the inclusion of the four major NCDs[7] (cardiovascular diseases, diabetes, cancers and chronic respiratory diseases) and their related risk factors (smoking, unhealthy diet, physical inactivity and harmful use of alcohol) within primary health care, across all health system building blocks.

CURRENT LEVEL OF INTEGRATION: GLOBAL COMPARISON

The World Health Organization (WHO) periodically monitors Member States' capacity to respond to the NCD epidemic, through a global survey known as the NCD Country Capacity Survey (NCD CCS).[8] The global survey, undertaken since 2000, covers health system infrastructure; funding; policies, plans, and strategies; surveillance; and partnerships and multilateral collaboration. A specific set of questions assess national capacity for NCD management at the primary health-care level. This provides a useful course of information to compare between the WHO regions on the integration of NCDs within PHC.

TABLE 6.1   Necessary elements for NCD integration in PHC

Building block	Necessary for PHC integration
Governance	• National NCD plan that is financed and implemented including a Monitoring & Evaluation Framework
Finance	• NCD interventions included in the benefit package for PHC • Mixed payment methods including capitation and performance-based incentives
Health Workforce	• Multidisciplinary teams with a context-appropriate skill mix • Appropriate competencies including prevention, diagnosis, management, behavioural counselling, and integrated risk stratification • Trained to manage undifferentiated conditions and consider comprehensive health needs
Medical Products, Vaccines, and Technologies	• Availability of necessary NCD diagnostic modalities at the PHC level • NCD vaccines and medications included on the PHC formulary in accordance with national treatment protocols and guidelines
Health Information Systems	• Longitudinal patient record • NCD registries • NCD indicators monitored and evaluated at facility level at regular intervals, and reported through routine channels • Integrated information systems with referral levels of care
Service Delivery	• PHC services organized to be: First access; Comprehensive; Continuous; Coordinated; People-centred; and Family and community-oriented • Functioning referral and counter-referral mechanisms • Empanelment and proactive population management • Strategies to promote self-care, care plans, etc. • NCD guidelines and protocols • Quality and performance management capabilities at PHC level

Figures from 2015 illustrate challenges countries of the Eastern Mediterranean Region (EMR) face in carving comprehensive national responses for the prevention and control of NCDs, in comparison to the other WHO regions.[1] Of the six regions globally, the EMR has the lowest percentage of countries with funding for NCD activities at 65%, compared to 83%–100% of countries within the other regions.[9] Furthermore, this figure in the EMR was a marked decline from 2013 when 86% of countries reported having this funding available, a decrease which could be related to conflicts affecting the region. A similar story is true for governance, with only 36% of EMR countries reporting having an operational, integrated NCD plan that addresses the four main NCDs and risk factors, while other regions reported 55%–80% of countries had achieved this (Figure 6.1).

Regarding access to essential NCD medicines within PHC, a higher proportion of EMR countries reported having these available than in the Africa and South-East Asia regions, but a lower proportion than in Europe and the Americas. The least available drug is oral morphine; only 15% of countries have access to this in the EMR, similar to the 14% in Africa and 18% in South-East Asia. However, this is significantly lower than in Europe where 77% of countries have oral morphine available.[9]

Another important expected outcome of the integration of NCDs into PHC is the ability at PHC level to detect NCDs and related risk factors early and to manage them. In the field of cardiovascular prevention and control, WHO recommends a total risk approach, a process of stratifying people based on their likely risk of cardiovascular disease (CVD), integrating the identification of multiple risk factors such as tobacco use, hypertension, or diabetes, and targeting those at high risk with preventative risk-reduction measures. For example, some countries, such as the United Kingdom, advocate the use of statins as prophylaxis for patients who are considered at high risk.[10] However, both globally and in the EMR, only one in five countries reported having CVD risk stratification in at least 50% of their PHC centres. Comparatively,

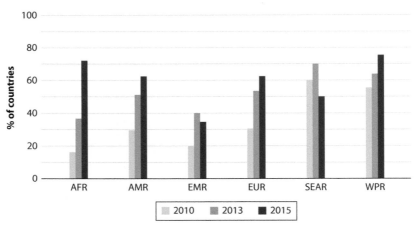

* Of 160 countries that responded to all 3 surveys.

FIGURE 6.1 Percentage of countries with an integrated national NCD policy, strategy, or action plan, by WHO region,[9] 2010, 2013, and 2015. (*Source*: WHO Assessing national capacity for the prevention and control of noncommunicable diseases global survey, 2015.)

in Europe, this is double at two in five countries, whereas in Africa it is a fraction with just one in 20 countries reportedly achieving this (Figure 6.2).[9]

These findings correlate with assessments at country level showing that health services have traditionally focused on communicable diseases, other acute conditions, and maternal and child health, with the absence or minimal integration of NCDs and their related risk factors. In countries were NCD integration took place, PHC services are too often arranged vertically and organized in siloes according to specific diseases or risk factors, with limited emphasis on developing a holistic appreciation of PHC visitors, the totality of their health conditions, and their lifestyle throughout the life course.

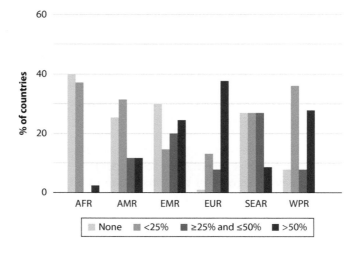

FIGURE 6.2 Percentage of primary health-care facilities offering cardiovascular risk stratification for the management of patients at high risk for heart attack and stroke, by WHO region. (*Source*: WHO assessing national capacity for the prevention and control of noncommunicable diseases global survey, 2015.[9])

CURRENT LEVEL OF INTEGRATION: VARIATION WITHIN THE REGION

While the global picture shows how the EMR is progressing compared to other WHO regions, substantial variation is present within the region itself. This can be best demonstrated by comparisons between the three country groups. The 22 countries are divided into these groups based on population health outcomes, health system performance, and level of health expenditure (Box 6.1).[11]

The Country Capacity Survey (CCS) results show stark variation by country group.[12] NCD action plans and funding are available for all the Group 1 countries, but less than half of the lowest income countries have these structures in place. This differentiation is seen for every indicator related to the integration of NCDs within PHC.

Any effort to integrate NCDs in PHC must, firstly, identify the key interventions and cost-effective services which can be implemented. This led to the 2010 launch of the WHO Package of Essential Non-communicable Disease Interventions (WHO PEN) for Primary Care in Low-Resource Settings. This WHO suite of tools identified an action-oriented set of cost-effective interventions that can be delivered to an acceptable quality of care, even in resource-poor settings. These tools enable early detection and management of cardiovascular diseases, diabetes, chronic respiratory diseases, and cancer to prevent life-threatening complications such as heart attacks, stroke, kidney failure, amputations, and blindness. Many countries across the world have derived national NCD guidelines based on WHO PEN. In the EMR, uptake and implementation of WHO PEN has been uneven, but most of the countries are making efforts in developing or adapting guidelines in order to standardize and improve NCD management.

All of the Group 1 countries had guidelines/protocols in place for the management and referral of the main NCDs within PHC. However, less than half of the Group 2 countries had these in place for the referral of cancers and respiratory diseases. Among the lower-income countries, just one of the six (Sudan) had guidelines in place for management within PHC, and none had guidelines or protocols for referral of their NCD patients.[12]

The region's Group 3 countries also are lacking in access to essential technologies and medicines for the management of NCDs within PHC. According to the 2015 survey, the least available medicines in the region were insulin, beta blockers, statins, oral morphine, and steroid inhalers. Furthermore, none of the low-income countries had achieved the indicator on "the provision of drug therapy, including glycaemic control, and counselling for eligible persons at high risk to prevent heart attacks and strokes".[12] This may be hindered by a lack of CVD risk stratification, which limits health practitioners' ability to identify those at high risk of cardiovascular disease.

BOX 6.1   MEMBER STATES OF THE WHO EASTERN MEDITERRANEAN REGION GROUPING

Group 1	Group 2	Group 3
Bahrain	Egypt	Afghanistan
Kuwait	Iran (Islamic Republic of)	Djibouti
Oman	Iraq	Pakistan
Qatar	Jordan	Somalia
Saudi Arabia	Lebanon	Sudan
United Arab Emirates	Libya	Yemen
	Morocco	
	Palestine	
	Syrian Arab Republic	
	Tunisia	

Early diagnosis of cancer patients is another key responsibility of primary health-care services. If diagnosed early, most cancers are amenable to treatment and mortality rates can be significantly reduced.[13] However, strategies for early detection of cancer have only been integrated into PHC in some countries of the region. Only two-fifths of countries had developed such programmes for cervical cancer within PHC. All Group 1 countries have integrated early diagnosis of breast, colon, and prostate cancer. Furthermore, only one of the six Group 3 countries (Sudan) had integrated any early detection programmes for cancer covering breast, cervical, and oral cancers.[12] Therefore, more efforts are needed to integrate early diagnosis into PHC in all countries of the region.

WHO REGIONAL INITIATIVE

As indicated above, effective NCD integration in PHC is contingent on wider actions aiming at strengthening health systems to achieve better health, universal health coverage (UHC), and equitable health financing policies.

The WHO 2016 "Framework on integrated, people-centred health services" emphasized the importance of organizing PHC around the comprehensive needs of people, rather than around a singular focus of specific diseases.[13] When combined with population wide preventative measures, people-centred PHC can prove very effective in tackling NCDs both at the population and at the individual level.

On a regional level, the WHO Regional Office for the Eastern Mediterranean (EMRO) also has adopted Family Practice as the best platform to address NCD and, beyond that, reaching the Sustainable Development Goals (SDG) target 3.8, which focuses on achieving universal health coverage.

The Regional Initiative on Strengthening the Integration and Management of NCDs in PHC in the EMR draws on and is aligned with the Regional Framework for Action on Advancing Universal Health Coverage (UHC) in the Eastern Mediterranean Region and the Regional Strategy to expand Family Practice in the EMR.[14,15]

In September 2014, WHO held a regional meeting to discuss strengthening the integration and management of NCDs in primary health care. Participants shared and discussed relevant challenges and proposed recommendations for a way forward.[16] WHO also visited several countries for specific meetings on NCD integration, including Kuwait, Sudan, Saudi Arabia, and Iran.

A number of key challenges were highlighted in relation to NCD integration. The health workforce was one of these issues. Countries reported having an inadequate number of health-care workers, some of whom are insufficiently trained and skilled, and inappropriately distributed across the health system.[16] However, it was suggested that a task-shifting approach may be a step forward in addressing this problem.

Other key challenges brought up supported the CCS data – inadequate access to essential medicines, insufficient CVD risk stratification, and a lack of secondary prevention within PHC. Further health system issues were highlighted regarding referral, follow-up, and patient adherence. Also, public education for self-referral is limited within the region.

The EMR also faces a number of further challenges relating to the emergency and humanitarian situations affecting a number of countries across the region.[17] Health systems have been disrupted in many of these countries and refugees and displaced people have insufficient access to health services. However, WHO is undertaking a separate programme of work specifically to provide NCD care in emergency contexts.[18]

The 2014 regional meeting was a key milestone in the regional initiative on the integration of NCDs in PHC. In addition to discussions regarding challenges, participants also developed a draft regional framework, which was published as an annex in the meeting report.[19] The framework covered all six of the WHO health system building blocks, in addition to a domain on Community and Self-Care. The tool allows a systematic review of health system readiness for NCD integration in PHC, proposing a set of strategic interventions across the seven areas. The framework has subsequently been trialled as a review tool in Iran, Kuwait, Saudi Arabia, and Sudan.[20]

Furthermore, WHO EMRO held an expert meeting in 2015 to progress further on NCD integration. However, the draft framework has yet to be endorsed by Member States and to become a formal working WHO document. Endorsement of the document for integration of NCDs could be a great step forward to support Member States on this topic.[21]

EXAMPLES OF COUNTRY PROGRESS

Although the need for more progress on NCD integration has been clearly highlighted, several countries in the region have been making substantial progress to integrate the management of NCDs into their PHC services. Examples of such progress are described below for three countries, representing one from each of the groups.

BOX 6.2 BAHRAIN, IRAN, AND SUDAN

BAHRAIN (EXAMPLE GROUP 1 COUNTRY)

The WHO Package of Essential NCD (PEN) interventions for primary health care[22] was implemented in Bahrain in 2009.[23] Initially piloted in four PHC centres, it was scaled up nationally. The multidisciplinary team consists of a family doctor (general practitioner), nurse, and a health educator. Together they support patients with NCDs to better manage their conditions. This includes analysing patients' 10-year CVD risk scores, and providing health promotion advice, in addition to improving availability of essential medicines. There is now an NCD clinic in all 27 PHC centres in the country, and the government has provided the financial support needed to staff them.

An inter-agency taskforce mission undertaken by the United Nations in 2017[24] found that NCDs have been well integrated into PHC, with very promising progress. However, it was also seen that some areas, such as cancer screening, had been over-implemented, incorporating a larger age range than recommended by WHO.[25] A strategy such as this, while well meaning, can actually result in overdiagnosis and overtreatment of benign cases, as well as being less cost-effective than focussing on the recommended age range.

IRAN (EXAMPLE GROUP 2 COUNTRY)

Iran has been showcased by WHO as a fast-track country to tackle NCDs as a result of their recent progress and dedication.[26] The government has committed substantial funds to NCDs, implemented a multi-sectoral action plan for 2015–2025, and developed an NCD committee to oversee national progress.[28]

In 2016, the WHO Package of Essential NCD (PEN) interventions for primary health care[22] was adapted and implemented in Iran – the IraPEN. It has now been successfully piloted in four regions of the country and national-level scale up is beginning.[30]

Within PHC, a good level of access to essential medicines has been developed with 11 of the 12 essential non-communicable disease medicines available through PHC, and most of the essential technologies. Multidisciplinary teams have been established within PHC, and NCD training has been developed for staff. Furthermore, staff perceived an increase in workload with

30% of cases in PHC perceived by staff as being related to the IraPEN, due to increased case-finding and follow-up.[30]

While full national implementation will take many years, the results of the pilot have been promising and demonstrate substantial progress on NCD integration.

SUDAN (EXAMPLE GROUP 3 COUNTRY)

Sudan has developed a new national health policy for 2017–2030, including a PHC expansion plan, and updates on NCD and cancer strategies.[31] A high level of political commitment has been demonstrated to progressively expand essential health services packages offered at PHC level, including a bundle of NCD services covering hypertension, diabetes, asthma, and oral health. An NCD facility readiness assessment was conducted in 2017 across the country covering 20 centres in 10 states.

The country adopted a step-wise approach to progressively integrate NCD as part of a PHC expansion, devising the exact content of the essential package to be added to the national insurance scheme and the health systems requirements identified for implementing and scaling up the agreed package.

The systematic approach adopted and the continued momentum in Sudan presents a positive example within a low-income country setting.

DISCUSSION

There are a number of health systems challenges affecting countries' abilities to integrate NCDs within PHC services (Table 6.2). These include insufficient funding for NCD national programmes in most of the low- and middle-income countries, a lack of implementation of NCD plans, a limited and insufficiently training workforce, and a lack of universal health coverage. However, these challenges are not insurmountable, and the development of an operational, multi-sectoral action plan on NCDs is important to ensure that a holistic, cost-effective, context-specific approach is taken.[27] Additionally, funding can be galvanized through fiscal interventions: according to the WHO Country Capacity Survey in 2015, 19 out of 21 countries are implementing taxation on tobacco, but none have earmarked specific funding to be utilised for NCDs.[12] This presents an opportunity for all countries of the region to consider.

Moreover, the current conflicts and humanitarian crises affecting several countries in the region, and the additional burden of refugees in neighbouring countries, are challenging already stretched health systems. Consequently, WHO has undertaken a programme of work on NCDs in emergencies, including the development of a brief for emergency planners and policy makers and development of a kit to guide Member States on the essential medicines and technologies required for NCDs during a conflict or humanitarian emergency.[17,32]

In addition to the broader challenges of governance, funding, and humanitarian crises, there are also a number of issues specific to NCD integration in PHC. These include: lack of NCD guidelines/protocols for diagnosis, management and referral of NCDs; inadequate access to the 12 essential NCD medicines, especially in the public sector; insufficient availability of essential technologies for the diagnosis and management of NCDs; limited CVD risk stratification to identify patients at high risk of CVD; and insufficient integration of cancer early diagnosis strategies into PHC.

The examples of countries that have worked through these challenges and successfully integrated NCDs into PHC within the region and globally, include high-, medium-, and low-income countries, and illustrate that with sufficient political will and dedicated funding, progress can be made in this field.

TABLE 6.2 Country Capacity Survey results in region related to NCD integration in PHC[12]

WHO Country Capacity Survey for NCDs (2015) – Results related to NCD integration in PHC		Group 1 countries (%)	Group 2 countries (%)	Group 3 countries (%)	All countries (%)
Funding for non-communicable disease and risk factor-related activities/functions	Primary prevention	100	80	17	68
	Health promotion	100	70	17	64
	Early detection/screening	100	80	33	73
	Health care and treatment	100	100	50	86
Integrated national non-communicable disease policy, strategy, or action plan		100	80	50	77
Availability of evidence-based national guidelines/protocols/standards for the management and referral of major NCDs at the primary care level, recognized/approved by government or competent authorities	Management (diagnosis and treatment)				
	CVD	100	80	17	68
	Cancer	83	60	17	55
	Respiratory diseases	100	30	17	45
	Diabetes	100	90	17	73
	Referral from PHC				
	CVD	83	60	0	55
	Cancer	100	40	0	41
	Respiratory diseases	100	20	0	36
	Diabetes	100	70	0	59
Availability of the 13 basic technologies for the early detection, diagnosis, and monitoring of NCDs at primary care facilities	Public sector	85	41	27	49
	Private sector	74	56	24	52
PHC service integration of early detection of cancers by means of rapid identification of the first symptoms	Breast	100	70	17	64
	Cervical	67	40	17	41
	Colon	100	10	0	32
	Prostate	100	0	0	27
	Oral	50	0	17	18

(Continued)

TABLE 6.2 (CONTINUED) Country Capacity Survey results in region related to NCD integration in PHC[12]

WHO Country Capacity Survey for NCDs (2015) – Results related to NCD integration in PHC		Group 1 countries (%)	Group 2 countries (%)	Group 3 countries (%)	All countries (%)
Availability of the 12 essential non-communicable disease medicines at the primary care facilities of the public health sector	Insulin	100	70	33	68
	Aspirin	100	80	50	77
	Metformin	100	90	50	82
	Thiazide diuretics	100	90	67	86
	ACE inhibitors	83	80	50	73
	Calcium Channel blockers	83	80	50	73
	Beta blockers	100	80	50	68
	Statins	100	60	50	50
	Oral morphine	50	30	33	18
	Steroid inhaler	83	10	0	55
	Bronchodilator	100	70	0	86
	Sulphonylurea(s)	100	80	83	73
Member State has provision of drug therapy, including glycaemic control, and counselling for eligible persons at high risk to prevent heart attacks and strokes, with emphasis on the primary care level	Fully achieved	100	20	0	36
	Partially achieved	0	50	0	23
	Not achieved	0	30	100	41

Furthermore, systematic monitoring of country progress on NCDs through the CCS is important to enable progress to be reviewed at the country, regional, and global level. This information can act as a lever to celebrate progress and to stimulate efforts in areas of NCD prevention and control that require more momentum.

CONCLUSION

It is clear that the level of NCD integration within PHC varies substantially across the region, and that EMR countries face multiple challenges in realizing an effective integration of NCDs into PHC. However, it is also evident that several countries at high-, medium-, and low-income levels have made significant progress on this topic and provide a great example to their neighbours.

Going forward, substantial progress could be made in the Eastern Mediterranean Region if the initiative on NCD integration in PHC continues to be developed by WHO, and if momentum can be built among Member States.

International commitment to NCDs has been evident since the UN high-level meeting[2,27] in 2011, and the development of the nine global voluntary targets on NCDs.[28,29] However, these targets are unlikely to be reached by 2025 without integration of NCDs into PHC. The next UN high-level meeting on NCDs will take place in 2018 and will be another milestone in global efforts to tackle this epidemic. Continued and enhanced commitment from countries of the Eastern Mediterranean Region is vital.

BOX 6.3 SUMMARY BULLET POINTS

- The Eastern Mediterranean shows slow progress integrating NCDs into PHC and more attention is required in this area.
- A number of challenges have been identified to NCD integration, including: lack of funding; lack of guidelines/protocols; insufficient number of staff and inadequate training; lack of public education; insufficient availability of essential NCD medicines and technologies; lack of early diagnosis programmes for cancer within PHC; and limited use of CVD risk stratification for prevention and case finding.
- Progress has been made by some countries in the region, including, through adaptation of the PEN, designation of funds to NCDs, and development of NCD clinics in PHC services.
- Integration approaches will need to be scaled up across the region for the countries to achieve the UN targets on NCDs by 2025.[32]

REFERENCES

1. *Declaration of Alma-Ata International Conference on Primary Health Care*, Alma-Ata, USSR, 6–12 September 1978. Available from: http://www.who.int/publications/almaata_declaration_en.pdf?ua=1 [Accessed 7 December 2017].
2. WHO. *Political declaration of the high-level meeting of the general assembly on the prevention and control of non-communicable diseases.* 2012. Available from: http://www.who.int/nmh/events/un_ncd_summit2011/political_declaration_en.pdf [Accessed 19 October, 2016].
3. WHO. *Noncommunicable Diseases Progress Monitor 2017.* Available from: http://apps.who.int/iris/bitstream/10665/258940/1/9789241513029-eng.pdf?ua=1 [Accessed 23 April 2018].
4. Boutayeb A, et al. Multi-morbidity of noncommunicable diseases and equity in WHO Eastern Mediterranean countries. *International Journal for Equity in Health*, 2013; 12: 60. Available from: https://equityhealthj.biomedcentral.com/articles/10.1186/1475-9276-12-60.

5. Chan M. Address to the regional committee for the Eastern Mediterranean, sixty-third session. 3 October 2016. Available from: emro.who.int/docs/Other_Speech_Messages_RC63_DG_ opening_2016_ EN_19100.pdf?ua=1 [Accessed 13 October 2016].

6. WHO Western Pacific Region. Health Services Development. The WHO Health Systems Framework. Available from: http://www.wpro.who.int/health_services/health_systems_framework/en/ [Accessed 7 December 2017].

7. Narain JP. Integrating services for noncommunicable disease prevention and control: use of a primary care approach. *Indian Journal of Community Medicine*, 2011; 36 (Supplement 1): 67–72. Available from: https://www.ncbi.nlm.nih.gov/pubmed/22628915.

8. WHO. *Noncommunicable disease and their risk factors: assessing national capacity for the prevention and control of NCDs*. Available from: http://www.who.int/ncds/surveillance/ncd-capacity/en/ [Accessed 15 December 2017].

9. WHO. *Report of the 2015 Global NCD Survey: assessing national capacity for the prevention and control of noncommunicable diseases global survey*. 2015. Available from: http://apps.who.int/iris/bitstream/handl e/10665/246223/9789241565363-eng.pdf?sequence=1 [Accessed 23 April 2018].

10. National Institute of Clinical Excellence (NICE). Cardiovascular disease: risk assessment and reduction, including lipid modification. Clinical guideline CG181, 2014. Available from: https://www.nice.org.uk/guidance/CG181 [Accessed 23 April 2018].

11. WHO Eastern Mediterranean Regional Office (EMRO). Regional Committee 59 Technical Paper, EM/RC59/R.3: *Health systems strengthening in countries of the Eastern Mediterranean Region: challenges, priorities and options for future action*. 2012. Available from: http://applications.emro.who.int/docs/RC_ Resolutions_2012_3_14693_EN.pdf?ua=1 [Accessed 15 December 2017].

12. WHO EMRO. *Assessing national capacity for the prevention and control of noncommunicable diseases: report of the 2015 country capacity survey in the Eastern Mediterranean Region*. 2015. Available from: http://applications.emro.who.int/dsaf/EMROPUB_2016_EN_19168.pdf?ua=1&ua=1 [Accessed 27 October 2017].

13. WHO website. *Framework on integrated, people-centred health services*. Available from: http://www.who.int/servicedeliverysafety/areas/people-centred-care/en/ [Accessed 28 January 2018].

14. WHO EMRO. *Framework for action on advancing UHC in the EMR*. 2016. Available from: http://applicat ions.emro.who.int/docs/Technical_Notes_EN_16287.pdf?ua=1 [Accessed 28 January 2018].

15. WHO EMRO. *Conceptual and strategic approach to family practice*. 2014. Available from: http://applicat ions.emro.who.int/dsaf/EMROPUB_2014_EN_1783.pdf [Accessed 28 January 2018].

16. WHO EMRO. *Report on the Regional meeting on strengthening the integration and management of noncommunicable diseases in primary health care*. 2014. Available from: http://applications.emro.who.int/do cs/IC_Meet_Rep_2014_EN_15646.pdf [Accessed 23 April 2018].

17. Slama S, et al. Care of non-communicable diseases in emergencies. *The Lancet*, 2017; 389(10066): 326–330. Available from: http://dx.doi.org/10.1016/S0140-6736(16)31404-0 [Accessed 23 April 2018].

18. WHO EMRO. Summary report on the Expert consultation on the development of a noncommunicable diseases emergency kit, Cairo, Egypt, 20 July 2016.

19. WHO EMRO. Noncommunicable diseases. Regional framework for action. 2015. Available from: http://www.emro.who.int/noncommunicable-diseases/framework-for-action/index.html [Accessed 17 February 2016].

20. WHO EMRO. Regional Committee for the Eastern Mediterranean. Sixty-fourth session. Provisional agenda item 3(a). *Regional framework for action on cancer prevention and control: Technical Paper*, September 2017. Available from: http://applications.emro.who.int/docs/RC_technical_papers_2017_3_ 20037_en.pdf?ua=1 [Accessed 6 December 2017].

21. WHO Regional Committee of the Eastern Mediterranean. Resolution EM/RC64/R.2. *Regional framework for action on cancer prevention and control*. Available from: http://applications.emro.who.int/docs/RC64_Resolutions_2017_R2_20127_EN.pdf?ua=1 [Accessed 6 December 2017].

22. WHO. Tools for implementing WHO PEN (Package of essential noncommunicable disease interventions). Available from: http://www.who.int/ncds/management/pen_tools/en/ [Accessed 15 December 2017].

23. Case study on non-communicable diseases management clinics in PHC Bahrain, Regional meeting on strengthening the integration and management of noncommunicable diseases in primary health care, Cairo, 8–10 September 2014.

24. UN Agency Task Force on NCDs. Joint Mission of the United Nations Interagency Task Force on the Prevention and Control of Noncommunicable Diseases, Bahrain, 15–17 May 2017. Available from: http://www.who.int/ncds/un-task-force/publications/bahrain-joint-mission-report-2017/en/ [Accessed 15 December 2017].

25. WHO EMRO. Policy statements and recommended actions for early detection of cancer in the Eastern Mediterranean Region. 2016. Available from: http://www.emro.who.int/noncommunicable-diseases/publications/policy-statements-ncds.html [Accessed 15 December 2017].

26. WHO website. Islamic Republic of Iran on a fast-track to beating noncommunicable diseases. 2017. Available from: http://www.who.int/features/2017/iran-noncommunicable-diseases/en/ [Accessed 15 December 2017].

27. WHO. Third United Nations High-level Meeting on NCDs. Available from: http://www.who.int/ncds/governance/third-un-meeting/en/ [Accessed 8 December 2017].

28. Peykari N, et al. National action plan for non-communicable diseases prevention and control in Iran; a response to emerging epidemic Iran. *Journal of Diabetes & Metabolic Disorders*, 2017; 16: 3. Available from: https://jdmdonline.biomedcentral.com/articles/10.1186/s40200–017-0288-4.

29. WHO webpage: About 9 voluntary global targets. Available from:http://www.who.int/nmh/ncd-tools/definition-targets/en/ [Accessed 8th December 2017].

30. Slama S. Review of IRA PEN pilot implementation in Shahreza, Isfahan Province & Maragheh, East Azerbaijan, 13–18 July 2016 (unpublished).

31. Slama S. NCD integration into primary health care in Sudan, WHO EMRO review mission, 15–19 October 2017 (unpublished).

32. UN Inter-Agency Task Force on Non Communicable Diseases. Policy Brief on Noncommunicable Diseases in Emergencies, 2016. Available from: http://apps.who.int/iris/bitstream/10665/204627/1/WHO_NMH_NVI_16.2_eng.pdf?ua=1 [Accessed 15 December 2017].

CHAPTER 7

Family practice workforce: Multidisciplinary teams

Fethiye Gülin Gedik, Arwa Oweis, and Merette Khalil

INTRODUCTION

While there is a commitment globally, and by the countries of the Eastern Mediterranean Region (EMR), to advance towards universal health coverage (UHC), access to quality health-care services remains a challenge. The pivotal role of primary care is well acknowledged in improving access to care, and efforts are being made to strengthen primary care systems in the region.

While the major challenges in primary care are around the availability of defined services and financial coverage for access to these services, the most critical input is the health workers who ensure that services are available and accessible. Efforts are ongoing to define health-service packages, and they are different from country to country, which also is reflected in the staffing pattern needed to deliver these packages in each country. In the EMR, many countries not only face an overall shortage of health workers, but also face challenges in attracting, recruiting, and retaining health professionals to work in primary care settings. This has a significant impact on the availability, accessibility, and quality of services provided in primary care settings, especially in rural and remote areas.

In efforts to move towards UHC, there is a global and regional trend towards implementing family practice-based primary care to address gaps in primary care. The family practice model promotes the availability of well-trained, multidisciplinary teams in providing primary care services. The composition of the team, how they are trained, and how they work vary among countries in the region. This chapter explores staffing patterns and challenges of implementing family practice in the EMR, and how to maximize the contribution of each professional in the family practice team to increase productivity. This chapter will also review the recruitment, employment, and retention challenges at the primary care level, and labour market implications. The chapter does not address the education and training of the family practice workforce as this is covered elsewhere in this book.

THE TEAM APPROACH IN FAMILY PRACTICE

Team-based care is now recognized as an essential feature of high-quality primary care. Comprehensive health services to individuals, families, and their communities should be provided by a multidisciplinary team of health professionals who work collaboratively along with patients, family caregivers, and community service providers on shared goals within and across settings to achieve care that is safe, effective, patient-centred, timely, efficient, and equitable.[1]

Family practice (FP) models emphasize the importance of the multidisciplinary team as a way to deliver comprehensive, continuous, coordinated, collaborative, and personal family and community-oriented services.[2,3] The composition of the team may vary among countries depending on the essential service package, structures, resources, and availability of human resources.

Family physicians are often the central members of the multidisciplinary primary care team, and thus are the health professionals that receive more attention, with regard to their training, scaling up, and deployment. There have been several initiatives to increase the production of family physicians, and build the capacities of existing practitioners, by offering short and long family practice courses for general practitioners (GPs) to support them to bridge their knowledge gaps. Such programmes are lacking in other team members, particularly from the nursing and midwifery workforce. This implies the need to scale up the numbers and qualifications of other health professionals, and to develop and institutionalize policies on building effective and efficient multi-disciplinary family practice teams.

The primary care team should include at least a family physician and a nurse; the inclusion of other health-care workers may be more context dependent. In one study of FP in the United States, over 52% of family physicians were working with a nurse practitioner and 39% were working with a physician assistant; 21% of FP teams included a mental health counsellor, and 12% included a psychiatrist, while other health professionals included pharmacists, social workers, midwives, and physical and occupational therapists, although these latter groups were present in fewer than 20% of family physician-led practice teams.[4] Many teams in other countries also include social workers, nutritionists, care coordinators, and lay health workers.[5]

Following are some examples from the EMR which indicate the variations of multidisciplinary team composition among countries of the region.

The Ministry of Health in Egypt has identified a team of health workers to work in a family health unit serving 750 to 1000 families, comprising a family physician, a dentist, five nurses (chief nurse, family physician clinic, dental clinic, emergency, and immunization), a pharmacist, a pharmacy assistant, a lab technician, health educator, social worker, and administrative staff.

A heath centre in Bahrain employs family physicians, nurses, a pharmacist, a pharmacy assistant, social workers, lab technicians, radiology technicians, dieticians, and administrative staff. However, there is no registration of patients to a particular family physician, and patients are seen by whomever is available. Family physicians also are further focused, or specialized, in certain areas such as diabetes and reproductive health, etc.

In Lebanon, primary care clinics offer care provided by a family physician and a registered nurse and/or nurse practitioner. The number and skill mix of staff depends on working hours, the number of families and their needs, as well as the number of unattached population members. In addition to the above, the primary care team may include social workers, psychologists, psychiatrists, pharmacists, community pharmacists, spiritual care providers, and other therapists.

In Iran, rural health centres are staffed by a general practitioner or family physician and cover three to five health houses in villages staffed by "behvarzes" (community-based health workers).[6] The urban health centres in Iran also include dentists and mental health workers. The policy is to expand the population coverage provided by family physicians.

In Iraq, the main Primary Health Care Centres (PHCCs) are staffed by doctors, dentists, pharmacists, nurses, medical assistants, laboratory technicians, and several administrative and support staff, while the smaller PHCCs located in rural areas are staffed by non-physician health-care providers.[7]

While moving towards family practice-based primary care is a priority in many EMR countries, policies clearly defining the team composition are mostly absent.

NEW COMPETENCIES FOR THE FAMILY PRACTICE WORKFORCE

Traditionally the training of health professionals emphasizes clinical knowledge and skills. We are now witnessing a paradigm shift, recognizing that some additional competencies are critical. Primary care professionals need to master certain core competencies to meet the needs of their communities. These may include building continuous relationships with individuals and communities, providing person-centred care, providing comprehensive care for individuals, families, and communities, and demonstrating inter-professional and practice management skills.[8]

Health professionals usually do not receive structured training to enable them to meet these competencies. Assertiveness, critical thinking, and decision-making are all skills learnt on the job by training and through daily practice. It is imperative to empower all staff by training them to acquire these skills, monitoring improvement, and addressing any deficiencies that challenge them.[9]

These requirements should be part and parcel of both undergraduate and postgraduate health professional education and training. Undergraduate education curricula should include adequate exposure to primary care facilities and community-based training, as well as addressing the above-mentioned competencies.[10]

HEALTH WORKFORCE SHORTAGES AND IMPLICATIONS
FOR FAMILY PRACTICE-BASED PRIMARY CARE

The Eastern Mediterranean Region faces shortages of the health workforce at varying levels, from critical shortage to shortage in some professional cadres. The overall production and availability of health workers is suboptimal and imbalanced. Inequitable geographical distribution is a daunting challenge in several Member States, and concerns abound in relation to the quality, relevance, and performance of health workers (Figure 7.1).

The shortages become more critical at the primary care level in most countries. Many physicians prefer to specialize and work in secondary and tertiary hospitals in urban areas, leading to shortages of GPs based in primary care facilities. For example, 40% of primary health-care centres in Iraq lack physicians,[11] while in Egypt, the PHC staff breakdown was 44% nurses, 18% auxiliary staff, and only 12% doctors.[12] In Lebanon and Iran, over 70% of physicians are specialized, leaving a shortage of general practitioners.

Many countries also face skill mix imbalances, especially shortages of nurses. The number of physicians exceeds the number of nurses in Pakistan, and in many countries the ratio of nurses to doctors is around one-to-one (Figure 7.2). Pakistan's basic health units are staffed with a physician and a lady health visitor, but the staffing does not include a nurse due to shortages. Almost all countries in the Eastern Mediterranean Region "have taken initiatives to improve basic nursing education through increasing the number of programmes, reorienting the curriculum

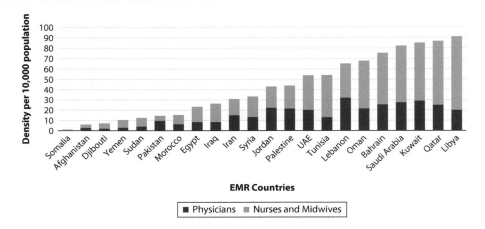

FIGURE 7.1 Density of physicians, nurses, and midwives in the EMR (2015). (*Source*: EMR Health Workforce Observatory, http://www.emro.who.int/health_workforce_observatory/index.html.)

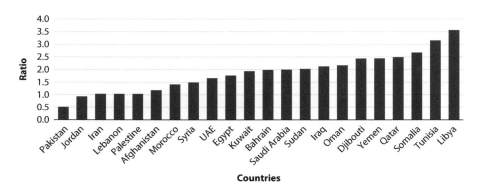

FIGURE 7.2 Ratio of nurses and midwives to doctors in the EMR (2015). (*Source*: EMRO Health Workforce Observatory, http://www.emro.who.int/health_workforce_observatory/index.html.)

towards the primary health care approach".[13] Postgraduate training in community health nursing has been introduced in Lebanon, Jordan, Egypt, Sudan, Iran, and Pakistan to improve the role and contribution of nurses at the primary care level.

These trends indicate that the shortages will continue and the preferences of health professionals towards specialization and working in hospital settings may be obstacles to strengthening primary care and moving towards a family practice-based model.

Countries with critical shortages of health workers may have difficulty in deploying adequate numbers of physicians and nurses to primary care facilities, especially in rural areas; in some cases, the primary care facilities will not be staffed with physicians at all. In the latter case, the family practice team can benefit from incorporating community-based health workers in the team as in the example of Brazil, thus allowing a limited number of professionals to extend the coverage to a larger catchment population. In such cases, the roles, functions, accountability, and supervision of community-based health workers should be well defined. The "behvarz" in Iran is a good example of the integration of community-based health workers in primary care in the EMR; they are part of the family practice team as the system moves towards family practice-based primary care.

LABOUR MARKETS AND ATTRACTING A HEALTH WORKFORCE TO PRIMARY CARE

Health workers are part of the labour market and their behaviours and preferences will have an impact on the availability of the workforce for family practice, as in other professions. Their preferences and behaviours will be dependent on their personal background, context, living and working conditions, and various incentives.

There is a major shortage in GPs across the region as mentioned above, especially in primary care settings and in rural areas, as most doctors who specialize remain in urban areas. In Northern Iraq, 84% of doctors are based in urban areas, 74% work in hospitals, and only 23% work in PHC centres.[14] In Somalia, only 9% of physicians are employed in rural settings.[15] In Sudan, 67% of health workers work in secondary and tertiary settings, and 65% of specialists are working in the capital, Khartoum.[16] In Afghanistan, 89% of specialists, 85% of dentists, and 84% of physiotherapists work in urban areas; this is likely due to the fact that pre-service training for some cadres was only available in the capital city.[17] In Iraq, a small number of family medicine specialists exist, but they are reported to be unwilling to work in primary health-care centres; a high proportion of specialists have also been reported to be working in urban PHC centres in Iraq as local hospitals are unable to accommodate the growing number of specialists.[7,14] In many EMR countries, such as Jordan, nurses and midwives are also concentrated mainly in hospitals with limited numbers working in the community.[18]

While there is an increasing trend towards urbanization globally and in the Eastern Mediterranean Region, it is important to note that the countries with the highest proportion of the population based in rural areas are mostly low-income countries. Almost 60% or above of the populations of low-income and low- to middle-income countries in the EMR live in rural areas (Figure 7.3). In addition to low economic standing, most of these countries are currently affected by crises, or graded emergencies as defined by the United Nations and WHO. This affects how these countries manage their human resources, especially as rural and remote areas tend be more vulnerable to poverty, scarcity, insecurity, and violence.

Ensuring adequate family practice-based primary care will require the introduction of necessary interventions and incentives to attract health professionals to work at the primary care level.

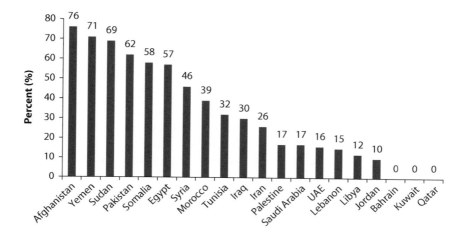

FIGURE 7.3 Proportion of rural population in the EMR. (*Source*: Framework for health information systems and core indicators for monitoring health situation and health system performance 2017.[19])

It is well known that some educational and regulatory interventions, financial incentives, as well as professional and personal support[20] may help to improve deployment and retention in rural and remote areas, leading to improved geographical distribution of health workers.

The decentralization of training institutions, for example in Sudan and Somali, has allowed recruitment of students locally with more possibility of them serving as health professionals in their own communities. Financial incentives are provided in many countries, most dispensing them in the form of rural hardship allowances, while some countries, such as Egypt, Lebanon, Pakistan, and Sudan, have also offered fringe benefits including housing subsidies, health insurance, car ownership, or tuition reimbursements as part of a recruitment and retention package.[21-24] In Iraq and Iran, physicians staffing primary health-care centres are primarily recent medical graduates who have to provide one year of obligatory work based in a rural PHC sub-centre.[7,14]

Attracting health professionals to primary care will require a combination of incentives. The payment mechanisms alone should not only present an attractive package, but also should be linked to performance. Working environment, job satisfaction, connection to a professional network, and being part of a collaborative team are other factors that need to be considered in designing the system.

SYSTEM CHANGES AND ENABLING WORKING ENVIRONMENT IN FAMILY PRACTICE

The transition to family practice-based primary care is critically important. Family practice-based primary care goes beyond training and introducing family physicians into the system in many cases. Significant attention and effort is often diverted to training and scaling up of family physicians, without enough attention paid to training the other members of the team.

Similarly, introducing system changes follows at a later stage, for example, in the way services are delivered and utilized. In many cases, primary care services are not adequately utilized, not just due to lack of trust in GPs, but also due to how the services are accessed and provided. For example, 90% of the population of Egypt has access to public sector primary care clinics, of which 88% are in rural areas and predominantly include family health units and rural health units;[12] however, the utilization rate is less than 10% in both rural and urban settings, due to perceived low quality, long waiting times, and overcrowding.[25] In Iraq, there is only a 20% utilization rate of primary care facilities, and 60% of rural households prefer to attend clinics run by private doctors.[14] Fifty-five percent of rural Egyptian women use private care providers, 19% use the public sector, and 25% receive no health care at all; the same study showed that 43% of Egyptian rural households were more likely to utilize private doctors as compared to 25% of urban households.[25]

Thus, system changes should aim to influence both provider and user behaviour while aiming to improve the quality of services. It is important to ensure adequate system changes occur to ensure the provision of the basic elements of family practice.

While interventions should facilitate easy access of the population to quality services which they trust, measures should be taken to attract health workers to work in primary care settings as well as increasing their motivation and job satisfaction. Working with assigned populations, being able to follow up their own patients, financial incentives, payment mechanisms to improve performance, a better working environment, and access to adequate medicines and supplies, are some important examples of system-related changes needed to accompany the provision of trained health professionals.

Unless system changes occur, the trained health workforce will not be able to see the benefits of additional qualifications. As a result, trained family physicians may either leave the country to work elsewhere, especially in the GCC countries as well as other developed countries, or they may move to the private sector. According to the Sudan Medical Specialties Board, over 800 family physicians have been trained, but nearly 450 of them have already migrated from the country.

THE WAY FORWARD

The family practice-based primary care model in the EMR is still fragmented, poorly staffed, and underutilized. Serious political efforts and financial investments are needed to strengthen family practice-based primary care towards building a sustainable interdisciplinary team able to respond to the needs of the population.

Establishing and strengthening family medicine and health professional education programmes is timely and imperative and should promote, encourage, and enable the education of health professionals collaboratively. It should also include clarifying and emphasizing the vital role and impact of the family doctor and the primary care team on the health of the community, and the effectiveness of the entire health-care system.

REFERENCES

1. Lowe F, O'Hara S. Multi-disciplinary team working in practice: Managing the transition. *J Interprof Care*. 2000;14(3): 269–79.
2. Rodriguez HP, Rogers WH, Marshall RE, Safran DG. Multidisciplinary primary care teams: Effects on the quality of the clinician-patient interactions and organizational features of care. *Med Care*. 2007;45(1): 19–27.
3. Schuetz B, Mann E, Everett W. Educating health professionals collaboratively for team-based primary care. *Health Aff (Millwood)*. 2010;29(8): 1476–80.
4. Bazemore A, Wingrove P, Peterson L, Petterson S. The diversity of providers on the family medicine team. *J Am Board Fam Med JABFM*. 2016;29(1): 8–9.
5. Wagner EH, Flinter M, Hsu C, Cromp D. Effective team-based primary care: Observations from innovative practices. *BMC Fam Pract*. 2017;18(1): 13.
6. Naderimagham S, Jamshidi H, Khajavi A, Pishgar F, Ardam A, Larijani B, et al. Impact of rural family physician program on child mortality rates in Iran: A time-series study. *Popul Health Metr*. 2017;15: 21. Available from: https://www.ncbi.nlm.nih.gov/pmc/articles/PMC5455106/ [Accessed 3 December 2017].
7. Shabila NP, Al-Tawil NG, Al-Hadithi TS, Sondorp E, Vaughan K. Iraqi primary care system in Kurdistan region: Providers' perspectives on problems and opportunities for improvement. *BMC Int Health Hum Rights*. 2012;12: 21.
8. Babiker A, El Husseini M, Al Nemri A, Al Frayh A, Al Juryyan N, Faki M, et al. Health care professional development: Working as a team to improve patient care. *Sudanese J Paediatrics*. 2014;14(2): 9–16.
9. Kringos DS, Boerma WG, Hutchinson A, van der Zee J, Groenewegen PP. The breadth of primary care: A systematic literature review of its core dimensions. *BMC Health Services Research*. 2010;10: 65.
10. Schuetz B, Mann E, Everett W. Educating health professionals collaboratively for team-based primary care. *Health Aff (Millwood)*. 2010;29(8): 1476–80.
11. Al Hilfi TK, Lafta R, Burnham G. Health services in Iraq. *Lancet*. 2013;381(9870): 939–48.
12. Abo El-Ata GA. Health coverage for workers in Egypt. *Egypt J Occup Med*. 2014;38(1): 23–42. Available from: http://ejom.journals.ekb.eg/article_786_86038c890ed190ae517377c44bcb9ed0.pdf.
13. Kronfol NM. Historical development of health systems in the Arab countries: A review. *East Mediterr Health J*. 2012;18(11): 1151.
14. Shukor AR, Klazinga NS, Kringos DS. Primary care in an unstable security, humanitarian, economic and political context: The Kurdistan Region of Iraq. *BMC Health Serv Res*. 2017;17(1): 592.
15. WHO. *Strategic review of the Somali health sector: Challenges and prioritized actions*. Available from: http://moh.gov.so/en/images/publication/review_somali_Health_sector.pdf [Accessed 26 December 2017].
16. Federal Ministry of Health, Sudan. *National human resources for health: Strategic plan 2012-16* Available from: http://www.who.int/workforcealliance/countries/Sudan_HRHPlan_2012-16.pdf [Accessed 26 December 2017].

17. Afghanistan HRH plan 2012. Available from: http://www.who.int/workforcealliance/countries/Afghanistan_HRHplan_2012_draft_wlogos.pdf [Accessed 11 December 2017].

18. Maaitah RA, AbuAlRub RF. Exploration of priority actions for strengthening the role of nurses in achieving universal health coverage. *Revista Latino-Americana de Enfermagem.* 2017;25: e2819. Available from: http://doi.org/10.1590/1518-8345.1696.2819.

19. WHO. *Eastern Mediterranean Region Framework for health information systems and core indicators for monitoring health situation and health system performance.* Available from: http://applications.emro. who.int/docs/EMROPUB_2017_EN_16766.pdf?ua=1 [Accessed 5 March 2018].

20. WHO. *Increasing access to health workers in remote and rural areas through improved retention.* Available from: http://www.who.int/hrh/retention/guidelines/en/ [Accessed 18 January 2018].

21. Badr E, Mohamed NA, Afzal MM, Bile KM. Strengthening human resources for health through information, coordination and accountability mechanisms: The case of the Sudan. *Bull World Health Organ.* 2013;91(11): 868–73.

22. Fayssal M, Farahat MD P. Challenges facing female physicians in Egypt. *Arch Environ Occup Health.* 2009;64(2): 121–8.

23. Alameddine M, Khodr H, Mourad Y, Yassoub R. Upscaling the recruitment and retention of human resources for health at primary healthcare centres in Lebanon: A qualitative study. *Health Soc Care Community.* 2016;24(3): 353–62.

24. Shah SM, Zaidi S, Ahmed J, Rehman SU. Motivation and retention of physicians in primary healthcare facilities: A qualitative study from Abbottabad, Pakistan. *Int J Health Policy Manag.* 2016;5(8): 467–75.

25. Galal SB, Al-Gamal N. Health problems and the health care provider choices: A comparative study of urban and rural households in Egypt. *J Epidemiol Glob Health.* 2014;4(2): 141–9.

CHAPTER 8

Current status of family medicine education and training in the Eastern Mediterranean Region

Waris Qidwai and Gohar Wajid

INTRODUCTION

Family Medicine (FM) is witnessing expansion in most Member States of the Eastern Mediterranean Region (EMR) at a variable pace. However, its progress is hindered by lack of availability of trained human resources, mainly due to a shortage of training programs and lack of support from some policy makers for the specialty. There are few family practice (FP) models in the developed countries, while progress in this specialty has been unsatisfactory in several other countries.[1]

To date, there has been limited information available about undergraduate education in FM in the EMR. Moreover, there are no reliable estimates regarding postgraduate training programs in FM in the EMR. Therefore, the purpose of this chapter is to review the current status of FM education, training, and continuing professional development programs in the EMR. Moreover, it aims to identify perceptions about the role of nurses in family practice and the need for on-the-job short training courses in the specialty to enhance the knowledge and skills of practicing general practitioners (i.e. doctors working in primary health care without formal postgraduate training or qualifications in FM). Such information is extremely valuable in setting national and regional policies regarding building capacity in FP and to identify possible future challenges and their probable solutions.

At the undergraduate level, there is a lack of FM exposure by undergraduate medical students in medical schools of many countries of the region. There is a need to establish FM departments in all medical schools, in order to provide medical students with exposure and understanding about this specialty. Evidence suggests that more medical students select FM as their future career when exposed to the specialty at undergraduate level. In addition, there are several reasons that students do not select FM as their specialty. These include the specialty is perceived as less attractive compared to other specialties; not well known; comparatively less salary; the present health system does not fully support FM and there are few positions for family physicians at primary health-care facilities (health system structure based constraints) Moreover, there are no role models for medical students in FM; and inadequate training capacity in medical schools.[1] In the absence of FM teaching and learning infrastructure at the undergraduate level, students miss an important opportunity to gain experience in the concepts of FM at an early stage of their careers. Transformation of a general practitioner (GP) based system into an FP-based system requires that medical students are exposed to the concepts of FM as early as possible.

Most countries in the region face a shortage of postgraduate training programmes in FM. Numbers of graduates trained through these programs are insufficient to meet the current and future health-care needs of the countries in the region. A need exists for two- to four-year postgraduate training programs, with a robust family practice curriculum, and a focus on training in community settings. Presently most of the programs are based in the public sector and a need exists for more active participation within the private sector. Issues related to curriculum, assessment, and accreditation require urgent attention.[1]

Another major task for any government is the transformation of existing GPs into family physicians. On-the-job training in FM and building the capacities of GPs in the delivery of quality primary health-care services exist and are growing in the region. These programmes vary in duration from three months to two years of training and aim to improve the knowledge and skills of GPs in the management of diseases, based on local needs. A need has been identified for on-the-job training programs that are well-designed and facilitated by experienced faculty. By no means are these programmes a replacement for well-structured, longer duration training postgraduate training programs in family medicine, so they should be for an interim period to meet immediate short-term needs.[1]

Availability of Continuing Medical Education (CME) Programs for family physicians in the region is variable and far from satisfactory. Unfortunately, CME is not a mandatory requirement for licensing, credentialing, or recertification of health professionals. Well-designed and executed robust CME programs are needed across the region.[1]

The family practice approach requires teamwork. A family physician, nurse, and other health-care providers form essential members of the family practice team. In most countries in the region, such team-based approaches do not exist, and they will require well-trained nurses and other health-care providers, who are in short supply. Continuing Professional Development (CPD) opportunities for nurses and other health-care providers are lacking and need to be developed in the region.[1]

The EMR faces major gaps and challenges needing urgent attention from governments, policy makers, academic institutions, and all stakeholders including the World Health Organization (WHO). Availability of education and training opportunities in FM in the region is variable and far from satisfactory. A medium to long-term goal should be to ensure every medical school has a Family Medicine Department, and that a sufficient number of robust postgraduate training programs (mostly of two to four years duration) are available, to meet the needs for trained family physicians in the region. A short-to medium- term goal should be to have on-the-job training short courses in Family Medicine to improve the knowledge and skills of those already working in the health system. A shorter-term strategy should involve the development and implementation of robust and effective CME programs in the region. Steps should be taken to address the shortage of trained nurses and other health-care providers and provide them with CPD opportunities. The family practice team approach should be advocated and supported.[1]

Family medicine has evolved at different rates in different parts of the world. In 1966, the United Kingdom started a GP vocational training program. During the same decade, Canada, the United States, and several other countries initiated programs specifically designed to train family physicians. By 1995, at least 56 countries had developed specialty training programs in FM and many more have followed suit since. Many family practice training programs were established through partnerships with medical schools, community hospitals, and practicing physicians. Yet in many countries, FM is still not recognized or established as a distinct medical specialty. There are many examples of countries that have benefited from the FP model, including Brazil and Thailand.[2]

An optimal doctor to patient ratio requires one family physician for every 2000 people. With the population of more than 350 million, the Arab world within the EMR needs more than 175,000 family physicians. Therefore, decisions are necessary, and efforts need to be made in order to establish training programs, which produce more skilled family physicians. It has been recommended that 20% of all doctors in the six GCC Member States should be trained as specialists in family medicine over the next 10 years.[3] However, there is still an acute shortage of training programs to achieve these targets. Taking Bahrain as an example, with its production of an average of 16 family physicians per year, and with its immediate need for more than 600 family physicians (with less than 250 currently available); it will require more than 20 years to achieve the target.[3]

Limited information is available on education, training, and Continuing Medical Education (CME) programs for family physicians in the EMR. Family Medicine specialty training in the EMR started in 1979, with the establishment of a Department of Family Medicine at the American University of Beirut.[4] According to a report published in 2011, 31 FM residency programs existed in 13 countries across the region, graduating approximately 182 residents per year.[2,4] This was up from an earlier reported 20 programs graduating 150 residents each year in 2007 in the Arab world.[5] Further increases in the number of postgraduate training programs in FM in the region are taking place, but at a pace that will not be able to meet the needs for family physicians in the near future.[3]

The Arab Board for Medical Specialization was established in 1978 and has been advocating for FM.[3] The Arab Board of Family and Community Medicine aims to set standards for FM training programs in the Arab world and provides certification to eligible graduates.[3] It has offered assistance to any Arab state interested in establishing an FM discipline and training program. Despite that, and until the present time, unfortunately only a handful of Board-accredited programs have been established in the Arab world.[3] Very few family physicians, in comparison to the need, have been certified by the Board.

Family Medicine Postgraduate Training in Saudi Arabia started in 1983.[6] Subsequently, Fellowship, Arab Board, and Saudi Board in Family Medicine were introduced between 1988 and 1995.[6] The Saudi Diploma in Family Medicine (14 months duration) started in 2008.[7]

In 2013, Saudi Arabia reported to have 75 postgraduate training centres in FM with 150 trainers, 474 trainees and averaging 120 graduates annually, despite having a capacity to graduate 200.[7] A recent study, conducted to assess accreditation of primary health-care centres in Saudi Arabia for postgraduate training in FM, identified a number of challenges. A substantial need for improvement has been identified.[7]

The Kuwait Institute for Medical Specialization (KIMS) developed an FM residency program in 1983. During 2011, 45 out of 87 applicants to the Primary Health Care Residency program were accepted in Kuwait.[8]

The Family Practice Residency Program (FPRP) in Bahrain started in 1979, as a three-year postgraduate residency training program in FM, affiliated with the American University of Beirut (AUB).[9] The Arab Board Council for Family & Community Medicine recognized the program in 1989, as a postgraduate specialty program in family and community medicine. In 1996, the program was modified to four years training in affiliation with the Irish College of General Practitioners (ICGP) and The Royal College of Surgeons in Ireland (RCSI).[9]

Residency training in FM in Lebanon was reported to have graduated six residents in 2007, had a structure and duration similar to programs in the United States and prepared residents to provide in-patient care in addition to out-patient care.[4]

Residency training in the United Arab Emirates started in 1994, at Al Ain University, and now there are several programmes.[5]

Family Medicine residency training in Jordan started in 1981, and currently, there are four residency training programs accredited by the Jordan Medical Council.[5]

Qatar established an FM program in 1994, in response to the need for upgrading primary care and to attract physicians to the country.[4] Qatar recognized FM as a specialty in 1995 and as of 2011, there were 147 family physicians working in the country – 18% of its total physician workforce. A four-year FM residency program was established in the mid-1990s, and the inaugural class graduated in 1999. The establishment of Weill Cornell Medical College in Qatar in 2001 signalled the government's continued commitment to medicine and health care. Despite this, there is still a shortage of family physicians and a lack of academic capacity to produce sufficient numbers. These are both issues the government will need to address to provide quality health care for all in the future. Currently, Weill Cornell Medical College in Qatar offers undergraduate experience in FM.[10,11] Hamad Medical Corporation (HMC) is the largest health-care institution providing health-care services across Qatar and offers four-year residency training in FM.[12]

In Oman, the Department of Family and Community Medicine (FAMCO) was established in 1987 at the College of Medicine, Sultan Qaboos University to teach undergraduates. In 1994, a formal structured four-year postgraduate training program was started in FM. In 2001, this program was recognized by the Royal College of General Practitioners (UK) and Oman was the first country in the world to conduct the Membership of the Royal College of General Practitioners (International) MRCGP (INT) examination.[13,14]

A study conducted in Oman examined the ideal attributes of an FM residency training program.[15] In summary, an ideal FM residency training program could be built on a longitudinal model. Residents in this model would spend more time doing FM and less time in the hospital. Residents should be trained to be adult lifelong learners and faculty should be more of a facilitator. Thus, training would be more relevant to their future role as family physicians.[15] There are ongoing discussions and a pilot project in the United States, to see whether a three or four-year residency training is required in FM. Findings of this pilot will have repercussions on the duration of residency training in FM in the future.[16] Redesigning undergraduate medical programmes may also help in reducing the postgraduate training period.

In Pakistan, FM education at undergraduate level started at Aga Khan University in Karachi in 1986. Later, a postgraduate program in FM was developed in collaboration with the College of Physicians and Surgeons, Pakistan.[14] Currently, there is a four-year training program, offered at four accredited institutions in the country, but only four to five FM specialists are produced each year. Pakistan faces major challenges introducing family medicine at the undergraduate level, developing family medicine orientation programmes for its over 100,000 existing GPs, developing "train the trainer" programmes, and scaling up the production of postgraduate family physicians in order to bring major reforms to its family practice based primary healthcare approach.

Family Medicine is a sub-specialty established in 2013 at Hadramout Medical University in Yemen. The Yemeni Board for Medical Specializations planned to establish a four-year training program on FM with 20 trainees per year by 2015.

Iran has recognized the need for cost-effective and preventive health care and has also embarked on implementing the FM model, but faces a number of challenges including financial constraints and issues related to acceptance by the people. A two-year Master of Public Health Training, through multimedia and distance education, has been started in Iran.[17]

Sudan has multiple entry points for FM training. The Diploma in Family Medicine is of six months duration and offers career opportunities in Saudi Arabia after completion.[18] In addition, an in-service, two-year, Masters level program is offered in Sudan. It allows on-the-job physicians to get training and certification in Family Medicine.[19] Gezira University in Sudan participated in an African Family Medicine training project called "Primafamed" and as a result reached level four in 2010, which includes having a department/unit of FM, training facilities, written curriculum, postgraduate training, and acceptance of family medicine as a specialty by the Ministry of Health, and graduated family physicians working as part of the health-care system.[20,21]

Evaluation of ongoing training programs is important. Recently, an assessment of the Saudi Diploma program was conducted and offers opportunities to critically evaluate other training programs in the region. It reports that the context, input, process, and product approach (CIPP format) is useful in evaluating diploma training in FM. The duration of the diploma in FM needed revision to ensure the depth and quality of training. It was found that proper assessment methods need to be applied to assure the trainee's satisfactory performance. The study found the use of sophisticated technology (such as skills labs) were useful in improving the skills of trainees. It was noted that trainee feedback is important to ascertain the achievement of objectives, identification of barriers, and also better solutions. It was found that supervision is a fundamental issue in the learning process.[22]

Limited data is available on FM related CME activities in the region. A study in Oman found interactive, collaborative, co-operative small group learning was more effective than traditional didactic methods in providing a stimulating environment that motivates the learners, enhances lifelong learning skills, and is more enjoyable.[23] The Canadian model of practice-based small group learning may also be effective in the Omani context and for the region. Delivery of effective CME depends on support from stakeholders, an establishment recognition system, and adequate resources.[24]

FAMILY MEDICINE DEPARTMENTS AND UNDERGRADUATE MEDICAL EDUCATION

Undergraduate programs in FM are essential to serve as the foundation for the specialty. Medical students need to be exposed to FM and see it as a worthwhile career option. To meet this essential objective, FM departments are required in all medical schools. Studies indicate that, in the case of countries such as Bahrain and Saudi Arabia, there are substantially more medical graduates entering postgraduate training in FM, since they have departments of FM in their medical schools and teaching in FM at the undergraduate level. This is in contrast with countries such as Syria and Yemen, with substantially fewer medical graduates entering postgraduate training in FM. Medical education at the undergraduate level in most institutions in the EMR is substantially hospital-based, whereas it should be in combination with major exposure to community based activities.

POSTGRADUATE TRAINING IN FAMILY MEDICINE

In the EMR, there is a general shortage of training programs that could provide trained human resources to work in FM departments. Strategies can be drawn from existing models in which training in FM has been successfully achieved in a short period of time. The Primafamed project involved 10 universities in eight Sub-Saharan countries in training family physicians in a span of two and a half years. Primafamed has adopted a strategic approach, drawing on successful models from the developed world. This includes an overall framework, a network to enable sharing of information and resources, and local coordinators to ensure ongoing communication and implementation. They recognize the importance of a vertical progression from FM training in undergraduate curricula to postgraduate community-based training program, and a career pathway with sufficient and adequately remunerated positions for registrars and qualified family doctors. Promoting teamwork with other PHC workers is also a feature. Sudan is one EMR country to have already benefited from this model.[25]

Postgraduate training programs vary in number and duration of training across the countries of the EMR. If we look at the higher number of postgraduates coming out of four-year structured training programs, Saudi Arabia and Egypt stand out prominently. On the other hand, we have a majority of countries in the region, such as Afghanistan and Yemen, with major challenges in improving the number of postgraduates to provide the required human resource. It appears that countries such as Egypt and Saudi Arabia are doing well and producing a substantial number of postgraduates, with a varying number of years of training.

There is a need for a greater private sector role in initiating and running postgraduate training programs in FM. A need exists to ensure that training takes place in the community, along with some components that are hospital-based. Unfortunately, there are several programmes where the majority of the training takes place in hospitals.

Assessment of postgraduate training varies across the countries in the region. The WHO can play a role in bringing stakeholders together to ensure that the curriculum is need-based and relevant, and that assessment methods ensure that enough specialists in FM are produced to meet each country's needs. It is important, and a need has been identified, to ensure regular inspection and evaluation of training programs. A very important issue identified is that of accreditation of postgraduate training programs in each country.

Recently, a number of challenges have been identified and solutions explored in postgraduate training programs in Saudi Arabia. These have relevance for such programs across the region. These challenges are related to difficulties in health-care settings, involving trainers, trainees, health teams, patients, and the health system.[7] A recent study conducted in Saudi Arabia found that factors such as continuity of care, duration of work in PHC, the opportunity for discussion and evaluation of patients, and number of trainers, were associated with residents attaining their training objectives.[26] Such findings have practical implications for postgraduate training programs in the region.

SHORT TRAINING ON CAPACITY BUILDING OF GPs

Egypt, Iran, Iraq, Jordan, Oman, Pakistan, Saudi Arabia, the United Arab Emirates, and Yemen all claim to have short courses in FM for existing GPs, of up to a year in duration. A need for such short courses has been identified in FM. They are mostly run in the public sector and appear to fulfil short-term urgent needs. The private sector needs to also be involved in this endeavour. There are concerns whether family physicians are safe clinicians after going through these short courses. Curriculum, assessment, and accreditation issues need further strengthening. Accreditation of training programs can be either at a national level, such as Saudi Commission for Health Specialties in Saudi Arabia or the College of Physicians and Surgeons in Pakistan, or at the regional level such as the Arab Board of Family and Community Medicine. The WHO needs to advocate for short courses in improving the capacities of GPs to ensure that the quality of practice of those undertaking these courses is guaranteed, and that they are allowed for a limited period of time until a sufficient number of four-year training programs has been established.

The majority of respondents agree with a model where a nurse works with a family doctor as a team, but such a model doesn't fully exist as yet in EMR. There is a lack of trained nurses and a lack of continuing nursing education opportunities for nurses working in PHC in the region. The WHO can play a positive role in promoting such a model in the region.

We have most GPs practicing in the EMR without any postgraduate training or certification. In addition, those who have completed their postgraduate training need continued upgrading of their knowledge and skills. Therefore, a robust CME program is required for all practicing family physicians in the region. There is a need for CME programmes to be mandatory and linked to licensing, credentialing and, where appropriate, re-certification. CME programs should be convenient, relevant, and individualized; incorporate feedback with learning, and be interesting and well-planned and delivered. The WHO can provide guidance and support for such CME activities for family physicians in EMR.

EMR countries are divided into three groups. Group 1 consists of high income Gulf Cooperation Council (GCC) countries. Group 2 consists of middle and lower-middle-income countries (includes Egypt, Iran, Iraq, Jordan, Lebanon, Libya, Morocco, Palestine, Syria, and Tunisia). Group 3 consists of mainly lower-income countries (including Afghanistan, Djibouti, Pakistan, Somalia, Sudan, and Yemen).

Group 1 countries do not have as much of an issue regarding shortages of health workers, as they can always import health workers from other countries. At the same time, they are trying to develop their own health workforce. Group 2 countries have health workforce issues and all countries included in Group 3 have a significant shortage of doctors, nurses, and midwives.

GROUP 1 COUNTRIES

Group 1 includes Bahrain, Kuwait, Oman, Qatar, Saudi Arabia, and the United Arab Emirates. Taking Bahrain as an example from this group, it has an annual family physician production of 22. There are 228 family physicians working in primary health-care facilities, and currently, the country has 1.84 trained family physicians looking after every 10,000 members of the population. At its current rate of production by 2030, it will have 330 trained family physicians in the country with 558 working in primary health-care facilities, and therefore will be the only country in EMR to have exceeded the international benchmark of 3.4 trained family physicians for 10,000 members of the population. At the current rate of production, Kuwait, Oman, Qatar, Saudi Arabia, and the United Arab Emirates will have 1.49, 0.9, 1.16, 0.76, and 0.15 trained family physicians per 10,000 population, respectively, falling short of the international benchmark of 3 per 10,000 population. Table 8.1 provides the distribution and projections of family physicians in Group 1 countries of the region.

GROUP 2 COUNTRIES

Group 2 includes Egypt, Iran, Iraq, Jordon, Lebanon, Libya, Morocco, Palestine, Syria, and Tunisia. Taking Egypt as a case, it has an annual family physician production of 180, family physicians working in primary health-care facilities are 256, and currently, it has 0.05 trained family physicians looking after 10,000 population. At its current rate of production, by 2030, it will have 2700 trained family physicians in the country, or 0.29 trained family physicians for 10,000 population. At the current rate of production, Iran, Iraq, Jordon, Lebanon, Libya, Morocco, Palestine, Syria, and Tunisia will have 1.33. 0.52, 0.80, 0.82, 0.34, 0.19, 0.12, 0.17, and 1.07 trained family physicians per 10,000 population respectively, falling short of the international benchmark of 3 per 10,000 population. Table 8.2 provides the distribution and projections of family physicians in Group 2 countries of the region.

TABLE 8.1 Projection of family physician production to 2030 in Group 1 countries

Country	Annual family physician output (2015)	Family physicians/ 10,000 population (2015)	With current annual increase by 2030		With recommended annual increase by 2030	
			Cumulative trained family physicians	Family physicians/ 10,000 population	Cumulative trained family physicians	Family physicians/ 10,000 population
Bahrain	22	1.84	330	3.40	330	3.40
Kuwait	35	0.64	525	1.49	1223	2.93
Oman	20	0.4	300	0.90	1313	2.96
Qatar	12	0.64	180	1.16	657	2.88
Saudi Arabia	140	0.25	2100	0.76	12102	3.56
UAE	10	0.05	150	0.15	3767	3.08
Subtotal	239	0.31	3585	0.79	19392	3.34

TABLE 8.2 Projection of family physician production to 2030 in Group 2 countries

Country	Annual family physician output (2015)	Family physicians/ 10,000 population (2015)	With current annual increase by 2030		With recommended annual increase by 2030	
			Cumulative trained family physicians	Family physicians/ 10,000 population	Cumulative trained family physicians	Family physicians/ 10,000 population
Egypt	180	0.05	2700	0.29	35701	3.51
Iran	810	0.10	12150	1.33	28309	3.51
Iraq	120	0.27	1800	0.52	16453	3.39
Jordan	35	0.33	525	0.80	2760	3.19
Lebanon	27	0.09	405	0.82	1618	3.17
Libya	10	0.17	150	0.34	2175	3.05
Morocco	50	0.01	750	0.19	11921	3.04
Palestine	4	0.05	60	0.12	1995	3.11
Syria	20	0.10	300	0.17	9234	3.08
Tunisia	80	0.20	1200	1.07	3804	3.03
Subtotal	1336	0.11	20040	0.62	115399	3.25

GROUP 3 COUNTRIES

Group 3 includes Afghanistan, Djibouti, Pakistan, Somalia, Sudan, and Yemen. Taking Afghanistan as an example from this group, it has an annual family physician production of 6, family physicians working in primary health-care facilities are 20, and currently, it has 0.01 trained family physicians looking after 10,000 population. At its current rate of production by 2030, it will have 90 trained family physicians in the country and therefore, will have 0.03 trained family physicians for 10,000 population. At the current rate of production Djibouti, Pakistan, Somalia, Sudan, and Yemen will have 0.00, 0.00, 0,00, 0,00, 1.19, and 0.00 trained family physicians per 10,000 population respectively, falling short of the international benchmark of 3 per

TABLE 8.3 Projection of family physician production to 2030 in Group 3 countries

Country	Annual family physician output (2015)	Family physicians/ 10000 population (2015)	With current annual increase by 2030		With recommended annual increase by 2030	
			Cumulative trained family physicians	Family physicians/ 10000 population	Cumulative trained family physicians	Family physicians/ 10000 population
Afghanistan	6	0.01	90	0.03	12092	2.78
Djibouti	0	0.00	0	0.00	0	0.00
Pakistan	4	0.00	60	0.00	70686	3.05
Somalia	0	0.00	0	0.00	0	0.00
Sudan	435	0.13	6525	1.19	15203	2.77
Yemen	0	0.00	0	0.00	0	0.00
Subtotal	445	0.02	6675	0.18	97981	2.57

10,000 population. Table 8.3 provides the distribution and projections of family physicians in Group 3 countries of the region.

SHORT COURSE ON FAMILY MEDICINE, AN ON-THE-JOB TRAINING INITIATIVE BY THE WHO-EMRO

Most current general practitioners in the EMR are not familiar with the foundations and principles of FM. Orienting these GPs with the basic principles of FM is a major task for any government. A complementary strategy is to develop a national level bridging/orientation programme to familiarize current general practitioners with the basic principles and concepts of family medicine. WHO Regional Office for the Eastern Mediterranean (EMRO) has taken the initiative to develop a six-month online course with the help of American University of Beirut to orient and train general practitioners about the basic principles of family medicine. The programme helps GPs to understand their role as family physicians and how they contribute to the concepts of UHC. This course can be part of a national bridging programme and is not a replacement for the full postgraduate training of family physicians. The programme has been designed on the principles of adult learning, using blended learning strategies. Countries can modify the six-month programme to suit their family practice needs.

With a population of over 200 million and over 100,000 general physicians working both in public and private sectors, Pakistan has diverse challenges to promote family medicine. One major challenge is to provide orientation to over 100,000 practicing general practitioners to expose them to the basics of family practice so that they can be effectively integrated into the family practice system. The WHO-EMRO six month family medicine programme was carefully reviewed by family medicine experts at Khyber Medical University in Pakistan and is being upgraded to a one-year programme to meet the larger family practice needs of Pakistani family physicians. The programme can be adopted by other provinces in the future. The programme is being upgraded in collaboration with WHO and shall be implemented in early 2018.

CONCLUSION

Achieving Sustainable Development Goals and Universal Health Coverage targets require a sound primary care approach largely based on the family practice model. Most EMR Member States have significant deficiencies in human resources for health, especially in Family Medicine.

Member States need to make concerted efforts to introduce FM at the undergraduate, postgraduate, and continuing professional development levels. The team-based approach of family practice also requires the training and professional development of other health professionals. Most countries in the EMR will need to go through a major transformation to redesign and strengthen their health-care systems from hospital-based systems focusing on treating diseases, to community-based systems with a focus on providing comprehensive basic preventive, promotive, and curative health services to all their people. High-quality family physicians and other health professionals, sufficient in numbers, will play a central role in promoting such systems and delivering UHC to the people of the region.

REFERENCES

1. World Health Organization, Eastern Mediterranean Region Working Paper. Current Status of Family Medicine Education and Training in Eastern Mediterranean Region. 2014.
2. Kidd M. *The Contribution of Family Medicine to Improving Health Systems. A Guidebook from the World Organization of Family Doctors*, 2nd edition. 2013. New York: Radcliffe Publishing London.
3. Alnasir FAL. Family medicine in the Arab world? Is it a luxury? *Journal of the Bahrain Medical Society*. 2009; 21(1):191–192.
4. Osman H, Romani M, Hlais S. Family medicine in Arab countries. *Family Medicine*. 2011; 43(1):37–42.
5. Abyad A, Al-Baho AK, Unluoglu I, Tarawneh M, Al-Hilfy TKY. Development of family medicine in the Middle East. *Family Medicine*. 2007; 39(10):736–741.
6. Albar AA. Twenty years of family medicine education in Saudi Arabia. *Eastern Mediterranean Health Journal*. 1999; 5:589–596.
7. Al-Khaldi YM, AlDawood KM, AlBar AA, Al-Shmmari SA, Al-Ateeq MA, Al-Meqbel TI, Al-Yahya OA, Al-Dayel MA, Al-Ghamdi MS, Al-Badr BO. Challenges facing postgraduate training in family medicine in Saudi Arabia: Patterns and solutions. *Journal of Health Specialties*. 2014; 2:61–67.
8. Marwan Y, Adel Ayed A. Selection criteria of residents for residency programs in Kuwait. *BMC Medical Education*. 2013, 13:4.
9. Ministry of Health, Kingdom of Bahrain. Family Practice Residency Program-Overview. Available at: http://familymedicine.moh.gov.bh/Overview.aspx [Accessed 25 September 2014].
10. Cornell Weill University, Qatar. Available at: http://qatar-weill.cornell.edu/aboutUs/fa/bios/verjeeMohamud.html [Accessed 25 September 2014].
11. Verjee M. The future of family medicine in Qatar. *Marhaba*. 2013. Available at: http://marhaba.com.qa/the-future-of-family-medicine-in-qatar/ [Accessed 26 September 2014].
12. Hamad Medical Corporation. Applying for Residency Training Programs at HMC. Available at: http://med.hamad.qa/en/residency_program/residency_program.aspx [Accessed 26 September 2014].
13. Al-Shafaee M. Family medicine practice in Oman Present and future. *Sultan Qaboos University Medical Journal*. 2009; 9(2):116–118.
14. Haq CL, Qureshi AF, Zuberi RW, Inam SN, Bryant JH. Family medicine postgraduate training in Pakistan. *Journal of Pakistan Medical Association*. 1992; 42(3):69–73.
15. Almahrezi A, Al-Shafaee M. Attributes of an ideal family medicine residency training program. *Oman Medical Journal*. 2008; 23(1):7–8.
16. American Academy of Family Physicians. Should family medicine residents train for three years or four? *AAFP News*. 2012. Available at:http://www.aafp.org/news/education-professional-development/2012111 5lengthoftraining.html [Accessed 26 September 2014].
17. Majdzadeh R. Family physician implementation and preventive medicine; opportunities and challenges. *International Journal of Preventive Medicine*. 2012; 3(10):665–669.
18. University of Medical Sciences and Technology. Postgraduate Diploma in Family Medicine. Available at: umst-edu.com/FamilyMedicine.aspx [Accessed 28 September 2014].
19. Public Health Institute. Master of Family Medicine. Available at: www.phi.edu.sd/node/222 [Accessed 29 September 2014].
20. Flinkenflögel M, Essuman A, Patrick Chege P, Ayankogbe O, and Maeseneer JD. Family medicine training in sub-Saharan Africa: South–South cooperation in the Primafamed project as strategy for development. *Family Practice*, 2014; 31(4):427–436.

21. Mohamed KG, Hunskaar S, Abdelrahman SH, Malik EM. Scaling up family medicine training in Gezira, Sudan: A 2-year in-service master programme using modern information and communication technology: A survey study. *Human Resources for Health*. 2014; 12:3.
22. Al-Khathami AD. Evaluation of Saudi family medicine training program: The application of CIPP evaluation format. *Medical Teacher*. 2012; 34:S81–S89.
23. Anwar H, Batty H. Continuing medical education strategy for primary health care physicians in Oman: Lessons to be learnt. *Oman Medical Journal*. 2007; 22(3):33–35.
24. Ronald M. Harden. A new vision for distance learning and continuing medical education. *The Journal of Continuing Education in the Health Professions*. 2005; (25):43–51.
25. Goodyear-Smith F. Sub-Saharan Africa fast-tracks towards family medicine. *Family Practice*, 2014; 00(00):1–225.
26. Abu Zuhairah AR, Al-Dawood KM, Khamis AH. Factors affecting Family Medicine residents' perception of achievement of training objectives. *Journal of Health Specialties*. 2014; 2:114.

CHAPTER 9

Leveraging technology to transition general practitioners to the family practice model of care

Ghassan Hamadeh, Mona Osman, and Hossein Hamam

INTRODUCTION

Countries are taking different paths to achieve the United Nations' agreed upon Universal Health Coverage (UHC) Sustainable Development Goal 8.3, by 2030. This includes achieving universal health coverage, including financial risk protection, access to quality essential health-care services and access to safe, effective, quality, and affordable essential medicines and vaccines for all.[1,2]

A critical challenge in this endeavour is the shortage of well-trained primary care physicians who could contribute to building strong systems of primary health care (PHC) in each nation.[3] Graduating sufficient family physicians to relieve this shortage and ensure a strong new PHC model is particularly daunting using standard Family Medicine (FM) residency training programs in the Eastern Mediterranean Region (EMR).[3,4] Innovative ways to increase the numbers of physicians trained in Family Medicine are needed to accelerate the transition to UHC.

In this chapter, we describe the use of eLearning tools with experienced general practitioners (i.e. doctors without formal postgraduate training and qualifications) to transition them to the family practice model of care.[5] The on-the-job training described, uses the Moodle Learning Management System (LMS) in a blended supervision format.[6–8] The course content was based on a review of the curricula of the European Academy of Teachers in General Practice, the US. Accreditation Council for Graduate Medical Education, the Arab Board of Family Medicine, and a survey of PHC authorities and general practitioners (GPs) in 22 countries covered by WHO Eastern Mediterranean Region Office (EMRO).[9–11] The final curriculum included modifications to accommodate common country needs and resource limitations.

THE FAMILY PRACTICE MODEL

A succinct definition of Family Medicine is that discipline "concerned with the provision of personal, primary, preventive, comprehensive, continuing, and coordinated health care of the individual in relation to his or her family, community, and environment".[5]

Family medicine as a discipline was started by general practitioners on both sides of the Atlantic (the United States and the United Kingdom) in the 1960s as a counterculture to post-war medical specialization, which had resulted in a narrow biomedical focus and fragmentation of care.[12] In the United States, family practice was recognized as a specialty on February 8, 1969, and its first Board consisted of 15 members: five from the American Academy of General Practice, five from the Section on General Practice of the American Medical Association, and one each from the specialty boards of surgery, internal medicine, paediatrics, obstetrics-gynaecology, and psychiatry-neurology.[13] The American Academy of Family Physicians (AAFP) was set up in 1947 and reorganized to serve the academic needs of expert Family Physicians.[14]

Family practice is characterized by eight different attributes, namely the provision of general, first contact, continuous, comprehensive, coordinated, and collaborative care with an orientation towards the family and the community.[15] Taking these characteristics into consideration, the World Health Organization (WHO) Regional Office for the Eastern Mediterranean (EMRO) adopted the concept of family practice for the effective and efficient delivery of primary health-care services and achieving UHC in the 22 EMR countries.[16] UHC entails ensuring access by all people to, preventive, curative, rehabilitative, and palliative health services that are of sufficient quality to be effective and without exposing the people using these services to financial hardship.[17]

The World Organization of Family Doctors (WONCA) defined six main competencies that a general practitioner/family physician has to master. These competencies include the following: primary care management, person-centred care, specific problem-solving skills, comprehensive approach, community-orientation, and holistic approach.

These competencies cover the main characteristics of the discipline of general practice/family medicine; namely:

1. Acting as the first point of contact in the health-care system, dealing with all the health problems of the individuals regardless of their age and sex.
2. Coordinating care with other specialists, professionals, and health-care resources in an efficient way, taking an advocacy role for the patient when needed.
3. Developing a person-centred approach that is oriented to the individual within the context of his/her family and community.
4. Promoting patient empowerment.
5. Providing long-term continuity of care depending on the needs of the patient.
6. Applying a specific decision-making process as determined by the prevalence and incidence of the illness in the community.
7. Managing both acute and chronic health problems of individual patients.
8. Managing illnesses presenting in an undifferentiated way namely at an early stage of their development.
9. Promoting health and wellbeing through appropriate and effective intervention.
10. Assuming specific responsibility for the health of the community.
11. Dealing with health problems in their different physical, psychological, social, and cultural dimensions.

A curriculum for training general practitioners/family physicians is expected to facilitate the acquisition of the above six main core competencies rooted and nurtured by the "proper" attitude, scientific basis, and social context. The contextual features take into consideration the context of the physicians themselves (working conditions, community, culture, financial and regulatory frameworks); the attitudinal features cover the professional capabilities of the physicians in addition to the values and medical ethics of the profession; and the scientific features cover the application of a critical and research-based approach in practice through continuous learning and quality improvement

Such a curriculum was conceived from the early days of the establishment of the specialty of family medicine where it was perceived that the graduate training program should be structured on par with other specialties as a three-year residency program with more than 50% of training in out-patient settings, and subject matter to include internal medicine, paediatrics, surgery, psychiatry, obstetrics and gynaecology, community medicine, and social and behavioural sciences. In the United States, there were 30 such training programs (290 graduates per year) in 1969 and the number increased to 259 in six years (3705 graduates per year).[18] The United States also accommodated practicing physicians interested in becoming certified family physicians by allowing them to sit for certifying exams if they met "interim eligibility" criteria.[13] This was a common practice for new boards later on known as "grandfathering" or "bridging".[19]

It goes without saying that the model emphasizes the challenge of moving doctors towards the bio-psychosocial or community-oriented models of care.[20,21] These models rely on a team of health professionals and a health system that is patient-centred and supportive of primary care. The Patient-Centred Medical Home (PCMH) is one such re-incarnation of these models where a "family physician" plays a central role in care coordination and delivery.[21-23] This same primary care family physician will function as the facilitator for achieving UHC and communities will need to accurately assess their primary care workforce needs and develop programs to meet those needs.[24-26] This will include the need for changes in training content and an increase in the number of training programs, as well as modifications of the roles of health providers in primary care.[27-30]

BRIDGING PROFESSIONAL DEVELOPMENT PROGRAMS

The main challenge facing the implementation of family practice in the EMR region is the limited number of available family medicine training programs and subsequently the limited number of practicing family physicians.[31] Expanding the number of training programs is the preferred approach to this challenge, similar to what happened in the United States between 1969 and 1975 with a resulting 13-fold increase in the number of family physician graduates.[18] Should this approach be difficult to adopt, the alternative option for building the capacity to meet UHC requirements in the EMR region is to upgrade the skills of GPs in the family practice model through bridging professional development programs.[3]

Bridging programs are not uncommon when new specialties are created. Numerous countries have adopted programs leading to diplomas or certificates "designed to upgrade the standard of care in General Practice, and to increase awareness of the global trend towards the provision of continuing and comprehensive care by the family doctor".[32,33] The Academy of Family Physicians of Malaysia has been leading in this educational program for many years. Similar programs have been established in Sudan and in the Kingdom of Saudi Arabia.[34,35] The Kingdom of Saudi Arabia has currently 91 Family Medicine four-year training programs and 73 accelerated two-year programmes. Both are full-time residency programmes. While some may feel shorter full-time residency programs are acceptable to produce the competent Family Physicians described earlier, the majority of health educators feel full-time residency training of new graduates should be closer to 36 months.[18,36] At the moment, there is no comprehensive analysis of the time needed for a professional development program to transition experienced practitioners into the FM model while on the job. However, the model has been applied to a variety of countries and in different methodologies for more than 20 years.[4,33,34,37,38] Most of these professional advancement programs offer a mixture of live or online lecturing coupled with direct observation of work and audits.[32,34,38–40]

BLENDED LEARNING

Technological advances and Internet connectivity have revolutionized traditional methods of teaching by making it possible for educators to have virtual classrooms available to a larger audience according to the latter's time and location convenience. A teacher can communicate with students in real time in what is called synchronous communication (chatting or web conferencing) or in an asynchronous mode where messages or presentations are left for students to peruse at their convenience and assignments or questions posted to teachers for later feedback. Discussion forums, blogs, wikis, and email messages are examples of asynchronous communication.[41] This mode of learning is ideal for working professionals who are committed to their jobs during regular hours and would prefer to "study at their own pace" and review the content of online activities as frequently as they wish. This approach seems to be of equal benefit to face-to-face interaction.[42]

Not enough studies have been made to validate the exclusive use of online training without some form of face-to-face interaction, especially in the health sectors.[42] This may be why most universities continue the use of "blended learning" which merges web-based training with face-to-face activities.[43] In this format, teachers are able to share innumerable resources with their students: books, monographs, articles, videos, presentations, or any content that can be posted on the web, and at the same time plan live interactions for review and testing. One wonders if this modality of training not only will be the norm for work-based training but also the preferred modality in regular universities or schools as well. Blending is not only mixing live and web but can also extend to mixing instructional modalities, methods, and delivery media. The main purpose of this approach is making education more student-centric while paying due attention to mitigating risks of social isolation, up-front development costs, and technical problems.[8]

PROPOSED PROGRAM

The Department of Family Medicine at the American University of Beirut Medical Center (AUBMC) was approached by WHO-EMRO to develop tools that help advance the Family Practice Model in the region. One proposed program was an "Advanced General Practice" update course teaching the elements of the Family Medicine model. The course targets GPs who have not received any vocational or postgraduate training prior to entering practice. It complements the experience these practitioners have acquired in their career and hopes to re-focus them on the main components that are critical to a successful application of the FM model (Figure 9.1). This was in complete alignment as well with the vision of the Ministry of Public Health in Lebanon, which has been working on strengthening the role of primary care physicians and integrating family practice in the primary health-care centres in its network.

OBJECTIVES OF THE COURSE

The main objectives of the course are:

- To equip GPs with the knowledge, skills, and attitudes that are needed to provide comprehensive, continuous, and appropriate health care to individuals and families.
- To institutionalize continuous professional development among the practicing GPs in the region.

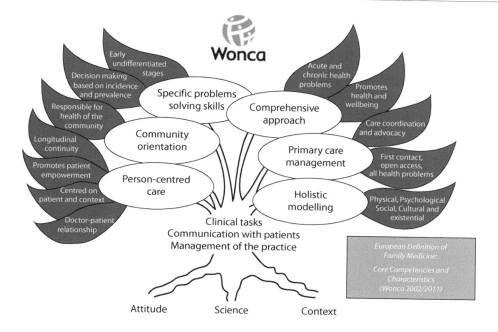

FIGURE 9.1 European definition of family medicine.

STRUCTURE OF THE COURSE

The course spans over a period of 24 weeks and it is offered in a blended format including both online and face-to-face live courses. It is intended to accommodate the work schedule of the practicing GPs. This format allows also continuous online interaction between the tutors and trainees. One tutor is assigned to a group of trainees; the ratio can range from 1:5 to 1:8 tutor to trainees.

The course includes an orientation session, four teaching blocks, and an exam period (Figure 9.2).

- The orientation session is the first face-to-face encounter with the trainees and it aims at providing them with a general overview of the course, hands-on for using Moodle as well as the introduction of other tasks that they are supposed to complete such as filling log book and completing assignments.

	Orientation	Block 1					Block 2					Block 3					Block 4					Exams		
Week	1	2	3	4	5	6	7	8	9	10	11	12	13	14	15	16	17	18	19	20	21	22	23	24
Orientation	♦																							
Self-study																								
Chat			♦	♦	♦	♦		♦	♦	♦	♦		♦	♦	♦	♦		♦	♦	♦	♦			
On-the-Job Training			♦	♦	♦	♦		♦	♦	♦	♦		♦	♦	♦	♦		♦	♦	♦	♦			
Live Review	♦					♦					♦					♦					♦			
Final Exam																								
tn																								

FIGURE 9.2 Advanced general practice course schedule.

- The four blocks are the main teaching period. The components and different activities of these blocks are detailed in Box 9.1.
- Exam period at the end of the course.

BOX 9.1   TEACHING MODALITIES OF THE COURSE

1. **Web-Based PowerPoint Presentations:** Forty-eight common topics are presented based both on the most common medical problems seen in primary care as reported in the literature and on the results of a learning needs assessment of GPs conducted by the consultant team. These PowerPoint presentations are also available with a voice over. Three PowerPoint presentations are to be posted weekly for four weeks each block. The topics are grouped along two themes derived from the WONCA core competencies:
   a. **Family Medicine Core Concepts:** Principles of family medicine, practice of family medicine, documentation and medical records, communication skills, professionalism, and evidence-based medicine.
   b. **Clinical Updates:** Covering 42 medical topics representing common problems encountered in primary care. These include: Abdominal pain, acne, anxiety disorders, asthma, cardiovascular diseases, risk assessment and prevention, chronic obstructive pulmonary disease, back pain, breast lump, chest pain, common skin problems, constipation, contraception, depression, dementia, diabetes mellitus type 2, diarrhea, dizziness, dyslipidaemia, dyspepsia, electrocardiograms, headache, haematuria, hypertension, insomnia, irrational use of medications, large joint pain, menopause, menstrual disorders, obesity, osteoarthritis, periodic health examination for adults, periodic health examination for children, pneumonia, prostate diseases, pulmonary tuberculosis, red eye, sexually transmitted infections, urinary tract infections, vaginitis.
2. **Online Discussions:** These discussions can be done using Moodle, Skype, or even WhatsApp; and they are to be conducted on a weekly basis with a tutor to cover different issues such as questions related to the PowerPoint presentations, review log book, and chart audits. The tutor and trainees would agree on a specific date and time to conduct these discussions.
3. **On-the-Job Training Sessions:** A total of eight on-the-job training sessions are to be done at the rate of two sessions per block. Tutors meet their group of trainees in their practice facilities or in an academic health centre. During these sessions, tutors observe trainees while seeing patients and discuss the management of these patients. Tutors can also discuss the assignments, the chart audits, and the log book with trainees during these sessions.
4. **Live Review Courses:** At the conclusion of each block, a "one-day release" is organized to bring the trainees together away from their work in one location for a review of the materials covered during that block. This time is also used to discuss cases seen in the clinic and review how trainees are documenting their practices. Four face-to-face sessions of 6 hours each (a total of 24 hours) are conducted. The sessions include board exam review style questions and case discussions.
5. **Log Book:** Trainees are required to keep a log book of the cases that they manage in their own practice over the period of the course. This should show the documentation of at least 8 visits per day with their respective International Classification of Diseases (ICD-10) diagnosis. Log book entries can be made on Moodle or on a regular excel sheet. They can be discussed online or during the day release activities.
6. **Chart Audit:** A total of 10 charts/medical records will be reviewed by tutors during the course duration for documentation and continuity of care according to a pre-defined checklist. These include, for example: 2 charts for people with diabetes mellitus, 2 for people with hypertension, 2 for children under 5, 2 for elderly patients above 65, and 2 for women aged between 20 and 50 years. The purpose of this audit is to introduce the concept of audits and checklists to the GPs and emphasize the importance of medical record documentation.
7. **Assignments:** Each trainee has to complete one assignment per block, which covers topics discussed during that block. This includes for example, a self-audit of medical records for preventive services, recording patient interview for communication skills assessment, etc.

BOX 9.2   ASSESSMENT OF TRAINEES IN "ADVANCED GENERAL PRACTICE" COURSE

1. **Formative Assessment:** Evaluation based on participation and completing the quizzes and the assignments. This evaluation covers the different online activities (quizzes, online discussions, and assignments) and the live review sessions.
2. **Summative Assessment:** Based on a final multiple choice question live exam and an objective-structured clinical examination (OSCE). The OSCE exam includes different stations that assess the practical skills and knowledge of the trainees in conducting physical examination, taking history, providing counselling as well as interpreting diagnostic tests such as electrocardiograms. For the OSCE, there is a need to prepare simulated patients and observers with defined checklists.

The evaluation of trainees is based on both a formative and summative assessments. These assessments are described in Box 9.2.

MANAGEMENT OF THE COURSE

There is a need to have a course director for the course. The role of the director is to oversee the online setup and content, as well as update the course material as needed; he/she will also manage trainees and tutors. It is important for the course directors to define the responsibilities of both tutors and trainees and follow them up accordingly. These responsibilities are depicted in Box 9.3.

The presence of information technology (IT) support is also needed while providing a course in a blended format. The IT specialist will help in setting up Moodle, adding the names of trainees, and addressing any potential technical difficulties that might face the tutors or trainees.

FIRST IMPLEMENTATION OF THE ADVANCED GENERAL PRACTICE COURSE

The course was first implemented in 2017 with 16 GPs working with the United Nations Relief and Works Agency (UNRWA) and based in different primary care centres across Lebanon. The

BOX 9.3   RESPONSIBILITIES OF TUTORS AND TRAINEES

1. Responsibilities of tutors
   - Manage the posting of the materials corresponding to each week
   - Supervise the progress of each trainee
   - Chat online with trainees once at the end of the week
   - Conduct the on-the-job training sessions
   - Correct the assignments and give feedback to the trainees

2. Responsibilities of trainees
   - Self-study three web-based topics (online presentations)
   - Do the online quiz for each topic (3 attempts are allowed; completion of the quiz is essential as a proof of completion of the topic)
   - Complete the additional readings and/or videos posted
   - Complete the online assignment per block
   - Chat online with the tutor once at the end of the week
   - Fill the log book
   - Participate actively in the on-the-job training sessions and the live review sessions

selection of GPs was on a volunteer basis. This first implementation enabled the identification of the actual challenges and the facilitating factors for optimal delivery of the course. Specifically, it allowed evaluation of the following:

- The comfort of GPs in the use of the Internet to review lectures.
- The proposed duration of 24 weeks and its acceptability in the context of GPs continuing their usual daily routines.
- The ideal ratio of tutor to trainees to allow for online communication and live interactions.

The course started with a one-day orientation session. Since most of the GPs had no experience with blended learning and had never used Moodle or any other learning management system (LMS) before, the orientation session included Moodle hands-on training. GPs were given guidance on whom to contact when facing problems with Moodle, and their laptops were assessed to ensure that all the needed software had been installed and updated for a smooth technical experience during this course. GPs were asked to complete a pre-course quiz in order to assess their current knowledge. The first week of the course did not include any lectures or assessments; instead, GPs were required to engage in online discussions and chatting regarding their personal expectations from attending this course. These activities were designed on purpose to further orient the GPs to this new environment before the start of any actual learning.

GPs were divided into three groups (five to six persons per group) with a tutor assigned to each group. The groups were selected based on the geographical location of its members in order to facilitate the on-the-job meetings. The role of the tutor was to follow-up with the trainees on a weekly basis either through Moodle discussions or through WhatsApp and to conduct the on-the-job training.

GPs were expected to complete online quizzes on a weekly basis and one assignment per block. At the conclusion of the course, GPs were evaluated through a written final exam and an Objective Structure Clinical Examination (OSCE).

The course implementation was smooth and the feedback from GPs revealed great satisfaction with the content and modality of training. A challenge faced by some GPs was Internet interruptions, especially in remote areas. This resulted in delayed studying times due to interruptions and extended download times of course materials. To counter this, GPs started downloading the materials for each week once they were made available on Moodle. For future iterations, and depending on the geographical locations of the GPs, course materials could be shared on a flash drive during the orientation session. The ratio of one tutor to six trainees proved to be ideal, as tutors reported that the time spent in the course matched their initial expectations, and trainees reported satisfaction with the tutor to trainee communication.

It's worth noting that the course offered multiple channels of communication. GPs were in contact with the tutors through Moodle discussions, email, WhatsApp, on-the-job training, and during the live review sessions. This array of communication channels offered tutors continuous and reliable supervising methods that facilitated tracking the performance and assessing the progress of their trainees. In addition, the course on Moodle was completely ready before the course start date in order to reduce, and in some cases eliminate, any time needed from the tutors to upload materials or grade assessments, thus freeing tutors to focus on the learning process rather than technical aspects related to course design. For instance, the weekly formative assessments were built using the Moodle Quiz activity which automatically grades the attempts of the trainees.

CONCLUSION

Technology is a viable method to transition general practitioners into the family practice model of care. The outlined course adopts the blended learning model. It expands on the traditional learning model of clinical supervision and didactic teaching by adding trainee-centred activities (e.g. online discussions, documentation of clinical activity, face-to-face case discussions based on prior experience). More iterations of the course are needed in order to evaluate its cost-effectiveness, impact, and the criteria used for the recruitment of participants.

In its current form, this course is offered as a university-based structured continuous professional development in general practice. Moving forward, and to accelerate the transition to the Family Practice Model across the Eastern Mediterranean Region, a full bridging programme should be adopted by specialty licensing bodies until a satisfactory number of full-fledged residency training programs has been established.

REFERENCES

1. Ghebreyesus, T.A., All roads lead to universal health coverage. *Lancet Global Health*, 2017. **5**(9):e839–e840.
2. Reich, M.R., et al., Moving towards universal health coverage: Lessons from 11 country studies. *Lancet*, 2016. **387**(10020):811–816.
3. EMRO. *Scaling up family practice: Progressing towards universal health coverage.* Regional Committee for the Eastern Mediterranean - Technical Papers 2016; EM/RC63/Tech.Disc.1 Rev.1 [Accessed 17 November 2017].
4. Zarbailov, N., et al., Strengthening general practice/family medicine in Europe–Advice from professionals from 30 European countries. *BMC Family Practice*, 2017. **18**(1):80.
5. WONCA. *The European Definition of General Practice/Family Medicine.* 2011 [Accessed 17 November 2017].
6. *About Moodle.* Available from: https://docs.moodle.org/34/en/About_Moodle [Accessed 17 November 2017].
7. Cole, J.R., *Using Moodle: Teaching with the Popular Open Source Course Management System.* 1st ed. 2005, Sebastopol, CA: O'Reilly Community Press. xv, 219.
8. de Jong, N., et al., Blended learning in health education: Three case studies. *Perspectives on Medical Education*, 2014. **3**(4):278–288.
9. Eyrman, J., *EURACT Educational Agenda*, J. Heyrman, Editor. 2005, European Academy of Teachers in General Practice EURACT: Leuven.
10. ACGME. *Accreditation Council for Graduate Medical Education–Family Medicine Requirements.* 2017; Available from: http://www.acgme.org/Specialties/Overview/pfcatid/8/Family-Medicine [Accessed 17 November 2017].
11. ABHS. *Distribution of the Training Program - Family Medicine.* 2017; Available at: http://arab-board.org/en/content/family-medicine [Accessed 17 November 2017].
12. Stephens, G.G., Family medicine as counterculture. 1979. *Family Medicine*, 1998. **30**(9): 629–636.
13. Walsh, J.G., New specialty--family practice. *JAMA*, 1970. **212**(7):1191–1195.
14. ABFM. American Board of Family Medicine. *History of the Specialty.* 2017; Available from: https://www.theabfm.org/about/history.aspx.
15. Kidd, M.R. and World Organization of National Colleges Academies and Academic Associations of General Practitioners/Family Physicians., *The Contribution of Family Medicine to Improving Health Systems: A guidebook from the World Organization of Family Doctors.* 2nd ed. 2013, London, New York: Radcliffe Pub. xxvii, 293 p.
16. EMRO. *Conceptual and strategic approach to family practice: Towards universal health coverage through family practice in the Eastern Mediterranean Region.* 2014; Available from: http://applications.emro.who.int/dsaf/EMROPUB_2014_EN_1783.pdf [Accessed 17 November 2017].
17. Etienne, C., *The World Health Report: Health Systems Financing: The Path to Universal Coverage*, C. Etienne, Editor. 2010, WHO.
18. Carek, P.J., et al., Residency training in family medicine: A history of innovation and program support. Family Medicine, 2017. **49**(4):275–281.

19. Merriam-Webster. *Grandfather Clause*. 2017; Available from: https://www.merriam-webster.com/dictionary/grandfather%20clause [Accessed 17 November 2017].

20. Engel, G.L., The biopsychosocial model and family medicine. *Journal of Family Practice*, 1983. **16**(2): 409, 412–413.

21. Ibid.

22. Kieber-Emmons, A.M. and W.L. Miller, The Patient-Centered Medical Home (PCMH) framing typology for understanding the structure, function, and outcomes of PCMHs. *Journal of the American Board of Family Medicine*, 2017. **30**(4): 472–479.

23. Chandran, R., et al., Training family medicine residents to build and remodel a patient centered medical home in Rhode Island: A team based approach to PCMH education. *Rhode Island Medical Journal* (2013), 2014. **98**(4):35–41.

24. Stigler, F.L., et al., No universal health coverage without primary health care. *Lancet*, 2016. **387**(10030): 1811.

25. Rahman, S.M., et al., Role of family medicine education in India's step toward Universal Health Coverage. *Journal of Family Medicine and Primary Care*, 2014. **3**(3):180–182.

26. Caley, M., Remember Barbara Starfield: Primary care is the health system's bedrock. *BMJ*, 2013. **347**:f4627.

27. Cunningham, P.R., E.G. Baxley, and H.G. Garrison, Transforming medical education is the key to meeting North Carolina's physician workforce needs. *North Carolina Medical Journal*, 2016. **77**(2):115–120.

28. Jackson, A., et al., Addressing the nation's physician workforce needs: The Society of General Internal Medicine (SGIM) recommendations on graduate medical education reform. *Journal of General Internal Medicine*, 2014. **29**(11):1546–1551.

29. Brown, J.B., et al., Sustaining primary health care teams: What is needed? *Journal of Interprofessional Care*, 2010. **24**(4):463–465.

30. Geyman, J.P., How many family physicians are needed? *Journal of Family Practice*, 1978. **7**(2):257–260.

31. MRO. *Regional consultation on strengthening service provision through the family practice approach*. 2014; WHO-EM/PHC/165/E/02.15:Availablefrom:http://applications.emro.who.int/docs/IC_meet_rep_2015_EN_16267.pdf?ua=1.

32. Malaysia, A.O.F.P.O. *Graduate Certificate in Family Medicine (GCFM)*. 2017; Available from: https://www.afpm.org.my/programmegcfm.

33. WONCA. *Report for Wonca Asia Pacific Council meeting May 2012*; Available from: http://www.globalfamilydoctor.com/site/DefaultSite/filesystem/documents/regionDocs/APR%20reports/Malaysia.pdf [Accessed 17 November 2017].

34. Mohamed, K.G., et al., Scaling up family medicine training in Gezira, Sudan – a 2-year in-service master programme using modern information and communication technology: A survey study. *Human Resources for Health*, 2014. **12**:3.

35. SCFHS. *The accredited training centers for Saudi Board programs*. 2017; Available from: https://www.scfhs.org.sa/en/MESPS/Statistics/Pages/default.aspx.

36. Carek, P.J., The length of training pilot: Does anyone really know what time it takes? *Family Medicine*, 2013. **45**(3):171–172.

37. Zhao, Y., et al., General practice on-the-job training in Chinese urban community: A qualitative study on needs and challenges. *PLoS One*, 2014. **9**(4):e94301.

38. Piterman, L., A graduate diploma in family medicine by distance education. *Medical Journal of Australia*, 1992. **157**(3):178–181.

39. Schattner, P., et al., Impact of master of family medicine degree by distance learning on general practitioners' career options. *Med Teach*, 2007. 29(4):e85–e92.

40. Zarif Sanaiey, N., S. Karamnejad, and R. Rezaee, Educational needs of family physicians in the domains of health and conformity with continuing education in Fasa University of Medical Sciences. *Journal of Advances in Medical Education & Professionalism*, 2015. 3(2):84–89.

41. Inclair, P.M., et al., The effectiveness of Internet-based e-learning on clinician behaviour and patient outcomes: A systematic review. *International Journal of Nursing Studies*, 2016. **57**:70–81.

42. McCutcheon, K., et al., A systematic review evaluating the impact of online or blended learning vs. face-to-face learning of clinical skills in undergraduate nurse education. *Journal of Advanced Nursing*, 2015. **71**(2):255–270.

43. Marrinan, H., et al., Let's take it to the clouds: The potential of educational innovations, including blended learning, for capacity building in developing countries. *International Journal of Health Policy and Management*, 2015. **4**(9):571–573.

CHAPTER 10

Measuring the quality of primary health care: A regional initiative in the Eastern Mediterranean Region

Mondher Letaief, Lisa Hirschhorn, Aziz Sheikh, and Sameen Siddiqi

INTRODUCTION

High-quality primary health care (PHC) has a pivotal role in ensuring that planned service developments align with the Universal Health Coverage (UHC) agenda whilst at the same time meeting the goals of improving population health and contributing to progress towards meeting the Sustainable Development Goals (SDGs).[1,2] This revival in the focus on primary health care as core to achieving People-Centred Integrated Health Services and creating resilient health-care systems able to deliver quality effective care in good times and during crises, whether due to conflicts, outbreaks of infectious disease, population migration, or natural disasters, is very welcome.[3,4] In response, the Regional Committee of the World Health Organization Eastern Mediterranean Region (WHO EMRO) has urged their Member States to "develop an essential package of health services at the primary health care level" and "improve the quality and safety of care in health facilities".[5]

This work is even more important given the changing epidemiology across the region and the challenges related to finding measures which have cross-national relevance. The Global Burden of Disease (GBD) study found that there is increasing morbidity and mortality related to non-communicable diseases (NCDs), with ischemic heart disease the leading cause of death in 2013 in the region (90.3 deaths per 100,000 people), representing a 17% increase from 1990.[6] However, significant regional variability also was seen with diarrheal disease, which was the leading cause of death in Somalia. The main causes of disability-adjusted life years (DALYs) included hypertension (83% increase since 1990), with NCDs contributing the most in higher-income countries, while childhood wasting was the leading cause in Afghanistan, Somalia, and Yemen. The authors also estimated that in countries including Egypt, Libya, Syria, and Yemen, the increase in NCDs also resulted in a decline in life expectancy in men and women. Additional challenges from conflict in the region also contribute to the evolving spectrum of diseases. Evidence from Syria indicates a growing proportion of PHC facilities that are no longer functional and the re-emergence of communicable diseases like measles, pertussis, and polio.[7] These data suggest that a stronger PHC system would be effective in reducing mortality and morbidity across the region as many of the leading causes, whether infectious diseases or NCDs, can be prevented or treated through a strong high quality and a people-centred health-care delivery system centred at the PHC level.

However, considerable work still needs to be done to develop feasible and effective approaches to measure and strengthen PHC that reflect both global concepts of quality, as well as national and sub-national contextual realities. The Primary Health Care Performance Initiative (PHCPI), jointly launched by the Bill & Melinda Gates Foundation (BMGF), World Bank Group, and WHO, as well as work of the Organization for Economic Cooperation and Development (OECD) and others, is contributing considerable knowledge on frameworks which can be used to guide measurement.[8–11] The World Organization of Family Doctors (WONCA) has recently called for action on developing global primary care indicators to achieve the aims associated with the post-2015 development agenda and, in particular, the SDGs. A focus on core shared indicators reflects the potential benefits of comparable measures which help countries benchmark their performance and identify countries in their region that can offer lessons which can help accelerate change at sub-national, national, and regional levels.

For example, the OECD has worked across over 25 countries to design and implement a cross-national performance measurement initiative, across multiple levels of the health-care system that has allowed countries to assess their own performance and learn from each other.[12] One of the measurements has shown that the range of hospitalizations for asthma and chronic obstructive pulmonary disease (COPD) differs by a factor of 10, offering the chance for countries to determine areas where their improvement efforts should be focused.[13] PHCPI was done through a process of background research and expert input to develop a core set of indicators building on existing data sources which will allow low- and middle-income countries (LMICs) to assess the current status of their PHC systems and benchmark within a region, economic group or globally.[10] These initiatives need to be balanced by the challenges of applicability of measures which reflect local context and are able to be measured at the needed sub-national levels to identify gaps and drive change.

There is growing evidence of the strengths and challenges of PHC and related health outcomes in the countries of the Eastern Mediterranean Region (EMR), which is also impacted by epidemiological shifts as well as political and other challenges. A review of quality of care in the region has found major gaps in processes of technical care delivery, along with variable results in patient satisfaction related to factors such as time spent with the patient and the communication skills of health-care providers.[14] Gaps in the continuity of care have also been noted, including low rates of referrals, with many of these gaps representing poor care quality.

To strengthen the measurement of PHC to drive change, the WHO Regional Office for the Eastern Mediterranean Region (EMRO) embarked on a process to identify and test a core set of indicators which could be implemented as part of an initiative across the region to improve the quality of health-care delivery through better measurement to drive improvement. This chapter provides an overview of the process undertaken, which was designed to ensure regional engagement and ownership while leveraging expertise from within and beyond the region. The process included a strategic series of activities including literature review, expert input, pilot testing, regional conferences for sharing information, and iteration of the set of core measures.

METHODS

The development and testing of the core set of measures involved the series of steps described below:

Framework:

To organize the work and measurement, a conceptual framework was developed which focused on the continuum of health care from promotion and prevention to the diagnostic and therapeutic services of PHC, and on Donabedian's classic framework on structure, process, and outcomes.[15] This framework, which encompasses population and individual health, was then overlaid with core dimensions of quality including the six domains of health quality identified by the Institute of Medicine – namely, access, equity, safety, efficiency, effectiveness, and patient-centredness.[16]

Quality of Care Indicator Selection:

The goal of the overall indicator selection was to provide health-care facilities and health systems in the region with a means to measure and compare the quality of care at the primary care level and provide a benchmark for improvement. The choice of indicators was informed by the five regional strategic health-care priorities including health system strengthening, maternal and child health, NCDs, emergency and preparedness, and global health security.[17] The process also incorporated lessons from the OECD Health Care Quality Indicator Project.[18] The process also considered three critical characteristics of any indicator: importance (including relevance), its scientific validity, and feasibility for measurement in the region. This selection process included a number of steps that are described below.

Initial Indicator Selection

The methodology underlying the initial development of indicators and the consultation exercise conducted by the WHO EMRO consisted of two elements:

1. A rapid scoping review of the existing literature

   The objective of the review was to identify relevant available information on the current thinking on the measurement of quality of care at the primary care level to facilitate developing a robust set of indicator options for the standardized measurement of quality of care at the primary care level in the countries of the EMR. The literature search was conducted using PubMed and Google Scholar to identify articles and existing reviews. The search terms were "quality of care", "indicators", and "measures". Eligible articles from 2000 onwards were screened and selected if they described an existing set of PHC measures of quality used at a national or regional level. A total of 17 papers were included in the review.

2. Development of a candidate indicator matrix

   The review of the literature was supplemented by input from experts in the area of quality of care and primary care across the EMR. This work resulted in the identification of a broad list of 83 indicators. These ranged from process (such as blood pressure measurement, screening), structure (e.g. stock outs, emergency rooms equipped) to outcomes (such as NCD control and prevalence) and across delivery areas including Maternal and Child Health (such as immunization, antenatal care coverage) to NCDs (such as blood pressure measurement and control, smoking cessation) and covered the six domains of quality and included safety infection control practices, medication management, patient-centredness (participation in care decisions), and others.

eDelphi Process

An eDelphi process modified from similar efforts to choose appropriate PHC indicator was done involving 27 experts external to and from the region to review the candidate indicators.[19] The eDelphi survey included background on the goals of the initiative, definitions of the proposed indicators and experts were then asked to score the indicators on a five-point Likert scale ("strongly rejected" to "strongly supported") by scientific strength, relevance and importance for the region, and feasibility. Scientific strength was defined as face and content validity, importance, and relevance as the potential for the gap in the areas measured to be identified and the potential for improvement and impact on health and health expenditures. Feasibility (scored from "highly unlikely" to "highly likely") related to the availability of existing data and costs for new collection. Indicators were included based on importance and relevance as well as scientific strength if they were rated at four or five by 70% or more of the experts, and feasibility at four or five by 50% or more. Based on the results, 34 indicators were identified for further testing.

Small-Scale Pilot Testing

Small-scale testing was then conducted to field test the eDelphi identified indicators. Specific goals were to determine validity and reliability issues in relation to data collection, the utility of the indicators for improvement in quality and care, reliability and quality of available data, and what adaptations and additional measures are needed. Two small field tests of the indicators were completed in three PHC facilities in Egypt and two United Nations Relief and Works Agency for Palestine Refugees (UNRWA) PHC centres in Jordan. The work led to refining the set of priority indicators as well as suggested modifications on operational definitions.

Follow-on Expert Opinion

The draft list of indicators and experience with small-scale testing were shared with the focal points of the different program areas in the WHO EMRO and experts in Cairo in May 2015 seeking their feedback including if indicators reflected the key priorities and eliciting additional suggestions for change. In addition, a meeting was held in Tunis in June 2015 with national focal points from 19 countries in the region and additional experts from the quality of care and PHC communities to review the refined list. Based on this feedback, a final list of 34 indicators, covering six domains of quality (access, equity, safety, efficiency, effectiveness, and patient-centredness) with each domain split into three sub-categories (structure, process, and outcomes), was developed for broader testing (Table 10.1). While indicator definitions were developed, details on the proposed data sources were not specified to reflect the variability of health information systems in each country.

Toolkit Development and Pilot Testing in Four Countries

Following the initial consultation meeting, a toolkit was developed to further test the feasibility of indicator measurement, data availability, and challenges and gaps. The toolkit was designed to help with the planning, implementation, and analysis of the measurement work and included definitions of the 34 indicators (metadata dictionary) as well as a template for data collection. The toolkit also was designed to inform optimization of a final PHC assessment tool for broader use, while the results of the data collection would provide initial insights into PHC gaps in the region. The measurement of the identified indicator set using the toolkit was implemented through a five-step process in 10 facilities in each of four countries (Iran, Jordan Oman, Tunisia) and through facilities run by UNRWA. The work was led by identified focal points in each country who were briefed by EMRO to ensure a common understanding of the indicators and data collection methods detailed

TABLE 10.1 Shortlisted quality indicators by domains

Domains	Indicators
Access and Equity	1. % of catchment population eligible to register with the facility
	2. % of patients reporting to PHC per month who are being managed for common mental disorders disaggregated by diagnosis
	3. % of pregnant women with first visit at the first trimester
Safety	4. % of Individual patient file with unique identifier within the health-care facility
	5. % of health facility staff immunized for hepatitis B (3 doses)
	6. % of safe injections in the health-care facility
	7. % of staff who have attended continuous training about quality and patient safety during the last year
	8. % compliance with hand hygiene guidelines
	9. Number of adverse events reported (immunization/medication)
Efficiency	10. % of prescriptions that include antibiotics in out-patient clinics
	11. Number of days of stock outs per year for identified 15 essential medicines in the available essential drug list (EDL) in the facility
	12. % of the 11 essential non-communicable disease (NCD) medicines with no stock out in last 3 months
Effectiveness	13. % of registered NCD patients with 10 years cardiovascular risk recorded in past 1 year
	14. % of registered hypertension patients with BP <140/90 at the last follow-up visit
	15. % of registered NCD patients with blood pressure recorded twice at last follow-up visit
	16. % of children assessed for anaemia
	17. % of women received family planning counselling
	18. % of women who delivered and received at least three postnatal care visits within the first 6 weeks
	19. % of substance users including tobacco users in receipt of brief intervention
	20. % of under 23 months children fully immunized according to the national protocol
	21. % of high-risk group immunized against influenza
	22. % of pregnant women appropriately vaccinated against tetanus
	23. % of diabetic patients with HbA1C less than 7%, or % of registered diabetic patients with fasting blood sugar controlled at last 2 follow-up visits*
	24. % of diabetes mellitus patients who had fundus eye examination during the last 12 months
	25. % of pregnant women received at least 4 antenatal care visits
	26. % of pregnant women who received health education (nutritional care, anaemia, sanitation, and high-risk pregnancy signs)
	27. % of children under 5 that had weight for age measured in the past 1 year
	28. % of infants who are exclusively breastfed for the first six months
	29. % of children with pneumonia who are prescribed antibiotic treatment correctly
People-Centredness	30. % of patients informed about patients' rights and responsibilities
	31. Staff satisfaction rate (%)
	32. User satisfaction rate (%)
	33. % of appropriate (upward) referrals during the last 6 months (by specific conditions)
	34. Average waiting time at out-patient clinics (days)

in the toolkit. The goal was to use the results of both implementation of measurement (such as feasibility, adaptations to the toolkit, measurement process, and indicators) and the preliminary results in a regional consultation to be able to identify a final set of PHC indicators for broader implementation and inform future development of the PHC assessment toolkit to support the work.

RESULTS FROM THE TESTING IN FOUR COUNTRIES AND UNRWA

The testing was successfully completed by the four countries and UNRWA using key steps including stakeholder engagement, the assembling of a team, training, and mapping of data sources (Table 10.2). Of note, each country adopted the implementation of the measurement to reflect local capacity and data sources. This represented a challenge to comparability, balancing the goal of regional comparison by using the same indicators with feasibility reflecting the capacity and data systems in each country.

Wide variability was seen between and within countries on both data availability and the results (Table 10.3). For example, staff satisfaction was only assessed in 21 out of the total 40 facilities and the average percentage of catchment population registered with the health-care facility ranged between 16% and 100%. In terms of patient-centredness, only two countries had enough data, with rates of 44% and 64%, while 53% and 77% in those same countries were aware of patients' rights and responsibilities. Three countries were able to report average waiting time at out-patient clinics, with Iran and Oman reporting times of about 20 minutes, and Tunisia finding an average of 75 minutes. Other areas of marked variability included a measure of timely access to antenatal care, with an overall average of 70% of pregnant women with the first visit at the first trimester, but a range from 10% to 100%. While some of this variability may reflect health-care delivery, the use of different data collection methods and unknown data quality could also have contributed to within and across country variability.

Effectiveness was measured by 16 indicators including NCD management and maternal and child health. While immunization rates for children under 23 months were generally high (82% to 100%), influenza vaccination was much lower. Many of the indicators in this domain focused on NCD care. Percentage of registered hypertension patients with BP <140/90 at last 2 follow-up visits was 32% to 73%, and percentage of registered diabetic patients with HbA1C under 7% ranged from 16% to 56%. The percentage of diabetes mellitus patients who had fundus eye examination during the last 12 months or the percentage of registered NCD patients with blood pressure recorded twice at last follow-up visit were on average 45% and 40%. No facility appeared to have adequate data on the percentage of smokers attending smoking cessation counselling (Figure 10.1).

The intra-country variability in the selected primary health-care centres in Oman and Tunisia is summarized in Table 10.4.

We noted that variability was also seen within a single country even given the relatively small number of sites studied (Table 10.5). For example, timely initiation of antenatal care ranged from 31% to 90% in Oman and 11% to 98% in Tunisia. Similarly, broad ranges were seen with control of diabetes in Oman (7% to 90%), immunization of children in Tunisia (42% to 99%) and average wait times which had a four- to six-fold difference across the facilities surveyed. This variability highlighted the need for local as well as national level measurements to understand overall performance as well as areas where disparities in quality occur. Further analysis is needed to understand if the variability was from sites which were overall high or low performers or whether variability in performance varied within a site depending on the areas measured.

There were several cross-cutting challenges and recommendations from the countries related to measurement. These included the absence of tools that could reliably measure some core areas in the local contexts, data availability from routinely collected sources, and gaps in

TABLE 10.2 Implementation of pilot testing of the assessment tool and indicators

	Tunisia	Iran	Oman	Jordan and Jordan UNRWA
Stakeholder involvement	Basic health-care directorate of the Ministry of Health (MoH), regional officials	Director and team from Tabriz district network, directors from provincial health centre, information technology leads	Focal point from governorate, DG PHC services, and supervisors for selected PHC	Engagement with the basic health-care directorate of the MoH, regional officials and basic health services in choosing the sites, pilot testing, and review of the resulting data
Sites	10 PHC sites across 5 governorates	Tabriz district: 4 public urban HCs, 4 private urban HCs, and 2 rural HCs	10 PHC sites across 7 directorates. Urban/rural mix	5 MoH clinics 5 UNRWA clinics
Pre-data collection	Reviewed existing data and developed additional data collection tools. Training of data collectors	Development and testing additional 4 data collection tools (such as safe injection checklist); training of data collectors	Development and testing additional data collection tools, training for collection	Additional tools for hand hygiene and patient exit surveys developed to complement EMRO tools and unstructured interviews
Team	2 physicians, 2 technicians, driver and secretary	10 data collectors with experience in PHC (physicians, nurses, pharmacists, managers)	Focal point from governorates	Consultant and one Ministry of Health (MoH) representative
Existing Routine Health Management Information System (RHMIS)	Routine data collection for routine curative and preventive activities	Existing household file and Heath Information System	Electronic Medical Record (EMR) at each site	National system for performance indicators (MoH). UNRWA e-Health programme including performance indicators
Time at sites	½ day	3 days	4–8 weeks/centre	2 or more dates

some service availability (overall or at the PHC level); these made it difficult to measure quality. The challenges of data availability and measurement tools were seen in the frequency of results. While every indicator had results from at least one country, a number had some data from only two, while others had only one country with at least 50% of sites able to provide data. While some data availability gaps were related to the capture of existing data in reliable sources, the countries also identified a need to develop, or adapt for local use, measurement tools to capture a number of indicators including staff satisfaction, standards for safe injection and hand hygiene, waiting times, tracking upwards referrals, awareness about patient rights, and patient satisfaction. Some countries had already started to develop some of these tools which will be important to include in a toolkit. For example, the team in Iran had developed a five-item checklist for injection safety and had used the short-form of the Minnesota Satisfaction Questionnaire (20 + 8 questions) for staff satisfaction and the short-form of the Patient Satisfaction Questionnaire (PSQ-18) for patient satisfaction. They also used a 12-item questionnaire for the patient rights assessment.

In addition to the need to develop new tools or adapt tools from existing validated ones to measure a number of areas, a range of other challenges in performance measurement were

TABLE 10.3 Tested indicators and results from the four-country pilot testings (ten clinics were chosen in each country)

Level	Indicators	Tunisia (%)	Iran (%)	Oman (%)	Jordan PHC sites (%)	Jordan UNRWA %
Access and equity	Structure	% of catchment population registered with the facility	<25	>75	>75	25–50	–
	Process	Proportion of patients reporting to PHC per month who are being managed for mental health conditions	<25	–	–	–	–
	Outcome	Staff satisfaction rate	51–75	–	51–75	–	–
		% of pregnant women with first visit at the first trimester	51–75	51–75	51–75	51–75	>75
Safety	Structure	% of individual patient file with unique identifier within the health-care facility	>75	>75	>75	>75	>75
	Process	% of health facility staff immunized for hepatitis B (3 doses)	25–50	>75	>75	>75	–
		% of safe injections in the health-care facility	<25	>75	>75	>75	>75
		% of staff who have attended continuous training about quality and patient safety during the last year	<25	25–50	<25	–	–
		% injections given with a new sterile standard safety syringe	>75	>75	>75	>75	>75
		% injections in which the used device was disposed of immediately	>75	>75	>75	>75	>75
		% compliance with Hand Hygiene guidelines	<25	>75	51–75	–	–
	Outcome	Number of adverse events reported (immunization/medication)	<25*	<25*	–	–	–
Efficiency	Process	% of prescriptions that include antibiotics in out-patient clinics	51–75	<25	25–50	51–75	<25
	Outcome	Number of days of stock-outs per year for identified 15 essential medicines in the facility	<25	0	0	–	–
		% of the 8 essential CVD and DM medicines with no stock out in last 3 months	>75	>75	>75	–	–
	Process	% registered hypertension patients with Initial laboratory investigations	79	>75	51–75	–	>75
		% of registered hypertension patients with blood pressure (BP) <140/90 at last 2 follow-up visits	25–50	51–75	25–50	–	51–75

(Continued)

TABLE 10.3 (CONTINUED) Tested indicators and results from the four-country pilot testing (ten clinics were chosen in each country)

Level	Indicators	Tunisia (%)	Iran (%)	Oman (%)	Jordan PHC sites (%)	Jordan UNRWA %
Effectiveness	% of registered diabetic patients with fasting blood sugar controlled at last 2 follow-up visits	>75	25–50	25–50	–	25–50
	% of registered NCD patients with 10 years cardiovascular risk recorded in past 1 year		51–75	–	–	25–50
	% of registered NCD patients with blood pressure recorded twice at last follow-up visit		>75	–	–	–
	% of children screened for anaemia	<25*	51–75	–	75*	>75
	% of smokers attending cessation counselling	0	–	–	–	–
Outcome	% of children under 23 months immunized according to the national protocol	>75	>75	>75	>75*	>75
	% of high-risk group immunized against influenza	<25	25–50*	–	–	–
	% of pregnant women fully vaccinated against tetanus	>75	51–75	>75	>75*	>75
	% of diabetic patients with HbA1C less than 7%	<25	25–50*	51–75	–	–
	% of diabetes mellitus patients who had fundus eye examination during the last 12 months	<25	>75	–	–	–
	% of pregnant women received at least 4 antenatal care visits	25–50	>75	>75	>75*	>75
	% of pregnant women who received health education (nutritional care, anaemia, sanitation, and high-risk pregnancy signs)	>75	>75	>75	>75*	>75
	% of children under 5 that had weight and height measured in past 1 year	51–75	51–75	>75	>75*	>75
Patients Centredness Outcome	% of patients aware about patients' rights and responsibilities	>75	–	51–75	–	–
Process	Patient satisfaction rate (%)	51–75	–	25–50	–	–
	% of appropriate (upward) referrals during the last 6 months (by specific conditions)	<25	25–50*	<25	–	–
	Average waiting time (min) at out-patient clinics	>75	<25	<25	–	–

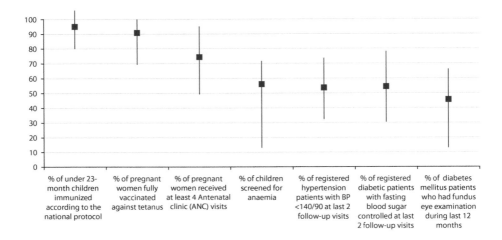

FIGURE 10.1 Range in effectiveness indicator results across the five pilot countries (countries without data excluded).

TABLE 10.4 Intra-country variability in the EMRO Primary Health Care Core Indicator pilot testing in Oman and Tunisia

	Oman	Tunisia
% pregnant women with 1st ANC in 1st trimester	31–90% (4 ANC: 57–100%)	11–98% (4 ANC: 15–84%)
% Hypertension patients with initial labs	23–100%	62–98%
% Hypertension patients with BP<140/90	26–91%	41–71%
% patients with diabetes with controlled fasting blood sugar (FBS)	7–90% (A1C<7%: 3–70%)	66–97%
% children fully immunized	98–100%	41–99 (1 >100%)
% of appropriate (upward) referrals during the last 6 months (by specific conditions)	7–100%	14–49%
Average wait time	10–60 minutes	39–111 minutes

TABLE 10.5 Variability across facility types in Iran

Quality indicators	Urban public health centres (%)	Rural public health centres (%)	Urban private health centres (%)
Staff satisfaction rate	68.0	83.2	71.3
% of pregnant women with first visit at the first trimester	42	71.4	85.8
% of health facility staff immunized for hepatitis B (3 doses)	77.5	63.2	74.3
% of prescriptions that include antibiotics in out-patient clinics	45.9	56.7	39.2
% of pregnant women received at least 4 ANC visits	74.2	95.9	83
% of patients aware about patients' rights and responsibilities	56.5	64.2	43.9
Patient satisfaction rate	38.2	28.17	43.3

identified and These included a number of indicators not recorded (ever or reliably), differences in quality standards across sites within a country, and an absence of specific services or standards (such as safe injection, adverse medication event documentation, anaemia screening, smoking cessation, comprehensive cardiovascular risk assessment, and the list of 17 essential drugs). In addition, there were challenges with feasibility, including the time needed to collect some indicators and to identify unique patients to calculate denominators.

Lessons learned in implementing the measurement work included the need to engage relevant stakeholders, the critical role of support from leadership, the preparation of teams, and allowing additions to the core list to adapt to national priorities. The country teams also made some recommendations for further refinement of the toolkit to include more detailed definitions of some indicators, guidance on sample size or sampling methods, and development of tools to measure some of the challenging areas noted above. Finally, they noted that e-health holds promise in helping with the measurement initiative, but more work is needed in all the countries for this to become a reality.

REGIONAL CONSULTATION

Following completion of the field testing in May 2016, a group of country key stakeholders, and regional and global experts in PHC delivery, quality of care measurement and improvement was convened in Amman, Jordan, to review the results of the four country experience and provide input into further adaptations needed for the indicators, toolkit, and processes.[20] The results from the four countries were reviewed as well as input from other initiatives working to measure and improve PHC. The indicator list was further refined to modify some existing ones (for example, expanding from smoking cessation to broader substance use counselling) and adding selected ones including anaemia for testing for children under five years of age, percentage of infants who are exclusively breastfed for the first six months, percentage of women who received family planning counselling, and proportion of children with pneumonia who are prescribed antibiotic treatment correctly. The final list is included in Table 10.1.

Key conclusions from the meeting included the need to adapt the indicators for adoption into existing country contexts, the recognition of current challenges to the full measurement of the core indicators, and that planned measurement work needed to include capacity building for data collection and use, including supervision.

Despite these challenges, there was general agreement that the core indicators and accompanying tool represented a valuable opportunity for within-country measurement for improvement in PHC, as well as benchmarking across the region, and provided a common framework to identify successful models for spread within and between countries. It was also recognized that given the wide range in current strengths and challenges faced by PHC systems within the region, that some modifications might be needed and that the goal of full measurement across the region would take time, resources and further strengthening of PHC delivery. Other key areas of focus identified including the need for national commitment and leadership to support measurement and improvement of PHC quality, including the adoption of a high-level structure empowered to move the work forward, and better community engagement and empowerment.

Above all, future work needs to build on existing activities and engage the range of stakeholders and partners working in PHC delivery and improvement, with a goal to begin implementation of broader measurement and link this to improvement. Future steps planned included further refinement of the data collection tools, capacity building and initial measurement across a broader number of countries. This will also include initiation of local work to address identified gaps and broader regional sharing of further lessons learned by mid-2018. Recommendations from the countries for WHO included the WHO continuing to serve as a technical advisor and importantly in its convening role and as a facilitator for the exchange of experiences and tools, within and beyond the region, to continue the progress to better measurement and improved delivery of PHC.

ONGOING PROGRESS AFTER THE REGIONAL MEETING

Following the meeting, a number of countries continued their commitment and engagement in the process of PHC quality measurement: Iran has established a national committee which is working on next steps; Oman started with field implementation of the indicators, specifically by addressing the data collection gaps identified through the pilot implementation exercise, and building local capacity on data collection and reporting; Sudan has translated the indicators with adaptation to the local context, trained local focal points from the state levels, identified provinces to establish demonstration projects, and added some additional indicators to reflect country priorities not included in the core set, with this final set being integrated with the National Quality Policy and Strategy to ensure they are included in the national priorities for health.

The Regional Committee of the EMR at its 63rd meeting in 2016 approved a resolution on adopting quality indicators for improving the quality of care at the primary care level, facilitating broader support, and providing endorsement to moving forward on national and regional efforts.[21] The framework has also been shared with other global PHC measurement initiatives including PHCPI and the WHO Health Data Collaborative, and the process has informed discussions on how to balance local ownership with the value of regional benchmarking and peer learning.

DISCUSSION

Measurement of quality is a critical step towards identifying areas for strengthening, as well as needed strategies and interventions. This needs to occur within and across countries for local action and regional benchmarking.[22] This work has resulted in a number of findings and recommendations for work within WHO EMRO and beyond:

1. *Feasibility of creating a regional indicator set*: Despite the vast differences in resources and strengths of primary health care systems across countries of the EMR, we were able to collectively identify a set of core indicators to measure the quality of PHC at a national and regional levels.
2. *Importance of stakeholder engagement*: Active engagement of country-led teams along with the step-wise approach was important to ensure regional engagement and ownership by each country at the same time. As a result, the formative stage has been led by countries which are willing and able to test and share the results of initial measurements to drive further iteration.
3. *Build on existing work and measures but allow local adaptation*: The measures were drawn from existing experience in high-income countries, as well as global measurement sets, such as the 100 core health indicators, PHCPI, and the OECD.[10,23,24] The incorporation of selected measures, as well as the adoption of the strategy of common measures, was designed to facilitate peer-to-peer learning between countries through the use of comparable indicators.
4. *Measure what matters*: This set of measures was developed for several reasons. It has become increasingly evident that simply providing services without ensuring quality will fall short of the goal of reducing morbidity and mortality through strong and effective PHC systems.[25] The measures included effective coverage, rather than simply the

proportion of people served. The set also incorporated the six domains of quality as defined by the Institute of Medicine (Table 10.6) and moved beyond inputs and processes into outcomes.

5. *Ensure people-centredness in indicators:* Even during the pilot phase, the set of measures included three measures of people-centredness; two patient-level measures (awareness of their rights and patient-centredness) and one staff level measure (satisfaction). This work is informed by the growing demand to ensure that PHC is people-centred, meeting the needs of patients and their providers.

There were a number of challenges recognized which some of the countries have already begun to address and recommendations for future work:

1. *Include all sectors in the national quality measurement work:* Many quality measurement initiatives exclude the private sector, but it is a major growing provider of PHC in countries in the region. In spite of this recognition, only one country piloted in that sector and ongoing discussions are needed on how to engage with private providers to include them, either voluntarily or through mandates, to measure quality, share their results, and increase accountability regardless of provider type.

2. *Address measuring quality in the context of conflict:* The region includes countries with significant crises, including population displacement and natural or manmade disasters. The group identified a need for better understanding on how to measure PHC during times of acute or chronic crisis, an emerging area of focus globally.[26] Questions included: What are the optimal measures? How is effective quality PHC defined when population movement threatens continuity? How do countries prioritize what to measure and improve in fragile states?

3. *Be willing to measure aspirational goals and ensure flexibility to cover priorities across a diverse set of health systems:* Despite the work to test in a range of settings and generate broad consensus, it was also clear that some of the non-communicable disease measures would serve more as aspirational rather than measuring the quality of available care, while some of the maternal health and child measures were less relevant to countries where quality and effective coverage in those areas has already been achieved. Developing a set of common measures across the variety of countries requires flexibility, and willingness of some countries to have measures which did not yet reflect services being delivered but recognizing that these indicators could serve to drive increased comprehensiveness of care (a core component of PHC), and ensure that services deliver quality care as they are initiated and then scaled up.

4. *Continue work to adapt or develop better tools:* The need was identified for better and more feasible measures, which could be implemented across settings, including

TABLE 10.6   Distribution of the 34 PHC quality indicators used in the four country pilot testing

	Access and equity	Safety	Efficiency	Effectiveness	People-centredness	Total
Structure	1	1	–	–	–	2
Process	1	6	1	6	2	16
Outcome	1	1	2	9	3	16
Total	**3**	**8**	**3**	**15**	**5**	**34**

measurement of patient-reported experience rather than relying only on satisfaction. The participating countries also recognized that they would need to add more measures to reflect the local context and national and sub-national demands. For example, Iran added additional measures for safety and adapted existing surveys to measure patient and staff satisfaction.

As a result of the expert meeting, a number of concrete recommendations were developed for Member States and the WHO and agreed upon along with a specific time frame. These include:

To the Member States:

1. Establish/use existing steering committees or available high-level structures, chaired by a senior official at the Ministry of Health, and involving membership of all priority program managers, to plan and oversee assessment and improvement of quality of care at primary care level and report progress of this work to the Minister of Health (and other relevant stakeholders) on a regular basis.
2. Build on existing relevant activities and programs, reviewing the ongoing quality of care activities and interventions at the country level, identifying major challenges, opportunities, and priorities for implementing Phase 1 of the WHO framework for assessment and improvement for quality of care at primary care level.
3. Through the steering committee, strengthen coordination, partnership, and alignment with major stakeholders and different care providers at the national and subnational levels including private sector providers, other public health-care providers, NGOs, patients, and communities.
4. Adapt the WHO framework of action, adding indicators if necessary, but ensuring collection of the agreed 34 core indicators to ensure assessment and improvement of the quality of care at primary care level based on health system infrastructure, national and local capacities, community needs and priorities, cost-effectiveness, and burden of diseases.
5. Preparations in advance of broader measurement should include finalizing data collection tools and procedures, as well as building the capacity of teams at different levels to oversee and manage the assessment, integration, and improvement of the quality of care at the PHC facility level. This preparation should also include updating guidelines, standards, and protocols for service delivery at the primary care level as needed.
6. Start with a first phase of implementation to identify areas where adaption is needed.
7. Following finalization of indicators and collection tools and procedures, collect and analyze data to identify gaps in the delivery of quality PHC services and to inform local interventions to improve quality of care at structure, process, and outcomes levels related to the main domains of quality: Access and Equity, Safety, Efficiency, Effectiveness, People-Centredness, and Timeline.
8. Plan for continuous monitoring and supportive supervision, and correct actions based on findings, documentation and evidence building.
9. Disseminate the findings from the initial and broader measurement, as well as improvements and lessons learned, to stakeholders including national and subnational policy makers and stakeholders to inform plans for scaling up of quality PHC.
10. Facilitate peer-to-peer learning between facilities.

For WHO:

1. Support further development of an expanded list of indicators for countries looking for broader measurement.
2. Take an active convening role in briefing policy makers and coordination with partners at the regional and national levels based on the needs and priorities of countries.
3. Participate and contribute in national and sub-national capacity building activities using the expertise in the region.
4. Facilitate the exchange of experiences between countries and establish a share point/website/platform for uploading tools, standards, and guidelines that can assist Member States moving ahead with their national plans to strengthen PHC.
5. Facilitate intercountry/cross-country collaborations within and outside the region on ways to improve quality of care at the PHC level.
6. Monitor implementation, collect progress reports, and develop a technical paper to be presented in the 65th session of the Regional Committee in October 2018.

CONCLUSION

In conclusion, a step-wise approach incorporating a strong strategy of country engagement, formative testing, and willingness to adapt based on field experience was shown to be successful in developing an initial core set of quality of PHC measures that can be implemented across the Eastern Mediterranean Region. The willingness of countries to share experiences and results and to openly discuss challenges was also critical to the level of ownership and national level commitment to implement the measures as a next step in strengthening PHC delivery in the individual countries and across the region. Ongoing evaluation of the implementation challenges and successes, as well as their effectiveness in driving improvement, is a critical next step.

ACKNOWLEDGEMENTS

We are grateful for the valuable input provided by the regional and international experts, especially: Dr Nabil Fouad Abu-Ghazalah, Dr Ishtaiwi Abu Zaied, Dr Riham Al Asady, Dr Ahmed Al Mandhari, Dr Buthaina A AlMudhaf, Prof Mahi Altehewy, Dr Salem Alwahabi, Dr Seita Ashiro, Dr Najoua Belkaab, Dr Shannon Barkley, Prof Abdelmejid Ben Hmida, Mrs Kathrin Cresswell, Dr Rafla Dallagi, Dr Ahmed Elmuez Altayeb, Dr Sihem Essaafi, Mrs Salma Jaouni, Dr Naser Kalantari, Dr Ali Khader, Prof Tawfik Khoja, Dr Rajaa Khater, Mrs Kid Kohl, Dr Iciar Larizgoitia, Dr Rashad Messaoud, Dr Fouad Nasereddine, Dr Safa Qsoos, Prof Fauziah Rabbani, Dr Charles Shaw, Dr Jaafar Tabrizi, Dr Ayda Taha, and Dr Mohammed Ibrahim Tarawneh.

REFERENCES

1. WHO. Why quality UHC?. WHO. Available from: http://www.who.int/servicedeliverysafety/areas/qhc/quality-uhc/en/ [Accessed 6 February 2017].
2. Bitton A, Ratcliffe HL, Veillard JH, Kress DH, Barkley S, Kimball M, et al. Primary health care as a foundation for strengthening health systems in low- and middle-income countries. *Journal of General Internal Medicine.* 2017;32(5):566–571. Available from: https://link.springer.com/article/10.1007%2Fs11606-016-3898-5.
3. WHO. WHO Framework on Integrated People-Centred Health Services. Available from: http://www.who.int/servicedeliverysafety/areas/people-centred-care/en/[Accessed 14 March 2018].
4. Kruk, ME, Larson, E, Twum-Danso NAY. Time for a quality revolution in global health. *Lancet Global Health. 2016*; 4(9):e594–596. Available from: https://www.thelancet.com/journals/langlo/article/PIIS2214-109X(16)30131-0/fulltext.

5. WHO EMRO. Expert Consultation on Improving the Quality of Care at Primary Health Care Level through the Implementation of Quality Indicators and Standards. Available from: http://applications.emro.who.int/docs/IC_Meet_Rep_2016_EN_18951.pdf?ua=1EASP [Accessed 19 May 2017].

6. Mokdad AH, Forouzanfar MH, Daoud F, El Bcheraoui C, Moradi-Lakeh M, Khalil I, et al. Health in times of uncertainty in the eastern Mediterranean region, 1990–2013: A systematic analysis for the Global Burden of Disease Study 2013. *Lancet Global Health*. 2016;4(10):e704–e713. Available from: https://www.thelancet.com/journals/langlo/article/PIIS2214-109X(16)30168-1/fulltext.

7. WHO. The cost of war. Available from: http://www.who.int/mediacentre/commentaries/war-cost/en/ [Accessed 13 February 2017].

8. WHO Collaborating Centre for Integrated Health Services based on Primary Care. Available from: http://www.integratedcare4people.org/ [Accessed 4 April 2017].

9. Health Data Collaborative. 100 Core health indicators. Available from: https://www.healthdatacollaborative.org/resources/100-core-health-indicators/ [Accessed 17 Mar 2017].

10. PHCPI. *PHCPI*. Available from: http://phcperformanceinitiative.org/[Accessed 17 June 2017].

11. OECD. Health Care Quality Indicators - Primary Care. Available from: http://www.oecd.org/els/health-systems/hcqi-primary-care.htm [Accessed 1 August 2017].

12. Forde I, Morgan D, Klazinga NS. Resolving the challenges in the international comparison of health systems: the must do's and the trade-offs. *Health Policy*. 2013;112(1–2):4–8.

13. Kidd MR, Anderson MIP, Obazee EM, Prasad PN, Pettigrew LM, World Organization of Family Doctors' executive committee. The need for global primary care development indicators. *Lancet*. 2015;386(9995):737. Available from: https://www.thelancet.com/journals/lancet/article/PIIS0140-6736(15)61532-X/fulltext.

14. Saleh S, Alameddine M, Mourad Y, Natafgi N. Quality of care in primary health care settings in the Eastern Mediterranean region: A systematic review of the literature. *International Journal of Quality Health Care*. 2015;27(2):79–88. Available from: https://academic.oup.com/intqhc/article/27/2/79/1787554.

15. Donabedian A. The quality of care. How can it be assessed? *JAMA*. 1988;260(12):1743–1748.

16. Institute of Medicine (US) Committee on Quality of Health Care in America. *Crossing the Quality Chasm: A New Health System for the 21st Century*. Washington (DC): National Academies Press (US); 2001. Available from: http://www.ncbi.nlm.nih.gov/books/NBK222274/ [Accessed 20 March 2017].

17. WHO EMRO. Introduction and highlights of the report, 2015, Annual report. Available from: http://www.emro.who.int/annual-report/2015/introduction.html [Accessed 11 February 2017].

18. Arah OA, Westert GP, Hurst J, Klazinga NS. A conceptual framework for the OECD Health Care Quality Indicators Project. *International Journal of Quality Health Care*. 2006;18 Suppl 1:5–13.

19. Refinement of indicators and criteria in a quality tool for assessing quality in primary care in Canada: a Delphi Panel study. Available from: https://pdfs.semanticscholar.org/3b92/ab32d4c42ea92e8613f46702707ae2336fd8.pdf [Accessed 2 March 2017].

20. WHO EMRO. Regional meeting on tools and standards to assess and improve quality of care at the primary care level. Available from: http://applications.emro.who.int/docs/IC_Meet_Rep_2016_EN_18951.pdf?ua=1 [Accessed 9 February 2017].

21. WHO EMRO. Scaling up family practice: progressing towards universal health coverage. RC63_Resolutions_2016_R2_19197_EN.pdf]. Available from: http://applications.emro.who.int/docs/RC63_Resolutions_2016_R2_19197_EN.pdf.

22. WHO. Quality of care: measuring a neglected driver of improved health. Available from: http://www.who.int/bulletin/volumes/95/6/16-180190/en/ [Accessed 9 February 2017].

23. WHO. Global Reference list of 100 core health indicators. Available from: http://apps.who.int/iris/bitstream/10665/173589/1/WHO_HIS_HSI_2015.3_eng.pdf?ua=1 [Accessed 17 February 2017].

24. Carinci F, Van Gool K, Mainz J, Veillard J, Pichora EC, Januel JM, et al. Towards actionable international comparisons of health system performance: Expert revision of the OECD framework and quality indicators. *International Journal of Quality Health Care*. 2015;27(2):137–146. Available from: https://academic.oup.com/intqhc/article/27/2/137/1787909.

25. Powell-Jackson T, Mazumdar S, Mills A. Financial incentives in health: New evidence from India's Janani Suraksha Yojana. *Journal of Health Economics*. 2015;43:154–169. Available from: http://dx.doi.org/10.2139/ssrn.1935442.

26. Kersten R, Bosse G, Dörner F, Slavuckij A, Fernandez G, Marx M. Too complicated for the field? Measuring quality of care in humanitarian aid settings. *Glob Health Action*. 2013;6. Available from: http://www.ncbi.nlm.nih.gov/pmc/articles/PMC3657069/ [Accessed 9 February 2017].

CHAPTER 11

The challenge of providing primary health care services in crisis countries in the Eastern Mediterranean Region

Xavier Mòdol

INTRODUCTION

The Eastern Mediterranean Region (EMR) is now characterized by conflict and political unrest. Out of the 10 countries* listed as the highest risk for crises in 2017, six belong to the EMR.[1] Out of the 22 countries composing the region, over one-third have been in permanent conflict for the last five years or more, and a few more witness intermittent turmoil in at least part of their territory.[2]

The EMR also is the sole region with a United Nations Agency devoted to supporting refugees on a permanent basis: the United Nations Relief and Works Agency for Palestinian Refugees in the Near East (UNRWA) has been providing essential services to Palestinian refugees for over 60 years, often in a context of conflict.

Therefore, there is no shortage of examples of health systems that are expected to deliver Primary Health Care (PHC) services in the context of vast health network destruction, fleeing staff, disrupted supply chains, underperforming information systems, and massive population displacement.

This chapter describes and analyzes the approach to providing PHC services in some crises countries of the region. The chapter begins with a summary of the effects of conflict and crisis on the health of the population and the health system's capacity to deliver essential services. The following sections describe how PHC services are organized, how benefits and entitlement are decided, financing models to fund PHC, as well as the human resources involved in providing those services, with particular attention to Physicians and Community Health Workers.

---

* Afghanistan, Central African Republic, Democratic Republic of Congo, Iraq, Libya, Nigeria, Somalia, South Sudan, Syria, and Yemen.

The final section draws some conclusions from practical cases. It also qualifies the different approaches according to their effect on granting Universal Health Coverage to the countries' populations.

Sources of information include mainstream journals, unpublished reports, and the author's own experience.

EFFECTS OF CONFLICT AND CRISES ON HEALTH AND HEALTH CARE

The health impact most closely associated with conflict situations traditionally include increased morbidity and mortality as a consequence of violence.[3] However, wars and conflict have increasingly become protracted, targeting civilians as well as socio-economic infrastructure, and creating mass population displacement that often settles in urban settings, among the regular dwellers rather than in refugee/IDP (internally displaced people) camps.[4] Although the functions assigned to each agency may be contested, Blanchet et al.'s framework illustrates the complexity of the resulting contexts (Table 11.1).[5] Users' mobility may be affected further through the imposition of curfews and other displacement barriers. Refugees living in well-organized camps show malnutrition rates comparable to those of the host population and mortality rates below those of IDPs and host populations.[6,7]

Long periods of low-intensity conflict tend to produce fewer violent deaths but more long-term health effects.[8] Evidence has been found of increased prevalence of mental health conditions – particularly post-traumatic stress disorder – in children and adolescents, which may exceed one-third of people in these age groups.[9,10] Other conditions, such as tuberculosis, respiratory infections, or non-communicable diseases are also reported in greater numbers.[11,12,13] A worrisome finding is the re-emergence of communicable diseases, of which the region had been free for more than a decade, such as poliomyelitis (Syria, Iraq) and diphtheria (Yemen), this reflects the collapse of routine immunization systems.[14] System collapse also is at the roots of the occurrence in Yemen of a cholera epidemic of unprecedented dimensions.

A more systematic review of the conditions that contribute to Disability-Adjusted Life Years (DALYs), one of the tools to assess burden of disease shows that even in countries such as Afghanistan, Iraq, Syria, and Yemen, where war and violence are the leading causes of DALYs, respiratory infections, neonatal issues and non-communicable diseases (NCDs) are listed among the main health challenges (Table 11.2).[15] The crises in Egypt, Yemen, Libya, and Syria

TABLE 11.1 The fragmented structure of the Lebanon Health System by population group in 2016

| Functions of health system | Population groups | | | | | |
| | Non-poor | | Vulnerable | | | |
	Socially insured	Privately insured	Vulnerable lebanese	Palestinian in lebanon	Palestinian refugees from Syria	Syrian refugees
Stewardship	MoH	Private sector	MoH	UNRWA	UNRWA	UNHCR
Financing	National Social Security Fund (NSSF)	Insurance premiums	Taxes	International	International	International
Delivery	Public sector	Private sector	Public Services	Humanitarian sector	Public services, NGO and private sector	Public services, NGO and private sector

Source: Blanchet et al., 2016 (adapted from Londono and Frenk).

TABLE 11.2 Leading ten causes of DALYs in selected EMR countries

Country	1	2	3	4	5	6	7	8	9	10
Afghanistan	War	LR	IHD	Congenital	Stroke	NN Preterm	Road Injuries	Other unint.	Diarrhea	Violence
Iraq	War	IHD	Congenital	NN Preterm	Diabetes	Stroke	NN Sepsis	Road Injuries	Neck & Back	LRI
Libya	War	IHD	Neck & Back	Congenital	Road Injuries	Stroke	Diabetes	NN Preterm	Depression	Other unint
Palestine	IHD	NN Preterm	Congenital	Neck & Back	Depression	Road Injuries	Stroke	LRI	Skin	CKD
Somalia	Diarrhea	LRI	Malnutrition	Tuberculosis	NN Preterm	Anemia	Malaria	Congenital	Meningitis	War
Sudan	NN Preterm	Congenita	IHD	LRI	Road Injuries	Diarrhea	Stroke	Neck & Back	Anemia	Diabetes
Syria	War	IHD	Stroke	Neck & Back	Congenital	Depression	LRI	Sense	Road Injuries	Skin
Yemen	War	NN Preterm	IHD	Congenital	Road Injuries	LRI	Stroke	Diarrhea	Neck & Back	Diabetes
MENA	*IHD*	*War*	*Congenital*	*NN Preterm*	*Road Injuries*	*Neck & Back*	*Stroke*	*LRI*	*Diabetes*	*Depression*

LRI, Lower Respiratory Infection; IHD, Ischemic Heart Disease; Other unint, other unintentional injuries; CKD, Chronic Kidney Disease; Sense, Sense organ diseases; NN, neonatal; MENA, Middle East and North Africa.
Source: Global Burden of Disease 2015.

are believed to have resulted in a reduction in life expectancy, in a new pattern that may continue for years.[16]

At least as determinant as the conditions themselves may be how conflict affects access to health services and their capacity to deliver the necessary care. Conflict may reduce the system's capacity through different mechanisms, including the actual destruction of the health facility, the disruption of supply chains, or the displacement of skilled health workers.[4,8,13]

The Health Resources Availability Mapping System (HeRAMS) is an emergency-oriented health facility assessment tool which helps establish the delivery capacity of the health system. In recent HeRAMS surveys conducted in North Syria and Yemen, the number of at least partially damaged facilities exceeded 22% in Syria and 8% in Yemen.[17,18] In the later, however, less than half of the health facilities (47%) were fully functional, reflecting the impact of conflict on the ability of the health network to function.

Health facilities and personnel are becoming targets in increasingly sickening conflicts.[19] Reports show an escalation of attacks in recent years; 63 in Afghanistan in 2015, 61 in Iraq and a record high of 122 in Syria the same year.[20,21] In Libya, more than 80% of nursing staff, many of whom were expatriates, were evacuated in 2014. By December 2015, 40% of the health facilities in that country were closed. Attacks are not always the result of open conflict between two warring parties; the Palestine Red Crescent Society reported more than 300 attacks on its infrastructure, ambulances, and personnel between October 2015 and January 2016.[20]

Security is not the only concern for the capacity to deliver health services. Financial uncertainty and insufficiency may have the same effect of preventing access to necessary health care. Global reduction of oil prices forced the Iraq government to limit health allocations to the bare necessities to absorb salaries. UNRWA has experienced recurrent financial crises which may end up soon in a humanitarian crisis of "epic" dimensions.[22,23] Also, the care provided to affected populations may be not adapted to their actual needs and expectations, as reported by international non-governmental organizations (NGOs) working in conflict countries as well as by country health systems supporting refugees[24,25] Often, the care provided is composed of traditional humanitarian interventions focusing on communicable diseases, while what is required is the management of NCDs and other routine health services, as well as higher-level interventions, such as cancer treatment or haemodialysis, which were readily available in pre-conflict days in medium-level income countries such as Iraq or Syria.

ORGANIZING PHC SERVICE DELIVERY: WHAT IS BEST AND WHAT IS POSSIBLE

The classic District Health System – composed by an ensemble of PHC facilities, a referral facility, and a health management team – is still the preferred model in many EMR countries. However, the combination of new health needs (e.g. the NCD epidemic), people's expectations about their health and their entitlement to health care, and increased capacity of the involved human resources, all requires reform towards a system that offers a long-term relationship between patients and their preferred provider, and where PHC teams play an active role in coordinating care delivered by other providers to their registered population.[26]

Thus, 30 years after Alma Ata, PHC aimed at "putting people at the centre of health care", by responding to health needs and social expectations, which is still the objective today.[26] How do health systems struggling with conflict-enhanced needs and weakened capacities address this challenge?

Crises tend to be protracted events, alternating, often erratically, phases of open conflict with periods of relative calm, before something similar to stabilization is achieved. Each of these arbitrarily defined periods may require a specific approach to PHC service provision. The situation is compounded by the fact that different areas of the country may be administered by different warring parties with different priorities. A split that may be temporary (as in Syria, Libya, or Yemen, where open conflict is still ongoing) or definitive, as in the Kurdistan Autonomous Region in Iraq, or the split of Somalia into three de facto countries.

The open conflict phase is often characterized by the presence on the ground of different actors with different agendas and priorities, who do not always recognize the coordinating role of the local health authorities. NGOs, local and international, are present as service providers or intermediaries between donors and public or private providers in most crisis scenarios. NGOs remain the main PHC service providers in Afghanistan and are essential players in Yemen and some areas of Syria. In the latter, so-called "field hospitals" – which are in fact makeshift clinics where limited PHC services are provided -have been operating in certain areas.[27]

Another feature of the open-conflict phase is that support is usually provided to individual facilities, rather than to local health systems. With no resources to distribute and little reliable information to share, local health systems and their management teams are often by-passed or plainly ignored.[13] Coordination moves to internationally sponsored and managed bodies, such as the Health Cluster.*

The open-conflict phase is also when most refugees and internally displaced people are generated. As a result, a large part of the PHC provision is actually delivered outside the country, by health systems that may themselves be under stress. Hundreds of thousands of Syrian refugees are hosted in Lebanon and Jordan, imposing a heavy burden on these small countries and their health systems. Also, this case assistance usually comes in the form of non-governmental partners, who may be providing care not according to people's expectations in the normal context.[25]

PHC service provision in this phase usually is limited to a selection of services (e.g. mother-and-child care, nutrition, control of communicable diseases), often delivered in a vertical approach, led by usually fragmented and inconsistent information systems.[4]

Once violence recedes, even if temporarily, country health systems attempt to rebuild their infrastructure and functions. Countries with stronger health systems before the crisis and sufficient resources may try to reconstruct the system in its former shape. Iraq, whose hospital-oriented health system has not been modernized for decades, expanded its PHC network by 60% between 2002 and 2013, while still maintaining the split between levels that prevent a proper referral system to operate.[28] Along with the Kurdistan Region, Iraq has adopted Family Practice as its service delivery model, although large limitations in implementation and governance remain.[29,30] As with most EMR countries, little is known about its private sector, besides its large size (there are more than 12,000 private facilities in Iraq) and the assumption that users prefer those facilities to the public ones.

In other countries, the initial reconstruction has brought a change of paradigm, usually in the direction of introducing contracting schemes. Involvement of international partners is instrumental for this reform approach.[31] Afghanistan moved to PHC provision almost exclusively contracted to NGOs with external funding and very little government financing.[32] Somalia, with very little fiscal capacity, relies on a combination of NGO-managed facilities, and others formally belonging to the public sector but managed privately and funded by external remittances or user fees.[33] In the Darfur region of Sudan, PHC to displaced populations was provided by a myriad of NGOs 10 years after the conflict onset. There is often a lack of relationship between service providers and local health authorities when implementing NGO-based systems, resulting in flawed governance and blurred accountability.[32,34]

---

* Health Clusters are coordinating mechanisms; national and international organizations – from NGOs to UN Agencies – meet to decide the role of the non-government health sector in some selected emergency contexts. The MoH and WHO act as co-chairs. Out of the 23 clusters currently active, eight are located in EMR countries, the largest number after Africa.

In Syria and Yemen, the security situation is still too fluid to offer a clear path. The fragmentation in Syria in areas administered by opposing parties has resulted in the adoption of different models, from the traditional, if reduced, public health system, to an informal network of providers delivering irregularly different combinations of services.[35] In Yemen, the public health system remains formally in place, but migration of health workers, associated with a break in public expenditure, including lack of salary payments lasting more than one year, and non-functional supply chains, has resulted in a PHC system that works haphazardly, resorting to user fees and the intermediation of NGOs to access external funding, and where local health authorities are side-lined by all but a handful of organizations and United Nations' agencies.

In Palestine, the PHC public network was built through the absorption of the Israel-managed system. Some of the many local NGOs are active in the sector. Basic PHC services are provided by the public sector, complemented by private providers and UNRWA, while NGOs focus on vulnerable people and areas barred to Palestine government services.[36] The country endures a very specific type of conflict, requiring tailored responses, including the very structure of the PHC network (Box 11.1).

UNRWA runs one of the most stable PHC systems in the region. This UN agency provides PHC services through a network of 143 PHC facilities in five fields of operation spread across four countries. Over the years, the health programme had become barely sustainable, inefficient, and insufficiently coordinated with the host health systems.[37] Recent reforms have included the introduction of the Family Health Team (FHT) approach, consisting of the reorganization of teams (formerly structured in vertical services) and registration of users with a preferred provider. The FHT is now present in almost all UNRWA health centres, including most of those in Syria.[38]

Periods of relative peace, or when displacement to another country allows interacting with less stressed health systems, are also when the integration of services regarded as less urgent or more complex is attempted. The two service components most often mentioned are Mental Health and NCD management. The first condition is usually addressed through the training of existing health professionals, while NCD management also requires interventions to ensure the supply of the abundant medicines utilized.[39,40,41,42,43] Only relatively stable countries such as Palestine have attempted the implementation of more structured approaches, such as the Package of Essential NCD interventions (PEN) and the Total Risk Management for NCD strategy.*,[44]

Slowly, the restoration of routine health services is accompanied by actions to revitalize systemic components, such as Health Management Information Systems (HMIS) or efficient drugs

---

BOX 11.1   FIGHTING ACCESS BARRIERS IN THE WEST BANK (WB)

According to the Palestine MoH [64], in 2015 there were 422 government PHC clinics in the West Bank and 49 in the Gaza Strip (GS), resulting in availability of 6,166 people per clinic in the WB and 37,142 in the GS. Differently to what could be expected, the comparatively lower availability in Gaza does not respond to dissimilar prioritization, as reflected in the fact that the GS has better availability of PHC physicians.

Virtually all West Bank villages have a clinic, operating between 1 and 5 days per week. Besides the urbanization pattern, the MoH keeps this comparatively costly approach to ensure that in the event of the frequent closures and curfews, every village has the capacity to offer at least basic health services [36].

---

* The Package of Essential Non-communicable disease interventions is designed to expand NCD diagnosis and management in low-resource settings.

procurement and distribution systems, which require uninterrupted efforts over long periods. In Afghanistan, despite a routine HMIS having been operating for years, only indicators obtained from population surveys are considered, while all attempts at creating a centralized drug procurement agency have failed, and drug supply relies on multiple, inefficient supply schemes.[32] In Yemen, the last Ministry of Health Annual Report compiled with routine HMIS before the most recent outburst of violence lacks information on more than half the public hospitals. UNRWA has been developing in-house an electronic clinical record since 2009; a still-unfinished version of the tool is now operational in more than 110 health centres.

WHICH SERVICES SHOULD BE PROVIDED?

Most health systems struggle with spiralling costs of health care, fuelled by technology and expanded access to an undefined range of services. Essential Packages of Health Services (EPHS), usually composed of PHC interventions and selected first-referral services, are promoted as an effective, efficient, and standardised way of scaling up service delivery, often as a part of a sector reform process.[45] Conceptually, EPHS are a statement of entitlement: people are entitled only to the services included in the package but are entitled to all the services in the package.

One of the first decisions service providers in conflict settings have to make is the range of services that should be delivered. Two of the most popular sources of guidance are the Sphere Project and the Minimum Initial Service Package (MISP). The Sphere Project lists the minimum standards in humanitarian response, including the availability of health facilities and human resources.[46] The standards cover the following services: identification, prevention and management of communicable diseases, child health, sexual and reproductive health, injury care, mental health, and NCDs. Although a reference among humanitarian actors, it is little known among the governments that should implement the standards.

The MISP (for reproductive health in crisis situations) is a list of essential sexual and reproductive services, including prevention and management of sexual violence, reduction in transmission of HIV, and prevention of excess neonatal and maternal morbidity and mortality, developed by the Inter-Agency Working Group for Reproductive Health in Refugee Situations and integrated with the Sphere Project. It has been found that relatively solid health systems already include some of the MISP components, but they often fail to integrate those related to sexual violence and HIV.[47]

Despite the existence of these crisis-oriented tools, most EMR countries in crisis have developed their own EPHS, and mostly when the country was already enduring the hardships of conflict situations. At least seven countries in crisis (Afghanistan, Iraq, Pakistan [selected provinces], Somalia, Sudan [service standards], Syria [North], and Yemen) have designed and adopted an EPHS.

In crisis countries, as in less strained settings, the EPHS often is too ambitious for the capacities of the health system, despite the time and efforts undertaken in its design.[45] It is seldom used for any practical purposes. Rather than a statement of entitlement, the package is used as an advocacy tool, particularly when associated with a costing exercise showing the additional financial needs that its implementation would entail.

There are exceptions, however. In Afghanistan and Somalia, the EPHS has become a tool to facilitate contracting NGOs for service delivery, although the implementation is far from homogeneous.[32,48] North Syria also is moving in that direction. Yemen has recently designed a package tailored to the crisis situation (Box 11.2) and is piloting its implementation by the public PHC system.

Entitlement is understood as the right of individuals to access health services. Of all the EMR crisis countries, only Palestine has a formal Social Health Insurance (SHI) scheme, whose membership determines the entitlement of registered users to benefit from public health services.

BOX 11.2   YEMEN, A MINIMUM SERVICE PACKAGE
TO RESTORE PHC SERVICE DELIVERY

In 2004, following the inception of a National Health Sector Reform strategy, the Yemen Ministry of Public Health and Population produced the "Essential Service Package for the District Health System" (ESP). The ESP was never implemented in its totality, but it remained as a reference point for an aspirational package of health services.

With the humanitarian crisis affecting the whole country, in 2017, WHO helped to adapt the ESP to a short-term practical tool consisting of life-saving health interventions[68] that the national public health system must be able to provide in a relatively short period of time.

Instead of non-existing epidemiological information and protracted discussions, Global Burden of Disease estimates and recommendations from the Diseases Control Priorities version 3 were used in the selection of priority interventions for the ESP.

Following the decline of the cholera outbreak in Yemen, the Minimum Service Package is to be piloted in selected areas, in a novel approach that focuses on the restoration of public services, including the revitalization of the local health authorities and their role in managing the PHC network.

TABLE 11.3   Coverage of selected PHC services, by socio-economic characteristics: Somaliland, MICS 2011

Service component	Residence		Mother's education		Wealth Quintile		
	Urban (%)	Rural (%)	None (%)	Secondary+ (%)	Poorest (%)	Richest (%)	Total (%)
DTP-3 vaccine	16	11	12	39	6	18	*13*
Care for Pneumonia	47	15	26	40	8	64	*31*
Antenatal Care 4+	24	6	12	41	3	31	*15*
Institutional Delivery	54	9	25	73	4	73	*31*

Even in this country, public PHC services are generally accessible to the whole population, regardless of their SHI status. In all other countries, access to public PHC services is open to all nationals without restriction, although in many cases service utilization is only granted in exchange for user fees.

However, the combination of universal entitlement and the adoption of a standard package of services does not necessarily translate into universal and equitable access and utilization of health services. As shown by the most recent Multiple-Indicators Country Survey (MICS) conducted in Somaliland (Table 11.3), important inequities remain in PHC service utilization across socio-economic layers of society, and this is common to most countries in crisis.[49] Also, substantial territorial inequalities exist in the availability and utilization of health services. The overall low service coverage, even of the most basic services, added to the identified imbalances, makes it questionable that the package of services is actually being provided.

UNIVERSAL HEALTH COVERAGE IN A CRISIS COUNTRY?

The health financing combination that best serves the purpose of Universal Health Coverage (UHC) is a pre-payment scheme, either tax-based or through Social Health Insurance; a unified pooling mechanism allocating sufficient funds according to explicit criteria that promote equity and efficiency; and a purchasing tool linked to performance. Among the variety of provider payment mechanisms available, capitation, with some adjustment for the characteristics of the population to be served, is probably the best.

Crisis situations coincide with reduced fiscal space of the involved government, either because of the downsizing of the economy as a result of conflict, or because of re-oriented priorities, usually towards the security sector. All this results in reduced government allocation to the health sector. When the government fails to fulfil its role, a myriad of other funding sources usually appears, with variable degrees of inefficiency.

The main alternatives for unavailable government funding are external resources and out-of-pocket (OOP) expenditure. The Global Health Expenditure Database gives levels of OOP of 76% of total health expenditure in Yemen and Sudan, 64% in Afghanistan, and 54% in Syria, compared to 20% in Jordan, 35% in Tunisia, and 15% in Saudi Arabia. In Iraq, the crisis generated by lower oil prices and additional security expenditure to fight ISIS forced the health sector to re-introduce user fees as the sole mechanism to fund the supply of medicines and consumables. In Afghanistan, OOP expenditure to purchase medicines, prescribed at facilities contracted for the delivery of the Basic Package of Health Services, exceeds the amount disbursed by donors to cover those contracts.[32] In Yemen, most government health expenditure, including that for salaries of government workers in any sector, stopped by late 2016; user fees levied on an impoverished population became the only source of funding, barely enough to cover some staff compensation, as low as 10% of the regular salaries, for the staff irregularly present at the facilities. In Somalia, government health expenditure is negligible or absent, and service provision is supported by a combination of external funding (partly channelled to contracting NGOs), remittances, and user fees.

Donor funding has been instrumental in maintaining service delivery in Afghanistan, Somalia, and Darfur, for example, and is presently contributing to keeping the system alive in Yemen. Establishing a pattern of donor support is very difficult because of the political nature of some of these contributions, which may favour one or other warring party, and also because the region is a preferred target for the so-called non-traditional donors, e.g. Turkey, Gulf Countries, China, and Russia, who do not always provide information to global financial data repositories.

Although occasionally involved in funding routine operations, donor funding can be more often found in infrastructure projects and, in PHC, in the contracting of NGOs for service delivery (Box 11.3). External funds are also involved in innovative approaches, such as funding

BOX 11.3   CONTRACTING NGOs IN AFGHANISTAN

In 2002, shortly after the fall of the Taliban, the decision was made to change completely the paradigm of PHC service delivery in Afghanistan. At that point, most services were provided by NGOs with external funding. Government health services had been shrinking during the Taliban regime, due to low prioritization and insufficient funding.

Three donors, the World Bank, USAID and the European Union, have been financing contracts with NGOs for the delivery of the Basic Package of Health Services. Each contract covers the whole PHC system of a province, including District Hospitals. Contract award follows a competitive process where the invited NGOs submit a detailed project proposal tailored to the situation of the relevant province. The provider payment mechanism consists of global budgets with limited flexibility. Per capita expenditure with NGO contracts varies significantly across provinces; with average figures lower than US$5, effective service availability requires substantial OOP expenditure. Service coverage indicators also vary between territories and services.[32]

Social Health Insurance membership for vulnerable populations in a post-conflict setting in Darfur.[50]

Social Health Insurance (SHI) is an uncommon pre-payment scheme in EMR crisis countries. In Palestine, the only setting with a sizeable SHI, the scheme is in fact a tax that reverts to the government general budget, with no relation with government health allocations or payment to providers.[36]

With some exceptions, such as NGO contracts, providers are paid through line-item budgets, preventing any meaningful management autonomy. Rather than financial allocations, budgets are usually converted to physical items, distributed to health facilities according to some criterion. Local health authorities seldom participate in managing these resources, even when the source is their own government.

PRIMARY HEALTH CARE IS ABOUT TEAMWORK

Delivering the combination of services that comprise PHC requires that the right combination of skills operates in the right locations. No one single category can provide the whole range of services; instead, basic teams, usually composed of physicians (and medical assistants in some settings), nurses, and midwives, and with contributions from specialized and support staff, deliver PHC services while acting as gatekeepers and coordinate access to other levels of care.

Country health systems should ensure proper supply, adequate distribution and performance-informed management of staff for these basic teams to be able to perform their duties.[51] Training institutions need to be of certified quality and accessible to prospective trainees, adequate funding is needed to allow the recruitment of necessary personnel, updated information is required to facilitate the proper distribution of the health workforce, and tools have to be available to enable local managers to assess and reward staff performance. These requirements are universally recognized as essential but are not always present.[52]

Some of the factors influencing the performance of health care workers, such as knowledge and skills, motivation, availability of updated clinical guidelines, availability of equipment, medicines, and supplies, and supportive evaluation, are not easy to access and enforce, particularly in challenging contexts.[53] According to Witter, in selected post-conflict settings, *"problems are well understood [...] but core issues – such as adequate pay, effective distribution and Human Resources for Health (HRH) management – are to a greater or lesser degree unresolved".*[54]

Training capacity, and particularly the standards of training quality, are among the first casualties in a conflict situation. Private production often replaces public training. Attrition of cadres of health-care workers, and even migration to safer contexts, is high during the first phases of the crisis, but also substantial is their replacement by foreign and volunteer humanitarian workers.[2] PHC systems in rural areas, often staffed by small teams and working in isolation, are likely to be abandoned, while hospitals and urban PHC facilities become recipients of foreign humanitarian workers. In addition to the regional market that Gulf countries represent, and which act as a magnet for health workers anxious to leave unsafe settings, PHC services offered to refugees in neighbouring countries (e.g. Lebanon or Jordan for Syrian and Iraqi refugees) are also a source of employment, although often in informal arrangements, and a reason for health-care worker migration.[2,52]

Adequate distribution of the health-care workforce is hindered by insecurity, low salaries, and lack of appealing retention packages. Information systems are often unable to update the location of staff, let alone help assess their performance. As a result, staff distribution is based on standard teams by facility type or according to population: staff ratios. However, since other factors often have a greater effect, staff distribution seldom follows the adopted standard, as proven in the Iraq distribution of General Practitioners (GPs) shown in Figure 11.1. In Yemen,

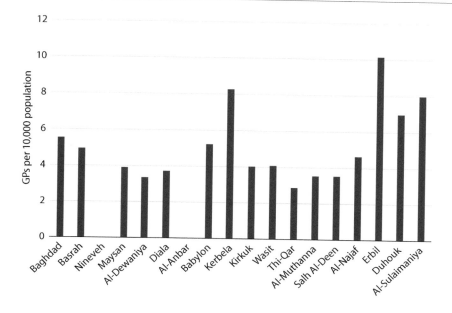

FIGURE 11.1 Availability of GPs per 10,000 population, by province. Iraq, 2015. (*Source*: MoH Annual Report 2015.)

the median team in Ministry of Health Centres found in the HeRAMS survey 2016 was one-third of the approved standard, with the scarce presence of physicians.[18] In both places, also in Darfur, staff presence is disproportionally skewed towards urban areas.[55]

Funding shortages to grant adequate staff pay are addressed differently. In Iraq, budget constraints brought by the reduction in oil prices forced the Ministry of Health to concentrate all funding on salary payment, while all other costs had to be shouldered by increasing user fees. In Yemen, no salary has been paid for more than one year, and staff get some compensation from user fees. In Yemen, external partners are also an attractive source of staff "incentives", but no common salary scale has been agreed so far. In Afghanistan, a harmonized salary scale was agreed in the run-up to establishing contract arrangements with NGOs and is complemented by supplements that grow with the instability of the province and the distance of the facility where the staff member is deployed to the provincial capital.[32] In the Gaza Strip, staff received the equivalent to 40% of their monthly salary every 50 days. Everywhere, this translates into low staff morale, absenteeism and "double practice", with staff working more than one role at the same time, as coping strategies.

The adoption by many countries of the Family Practice (FP) approach has linked this strategy to the presence of a specialized health-care worker, the Family Medicine (FM) specialist. This presents the double challenge of developing a training and certification package that can be appealing to some of the best physicians in the country, and finding a solution for the many doctors, often numbering thousands in a country, who have been working in PHC and cannot, or will not, engage in such demanding training, especially given that average family medicine specialist training programmes last between three and four years. There are several FM programmes in EMR countries; however, there has been a reduced output of certified specialists.[56] Only the Gaza Strip and Iraq, among the crisis countries, are implementing the FM specialist training program. In Palestine, the complementary approach is to provide training on essential FP components, coinciding with the introduction of the PEN strategy.[44] UNRWA has adopted

---

BOX 11.4 PAKISTAN'S LADY HEALTH WORKER (LHW) PROGRAMME

The programme was launched in 1994. Working from their own houses, LHWs provide door-step services, including basic curative care, promotion of healthy habits, immunization, and antenatal care (delivered by the nearest public health facilities) and referral to formal health services.

There is a standard 1000 population per LHW, and it is estimated that the programme covers above 60% of the rural population of the country. LHW-covered areas reportedly show better coverage and health status indicators than those areas without coverage.

Since 2013, LHWs have received regular salaries, covered by the government, and are offered career paths. The estimated annual cost per LHW exceeds US$700.

Among the many challenges faced by the programme, the most daunting are the variable quality of local training, recruitment among urban rather than rural candidates, support from sub-optimal functional health facilities, poor access to referral services, financial constraints, and political interference from local authorities[60-63].

---

the so-called Family Health Team approach and combines in-house training with the piloting of Diploma courses on Family Medicine, run in both Gaza and Lebanon.

In countries where access to basic health services is not guaranteed by formal delivery systems, new cadres may be created, recruited, and trained to operate in the remotest, most insecure locations. In Afghanistan, training and recruitment of Community Midwives have been accelerated to increase skilled deliveries in remote areas where no urban-trained professional would accept a position.[32]

Community Health Workers (CHW) have been used as a replacement for the provision of at least some PHC components. CHWs have demonstrated their effectiveness in simple tasks that increase immunization uptake and even in the screening of risk of cardiovascular disease, but their scope of work often expands from initial limited preventive tasks to complex curative activities.[57,58] In Afghanistan, the combination of a perceived historical debt and lack of alternatives to provide services to scattered and nomad populations has contributed to the creation of a workforce of over 20,000 CHWs that play a substantial role.[59] In 2014, CHWs were responsible for 20% of the total outpatient contacts attended in Afghanistan public facilities and referred 25% to 30% of all the deliveries reported through the HMIS.[32] By 2014, Pakistan had deployed more than 100,000 Lady Health Workers, focusing on mother and child PHC services (Box 11.4).[60] However, CHWs may impose a heavy burden on otherwise weak health systems.

To be effective, CHWs require focused tasks, adequate remuneration, training, supportive supervision and active involvement of the community, in addition to reliable supplies.[61] CHW programs also require the design and implementation of adequate incentives and imaginative combinations of funding sources, from donors and communities, that inherently have local features and therefore vary across the territory.[62] Supporting dozens of CHWs may be perhaps too ambitious for district health systems barely able to supervise and supply a few health facilities.[63]

CONCLUSION

The boundary between PHC and hospital care in a crisis context is blurred. Probably, providing PHC in Yemen shares more problems with hospital care provision in Somalia than with delivering PHC in Tunisia.

Conflict has deleterious effects on the health of the affected population. However, a large part of the health impact can be attributed to the limits conflict imposes on the capacity of the health system to provide accessible health care.

Traditional models of PHC provision are disregarded in the first phases of a crisis. Service delivery becomes opportunistic and where, when, what, and by whom, services are provided is not decided by local health authorities. Recovery efforts may replicate often inadequate old patterns of health care or may move to more "modern" paradigms. Multiple interests, not always in the best interest of the population, may influence the final outcome. Whatever the approach taken, the role of local health authorities is essential and should be strengthened.

In general, entitlement to using public PHC services is unrestricted. However, limited geographic access, inadequate service availability, insufficient presence of skilled personnel, inappropriate drug supply, and sometimes unaffordable user fees, mean that the right to health is often compromised. Service packages have only proved their value when used as a contracting or advocacy tool. There is, however, some potential for service packages to be used as instruments of coordination to facilitate agreement among partners in need of guidance.

Prevalent health financing schemes are far from optimal. The pervasive presence of user fees signals the distance between current practices and effective universal health coverage. Nonetheless, substantial funds, even if fragmented, are devoted to financing PHC services in crisis situations. The challenge is finding how to solve the challenge, using the most flexible sources of funds, to fill the gaps left by the most orthodox funding schemes.

Few, if any, crisis contexts offer the regular PHC teams required for the provision of modern PHC services. Rarely available physicians get employment in urban areas, large hospitals, or international humanitarian organizations, where security is better and prospects of obtaining a decent salary higher. Community Health Workers have been used as a replacement in many countries, often without assessing properly the challenge of providing thousands of workers with the necessary training, sustainable compensation, sufficient drug supply, and adequate supervision.

Each crisis requires a tailored approach to delivering PHC. Time and again, resilient health systems bounce back to provide the closest they can to a standard range of PHC services. Blueprints and models do not work; the focus should be on how to adapt to a changing situation, rather than on how to apply a defined model. Having a structured vision for the future may help navigate the stormy waters of the present, but appropriate adjustment should happen almost on a daily basis.

NOTES

1. Assessment Capacities Project, *Crisis Overview 2016. Humanitarian Trends and Risks for 2017*, ACAPS, 2016.
2. E. Pavignani, Human Resources for Health Under Stress in the Eastern Mediterranean Region, *World Health Organization*, 2017.
3. C. Murray, G. King, A. Lopez, N. Tomijima and E. Krug, Armed conflict as a public health problem, *British Medical Journal*, vol. 324: 346–349, 2002.
4. P. Spiegel, F. Checchi, S. Colombo and E. Paik, Health-care needs of people affected by conflict: Future trends and changing frameworks, *Lancet*, vol. 375: 341–345, 2010.
5. K. Blanchet, F. Fouad and T. Pherali, Syrian refugees in Lebanon: The search for universal health coverage, *Conflict and Health*, vol. 10: 12, 2016.
6. K. Blanchet, F. Fouad and T. Pherali, Syrian refugees in Lebanon: The search for universal health coverage, *Conflict and Health*, vol. 10: 12, 2016.
7. P. Heudtlass, N. Speybroeck and G.-S. D, Excess mortality in refugees, internally displaced persons and resident populations in complex humanitarian emergencies (1998–2012) – insights from operational data, *Conflict and Health*, vol. 10: 15, 2016.
8. E. Pavignani and A. Colombo, *Analysing Disrupted Health Sectors. A Modular Manual*, Geneva: World Health Organization, 2009.
9. L. Dimitry, A systematic review on the mental health of children and adolescents in areas of armed conflict in the Middle East, *Child: Care, Health and Development*, vol. 38(2): 153–161, 2011.

10. A. Al-Jawadi and S. Abdul-Rhman, Prevalence of childhood and early adolescence mental disorders among children attending primary health care centres in Mosul, Iraq: A cross-sectional study, *BMC Public Health*, vol. 7: 274, 2007.

11. A. Gele and G. Bjune, Armed conflicts have an impact on the spread of tuberculosis: The case of the Somali Regional State of Ethiopia, *Conflict and Health*, vol. 4: 1, 2010.

12. A. Bellos, K. Mulholland, K. O'Brien, S. Qazi, M. Gayer and F. Checchi, The burden of acute respiratory infections in crisis-affected populations: A systematic review, *Conflict and Health*, vol. 4: 3, 2010.

13. M. Kherallah, T. Alahfez, Z. Sahloul, K. Eddin and G. Jamil, Health care in Syria before and during the crisis, *Avicenna Journal of Medicine*, vol. 2(3): 51–53, 2012.

14. R. Raslan, S. El Sayegh, S. Chams, N. Chams, A. Leone and I. Hussein, Re-emerging vaccine-preventable diseases in war-affected peoples of the eastern Mediterranean Region—an update, *Frontiers in Public Health*, vol. 5, 2017.

15. GBD 2015 DALYs and HALE Collaborators, Global, regional, and national disability-adjusted life-years (DALYs) for 315 diseases and injuries and healthy life expectancy (HALE), 1990–2015: A systematic analysis for the Global Burden of Disease Study 2015, *Lancet*, vol. 388: 1603–1658, 2016.

16. A. Mokdad et al., Health in times of uncertainty in the eastern Mediterranean region, 1990–2013: A systematic analysis for the Global Burden of Disease Study 2013, *Lancet Global Health*, vol. 4: e704–e713, 2016.

17. Health Cluster Turkey, Health Resources Availability Mapping System (HeRAMS) Health Facilities Report. Assessment of 254 facilities in 9 Governorates in Syria, *World Health Organization*, Gaziantep, 2015.

18. Ministry of Public Health and Population; World Health Organization, Service Availability and Health Facilities Functionality in 16 Governorates, *World Health Organization*, Sana'a, 2016.

19. S. Colombo and E. Pavignani, Recurrent failings of medical humanitarianism: Intractable, ignored, or just exaggerated? *Lancet*, 2017. Available from: https://www.thelancet.com/journals/lancet/article/PIIS0 140-6736(17)31277-1/abstract.

20. No protection, no respect. Health workers and health facilities under attack. 2015 and early 2016, *Safeguarding Health in Conflict*, 2016.

21. M. Heisler, E. Baker and D. McKay, Attacks on health care in Syria — Normalizing violations of medical neutrality? *New England Journal of Medicine*, vol. 373(26): 2489–2491, 2015.

22. Update to the Special Report of 3 August 2015 of the Commissioner-General of the United Nations Relief and Works Agency for Palestine Refugees in the Near East on the Financial Crisis of the Agency, *UNRWA*, 2016.

23. United Nations, Epic Humanitarian Crisis Looms Should Palestine Refugee Agency Be Compelled to Scale Back Services, Delegates Warn as Fourth Committee Debate Continues, 2016. Available from: https://www.un.org/press/en/2017/gaspd654.doc.htm [Accessed 24 January 2017].

24. J. Whittall, The "new humanitarian aid landscape" Case study: MSF interaction with non-traditional and emerging aid actors in Syria 2013-14, *Medecins Sans Frontieres*, 2014.

25. Z. El-Khatib, D. Scales, J. Vearey and B. Forsberg, Syrian refugees, between rocky crisis in Syria and hard inaccessibility to healthcare services in Lebanon and Jordan, *Conflict and Health*, vol. 7: 18, 2013.

26. World Health Organization, *The World Health Report 2008. Primary Health Care. Now More than Ever*, Geneva: World Health Organization, 2008.

27. F. Alahdab, M. Omar, S. Alsakka, A. Al-Moujahed and B. Atassi, Syrians' alternative to a health care system: "field hospitals", *Avicenna Journal of Medicine*, vol. 4(3):51–52, 2014.

28. V. Cetorelli and N. Shabila, Expansion of health facilities in Iraq a decade after the US-led invasion, 2003–2012, *Conflict and Health*, vol. 8: 16, 2014.

29. A. Shukor, N. Klazinga and K. DS, Primary care in an unstable security, humanitarian, economic and political context: The Kurdistan Region of Iraq, *BMC Health Services Research*, vol. 17: 592, 2017.

30. M. Moore, C. Anthony, Y. Lim, S. Jones, A. Overton and J. Yoong, The Future of Health Care in the Kurdistan Region—Iraq. Toward an Effective, High-Quality System with an Emphasis on Primary Care. Sponsored by the Kurdistan Regional Government, *The RAND Corporation*, 2014.

31. L. Strong, A. Wali and E. Sondorp, *Health Policy in Afghanistan: Two years of rapid change. A review of the process from 2001 to 2003*, London School of Hygiene and Tropical Medicine, London, 2005.

32. X. Mòdol, *Afghanistan Joint Health Sector Review and Strategic Plan Implementation Assessment*, European Union; Ministry of Public Health of Afghanistan, Kabul, 2015.

33. E. Pavignani, The multiform Somali healthcare arena, *World Bank*, 2016.

34. Z. Anwari, M. Shukla, B. Maseed, G. Wardak, S. Sardar, J. Matin, G. Rashed, S. Hamedi, H. Sahak, A. Aziz, M. Boyd-Boffa and R. Trasi, Implementing people-centred health systems governance in 3 provinces and 11 districts of Afghanistan: A case study, *Conflict and Health*, vol. 9: 2, 2015.

35. E. Pavignani and S. Colombo, *Health policy and planning in turbulent settings A consultative workshop, with a focus on the Whole of Syria Amman*, 2-5 December 2017, World Health Organization, Amman, 2018.

36. X. Mòdol, *Assessment of the MoH Primary Health Care System in the West Bank A baseline exploration of issues relevant to the introduction of Family Health Care in the oPt*, World Health Organization, Jerusalem, 2013.

37. E. Pavignani, External assessment of the UNRWA Health Programme, *UNRWA*, 2009.

38. UNRWA, Health Department Annual Report 2016, *UNRWA*, 2017.

39. S. Sadik, S. Abdulrahman, M. Bradley and R. Jenkins, Integrating mental health into primary health care in Iraq, *Mental Health in Family Medicine*, vol. 8: 39–49, 2011.

40. R. Renato Souza, S. Yasuda and S. Cristofani, Mental health treatment outcomes in a humanitarian emergency: A pilot model for the integration of mental health into primary care in Habilla, Darfur, *International Journal of Mental Health Systems*, vol. 3: 17, 2009.

41. Shannon Doocy, Emily Lyles, Baptiste Hanquart, The LHAS Study Team and Michael Woodman, Prevalence, care-seeking, and health service utilization for non-communicable diseases among Syrian refugees and host communities in Lebanon, *Conflict and Health*, vol. 10: 21, 2016.

42. D. Collins, K. Jobanputra, T. Frost, S. Muhammed, A. Ward, A. Shafei, T. Fardous, S. Gabashneh and C. Heneghan, Cardiovascular disease risk and prevention amongst Syrian refugees: Mixed methods study of Médecins Sans Frontières programme in Jordan, *Conflict and Health*, vol. 11: 17, 2017.

43. A. Mansour, Patients' opinion on the barriers to diabetes control in areas of conflicts: The Iraqi example, *Conflict and Health*, vol. 2: 7, 2008.

44. R. Dwekat, N. Barghothi, I. Shmasna and W. Venter, *Introducing the PEN in Palestine. Implementation of the WHO Package of Essential Noncommunicable Disease (PEN) Interventions for Primary Health Care in Salfit District: A review of the pilot*, Palestine Ministry of Health & World Health Organization Palestine Office, 2013.

45. X. Mòdol and S. Colombo, The Essential Package of Health Services in Humanitarian Crises: A review, *World Health Organization*, 2017.

46. The Sphere Project, *Humanitarian Charter and Minimum Standards in Humanitarian Response*, The Sphere Project, 2011.

47. S. Krause, H. Williams, M. Onyango, S. Sami, W. Doedens, N. Giga, E. Stone and B. Tomczyk, Reproductive health services for Syrian refugees in Zaatri Camp and Irbid City, Hashemite Kingdom of Jordan: An evaluation of the Minimum Initial Services Package, *Conflict and Health*, vol. 9 (Suppl1):S4, 2015.

48. N. Pearson and S. Khan, *Somali Package of Health Services, more essential than ever. Review of the implementation of the essential package of health services in Sahil region of Somaliland, Kaarkar region of Puntland and Gedo region of South Central Somalia*, Health Consortium for Somalia/UKAid, 2013.

49. UNICEF Somalia and Somaliland Ministry of Planning and National Development, Somaliland Multiple Indicator Cluster Survey 2011, Final Report, *UNICEF*, Somalia and Somaliland Ministry of Planning and National Development, Somaliland, Nairobi, Kenya, 2014.

50. S. Witter and NHIF Team, Expanding access, utilisation and financial protection in a post-conflict setting: Results of a pilot project with the NHIF in Darfur, 2015. [Online]. Available from: https://www.res earchgate.net/profile/Sophie_Witter/publication/307866089_Expanding_access_utilisation_and_fina ncial_protection_in_a_post-conflict_setting_results_of_a_pilot_project_with_the_NHIF_in_Darfur/ links/57cfe8ce08ae83b374643a65/Expanding-access-utilisation-and-financial-protection-in-a-post-conflict-setting-results-of-a-pilot-project-with-the-NHIF-in-Darfur.pdf.

51. E. Roome, J. Raven and T. Martineau, Human resource management in post-conflict health systems: Review of research and knowledge gaps, *Conflict and Health*, vol. 8:18, 2014.

52. F. El-Jardali, D. Jamal, A. Abdallah and K. Kassak, Human resources for health planning and management in the Eastern Mediterranean region: Facts, gaps and forward thinking for research and policy, *Human Resources for Health*, vol. 5: 9, 2007.

53. A. Rowe, D. de Savigny, C. Lanata and C. Victora, How can we achieve and maintain high-quality performance of health workers in low-resource settings? *Lancet*, vol. 366: 1026–1035, 2005.

54. S. Witter, M. Bertone, Y. Chirwa, J. Namakula, S. So and H. Wurie, Evolution of policies on human resources for health: Opportunities and constraints in four post-conflict and post-crisis settings, *Conflict and Health*, vol. 10:31, 2016.

55. X. Mòdol et al., Health and nutrition facility mapping and prospective investment planning study. Greater Darfur summary, *World Bank*, 2013.

56. A. Abyad, A. Al-Baho, I. Unluoglu, M. Tarawneh and T. Al Hilfy, Development of family medicine in the middle east, *Family Medicine*, vol. 39(10): 736–741, 2007.

57. S. Lewin, S. Babigumira, X. Bosch-Capblanch, G. Aja, B. van Wyk, C. Glenton, I. Scheel, Z. M and K. Daniels, Lay health workers in primary and community health care: A systematic review of trials, *London School of Hygiene and Tropical Medicine*, 2006.

58. T. Gaziano, S. Abrahams-Gessel, C. Denman, C. Mendoza Montano, M. Khanam, T. Puoane and N. Levitt, An assessment of community health workers' ability to screen for cardiovascular disease risk with a simple, non-invasive risk assessment instrument in Bangladesh, Guatemala, Mexico, and South Africa: An observational study, *Lancet Global Health*, vol. 3: e556–e563, 2015.

59. S. Najafizada, R. Labonté and I. Bourgeault, Community health workers of Afghanistan: A qualitative study of a national program, *Conflict and Health*, vol. 8: 26, 2014.

60. N. Zhu, E. Allen, A. Kearns, J. Caglia and R. Atun, Lady Health Workers in Pakistan Improving access to health care for rural women and families, *Harvard School of Public Health*, Integrare, Maternal Health Task Force, 2014.

61. A. Haines, D. Sanders, U. Lehmann, A. Rowe, J. Lawn, S. Jan, D. Walker and Z. Bhutta, Achieving child survival goals: Potential contribution of community health workers, *Lancet*, vol. 369: 2121–2131, 2007.

62. K. Bhattacharyya, P. Winch, K. LeBan and M. Tien, Community Health Worker Incentives and Disincentives: How They Affect Motivation, Retention, and Sustainability, Basic Support for Institutionalizing Child Survival Project (BASICS II) – *USAID*, 2001.

63. A. Hafeez, B. Mohamud, M. Shiekh, S. Shah and R. Jooma, Lady health workers programme in Pakistan: challenges, achievements and the way forward, *JPMA*, 2011. Available from: http://jpma.org.pk/full_article_text.php?article_id=2633 [Accessed 20 January 2018].

64. Ministry of Health, PHIC, "Health Annual Report. Palestine 2015," Ministry of Health, 2016.

CHAPTER 12

Public–private partnerships: The Mazandaran experience on contracting with private family physicians, Islamic Republic of Iran

Mohsen A'arabi, Mohsen Asadi-Lari, and Ghasem Janbabaei

INTRODUCTION

Mazandaran province is located in northern Iran on the coast of the Caspian Sea (Figure 12.1). The population of the province was 3,283,582 people, based on the 2016 census, with 1,756,456 of those people living in urban areas.[1]

The Rural Family Medicine Programme began in the rural areas of Mazandaran province in 2005, as in other parts of the country, serving a population of 1.5 million people living in villages and in cities of under 20,000 people in the province. The programme included health houses (rural village health posts), and rural family physicians and midwives based in rural health centres. In this programme each rural health centre is staffed by at least one rural family physician and midwife and, for every 4000 people, one extra physician is added.

Behvarzes, community health workers based in the village health houses, are responsible for providing health service packages to all people. For those that need to be seen by a family physician, a referral system is in place between the village health house and the rural health centre. All the health team members are employees of the public sector and receive their salary from the District Health Centre (DHC) by a mixed payment method. Family physician and midwife salaries are calculated on a per capita basis. The service delivery structure is shown in Figure 12.2.

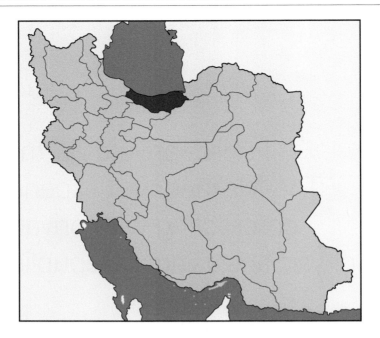

FIGURE 12.1 Mazandaran province (in black), Islamic Republic of Iran.

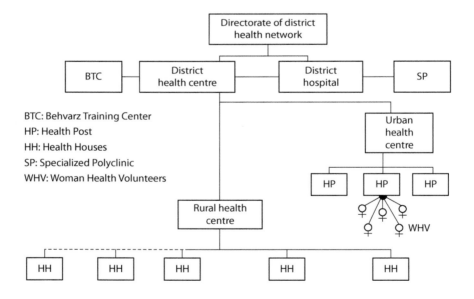

FIGURE 12.2 Primary health-care system in the Islamic Republic of Iran.

Service delivery in cities with a population of over 20,000 was not carried out as a whole by family physicians. In these larger cities only some patients were attended by physicians who worked in urban health centres. In addition, the provision of services based on the burden of non-communicable diseases (e.g. diabetes, hypertension, hyperlipidaemia) and nutritional and mental health problems was not integrated at this time. Therefore, the need for a family physician-based approach for service delivery for urban areas, as well as in rural areas, was considered by policymakers and members of Parliament.

POLITICAL COMMITMENTS

The Urban Family Physicians Programme in Mazandaran province began in the year 2012, with governmental approval (Decree No. 10362/T47971/H) provided by the Cabinet of Ministers on April 14, 2012.[2] In the Islamic Republic of Iran, health is considered a right, which has been emphasized in several principles in the constitution. In the country's Fifth Social, Economic, and Cultural Development Plan, the expansion of the family physician programme and the referral system was emphasized as the duty of the Government.

To establish this urban programme, there was very strong cooperation at a national level between the Ministry of Health, alongside the Ministry of Cooperation, Work, and Social Welfare. For this programme to be carried out, there also was close and serious cooperation between the Mazandaran University of Medical Sciences, the health insurance organization, the social security insurance organization, and the Imam Khomeini Relief Committee Insurance at the provincial level. In the presence of the heads of insurance organizations as the programme's main stakeholders, a provincial executive committee led the establishment and implementation of the programme. In addition, a provincial steering committee was established with the Governor, the Chancellor of the University of Medical Sciences, heads of the insurance organizations, and a representative of the Medical Council.

In each district there was also a City Executive Committee set up with the heads of the insurance companies, the head of the DHC, the Head of the District Medical Council, and the governor of the district.

In the country's Sixth Social, Economic, and Cultural Development Plan, there was also an emphasis on the implementation of the family physician programme and the referral system.

THE PROCESS OF DEVELOPING CONTRACTS WITH PRIVATE PROVIDERS

Private sector physicians interested in working as urban family physicians apply to the DHC. In the application form, the physician declares readiness to start working as a family physician for a specific population. They also pledge to work only as a family physician and not to have any dual practice. In addition, they are obligated to employ a midwife/nurse to work in their office.

The DHC examines the applicant's documents and sends an expert to inspect the proposed office. If the city requires a family physician, the standards are met and the documents are complete, the Director of the DHC accepts the application and sends a letter with the certified documents to the Provincial Health Centre (PHC).

The Provincial Health Centre also, if the documents are complete and approved, submits the family physician's request to the Provincial Health Insurance Organization and the Provincial Social Security Insurance Organization. Both insurance organizations announce their acceptance or rejection of the applicant within one week of receiving the application and after having examined the documentation.

In the next stage, insurance organizations sign a contract with the accepted physician to provide services based on the instructions of the Ministry of Health and Medical Education. In all the contracts, the director of the health centre of each district is known as a contract observer for the provision of services to all family physicians in that city. As a result, the director of the health centre cannot work as a family physician. All payments are made directly to family physicians in accordance with the guidelines of the Board of Governors who are responsible for the health team. Over the past five years, more than 78% of 637 family physicians have had contracts with insurance agencies for more than three years.[3]

RATIO OF POPULATION PER PHYSICIAN

The population covered by each full-time family physician post is 2500 people for eight hours' service delivery per day. The working hours are 08:00 to 12:00 and 16:00 to 20:00. This has increased people's access to services, since public sector working hours are only in the mornings.

Physicians who cannot or do not want to work full-time in the family physician programme can take part by reducing the number of population covered. In this case, their working hours will be halved and the population covered by them will be 1250 people.

In each city, for every 30,000–50,000 people there is an urban comprehensive health centre that operates in the mornings. At these centres, one or more general practitioners (GPs) are employed by the public sector; the staff also includes a nutritionist, a clinical psychologist, a midwife, a person for laboratory sampling, a dentist, an environmental health expert, and at least one health expert. The health expert is the first person who provides service to the population in urban areas; most of them are midwives, but nurses and other graduates with a bachelor degree in public health also are employed in this role.

The family physician director of the urban centre provides care for 2000 people. The director also holds meetings with other family physicians in the area and acts as a point of coordination and support between them and the DHC. The support includes arranging delivery of pharmaceutical supplements (vitamins) and educational materials to them. In addition, the director collects data from the family physicians, and conducts monthly visits to monitor their activities. In some of these centres, where there is enough space, family physicians work part-time in the afternoons.

All people in the cities of the province have access to their own family physician. In a study of 1768 randomly selected families within the province, the average time required to reach the family physician was reported as 16.3 minutes (SD = 12.7) on foot, or 5.6 minutes (SD = 4.7) by car.[4]

THE CONCEPT BEHIND CONTRACTING WITH PRIVATE PROVIDERS

In the beginning, there was a shortage of physicians working in the public sector. As a result, only 20% of the population were covered by these physicians. One of the characteristics of outpatient services in the country and in Mazandaran province is that the private sector has a special role to play in providing services; it tends to be more trusted by the people. In addition, the general condition of physicians' private offices was better than those in public centres.

Using the private sector's capacity to cover the population was one of the best available solutions, because there was no need for governmental investment in the construction and equipping of new offices, or the employment of extra human resources.

However, due to their low level of familiarity with the concept of family physician service delivery, physicians in the private sector needed training and empowerment through the provision of health-care education packages.

CRITERIA FOR SELECTION OF PRIVATE PROVIDERS

Having a medical degree in general medicine and a license to practice as a physician for the requested city is the first requirement; in addition, the physician must have completed their two years of legal work experience following graduation from medical school.

The obligations of physicians at the beginning of their contract are compliance with the standards announced for the job, passing training courses, and providing health services to the population based on the declared services package.

At the start of the contract, physicians need to have a suitable physical space, with an area of at least 40 m², and the equipment required by the standard list. The family physician should also nominate a locum physician in case of absence, to ensure continuity of care. For part-time family physicians, a locum physician for both morning and afternoon shifts is required. However, it is preferred that a part-time family physician coordinate with another part-time colleague to provide, between them, full coverage in one place. This has been done to ensure full population access to their family physicians in all circumstances.

The introduction of a midwife or nurse to work with a family physician is carried out at the beginning of the contract by providing her license. She must have at least two years of work experience and must attend the health services package training course held by the city health centre. Interested paediatricians, internists, infectious disease, and social medicine specialists are able to serve the population with the same per-capita payment and roles defined for the family physicians. Specialist physicians who are contracted as family physicians are not allowed to refer patients to themselves (as second level physicians).

OUTLINE OF THE CONTRACT WITH PRIVATE PROVIDERS

Prior to the start of the project, all general physicians were informed of the details by the Medical Council. Introductory meetings were held in each of the province's cities, attended by the director of the provincial health insurance organization, the director of the provincial social security insurance, and the director of the PHC.

An electronic system was launched for the initial registration of the applicant physicians. Each applicant also advised the geographic location where they were to establish their own office; a number of them were already practicing family medicine, but not as family physicians.

In addition, insurance companies shared their information through their communication channels with all general practitioners.

MONITORING AND EVALUATION OF PROVIDER PERFORMANCE

Monitoring of family physician performance is done at two levels. The first level is carried out by family physicians and health experts from the comprehensive health centre in the family physician's area. The second level is implemented by the insurance organizations and the city health centre. Usually, these experts come as a team to the family physician's post. The monitoring is based on a pre-designed checklist. At the end of each monitoring, the checklist is signed by the inspector and the family physician, and a copy is delivered to the latter.

In each city, a monitoring and evaluation committee meets monthly to review the results of each physician's monitoring in the presence of representatives of insurance organizations in the city and the DHC. Every three months, a monitoring committee meeting is held at the provincial level. Representatives of each DHC are present at these meetings, and the results of the three-month monitoring of each physician are evaluated. In addition to the monthly monitoring report, the results of the family physician's medicine prescriptions are also provided by the insurance organizations at the meeting, including the percentage of injections, antibiotics, and corticosteroids prescribed.

The results of the provincial monitoring committee are presented every three months to the provincial executive committee and, after approval, are announced to insurance organizations. Each physician's three-month monitoring feedback is sent to them in the shape of a form, signed by the heads of the provincial health insurance and health centre.

In the case of family physicians who have worked very well, with the approval of the monitoring committee, the percentage per-capita payment received is increased as a reward, up to 20%. For physicians whose performance is deemed inadequate, in addition to a per-capita payment reduction, the following actions can be taken with the approval of the monitoring committee: oral warning, written warning, meeting with the physician and obtaining a written statement, discontinuing the per-capita payment, and cancelling the contract.

OUTLINE FOR THE ESSENTIAL PACKAGE OF HEALTH SERVICES (EPHS) (SERVICES EXPECTED TO BE PROVIDED BY PRIVATE PROVIDERS)

First-level health service packages are provided by the Ministry of Health and Medical Education, based on the age of the covered population, and notified to all family physicians. These age groups include neonates, children, adolescents, youth, middle-aged, elderly, and pregnant and lactating mothers.

Children (up to 6 years)

At each visit, care assessments are conducted, as detailed below, and recommendations are made and action taken.

- Neonatal care: at 3–5 days, 14–15 days, and 30–45 days
- Caring for healthy children: at 2, 4, 6, 7, 9, 12, 15, and 18 months; then annually till age 6

Integrated health care for adolescents (aged 6–18 years)

Assessments, based on clinical guidelines, are made at the age of 6, 9, 12, 15, and 18 years, emphasizing the prevention of diseases, proper education of the individual and their parents, correct and timely diagnosis and treatment of any diseases and disorders, prevention of complications and possible disabilities, treatment of any complications, timely referral to higher levels where appropriate, and follow-up as required.

Integrated youth health care (aged 18–29)

This care focuses on the prevention of diseases, based on the most common dangers during youth years, and includes proper education of the individual and their parents if appropriate, proper diagnosis and treatment of any illnesses and disorders, prevention of possible complications and disabilities, treatment of any complications, timely referral to higher levels of care, and follow-up as appropriate.

Integrated middle-aged health care (aged 30–59 years)

Care for this age group focuses on the prevention of diseases, based on the most common ailments during the middle-aged years, and includes education of the individual and their family members and community, proper diagnosis and treatment of any illnesses and disorders, prevention of possible complications and disabilities, treatment of any complications, timely referral to higher levels of care, and follow-up as appropriate.

Integrated health care for the elderly (aged 60 and older)

Care for the elderly focuses on the prevention of diseases, based on the most common problems of ageing, and includes proper education of the individual and their family members and community, proper and timely diagnosis and treatment of any diseases and disorders, prevention of possible complications and disabilities, treatment of any complications, timely referral to higher levels of care, and follow-up as appropriate.

Health care of pregnant mothers (prenatal care until after delivery)

Pre-pregnancy, pregnancy, and postpartum care play a very important role in the early diagnosis and timely and effective treatment of any complications of pregnancy and the postpartum period. This includes examining maternal and fetal health status, determining the gestational age, conducting clinical examinations and early diagnosis of risk symptoms, and assessment for conditions such as high blood pressure, anaemia, diabetes, infectious diseases, blood malformations between mother and fetus, inappropriate weight gain, and common psychiatric disorders occurring during pregnancy and the postpartum period. The aim is a pregnancy with minimal complications.

Integrated care for reproductive health

Integrated care for fertility and childbearing health includes education and services to support establishing and consolidating the family foundation and the provision of healthy fertility services to simultaneously promote overall fertility rates and maintain and promote the health of mothers and children.

Provider satisfaction

In a study of 96 urban family physicians, the overall satisfaction of physicians involved in the programme was 3.37 out of 5 (SD = 0.56).[4] The average satisfaction of the support and cooperation provided by the city health centre, insurance organizations, and specialist physicians was 3.2, 3, and 3, respectively. The family physicians' satisfaction with the collaboration and participation of the population covered was 3.25, and the health-care function of the health team was 4.5. Generally, family physicians' satisfaction in small cities was greater than in large cities.

In this study, the satisfaction of 95 health experts was evaluated as well. Satisfaction with family physicians and the cooperation and participation of the population were 4 and 3.25 out of 5, respectively.

Patient satisfaction

In a survey of 888 people in 2016, who were randomly selected in the province, 207 (23.8%) had changed their family physician once and 24 (2.8%) had changed their physicians twice or more during the past 12 months.[4] With regard to satisfaction with the services provided, 62.8% were satisfied and 37.2% were dissatisfied.

FAMILY MEDICINE TRAINING OF GENERAL PRACTITIONERS (GPS)

The training of family physicians has been conducted in two main areas. The first area deals with service packages provided to those age groups that the private sector had no previous role in providing health services to; and the second deals with prevention and the care of patients with chronic diseases such as diabetes, high blood pressure, high blood lipids, asthma, and chronic obstructive pulmonary disease (COPD), as well as depression and anxiety.

One of the most valuable experiences is team-based learning, in which family physicians in groups of three to seven review clinical guidelines, then, in subsequent sessions, use the guidelines to discuss patient management in the form of case reviews. Finally, with clinical specialists acting as coaches, family physician questions are answered and the training is complete. In a study of the educational needs of family physicians, the items listed in Table 12.1 have been identified as educational priorities. [4]

The educational programme for health experts was conducted and involved 147 hours of theory and 443 hours of practical training by the Behvarzi Education Centre in each city.

In examining the educational needs of health experts, the items listed in Table 12.2 have been identified as educational priorities.

TABLE 12.1 Educational needs of family physicians ($n=96$)

Title	Percentage
Prevention and control of high blood pressure	43.8
Prevention and control of diabetes	33.3
Diagnosis and treatment of psychiatric disorders	0
Cardiac and pulmonary resuscitation (CPR)	26
Prevention and control of overweight and obesity	25
ECG interpretation	21.9
Growth and development of children	20.8
Substance abuse and addiction treatment	18.8
Sexually transmitted diseases	18.8
Prevention and control of hyperlipidaemia	17.7
Principles of consultation	15

TABLE 12.2 Needs of health-care experts ($n=95$)

Title	Percentage
1. Pregnancy ultrasound interpretation	88.5
2. Screening of fetal abnormalities	87.5
3. Performing and interpreting ECGs	84.5
4. Preparation for physiological delivery	77.1
5. Interpretation of routine pregnancy tests	72.9
6. Sickness and hearing impairment	70.8
7. Principles of consultation	68.8
8. Life skills education	59.4
9. Familiarity with work of non-government organizations	56.3
10. High-risk pregnancy control	14.4

CHALLENGES FACING IMPLEMENTATION

During the implementation of this programme, several problems came to light:

- *Insurance companies*: A lack of equivalent funds provided by insurance organizations; differences in payment processes between insurance organizations; non-entry of individuals into the programme if covered by armed forces insurance and private bank insurance.
- *Health team*: A lack of competencies among family physicians in providing health promotion services and primary prevention; unwillingness of specialists to play their role and provide advice and feedback to family physicians; challenges for solo family physicians; a significant increase in workload after the establishment of the programme due to increased patient visits; job burnout of family physicians due to long working hours (8–12 or 16–20 hours every day); different programmes in rural areas and cities with a population less than 20,000.
- *Salaries*: Delays in monthly per-capita payments to family physicians; incomplete pay-for-performance payment system; low payments to the health experts; inadequate annual increase of per-capita tariffs over the years of implementation; fee-for-service programmes in other provinces.

- *Patient attitude*: Low awareness and cultural acceptance of family physician services among the population.
- *Referrals*: Increased demand at levels two and three for a referral form from level one; a payment system based on the number of patient visits to the second and third levels of care (fee charged for services); the absence of a contract for a number of specialists.
- Incomplete monitoring and evaluation programmes.
- *Health records*: Delay in access to efficient electronic health record software.
- Lack of planning for laboratory and imaging services.

PLAN FOR FUTURE ROLLOUT OF THIS PROGRAMME

After nearly five years of experience since the implementation of the urban family physician programme in Mazandaran province, the following initiatives are being developed in order to improve the performance:

- Applying a complete performance-based payment system
- Encouraging family physicians to work in a group instead of solo
- Raising the competencies of family physicians and health experts through education
- Using team-based training models for family physician team education
- Advocacy for access to sustainable financial resources and regular payments
- Establishment of similar family physician programmes in urban and rural areas
- Advocacy for reform in payment systems for specialist and sub-specialist physicians
- Educating the population about the benefits of receiving services from family physicians

ACKNOWLEDGEMENTS

Data and information are received from the Social Security Insurance Organization (SSIO) and the Iran Health Insurance Organization (IHIO) in Mazandaran province. The authors would like to emphasize their appreciation to the heads of both provincial insurance organizations, Dr Mohammad Khorshidi and Dr Rasoul Zafarmand respectively. The authors acknowledge Dr Ghasem Oveis and Dr Adel Tabarestani and Dr Adel Hadidi who provided invaluable information and comments regarding the monitoring and evaluation process and feedback. Special thanks to Dr Omidreza Alaei and to the team of experts who have taken care of the administrative jobs for the urban family physician programme in Mazandaran Province.

REFERENCES

1. Population and Housing Censuses. Islamic Republic of Iran: Statistical Center of Iran; 2017. *Population by Age Groups and Sex and Province*; Available from: https://www.amar.org.ir/english/Population-and-Housing-Censuses [Accessed 6 March 2018].
2. National Executive Committee of Family Physician and Referral System Program. *Instruction of Family Physician Program and Referral System in Urban Areas – Version 02*. 1st. Tehran: Ministry of Health and Medical Education; 2012: 96.
3. Aarabi M, Oveis G, Alaei O. *Urban Family Physician in Mazandaran Province*. Sary, Mazandaran (Iran): Mazandaran University of Medical Sciences and Health Services, Deputy of Public Health; 2017: 14 pages. Report No.: 3.
4. Nasrollahpour Shirvani SD, Kabir MJ, Ashrafian Amiri H, Rabiei SM, Keshavarzi A, Farzin K. *Experience of Implementing the Program of the Urban Family Physician in Iran*. 1st edition. Tehran: Iran Health Organization; 2017: 93.

CHAPTER 13

Afghanistan

Bashir Noormal, Najibullah Safi,
and Shafiqullah Hemat

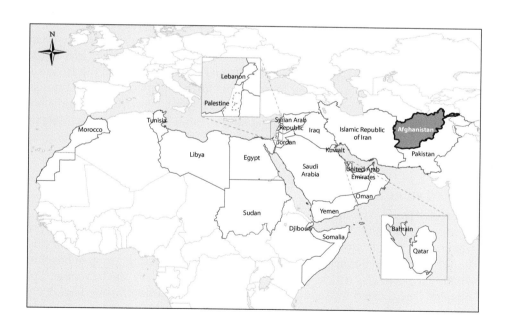

INTRODUCTION

Total number of primary health-care (PHC) facilities	2067
Number of general practitioners working in public PHC facilities	2941
Number of certified family physicians working in PHC facilities	70
Average number of family physician graduates/year	8
Number of medical schools	37 (public 9, private 28)
Number of family medicine departments in medical schools	2

Afghanistan is a landlocked country located within South Asia and Central Asia, with a population of approximately 30 million (United Nations estimate 2014), making it the forty-second most populous country in the world.[1] It is bordered by Pakistan in the south and east and Iran in the west. Turkmenistan, Uzbekistan, and Tajikistan share its northern border, while China lies in the far northeast.

As of 2015, roughly 2.7 million Afghan refugees were still living in Pakistan and Iran. In 2013, 46% of Afghanistan's population was under 15 years of age and 74% of the population lived in rural areas. The current total fertility rate in Afghanistan is 5.3 children per woman, and the infant mortality rate is 45 deaths per 1000 live births.[2] Life expectancy was 60 years in 2013.[3]

Like many of its neighbouring countries, Afghanistan has an ethnically, linguistically, and religiously diverse population. In 1999 around 79% of the country's population lived in rural areas compared to approximately 74% in 2014. The only city with over 4 million residents is its capital, Kabul. Other large cities in the country are, in order of population size, Kandahar, Herat, Mazar-i-Sharif, Kunduz, Jalalabad, Lashkar Gah, Taloqan, Khost, Sheberghan, and Ghazni. The Afghanistan population is estimated to increase to around 56 million by 2050.[4]

Afghanistan is an Islamic republic consisting of three branches, the executive, legislative, and judicial. The nation is led by the president. The National Assembly is the legislature, a bicameral body having two chambers, the House of the People (lower house) and the House of Elders (upper house). The Supreme Court is led by the Chief Justice. Afghanistan is administratively divided into 34 provinces (wilayats), with each province having its own capital and a provincial administration. The provinces are further divided into about 398 districts (woloswalies), each of which normally covers a city or a number of villages. Each district is represented by a district governor.[5]

AFGHANISTAN HEALTH SYSTEM

The Afghanistan Health System has the Basic Package of Health Services (BPHS) and the Essential Package of Hospital Services (EPHS). The BPHS provides primary care and preventive services whereas the EPHS consists of hospital-level services. District hospitals have elements of both categories of services. Besides these two packages, there is another group of hospitals called speciality/national hospitals, which are referral centres for tertiary medical care. Speciality/national hospitals are located in Kabul, provide specialized training for medical doctors, and act as referral hospitals for the provincial and regional hospitals (EPHS, 2005).[6] The service mix provided at different levels is described in Table 13.1.

A clear increase in access to health services since 2002 has taken place in Afghanistan: an estimated 87% of the population can reach a health facility within two hours using any means of transportation, up from only 9% in 2002.[7] Nevertheless, health service quality often suffers due to low staff competency and lack of supplies. Also, chronic malnutrition continues to undermine the country's future level of educational achievement and, ultimately, economic productivity. BPHS and EPHS delivery is funded and contracted through the Government of Islamic Republic

TABLE 13.1   Health services provided according to level of health facility

Coverage population	Type of service	Health facility
Not available	Assessing, diagnosing, stabilizing, treating, or referring back to a lower-level hospital	Regional hospital
200,000–500,000	In-patient care	Provincial hospital
100,000–300,000	Preventive and curative out-patient and in-patient care	District hospital
30,000–60,000	Preventive and curative (mostly out-patient) care	Comprehensive health centre
15,000–30,000	Preventive and curative (mostly out-patient) care	Basic health centre
Variable, depending the size of target villages	Preventive and selected curative (mostly out-patient) care	Mobile health centres
3000–7000	Preventive and selected curative (mostly out-patient) care	Health sub-centre
100–150 families or 1000–1500 individuals	Preventive and selected curative care	Health post

Afghanistan (GoIRA) health systems and accompanied by technical assistance to the Ministry of Public Health (MoPH) by multiple development partners. The GoIRA directs the delivery of health services, but delivery itself is accomplished largely by non-governmental organizations (NGOs), while private sector providers are an emerging resource.

Funding for the public health system comes almost exclusively from external resources. For more than 10 years, health service delivery has depended strongly on donor funds from the World Bank, United States Agency for International Development (USAID), and the European Union. Over time, the GoIRA will gradually need to become the principal provider of funds to the health sector. Donors will continue to fund delivery of the BPHS and EPHS across all 34 provinces of the country to year 2021. The provision of essential health services to the Afghan population has been a critical driver of the substantial gains in health.[8]

Vaccine campaign

To start work on creating a more self-sufficient health system, the GoIRA has developed a National Health Strategy (NHS 2016–2020).[8] This strategy has the goal to attain strengthened, expanded, efficient, and sustained performance by the health system, thus ensuring enhanced and equitable access to quality health-care services in an affordable manner, and resulting in the improved overall health and nutrition status of all populations, especially women, children, and members of vulnerable groups. The MoPH is leading the implementation of the NHS 2016–2020, with specific roles and responsibilities at different levels. The MoPH departments at both central and provincial levels develop annual action/operational plans for implementation of this strategy.

However, the Ministry of Public Health still recognizes substantial challenges to implementation of the NHS 2016–2020, including:

- Weak evidence-based policy, planning, and regulatory capacity of the MoPH at all levels
- Inadequate regulatory enforcement mechanisms, capacity, and practices
- Heavy donor dependence and high staff turnover
- Weak MoPH capacity for effective public and political advocacy
- Inadequate number of female health workers in rural areas, including the management teams of provincial public health offices (PPHOs)
- Weak coordination and collaboration among various stakeholders

Articles 52, 53, and 54 of the Afghan Constitution lay out the basic mandates and fundamental basis for health and related rights and services for the population of the country.[10]

The MoPH is the lead state institution responsible for the health of the entire population. A number of other government ministries and agencies also implement activities that either directly or indirectly impact the health of the people. Development partners, NGOs, professional associations, regulatory bodies, and the private sector also are key stakeholders in health.

To ensure rapid expansion of basic health services for under-served and badly affected populations after the collapse of the Taliban in 2001, the MoPH developed packages of basic services — the Basic Package of Health Services (BPHS) and the Essential Package of Hospital Services (EPHS). In addition, the MoPH introduced a contracting modality whereby NGOs are commissioned by the MoPH to provide the BPHS and EPHS in 31 provinces, while in three provinces the MoPH continues to provide these services. This strategic choice allowed the MoPH to focus on strengthening the governance of the health sector and the institutional development of the Ministry as a state institution. This comprehensive approach was intended to lay the foundations of a health sector that had the health of the people at its core.[11]

Out of the nearly 2600 health facilities, the majority are delivering BPHS, less than 30 are delivering EPHS, and less than 20 are delivering specialized services. Aside from the public health sector, there is a large private sector which is largely unregulated and informal. Despite past efforts, there is still a long way to go before sufficient regulations are enforced and synergies between the government and private sector are secured through effective public–private partnerships (Table 13.2).

The MoPH has 10 operating principles:

1. Country-owned and country-led development
2. Good governance, including effective transparency and accountability[12]
3. The right to health for all, especially women, children, and members of vulnerable groups
4. Gender balance
5. Leverage strengths through internal and external partnerships and coordination

TABLE 13.2 Types of health facilities[12]

Service facility type	Number
Regional and national hospital	6
Provincial hospital	28
District hospital	80
Special hospital	29
Comprehensive health centre	413
Basic health centre	849
Sub-health centre	652
Mobile health team	153
Health post	15 175

6. Effective community involvement and participation
7. Culture of evidence-based planning, decision making, results orientation, and results-based management
8. The promotion of "systems thinking" at all levels
9. A culture of togetherness and team and cross-functional work
10. Emphasis on health promotion and prevention[14]

This improved access and expansion of coverage has led to some impressive results. The infant mortality ratio (IMR) has declined from 66 deaths per 1000 live births in 2005 to 45 in 2017. During the same period, neonatal mortality has dropped from 31 to 22, under-five mortality from 87 to 55 per 1000 live births, and skilled birth attendance has increased from 14% in 2003 to more than 50% in 2017.[7]

The decline in the maternal mortality rate (MMR) also has been dramatic, falling from 1600 to 396 per 100,000 live births.[7] There has also been a significant increase in the coverage of key maternal and child health service indicators; antenatal coverage increased from 16% to 59%, the contraceptive prevalence rate rose from 10% to 23%, institutional deliveries from under 15% to 48%, and DPT3/Penta 3 coverage for children of ages 0 to 23 months increased from 30% to 58%.[2]

The MoPH also has successfully launched other interventions to strengthen health services and public health interventions, particularly training community midwives and nurses, developing information and education materials and strengthening health infrastructure. In addition to public sector efforts, private sector engagement in health, including by national NGOs, also has been increasing progressively. As the Afghanistan National Development Strategy (ANDS) 2008–2013 assessment conducted in June 2014 noted, about 88% of the targets set were achieved during the ANDS implementation period, making health the most successful sector in Afghanistan's development efforts.

The core values of the Ministry of Public Health have been highlighted in the National Health and Nutrition Policy 2012–2020, which includes: right to health, partnership and collaboration, equity, community participation and ownership, evidence-based decision making, promoting a results-oriented culture, quality, transparency, sustainability, dignity, and respect.

In order to target specific health issues, a population-based approach will be adopted for planning health promotion initiatives. Priority will be given to the most vulnerable groups including women, children, youth, internally displaced people, returnees, and nomads.

The Afghanistan Health Promotion strategy has been designed with reference to the relevant international charters and declarations (1986 Ottawa Charter of Health, 1997 Jakarta Declaration on Leading Health Promotion, the 2005 Bangkok Charter of Health Promotion).[15–17] The strategy directly relates to the Millennium Development Goals (MDGs) and the overall health and well-being of communities. The strategy aims not only to promote health, but to remove or reduce the obstacles to health inherent in Afghan social structures. It aims to adopt the following actions: implementation of health promotion activities across the whole population, not just those at risk of specific diseases, improvement of people's ability to control the factors determining their health, and integration of a mix of individual and population-level interventions from several stakeholders, which aim to improve health.

In Afghanistan, social structures and social support networks, such as family, relatives, tribes, and communities, strongly affect personal health practices and behaviour. Health promotion is the most effective tool for addressing these social determinants of health. Health promotion is emphasized in the MoPH National Health Policy (NHP) 2015–2020 as one of the most important components of the MoPH.[18] As indicated in the NHP, MoPH perceives the health system as an interaction between two systems: the system of care and the system of health promotion. Both systems are working towards the goals of good health, of being responsive to the expectations of the people of Afghanistan, and of fairness of financial contribution.

The policy of the MoPH on health promotion is to have a participatory approach in promoting and understanding the causes of ill-health, taking action, and capacity building to better address issues at the community level. This is in recognition that health promotion is one the most cost-effective strategies to improve and maintain the health of individuals, families, and communities. When people are empowered with correct knowledge on healthy habits they can make decisions about their personal and families' health that can make a difference. The Afghanistan government, along with its partners, has worked towards a significant improvement in health outcomes by rebuilding and developing a sustainable health-care system. To date, a broad range of health promotion interventions/programmes have been deployed in both rural and urban settings.[19]

Effective health promotion must actively influence the social factors determining the health of people and the range of choices available to them. It is obvious that most of the global burden of diseases and the bulk of health inequalities are caused by the social determinants of health.

Figure 13.1 indicates the contextualization of factors that determine health in Afghanistan. As mentioned earlier, social structure and social support networks such as families, relatives, tribes, and communities strongly affect personal health practices and coping skills in Afghanistan.

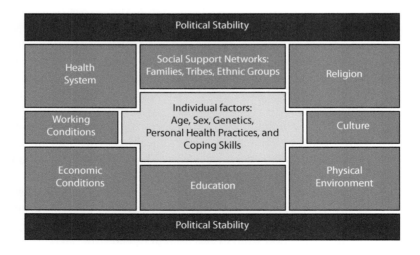

FIGURE 13.1 Factors determining health in Afghanistan.

Beliefs and health practices of the Afghans are fundamentally constructed by religion (Islam). Islam gives tremendous value to health and healthy behaviours and urges human beings to have healthy lifestyles. It must be noted that political and economic instability has historically impacted the health of Afghan population.

The MoPH is committed to promoting the health of individuals, families, and communities throughout their life course by working on social determinants of health through strengthening institutional and organizational capacity, community actions, adopting a health in all policies approach, creating supportive environments, and re-orienting health services. Health workers in addition to providing health-care services, also strive for improving family practices among the general public through interpersonal communication and counselling at health-care facilities and periodic house-to-house visits.

The MoPH is working to strengthen effective mechanisms of collaboration and coordination with public, private, national, and international organizations, as well as with civil society, for creating and supporting sustainable health promotion actions.

The MoPH is working with the Ministry of Finance (MoF) to develop a sustainable financial system using taxes on tobacco and other hazardous goods to support health promotion to ensure long-term sustainability of the health promotion programme in the country.[20]

PRIORITY HEALTH ISSUES

The targeted areas for health promotion were identified by reviewing relevant literature including policies, strategies, and through several consultative meetings with representatives of relevant ministries, donors, UN agencies, NGOs, and civil society. As result, the following targeted areas were identified for health promotion:

1. Maternal and newborn health, including family planning
2. Child health
3. Public nutrition
4. Sanitation and hygiene
5. Non-communicable diseases
6. Communicable diseases
7. Disability, injury prevention, and road safety
8. Environmental health
9. Population growth
10. Mental health
11. Occupational health
12. Substance abuse
13. Pharmaceutical affairs

MoPH Strategic Directions are:

Strategic Direction 1: Healthy Public Policy/Health in All Policies

The MoPH works with other sectors to raise awareness of the health consequences of their policies and to encourage accepting responsibilities for health. The MoPH also advocates for a legislative setting to ensure safer and better goods and services, increase prices and controls on the marketing of unhealthy products, incentives for healthy behaviour, and a less hazardous environment.

Strategic Direction 2: Supportive Environment

The MoPH works with other sectors to systematically assess the health impact of a rapidly changing environment, with increased urbanization, use of technology and growing food, beverage, and tobacco industries, and takes steps to minimize the negative impact on health. The MoPH also engages with communities to promote cultural and social norms towards improving public health and tolerance for programmes that empower women to improve their own and their children's health.

Strategic Direction 3: Community Actions

The MoPH works to enable communities and their leaders to take ownership and control of their population's health and wellbeing by being engaged in setting priorities, making decisions, planning and implementing strategies.[7]

Strategic Direction 4: Develop Personal Skills

The MoPH works to enable individuals and families to take ownership and control of their health through a comprehensive media and face-to-face communication approach for provision of information, education for health, and enhancing life skills to support personal and social development.

Pharmacist with patient

Strategic Direction 5: Reorient Health Services

The MoPH works with health professionals and institutions, and various government departments, towards developing a health-care system which promotes health beyond its traditional responsibility for the provision of clinical and curative services, increases screening and preventive services, assesses health status and risk factors at the population level, and assigns responsibilities for health of entire populations.

Strategic Direction 6: Capacity Building

The MoPH strives to enhance institutional and organizational capacity for health promotion at all levels of the MoPH.

Strategic Direction 7: Coordination and Partnership

The various departments of the MoPH work closely to make sure that work plans and campaigns are developed in a consultative manner. The MoPH established strategic partnerships in planning, monitoring, and strengthening inter-sector health promotion programmes with key ministries including Ministry of Education, Ministry of

Higher Education, Ministry of Labour, Social Affairs, Martyrs and Disabled, Ministry of Agriculture, Livestock and Irrigation, Ministry of Women Affairs, Ministry of Hajj and Religious Affairs, Ministry of Information and Culture, and Ministry of Rural Rehabilitation and Development.

AFGHANISTAN'S EXPERIENCE IN ADDRESSING THE SHORTAGE OF FEMALE HEALTH-CARE PROVIDERS

Afghanistan has a critical shortage of health workers, the second lowest health workforce density, and the highest level of rural residing population in the Eastern Mediterranean Region (EMR) (National HRH Strategy 2013–2020). In Afghanistan, the ongoing insecurity, in addition to geographic, economic, social, and cultural barriers have contributed to the shortage of health workers, particularly in rural and remote areas accompanied with shortage of female health workers, which is necessary to achieve UHC and improve health.

To address its critical shortage, gender and geographic imbalances, Afghanistan implemented a bundle of interventions to ensure recruitment and retention in rural and remote areas. Afghanistan established training institutions in remote provinces and introduced new cadres such as community health workers, community midwives and community health nurses, strategically recruited and deployed to rural areas, to deliver the basic package of health services and strengthen primary care delivery. Other interventions included financial incentives (hardship allowance) and addressing personal and environmental factors through cultural and gender-appropriate measures. Through these interventions, Afghanistan has made progress towards a gender-balanced workforce with increased availability of health-care providers in rural areas. These successes surely have strong implications on improving service delivery and health outcomes.

The challenges of attraction, recruitment, and retention of the health workforce in rural and remote areas are not unique to Afghanistan (Table 13.2).[21]

TABLE 13.2 Categories of interventions used to improve attraction, recruitment, and retention of health workers in remote and rural areas, globally, and in Afghanistan

Category of intervention	Examples from the global recommendations	Examples in Afghanistan
Education	• Students from rural background • Health professional schools outside of major cities • Clinical rotations in rural areas • Curricula that reflects rural health issues • Continuous professional development for rural health workers	• Recruiting students from rural backgrounds (through CME, CHNE) • Increasing more training institutes in remote provinces (through IHS/CME) • National midwifery accreditation programme (tailored to rural deployment) • CHW/CHN/CM curricula are based on rural health issues • Continuous professional development (refresher courses for CHW) • Consideration of preferential admission to meet quotas and rural rotations
Regulation	• Enhanced scope of practice • Different types of health workers • Compulsory service • Subsidized education for return of service	• Introducing new cadres • Enhancing scope of practice, especially for CHN, CM

(Continued)

TABLE 13.2 (CONTINUED)   Categories of interventions used to improve attraction, recruitment, and retention of health workers in remote and rural areas, globally, and in Afghanistan

Category of intervention	Examples from the global recommendations	Examples in Afghanistan
Financial	• Appropriate financial incentives	• Hardship allowances (double for women in rural care)
Professional/ Personal	• Better living conditions • Safe and supporting working environment • Outreach support • Career development programmes • Professional networks • Public recognition	• Providing opportunities to male family members • Public recognition measures • Afghan Midwifery Association (CPD, network)

CHALLENGES

Afghanistan faces the serious challenges of a fragile political environment, continued threats from insurgencies and local power holders, economic downturn, diminishing aid flows, widespread corruption, and regional relationships that continue to exacerbate conflict. These complex factors and associated dynamics have had significant adverse impacts on state effectiveness and all aspects of Afghanistan's development, including in the health sector.

One of the critical overarching challenges facing Afghanistan's health sector is the country's insecurity. It results in many parts of the country being inaccessible to health services and puts health workers at high risk of being the victims of crimes and acts of terrorism. This often makes it impossible for rural inhabitants to access health services without walking long distances.

Afghanistan has the highest total fertility rate in Asia, at 5.3 children born/woman; its population is now growing by almost 1 million people annually.[2,22] The high rate of population growth results in increased demand for health. The combination of rapidly increasing demand for health services, decreasing foreign aid, and a slowing economy represent major challenges to scaling up health services and their sustainability.

In general, Afghanistan's "hard infrastructure", including roads and reliable supplies of water and power, is inadequate to support expanded and effective health service delivery and access. There is a nationwide shortage of qualified health workers in the public sector, particularly female medical personnel. The lack of female providers hinders the efforts of the MoPH to reduce maternal and child mortality, especially in rural areas. In addition to an unbalanced gender composition, the health workforce also is poorly distributed around the country and overly concentrated in large urban areas. Due to lack of regulations, different categories of health workers graduating from private education institutes are of a low standard. Poor personnel management, operational policies and procedures result in inequitable pay scales, urban concentration of staff, favouritism, low morale, and low retention rates. The referral system is not functioning well, and district hospitals are underutilized, leading to wasteful inefficiencies in service provision while overburdening facilities at higher levels.

The health status of maternal, newborn, and child health (MNCH) in Afghanistan is among the worst in the world. Achieving a reduction of child and maternal mortality are two of the top national health priorities for Afghanistan (National Health Policy 2005–2009 and National Health Strategy 2005–2006) and the improvement of children and mothers' survival has thus been highlighted as one of the most pressing goals of all major national policy documents, including the Afghanistan Millennium Development Goals Country Report 2005-Vision

2020.[20,23] Afghanistan's infant mortality rate is 74 per 1000 live births and the under-five mortality rate is 102 per 1000 live births.[7] Acute respiratory infections, mainly pneumonia, account for almost a quarter (23%) of all under-five deaths. Only 18% of children aged 12 to 23 months have received the full series of eight recommended vaccinations, while 15% have never been vaccinated at all.[22]

Malnutrition is a serious problem in Afghanistan. According to a recent report by UNICEF, 59% of children in Afghanistan suffer from childhood stunting, making it the worst in the world. In addition to stunting, millions of children suffer from other forms of malnutrition, such as low birth weight, underweight, vitamin A and iodine deficiency, and anaemia. Despite a significant reduction in maternal mortality during the last decade, it still remains very high at 327 maternal deaths per 100,000 live births.[24] While approximately 60% of women received antenatal care during pregnancy from a skilled birth attendant, only 16% of women attend all four recommended visits. Only one-third of women deliver with the assistance of health personnel and less than a quarter of women receive postnatal care from a medically trained professional in the 48 hours following birth.[7] Despite relatively good awareness of contraceptives among women (91% of women report hearing about any contraceptive method), only 22% of women are using some form of family planning method.

The three major causes of death in Afghanistan are non-communicable diseases, infections, and injuries. About 35% of deaths in Afghanistan are due to non-communicable diseases (NCDs), such as cardiovascular disease, cancer, and diabetes. Non-communicable diseases presently result in 37% of all female deaths of which 18% are due to cardiovascular disease.[24] Obesity, a major risk factor for NCDs, is now prevalent in Kabul. As the Afghan economy develops and populations become more urban, the burden of NCDs could become enormous due to increasing rates of obesity and tobacco use that usually accompany such development.[7]

Article 54 of the Constitution of Afghanistan (2004) stipulates that "family is the fundamental unit of society and is protected by the state. The state shall adopt necessary measures to ensure (the) physical and psychological wellbeing of family, especially of child and mother". In addition, article 22 states that "any kind of discrimination between and privilege among the citizens of Afghanistan is prohibited. The citizens of Afghanistan have equal rights and duties, as per the law".[2]

The new strategy will inform the future direction and focus for the MoPH. Additionally, it will provide a resource and guide for relevant partners, statutory and non-statutory, concerned with promoting positive health in the new millennium. The National Health Promotion Strategy will provide a platform to foster an inter-sector approach for addressing the major determinants of health. This National Health Promotion Strategy for Afghanistan provides the strategic direction to contribute to this global health improvement agenda.

Programmes promoting healthy lifestyles and prevention are underfunded. The problem is complicated by the proportional rise in non-communicable diseases as major causes of morbidity and mortality. Moreover, there is also a serious lack of quality tertiary health services; combined with a lack of trust by citizens in public sector health services, which is resulting in significant medical tourism to countries in the region.[25] The lack of routine information readily available through functioning health management information systems negatively affects drug supply-chain performance and quality control, and also adversely affects a variety of other critical MoPH functions.

Health expenditures in the country are tilted towards out-of-pocket spending by families; they account for 74% of all spending. High outlays mean that low-income families are especially vulnerable to catastrophic health expenditures perpetuating the poverty cycle.

REFERENCES

1. Central Statistics Organization (CSO), *Estimated Population of Afghanistan* 2012–13.
2. Central Statistics Organization (CSO), Ministry of Public Health (MoPH), and ICF. *Afghanistan Demographic and Health Survey 2015*. Kabul, Afghanistan, and Rockville, Maryland, USA. 2017.
3. World Health Organization (WHO), *Life expectancy at birth m/f (years) 59/61*. 2013.
4. Population Pyramids of the World from 1950 to 2100. Available from: https://www.populationpyramid.net/afghanistan/2050/ [Accessed 29 January 2018].
5. Afghanistan Online. Available from: http://www.afghan-web.com/politics/government.html [Accessed 29 January 2018]
6. Essential Package of Health Services for Afghanistan, 2005.
7. Central Statistics Organization. *National Risk and Vulnerability Assessment 2011–12. Afghanistan Living Condition Survey*. Kabul, CSO. 2012.
8. Afghan Public Health Institute, Ministry of Public Health (APHI/MoPH), Central Statistics Organization (CSO), ICF Macro, Indian Institute of Health Management Research, (IIHMR), and World Health Organization Regional Office for the Eastern Mediterranean (WHO/EMRO). *Afghanistan Mortality Survey 2010*. 2011. Available from: https://dhsprogram.com/pubs/pdf/FR248/FR248.pdf [Accessed 29 January 2018].
9. National Health and Nutrition Policy 2012–2020. *Islamic Republic of Afghanistan Ministry of Public Health National*. September 2012.
10. Islamic Republic of Afghanistan. *The Constitution of Afghanistan*, (Ratified). Kabul, Afghanistan 2004.
11. Ministry of Public Health. *Interim Health Strategy 2002–2004*. Available from: http://moph.gov.af/Content/Media/Documents/Monitoring-Evaluation-Policy-Strategy2912201016288921.pdf [Accessed 29 January 2018].
12. Ministry of Public Health, *Health Management Information System (HMIS) data*. 2014.
13. Ministry of Public Health. *Statement on Good Governance of the Health Sector, April 2015 and the Ministry of Public Health Briefing Note on Accountability*, June 2015.
14. Ministry of Public Health. *Afghanistan Health Indicators Fact Sheet*. 2014. Available from: http://moph.gov.af/Content/Media/Documents/AfghanistanHealthIndicatorsFactsheetFeb201461220141026165 1553325325.pdf [Accessed 31 January 2018].
15. World Health Organization. *Ottawa charter for health promotion: First international conference on health promotion*. Ottawa. 1986. Available from: http://www.who.int/healthpromotion/conferences/previous/ottawa/en/ [Accessed 31 January 2018].
16. World Health Organization. *Jakarta declaration on leading health promotion*. Jakarta. 1997. Available from: http://www.who.int/healthpromotion/conferences/previous/jakarta/declaration/en/ [Accessed 31 January 2018].
17. Ministry of Public Health. *Strategic plan for the ministry of public health 2011-2015*. Kabul.2011. Available from: http://moph.gov.af/en/Documents?DID=144 [Accessed 29 January 2018].
18. Ministry of Public Health. *National Health Policy 2015–2020*. Kabul. 2015. Available from: http://moph.gov.af/Content/files/National%20health%20policy%202015-2020.pdf [Accessed 29 January 2018].
19. World Health Organization. Bangkok charter of health promotion. Bangkok, 2005
20. Ministry of Public Health. *National Health Policy 2005–2009: A policy and strategy to accelerate implementation*. Kabul, 2005.
21. WHO | Increasing access to health workers in remote and rural areas through improved retention." *WHO*, http://www.who.int/hrh/retention/guidelines/en/ [Accessed 16 December 2017].
22. World Bank. *Afghanistan Development Indicators*. Washington, DC. 2016. Available from: http://databank.worldbank.org/data/reports.aspx?source=2&country=AFG&series=&period [Accessed 29 January 2018].
23. Central Statistics Organisation (CSO) and UNICEF. *Afghanistan Multiple Indicator Cluster Survey 2010–2011: Final Report*. Kabul. CSO and UNICEF. 2012.
24. Afghanistan Mortality Survey 2010. Available from: https://dhsprogram.com/pubs/pdf/FR248/FR248.pdf [Accessed 29 January 2018].
25. Ministry of Public Health. Ministry of Public Health sector review report. 2015.

CHAPTER 14

Bahrain

Faisal Abdullatif Alnasir and Adel Al-Sayyad

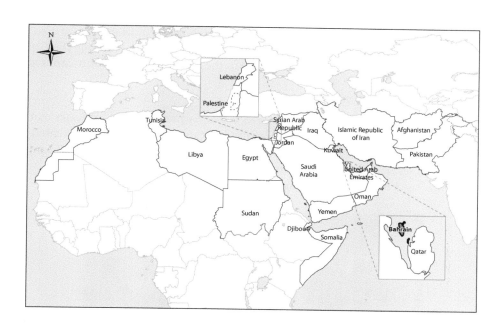

Total number of PHC facilities	28
Number of general practitioners working in public PHC facilities	98
Number of certified family physicians working in PHC facilities	228
Average number of family physician graduates/year	22
Number of medical schools	2
Number of family medicine departments	1

INTRODUCTION

The Kingdom of Bahrain is an island in the heart of the Arabian Gulf with a land area of 777 square km and a total population of around 1,423,726 Bahrainis and residents.[1,2] The word Bahrain in Arabic means "two seas", as in ancient times it was believed that under the salty water of the sea there are streams of fresh water. Over 4000 years ago, the country was considered the most important commercial crossroads in the Gulf region. Now its main income is from oil and petrochemicals, as well as from other sources such as manufacturing aluminium, provision of dry dock for repair and maintenance of supertankers, banking, telecommunication, and commercial services. Bahrain was the first Gulf country where oil was discovered during 1932 and its annual real GDP growth ranged between 2.1% and 8.3% over the period.[3] These factors, along with its geographical location, have attracted many multinational firms to be based in Bahrain while running their businesses in the Gulf region.[4,5]

For a long time, Bahrain has been well known in the region for its excellent health and education systems with an adult literacy rate of 87.7% and good health indicators.[4,6,7] It also was the first country in the region to start both these services. It is reported that among the Gulf countries, the health services in Bahrain have been one of the most advanced health-care systems.[6]

HEALTH SERVICES

The first clinic in Bahrain was established in 1888 by Mr Samuel Zwemer, an American scholar and medical student who frequently stopped over in Bahrain. On Dec 7, 1882, he rented a room, which led to the opening of a medical dispensary in the old Souk of Bahrain in 1883, igniting the vision of the health services that led to the foundation in 1902 of the first hospital, "the American Mission Hospital", as a non-profit health-care institution.[8]

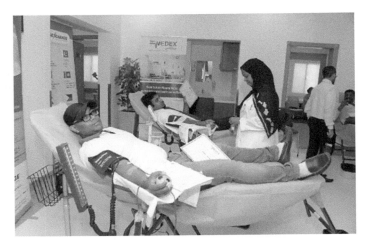

PHC facility in Bahrain

In 1960, the government decided to launch its health service to be available and free for all the people living on the island, with a system of primary health-care centres and modern hospital facilities.[1] According to the Ministry of Health, Bahrain has adopted a "Health for All" policy since 1979 through many governmental hospitals and around 26 primary health-care centres and three clinics that are distributed all over the country.

The country has one of the highest levels of health expenditure and is also among the healthiest nations in the Gulf. Bahrain's government allocated 8% of its over-all spending towards healthcare in the 2015 budgets. As of 2015, there were more than 4672 people working in the private health-care sector and 9685 in the public health-care sector, 79.1% of which are Bahraini nationals.[9,10]

Bahrain fulfilled the United Nation's Millennium Development Goals (MDGs) in the health sector five years before the agreed schedule of 2015.[6] The life expectancy rate in the Kingdom had significantly increased, reaching 77.2 years in 2015, compared to 73.4 years in 2000.[10] This has led to an increase in the population of elderly people who have more health-care needs.[11] Worldwide health services are becoming complex and expensive and the number of people is rising, especially the older population. This is particularly the case in the Eastern Mediterranean Region where it has put much pressure and constraints on certain countries and limited the provision of universal health coverage.[11] Non-communicable diseases (NCDs), which include hypertension, dyslipidae-mia, diabetes, chronic respiratory diseases, cardiovascular diseases, and cancer, are becoming a serious threat to the overall health system in the countries of the Eastern Mediterranean Region (EMR) including Bahrain. NCDs are considered the principal cause of death and their compli-cations pose an economic burden on the country as a result of high treatment expenditure due to prolonged periods of treatment and the negative impact of ill-health on the productivity of individuals, which adversely affects the progress of society. Another serious problem in Bahrain is obesity. In the year 2000, it was reported that among children 29.9% of boys and 42.4% of girls were overweight in Bahrain.[12–17] The country also has one of the highest prevalence rate of dia-betes in the world (fifth), with diabetes affecting more than 15% of the Bahraini population and accounting for 5% of all deaths.

The Ministry of Health has adopted a strategy to sustain the population's health through con-tinuous health promotion and prevention programmes. Improving the health of the population has been a national priority to be accomplished through the ministry's efforts in enhancing the capacity of primary care services. The goal is not only to provide curative services but also to promote health and increase the awareness of people about the benefits of healthy lifestyle habits, through a greater focus on health screening programmes and the development and enforcement of public policies.[9] Therefore, Family Medicine, with its major role in prevention, health promo-tion, and patient-centred care, has been advocated to achieve these goals.[12–14]

THE NUMBER OF MEDICAL SCHOOLS AND FAMILY MEDICINE DEPARTMENTS

Bahrain has two medical colleges: the College of Medicine and Medical Sciences of the Arabian Gulf University, and the Royal College of Surgeons in Ireland, Bahrain. In addition, there is a College of Health Sciences at Bahrain University that has bachelor programmes for nursing and other allied health specialties.[6] Each of those medical schools has a department for family and community medicine (total of two in the country) that oversees the training of medical stu-dents in the public health sector. However, the Arabian Gulf University has developed extensive training programmes in family medicine that is being provided for medical students starting from year two until year five of medical studies.[15,16] The Ministry of Health has a large division of primary health care which includes family medicine and primary health-care services, and another department for public health.

A PHC facility

NUMBER OF FAMILY PHYSICIANS

According to 2015 statistics, the total number of medical doctors working in the Ministry of Health is 1270 of whom 82% are Bahraini nationals. Of these doctors, 445 are working in primary health-care centres, including 304 (68%) family physicians, who have graduated from the nation's Family Medicine residency programme.[10]

PRIMARY HEALTH CARE

Family Medicine and Primary Health Care services are being provided through 26 health centres and three clinics in Bahrain. Initially, the Health Centres were classified into three categories: A, B, and C that depends on the total population served by these centres within a certain geographic area. Type "A" serves around 35,000 people, type "B" serves from 15,000 to 25,000, and type "C" serves populations of less than 15,000 people. All the health centres are distributed within the four governorates of the country. Most of the essential facilities and services, including family medicine, are available within these health centres. In each specific health centre, only people within its geographical distribution are registered and people are not permitted to consult other health centres without a referral. The curative and preventive services that are provided by the centres are under the direct supervision of family physicians. More often, each family is assigned to a specific doctor (i.e. their own family physician). Up until one year ago, there was a family folder for each family that contained most of the information and the progress notes pertaining to each family member. However, recently electronic medical records (I-Seha) were introduced and within I-Seha the patient's information is saved to the server and can be shared, with permission, by different sections of the health system such as secondary care, tertiary care, and other health facilities.

Preventive services include maternal and child health services, such as antenatal services, periodic child screening, immunization, postnatal and post-abortion services, family planning, periodic women checkups, premarital services, and ultrasound examination for pregnant women. In addition, oral health services by a dental hygienist are provided and services include various preventive programmes like fissure sealant, fluoride application, educational activities, maternal and child dental services, and oral health services for people with diabetes, the elderly and other clients with special needs. Other supportive services also are available in certain health centres including physiotherapy and social services. Health promotion services are provided via community participation and health education by health promotion specialists.[17]

In addition to pharmacy and laboratory departments, large health centres have various other sections such as nursing stations, minor theatre, emergency room, community health services, specialized clinics for hypertension and diabetes, X-ray and ultrasound facilities, and dental clinics for general dental and ortho-dental services.

Patients can consult their doctors either by appointment or walk-in. Usually, the consultation for each patient runs around seven minutes and for investigations, patients may be referred to the laboratory or the X-ray departments where their request is electronically sent or they may go to the nursing room for further procedures including minor surgeries. On discharge, the patient may approach the pharmacy to receive their prescribed medications. Family physicians embrace the concept of continuous medical care which is a strategy that is being implemented in all the health centres. Hence, the family members are mostly seen by the same doctor whenever they attend for follow-up.

The primary health-care service is provided free of charge for Bahrainis and for a fee for expatriates if they are not insured. Within primary health care there is a good referral system for secondary care, should the patient need further investigation, treatment, or a second opinion. Later all the information is fed back to the referring doctor. Pregnant women are followed up regularly in the antenatal clinic by their family physicians. If they were at risk or developed complications, they will be referred to the obstetric clinic/ward in a hospital. After delivery, both the woman and her baby are referred back to the health centre for postnatal checkups, and the baby is referred to the well-baby clinic for follow-up and to receive vaccinations.

FAMILY PRACTICE RESIDENCY PROGRAM

The family medicine programme started in 1979, which was a milestone in health sector improvement. All credit goes to the courageous decision that was taken by a politician who was a strong believer and advocate for family medicine, former Minister of Health, Dr Ali Fakhroo, who had a vision for the health of the nation which proved to be the right one for the country. He believed in family medicine and thought that without it the health of the nation would be compromised. Therefore, the Family Practice Residency Programme (FPRP) was established to train family physicians. The training programme was initially for three years and later was changed to four years. It was founded in joint collaboration with the American University of Beirut and later in affiliation with the Irish College of General Practitioners and The Royal College of Surgeons in Ireland. The first batch of five doctors to join the programme graduated in 1983, and thereafter the intake capacity has increased to more than 18 candidates per annum. To join the programme, candidates must go through a complex selection process which requires critical assessment of their academic and personal characteristics via testing and interview.

During the first two months of the programme, residents attend a structured foundation course to orient them about the concepts of family and community medicine. Within the first three years, residents spend a portion of their time in the Health Centre while most of their training is carried out in various departments of the secondary care hospital. In the fourth year, the residents are trained fully in a primary health-care centre while being mentored under direct supervision of a tutor family physician. Also during this year, they take block courses in occupational health, environmental hazards, sexual health, therapeutics, health-care management, advanced medical ethics, dental health, common skin problems, and advance life support training. In order to pass from one stage to the other, the residents are assessed and evaluated regularly and if they are successful they can be promoted. Also during the course, the candidate is obliged to conduct a research project which is an integral part of the Community Medicine curriculum.

The research outcome is evaluated by a team of experts and the residents are encouraged to publish the results in a peer-reviewed journal. At the end of the fourth year, the candidate must pass a final written, clinical, and oral examination and those who are successful are allowed to sit for the Arab Board of Health specialty examination to be recognized as a certified family physician. Graduate family physicians are deployed to work in Bahrain's primary health-care centres while a few are selected to be future faculty in the residency programme.[18]

CHALLENGES

Although Bahrain was the first country in the Gulf region to start its residency programme in family medicine and to establish primary health-care services for its population, it faces many challenges that may prevent it from applying a full-fledged family medicine service. One of the most important obstacles is the shortage of family doctors produced to date, which is far less than is needed. The country with its present population requires 696 well-trained family doctors, while the available workforce is nearly half of that, making a family doctor to population ratio of 1 to 3580 which is far less than optimal. The second serious challenge, which is also related to the shortage of family physicians, is that the fully qualified family doctors are overloaded with patients during their day to day practice. Therefore, this does not allow the time required to implement ideal family medicine practice due to the shortage of time. All of these factors ultimately play a major role on the quality of health service provided and this may compromise the health of the nation as health promotion and prevention are as important as curative medicine.

RECOMMENDED ACTIONS

To overcome those challenges, a firm strategy must be adopted by policy makers that entails the following:

- The government should have a clear strategy of considering family medicine and primary health care as the foundation of the health system in the country.
- There should be an increase in the health-care budget which is allocated to the primary health-care services compared to the budget allocated to secondary and tertiary care services.
- Moreover, a brave decision ought to be taken to increase the number of specialized family physicians by increasing the number of residency programmes to more than one and by increasing the intake capacity of the existing programme to more than thirty doctors per year. The current production rate of 16 new family doctors graduating each year means it will take at least 22 years to produce the number of family physicians the country needs.

LESSON TO LEARN

Bahrain's experience in developing primary health care and family medicine has been proven to be appropriate and rewarding. Many health indicators have improved since the introduction of these services. It was noted from several examples from neighbouring countries that their health policies and decisions taken were inappropriate because they had invested tremendously in establishing specialized and sub-specialized secondary and tertiary care centres.

CONCLUSION

Family medicine is not only the medical discipline that provides care at a primary care level, but it encompasses the breadth of medical practice. It is the medical discipline that takes into consideration the whole family as one unit, providing them with holistic care rather than disease-centred care. Moreover, it looks after people of both genders and all ages from birth till death. Family medicine does not only manage problems, but it also investigates to detect those factors that affect the wellbeing of the patient, and other family members, be they medical, psychological, social, or economic. It is well known that all those factors interact when illness happens. It is the duty of the family doctor to be aware of them to help their patients and to prevent the development of related complications. It is not only organisms that are contagious, but harmful psycho-social problems can also spread to affect other family members while interacting with their beloved sick family member.

In order to be vigilant, one of the cornerstones of family medicine is the provision of continuous care. Family medicine without continuity of care would not be considered as family medicine, rather it would be just an incidental type of care which is removed from the concept of family medicine. Person-centred care, rather than disease-centred care, is another important element in family medicine. A study conducted in the Eastern Mediterranean region in 2012 indicated the importance of the person-centred approach stating that, "A well planned and evidence-based approach is the only way forward to ensure universal access to all populations in the Eastern Mediterranean Region. Provision of health-care services through a well-defined health system with a prime focus on a primary care model delivered by trained family doctors is the single most appropriate step to achieve health for all".[19]

Since the specialty of Family Medicine is growing rapidly across the Eastern Mediterranean region, there is also a need to develop leadership capabilities within family physicians in line with today's fast-moving changes in health care. This will also allow family medicine leaders to obtain due recognition in the health-care delivery system.[20]

Finally, family medicine is the branch of medicine that provides primary, continuous, regular, person-centred care for all people, in a way that no other branch of medicine can do.

NOTES

1. About Bahrain. Available from: http://www.encyclopedia.com/places/asia/arabian-peninsula-political geography/Bahrain #HEALTH [Accessed 22 September 2018].
2. Bahrain Open Data portal, www.data.gov.bh [Accessed 22 September 2018].
3. History of Bahrain. http://www.bahrain.com/en/About-Bahrain/Pages/History.aspx#. WfrRljtx3cs [Accessed 22 September 2018].
4. Health Profile System Bahrain, EMRO, 2007, Regional Health Systems Observatory. who.int/medicin edocs/documents/s17291e/s17291e.pdf [Accessed 22 September 2018].
5. Ministry of Information. http://www.mia.gov.bh/en/Kingdom-of-Bahrain/Pages/General_ Data. Aspx [Accessed 22 September 2018].
6. Bahrain Health Care. http://www.bahrain.com/en/bi/key-investment-sectors/Pages/Healthcare. aspx#. WfrUAztx3cs [Accessed 22 September 2018].
7. Education and Health, Ministry of Information. http://www.mia.gov.bh/en/Kingdom-of-Bahrain/P ages/Education-and-Health-Services.aspx [Accessed 22 September 2018].
8. History of American Mission Hospital. http://www.amh.org.bh/history/ [Accessed 22 September 2018].
9. Health Improvement Strategy 2015–2018. Ministry of health, www.moh.gov.bh/Content/Files/Health _Improvement_Strategy(2015-2018).pdf [Accessed 22 September 2018].
10. Ministry of Health statistics 2015. https://www.moh.gov.bh/Content/Files/Publications/statistics/HS20 15/hs2015_e.htm [Accessed 22 September 2018].
11. Alnasir Faisal "Ageing and Pattern of Population Changes in the Developing Countries". *The Middle East Journal of Age & Aging*. 2015: 12:2; 26–32.

12. W. Qidwai, K. Nanji, T.A.M. Khoja, S. Rawaf, N.Y. AlKurashi, F. Alnasir, et al. Health promotion, disease prevention and periodic health checks: Perceptions and practice among family physicians in Eastern Mediterranean Region. *Middle East Journal of Family Medicine.* 2015; 5; 44–51.

13. W. Qidwai, K. Nanji, T.A.M. Khoja, S. Rawaf, N.Y. AlKurashi, F. Alnasir, et al. Barriers, challenges and way forward for implementation of person-centered care model of patient and physician consultation: A survey of patients' perspective from Eastern Mediterranean Countries. *Middle East Journal of Family Medicine.* 2015; 3; 4–11.

14. W. Qidwai, K. Nanji, T.A.M. Khoja, S. Rawaf, N.Y. Al Kurashi, F. Alnasir, et al. Are we ready for a person-centered care model for patient-physician consultation? A survey from family physicians and their patients of East Mediterranean Region. *European Journal of Person Centered Medicine.* 2013: 2.

15. F.A. Alnasir and A.A.-K. Jaradat. The effect of training in primary health care centers on medical students' clinical skills. *ISRN Family Medicine.* 2013; Vol 2013, http://dx.doi.org/10.5402/2013/403181 [Accessed 22 September 2018].

16. F. Alnasir and A. Jaradat. Patient-centered care; physicians' view of obstacles against and ideas for implementation. *International Journal of Medical Research & Health Sciences.* 2016: 5, 4:161–168.

17. Ministry of Health. https://www.moh.gov.bh/Services/PrimaryHealthCare [Accessed 22 September 2018].

18. Family Medicine Residency Program. Ministry of Health. https://familymedicine.moh.gov.bh/SelectionProcess.aspx [Accessed 22 September 2018].

19. W. Qidwai, T. Ashfaq, T.A.M. Khoja, S. Rawaf, N. Kurashi, F. Alnasir, et al. Access to person-centered care: A perspective on status, barriers, opportunities, and challenges from the Eastern Mediterranean Region. *Middle East Journal of Family Medicine.* 2012: 6; 4–13.

20. S. Rawaf, W. Qidwai, T.A.M. Khoja, K. Nanji, N.Y. Kurashi, F. Alnasir, et al. New leadership model for family physicians in the Eastern Mediterranean Region: A pilot study across selected Countries. *Journal of Family Medicine.* 2017: 2; 1–8.

CHAPTER 15

Djibouti

Abdoulaye Konate

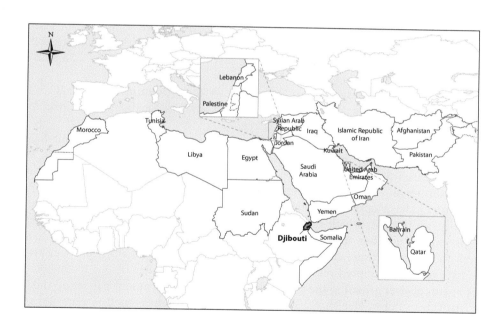

Total number of primary health-care facilities	71
Number of general practitioners working in public primary health-care institutions	51
Number of certified family doctors working in primary health-care institutions	0
Average number of family medicine graduates per year	0
Number of medical schools	1
Number of family medicine departments	0

INTRODUCTION

After gaining independence in 1977, the Republic of Djibouti made a choice in terms of health policy by joining the 1978 Declaration of Alma-Ata in 1980 with the aim of developing primary health care (PHC) and health for all. Subsequently, many international commitments have been made in the field of health. Various laws have also been enacted and documents have been drafted, particularly in relation to PHC.

One such example is Law no. 48/AN/99/4ème L, dating from 3 July 1999, on guidelines for national health policy. This law is in line with the 1978 Declaration of Alma-Ata adopted by the Republic of Djibouti. The priorities of the national health policy in chapter eight of this law are the availability and affordability of medicines, promoting prevention, and hygiene. Decree no. 2007 0155/PR/MS on the health map outlines the organization and operations of the health system based on the district health approach and the PHC strategy.

In 2002, the Strategic Health Development Framework (10-year development plan) was drawn up and approved for the period 2002–2011. At the end of the first five-year plan (for 2002–2006), the Ministry of Health (MoH) published the 2008–2012 National Health Development Plan. The 2013–2017 National Health Development Plan has just ended, and the 2018–2022 plan is being finalized.

In 2014, the MoH developed a National Strategy for Strengthening PHC. In 2015, Djibouti launched the Campaign on Accelerated Reduction of Maternal, Newborn, and Child Mortality in Africa (CARMMA).

In order to meet the population's PHC needs, the government organized public health care using a pyramid structure, with 61 health facilities: 14 health centres in urban areas, 39 health posts in rural areas, 5 university hospitals, and 3 centres specialized in maternal and neonatal care, as well as tuberculosis (TB) treatment.[1]

The government has stepped up efforts to increase the number of primary health-care facilities, especially health posts which rose from 22 in 2004 to 38 in 2016, a 73% increase. During the same period, the number of health centres rose from 8 to 15, an increase of 88%. In addition to the semi-public sector, there are 10 primary health-care facilities. Family practice and family medicine have not been adopted yet for implementation in Djibouti.

With the aim of strengthening the preventive sector, the government has set up the Djibouti National Institute of Public Health, facilities for priority health areas such as maternal and child health, immunization, malaria, TB, and human immunodeficiency virus (HIV), in addition to providing curative care.

All these government initiatives have helped to improve the PHC situation in Djibouti, although further efforts need to be made to reduce the burden of disease on the population.

Maternal and child health has seen an improvement, with the number of maternal deaths per 100,000 live births decreasing from 740 in 1996 to 383 in 2012, a reduction of almost 50%. The main causes of maternal morbidity and mortality are haemorrhage, septic shock, and eclampsia. The improvement in maternal health is highlighted in Figure 15.1, shown by an increase in the number of births assisted by qualified personnel.

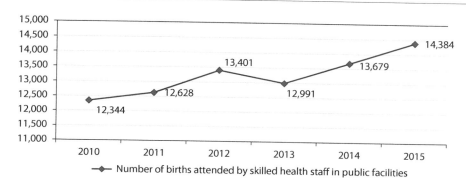

FIGURE 15.1 Number of births assisted by qualified personnel between 2010 and 2015. (*Source*: Statistical Yearbooks 2002 to 2015, routine data.)

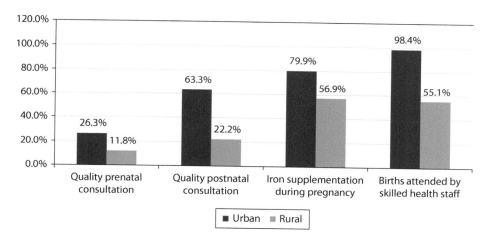

FIGURE 15.2 Coverage rate of main maternal health services. (*Source*: PAPFAM 2012.)

Figure 15.2 shows that the national coverage of maternal health care is not at an optimal level, particularly regarding pregnancy monitoring. In terms of equity, there is a significant gap in coverage between urban and rural areas for antenatal consultations and deliveries assisted by qualified personnel. Furthermore, national coverage of antenatal consultations between 2012 and 2015 shows a decrease in the use of antenatal health-care services, particularly on the third antenatal consultation. This is a concern in terms of the quality of prenatal care.

Between 2002 and 2012, infant and child mortality fell from 131 to 68 per 1000 live births, infant mortality fell from 108 to 68 per 1000 live births, and neonatal mortality fell from 45 to 36 per 1000 live births (PAPFAM 2002, 2012).[2]

The main causes of death in children under five are diarrhea, acute respiratory infections, and birth asphyxia, whereas the main causes of neonatal death are linked to prematurity, malnutrition, and neonatal infection. Forty-three percent of under-five deaths in Djibouti are linked to malnutrition, which is an underlying factor.

The prevalence of overall acute malnutrition has shown a downward trend. It fell from 12.55% in 2013 to 10.18% in 2015, while severe acute malnutrition fell from 5.32% to 4.94%. For the same period, moderate acute malnutrition dropped from 7.23% to 5.24%.

In 1984, malaria became a public health problem in Djibouti. Since then, the number of malaria cases has continued to rise. The epidemiological analysis suggests that malaria incidence has been increasing. As shown in Figure 15.3, the number of confirmed cases rocketed from 24 in 2012 to 13,804 in 2016, mainly due to poor coverage of interventions, with major outbreaks in 2013, 2014, and 2016 caused by the significant influx of people crossing the border.[3]

The prevalence of TB in 2014 was 906 cases per 100,000 inhabitants. Incidence has been decreasing, with 378 new cases per 100,000 inhabitants in 2015, down from 619 new cases in 2013. Despite this downward trend, Djibouti still has one of the highest rates of TB in the world. In 2015, the mortality rate stood at 39 cases per 100,000 inhabitants. Those aged 15–44 are the most at-risk group. The number of detected cases drops as you move away from the capital. In 2016, Djibouti City accounted for 89% of detected cases and the country's interior regions accounted for the remaining 11%.

The cohort analysis shows that cure rates are improving year-on-year. In fact, the cure rate went up from 78.8% in 2009, to 81% in 2014 and to 85% in 2015.

The cure rate for multi-resistant TB in the 2015 cohort was 36.11%. In total, 71 patients were given short course treatment (9 months) in 2016.

The Expanded Program on Immunization (EPI) was created in 1984 and is one of the main basic priority health programmes in the Republic of Djibouti. The diseases targeted by the EPI in Djibouti are: TB, diphtheria, tetanus, pertussis, polio, measles, hepatitis B, *Haemophilus influenzae* type b (Hib), pneumococcal infections, and diarrhea caused by rotavirus. Epidemiological surveillance is carried out on all vaccine-preventable diseases (VPDs) on a national scale.

No new cases of wild poliovirus have been recorded in Djibouti since 1999, and the country is currently at the certification stage of polio eradication.

As shown in Figure 15.4, the antigen coverage of VPDs saw a sharp increase between 1982 and 1990, before falling back by the millennium. After this, the upward trend resumed, with the majority of antigens reaching more than 80% coverage in the 2000s. Since 2010, the rate of routine immunization coverage has stayed relatively stable and was at around 80% in 2016. There is wide disparity between the capital and the largely rural areas, where coverage rates are lower. This shows the lack of equity in vaccination services.

Djibouti has experienced a generalized HIV epidemic, for which seroprevalence has been decreasing since 2012 (when it was 2.9%) and was estimated at 1.6% in 2016 (Spectrum 2016). In 2016, the number of people living with HIV in Djibouti was estimated at 6971, and the number of deaths due to AIDS stood at around 504 people (Spectrum 2016). There has been a so-called

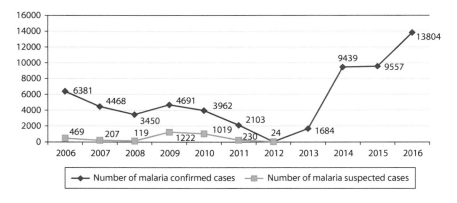

FIGURE 15.3 Incidence of malaria in Djibouti between 2006 and 2016. (*Source*: PNLP, the National Malaria Control Programme.)

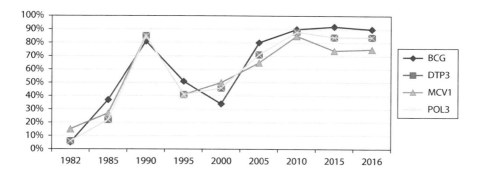

FIGURE 15.4 Immunization coverage of children aged 0–11 months (%) by antigen from 1982 to 2016. (*Source*: http://apps.who.int/immunization_monitoring/globalsummary/estimates?c=DJI.)

"feminization" of the epidemic, with 3812 women diagnosed with HIV in contrast to 2818 men (Spectrum 2016).

HIV prevalence is at 13% among female sex workers, 1% among truck drivers, and 1% among refugees. The prevalence of HIV among TB patients was at 6% in 2016. Analysis of patterns of the HIV epidemic using population groups shows the heterogeneity of the HIV epidemic in several ways.

Since 2006, sentinel surveillance of HIV in pregnant women has shown an almost constantly high prevalence in urban areas in comparison with rural ones. In terms of urban areas, it appears that certain localities in the capital such as Arhiba, Farah-Had, Khor-Bourhan, and Ali Sabieh had the highest prevalence rates (between 2% and 4%) until 2010.

The most common non-communicable diseases (NCDs) are cardiometabolic diseases (such as cardiovascular disease and diabetes) which are interlinked and share the same risk factors. The other most common NCDs include chronic kidney disease, cancer, chronic respiratory disease, and mental illness. Bodily injuries caused by accidents, particularly those occurring on public roads can be added to that list.

Smoking rates have decreased following the launch of government initiatives on tobacco use, implemented as part of the Framework Convention on Tobacco Control. However, in 2012, according to the results of the Djibouti Multiple Indicator Survey, 14% of young people aged 15–19 were smokers, and 42% of those aged younger than 15 had been exposed to tobacco smoke.

No studies have been performed to illustrate the prevalence, incidence, and patterns of NCDs in general. In early 2018, various hospitals observed a significant increase in the number of visits linked with NCDs. We found that non-communicable diseases are responsible for 40% of hospital admissions and one-third of hospital deaths at Hôpital Général Peltier in Djibouti City.

Neglected tropical diseases (NTDs) persist, despite interventions and some successful achievements. Djibouti has a heavy burden of one endemic NTD, leishmaniasis, although leprosy also needs to be closely monitored. The elimination of lymphatic filariasis and schistosomiasis must be monitored.

The Djibouti National Institute of Public Health (INSPD) monitors, prepares for, and responds to epidemic-prone diseases. In 2016, the institute received 12,433 reports of notifiable diseases. For the same year, the epidemiological data collected was characterized by an increase in the number of cases of influenza-like illness, acute watery diarrhea, severe acute malnutrition, severe acute respiratory infections, hepatitis, typhoid fever, malaria, dengue fever, meningitis, and acute bloody diarrhea. However, there was a decrease in the number of cases of neonatal tetanus and measles, compared to the previous year. No cases of leprosy, tetanus in adults, human rabies, viral haemorrhagic fever, or unknown or emerging diseases were recorded.

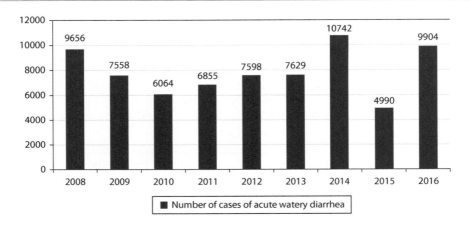

FIGURE 15.5 Cases of acute watery diarrhea in Djibouti from 2008 to 2016. (*Source*: INSPD.)

As shown in Figure 15.5, the number of cases of acute cholera-like watery diarrhea in Djibouti from 2008 to 2016 illustrates that it currently has an endemic nature.

INTEGRATION OF BASIC HEALTH SERVICES

The integration of basic health services has been one of the priorities of Djibouti's government for many years.[4] The country's health map, created in 2006, set out a Minimum Package of integrated services based on the types of facilities in the different levels of the health pyramid. The MoH has drawn up Integrated Management of Child Health (IMCI) guidelines.

However, further integration efforts need to be made in PHC, and screening, treatment, and monitoring of NCDs (hypertension, diabetes, mental illnesses, screening for breast and cervical cancer).

INFRASTRUCTURE OF PRIMARY HEALTH-CARE FACILITIES

The density of PHC institutions is estimated at 0.87 institutions per 10,000 inhabitants at national level. The highest density (1.64) is in the Arta region and the lowest is in Djibouti City (0.68), most probably due to its large population, accounting for two-thirds of the country's total population.

Physician with patient in PHC facility

According to the results of the Service Availability and Readiness Assessment (SARA) carried out in Djibouti in 2015, the availability index of health infrastructures on a national level is 38.9%. This percentage is even lower in some regions. In fact, two-thirds of the country's regions have not reached the national average.

The region of Arta has the highest rate of health infrastructure availability, with a score of 86%, followed by Obock, where the indicator is estimated at 46.5%.

Djibouti City, which has a large proportion of the country's health training programmes, has a score of 37.6%, one level below the national average.

In terms of the provision of health services, health-care facilities are organized in a pyramid structure, with three levels. It is governed by the health map, which is revised every five years based on the national health policy. The health map was created in 2006 and will be reviewed again in 2018–2019.

There are three health-care sub-sectors within this pyramid: public, semi-public, and private. In the semi-public sector, the first level is made up of health posts in rural areas and community health centres in Djibouti City. These health-care facilities are the population's first point of contact with the health system. They mainly provide services for the Expanded Program on Immunization (EPI), consultations for children under five, and reproductive health (ante/postnatal) consultations. The second level is composed of five university hospitals which play the dual role of district hospital and regional hospital in most regions. This second level mainly provides curative care for children and adults by a general practitioner, as well as standard biological tests, X-rays, patient hospitalization, and birth attendance by a skilled health worker.

In 2015, according to the SARA survey, the national availability index for health services was at 39.3%. This level is not high enough, and the same goes for all the regions except those in Djibouti City, where the level is 49.7% and in Arta, where the level is 47.8%.

Physician with patient in PHC facility

In terms of facilities, there were 10.68 in-patient hospital beds per 10,000 inhabitants. Of all the regions in Djibouti, Arta had the highest number of hospital beds per population at 21.37 per 10,000. Djibouti City reported 12.55 per 10,000. In the other regions, the indicator level was between 3.91 and 8.42 per 10,000 inhabitants. These results reflect a disparity in the availability of in-patient hospital beds between regions.

In 2016, only 249 in-patient hospital beds out of the 486 available on a national scale were usable, just 51%. The number of maternity beds available country-wide stands at 3.22 per 1000 pregnant women, compared to the WHO standard of 10. Among the various regions, only Arta had a satisfactory number of maternity beds, at 9.25 per 1000 pregnant women. In 2016, only 72 maternity beds out of the 122 available country-wide were usable, just 59%.

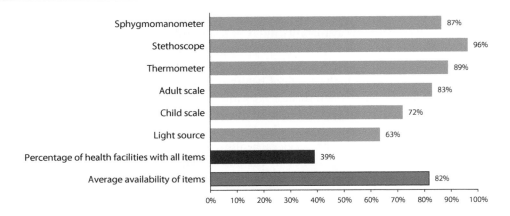

FIGURE 15.6 An availability index of basic equipment items in health facilities. (*Source*: SARA 2015.)

According to the 2015 SARA survey, 39% of health institutions had all the basic equipment items in 2015, and on average health institutions had five out of the six basic equipment items (Figure 15.6).

Each university hospital had standard X-ray equipment (except for Arta CMH), an ultrasound machine, and biomedical equipment.

There is no policy for maintaining facilities and biomedical equipment yet.

QUALITY, TREATMENT PROTOCOLS, AND REFERRAL SYSTEMS

Djibouti's MoH introduced mobile medical and surgical units in 2017, which provide high quality PHC services to populations living in remote areas with poor access to health facilities.

Djibouti still does not have a quality and accreditation programme for its health services. For most diseases there are no protocols harmonized on a national level, except for the health of under-fives with the development of IMCI guidelines, and the protocols for treating malaria, TB, and HIV.

It is essential that Djibouti develops protocols for all the other diseases, since the majority of the country's doctors studied at different universities, which had different treatment protocols.

There is a referral and counter-referral system between the different levels of the health pyramid. For maternal and child health, referrals are made from Level 1 to Level 3. Counter-referrals are made inversely from Level 3 to Level 1. This system makes direct admissions for patients easier, and treatment is free of charge. All reference materials are available and used properly. For adults, transfers and referrals are not as well-organized and are chargeable. The referral system follows hierarchical rules, except for emergency cases, which are directly transferred from Level 1 to Level 3. Counter-referrals are uncommon.

Telemedicine services are being brought into operation to ensure that populations can access high-quality services, regardless of where they live.

ESSENTIAL DRUG LIST (EDL)

In line with the PHC strategy, the health system has been making essential generic medicines available since 2003. The last update to the essential drug list (EDL) was made in 2016. The distribution of essential medicines in the public sector is organized by the Central Procurement Agency for Essential Medicines and Materials (CAMME), whose main responsibilities are to

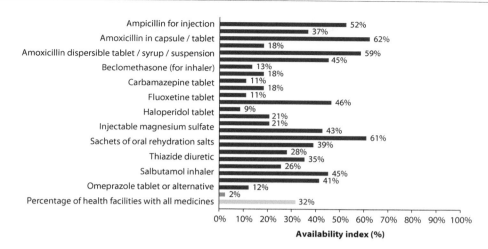

FIGURE 15.7 Availability of 14 essential tracer medicines (SARA 2015) and average scores.

provide, distribute, and sell essential medicines in the public and private sectors. However, the availability of essential medicines is still not adequate (Figure 15.7).

HUMAN RESOURCES FOR HEALTH

Human resources for health have seen a substantial increase, thanks to Djibouti's Faculty of Medicine established in 2007 and the new paramedical staff graduating from the "Institut Supérieur des Sciences de la Santé" (ISSS), who have been integrated into public service. The number of health-care staff has been steadily rising since 2008. In 2016, there were 1.06 general practitioners per 10,000 inhabitants, and 8.18 paramedical staff per 10,000 inhabitants.[5]

The health-care workforce rose from 1664 in 2008 to 3381 in 2017, an increase of more than 100% (Figure 15.8).

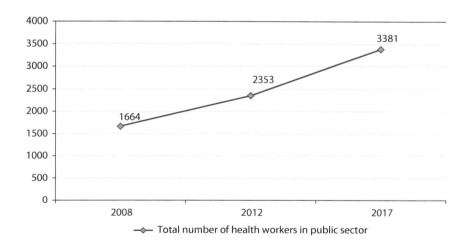

FIGURE 15.8 Health-care workforce from 2008 to 2017. (*Source*: DRHF — the Financial and Human Resources Department, 2017.)

In 2015, according to the SARA survey, the availability index for health-care staff on a national level was at 61.1%. In general, the index is below the national average in various regions, with the exception of Djibouti City which has a score of 84.1%. The lowest indicator is 20.9%, in the region of Dikhil.[6]

A continuing training strategy has yet to be developed for primary health-care staff. Only the staff within priority programmes such as HIV, maternal and child health, malaria, TB, and immunization, receive continuing training.

NATIONAL HEALTH INFORMATION SYSTEM

The National Health Information System (NHIS) incorporates various sub-systems: epidemiological surveillance, a routine information system for health services, information systems for special programmes, and an administrative information system.

The data used by these sub-systems mainly comes from weekly epidemiological surveillance bulletins on health training, monthly health training activity reports, personal data, surveys among health services, household surveys, censuses, specific studies, and research.

In terms of NHIS functionality, efforts are needed to strengthen the consolidation and validation of routine health data (annual statistical year book), and to address under-reporting of health data at all levels and poor coordination of data collecting. Data are not collected from the private sector.

The project for establishing the "District Health Information Software" in its second version (DHIS 2) is a good prospect for the future, which will mainly allow data to be reported in real time.

THE PRIVATE HEALTH SECTOR

The private health-care sector consists of 23 medical clinics and practices and 23 pharmacies. The private health sub-sector is restricted to Djibouti City. In most cases, private facilities offer curative care through general medical wards and emergency services, under the framework of PHC. In terms of prevention activities, it is mainly immunization services which are carried out by private facilities. However, the lack of price harmonization in the private sector has led to difficulties in terms of affordability for the population.

A public–private partnership is being developed in Djibouti. A centre has been set up by the MoH for awareness-raising activities on HIV, TB, and malaria. This centre is called the "PK 12 Prevention Centre". Integrating data from private facilities into the NHIS has not been effective.

There is no systematic reporting and sharing of health data from private health facilities. There are no statistics available except for those on immunization, with almost 5000 children vaccinated in the private sector in 2016.

For the time being, the private medical and pharmaceutical sector is not subject to any price regulations. There are ongoing negotiations for agreements with the National Social Health Insurance Fund (NSSF) in line with introducing Universal Health Insurance.

RECOMMENDED ACTIONS TO IMPROVE ACCESS TO QUALITY PRIMARY HEALTH SERVICES

There are several challenges to be overcome to provide high-quality services in public PHC institutions. In terms of organizing a health service provision system, the following actions are needed:

- Developing community health activities
- Adapting health care to patients' needs

- Extending a high-quality approach to hospitals and specialized centres
- Improving the coordination of emergency care
- Ensuring continuity of care between the different levels, from the community up (establishing a health-care network)
- Improving the preparedness of the health system to manage migration flows and humanitarian crises
- Increasing health-care access for rural and cut-off populations
- Developing an integrated strategy for health promotion
- Updating the minimum package of activities, with a focus on integrating services, particularly for non-communicable diseases

Regarding governance and leadership, the following actions are needed:

- Adapting legislation and regulations in view of the current issues and challenges faced by the health system
- Establishing a functional framework for inter and multisectoral coordination for the health sector
- Putting a decentralization and devolution policy into place in an effective and gradual manner, in line with the PHC policy
- Extending an accountability and results-focused management policy to all areas and to all levels of the health system
- Developing partnerships and contractual relationships

In terms of the health information system, the following actions are needed:

- Drawing up a roadmap for comprehensively reforming the health information system and implementing this reform with the involvement of all the stakeholders concerned
- Putting in place a functional and multisectoral coordination platform to improve data collection, analysis, and storage
- Producing key indicators for the health sector in a timely manner
- Integrating data from the private sector
- Putting the DHIS 2 platform in place and developing new information and communication technology (NICT) tools for producing and distributing health information

In terms of health products and other medical technology, infrastructure, and equipment, the following actions are needed:

- Introducing legislation, procedures, standards, protocols, and guidelines (on health products, infrastructure, and equipment)
- Coordinating the construction of new infrastructure in line with the requirements of the health map
- Ensuring the regular supply of medicines and other health products to health-care facilities
- Harmonizing biomedical equipment on a national level
- Establishing a multisectoral platform to fight against counterfeit and fake medicines
- Improving the quality of hygiene in hospitals
- Ensuring the maintenance of biomedical equipment and infrastructure

Concerning human resources for health, the following actions are needed:

- Drawing up a strategic development plan for human resources
- Ensuring that the quality and quantity of human resources is sufficient for the requirements of the health system
- Implementing accountability and results-focused human resources management
- Establishing a coordination platform with the Ministry of Higher Education for initial training of medical and paramedical staff
- Implementing information and communication systems
- Decentralizing human resources management

In terms of health financing, the challenges will lie in increasing the budget allocated to health care from the general budget, attracting funding from external sources, expanding the scope for Universal Health Insurance, and ensuring that it can be financed for the long term, and ensuring that strategic inputs from the health sector and the performance-based funding system can be financed for the long term.

REFERENCES

1. Final report, Service Availability and Readiness Assessment (SARA), Djibouti. 2015.
2. Survey final report, Pan Arab Project for Family Health (PAPFAM), Djibouti. 2012.
3. Annual Report of the National Malaria Control Programme, Djibouti. 2017.
4. National Health Statistics, Djibouti. 2016.
5. Annual Report of the Financial and Human Resources Department, Djibouti. 2017.
6. World Health Organization, *WHO vaccine-preventable diseases: Monitoring system. 2018 global summary*, 2018. Available from: http://apps.who.int/immunization_monitoring/globalsummary/estimates?c=DJI [Accessed 20 September 2018].

CHAPTER 16

Egypt

*Omaima El-Gibaly, Magdy Bakr,
Mona Hafez Mahmoud El Naka, Taghreed
Mohamed Farahat, and Nagwa Nashat Hegazy*

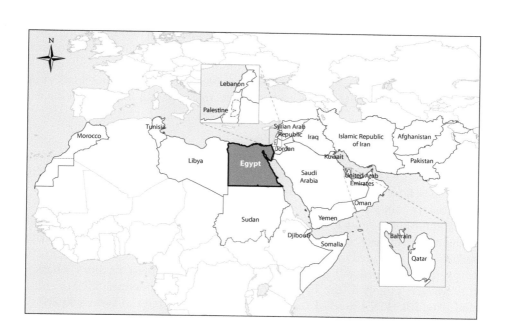

Total number of PHC facilities	5,391
Number of general practitioners working in public PHC facilities	14,973
Number of certified family physicians working in PHC facilities	256
Average number of family physician graduates/year	180
Number of medical schools	29
Number of family medicine departments	8

Egypt is administratively divided into 27 governorates which are further subdivided into 279 districts.

Primary health care (PHC) has been the primary focus of the Ministry of Health and Population (MoHP) since its establishment. Service is provided mainly through a network of MoHP PHC facilities distributed all over the country with a minimum of one PHC facility in a radius of five square kilometres with variable capacity, infrastructure, and coverage by physicians and other members of the health team.

MoHP has a total of 5391 PHC facilities in the country. Other facilities providing PHC services not counted in this figure belong to health insurance organizations, out-patient clinics providing PHC among other curative services, school clinics, and out-patient clinics belonging to private, non-governmental organizations (NGOs), universities, and other institutions and programmes which provide a wide range of PHC services including immunization.

PHC facilities in Egypt range between health offices, rural health units, maternal and child health facilities, school health facilities, and family health units and centres. Since 1999, with the initiation of a comprehensive Health Sector Reform Programme (HSRP) and the establishment of Egypt's Family Health Model (FHM), progressive development of PHC converted rural PHC facilities into family health units and centres following certain standards which will be explained later. Currently, 2957 PHC facilities are accredited and implement a family health model including 62% of rural health facilities. These provide a wide scope of public health, preventive, and curative PHC services including prevention and promotion.

As the Family Health Model is taken as Egypt's model for providing integrated, people-centred primary health care, further elaboration on PHC in Egypt will focus on giving a comprehensive account of the FHM.

EGYPT'S FAMILY HEALTH MODEL

Egypt's Family Practice (FP) was established in 1999 as one of Egypt's health sector reform programme strategies. It was structured as an integrated approach to providing basic health services and was commonly called the "Family Health Model". The FHM was designed as the first point of health care at the community level that provides quality primary health-care services based on "national planning standards and guidelines". Through the model, services are provided by PHC health facilities with reformed infrastructures, with staffing and training according to a standard "health team staffing pattern and training programme". Through these facilities, a basic package of health services is provided (the BBP) according to clinical guidelines (CGLs) and includes an essential drug list (EDL) derived from these CGLs, with a referral system to refer patients to higher levels of care when needed. A medical record (family folder) is created for each family with an information system to support it. Facilities enrolled in the FHM apply quality standards and are accredited through an accreditation system managed by the Ministry of Health and Population (MoHP). Facilities provide community services with community participation in facility management.[1]

As per its original design, the model has been an integrated approach to provide geographical coverage to families with basic services, including both health and population interventions. Each family physician, supported by a multidisciplinary health team, serves a roster of families within the catchment area of the health facility ranging between 5000 and 10,000 households. The catchment area is defined through a process of house enumeration with data collected on the households' living environments. The FHM has also helped ensure a first point of contact at the community level that provides quality, safe services, serves as a gatekeeper, and refers to higher levels of care as needed. The family physician and team are trained in new skills to assess, diagnose, treat, advise, and refer patients seeking care and aims to integrate the currently provided primary health-care delivery system.

Assessments of the FHM conducted after the first few years of its implementation found the model to be valid, viable, affordable, and popular. Since then, the model has been politically charted as the accepted norm for primary care in Egypt with a collective agreement that it needs refinement and further development.

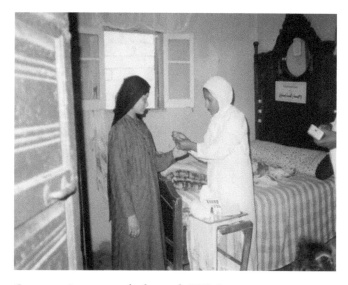

Community outreach through FHM

COMPONENTS OF EGYPT'S FAMILY HEALTH MODEL

The following account of components of the FHM in Egypt describes the original design of the model since its establishment in 1999 and further development for the following six to seven years. After this period, the model went through phases of development and phases of setbacks where improvement took place in some aspects of the model and deterioration took place in others.

At a more developed phase of implementation of the FHM, the District Health Authorities at five pilot sites were enhanced and strengthened their managerial capacities as a step for decentralization. The initiated organizational restructuring was tailored towards a purchaser/provider split. However, this model has not been sustainable, particularly failing to attract political will and support needed at the time.

The model was revised several times and improvements were introduced to it. The last review took place in 2014 with collaboration between the PHC sector of MoHP and Egypt's World

Health Organization (WHO) office. An account of the findings, recommendations of the 2014 assessment, and actions taken since then will be given.

The broad lines of the FHM components in Egypt are summarized into the model's infrastructure, human resources, operating system, and financing framework.

FHM INFRASTRUCTURE

Building standards

MoHP has established a standard architectural design for the family health units (FHUs) and family health centres (FHCs) which is used for building new facilities all over the country. This architectural design takes into consideration the size of facilities depending on the size of the catchment population to be served. This function has been institutionalized within the MoHP where a designated engineering unit, which is part of MoHP organizational structure, is established for this purpose. This unit not only delineates standards for architects but also works in commissioning and supervising the construction firms building these facilities. The design considers functional requirements for services provided in these facilities such as immunization, patient examination rooms, medical records rooms, laboratories, and other needs.

Patient flow

The architectural design of FHUs and FHCs considers circulation of the population visiting the facilities from reception and registration to waiting areas, to examination rooms, and so on, depending on the type of visits and services to be provided for each.

Equipment list and standards

Lists have been established for equipment and furniture for each of the facilities' rooms based on the contents of the basic benefit package.

HUMAN RESOURCES

Family health units and centres are staffed by new graduate physicians, dentists, pharmacists, nurses, and other cadres. All members of the family health team are important; nevertheless, family physicians are considered the core of the family health model workforce around which most family health (FH) standards are built.

Each year, some 10,500 physicians graduate from Egyptian universities, some 7500 of whom are enrolled in a two-year mandatory service period commonly called "takleef". The FHM supply of physicians comes from new graduates serving takleef. Annually, about 1500 takleef physicians are enrolled in a pre-service training programme qualifying them to serve in family health units and centres. The training programme started as a comprehensive seven to nine weeks training with a well-structured curriculum, but it was progressively downscaled and is now reduced to 12 days in response to limited resources.[2] On average, 180 newly family physicians graduate every year, most of them seeking employment abroad. MoHP has about 256 certified family physicians working in PHC/FH facilities nationwide.

Staffing pattern, organizational structure, and job description

Health teams working in FHUs and FHCs consist of physicians, dentists, pharmacists, nurses, laboratory technologists, social workers, sanitarians, clerks, janitors, and others. National planning standards and guidelines developed as part of the health sector reform programme have specifically defined the number and mix of these staff cadres for FHUs and FHCs. These standards and guidelines have been updated several times since its original design in 1999. According to these standards, numbers and cadres depend on the catchment population planned to be served by facilities. Standard organizational structures are developed for FHUs and FHCs with job descriptions for each staff category.

The numbers and mix of staff working in health units and centres have changed several times since the start of the model. Normally, one physician serves 1000 families, where an average family size is five persons. The human resource size of health facilities also depends on utilization where a new physician is added when the utilization rate is more than 30 persons/ physician/day. The minimum number of nurses serving in health facilities is five, serving in the examination room, vaccination, antenatal care, family planning, and the dental clinic, with one head nurse.

Deployment

Each year the Egyptian health system receives thousands of physicians (around 10,500), pharmacists (around 8800), dentists (around 5000), and nurses (around 11,000), who are pooled for the mandatory service period (one year) to be distributed among the different primary healthcare facilities all over Egypt. Frequent staff turnover and mal-distribution between Upper and Lower Egypt and urban versus rural areas are constant challenges for Egyptian primary healthcare provision.

Training

The MoHP implements several programmes for pre-service and on-the-job training of the different staff categories. An assessment of training streams provided for FHM workers conducted by the PHC sector of MoHP in collaboration with the WHO in 2015 revealed the need to strengthen these programmes, particularly for family practitioners. MoHP is currently working on implementing efficient pre-service training programmes to qualify this workforce to work in family health units and centres.

OPERATING SYSTEM

Enumeration of houses and household profiles

As a standard practice, houses in villages or districts lying in the catchment area of health facilities are enumerated and information recorded about the conditions of houses and the socio-economic profiles of the household members living in these houses. This serves to give an account of social determinants of health for inhabitants of the catchment area as well as a sort of epidemiological profile. Among the information collected are the presence of a source of running water, its garbage and sewage disposal, the presence of household animals, type of energy utilized, sources of income of the families, the presence of people with disability, and the social and economic conditions of the households. This information is recorded and kept in the family folder (medical record) of each family in the health facility serving this catchment area.

Catchment area definition/building rosters

The catchment area of each facility is determined based on houses' and enumeration records. A map of the catchment area served by the facility is drawn and posted at the facility entrance. Rosters of families assigned to each facility depend on the size of the facility and its manning by a health team members, particularly by physicians. The number of households assigned to each physician ranges from 5000 to 10,000.

Initial checkup for family members

The enrolment process includes an initial physical examination and basic laboratory work for all catchment area households. Information is recorded in designated forms and filed inside the family folder of each family.

Medical records/family folders

Each family folder contains medical records for each member of the family all kept in one folder and divided by separators. Family folders are given numbers that reflect the house number, family number, and other unique identifiers.

Medical records and family folders

Each family/family member is given a medical record card with household identification information and a medical record number. Medical records inside the health facility consist of registers that are kept in the medical records room, and family folders containing several standard forms for each member of the family. Registers are designed to record households' service utilization in the facilities. A procedure manual is written describing standards and usage of forms and registers and the flow and archiving of family folders. The family folder includes the following forms:

- Family identification data
- Socio-economic and environmental data
- History and physical examination form
- Significant data sheet
- Visit record sheet
- Diabetes care sheet (for diabetics)
- Hypertension care sheet (for hypertensives)
- Endemic diseases form
- Referral sheet
- Newborn sheet
- Antenatal care sheet
- Family planning sheet
- Dental care sheet

Medical Information System (MIS)

One of the main components of implementing the family health model is the availability of a strict system of medical registration of families and their members, represented in the family folder and family health files, and computerization of these folders.

At the outset of establishing the FHM, a computer application named a "Clinical Information System" (CIS) was developed consisting of modules covering all operational steps of work in family health units and centres. Through this application, clinical data are collected from the family health CISs at family health units and centres and operated to facilitate the measurement of performance level at these units, calculate bonuses, estimate the cost of delivered services, as well as other functions of this system.

After some time using the CIS, other similar computer applications were designed and implemented at some facilities over time, but none of these was scaled up to function in a sustainable way to be rolled out across all PHC/FHM facilities. The WHO has also supported the MoHP Information Centre in developing a computer application to manage health records at family health facilities, but the application was never implemented. A project for providing health services for the poor in Upper Egypt, funded by the World Bank, has also developed a computer application to trace utilization and financial transactions in health facilities enrolled in the project but this was never scaled beyond these facilities.

Integration of an essential health services package:
the Basic Benefits Package (BBP)

The development of a basic service package to be provided to all Egypt's population was one of the key components of Egypt's Health Sector Reform Programme initiated in 1997 – and was named the "Basic Benefits Package (BBP)". This was developed as one component of the family health model, consisting of a subset of core interventions to be provided through family health facilities at the primary health-care level which and selected to be a comprehensive set of services addressing all health problems.

Development of the package has taken into consideration some of the most prevalent health problems in Egypt requiring special attention such as high maternal mortality, poor antenatal care, and high rates of infectious, parasitic, malnutrition, and reproductive health problems. In addition, like many developing countries, Egypt is experiencing an epidemiological transition with the emergence of non-communicable diseases such as diabetes, hypertension, ischaemic heart disease and a high rate of injuries due to accidents. According to the PHC Sector of MoHP, in June 2017, 4754 PHC facilities have fully implementing BBP (88% of total PHC facilities).

BASIC BENEFITS PACKAGE IN EGYPT IS DIVIDED AT
THE FACILITY LEVEL INTO THE FOLLOWING

- Services targeting individuals which could be delivered through primary health services, such as vaccinations, follow-up growth stages, care in pregnancy, and early detection of cancer and other services.
- Services targeting families, delivered through primary health services at units or through the administrative board, such as health education and health consultancy.
- Services delivered to the community through main departments in the district/directorate or those responsible for health in family health units, such as water quality samples, supervision of food, smoking control, injury prevention, and others.
- Several vertical programmes were integrated through the BBP such as healthy mother and healthy child, family planning, DOTS, IMCI, schistosomiasis, and others.

BBP includes a core set of interventions to be provided through family health facilities at primary care level. It is not a comprehensive set of services addressing all health problems.

Clinical Guidelines (CGLs)

Clinical practice guidelines were developed for BBP interventions. Guidelines were put at the beginning of HSRP in the late 1990s through a consultative process led by MoHP with the participation of a group of expert professors in different medical specialties. It went through repeated rounds of revision and updates, the latest in 2013 in collaboration with WHO. Training on clinical practice guidelines is provided to family practitioners as part of family practice preservice training. Clinical practice guidelines are printed and disseminated to all family health facilities, and are considered part of accreditation standards for facilities enrolled into the model.

Essential drug list

A list of drugs that treat BBP interventions according to agreed clinical guidelines has been established. Drugs are listed in their generic formulae and should be made available in all family health facilities. Formulation of this drug list doesn't follow a health technology assessment (HTA) or economic studies but has been revised and updated several times randomly as well as part of a review of the basic benefits package and clinical guidelines. The last update took place in 2008.

Referral system

BBP consists of services that are provided at the level of family health units. Cases needing higher level care are referred to specialists in family health centres or district and general hospitals through an established "Referral System".

Staff working in family health facilities receive training on the referral system including what service to refer, where, and how to manage the referral. The FHM was built on the concept of letting the family physician be a "gatekeeper" for rationalizing the use of health-care services by the community it serves. Accordingly, secondary care services provided should "strictly" be provided to cases "referred" to these providers through the referral system.

According to the document on "Governorate Health Planning Standards and Guidelines for Facility-Based Services", certain standards were defined governing referral from FHU to higher levels as follows:

- Ideally, assignment of centres to receive referred cases from family health facilities is based on coverage of 50,000 to 100,000 population within the catchment area of the referral centre.
- A paved road and a standard means of transportation should be available between the centre and each facility assigned to it.
- Standard means of transportation implies that the drive between the unit and the referral centre is direct and complete. Patients should not need to use more than one transportation means to reach to the referral centre.
- The ideal distance (actual paved road) between the unit and the referral centre is between 5 and 10 km.
- In case of need for a specialist who is not present at the district hospital, referral from FHC or FHU to specialists at the general or specialized hospital (Level 4) is possible.
- Patients who turn up at an FHC or district hospital or general hospital without a referral from their assigned FHU will be provided with services/admitted only in cases of emergency or acute illness.

- The FH model specifies the referral from the FHU to out-patient in higher levels in three specialties, namely internal medicine, paediatrics, and obstetrics/gynaecology. Referral in the context of the referral system covers out-patient services other than these three specialties but is limited to services already provided in the out-patient departments of integrated, district, or general hospitals.
- Referral must be documented and referral forms archived in the patients' files.
- Referral system entails that each family health facility should implement a system to ensure and monitor the cycle of referral documentation with the centre/district hospital within its referral range.

A new social health insurance law mandates that family health units and centres are the first level of care acting as gatekeepers for higher levels. It mandates that secondary care services are provided only to cases referred from FH units and centres through a strict referral system.

Quality and accreditation

Improving the quality of services was a prime goal of Egypt's Health Sector Reform Programme. As part of the programme strategies, a "Quality Improvement Directorate" was established by "Ministerial Decree" (number 272 for the year 1998). The quality directorate developed a comprehensive programme to improve quality through designing and implementing an accreditation system. This included establishing standards for PHC facilities' accreditation with the development of MoHP accreditation trainers and surveyors. In the meantime, it started implementing a plan to enrol PHC facilities in the accreditation programme. The programme starts with an assessment of enrolled facilities, then developing an improvement plan for each, followed by field work to coach facilities to implement these standards, then finally undertake assessment and grant accreditation for facilities successfully passing these standards. Accreditation remains valid for two years then a re-assessment is done to renew it or give a grace period to qualify for it if a facility fails in the re-accreditation assessment.[3]

Accreditation has been used to lay the groundwork for a performance-based reimbursement system under the reform. Family health units and centres should be accredited first before they can contract with the "Family Health Fund" which was established as a pilot health insurance body to perform strategic purchasing at PHC level paying for services with a sort of "pay for performance" system.

In July 2007, the Egyptian accreditation standards for hospitals, ambulatory care, and PHC was accredited by the International Society for Quality in Health-care (ISQua) making Egypt the first country in the region to attain this certificate.

With further institutional development, the quality directorate was separated from accreditation where an executive committee for accreditation was established in MoHP which was concerned with assessing facilities for accreditation standards and granting accreditation when successfully passing these standards.

So far (June 2017), 2957 facilities are accredited and implement the family health model out of 5391 primary health-care facilities in total (62%). 4754 PHC facilities implement the full BBP and are ready to get accredited (88%).

Facility management, monitoring, and supervision

FHUs and FHCs are managed by family practitioners working in these facilities. These managers are usually selected based on their capacity and seniority.

Family health facilities are directly monitored and supervised by District Health Authorities through trained "district health teams". These teams have pre-determined performance indicators. A training programme for district teams is conducted as a standard practice and financial incentives are granted to staff in facilities achieving high performance and to district teams doing adequate monitoring and supervision. Monitoring and supervision are also done by PHC departments at the governorate-level health directorate as well as by the central ministry through dedicated teams from the PHC Sector.

Health promotion, education, and social services ("Family Club")

Health promotion and education are core services provided at family health units and centres. These are provided through routine patient visits to the facilities by the family practitioners, family nurses, immunization nurses, and others. It is also provided through a "Family Club" which is a dedicated service established in each family health facility. Social workers in these facilities and community health workers also conduct home visits to families in the catchment area of their facilities to have a clear picture about their residence and living environment and to raise awareness of family members about safety and hygiene and inform them about services provided at health facilities encouraging them to benefit from these services. Through this service, health promotion and education are given about health issues such as care of diabetes, hypertension, immunization, breastfeeding, family planning, environmental safety, infection control, and many other topics.

Community participation

Community participation is promoted through district level collaboration and participation with local authorities, stakeholders, and the community that is adequately involved in decisions and activities related to its own health. This helps to tackle important social determinants of health through a sustained intersectoral approach and methodology. Proactive members of the local community are included in the organizational structures of health facility boards, but their active role is variable and more theoretical in most instances.

FINANCING AND PAYMENT SYSTEM

As part of the health sector reform programme, the "Family Health Fund" (FHF) was established and developed through several ministerial decrees, to serve as a quality contracting and purchasing agency for primary health-care services on behalf of beneficiaries.

The FHF was established to be a purchaser of family health-care services included in the agreed Basic Benefit Package.[4] FHF is used to contract FH services from accredited public facilities and pays incentives to its staff according to agreed performance indicators, and provides medicines and other supplies to contracted facilities.[3] The FHF was further developed to include managing beneficiaries, collection and management of revenues, contracting with qualified facilities – directly or through district health authorities developed into a decentralized model called a "District Providers' Organization", paying them using agreed contracting and payment mechanisms, and ensuring that the service provided meets the agreed standards of quality specified in the contracts.

The FHF also contracted with accredited NGO facilities and facilities related to other sectors (universities and health insurance organizations) for the provision of FHM services through these facilities using contracting mechanisms ("per-capita" and "per-case"). FHF introduced separation between service provision and financing, introducing the co-payment concept to primary health-care MoH facilities, improving equity for underserved populations, raising awareness of family health-care services, implementing quality concepts, increasing patient satisfaction, and improving management capacity and technical efficiency.[3]

FHFs faced several major obstacles and challenges, the most important of which were lack of financial sustainability and weak institutionalization. There are four FHFs serving six governorates. They are contracted with a total of 641 family health facilities (in 2014).

Projections for the financial sustainability of accessible and affordable quality family health services have not been thoroughly studied. The FHF proves to be far from sustainable in financing FH services according to the current model. This area needs an extensive and multidisciplinary assessment which extends beyond this overall FH Model review work.[5]

CONTRIBUTIONS OF FAMILY PRACTICE TOWARD UNIVERSAL HEALTH COVERAGE

Egypt defined "Universal Health Coverage" (UHC) as its strategic health sector reform vision back in the late 1990s.[6] Since 2014, Universal Health Coverage was identified as Egypt's health sector vision and Social Health Insurance (SHI) was defined in the new Egyptian constitution and in the health pillar of the National Sustainable Development Strategy (SDS)-2030 as the means for achieving UHC. The new social health insurance explicitly mentions "Family Health Model" as the first level of service provided to families, and defines the family physician as the physician who has a post-graduate university degree or MoHP fellowship certificate in family medicine.

Since 2014, technical work is underway with strong WHO participation to finalize the new law with related organizational reform and to develop a plan to gradually implement it. The new law aims at extending coverage of health services to the entire population while improving service quality and ensuring financial sustainability and financial risk protection, and is based on the principles of separating health financing from provision.

Implementation and development of the FHM in Egypt is considered a strong contribution to UHC as it entails providing integrated and quality services to the entire population and considers their psychosocial well-being with well-defined social protection mechanisms where the poor and vulnerable populations members are covered by the state.

Improving quality and accessibility of the population at PHC level, which provides more than 75% of health needs to the public and enables early detection and management of serious illnesses, will reduce out-of-pocket spending on health and consequently reduce financial hardship and exposure to catastrophic health expenditures and impoverishment. Development of the FHM involves policies and strategies to improve human resources in health, improve accessibility and rational use of medicines, and improve information management as well as financial sustainability with improved efficiency. All this will positively contribute to progress towards achieving UHC which is clearly spelt out in the health sector vision of the Egypt Sustainable Development Strategy 2030.

SUMMARY NOTES FROM FHM ASSESSMENT IN 2014

The MoHP, in collaboration with the WHO, conducted a comprehensive assessment of the FHM in 2014. The first assessment was conducted after a few years of the model's implementation and found the model to be valid, viable, affordable, and popular. Since then, the model has been politically charted as the accepted norm for primary care in Egypt with a common agreement that it needs refinement and further development. The last FHM external assessment was done in 2014 and showed successes as well as several important challenges.

Over the last few years, drastic political, social, and economic changes have taken place which have further exacerbated the challenging situation of the model implementation. Still, there is strong political support for the FHM being the accepted norm for providing integrated people-centred PHC in Egypt. The following is a summary account of the assessment results[1]:

MAJOR CHALLENGES

1. As part of fragmentation of the whole health system, there's fragmentation in institutional and regulatory frameworks, and information management of the model.
2. There's a clear conceptual gap with a misunderstanding of the model's purpose and functions, especially among health professionals.
3. Many family health providers lack adequate knowledge about the BBP and its CGL.
4. One of the major challenges identified through the assessment is ensuring sufficient, well-educated, trained, adequately paid and motivated health teams in family health facilities.
5. There are recurrent shortages of medicines to support the service package.
6. Information management suffers from exhausting manual records, fragmentation, duplication, and lagging automation as well as weak information sharing and use.
7. A dysfunctional referral system with no institutional arrangements to govern service delivery and referrals can be found at PHC and hospital facilities.
8. The role of the district health authority is not adequate in terms of their organizational setup, capacity, and remuneration.
9. Community participation is rather "theoretical".

WAY FORWARD

Institutional and regulatory arrangements
- Revise, update, and standardize the model's institutional, regulatory, and financial frameworks.
- Address FHM /family practice conceptual gaps and the wider societal "conceptions/misconceptions" of general/family practitioner related to it.
- Revitalize accreditation to be a pre-requisite for enrolment into the Model and develop appropriate tools to improve the quality and safety of family health services.
- Enable District Health Authorities to manage health provision at their district boundaries through strengthening decentralization, organizational development, and provider autonomy.

Address human resources issues (not only physicians)
- Resolve or rectify the mandatory service (takleef) issue leading to better pay, attractive career path, effective on-the-job learning, better opportunities for postgraduate education, and an improved overall working and housing environment.
- A proposal to utilize existing hospital staff and to possibly contract staff from outside the public sector to fill human resource gaps.
- Possibly manage shortages in nursing and paramedical staff through task shifting and maximize utilization and employment of community health workers (CHWs) while setting standards for their training, supervision, and regulation to hold them accountable.
- Manage overstaffing to maximize facility performance through means such as re-deployment, working extra shifts, and other options, with rationalizing initial distribution.

Information management
- Rationalize medical records and registration, avoiding duplication and multiple streaming.

- Rationalize use of physical health records through automation.
- Improve performance monitoring system as part of the overall development of a health system monitoring framework. Ideas to do this include establishing a "dashboard" providing a view on selected indicators and milestones to jointly assess the model performance centrally and locally.

Service package
- Develop a well-balanced service package through systematic analysis of burden of disease and costing studies.
- Capacity building and improved monitoring of providers in compliance with clinical guidelines.
- Set standards and implement measures to ensure rational drug use (e.g. limiting the number of drugs per prescription, using generics, monitor antibiotic prescription practices).
- Measures to monitor medicine availability (recording and reporting drug-days out-of-stock).

Referral system
- Develop and implement solid institutional arrangements to mandate referral of clearly identified services (new social health insurance is expected to solve this problem, but measures need to be taken until its full implementation).
- Establish and enforce clear restrictions and incentives to ensure its implementation both to providers and clients with a strict system to monitor and link it with performance.

Funding and financing
- Assess the model's health financing structure.
- Advocate for giving priority to the model in resource allocation to ensure sustainable funding.
- Revisit the role of the FHF use in the experience and keep it as a subdivision of the new national social insurance fund given its acquired experience in strategic purchasing of PHC services.
- Implement strategic purchasing of FH services through contracts with appropriate provider payment mechanisms as an efficient way of using resources, improving provider performance and increase the quality of service.

Community engagement and partnership with the private sector
- Revisit Egypt's experience in piloting contracts with the private sector for the provision of a family health service.
- Enhance the role of the community through strengthening community-based initiatives (CBIs).
- Increase the share of outreach activities through nurses, community health workers particularly in immunization, family planning, and reproductive health services.

Research to support policy and planning
- Research areas include utilization reviews, costing, quality, customer satisfaction, level of financial risk protection, and others.
- Conduct regular internal and external assessment of the model.

FAMILY MEDICINE SPECIALTY

More than 20 years have passed since the start of the health sector reform and initiation of the Family Health Model in Egypt. Table 16.1 presents the number of students in the different

TABLE 16.1 Number of students in the different programme of family medicine in Egyptian universities 2017

University	Diploma*		Masters		Online Masters		Doctorate	
	Registered	Completed	Registered	Completed	Registered	Completed	Registered	Completed
Universities with established departments of family medicine								
Suez Canal from 1980–2016	180	180	13	222	212	353	33	52
Menofia	160	160	30	250	NA	NA		14
Cairo till 2016	NA	NA	100	36	NA	NA	44	13
Ain Shams					NA	NA		
Zagazig 2013			334	140	NA	NA	3	
Helwan started – 2017	NA	NA	–	–	NA	NA	–	–
Universities that have programmes but no established department								
Alexandria	NA	NA			NA	NA	NA	NA
El-Menia Started – 2017	NA	NA	4	–	NA	NA	NA	NA
Assiut	NA	NA	5	2	NA	NA	NA	NA
Sohag	–	3	10	1	NA	NA	1	NA
Aswan	NA	NA	–	–	NA	NA	NA	NA
Mansoura 2013	NA	NA			NA	NA	NA	Na

Universities without any postgraduate programme or department

Banha, Bani Sweif, Fayoum, Suez, Port Said, and South Valley (Qena)

* Diploma is no longer offered by Egyptian Faculties of Medicine.

Family Medicine programmes in Egyptian universities. Still, the deficit in the number of family doctors is significantly high due to several factors:

1. A recent study on the view of medical students towards family medicine as a specialty choice in Egypt shows that only 4.7% showed an intention to choose it as a future career, although 90.7% of students believed in the vital role that family medicine can play in Egypt's health-care system.[7]
2. Introducing Family Medicine in the undergraduate curriculum was lagging in many Egyptian universities. According to a recently issued Prime Minister's decree, by October 2018 all medical schools will follow the integrated medical curriculum in which family medicine is included in the undergraduate curriculum.
3. The career path for Family Medicine specialists has not been determined for Master's (MS) and doctoral degrees holders, including no financial benefits.
4. There has been a resistance to establishing Family Medicine as a specialty.
5. Many family physicians choose the specialty to be able to work in the rich Gulf countries after getting their degree in Egypt.

REFERENCES

1. Lie, DA, Boker, JR, Lenahan, PM, Dow, E, Scherger, JE. An international physician education program to support the recent introduction of family medicine in Egypt. *Family Medicine*, 2004; 36(10): 739–746.
2. Arab Republic of Egypt MoHP. *The Egyptian Board Training and Examination Guide*, 2nd edition. 2005.
3. Roadmap to achieve social justice in health care in Egypt. *World Bank*. 2015.
4. HIO medical audit guidelines for primary health care clinics and hospital. USAID. 2010.
5. Family Health Model assessment report 2014. MoHP.
6. Devi, S. Universal health coverage law approved in Egypt. *Lancet*, 2018; 391(10117): 194. Available from: https://www.thelancet.com/journals/lancet/article/PIIS0140-6736(18)30091-6/fulltext [Accessed 22 September 2018].
7. AlKot MM, Gouda MA, KhalafAllah MT, Zahran MS, Kallaf MM, Zayed AM. Family medicine in Egypt from medical students' perspective: a nationwide survey. *Teach Learn Med*, 2015; 27(3): 264–273.

CHAPTER 17

Islamic Republic of Iran

Mohammadreza Rahbar, Mohsen Asadi-Lari,
and Hasti Sanaei-Shoar

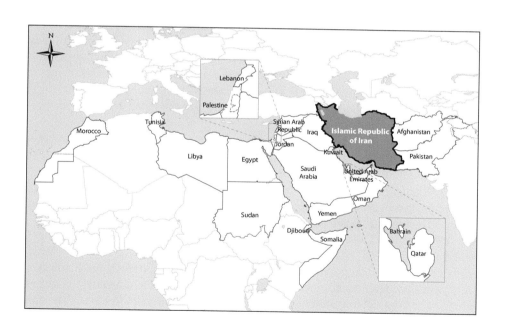

Total number of PHC facilities	27 173
Number of general practitioners working in public PHC facilities	9 500
Number of universities of medical sciences (public)	66
Number of medical schools	85
Number of family medicine departments	63
Number of general practitioners with MFM (Master of Family Medicine: 2-year course)	1 000
Number of family medicine residents	260
Number of medical universities engaged with training family medicine specialists	11

INTRODUCTION

The review of events leading to the establishment of a primary health-care (PHC) system towards developing family practice in Iran shows a transition through various phases to form the current health system. Events include legislation, designs, implementations, evaluations, and reforms. In this chapter, we have briefly reviewed the key episodes in three phases of development for PHC, family practice, and universal health coverage (UHC). The descriptions and explanations in this chapter are categorized into four major areas: legislation and governance, scaling up of family medicine training programmes, financing, and integration and quality assurance of health services.

Different plans and projects during a four-decade period shaped the current PHC network in Iran. The West Azerbaijan project was one of the most significant measures that led to the start of thinking about developing health services based on a social health vision for the first time.[1] The project started in 1971 based on an agreement between the Ministry of Health, Tehran University, and the World Health Organization (WHO) as a joint field study. It was implemented as a pilot design in a limited number of areas with no expansion plan, but it was a learning experience for the next phase of the PHC programme in the following years.[2] Referral and supervision were the two main issues that were considered in this programme. After the Islamic revolution in 1978, significant efforts were made by the government to develop a health network for the equitable allocation of resources and provision of essential services to the people.

The establishment of PHC networks in 1984 was the critical action of the government to ensure the right of citizens to basic health care with priority in rural and deprived areas. During the last decades the PHC networks have produced many valuable impacts; according to WHO report in 2008 "The Islamic Republic of Iran's health houses are responsible for a sharp drop in mortality over the last decades, with notifiable life expectancy increasing".[3] It was a highly successful policy in response to basic needs.

Between 1984 and 1991, over 8800 Health Houses (HHs), 600 Rural Health Centres (RHCs), 430 Urban Health Centres (UHCs), and 147 Behvarz Training Centres (BTCs) were built.[4] Today, in 2018, over 98% of the rural population are covered by PHC and family medicine services via the health networks which now comprise 17,884 HHs and 2644 RHCs. Almost the same services are delivered to the urban communities, with 4111 Health Posts and 2534 UHCs. The entire population of rural areas and cities under 20,000 is covered by the 6500 general practitioners (GPs); while the reforms and improvements in the health system are in the process of expanding family practice (FP) and UHC to the entire urban population. For the time being the health networks have 31,861 behvarzes (rural community health workers) and 205 Behvarz Training Centres. The table at the top of this chapter shows the other basic infrastructure for delivering PHC and family practice services.

In the years after the establishment of these health-care networks, different projects were designed and integrated into the health system to improve the infrastructure, make needed reforms and enable the system to incorporate FP. These projects have played a key role in promoting organizational culture, adapting the system to the current needs and future horizons, initiating a new discourse, and creating the tools and techniques needed to implement FP and UHC. A list of these projects is in Table 17.1.

GENERAL INFORMATION ABOUT HEALTH NETWORKS IN IRAN

The right of all citizens to access health care is embodied in the Constitution of the Islamic Republic of Iran which stipulates the rights of all citizens to health as well as an equitable distribution of health services. In practice, this has resulted in a strong focus on basic public health financed from the public budget and delivered to all Iranians through a public PHC delivery system run by the Ministry of Health and Medical Education (MoHME). Secondary and tertiary curative are financed, and sometimes directly provided, by the compulsory Social Security Organization (SSO) for formal sector employees and their dependents. The Armed Forces Medical Service Organization covers members of the military and their dependents, and the Health Insurance Organization (HIO) covers government employees, rural households, the self-employed, and "others" (for example, students, slum residents). In recent years, the comprehensive insurance plan has covered all rural residents

TABLE 17.1 List of projects to develop techniques for health system reforms from 2000 to present

Area	Project
Improving service provision strategies	Developing techniques for burden of diseases and risk factors
	Priority setting in health problems
	Integration of NCD plans
	Developing models for health programme planning
	Developing clinical guidelines and managed care
	Gatekeeping
	Community empowerment and participation
	Devolution of health services, service purchase and PPP
	Health informatics and management information system
	Developing integrated information system
	Developing disease and death registration system
Improving financing strategies	National health accounts
	Developing economic analysis in health programme planning
Improving human resource strategies	Developing instructional system design for on-job training
	Health workforce licensing
Improving governance and stewardship	Health-care accreditation and licensing
	Health governance
	Evidence-based policy making
	Decentralization
	Demographic health surveys and utilization studies
	Health technology assessment
	Improving models for monitoring and evaluation

according to the laws and regulations particularly after the nationwide Health Reform Plan started in 2014.

There is an integrated structure of the health-care system with medical universities, under the overarching umbrella of Ministry of Health and Medical Education (MoHME), with various deputy ministers including Public Health, and 66 medical universities throughout 31 provinces, with a defined population and catchment area, responsible for academic training and delivering services. Under the control of the universities, there are teaching and non-teaching hospitals, rural and urban health centres, and health posts. The integrated structure of the MoHME has resulted in easy channels for policy decisions.

DEVELOPING PHC IN IRAN: THE FIRST PHASE TOWARDS UHC

As stated above, the establishment of PHC was the first step in policy making for the development of equity and health-care effectiveness in the country. This started in 1984 with a broad government plan; priority was given to rural areas in the allocation of resources which led to the establishment of health networks that subsequently health plans were integrated into; likewise, structural reforms for the establishment of FP were conducted in this health system.

THE PHILOSOPHY BEHIND THE DEVELOPMENT OF PHC

PHC, as defined in the Alma-Ata Declaration, is not only a priority area service platform for the country but rather a philosophy, particularly after the Islamic Revolution. The way in which the government tried to influence a wide range of national policies, laws, regulations, by-laws, and practices in line with developing the PHC system had a great impact on the functioning and effectiveness of the health system and the achievement of health outcomes. This reflects the concern for human dignity, security, ethics, equity, and social justice, and the need to maximize health opportunities by tackling social and economic barriers to health and health care. The fundamental principles for developing PHC services in Iran are:

- Good health and wellbeing for all residents of the country throughout their lives
- An improvement in the health status of those currently disadvantaged
- Collaborative health promotion, and disease and injury prevention through the cooperation of all sectors
- Timely and equitable access for all to a comprehensive range of PHC services regardless of ability to pay

With these philosophies, the government tried to design a health network for delivering essential health-care services based on practical, scientifically sound, culturally appropriate, affordable, and socially acceptable methods.

POLICY AND STRATEGIC FRAMEWORK

The PHC system in Iran was designed based on principles, in which easy access (particularly in rural areas) was at its heart. From the very beginning, the following principles were declared as the main policies to construct the health networks and programmes:

- Priority of prevention over treatment
- Priority of remote and underprivileged rural over urban areas, with special consideration for vulnerable groups especially mothers and children

- Priority of out-patient over in-patient services, and
- Decentralization, aimed at forming self-sufficient regional and local facilities

PHC was blossoming as the leading strategy for attaining Health for All (HFA) by the Year 2000. The content and ideology behind PHC closely matched what the people expected: social justice, equity, human rights, universal access to services, giving priority to the most vulnerable and underprivileged groups.

MAJOR CHARACTERISTICS OF THE PHC NETWORK

There are important features in Iran's PHC system to ensure greater access to essential services. The first characteristic is the stratification of services and networking, where a client may be referred to a higher level if required. The distribution of facilities is implemented on different levels based on the needs of the population and the complexity of the needed services, according to the Master Plan, which defines the rules and standards for all facilities and functions.

The second characteristic is the integration of different services for the target groups. This means that a package of preventive and curative health interventions is utilized for a particular population group. Integrated Management of Childhood Illness (IMCI) and Maternal Care (MC) are the first experiences of the Iranian health system in providing integrated health care. MC tries to secure the patients' health by combating a group of diseases that endanger the well-being of the mother and her unborn baby. The services for prevention and control of iron deficiency, underlying systemic diseases, malnutrition, and eclampsia secure the mother's health; meanwhile, this integrated package tries to protect the fetus and neonate from neonatal tetanus, erythroblastosis fetalis, premature and low birth weight, birth trauma, asphyxia, hypothermia, and neonatal jaundice.

The third characteristic is the population allocated to each service unit. It should assure easy accessibility to every health service facility. Criteria for determining the population for each type of service delivery is based on available facilities, population distribution and geographical accessibility as well as administrative divisions. The plan for the development of health-care networks (The Master Plan) determines the population covered by each health unit, which is developed by local regional experts together with national experts in the MoHME.

The fourth characteristic is the standard protocol of action for service delivery especially in the first level of health services. The scientific departments within the MoHME are responsible for developing guidelines for health service provision at all levels; they are provided to health staff in the form of charts, handbooks, or training packages.

All of the above characteristics, together with the establishment of strong Behvarz Training Centres have provided the health networks with extensive facilities, where efficient female and male community health workers (behvarz) – frequently acclaimed for the quality of their work – are being trained.

HEALTH NETWORK STRUCTURE

To implement the policies, the District Health Centres (DHC) were selected as the independent administrative level for managing health programmes at the district level. The role of the DHCs is to realize the government's expectations and conduct governmental health strategies at the district level. The DHCs are responsible for the specific needs of their populations and funding is provided by the central government based on population size. They are also responsible for the logistic and administrative affairs of the district health network.

The Master Plan defines where the facilities should be located. The way in which the facilities are distributed depends on two main factors: first the size and location of the population, and second geographical accessibility.[5] To compile the Master Plan the experts of the DHCs gather information about the population and mark them on topographic maps showing geographical accessibility. The roads and pathways which people use are studied carefully. Thus, the Iranian government was able to provide PHC services for more than 98% of the population in rural areas, living in over 65,000 villages. The average population for each village is less than 350 and the average distance between villages is more than 25 kilometres.

Health House: The soul of the Iranian health system lies in its most peripheral facility – the Health House (HH) – which is run by community health workers (behvarz). The HH covers 1000 to 1500 people on average residing in one main village, or several satellite villages. A village on the way to urban areas, which is accessible to a larger population, is usually the site of the HH.[6]

The principal duty of the behvarz is the provision of PHC services for the covered population. They are multipotential community health workers (CHW). They have played a pivotal role in the success of the country's PHC networks so far. One major factor contributing to this success has been the intimate relationship between a behvarz and his/her community. It was exactly with this fact in mind that choosing behvarz strictly from their own target community was considered an essential policy from the outset. Behvarzes are totally familiar with the culture and traditions.[7]

A behvarz training mothers to cook food for their children

The two-year course for training the behvarz is a typical example of using appropriate technology and is delivered in a manner in total contrast to traditional pedagogy. The training packages are provided by the Deputy for Health and the course is completely task-oriented based on what the behvarz should do in the HH.[8]

Behvarz training

Health Post: The urban Health Posts (HPs) are responsible for delivering PHC to urban populations in a way similar to the HH in rural areas. The HP covers a population of about 12,000 individuals. Health-care experts accompanied by environmental and occupational health experts, a nurse, and a midwife staff each UHP.

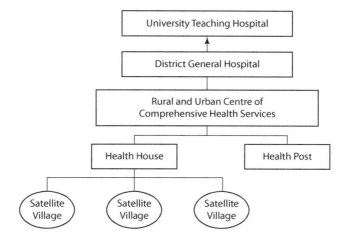

Rural and Urban Centres of Comprehensive Health Services (RCCHS and UCCHS): The RCCHS is a village-based facility that has one to five HHs under its supervision. It is staffed by a general practitioner, several health technicians, and administrative personnel. The UCCHS is functionally similar to the RCCHS, with three to five HPs under its control. General practitioners, mainly for supervising HPs and referral case management, work in each centre.[9]

Ministry of Health and Medical Education (MoHME): The MoHME is responsible for both health science education and provision of health services. In each province, a state university of medical sciences and health services is responsible for these activities. Therefore, in addition to district health networks, different faculties and teaching hospitals are also part of this organization in each province. As a result of this organizational unity, academic staff have been more involved in health system management, evaluation, research, and design. Close cooperation between scientific and executive bodies facilitates the movement of Iran's health system toward a more efficient, equitable, and sustainable service provision.

PHC Information System: The information system of the health networks is mainly based on data gathered from defined populations covered by health facilities. The Household Electronic Health Records has been designed and implemented in recent years. With the unique national identification (ID) code for every Iranian citizen all health information is recorded before birth and until death, and by using a password to ensure essential privacy, health information is accessible for by the client and their health care providers.

The largest project in this field was the launch of the integrated health information system called SIB. Besides the health profile of individuals, the online system collectively records structural information and service delivery processes.

Through conducting annual censuses, the facilities update their information about the population living within their catchment area. In addition to annual censuses, routine data are gathered using special tools. Additionally, periodic surveys are conducted in the country mainly to gather data related to coverage, household effects, and outcomes of health programmes, which are not collected through the registration system.

MOVING FROM PHC TOWARDS FP IN RURAL AREAS AND CITIES OF UNDER 20,000 POPULATION: THE SECOND PHASE TOWARDS UHC

During the course of PHC network formation, the system relied first on community healthcare providers, basic simple PHC elements, and GPs. In addition to expanding the number of service units and increasing population coverage, there was an improvement in the quality of health services and the integration of new health programmes in the health system. This upgrade was accompanied with applying higher-quality human resources. The existence of a functioning PHC system was pivotal in driving policy makers' decision to implement this phase of action.[10]

In terms of financing during the years of developing services in rural areas, all PHC services were provided free of charge to villagers, tribal populations, and urban areas. To reach UHC targets, the number of PHC services and the coverage of the population were scaled up. With the statutory requirement for rural health insurance, the government's commitment to a comprehensive referral system and the development towards a family practice approach accelerated. Along with health sector reform programmes, the quality of services was enhanced by the appointment of new staff, including nutritionists, mental health experts, and midwives.

Training courses for GPs were considered necessary to develop family and community-based services; therefore, the MoHME started training family physician specialists. In addition, with the implementation of health reform plans, the MoHME tried to expand health services for urban communities aiming at health market regulation.

HEALTH SYSTEM REFORMS

At the beginning of the health reforms, significant improvements were clear in health indicators. The PHC system was highly organized and efficient, resulting in a dramatic decrease in infant, maternal, and neonatal mortality rates, population growth, and increasing lifespan.[11] Nevertheless, Iran's health system has entered a new stage with its various strengths and challenges. These led policy makers to adopt specific approaches to plan and implement changes.

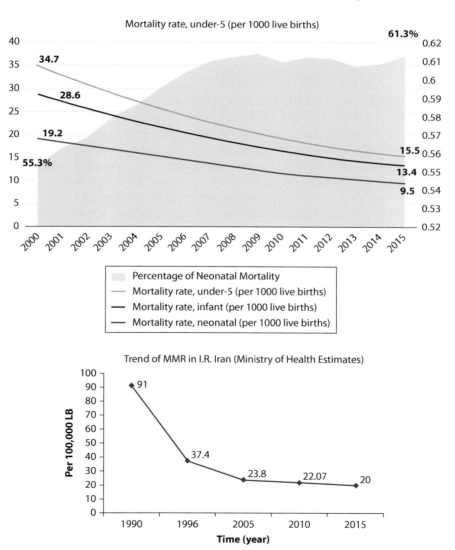

Source: Department for Family, Population and School Health, MoH, Iran

HEALTH SYSTEM STRENGTHS

These include:

- A large efficient and equitable health network for delivering PHC services
- An efficient and decentralized model of Community Health Worker (behvarz) training in health networks
- Merging medical education with public health affairs so that an integrated health system within the MoHME links the two sectors of medical education and public health closely and effectively
- Setting up scientific councils to integrate and develop health programmes in the PHC network
- Active continuing education of personnel within the health network
- Training medical students in the health networks through Community-Oriented Medical Education (COME) in Universities of Medical Sciences
- Providing potentials for applied research, to promote Community-Based Research (CBR) and learning-by-doing

HEALTH SYSTEM CHALLENGES: THE NEED FOR IMPLEMENTING A FAMILY PRACTICE SYSTEM

Iran, like many other societies, is experiencing rapid changes in all aspects of social life, such as urbanization and lifestyle changes, demographic changes, and a changing socioeconomic environment. The pattern of diseases has changed. The burden of disease attributable to communicable diseases (2012) is 9.7%, to non-communicable diseases 76.4%, and injuries 14.0%. Among non-communicable diseases (NCDs), cardiovascular diseases account for 45.7%, cancers 13.5%, respiratory diseases 3.8%, and diabetes mellitus 2.2%. It is expected 17% of adults aged 30 to 70 years will die from one of the four main NCDs.[12] More than 17.5% of adolescents (13–15 years of age) have smoked cigarettes at some point.[13] The prevalence rate of physical inactivity among people aged 15 to 64 years old is 40.1%.[14] These means that the health network in Iran is confronted with a significant weight of chronic diseases and risk factors that should be managed at higher costs. The health system should respond to these changes in time while trying to meet efficiency, equity, and sustainability criteria. As a result of these changes, Iran's health system is facing problems in meeting health needs. The most important challenges are below:

- Demographic transition with An increase in the elderly population and higher burden of disease
- Disease pattern transition and developing NCDs
- An increase in the population's expectations from the health system
- Limitations in financing a health system with new patterns of disease and client expectations
- Increased marginalization and lack of adequate health coverage
- Lack of adequate coverage of preventive health services in urban areas
- Factors increasing the susceptibility of the health market to failure:
  - Growing health inequity in the utilization of curative services from the private sector
  - Increasing out-of-pocket payments
  - Increasing provider induced demands in the private sector
  - Inequity in financial earnings for health staff, especially physicians
  - Increasing catastrophic payments

- Introduction of diagnostic and therapeutic health technologies with low cost-effectiveness
- The desire of health-care professionals to create a monopoly in the health market, and
- Excessive demand for sub-specialized services and the weakening of generalism

MACRO POLICIES

In order to regulate the health market, the referral system and family practice need to be strengthened. An effective family practice programme requires close coordination between the different executive and legislative bodies. Firstly, we require transparency in health policies and programmes to conduct the needed reforms sustainably. Secondly, we need to improve health information systems, as well as monitoring and evaluation systems. The disintegration of different levels of health service delivery could produce failures in the referral system. Sustainable financing should be provided mainly through insurance. In addition, new services should be implemented to address changing needs, particularly for NCDs. Finally, reforms in the recruitment and training of human resources are essential.

LEGISLATION FOR FAMILY PRACTICE

In Iran, the right to health has been stipulated in Articles 3, 21, 29, and 43 of the Constitution. Article 29 emphasizes that the provision of fair access to health services is the government's responsibility. It states: "The right to health and medical care in the form of insurance, and so on, is the government's task. It should be provided through public revenues. All people should have financial support for health." Article 43 of the constitution states that the provision of health and treatment needs for all people in the country is obligatory.

Provision of social justice and health for all has been emphasized in the national macro policies in the first to sixth development plans. The health sector reforms began with the third development plan and continued in the fourth, fifth, and sixth. The key point was rural health insurance in the fourth programme of development.

The parliamentary decision on the allocation of financial resources for rural health insurance was made in 2005. This action created an opportunity to begin the reform using the available resources from insurance organizations. Article 92 of the law emphasized that the share of people's contribution to health expenditure, which at that time was more than 55%, should be reduced to a maximum of 30%. Article 96 of the fourth development plan emphasizes that during the fourth Five Year Plan, universal health insurance should be gradually increased to 100%. In 2005, the HIO was obliged to issue health insurance cards for all residents of rural areas and urban communities with a population under 20,000. These services should be implemented in the framework of the family practice and referral system.[15] On this basis, the Ministry of Health and the Ministry of Welfare agreed to establish common memoranda. Following this, the HIO determined the cost per capita for inhabitants of each urban area according to the coefficients of exclusion.

GOVERNANCE

Health-care providers' accreditation and licensing is the most important issue in governance, where the key question is "Who is the family physician in Iran?" A family doctor is a person with a minimum degree of general practice and medical registration who has passed training courses. He/she is contracted to work in a health centre. The duties of the family physician are determined based on health-care packages. The responsibility of delivering comprehensive health services and managing the health team are the tasks of the family physician.

The second issue is the composition of the health team. It includes a physician, a dentist, a midwife, a nurse, as well as experts in family health, disease control, environmental and occupational health, laboratory sciences, radiology, and others who work together in the Centre of Comprehensive Health Services.

In order to operate the rural insurance programme and family practice at the national, university, and district levels, different committees are established. They have different tasks including designing operational programmes, providing technical assistance and support to lower levels, monitoring performance, and regulating the flow of financial resources and other governance activities.

THE HEALTH TEAM

The criteria for determining the size of the health team is based on the population covered by the centre.[16]

1. *Physician*: For each Centre of Comprehensive Health Services (CCHS), the physician–population ratio is 1:4000; increasing at a rate of one extra physician for every 4000 people or fraction.
2. *Midwife*: The ratio should be 1:7000.
3. *Dentist/oral health expert*: 1:15,000.
4. *Laboratory expert*: 1:7000.
5. Radiology may be assigned to the Centre of Comprehensive Health Services externally.

All health staff have contracts. Meanwhile, in order to increase the access of rural insurers to pharmaceutical services, the CCHSs in urban areas can contract with nongovernmental pharmacies.

FAMILY MEDICINE TRAINING PROGRAMMES

To increase the number of licensed family physicians, the discipline of family medicine needs to be established and strengthened. As a transitional arrangement, suitable bridging programmes and new courses are needed to upgrade GPs to family physicians.

Various programmes have been developed to enhance the ability of family physicians as well as members of the health team. These programmes included reviewing the syllabus of health staff especially physicians and compiling new academic disciplines and on the job training.

The training is directed at the GPs. In order to improve GPs' capabilities, a review of the GP syllabus was considered the first step and was subsequently carried out several times. The result of the revisions was improving social medicine and family practice subjects, with a value of 9.5 credits (equal to 171 hours of training). The subjects covered in the course are as follows: principles of health services delivery, epidemiology and medical statistics, evidence-based research and evidence-based medicine, epidemiology of communicable and non-communicable diseases, demographics and family health, and health psychology. Additionally, field practice in social and family medicine was added in two separate one-month periods.[17]

Additional graduate courses have been designed and implemented. These include:

- Master of Family Medicine (MFM) Virtual Modular Course
- Family medicine bridging programme, and
- Family medicine specialty programme

MASTER OF FAMILY MEDICINE VIRTUAL MODULAR COURSE

This is a cost-effective, two-year virtual course for training GPs who are working in the field. The country has plans to cover all GPs with this course over the next 10 years.

The course consists of:[18]

1. General Practice
   - Out-patient Management of Common Diseases in Adults
   - Out-patient Management of Common Paediatric Diseases
   - Out-patient Management of Common Gynaecology and Obstetric Diseases
   - Out-patient Management of Common Geriatric Diseases
   - Out-patient Management of Common Psychiatric Diseases
2. Comprehensive Care Approach
   - Preventive Medicine and Management of Common Risk Factors
   - Symptomatic and Palliative Treatment of Common Complaints
   - Rehabilitation of Common Diseases and Conditions
3. First Contact Care
   - The Health Care Delivery System and Managed Care
   - Family Physicians: Definition and Function
4. Coordination of Care
   - Principles of Case Management
   - Leadership Concepts and Skills
5. Continuity of Care
   - Referral Indications for Common Diseases
6. Family-Oriented Approach
   - Home Care for Common Diseases and Conditions in Iran
7. Community-Oriented Approach
   - Principles of Disease Management
   - Principles of Health Risk Management
8. System-Based Approach
   - Health System Structure and Functions
   - Evidence-Based Medicine
   - Rational Drug Use
   - Rational Imaging Investigation
   - Rational Laboratory Order
   - Principles of Utilization Management

BRIDGING PROGRAMME FOR BUILDING CAPACITIES OF GPS IN FAMILY MEDICINE

This is a six-month course which will be conducted through a national Learning Management System (LMS). The main objective is to empower all GPs working as family physicians to:

- Focus their approaches to the patient and community on family-oriented health care, and
- Provide essential care and service according to the national health protocols and guidelines

The expected outcomes are as follows:

- By the end of March 2019, all modules will be prepared and visible on the national LMS.

- At least 250 trainers in 25 medical universities will be trained and recruited by the end of 2019.
- By the end of 2021, a total number of 9000 GPs will be trained in the programme.

The programme is run in a blended format including online, face-to-face live, and hands-on experiences in ambulatory care service (CCHSs). It is intended to fit in with the work schedule of practising GPs. The programme includes five modules designed according to the major determinants of the burden of diseases of our country and the content of our service packages. Also, they are arranged around defined age groups. The content will cover national guidelines in the health system. The total duration of the programme is 24 weeks and includes the following modules:

- *Module I*: Basics of family practice
- *Module II*: Child care
- *Module III*: Adolescence and youth care
- *Module IV*: Adult and elderly care
- *Module V*: Reproductive health and prenatal care

FAMILY PHYSICIAN SPECIALTY

The curriculum of the family physician specialty was approved in 2011 by MoHME and the first resident admission for it was in 2014. The programme is based on the expected vision for the health system. With the training of family medicine specialists, within a 10-year period, it is expected that they will have a dominant role in the health market. They will act as the first contact to manage most common health problems and will be capable of carrying out most common interventions.

The length of the medical specialist's education is expected to be three years or two years for those who have passed the MFM Virtual Modular Course. Residents will be trained in various specialized clinics, as well as family medicine and emergency clinics.

FINANCING

The Iranian health system needs to increase its financing, undertake the costing of essential health services packages and practice strategic purchasing. According to Article 12 of the General Health Insurance Law of the country, all villagers, nomads, and residents of cities with a population below 20,000 should benefit from the rural and nomadic fund. They receive health insurance through a health insurance package and out-patient and hospital services will be provided for them through the referral system and family practice programme. The premium for this group is fully paid by the government. Financing the family physician programme in rural areas and cities with a population under 20,000 is provided from two sources including this fund and one percentage of the value added tax. These two are collected in a fund for HIO in order to purchase health services based on an agreement between the MoHME and the HIO. This purchase includes PHC services and patients visits, drugs, laboratory, and radiology services.

Funding for PHC services in cities over 20,000 people is provided through the general government budget that is allocated by the Organization of Planning and Budget, through various insurance schemes, such as Social Security Organization (SSO), HIO, and Armed Forces Medical Service Organization.

Payments to members of the health team, including family physicians and other staff, are mostly based on their covered population; however, different variables such as the deprivation score of the covered region and the performance of the team members are considered in the payment formula.

INTEGRATION AND QUALITY ASSURANCE OF SERVICES

A range of well-selected, quality assured health services should be provided in an integrated manner through family practice backed up by a robust referral system. The period of two decades of successive design and implementation of health programmes in the country has given us rich opportunities to understand the critical issues, strengths, and weaknesses for health programme planning. Based on the experience gained in designing health programmes over the past decades, the design and development of health programmes have been done in five steps:

1. Priority setting of health problems
2. Choosing the most appropriate strategy to solve the health problem
3. Designing the model of integration considering the chosen strategy
4. Designing a model for community participation, and
5. Designing a model for evaluation and development

The burden of diseases was calculated based on various health data in Iran. Relying on the incidence, prevalence, and severity of health problems, and considering the existence of proper intervention, effectiveness, and feasibility of actions, the scientific experts were able to design new health programmes and integrate them into the health networks. These actions played a key role in the development of health care and providing new service packages for family physicians and health team members.

Since the 1960s, the Islamic Republic of Iran's urban population has tripled, and life expectancy has risen. This has increased people's exposure to tobacco, unhealthy diets, and physical inactivity. Evidence indicates that the Iranian people have been affected by NCDs during recent decades. Therefore, the plan for tackling NCDs is the priority in delivering family practice services. In recent years the Iranian Package of essential NCD interventions for PHC (IraPEN) has been successfully piloted and its nationwide scale up has begun in at least one district per province. Cancer, diabetes, heart disease, stroke, and chronic respiratory disease are the target diseases for this programme, and reducing risk factors is one of the priorities of the health system.[19]

To be accessible to different target groups, new services were integrated into target group service packages. In order to optimize the effectiveness of these services, family physicians and health teams are trained on the new service packages. In addition, new members have been added to the health team including nutrition and mental health experts. Scientific groups in the MoHME develop these new service packages and provide them for family physicians and health teams. New service packages focus on the following issues:

- Smoking cessation
- Improving nutrition
- Reducing the incidence and impact of traffic accidents
- Increasing the level of physical activity
- Reducing the incidence and impact of cancers
- Reducing the incidence and impact of cardiovascular disease
- Reducing the incidence and impact of diabetes
- Improving oral health
- Reducing the incidence of mental illness and improving the health status of people with mental illnesses

Elderly health care and anthropometry for a patient with knee osteoarthritis at home, in one of the satellite villages. The behvarz is measuring weight; the family physician is recording data in the integrated health information system.

The first step of action for the family physician and health team is population identification in the catchment area followed by filling out a health record for each person. All the data should be recorded on the integrated health information system. An annual visit is required for all people in the health unit. The family physician should have a weekly visit to HHs with a population less than 2000, and a twice-weekly visit to the HHs with a population over 2000. Also, once a month, he should deliver services to the people in the satellite villages.

TOWARDS DEVELOPING FP IN SUBURBAN AREAS AND CITIES OF OVER 20,000 POPULATION: THE THIRD PHASE TOWARDS UHC

The target population of the programme includes the populations living in urban areas including the marginal population around cities and cities with more than 20,000 people. The total population for these areas in Iran is estimated at 10.2 million and 43 million (without considering marginal population) respectively. The programme aims to develop UHC all over the country.[20] This programme is based on public–private partnerships (PPP), and devolution of services to the nongovernmental sector.

The CHSCs accept referrals from health posts (HPs). Nutrition counselling, dietary regulation, mental health, control of substance abuse, oral health, genetic counselling, management of child developmental disorders, and environmental and occupational health services are being delivered in the urban CHSCs.

The members of the health team in this programme include a family physician, health-care provider, environmental health specialist, occupational health specialist, nutritionist, mental health expert, nurse, midwife, dentist, oral health-care provider, and laboratory staff. The payment in this programme is per capita adjusted by service.

REFERENCES

1. King M. *An Iranian Experiment in Primary Health Care: The West Azerbaijan Project.* New York: Oxford University Press; 1983.
2. Malekafzali H. Primary health care in the rural area of the Islamic Republic of Iran. *Iranian Journal of Public Health.* 2009;38(Suppl 1): 69–70. Available from: http://citeseerx.ist.psu.edu/viewdoc/download? doi=10.1.1.607.357&rep=rep1&type=pdf [Accessed 22 September 2018].
3. WHO. *The World Health Report 2008 - Primary Health Care (Now More Than Ever).* Available from: http://www.who.int/whr/2008/en/ [Accessed 22 September 2018].
4. Shadpour K. *The PHC Experience in Iran.* Tehran: UNICEF; 1994.
5. Pileroudi C. *The District Primary Health Care Networks in Iran.* 2nd ed. Tehran: UNICEF; 1999.
6. Shadpour K. Primary health care networks in the Islamic Republic of Iran. *East Mediterranean Health Journal.* 2000;6(4): 822–825.
7. WHO. *Iranian health houses open the door to primary care.* Bulletin of the World Health Organization. 2008. Available from: http://www.who.int/bulletin/volumes/86/8/08-030808/en/ [Accessed 22 September 2018].
8. Rahbar MR, Ahmadi M. Lessons learnt from the model of instructional system for training community health workers in Rural Health Houses of Iran. *Iran Red Crescent Medical Journal.* 2015;17(2): e2145.
9. Ministry of Health and Medical Education. *Health Network Standards.* 2017.
10. Takian A, Doshmangir L, Rashidian A. Implementing family physician programme in rural Iran: Exploring the role of an existing primary health care network. *Family Practice.* 2013;30(5): 551–559.
11. Asadi-Lari M, Sayyari A.A, Akbari M.E, Gray D. Public health improvement in Iran-lessons from the last 20 years. *Public Health.* 2004;118(6): 395–402.
12. WHO. *Noncommunicable diseases country profiles.* 2014. Available from: http://apps.who.int/iris/bitst ream/handle/10665/128038/9789241507509_eng.pdf?sequence=1 [Accessed 22 September 2018].
13. WHO. *Global youth tobacco survey.* 2010. Available from: http://www.emro.who.int/images/stories/tfi/do cuments/GYTS_FS_IRI_R2.pdf?ua=1 [Accessed 22 September 2018].
14. Ministry of Health and Medical Education. Tehran. *NCD Surveillance System Survey.* 2011.
15. Ministry of Health and Medical Education. *Evaluation Study of Family Physician Programme in Rural Areas and Cities under 20 Thousand Population.* Tehran: Noavaran Sina Press; 2013.
16. Ministry of Health and Medical Education. *Executive Order for Family Practice and Rural Health Insurance.* 2017.
17. Ministry of Health and Medical Education of Iran. *Educational programme of general practitioners.*
18. Ministry of Health and Medical Education of Iran. *Educational programme of MFM for General practitioners.* Approved 2008.
19. WHO. *Islamic Republic of Iran on a fast-track to beating non-communicable diseases.* 2017. Available from: http://www.who.int/features/2017/iran-noncommunicable-diseases/en/ [Accessed 22 September 2018].
20. Ministry of Health and Medical Education of Iran. *Promotion Plan in the Health System.* Tehran: Bamshad Sabz Press; 2017.

CHAPTER 18

Iraq

Abdul Munem Al Dabbagh, Ghaith Sabri Mohammed,
and Thamer Al Hilfi

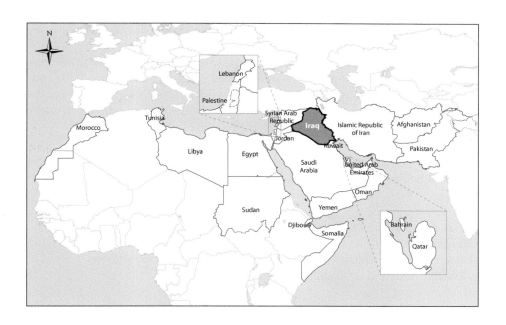

Total number of PHC facilities	2600
Number of general practitioners working in public PHC facilities	2362*
Number of certified family physicians working in PHC facilities	350
Average number of family physician graduates/year	80–90
Number of medical schools	27
Number of family medicine departments	27

* Excluding the Kurdistan Region.

INTRODUCTION

In Iraq, there are about 2600 Primary Health-Care Centres (PHCCs),[1] mostly located in population centres, but some are located in rural and peri-urban areas. Slightly more than 1400 PHCCs are staffed by doctors and are identified as Main Health-Care Centres (MHCCs). Around 1200 PHCCs are called Health Sub-Centres (HSCs).[2] Previously some, though not all, of these sub-centres were managed by nurses. Given the acute shortage of nurses in Iraq, almost all remaining nurses were reassigned to hospitals, leaving staffing of many facilities entirely in the hands of medical auxiliaries.[3] In some PHCCs doctors work alone, while other facilities may have up to 20 doctors. The number of doctors present is not necessarily based on workload or need, but more commonly on where doctors wish to live and the proximity of the PHCC to their house or their own private clinic. Difficulties with transportation, curfews, and numerous checkpoints exacerbate this practice.[1]

Most donor attention concerned with rebuilding health services in Iraq, following the invasion in 2003, has focused on the problems of hospitals. Interest in primary health-care services has come about mainly in the past 10 years.[4]

Essential health service packages (EHSP) are well integrated at the level of the main health-care centres which are managed mostly by well-trained general practitioners (GPs) and in some cases by certified family physicians; however, these services are not well integrated at the level of health sub-centres which are managed by medical auxiliaries whose sole duty is to manage acute emergencies. The EHSP offered at the MHCCs includes the following services:

- Family health, antenatal care, delivery and newborn care, postnatal care, family planning, child health, integrated management of childhood illness (IMCI), growth-monitoring and essential nutrition actions, immunization, and adolescent reproductive health
- Basic curative care and treatment of major chronic conditions
- Hygiene and environmental health (N.B. this excludes the provision of mass sanitation and water supplies, which is the responsibility of a different sector), and
- Health education and communication

Most of the MHCCs have good infrastructure, are medically fairly well equipped, well staffed with physicians, trained nurses and medical auxiliaries, and follow medical protocols. However, most of the facilities are facing shortages of essential drugs because of the economic difficulties the country is facing.

Antenatal care

Those centres which follow the family medicine model (around 230 centres) have well-established family files, referral systems, and ongoing training programmes.[5] Nine centres have been chosen by the World Health Organization (WHO) to follow the family health practice approach and are using the electronic health information system; they are under strict quality assurance and accreditation processes.

There is widespread satisfaction with primary health-care services, and levels do not differ appreciably between public and private sectors. The public sector PHCC services are preferentially used by poorer populations to whom they are important providers. PHCC services are free, with little evidence of informal payments to providers.[2]

There are 375 PHCCs in areas without access to hospitals, which are equipped with delivery rooms and an emergency room. Some of these PHCCs are designated as training centres, and 140 are fully updated and fully equipped facilities with staff who have received additional training through donor funds.[6] New PHCCs are being constructed and about 10% of HSCs are being upgraded to PHCCs in an effort to better distribute services according to population needs. The shortage of human resources limits the number of facilities that can be upgraded. Staffing of the underserved areas with qualified doctors requires incentives to make this a desirable career option. A more extensive programme has been developed to train community mental health workers in all 18 of Iraq's governorates.[7,8]

The key challenges to accessing quality health services in the PHHCs are a lack of political commitment, a shortage of certified family physicians and essential drugs, and poor community awareness towards the importance of primary care centres as an essential – and not a cheap – form of health care.[9]

FAMILY PRACTICE

The Ministry of Health is supporting the expansion of family practice in Iraq by increasing the number of primary care centres using the family practice approach and increasing the number of family doctors after academic training.

The increase in the number of family health centres is achieved by converting some preexisting centres after fulfilling certain infrastructure requirements, or by building new family centres. One major problem here is that the number of family doctors is much fewer than required. The mismatch is also encountered because of the time-consuming process for the graduation of qualifying family physicians. The reasons for the limited production of family physicians in Iraq are outlined here.

- There is only one Iraqi residency programme in family medicine which is capable of graduating no more than 30 to 40 candidates per year. Since starting in 1995, the number of certified family physicians graduated out of this programme has not exceeded 200 candidates.
- Iraqi Arab Board Residency Programme graduates, since 2008, is 150.
- The "brain drain" and emigration have added to the shortage of available family physicians.

Family practice has been integrated within the national public health initiative within the last 15 years, and there has been a gradual increase in the number of family medicine centres and family practitioners contributing to the provision of family health services at primary care level. After the participation of family doctors at primary care level, there was a noticeable improvement in the quality of care especially in certain primary care programmes such as screening for hypertension and diabetes and the integrated management of neonatal and childhood health. However, there is still a long way to go before family physicians can lead primary care services in Iraq. For example, in the largest health directorate in Baghdad, there are 110 primary care centres, but only 22 of them are family practice centres that provide a higher quality of care for the public. Therefore, the gap is still too big to be filled in the coming years.

Family practice is linked with other initiatives like hospitals and secondary care specialists through many channels such as:

- A referral system by which family physicians establish contact with hospital doctors (secondary care doctors), receive feedback from them, and adapt the management of their patients collaboratively
- Fellowship training for family medicine students offered in some of the training hospitals
- Frequent joint scientific activities conducted within the training programmes of the family health centres, inviting secondary care physicians to discuss recent advances and updates in their specialties

Family practice has contributed a lot towards universal health coverage in the country. This is best illustrated through the implementation of specific nationally designed programmes within the context of primary health-care services. Family doctors are playing a leadership role in this process by training and monitoring the implementation of these programmes, besides direct involvement in providing services in the field.

One example is the extended programme of immunization, including the use of phone calls to enhance compliance with vaccination schedule dates. Another example is the provision of screening programmes for hypertension and diabetes, which is one of the initiatives for the control of non-communicable diseases. All these programmes have benefited from the sound and up-to-date knowledge of family doctors, and their approach to follow up has ensured compliance and correct implementation. Unfortunately, this is still limited to a small number of primary care family centres and has not yet become nationwide practice.

Family practice teams are in their early first steps in PHCCs in the country. Only family health centres have separate family health units where a family doctor, a nurse, and a community worker work together to provide health services. There are very limited numbers of family health centres in the capital, only nine out of about 230 PHCCs. It should be mentioned that midwifery services are not an integral part of PHC services in central cities, but these services are only available in primary care centres on the outskirts of big cities and rural areas that lack family practice services at the present time.

Currently, family health services have yet to arrive in rural areas. This should be understood in the context of the shortage of family doctors, nurses, and health workers. There are about 3000 GPs versus less than 350 family physicians. Efforts are being made by the Ministry of Health (MoH) and Ministry of Higher Education (MoHE) to increase the number of certified family physicians and upgrade the available GPs to meet this shortage and extend family health services to rural areas.

Providing vulnerable and marginalized groups in the community with proper health services is an integral role of the majority of primary care centres. The presence of family doctors to supervise, manage, and provide such services has contributed to better quality of care through the utilization of the family health approach that led to better coverage and follow-up. One of the best examples in this regard was the introduction of elderly-friendly health facilities in those centres that follow the family health approach.

Despite requiring specialty degree qualifications, all primary care personnel are paid the same salary. There is no special financial privilege offered by the MoH for being a family physician. This is one of the obstacles towards encouraging newly graduated doctors to choose family medicine as a specialty. There is now a proposed draft law before the higher authorities to add financial incentives for family physicians to overcome this barrier.

Much research has been conducted addressing the issue of family health practice, some of it evaluating the services in the centres applying the practice and some addressing clients' and physicians' satisfaction with the services. All concluded that applying family health practice helped in improvement of the quality of care in these centres and attracted the clients to choose the centres rather than the overburdened hospitals for better health care.[10,11]

The key challenges facing family health practice can be summarized in the following:

1. Primary care financing, in general, is a major problem. Iraq has almost free health services but the quality and availability of some of these services are unreliable and unsustainable. Health personnel are paid equally by the government irrespective of the variable workload, which creates a feeling of lack of fairness among health workers.

Family physician with patient

2. There is a huge gap between the required and available government funding. One example of this is antihypertensive medications provided by the screening programme, which were subjected to a marked reduction in supply due to insufficient government funding. This shortage led to a drop in the follow-up rate of patients with hypertension at the primary care level.
3. A huge gap is also present between the required and the available number of certified family physicians; but this could be solved in the long term as the training process for new family doctors is ongoing.
4. There is poor community awareness about family medicine.
5. Poor motivation for junior doctors and GPs to pursue family medicine as a specialty is an issue, which might be due to lack of incentives.
6. The brain drain and emigration are problems, due to the unstable security situation in the country exacerbated by the attractive incentives for family physicians in some of the neighbouring countries. The migration of experienced doctors from Iraq has created concerns about the quality of health services, and the ability of training facilities to replace those migrating, especially those with advanced specialty training.[12,13]

The success of family practice is clear in the centres where it is available. The approach in which each family doctor is assigned to serve a specific number of families within a well-defined geographical area has tremendously improved coverage rate and regular follow-up of medical problems, with the use of scheduled phone calls. It is in such health centres that detailed records for all families including sociodemographic data, as well as health data, are kept available for use when necessary. Two successful examples of health facilities implementing family practice are:

- The improvement in the vaccination coverage rate to reach up to 98% of targets, for example, Bab Al Moathem Family Health Centre
- The increase in the number of people screened for hypertension and diabetes, to involve almost all those targeted

In another development, some of these centres have started using electronic health information systems for their data records. This helped in better evaluation and monitoring of the services. The information systems already applied in Bab Al Moathem PHC training centre, Al Russafah sector, and Al Mansour PHC training centre, Al Kurkh sector – both are in Baghdad.

FAMILY MEDICINE

The Iraqi residency programme in family medicine started in 1989 as a joint programme of Family and Community Medicine with those candidates passing the programme being awarded a Fellowship in Family and Community Medicine (FAMCO). In 1995 a separate residency programme in family medicine was established as a four-year programme including a theoretical component, training in major hospitals and a full year training in special primary health centres geared for training. In 2008 the first Iraqi residents joined the Arab Board in Family Medicine which has a similar four-year residency programme.

Furthermore, and to meet the shortage in family physicians, higher diplomas in family medicine – a two-year training programme – were established in many medical schools.

Recently the MoH and MoHE are planning to approve a bridging programme to upgrade GPs already working in PHHCs; this was proposed by WHO in collaboration with the American University of Beirut aiming at graduating at least 100 certified family physicians per year, and for the coming five years, to meet the shortage. It will be a one-year blended training programme incorporating electronic media in training for the first time in Iraq.

Unfortunately, few of the available 25 medical schools in Iraq are incorporating family medicine training in their curriculums and tremendous efforts are being made to fill the gap in the undergraduate training programme towards the importance of the concept of family medicine.

PRIVATE HEALTH SECTOR

The private sector in Iraq is participating actively in delivering health services whether primary, secondary, or tertiary services. Iraqi physicians have the right to have their own private clinics whether they are working in government settings or not. As a matter of fact, wealthy people prefer private sector providers for their health care to avoid the heavily loaded hospitals and PHCCs, and the shortage in essential drugs and medical equipment these settings are facing.

All health services are delivered in private clinics, particularly curative services. However preventive and promotive services are also delivered in some of the private clinics like antenatal and postnatal services, health education, and physical and mental rehabilitation.

The only challenge facing the health authorities is to establish sustainable coordination between the public and private sectors to complement each other. The best example in this regard is the management of tuberculosis (TB) patients where private clinics should provide full documents on their patients to TB centres in PHCCs so that they take the necessary steps in actively examine their close contacts and register the cases for follow-up.

Family physicians are actively participating in providing health services in the private sector, but because of the shortage of certified family physicians, a long time is needed before the importance of their role is acknowledged.

The private sector is serving a sizable proportion of patients in Iraq but unfortunately and because of the lack of coordination between the public and private sector, there is no official data estimating the percentage of patients using the private sector for their health care.

The private sector can play an important role in universal health coverage in Iraq because it has expanded tremendously, especially in recent years. Hence, the MoH is now adopting a new health system reform with the support of WHO and other international agencies incorporating the private sector as an active partner in universal health coverage and setting up new regulations to shape up a coordination system between the public and private.

REFERENCES

1. Ministry of Health, Government of Iraq. *Annual Statistical Report 2017*: 77–80.
2. Burnham G, et al. Perceptions and utilization of primary health care services in Iraq: findings from a national household survey. *BMC International Health and Human Rights*, 2011; 11: 15. Available from: https://bmcinthealthhumrights.biomedcentral.com/articles/10.1186/1472-698X-11-15.
3. Dorell O. Medical exodus worsens Iraq's ills. *USA Today*, 2007. Available from: http://www.usatoday.com/news/world/iraq/2007-08-17-medical-exodus_N.htm [Accessed 15 October 2017].
4. Ministry of Health, Government of Iraq. Health systems based on primary health care in Iraq. *International Conference on Primary Health Care*. 2008. Doha, Qatar.
5. Ministry of Health, Government of Iraq, Directorate General of Public Health. Personal communication.
6. USAID/Primary Health Care project in Iraq (USAID/PHCI) Annual Report. 2012. Available from: http://phciraq.org/sites/phciraq.org/files/Annual%20Report%202012.pdf.
7. Sadik S, Abdulrahman S, Bradley M, Jenkins R. Integrating mental health into primary health care in Iraq. *Mental Health in Family Medicine*, 2011; 8(1): 39–49.
8. Heartland Alliance International. Iraq: community mental health worker programme. Available from: https://www.heartlandalliance.org/international/about-hai/middle-east-north-africa/iraq/#Mental Health.

9. Hall JJ, Taylor R. Health for all beyond 2000: The demise of the Alma-Ata Declaration and primary health care in developing countries. *Medical Journal of Australia*, 2003; 178(1): 17–20. Available from: https://pdfs.semanticscholar.org/c134/d51110ed27488860884ddc3f2e8241d9c0bf.pdf.

10. Ahmed SM. Expectations of physicians working in Erbil city about the role of family medicine practice. *WONCA World Conference*. Prague. 2013.

11. Issa S. Family doctors' satisfaction: a sample from Baghdad. *Iraqi Postgraduate Medical Journal*, 2016(3); 109: 15–18.

12. MEDACT. The Iraq health crisis. *Report of a One-Day Conference Organized by the Iraq Medical Association in Collaboration with MEDACT*. 2007. Available from: http://www.medact.org/content/wmd_and_conflict/Iraq%20Health%20Crisis%20Conference%20Report%20final.doc [Accessed 16 November 2017].

13. Burnham G, Malik S, Al-Shibli A, Mahjoub A, Baqer AQ, Baqer ZQ, Al Qaraghuli F, Doocy S. Understanding the impact of conflict on health services in Iraq: information from 401 Iraqi refugee doctors in Jordan. *International Journal of Health Planning and Management*, 2012; 27(1): e51–e64. Available from: https://doi.org/10.1002/hpm.1091.

CHAPTER 19

Jordan

Oraib Alsmadi, Mohammed Rasoul Tarawneh, and May Hani Al Hadidi

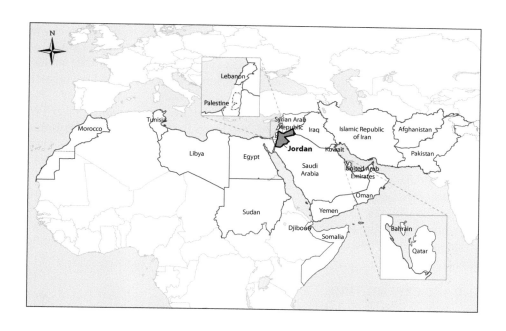

	Ministry of Health (MoH)	Royal Medical Services (RMS)	Universities	UNRWA
Total number of PHC facilities	• Comprehensive HC: 102 • Primary HC: 380 • Village HC: 194	12	4	25
Average number of family physician graduates/year	20 since 1993	2–3 since 1985	4–5 since 1999	–
Number of general practitioners working in public PHC facilities	1645			
Number of certified family physicians working in PHC facilities	115 (total of 210 are working in MoH)			
Number of medical schools	6			
Number of family medicine departments	3			

INTRODUCTION

Jordan is a small, upper-middle-income country with limited natural resources and scarce fresh water supplies (one of the world's 10 most water-stressed countries), with a population of 10 million of which 6.6 are Jordanian. Jordan has one of the most modern health-care infrastructures in the Middle East.

The health system is a complex amalgam of three major sectors: public, private, and donor driven. The public sector consists of two major public programmes that finance as well as deliver care: the Ministry of Health (MOH) and Royal Medical Services (RMS). Other smaller public programmes include several university-based programmes, such as Jordan University Hospital (JUH) in Amman and King Abdullah Hospital (KAH) in Irbid.

The extensive private sector includes 62 hospitals and many private clinics. Over 1.6 million Palestinian refugees in Jordan access primary care through the United Nations Relief Works Agency (UNRWA). In addition, according to the 2015 census more than 1.3 million Syrian refugees are living in Jordan requiring health services. Each of the health-care sub-sectors has its own financing and delivery system.[1]

The ratio of physicians to the population has decreased in recent years; in 2010 it was 26.5:10,000 people while in 2016 it was 14.1:10,000. Supply, personnel, health insurance, health information, and accounting departments are substantially computerized. Government institutions include the Jordan Food and Drug Agency (JFDA) and the Department for Unified Drug Procurement.

HEALTH-CARE EXPENDITURE

Health care in Jordan is provided through both the private and public sectors, with private expenditure on health making up 31.4% of the total in 2015, and the remainder being supplied by the Government. In 2015, Jordan spent approximately JD 2.2 billion (US$3.2 billion) on health, or JD 236 (US$332) per capita. As a percentage of gross domestic product (GDP), total expenditure on health amounted to 7.58% in 2012 according to Jordan National Health

Accounts (NHA), surpassing the average level of expenditure in the Middle East, which stood at 4.5% that year.[2]

Regarding public sector spending, the Jordanian Government's expenditure on health as a percentage of total government expenditure amounted to 18.6%, substantially higher than the next highest country in the region, Bahrain at 11.4%, and falling only slightly short of the 22.4% government expenditure in the United States.

Given the continued growth in the population, not to mention the number of refugees from Palestine, Syria, and Iraq, and the surge in cases of chronic health conditions, the current level of government expenditure on health care as a percentage of GDP is likely unsustainable.

Rising oil prices and inflation, alongside the Kingdom's weak economic performance and the rising and already-stretched government budget, foretell a decline in the level and quality of services provided in the longer term, unless private sector participation, both in terms of health-care provision and health insurance, rises sufficiently to compensate for the increased health-care demand.

PRIMARY HEALTH CARE

Primary health-care (PHC) services are provided mainly by the Ministry of Health (MoH), through an extensive PHC network, consisting of 102 comprehensive health centres, 380 primary health-care centres, and 194 village clinics. The total number of health centres rose sharply over the past decade, particularly with regard to maternal and child health (MCH) centres and dental clinics. A wide range of PHC services are provided in health centres, including general medical care, care of children, family planning, obstetric care, perinatal care, first aid, dispensing of pharmaceutical prescriptions, and dental care. The health centres are also responsible for public health activities not directly related to patient care and for health data collection/information systems at the local level. Public health activities (immunization, screening, health promotion, water safety, sanitation, food quality control, pest control, etc.) are usually performed by paramedical staff at the PHC level, under the supervision of the doctor in charge.

The following is a brief description of the respective roles and package of services provided at the different levels of PHC services within the MoH:

- *Primary Health Centre*: A primary health centre, generally headed by a general practitioner, provides both curative and preventive health services including dental services and school health. The staff also performs food inspections, health promotion activities, and simple epidemiological investigations.
- *Comprehensive Health Centre (CHC)*: In addition to all the services provided by the primary health centres, the comprehensive health centre provides specialty care in the areas of paediatrics, gynaecology, internal medicine, orthopaedics, ENT, ophthalmology, dermatology, and dentistry.
- *Village Health Centre*: Village health centres provide health promotion in villages and maintain simple information about births, deaths, etc. Their current functions are presently not in line with the original intention, being more focused on simple curative care rather than prevention. General practitioners (GPs) are the main medical providers in village health clinics as part-time staff.

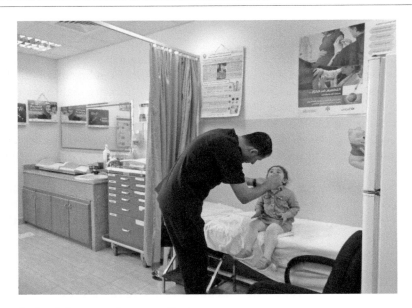

A physician examines a patient

Additional PHC services are provided by other health-care providers:

- *Royal Medical Services*: Twelve PHC clinics are distributed across the country. These facilities provide health services to soldiers, officers, and their dependents, referring patients if needed to one of the 15 military hospitals; at least one military hospital is located in most of Jordan's governorates.
- *Universities*: Jordan University, Jordan University of Science and Technology, Mutah University, and the Hashemite University each have a comprehensive training health centre facility and provide health-care services to the university students, employees of the university and their families, and other patients who buy these services, referring patients if needed, usually to the hospital belonging to each university.
- *United Nations Relief and Works Agency* (UNRWA): UNRWA has 25 PHC clinics distributed across the country, mainly in the refugee camps. They provide a wide range of primary health services using a family practice approach and a package of integrated essential health services.

A key goal of the government is to provide universal health coverage to the entire population. According to the 2015 census, 68% of the population had health insurance, with 8.5% insured by more than one party. The MoH insurance is the most prevalent, covering 44.5% of the population. A further 38% of the population is insured through RMS, and 17.5% of Jordanians are insured by others (university hospitals and the private sector).[3]

The Civil Health Insurance programme provides direct coverage for public sector employees, but also allows non-public sector employees to buy into the programme. Moreover, other individuals deemed eligible may also receive health services under the programme, with payment for the services being provided by the Royal Court.

With respect to clinic visits, in 2014 public sector services attracted the larger part of the patient market, but the private sector gained ground in its share of surgeries and births, at 38.6% and 32.4% of total clinic visits, respectively.

In 2015, the World Organization of Family Doctors (WONCA) and WHO/EMR conducted a collaborative assessment of 15 MoH health centres in Balqa Governorate. Based on the results of this assessment, there is an evident need to ensure technical support in many areas such as the essential health services package (EHSP), essential drug list (EDL), referral system and quality assurance, as well as engagement of the local community. The mechanisms necessary for patient follow-up vary from one health centre to another. Strengthening existing systems is crucial, including establishment of the catchment area and family rosters. Treatment protocols are available; however, compliance needs more observation. The accreditation programme is implemented in some health centres and would support the scale up of family practice.

There is a well-defined and implemented EHSP for all health centres, and the staff are trained in delivery. The EDL is available in all health centres based on the classification of the health centre (primary or comprehensive). The EHSP includes maternal and newborn services, child health and immunizations, communicable and non-communicable diseases (NCDs), health education and nutrition, food safety, environmental and school health, mental health (in a limited number of PHCs), emergency services and first aid, and pharmacy and laboratory services.

All health centres have a well-defined catchment area as a requirement for accreditation. However, because the health system in Jordan is composed of different sectors such as MoH, RMS, and others with no link between these health sectors, there is often duplication of medical records and sometimes the catchment area for a given PHC facility cannot be easily determined. Since the majority of Jordanian families have at least one member in the army, the system allows this individual to seek care in RMS facilities and all RMS hospitals across the country.

Guidelines are available at all health facilities; however, they are not updated, and the treatment protocols are not accessible to all staff. Staff are using the treatment protocols and clinical pathways in some areas on a regular basis. Most facilities have some of the following clinical guidelines and clinical pathways: antenatal, postnatal, child health, diabetes mellitus, hypertension, anaemia in children, maternal anaemia, and family planning. The quantity and distribution of the workforce does not fit the client load in many cases.

Regarding training, there are written training plans included in the directorate operational plans; however, some of these plans are not implemented due to financial challenges. The top challenges facing human resources include: work overload not allowing some health staff to participate in on-job training, financial issues in providing training, shortages of transportation, and shortages in training centres.

The accreditation programme in Jordan has been implemented in MoH PHC settings since 2010. In response to the accreditation standards, a patient should have one unique medical record and one number. All health centres are using the personal identification (ID) number for medical records. The principle of each family is assigned to one specific family doctor or GP is not applied. Also, the Hakeem system (electronic medical records) is not applied in all health centres.

The referral system and the feedback referral mechanism are both very weak, and the mechanism for follow-up is not clear. Usually the referral and feedback referral lists are sent to the district health authority and then to the central MoH. Patient satisfaction with the quality of service delivery is assessed regularly in the accredited health centres. They have a questionnaire to be filled by clients within a regular period ranging from six months to one year to reflect the client satisfaction regarding the services received. Most clients of PHC facilities are satisfied by the quality of services they receive and by the waiting time before seeing their doctor.

KEY CHALLENGES TO ACCESSIBLE, QUALITY SERVICE DELIVERY IN PUBLIC PRIMARY CARE FACILITIES

The challenges are as follows:

- Demographic changes, including a rapid increase in population due to refugees and higher life expectancy.
- A shortage and high turnover of GPs in the Ministry of Health.
- A shortage of family physicians and other key staff: Despite a political commitment to accelerate production of family physicians in the country, all the family medicine residency programmes have failed to produce sufficient numbers of family physicians to cover the minimum PHC facility needs due to insufficient capacities in these programmes to accommodate more residents (for example, lack of trainers). The MoH in the last two years has been actively recruiting more general practitioners into the family medicine residency programme, creating more training PC centres and trainers.
- Very limited places in medical schools to recruit postgraduate doctors: The MoH in collaboration with WHO EMRO initiated an online training of trainers' programme for GPs on family medicine which will help close the current gap for implementing a family practice approach to achieve universal health coverage in the country.
- Insufficient private sector engagement in the family practice approach.
- Limited availability of data on all aspects of health systems.
- Inadequate coordination between the public sector and the increasingly significant private sector.
- Lack of effective systems for monitoring and auditing clinical practice.

FAMILY PRACTICE

Background

Family practice (FP) is defined as the health-care services provided by family doctors often supported by a multidisciplinary team. It is characterized by comprehensive, continuous, coordinated, collaborative, personal, family, and community-oriented services, providing medical care with a particular emphasis on the family unit. Family practice is distinguished by two main characteristics that make it unique: its holistic and people-centred approaches. A holistic approach means that care delivered by the family physician team should be bio-psycho-social; the three dimensions of care – biomedical, psychological, and social – should be integrated, implying that not only should care be delivered encompassing all elements but that decisions made in one of these domains should explicitly be influenced by due consideration to the features of the other two. A people-centred approach means that people are free to seek their health-care services from any physician they prefer.

The government of Jordan is committed to implementing family practice in the country, but the primary care private sector is not involved. The overall commitment of the MoH regarding the implementation of FP was stated in the National Health Reform Plan 2018–2022 and MoH strategies for the years 2008–2012 (replacing general practitioners working in health facilities with family doctors). The MoH developed the strategic plan for the family practice approach, as the main health services provider at PHC levels. However, there were no specific activities, no funds allocated, and no indicators to measure implementation.[4]

In the updated version of the MoH Strategic Plan 2013–2017, the strategy to replace GPs with family doctors does not appear. However, in the modified version, the MOH will update it to include the implementation of FP with specific activities, indicators, and allocated funds. There is no clear future plan to expand the family medicine programme, but the MoH recruited 45 residents who joined the FM residency programme in 2014 and 30 residents in 2015.

The private sector is not involved in provision of integrated PHC services and is not providing these services in partnership with the public sector. At the same time there is a multitude of private GP clinics and centres spread all over the country, with GPs providing basic curative care. In the RMS, FP is provided in some health centres, as well as some units at Jordan University and Jordan University for Science and Technology. In MoH health facilities, FP is implemented in most comprehensive health-care facilities and in some primary health-care facilities.

In Jordan, the primary health-care centres refer patients if needed to the comprehensive health centres and then the comprehensive centres refer patients to hospitals as necessary. Comprehensive health centres offer specialties (most on an appointment basis) such as internal medicine, obstetrics and gynaecology, paediatrics, dermatology, and ophthalmology; they receive internal referrals from the FP. The referral system is functioning in all health centres with very weak feedback mechanisms. The MoH does not provide home health care through any health centres except for individual initiatives through community engagement and effective actions of community health committees and for individual specific cases such as elderly people. In the private sector, some family physicians provide home care.

The national health strategy 2016–2020 proposes two main ways to achieve universal health coverage (UHC):

- The long-term solution is to increase the production of family physicians. Achieving this goal is difficult given that all programmes have failed to date to produce sufficient family physicians to cover the country. According to WHO recommendations, 3 family physicians per 10,000 population are needed.[5,6]
- The short-term solution is to decrease the gap in producing family physicians by improving the capacities of GPs in the public sector by providing them with online training. The MoH has about 1645 GPs covering about 676 PHC facilities across the country; this online learning will fill the gap temporarily until better conditions will facilitate the introduction of more FP to suit the country demand for this specialty. A high level of commitment to scale-up family practice in Jordan was clear from the policy makers interviewed at all levels in addition to the willingness and readiness of health-care providers in the field to improve the quality of primary services. In addition to the nationwide movement towards UHC, all these factors obviously will push towards scaling up family practice in Jordan.

The family health team (FHT) concept was implemented in the UNRWA clinics with well-defined roles and responsibilities, in response to the change in the health needs of the Palestinian refugee population. Late in 2011 UNRWA launched a health reform package based on the FHT approach.[7] Through this model, UNRWA health services are organized to provide comprehensive and holistic primary health care for the entire family, emphasizing long-term provider–patient/family relationships and designed to improve the quality, efficiency, and effectiveness of health services, particularly with regard to NCDs.

Under the FHT approach families are registered and assigned to a team of health professionals which consists of a doctor, nurse, and midwife. The provider team is responsible for all health-care needs of the family through all stages of the lifecycle.

The FHT approach is supported by the concurrent introduction of electronic medical records (e-Health) and the necessary infrastructure upgrade. Before the end of 2016, the FHT approach was operational in 135 health centres serving 95% of the population served by UNRWA in Gaza, Lebanon, the West Bank, Jordan, and Syria.

An important dimension of the FHT reform is continuous capacity building of health professionals. Most of the physicians working in UNRWA primary health-care facilities are GPs who are certified to work without further specialized training after graduation. In 2016, jointly with local partners (Al-Azhar University, the Hashemite University, Al-Najah University, and the American University of Beirut) and international partners (RILA Institute of Health Sciences, Imperial College, Middlesex University, and Plymouth University in the United Kingdom), 15 doctors in Gaza were graduated with a 1-year diploma in family medicine from Middlesex University. In 2017 another 54 doctors were enrolled in this diploma course.

A patient and his physician

The broad geographical coverage of MoH PHC centres has penetrated all rural areas, complemented by the Village Health Centres that are currently only partially functioning as arms of the family practice approach, since they offer only basic curative care.

There are community outreach programmes implemented by donors and NGOs; these programmes aim to increase awareness of the services related to MoH and NGOs through conducting home visits. In order to strengthen the role of communities, the MoH established community health committees composed of members from the local communities in the catchment areas of health centres, in addition to members from health centres such as midwives. They function as health promoters, mobilizing communities around health facilities to conduct activities aimed at increasing awareness through lectures inside and outside health centres, social media groups, support group workshops, fliers, and health promotion tools. They also conduct screening activities (anaemia, body mass index [BMI], chronic disease) at the community level.

Reaching underserved areas is accomplished through PHC facilities by implementing elements of MCH and other services in village health facilities; services offered include counselling programmes for breast feeding, using available advocacy materials to promote it. A range of modern methods are available for family planning, with higher uptake in urban areas; an average of 50% and more of couples use modern contraceptives within the catchment area of the PHC facilities. No births take place in PHC facilities except for emergency cases; however, the referral channel is available. The staff have received training and workshops on MCH including antenatal care. The Integrated Management of Child Illnesses (IMCI) protocol is partially implemented; anaemia screening is done for all pregnant women. The coverage of immunization is close to 100%; the cold chain is in place and vaccines are available six days a week, except in rural health centres where they schedule children on certain days.

However, screening of individuals above 40 is not routine, especially for blood pressure and diabetes. Client satisfaction surveys are carried out twice a year with average satisfaction for most of the participating HCs. Ninety percent of diabetic and 80% of hypertensive patients receive treatment based on the national protocols; all diabetic and hypertensive patients are registered in a specific registry. Referral to hospitals, which occurs in 15%–20% of cases, is also based on protocols but feedback on referral is weak; in addition, the patient can go to hospitals without referral in many cases. Tobacco cessation clinics are rarely available although there are three clinics in the MoH and one in the RMS King Hussain Centre.

All staff are aware and have been trained in infection control policies and procedures for reducing the risk of health-care-associated infections, and there was an infection control officer in all health centres visited for the assessment. There is a defined and implemented essential health services package (EHSP) with an average of 50% for most health centres visited, and the staff are trained to deliver the EHSP; also the essential drug list (EDL) is available in all health centres based on the classification of the health centre (primary or comprehensive).

WONCA and WHO conducted an assessment in 2015 to scale-up family practices.[8] The main recommendations were as follows:

- Unify resources to improve health-care delivery
- Take full advantage of the comprehensive role of the family physician
- Enhance the proper training of the family physician team
- Create a supportive environment for families seeking heath care

KEY CHALLENGES IN THE IMPLEMENTATION OF FAMILY PRACTICE

There are many challenges in ensuring access to high-quality services using a family practice approach, including[9]:

- Major gaps in human resources capacity, financing, and organization
- Policy makers with limited awareness of the concept of family practice and an increasing tendency to rely on expensive technology
- Poor logistics management and distribution of health facilities and workforce
- A lack of public–private partnerships
- A shortage of resources and incentives to ensure proper implementation of family practice programmes
- A shortage of trained family physicians and the failure of existing training programmes to meet the enormous need for those practitioners to support primary care
- The limited legal and financial support to implement family practice with no dedicated funds allocated to promote the family practice approach
- Insufficient capacity to expand family practice and partnership development

Proposed priorities to scale-up the family practice programme in Jordan:

- Maintain high-level political commitment
- Restructure the health system to accommodate trained and certified family physicians
- Establish family medicine departments in all medical faculties
- Ensure exposure of medical students to family medicine at the undergraduate level

- Ensure availability of on-job capacity building short courses for practicing GPs
- Encourage population registration and patient rosters
- Improve the referral system and feedback mechanisms
- Support the active engagement of the private sector in implementation of family practice programmes
- Enhance the capacities of PHC facilities in delivering NCD-related services
- Build national capacities to expand family practice and partnership development
- Focus on client satisfaction and community perception of family practice
- Develop a national roadmap to enhance family practice

FAMILY MEDICINE IN JORDAN

Realizing the need for this specialty in the country, the Royal Medical Services (RMS) started a three-year residency programme in family medicine in 1981, which was accredited in 1986 by the Jordan Medical Council (JMC). Subsequently the MOH started a similar programme in 1989, followed by Jordan University (JU) and Jordan University of Science Technology (JUST) in 1995, and the Hashemite University will start its programme in 2018. There are six medical schools in the country with only three family medicine departments. The JMC is responsible for all medical specialties, including family medicine; in 1995, it extended the three-year period of residency to four years; the criterion for the specialty is to pass the Jordanian Board (JB) exam part 1 and part 2 successfully. In 1995 the JMC Scientific Committee adopted a job description of a family medicine specialist as: "a licensed medical graduate who gives care to individuals, irrespective of age, sex, and illness, who attends his patients in his consulting room and in their homes and sometimes in a hospital" (job description updated in 2017).

Currently, there are four training programmes of family medicine residency; the MoH, JU, JUST, and RMS. A diploma in family medicine does not exist in Jordan; however, an academic master's degree from JUST is provided.

The residency training programmes are of four years' duration; the total number of graduates from the different programmes since the first training programme was founded in 1981 is less than 700 family doctors. Family medicine is adopted in the national health policy in Jordan. The MoH is the main source of funding for programme implementation.

Around 210 family physician specialists are working in MoH health facilities mainly in comprehensive health centres and a few family physicians are taking a management role in the central MoH.[10] The curriculum of the residency is composed of three years of practice in a training hospital and the fourth year at an accredited community training health-care centre. Improvements in the quality of care provided by family physicians are likely to result in increased requirements for material and manpower at the primary care level due to the increase in workload. This, in turn, will require new administrative structures to monitor and ensure provision of adequate resources in these settings. Patient acceptance of this specialty is also important and will require efforts on the part of family medicine to educate patients on their roles and responsibilities within the system.

PRIVATE HEALTH SECTOR

The private health sector operates 62 hospitals with 4345 beds that make up about 38% of total beds in Jordan. Also 2600 medical clinics (with GPs) and 1900 specialized medical clinics are operating in the private sector. Amman has more than 80% of all private beds. The average hospital bed capacity in the private sector is 64 beds while the national average is 103 beds. About 60% of physicians, 98% of dentists, 93% of pharmacists, and 40% of nurses work in the private health sector. The private sector is the main employer of health workers (60%), followed by the MoH (26%), RMS (10%), and universities (4%).[11]

The private sector is active in curative primary care, accounting for nearly 40% of all initial patient contacts (26% for profit, 5% not-for-profit, and 9% private pharmacies). Private practice is mainly confined to urban areas and caters to wealthier Jordanians who can afford private sector fees. Thirty-six percent of private clinics are located in the capital, Amman. For the time being, there is no role for private family doctors in the national health insurance scheme, they are not considered as partners of PHC in the country.

There is no real partnership between the public and private sector. There is continuous improvement in family medicine practice in the country in both the private and public sectors; however, the concept of buying health services from private family physicians especially in communities where no public family practice exists, is not mature yet.

REFERENCES

1. WHO/MOH. *Health System Review 2013.*
2. High Health Council, Jordan. *National Health Accounts 2013.* Available from: http://www.hhc.gov.jo/uploadedimages/NHA%202013.pdf.
3. *National Health Reform, Jordan.* 2018.
4. High Health Council, Jordan. *National Health Strategy 2016.* Available from: http://www.hhc.gov.jo/uploadedimages/1fe9eeb0-590b-4b51-82e8-7013e98178de.pdf.
5. WHO EMRO, 63rd RC 2016. *Scaling up family practice: progressing towards universal health coverage.* EM/RC63/Tech.Disc.1. Available from: http://www.emro.who.int/about-who/rc63/documentation.html.
6. WHO EMRO, 63rd RC 2016. *Scaling up family practice: progressing towards universal health coverage.* Available from: http://applications.emro.who.int/docs/RC63_Resolutions_2016_R2_19197_EN.pdf?ua=1.
7. Dr Musa Ajlouni. *Jordan health system profile, 2010.* Available from: https://www.researchgate.net/publication/292135260_Jordan_Health_System_Profile2010.
8. WHO EMRO 2016. *Family Practice in the Countries of Eastern Mediterranean Region: A Preliminary Assessment.*
9. WHO EMRO. *Report on the Regional consultation on strengthening service provision through the family practice approach.* Cairo, Egypt 18–20 November 2014. WHO-EM/PHC/165/E. Available from: http://apps.who.int/iris/bitstream/handle/10665/253400/IC_meet_rep_2015_EN_16267.pdf?sequence=1&isAllowed=y.
10. Ministry of Health, Jordan. *Statistical Book 2016.* Available from: http://www.moh.gov.jo/Echobusv3.0/SystemAssets/3088f91a-96cc-49e2-82c5-86951ace3ebd.pdf.
11. Ministry of Health, Jordan. *Statistical Book 2017.* Available from: http://www.moh.gov.jo/Echobusv3.0/SystemAssets/b14dc747-8d28-46d2-b14b-53af5d504152.pdf.

CHAPTER 20

Kuwait

Huda Al-Duwaisan and Fatemah Ahmed Bendhafari

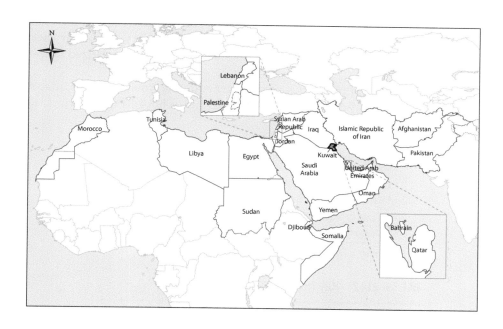

Total number of PHC facilities	103
Number of general practitioners working in public PHC facilities	832
Number of certified family physicians working in PHC facilities	194
Number of certified family physicians in PHC facilities	410
Average number of family physician graduates/year	35

INTRODUCTION

The State of Kuwait is a constitutional emirate with a surface area of 17,188 kilometres spread over six governorates: Asimah, Hawali, Farwaniya, Jahra, Ahmadi, and Mubarak Al-Kabeer. The total population was estimated to be around 4.1 million, with Kuwaiti nationals constituting about 30%.[1] Kuwait's Human Development Index score was 0.8, as shown in Table 20.1, which puts the country in the high human development category with a ranking of 51 out of 188 countries.[2]

The burden of disease (2012) attributable to communicable diseases is 16.1%, non-communicable diseases 72.9%, and injuries 11.0%. The share of out-of-pocket expenditure is 15.7% (2013). The health workforce density (2014) is 24 physicians and 59 nurses and midwives per 10,000 population (Table 20.2).[3]

CURRENT HEALTH SYSTEM

Kuwait has one of the most modern health-care infrastructures in the region. An overwhelming share of health services is provided by the public sector, but there is a growing private sector as well. The public health system is built in accordance with primary health care principles with three levels of health-care delivery: primary, secondary, and tertiary. The first level health services are provided by primary health care centres (PHCCs). Secondary and tertiary health care is provided through six general hospitals and a number of national specialized hospitals and clinics.

In the six health regions, the PHCCs provide general, maternal and child, diabetic, and dental clinics. The centres also offer preventive care and school health services. Recently,

TABLE 20.1 Kuwait's human development index

Life expectancy at birth	74.5
Expected years of schooling	13.3
Mean years of schooling	7.3
GNI per capita (2011 PPP$)	76 075
HDI value	0.800

Source: UNDP Human Development Report 2016.

TABLE 20.2 Key health-related statistics

Total health expenditure (% of general government expenditure)	5.8
Maternal mortality ratio (per 100,000 live births)	4
Primary health-care units and centres (per 10,000 population)	0.2
Total life expectancy at birth (years)	74.7

Source: Country statistical profiles 2016.

mental health care services have also been added. In addition, the records and data are computerized, and it is planned that they will be connected to the secondary and tertiary hospitals network.

One of the main challenges in health service delivery is to reduce the waiting time for patients due to high patient load and over-extension of medical staff. To overcome this, the government is planning to build more hospitals, more PHCCs, and renovate and build more medical laboratories and expand dental clinics during the 2015–2019 national development plan.[4] Other challenges include the following:

- The need for systematic assessment of the quality of services delivered by the PHCCs, hospitals, and specialized clinics at regular intervals
- Improving the referral and follow-up system
- Implementing continuous training and development of health promoters
- Strengthening of home-based and community-based care and community health promotion

The Supreme Council of Planning developed a framework for the five-year national plan for all ministries, including the Ministry of Health (MoH).[5] The strategic priority areas in national health services that are relevant to primary health care are:

- Establishing a family practice-based PHC approach across the country (focusing on the composition of multidisciplinary teams, catchment population, family folders etc.) and a well-functioning referral and counter-referral system between primary, secondary, and tertiary care
- Ensuring interoperable electronic health records across care interfaces and developing accompanying data science capabilities to allow the progressive move to a data-informed pay-for-performance model of care, and
- Developing health service research capacity to enable continuous cycles of evaluation and improvement

THE HISTORY OF PHCCs AND FAMILY MEDICINE

The first government health clinic in Kuwait was opened in 1939.[6] This was followed by a traditional system of primary care based on local clinics that provided basic health services to approximately 90,000 people administered by general practitioners. The basic system at that time was to some extent similar to the current family practice system. The family centre was run by a family practitioner. Every family doctor worked day and evening shifts to guarantee continuous care with clinical services covering all family medicine aspects, with referral to hospital limited to complicated cases. Later, such family practice centres shifted to a more general practice model for several reasons; the increase in population with people of mixed cultures; the increased urbanization which necessitated the segregation of female clinics from male and separate paediatric clinics leading to the loss of the family file structure; the shortage of qualified family practitioners. Another reason was reducing the work time for doctors in the primary centres to only one shift, which led to the loss of continuity of care.

The general practice system continued until a decision was made in 1983 with the partnership of the Royal College of General Practitioners (RCGP), which developed once again the family practice model as the basis of a patient-centred approach to primary care. The main goal was to develop a family doctor fellowship programme, which was the first RCGP international fellowship.[6] The objectives were stated as follows:

- The long-term aim was to make family practice the cornerstone of a fully integrated health care system.
- The medium term aim was to develop self-sufficient educational and training programmes for family practice within Kuwait.
- The short-term aim was to introduce a postgraduate qualification in family practice in Kuwait, equivalent to the Membership of the RCGP.

THE CURRENT PRIMARY AND FAMILY HEALTH-CARE SYSTEM IN KUWAIT

Currently, the total number of PHCCs under the Ministry of Health (MoH) is 103 distributed among all areas. Some of these centres apply the 13 elements of family medicine; others vary in this application, which leads to having both family and general health centres. Each centre provides health services for a population of about 40,000. The services provided are general practice and family medicine, maternal health, child health, dental services, vaccination, and preventive health services. The PHCCs also include diabetic care clinics, chronic disease follow-up, mental health clinics, laboratories, pharmacies, X-ray facilities, and nursing. There are also well-baby clinics and smoking cessation clinics.

All health centres include walk-in clinics and recently a system for an appointment-based general clinic was introduced in a family health centre as a pilot.

Open day for community, Yarmouk Centre

The drug list available in PHCC pharmacies has been expanded recently to include new medications. The list now includes more than 200 different medications for paediatrics, adults, and geriatrics. The expansion also included the medications for chronic diseases to take the burden off central hospitals.

PHC facilities use the electronic file system Primary Care Information System (PCIS) for registering patient health information. The system includes risk factors for chronic non-communicable diseases. Currently it covers all PHCCs and linking the system with hospitals will be implemented soon.

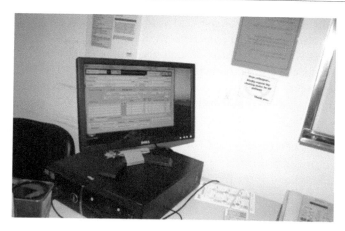

Primary Care Information System

Primary and family health-care centres follow treatment protocols, work policies, and quality standards according to the World Health Organization (WHO) guidelines. Applying quality protocols to get international accreditation has been started in collaboration with the Canadian Accreditation Council.

The primary and family health care system of the MoH is considered a unique and ideal system and has been highly supported by WHO as it provides a complete coverage of all populated areas in Kuwait. In planning new residential areas, an easy to reach PHCC is always included, rendering the health service available around the clock or at least till midnight. Among 63 centres, 65% of them are working till midnight.

Recent developments have led the government to promote insurance packages for specific sectors within the community aiming at better utilization of resources and optimization of the level of services. These include:

- Afya, which was introduced in 2016 to cover retired Kuwaiti citizens, managed by a private insurance company and funded by the government.
- Daman, which was introduced to cover all expatriates against a fixed payment paid by their employers to enable them to use health services at the Ministry of Health facilities.
- Others insurance packages where some private sector companies provide health insurance for their employees.

THE FACULTY OF PRIMARY HEALTH CARE

The Faculty of Primary Health Care is under the Kuwait Institute for Medical Specializations (KIMS), which was established in 1984. Since then, KIMS has been responsible for the education and training of physicians and dentists alike. Under the authority of the MoH, KIMS is the leading educational institution dedicated to the medical training of various specialties. KIMS strives to advance Kuwaiti society's health through expert medical training and education.[7]

The institute has 25 faculties with residency training programmes, which run for a period of five years. The programmes are comprised of structured medical training and a number of examinations. Furthermore, KIMS offers seven fellowship programmes (subspecialties). The approximate number of residents and fellows currently enrolled in KIMS programmes is 735.[7]

The vision at the Kuwait Family Medicine Academic Programme is to improve the health of the people of Kuwait through leadership in family medicine education, clinical practice, and research. To fulfil this vision, the faculty aims to develop and maintain exemplary family medicine educational programmes for medical students, resident physicians, physician assistants, other faculty and practicing physicians who train health-care providers for Kuwait. Furthermore, the faculty strives to provide comprehensive, high-quality, cost-effective, and humanistic health care in the family medicine clinical education centres through interdisciplinary cooperation. The objective is to promote the discovery and dissemination of knowledge that is important to teaching, clinical practice, and organization of health care.

THE DEVELOPMENT OF THE FAMILY MEDICINE FORMAL TRAINING PROGRAMME

Kuwait has long recognized family medicine as a key element to the health care system in the country and is considered one of the pioneers in the Middle East region to realize the necessity of vocational training programmes in family medicine. KIMS established the Family Practice Specialty Training Programme (FPSTP) to train family physicians in 1983 in affiliation with the RCGP as a three-year vocational training programme. Since then the programme has passed through a process of evolution. In 2001 the programme was extended to a four-year training and in 2002 a system was developed for enhanced evaluations and assessment of residents. The Kuwait Board of Family Medicine Exam achieved the MRCGP (INT) accreditation in 2005.

Currently, the Family Medicine Residency Programme (FMRP) is considered the predominant postgraduate residency programme with around 200 residents at different levels of training, and it is by far one of the most popular among the KIMS programmes.[7] The programme went through another stage of evolution in which it transformed from a four-year training to a five-year residency starting in 2010. The programme is reviewed every three years by the Faculty of Primary Care in collaboration with the RCGP, with the last review done in 2015.

The FMRP is designed to prepare the medical school graduate for the delivery of comprehensive health care to patients of all ages. The programme has a strong base in the main medical specialties with excellent training facilities that provide diverse training opportunities for residents. The underlying goal is to ensure that the graduate will be an exceptional family physician.

The Kuwait Family Medicine Competency Framework for the residents describes the different competencies, skills, and professional attitudes that residents in the family medicine residency programme need to acquire and develop during their five residency years. It is a result of an extensive review of internationally well-acclaimed curricula.

Upon completion of the five-year residency, see Figure 20.1, the resident should be able to demonstrate an understanding of all the competencies essential to family physicians. The total number of family medicine residency programme graduates from 1987 to 2017 was 410 physicians (Table 20.3).

Note: PGR 4/5 candidates have a chance to do a two-month elective rotation in Kuwait or abroad.

GENERAL PRACTITIONER PROFESSIONAL DEVELOPMENT PROGRAMME (GPPDP)

GPPDP was introduced to train the current PHCPs to be more competent in the diagnosis, assessment, and management of common medical conditions encountered in primary care settings. GPPDP is intended to equip GPs with core clinical skills and the ability to assess and address their learning needs over a professional lifetime. See Figure 20.2 for the Kuwait Family Medicine Competency Framework.

Currently, most primary care services in Kuwait are provided by GPs representing 64% of the total number of doctors working in primary care. Qualified family practitioners comprise the remaining 36%. National strategies and operational plans within KIMS are driven to increase

PGR1	Family Medicine Foundation 4 months		Emergency Medicine 2 months		Paediatrics 3 months		Family Medicine 2 months
PGR2	Internal Medicine 4 months		Obs/Gyn 2 months		Orthop 1 month	Surgery/ Urology 2 months	Family Medicine 2 months
PGR3	Psych. 2 months	Ophth. 1 month	Derma. 1 month	Ent. 1 month	Neonates 1 week	Palliative 2 weeks	Paediatric Surgery 1 week	Family Medicine 4.5 months
PGR4	Family Medicine 9 months						Audit Project	
PGR5	Family Medicine 11 months							

FIGURE 20.1 Components of the Family Medicine Residency Programme (FMRP). Note: PGR 4/5 candidates have a chance to do a two-month elective rotation in Kuwait or abroad.

TABLE 20.3 Statistics of the Family Medicine Residency Programme (FMRP)

Annual recruited residents	40–45 per year
Recruits accepted into the 2018/2019 programme	50
Residents currently enrolled	150
20 years FM graduates	410
Family medicine trainers	37
Family medicine examiners	28
Current potential trainers	9

FIGURE 20.2 Kuwait Family Medicine Competency Framework.

the number of well-trained GPs with the Family Medicine Diploma (two years' duration) and increase the number of family practitioners with Kuwait Board in Family Medicine qualification (five years' duration). The vision of the GPPDP programme is to be internationally accredited as a programme to train GPs and to have a well-established training programme. This will result in the improvement of the primary health care system through producing highly qualified GPs who be able to provide comprehensive health care of the highest standards.

FELLOWSHIP TRAINING PROGRAMME

The fellowship training programme aims to upgrade the primary care doctor's knowledge and skills by expanding and improving teaching in the care of the people through a well-structured, comprehensive, scientifically based, and clinically oriented approach. The fellowship covers geriatrics, chronic disease, and dietetics; future areas will include mental health, adolescent health, and trauma.

TRAINING OF TRAINERS' (TOT) PROGRAMME

The goal is to develop a team of professional clinical educators and clinical trainers who are highly motivated, confident, and highly competent in their abilities and skills to deliver and implement effective training. The TOT programme for the family practitioner trainer comprises three modules, each of six months' duration, with a total duration of 18 months. For the clinical educator, the programme comprises three modules each of four months' duration, with a total duration of 12 months. Each module in both programmes covers different aspects of training and consists of lectures, workshops, and assignments. The total number of family practitioner trainers is now 37, while the total number of general practitioner trainers is 15. The total number of examiners is 28 for the family medicine programme.

Training program, Yarmouk Centre

UNDERGRADUATE TRAINING PROGRAMMES

The undergraduate training programme aims to promote family medicine as a discipline of choice for medical students and residents and as a fulfilling career for practicing family physicians and GPs.

RESEARCH

The Faculty of Primary Health Care Research Committee (FPHCRC) works to improve the level of scientific epidemiological research of non-communicable diseases in primary health care, aiming to achieve international standards. Research projects are encouraged to allow cooperation between researchers in primary, secondary, and tertiary care, and between researchers in the MoH, medical faculties and other specialized research organizations, together with international and global partners.

KUWAIT ASSOCIATION FOR FAMILY PHYSICIANS AND GENERAL PRACTITIONERS (KAFPGP)

The association was formed by a group of family doctors in 2015 as part of the Kuwait Medical Association. It focuses on improving the performance of family doctors and general practitioners to provide integrated community medical care. It aims to enhance the overall status of family doctors and general practitioners, to encourage cooperation with local and international institutions, and to participate effectively in the formulation of policies for family medicine and general practice.

The association has been a full member of the World Organization of Family Doctors (WONCA) in the Eastern Mediterranean Region (EMR) since 2015. The association succeeded in hosting the 2018 WONCA EMR annual conference. It was instrumental in improving the job descriptions of family practitioners at the MoH. It is a key player in working towards the goal of having one family practitioner for the whole family.

The KAFPGP regularly organizes workshops, events, and produces publications dedicated to achieving a visible improvement in the performance of family doctors. Members of the association actively participate in regional and international meetings.

COUNTRY SUCCESSFUL EXPERIENCE: YARMOUK FAMILY HEALTH CENTRE

The Yarmouk District is located in the Asimah Governorate of Kuwait, with an area of around 2.5 square kilometres, and a population of around 24,000. There are six schools in Yarmouk, a main cooperative society with branches in each block, a Society Development Centre, and a state-of-the-art modern health centre (Yarmouk Family Health Centre). See Figure 20.3 for the major stakeholders in Yarmouk District.

Yarmouk Family Health Centre was established in 1989. An extension building was constructed and inaugurated in March 2010, with donations from Abdulla Al-Abdulhadi. Hence, the centre was named Al-Abdulhadi Centre.

Yarmouk Family Health Centre is a leading player in community development. It is heavily engaged in local activities, where it is considered a pillar in initiating wellbeing and progressive plans and projects. Many activities are undertaken in collaboration with different stakeholders that are invited to become partners in successful implementation. A schematic of the major stakeholders, as shown in Figure 20.3, shows the presence of government and private agencies, together with non-governmental organizations (NGOs). It should be mentioned that with such a high level of community achievement, WHO recently recognized Yarmouk as the first healthy district in Kuwait.

The various clinics and services provided by Yarmouk Centre are shown in Figure 20.4. It is staffed by 6 family doctors, 4 GPs, 34 nurses, and 37 administration and support staff. The total number of patients reached 177,047 in 2016, around 400 to 600 patients a day. The doctor/patient ratio is 1:2500 and the plan is to reach the international ratio which is 1:1600.

Yarmouk Centre is also one of the accredited educational facilities that supports and hosts medical students from the Faculty of Medicine and trainees from the Faculty of Primary

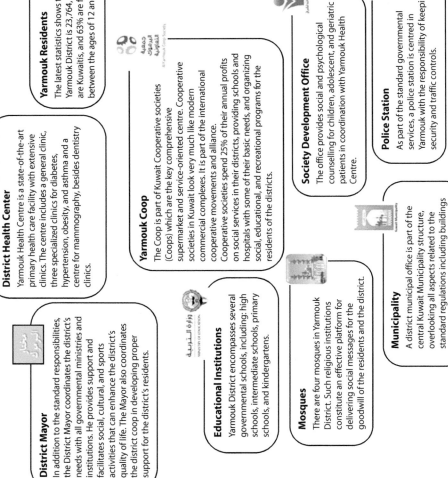

District Mayor

In addition to the standard responsibilities, the District Mayor coordinates the district's needs with all governmental ministries and institutions. He provides support and facilitates social, cultural, and sports activities that can enhance the district's quality of life. The Mayor also coordinates the district coop in developing proper support for the district's residents.

District Health Center

Yarmouk Health Centre is a state-of-the-art primary health care facility with extensive clinics. The centre includes a general clinic, three specialized clinics for diabetes, hypertension, obesity, and asthma and a centre for mammography, besides dentistry clinics.

Yarmouk Residents

The latest statistics shows that the population in the Yarmouk District is 23,764, out of which 76% are Kuwaitis, and 63% are females. 71% are between the ages of 12 and 65.

Educational Institutions

Yarmouk District encompasses several governmental schools, including: high schools, intermediate schools, primary schools, and kindergartens.

Yarmouk Coop

The Coop is part of Kuwait Cooperative societies (Coops) which are the key comprehensive supermarket and service-oriented centre. Cooperative societies in Kuwait look very much like modern commercial complexes. It is part of the international cooperative movements and alliance. Cooperative societies spend 25% of their annual profits on social services in their districts, providing schools and hospitals with some of their basic needs, and organizing social, educational, and recreational programs for the residents of the districts.

Society Development Office

The office provides social and psychological counselling for children, adolescent, and geriatric patients in coordination with Yarmouk Health Centre.

Mosques

There are four mosques in Yarmouk District. Such religious institutions constitute an effective platform for delivering social messages for the goodwill of the residents and the district.

Municipality

A district municipal office is part of the central Kuwait Municipality structure, overlooking all aspects related to the standard regulations including buildings and cleanliness.

Police Station

As part of the standard governmental services, a police station is centred in Yarmouk with the responsibility of keeping security and traffic controls.

FIGURE 20.3 Major stakeholders in the Yarmouk District.

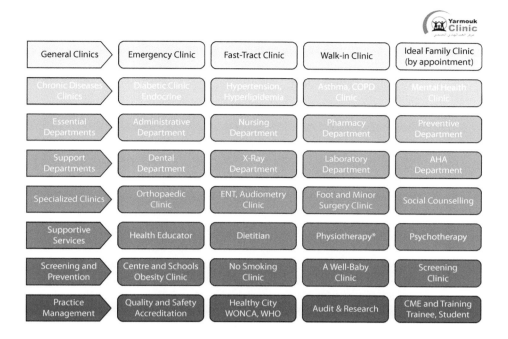

FIGURE 20.4 Units and services in the Yarmouk PHC Centre.

Health Care, family medicine training programmes and from other programmes at KIMS. Furthermore, the centre is one of the busiest hosts of training and capacity building workshops, held by regional and international partners including WHO and the World Organization of National Colleges, Academies and Academic Associations of General Practitioners/Family Physicians (WONCA).

The Yarmouk team believes strongly in pushing the boundaries of their role, to constantly improve practice to enhance services. As a result, they have engaged partners to introduce quality control and quality assurance procedures in their practice. Work is in progress to integrate Canadian accreditation at the centre. It has been recognized as the best PHCC in the capital as a result.

The team has broadened its target to implement the WHO 13 elements of family practice; essential health services, essential drug list, family folder, referral system, community participation, treatment protocol, and continuous medical education. In a joint effort with WHO EMRO, Yarmouk counted three successful rounds of training of trainers for PHC focal persons from 13 countries in 2015–2017. The training developed core family practice master trainers to lead the rolling out of family practice programmes in their own countries.

To foster community participation, the Yarmouk team have partnered with the District Community Council (DCC) to include health promotion campaigns in their activities. There have been many successful health and wellbeing campaigns in the past few years.

Examples include:

- Obesity prevention in schools
- Healthy eating and promoting physical activity
- Public campaigns on communicable and non-communicable diseases

- Promoting care of the environment and the culture of recycling, and
- Community safety campaigns such as the American Heart Association lifesaving training programme and community emergency and evacuation plans

Yarmouk has been designated the first "healthy district" in Kuwait as result of the cooperation with the DCC.

Yarmouk Centre is particularly proud of its mental health services, offered since 2011, which have received good feedback from patients and international psychiatrists alike. It aims to promote mental wellbeing as a primary concern of all public health services by 2020.

Finally, electronic administrative health services will be introduced in 2018 to Yarmouk Centre to facilitate client registration and follow-up, to reduce patient complaints.

THE ROAD FORWARD

The State of Kuwait continues its endeavours to follow best practice in sustaining primary health care and family medicine practice. The effective introduction of new initiatives relies on champions in PHCCs and within the MoH. As proven in the last two decades, collaborating with international partners is a major pillar contributing to a high level of success. Kuwait will continue efforts to adopt WHO and WONCA strategies and policies. The challenges of optimizing resources to achieve excellence in PHC services and academic education facilities persist. However, the state will continue with sustainable health initiatives together with all stakeholders to achieve the most important goal, which is that each family be assigned a highly qualified, available family practitioner.

The authors would like to acknowledge the support of Ms. Hayfaa Almudhaf in data collection and layout design of this chapter.

REFERENCES

1. State of Kuwait Central Statistical Bureau. *Population Estimates 2017*. Available from: https://www.csb.gov.kw/Socan_Statistic_EN.aspx?ID=67 [September 22, 2018].
2. United Nations Development Programme. *Human Development Report 2016*. Available from: http://hdr.undp.org/sites/default/files/2016_human_development_report.pdf [September 22, 2018].
3. Kuwait Ministry of Health, Central Department for Primary Health Care. Available from: https://www.moh.gov.kw/en/Departments/5/5-2/5-2-2 [September 22, 2018].
4. *Kuwait National Development Plan 2035*. Available from: http://www.newkuwait.gov.kw/en/plan/ [September 22, 2018].
5. WHO Report 2017. *Development of a New National Health Sector Strategy for the State of Kuwait (2018–2022)*.
6. Fraser RC. Developing family practice in Kuwait. *British Journal of General Practice*. 1995;45:102–106.
7. Kuwait Institute for Medical Specialization. *Family Practice Specialty Training Programme Curriculum*. 2016.

CHAPTER 21

Lebanon

Walid Ammar and Alissar Rady

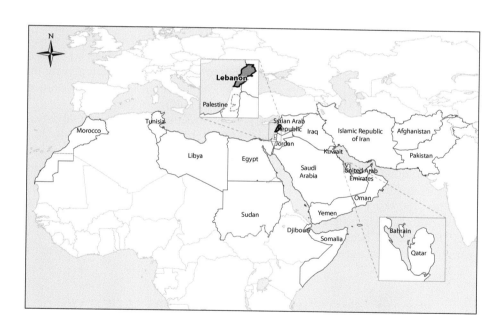

Total number of PHC facilities	205 PHC centres in the National MoPH network out of total 1100 dispensaries*
Number of general practitioners working in public PHC facilities**	Not Available
Number of certified family physicians working in PHC facilities	31 (in 2017)
Average number of family physicians graduates/year	10
Number of medical schools	6
Number of family medicine departments	2

* More than 95% of PHC centres are owned and managed by NGOs; very few are owned or managed by the Ministry of Public Health (MoPH) or Ministry of Social Affairs (MoSA).
** The number of GPs fluctuates as there is a high turnover.

INTRODUCTION

Lebanon became independent in 1943. Its recent history has been marked by two conflicts, the Lebanese Civil War 1975–1990, and the 2006 war on Lebanon. Since 2011, the country has been heavily affected by the Syrian crisis. In addition to hosting 1.5 million Syrian refugees (25% of its resident population), Lebanon also has 0.5 million Palestinian refugees.

THE HEALTH SYSTEM

Over the past two decades, the health system in Lebanon has been characterized by a long-standing public–private partnership, a dynamic civil society, a flourishing private sector, and a public sector that is progressively regaining its leadership and regulatory role. The Ministry of Public Health (MoPH) covers hospital stays and expensive medicines for Lebanese who are not insured through the program on catastrophic illnesses. The National Social Security Fund and the Government Employee Funds cover around 40% of the population; private insurance covers around 8%. For the 52% of the population that is not covered by health insurance, health services are purchased by the MoPH from the private and public sectors.

It is estimated that there are around 9000 private physician clinics, some 6000 private pharmacies and around 6000 dental clinics in the private sector. The syndicate of labs counts 150 medical labs that are hospital-based, and some 250 labs that are not within a hospital setting, either private standalone or affiliated to a primary health care (PHC) dispensary. The total hospital bed capacity is 20.3 beds per 10,000 population (a total of 12,000 beds), provided by 150 private hospitals (130 short stay and 20 long stay) and 28 operational public hospitals. Health facilities are concentrated in large cities (Box 21.1).

The MoPH purchases health services from private hospitals, based on a quota and flat rates, through contractual agreements. The MoPH partially subsidizes public hospitals, and

---

BOX 21.1   SELECTED COUNTRY INDICATORS AS OF 2017

- Per capita total health expenditures (THE): US$569
- General government expenditure on health as % of general government expenditure: 10.1%
- Out-of-pocket expenditure has dropped from 68% in 1998 to 36.4% in 2017
- Life expectancy at birth: total: 81.2; male: 80.3; female: 82.1
- Under-five mortality rate: 8.5/1000 live births
- Age-standardized mortality rates by cause: communicable diseases, 30/100,000 population; noncommunicable diseases, 385/100,000 population; injuries; 41/100,000 population
- Maternal mortality ratio: 20.9/100,000 live births

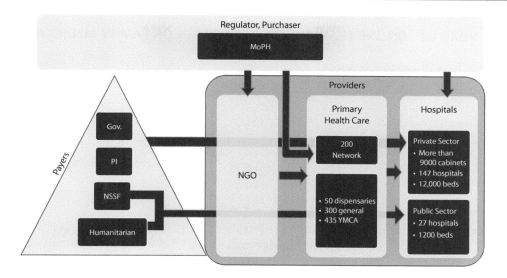

FIGURE 21.1 Overview of the Lebanese health system. (From Humanitarian Response report 2015-2016; WHOCO Lebanon.)

also purchases services from them (Law of Autonomy); the MoPH, through in-kind contribution of medicines, vaccines, and trainings, supports PHC services.

THE FAMILY PHYSICIAN AND HUMAN RESOURCES FOR HEALTH

The health system is also characterized by a surplus of medical doctors and a severe shortage in nurses and paramedical staff, with the following estimates: physicians, 31.0/10,000 population; nurses and midwives, 34.2/10,000 population; pharmacists, 18.2/10,000 population; and dentists, 15.1/10,000 population. Around 30% of practicing physicians are general practitioners.[1] Data from the Family Medicine Society indicates that there are 198 family doctors registered with formal training in Family Medicine (177 family physicians registered at the Lebanese Order of Physicians in Beirut, and 16 registered at the Lebanese Order of Physicians in the North). Of these registered family physicians, 49.2% are women; around half are affiliated to hospitals. Only 31 family doctors are recruited at the national PHC network. A few family physicians are recruited by insurance companies, mainly for administrative work, and a few others have additional degrees/subspecialties such as public health, geriatric medicine or maternal health.[2]

Two medical schools in Lebanon have family medicine residency programs that graduate a total of around 6 to 10 family doctors per year. The oldest program, established over 40 years ago, follows the North American curriculum and is offered over three years by the American University of Beirut (AUB). A more recent one has been offered by the Université Saint-Joseph for about 15 years, following the European curriculum. Lebanese American University, recently established, has introduced the community medicine approach in its medical school curriculum. Continuing education is poorly structured and mainly provided by the Lebanese Society of Family Medicine through lectures funded by pharmaceutical companies. There is no national board certification, but some family physicians are accredited by the Arab Board in Family and Community Medicine and a few are accredited by the American Board of Family Medicine.[3]

During 2015 and 2016, with funds from the European Union (EU) and under the Instrument for Stability projects, the World Health Organization (WHO) developed a national guidebook

BOX 21.2 ONLINE TRAINING COURSE FOR GPs ON FAMILY MEDICINE

- Duration of the course is 24 weeks; the total number of online hours is 45 hours at a rate of 3 hours per week of online self-study for candidates.
- A certificate (with credit hours) is issued by the American University of Beirut, hosting the online course
- Includes two modules:
  - Introduction to Family Practice
  - Clinical updates
- A guide for practical training at hospitals or emergency units of the participants' countries will be ready in 2018

for management of the 30 most common conditions encountered at PHC level. WHO was able to adapt the Guidebook on Integrated Management of Childhood Diseases. Intensive training was given to more than 200 medical doctors (general practitioners, family doctors, internists) and some 250 nurses working in the PHC network centres on these two guidebooks. In 2017, the Family Medicine Department at AUB, supported by WHO's Regional Office for the Eastern Mediterranean (EMRO), transformed this guidebook into an online training course targeting general practitioners (GPs) (Box 21.2). The online training course is hosted at AUB and is coupled with in-service observation. In 2017, the first cohort of GPs from the United Nations Relief Works Assistance for Palestinian refugees in Lebanon (UNRWA) clinics completed the online training.

PRIMARY HEALTH CARE

Lebanon has a long-standing history with PHC and conceptualizing family practice. A first important landmark was in 1983 when the first recommendations to regulate PHC were issued based on the Alma-Ata Declaration. PHC had become a necessity during the years of the Civil War (1975–1989). In 1991, immediately after the war ended, a national health conference was held to develop a consensus on national health priorities. The three main recommendations of the conference were: to develop a national PHC strategy that covered all of Lebanon; to develop the health infrastructure needed for it, and to introduce PHC concepts in medical and paramedical education. Since then, the MoPH has steadily reinforced PHC. The first national strategy for PHC was elaborated in 1994, then updated in 2004 and revised in 2014.

Patients in PHC centre

The PHC Unit at the MoPH was created on August 15, 1996, through decree no. 8908 under the Preventive Directorate of the Ministry of Public Health. It included the establishment of two subunits: a Health Centres Administrative section and Program Management section, which consisted of four programmes: community health, mother/child/family health, prevention/treatment, and essential drugs. Between May 2001 and 2006, based on a revised approach, the PHC Department, Ministry of Public Health, focused its main interventions on:

- Increasing coverage by contracting with more primary health-care centres
- Expanding the PHC package to include mental health, elderly care, emergency services, community-based rehabilitation, and the health village concept
- Developing a health information system and the analysis of generated outcomes
- Continuous review and awareness of the essential drug list
- Training for primary health-care workers at central and health centre levels
- Preparing indicators and auditing activities for quality control

After the war on Lebanon, in July 2006, the PHC strategy was redirected towards ensuring high-quality primary care and creating a gatekeeping (referral) system that would control costs, avoid reliance on out-of-pocket payment, and satisfy the public. The main focus was on the following activities:

- Gradually expanding the network of primary health centres working under an agreement with the MoPH; this would require about 150 centres, each serving an average of 30,000 persons.
- Improving service delivery by rehabilitating and equipping facilities and training staff on the implementation of standard practice.
- Revising and finalizing the list of basic services and PHC programs.
- Developing a referral system that links PHC to hospital services.
- Marketing and advocacy to support the PHC development strategy.
- Developing an accreditation system to ensure the quality and safety of care provided.
- Establishing payment mechanisms for PHC.
- Implementing the system for monitoring performance of facilities to ensure that they meet development objectives.
- Evolving and expanding PHC Management Information Systems in functionalities and capacity.

MAIN ACHIEVEMENTS IN PROVIDING PHC

Over the past three decades, the MoPH has developed options for provider payment reforms in ambulatory care and initiated a system of accreditation for PHC including standard setting guidelines, requirements for physical facilities, and manpower, equipment, and operational systems. It also has established a national network of PHC centres that has progressively expanded over the years to cover most geographical areas in the country, with more focus on areas with vulnerable populations. This national network of PHCs provides essential drugs and essential health services such as paediatrics, family medicine, oral health, reproductive health, cardiology, and vaccination. The mechanism for coordination between MoPH and non-governmental organizations (NGOs) is well-established, and there are attempts at improving quality audit and reviews.[4]

BOX 21.3 DEFINITIONS

Dispensary: Any not-for-profit health centre other than a private clinic that offers a set of free or sub-sidized basic services.

Primary Health Centre (PHCC): A not-for-profit health centre that has an agreement with the MoPH to deliver a set of health services within the national primary health-care network.

Currently, there are around 1100 dispensaries and not for profit health centres that provide packages of health services varying from simple drug dispensing to comprehensive services that include vaccination, management of childhood illnesses, reproductive health, non-communicable diseases, mental health, and various acute conditions (Box 21.3). The great majority of these dispensaries and not for profit centres are owned and managed by NGOs, with a few owned and co-managed by municipalities or the MoPH or Ministry of Social Affairs (MoSA). The MoSA has a network of around 250 Social Development Centres that provide some general and basic health services in addition to some social services (such as care for elderly and people with special needs, illiteracy eradication, vocational training). In 2017, a total of 205 of these dispensaries and not for profit health centres were part of to the national network of PHC supported by the MoPH and providing a more comprehensive set of services. These 205 centres are referred to as PHC centres: they benefit from all MoPH capacity building activities and are given priority for enrolment in the accreditation programme.

Since 2016, 75 centres of the 205 PHC facilities are enrolled in a project for providing defined preventive and curative packages of health services: the Emergency Primary Healthcare Restoration Project (EPHRP) was set up at the Lebanese MoPH with a grant from the World Bank Group. The primary objective of the project is to restore access to essential health-care services for poor Lebanese affected by the influx of Syrian refugees.[5-7]

The project included three components: provision of a subsidized package of essential health-care services to eligible poor beneficiaries; capacity building of contracted service providers; and project management and monitoring. Five core categories of indicators are designed including utilization, disease/condition, patient experience, equity, and quality. In addition, there are two program indicators to measure contracting and delivering, design, and sustainability.

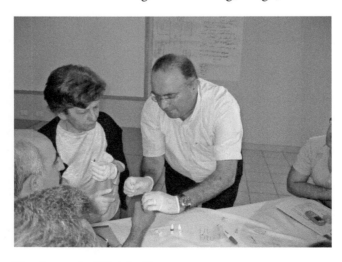

Blood sample, PHC facility

Referred to as "wellness packages", and including maternal and child health, noncommunicable disease, and mental health services, these prepaid sets of services, are to be delivered through the PHC network. They will reach out, over a pilot period of three years, to the most vulnerable 150,000 Lebanese identified across the country by the National Poverty Targeting Program.

Over the last 18 months of implementation, the project has already enrolled 18% of the planned target enrolees: 6.6% are elderly, 56.3% are children and 37.1 are adults. A patient satisfaction survey conducted at the PHC enrolled in the project indicated a high level of satisfaction by beneficiaries: 95% reported being treated well and approved of nurse– and doctor–patient exchange (94% and 83%, respectively).[8,9] The PHC team is working on addressing regional differences in service delivery and enrolment, evaluation of the basic benefits package cost, revision of certain indicators and associated targets, and laboratory material purchasing. In 2017, the project conducted a user satisfaction questionnaire to 1200 project beneficiaries (300 each quarter). A very high user satisfaction score (above 97%) was maintained throughout the year, and the overall user experience was found to be positive. The only area that showed issues with the perceived quality of visit was the perceived adequacy of user education as shown in Table 21.1 below.

Around 420 of the dispensaries and not-for-profit health centres, including the PHC centres of the national PHC network, are adherent to the National Chronic Medications Program operated by the Young Men's Christian Association (YMCA) for the MoPH since 1997. The program provides medications at a nominal cost for around 160 000 vulnerable and poor Lebanese and some 15,000 refugees, who suffer from non-communicable diseases (NCDs).

As dual private and public practice is allowed in the country, all the physicians working in the PHC network and/or in the dispensaries have private practices. Services in the private sector are based on fee for service. It is rare to encounter a PHC or dispensary with a full-time GP or family physician, except in the UNRWA-run clinics.

TABLE 21.1 PHC user experience October 2011

Question	Agree %	Disagree %	N/A %	Neutral %
Trust in skills (nurse)	98%	1%	0.5%	0.5%
Adequate time given (nurse)	98%	0.5%	1%	0.5%
Adequate explanation (nurse)	95%	3%	1%	1%
Trust in skills (doctor)	90%	3%	5%	2%
Adequate time given (doctor)	91%	3%	5%	1%
Adequate explanation (doctor)	91%	3%	5%	1%
User education adequate	70%	26%	3%	1%

Source: Reproduced from MoPH report 2017.

BOX 21.4   SUCCESS STORY: THE WADI KHALED MCH INITIATIVE

Wadi Khaled is a group of 24 villages located in the northeast of the governorate of North Lebanon. It is a pocket of poverty with higher maternal and child mortality than most of the country.

In 2003, the MoPH and the Al-Makassed Philanthropic Association signed a joint agreement aiming to start operations in Wadi Khaled Health Care centre, a PHC centre owned by the MoPH and managed by Makassed. The intervention of Makassed aims to ensure maternal-child health (MCH) services and essential health care for the population.

The MCH initiative covered 31 villages. It consisted of reaching out at community level to all women of childbearing age within the catchment area of the PHC centre, referring them to the PHC centre for preconception, antenatal and postnatal care, and normal vaginal delivery. The initiative also offers a set of preventive and well-baby services for children up to two years of age.

The Makassed has established a team of health workers at the Wadi Khaled PHC centre, headed by a GP/ family physician, with a nurse, a social worker, and a midwife. The team is backed up by a gynaecologist. The initiative is based on a people-centred approach, using capitation as a model of financing. A house-to-house survey conducted in 2007 revealed the drop of neonatal mortality rate from 10.8% to 2.66%, infant mortality rate from 18.6% to 5.29%, and C-section from 47% to 17.3%.

The initiative has operated over the last 15 years with no maternal deaths reported. Using humanitarian funds from the EU, it has been replicated with support from WHO in two other low-income areas: Tripoli and in the outskirts of Beirut.

PHC ACCREDITATION

In 2008, the MoPH initiated work on an accreditation mechanism for primary health care corporations (PHCCs), as a method to monitor and ensure quality. The accreditation program is fully funded by MoPH and implemented by the PHC department, with technical support from Accreditation Canada. The accreditation standards were developed with technical support from WHO; they classify the accredited PHC centre as basic, advanced, or excellent.

ACCREDITATION PROCESS

The accreditation process is as follows: (i) PHCC receives basic accreditation training; (ii) PHCC receives refresher training on various topics related to accreditation; (iii) PHCC conducts a self-assessment in preparation for mock survey; (iv) MoPH in collaboration with Accreditation Canada conducts mock survey visit to the PHCC and offers recommendations; (v) MoPH in collaboration with Accreditation Canada conducts actual survey visit; (vi) MoPH accredits PHCC based on the results of the actual survey visit; (vii) MoPH conducts accreditation post-monitoring visits to accredited PHCC 1-2 times per year; (viii) MoPH conducts accreditation survey visit every three years to renew accreditation status.[10]

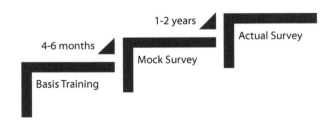

On average, it takes the PHCCs two years to go through the entire accreditation process from basic training to final accreditation. More than half of the PHCCs in the network have received basic accreditation training. However, by end of 2017 a total of 31 PHC facilities were accredited.

FAMILY PRACTICE WITHIN THE HEALTH SYSTEM STRUCTURE

Over the past decade, the political commitment of the MoPH to Family Practice was expressed by the adoption of the people-centred approach to PHC. An old Lebanese law requiring that all newly graduated GPs or family physicians practice in rural areas for at least one year after graduation was reactivated, but it has not been enforced, basically because of the heavier distribution of medical doctors in rural and semi-urban areas. More recent attempts at upgrading the capacities of GPs towards a more comprehensive family practice approach have been made in consultation with main academic institutions. A new law was issued to establish a two-year program for GPs, but financial constraints have kept the law from being enforced. As an alternative, the Family Medicine Department at UAB, with support from the WHO, developed an online course to introduce the family medicine approach to GPs. Participation of the Lebanese physicians remains limited; this is partially due to the fact that the course is optional, is not a prerequisite to be recruited by the PHCs, and offers no additional financial or other incentives. In 2016–2017, the UNRWA enrolled 16 of its GPs in this online training course and plans to enrol 16 more in 2018.

A few attempts have been made to introduce the gatekeeping mechanism through the family doctor/trained GP but these have not been sustained because of the lack of incentives to the physicians, inadequate regulations, and poorly defined catchment areas, as well as the long-standing culture of freedom of choice in physicians and health facilities. However, it is very common for a Lebanese to refer to his or her "family doctor", meaning, quite often, a specialist rather than a GP or family physician that he/she consults for every medical problem. In the same context, a study in 2015 (Ayoub F et al) indicated that the idealized perception of a doctor as a caregiving, compassionate, knowledgeable, and healthy role model still holds true within the Lebanese community.

KEY CHALLENGES

Promoting family medicine

Attracting GPs to get formal training in family medicine is a main barrier to introducing the family medicine/people-centred approach; in an era where medicine is moving towards narrow and advanced specialization, comprehensive, holistic people-centred medicine is not appealing to many fresh graduates in medicine. Moreover, Lebanon has no regulations limiting the number of specialists and no "carte sanitaire" for their distribution within specialties and within geographic areas. A recent survey of practicing family physicians in Lebanon indicates that family doctors suffer from heavy workloads, too many bureaucratic tasks, and demanding patients.[11] They also are under-valued by specialists, and their incomes cannot compete with those of other specialists. In the absence of financial incentives, and with limited career perspectives, most physicians who elect to specialize in family medicine do so with the perspective of establishing a private, individual practice. This makes attracting and retaining family doctors in the PHC network a challenge.

Adapting health service delivery to a family practice approach in PHCs

The current service delivery model at the PHC network at the MoPH is not fully adapted to the role of the family doctor as described in the people-centred approach; the family doctor has limited decision-making authority in the organization of health care. Community outreach is also limited. Moreover, without a well-defined population or geographic catchment areas, the distribution of workload can be an important challenge.

Changing the culture of specialty care

Lebanon is perhaps one of the few countries in the region where access to specialty care is readily available; promoting basic family practice comprehensive care requires effort. It needs pre-paid services and regulations for third party payers. However, this would risk raising discontent and the feeling of inequity as family/basic care is perceived by the Lebanese as lower quality care.

Getting stakeholder buy in for the integration of family physicians

With the adoption of the family medicine approach, specialists stand to reduce caseloads in private clinics and lose income. Neutralizing their counter-promotion of the family medicine approach is an important challenge. Moreover, other stakeholders such as third-party payers may be reluctant to pay for two consultations (initial family medicine consultation and the referral consultation for the specialist). There are no national studies related to these financial aspects of gatekeeping mechanisms and their cost-effectiveness, so there is little evidence to support promotion of such a paradigm shift in service delivery organization.

TOWARDS UNIVERSAL HEALTH COVERAGE: THE WAY FORWARD

Despite these challenges and limitations, there is a strong momentum for moving forward to reinforce PHC. It requires a paradigm shift for family physicians to be at the heart of a people-centred PHC system. There is ample room for more stakeholders to actively participate in this shift.

Recommendations include:

- To widen the structure of the primary health care committee to encompass all major players, including representatives from professional societies of GPs and family physicians, along with some key municipalities
- To reposition the family physician at the centre of a gatekeeping mechanism within the PHC national network, coordinating comprehensive, holistic patient care rather than a limited set of packages
- To supervise a clear referral system for secondary and tertiary care with MoPH co-funding mechanisms, and to oversee community-oriented interventions (such as awareness and home care) based on periodic needs assessments and community health needs and trends
- To open the door to private practice centres/family physicians' clinics to contribute to the primary care effort and to encourage the MoPH to experiment with capitation schemes
- To work towards PHC through a more comprehensive approach, such as the development of the healthy cities/healthy villages concepts

REFERENCES

1. Ministry of Public Health. Family Practice Profile 2016, Lebanon; unpublished.
2. Ministry of Public Health. Family Practice Profile 2017, Lebanon; unpublished.
3. Kronfol N. Healthcare systems and family medicine in the Arab World; unpublished.
4. Ministry of Public Health. Strategic Plan for the medium term (2016 to 2020). Lebanon; 2016. Available from: https://www.moph.gov.lb/userfiles/files/%D9%90Announcement/Final-StrategicPlanHealth2017. pdf [Accessed 19 April 2018].
5. World Bank. *Lebanon—Health Resilience Project (English)*. Washington, DC: World Bank Group; 2017. Available from: http://documents.worldbank.org/curated/en/616901498701694043/Lebanon-Health-Res ilience-Project [Accessed 19 April 2018].
6. Khalife J. Emergency Primary Healthcare Restoration Project (EPHRP) External evaluation report; June 2017; unpublished.
7. Emergency Primary Healthcare Restoration Project. User Experience, User Satisfaction & Data Verification; unpublished.
8. Akl EA, El-Asmar K, Khater-Menassa B, Maroun N, Adib S. Characteristics of physicians practicing in Lebanon: a survey. *Eastern Mediterranean Health Journal*. 2012;18(7):712–7. Available from: http://www .who.int/iris/handle/10665/118174 [Accessed 22 September 2018].

9. Ayoub F, Fares Y, Fares J. The psychological attitude of patients toward health practitioners in Lebanon. *North American Journal of Medical Sciences*. 2015;7(10):452-8. Available from: http://www.najms.org/article.asp?issn=1947-2714;year=2015;volume=7;issue=10;spage=452;epage=458;aulast=Ayoub [Accessed 22 September 2018].

10. Ministry of Public Health. Accreditation of primary health care centers and quality of care; 2016, unpublished.

11. Helou, M, Rizk, GA. State of family medicine practice in Lebanon. 2016; *Journal of Family Medicine and Primary Care*. 2016;5(1):51–5. Available from: https://www.ncbi.nlm.nih.gov/pubmed/27453843 [Accessed 22 September 2018].

CHAPTER 22

Libya

Syed Jaffar Hussain

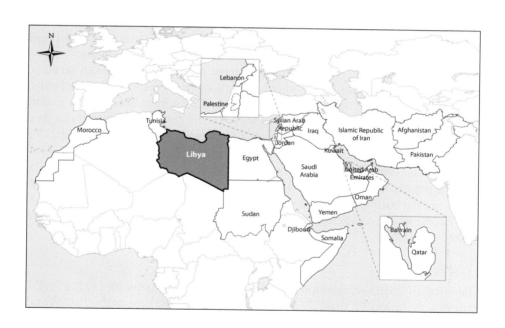

Total number of PHC facilities	1355 of which 273 are closed as a result of the conflict
Number of general practitioners working in public PHC facilities	2135
Number of certified family physicians working in PHC facilities	30
Average number of family physician graduates/year	10
Number of medical schools	14
Number of family medicine departments	10

INTRODUCTION

Libya is an oil-rich country in the Eastern Mediterranean Region. Mostly desert, it is one of the largest countries in Africa, with 1.77 million square kilometres. Its population is 6.3 million. The toppling of long-term leader Muammar Gaddafi in 2011 led to a power vacuum and instability, with no authority in full control. Since then the economy and social service delivery systems have been severely disrupted and the situation has worsened as conflict between militias has escalated.

While the 2009 Millennium Development Goals (MDG) Report for Libya stated that the country was on track to attain the MDGs by 2015, in 2017, amidst chronic insecurity fuelled by regional violent extremism, 1.3 million Libyans (20% of the country's population) needed humanitarian assistance. Public service infrastructure – especially electricity, banking, and health services – is collapsing throughout the country. Households are struggling to make ends meet, with rapidly soaring inflation. A deterioration of the educational system, whose progress was earlier a point of pride for the country, now poses the risk of losing a generation.

Armed conflict has disrupted the provision of most of the essential health services needed by Libyans, especially the vulnerable. Without enough supplies, manpower, or electricity, many medical centres and private hospitals in conflict-affected areas have been closed, making it difficult for citizens to receive the health care they need. The recently published Service Availability and Readiness Assessment (SARA 2) report of 2017 shows that 17 hospitals and 273 primary health-care facilities are closed.[1]

The burden of diseases in Libya is largely preventable if robust and effective PHC services are delivered to the population. Non-Communicable Diseases (NCDs) represent 77% of the burden of disease and are the leading cause of death in Libya. Smoking among adults exceeds 34% of the population. Excess weight, diabetes, and cancer are widespread and inadequately addressed by the weak PHC system.[1,2]

PHC IN LIBYA

Primary health care (PHC) services are delivered through a wide network of 1355 PHC facilities (units, centres, polyclinics). Of these, 273 (20%) were closed at the time of the 2017 World Health Organization (WHO)/Ministry of Health (MoH) Service Availability and Readiness Assessment (SARA). PHC services are perceived by many Libyans to have little to offer patients and, as a result, people tend to bypass the PHC level because of its limited quality of services; they find their way directly to the out-patient clinics or emergency services of secondary or tertiary care hospitals. Many PHC centres have no full-time doctors, and when they do, the doctors are usually young and not very experienced.

Primary health care in Libya is provided across the 23 districts (Governorates, Shabia). Each PHC unit serves 1000–5000 citizens and each PHC centre serves 10,000–26,000 citizens. There are 37 polyclinics; each of them serves 50,000–60,000 citizens. The survey on the availability and accessibility of PHC services conducted by the WHO and MoH in August 2012 showed that only one-third of primary care facilities were fully functioning and 44% were partially functioning. Around 23% of facilities were either not functioning or under rehabilitation; a higher percentage (30%) of PHC units were not functioning or under rehabilitation. This is in addition to 111 not included in the survey due to closure.

The level of functioning health centres and units varies greatly between Shabiat and Tripoli, which has the greatest number of functioning facilities. Fully functioning and available does not mean that the services are utilized. As an example, one of the fully functioning centres in Tripoli is located in the heart of a well-populated area. On in-depth analysis, we found that 70% of the medicines from the essential medicine list were not available: the doctors encouraged patients to buy medicine privately or to shop around in other centres, polyclinics, or hospitals. The dental chair had been dysfunctional for many months and 10 dentists sat idle; the laboratory diagnostic equipment was not working. In our assessment we found that the centre, although classified as "fully functioning", was, in reality, working at less than 50% capacity, taking into account public health activities of screening, immunization, and health promotion. Furthermore, staff capacity was weak: none had trained in family medicine, they had no supervision, and were not involved in any continuing professional development (CPD). We concluded that quality of care and patient safety were questionable. The unwillingness of many Libyan doctors to work in remote areas and the large size of the country limit ability to deliver effective health care. We are confident that all other "functional" centres and units are suffering from the same problem of poor management. If the government and the MoH want to increase public confidence in the national health services, primary care, as the first line of contact with the health system, should be at its best.

In most of the PHC facilities, stock outs of essential medicines are not uncommon, so people are not satisfied with the services delivered at this level. There are no electronic or paper medical records in most facilities that keep essential information on people in the catchment areas. As a result, patients are seen by different health professionals without accurate or complete health records. PHC facility hygiene, including the toilets and sanitation, are often seen as deficient.

PHC facilities in Libya lack standardized design and have no essential list of the equipment and lab facilities that enable the facility to deliver high-quality care. It is believed that for any serious health problem, the outcome of using the PHC would be referral, so that skipping PHC speeds up the process. PHC facilities are known to be open three to four hours a day, which discourages regular use. As in most countries in the region, PHC in Libya has been neglected, underfunded, and seen as a lower-level specialty.

The burden of disease attributable to communicable disease in Libya was 9.8%, to non-communicable diseases 77.8%, and to injuries 12.3%. The share of out-of-pocket expenditure in 2013 was 29.7%.[2] There was an imbalance of human resources and a shortage of specialized staff across the country. The readiness of the health services needed to be improved and service providers needed training on service quality and clinical guidelines; additionally, standard operating procedures were needed for each specific and specialized service. Overall, investment in developing the health workforce and institutional capacities remains a high prioritiy in Libya.

The SARA 2 survey noted that the total number of general practitioners in the country was 2135 and the total number of specialists was 1633. Overall there were 24,818 nurses and 552 midwives working in primary health-care facilities. A total of 4951 dentists and 2618 pharmacists also contribute to the workforce of primary health-care facilities. See Figure 22.1 for the health facilities infrastructure.

SARA results show that the general service readiness index mean score for the public health primary health care facilities was 36.8%, which is significantly compromised. Further analysis

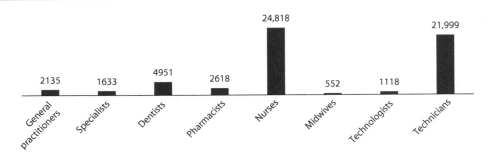

FIGURE 22.1 Health Facilities infrastructure. (The Service Availability and Readiness Assessment survey in Libya, 2017).

shows that the overall general service readiness mean score for PHCs was less than the target in all regions and all districts.

In Libya, there is a mixed system of public and private health care, rather than a purely state-run model. The health care delivery system operated on three levels:

1. The first level consisted of the PHC units (providing curative and preventive services for 5000–10,000 citizens); PHC centres (serving from 10,000 to 26,000 citizens); and polyclinics (serving approximately 50,000–60,000 citizens), containing laboratories as well as radiological services and a pharmacy, and staffed by specialist physicians.
2. The second level included general hospitals in rural and urban areas where care was provided to those referred from the first level.
3. The third level comprised of tertiary care specialized hospitals.

Libyan health services are largely perceived as seriously fragmented and inadequate overall – not just at primary care level. Several hospitals in Benghazi remain closed (the Hawari Hospital is in a state of collapse, as are many other major hospitals in country); Misrata's main hospital remains unfinished; hospitals in the south are without staff, medical equipment, medications or money; and medical facilities in Tripoli are dismissed as inadequate and incompetent. Those who can afford it seek health-care services they need from neighbouring countries like Tunisia, Turkey, or Jordan.

LIBYA'S HEALTH CARE IN DRAMATIC DECLINE

SARA is a systematic survey which aims to provide reliable information on the availability and readiness of service delivery.[3] The first SARA survey was conducted in 2012. The latest SARA survey was conducted as a census covering all 1656 public health facilities. It was a collaborative effort between WHO and the MoH. The survey for the hospitals started in August and ended in mid-December 2016, while the survey for PHCs data started in September 2016 and ended in February 2017. The population estimates for 2017 based on 22 districts were provided by the Bureau of Statistics, Libya.

LIBYA'S EXPERIENCE WITH PHC

Primary health care (PHC) has been the main cornerstone of health-care provision to Libyan people. During the revolution and the subsequent conflict in 2014, PHC service availability was limited. However, key services (preventive and curative) were offered in a sustained manner, albeit with diminishing outreach. Some of the major successful stories of PHC during this period, supported mainly by WHO, include:

- *Immunization*: Immunization throughout Libya is provided through fixed centres (mainly PHC centres) and there is no outreach mechanism in the country. Before the revolution, the immunization services had coverage of above 90%, which saw a sustained decline after the revolution and the mass exodus of expatriate health workers. However, in 2016–2017 immunization outreach improved again with support from WHO. For example, the MoH has successfully conducted four rounds of polio national immunization days through the PHC network, targeting 1.3 million children in each round (including migrants' children). The final round in September 2017 was also combined with measles, mumps, and rubella (MMR) vaccines.
- *Mobile outreach PHC services*: Realizing that many Libyans and migrants do not have access to PHC services due to the shortage of health workers, damage to PHC centres, and an acute shortage of essential medicines, the MoH and WHO set up an aggressive mobile outreach mechanism to provide PHC (preventive and curative) services to the most vulnerable populations. Currently, there are 13 mobile outreach teams working across Libya (more in the south and in recently liberated areas). These provide round-the-clock PHC services.

HEALTH SYSTEM CHALLENGES

Even prior to the conflict, the health system in Libya was weak and its overall performance had limitations, including:

- Lack of a technical health policy and planning function inside the planning department[4]
- Overall weak institutional capacity to plan and implement health programmes at national and sub-national levels
- Inadequate and fragmented national health information systems in areas of data required for decision making, ICT, and the development of e-records for the health sector
- The absence of a health-care financing policy and universal coverage schemes options
- An unclear national human resources development plan, policy, and strategy and lack of a comprehensive system for continuous professional development
- Inadequate health systems research as an integral part of national health development
- Fragmented and novice management of medicine supply and distribution
- No national model of PHC and generally low quality of care with an absence of referral pathways
- Sub-optimal levels of facility management and leadership

With a destructive civil war in many parts of the country, the situation is more complex. The vast majority of key informants in the country reported that people in their communities paid for medical services and medicines out of pocket. Additional health sector challenges include:

- A fragile and fragmented public health sector with lack of sector leadership and effective governance

- Very deficient institutional capacity, especially in policy development, strategic planning, programme management, monitoring, forecasting, and evidence-based decision making
- A significant number of foreign health workers have left the country, which has had a serious impact on the health response capacity and the functionality of health facilities
- A mushrooming and unregulated private sector
- Security constraints, which have rendered some facilities inaccessible, and conflict-related damage or looting of facilities
- A debilitated PHC network, with dysfunctional referral to higher levels of care
- Sending Libyans for treatment abroad, which consumes a substantial part of health expenditure
- Marginalized health services in some areas, predominantly in Southern Libya

POLITICAL COMMITMENT TO FAMILY PRACTICE

Libya has adopted the approach of improving primary health care through incremental strengthening of the family health model. There is political commitment to scale-up family medicine despite the enormous challenges and the disruption of the health system, with some financial allocations for the national programme.

To train and produce skilled and qualified family physicians to transform service delivery and scale-up this evidence-based approach, Libya has included the specialty of family medicine in the Libyan Board of Medical Specialties. Family physicians need to complete an undergraduate degree, medical school, and three to five more years of specialized medical residency training in family medicine. Their residency training includes rotations in internal medicine, paediatrics, obstetrics-gynaecology, psychiatry, surgery, emergency medicine, and geriatrics. Residents also must provide care for a panel of continuity patients in an out-patient "model practice" for the entire period of the residency. The specialty focuses on treating the whole person, acknowledging the effects of all outside influences, through all stages of life. Family physicians will see anyone with a medical issue but are experts in common problems. Many family physicians deliver babies in addition to taking care of patients of all ages. In order to become board certified, family physicians must complete a residency in family medicine, possess a full and unrestricted medical license, and take a written examination. Family medicine is part of community medicine in undergraduate examinations. Postgraduate training in family medicine is a four-year programme:

- *First year*: 11 modules in community medicine and rotations in different specialties followed by a part one exam
- *Second, third, and fourth years*: Rotations in gynaecology, surgery, ophthalmology, paediatrics, ENT, medicine, and psychiatry, with a part two exam followed by a thesis

FAMILY PRACTICE AND NATIONAL PUBLIC HEALTH INITIATIVES

Five years of armed conflict and political instability have affected almost every part of Libya, claiming thousands of lives and leaving thousands more injured; there are 435,000 internally displaced persons (IDPs) in the country, many of whom have endured multiple displacements and lost homes, livelihoods, and loved ones. Those affected but not displaced by the conflict include an additional 1.75 million people.

Long after the eruption of hostilities, the indirect impact of conflict includes the disruption of livelihoods, inadequate food and water quality, the destruction of health systems, and prolonged insecurity. These continue to erode public health. Yet conflict damage to public health systems is also due to the destruction of infrastructure, the exodus of the skilled health workforce, shortages of medicines and supplies, and the effect on health-care delivery at large. While there has already been significant emigration from Libya, there is no data yet on who has left the country or what the long-term effect on the health-care workforce will be. Various scenarios are possible, but based on the experience of other African countries, the longer a conflict endures, the more the health-care system narrows to focus on acute needs and delivery of care to support the conflict, at the expense of all other domains of health.[5]

Family medicine provides the right foundation for addressing public health issues and promotes initiatives that could add value and improve the health and well-being of the Libyan population and migrants during this transition of conflict and disrupted service delivery. For example, in the immunization programme led by WHO and the MoH, family physicians and general practitioners play a central role, directly promoting and implementing the programme to reach every child and leave no one behind.

The Ministry of Health recognizes four levels at which PHC/family practice operates, these are:

- *Home*: Practiced primarily by individuals on their own or within their families or other close social networks, or people from the neighbourhood; community workers may also be involved in this level of care and interact with individuals and the family through home visits.
- *Community*: This concerns the health of a whole community and involves the voluntary efforts of individual community members, community groups, and community workers. Activity is related to health promotion, public information, and the planning/implementation of communal health activities.
- *First health facility*: The first level at which a trained health professional and clinical facilities are available; acting at this level may involve a support role in training and supervising a variety of community health workers.
- *First referral*: This level concerns the administrative or clinical referral of a health threat or problem to secondary health-care services or to planners and managers and others with responsibility for ensuring, for example, the enforcement of environmental safety regulations.

CONTRIBUTIONS OF FAMILY PRACTICE TO UNIVERSAL HEALTH COVERAGE

The WHO report on Libya noted that recognizing the fact that the inherited weaknesses in the PHC network are contributing to deficiencies in delivering the essential package of health services, as well as increasing the burden on hospitals in areas with non-functional or poorly functioning PHC services, the first priority is to strengthen PHC service delivery.[6] This can include enhancing the PHC network and strengthening the outreach team strategy. The aim is to establish a strong network of PHC facilities that offer a comprehensive package of essential services, including reproductive health, prevention, screening, and management of NCDs, the establishment of a functional referral system, and mobile clinics. All levels of the health-care system should provide promotive, curative, and rehabilitative activities supporting people with disabilities.

Attempts to modernize health service delivery are facing serious security, political, financial, workforce, and resistance-to-change obstacles. Availability of health information, combined with advances in patient engagement technology, are creating better informed and more demanding patients. Patients expect more from their care as they are better informed about diseases and the availability of care. Currently, health services in Libya are severely challenged for many reasons. Modern approaches and advances on the technical side of the health service have not been matched by developments in health service and management processes; beneath the surface, there lies a less developed health service of paternalism and bureaucracy. This unique situation produces a number of questions which require answers in order for Libya to evolve into the role of the 21st-century country that the government and population desire.

WHO's conceptual and strategic approach to family practice ensures that taking the family practice approach will effectively lead to the attainment of universal health coverage. Experience from across the world has shown that the family practice approach can increase households' access to a defined package of services at an affordable cost, through trained and motivated family practice teams which can ensure high-quality, continuing, and comprehensive primary care services for the individual and family across all ages and both sexes. The fundamental characteristics of family practice and its derivative attributes allow the family physician to contribute substantially to health-care systems in all countries, despite differences in the way these systems are planned, organized, and managed.

FAMILY PRACTICE TEAMS

MoH and WHO are focusing on building the capacity of PHC facilities and training the healthcare team on the family health approach. This model is a coherent package of preventive, promotive, diagnostic, and therapeutic services that put people at the centre of the health-care package. Quality of service is the cornerstone of the service cycle and procedures, and the health-care team is trained and motivated to follow best practices.

PHC Centre, Tajoura

MoH and WHO are working together to build the capacity of 1000 PHC service providers, covering a good proportion of the PHC workforce in targeted districts: 300 doctors, 600 nurses, and 100 district management staff persons are being trained on effective planning, service delivery, and management of primary health-care services.

A number of ongoing projects are focusing on strengthening PHC staff capacity to function as a team. This capacity-building programme addresses knowledge gaps, providing appropriate skills and best practices to the team. The system needs trained staff who can take responsibility for the health needs of families living in the catchment areas of the PHC facilities. The PHC team should have the skills needed to assess health needs, providing an integrated package of preventive, promotive, curative, and rehabilitation services that meet the needs of the community.

The family health model in Libya is adopting an overall reform agenda so that:

- The MoH is responsible for all primary care service and provision is free to all those working and living in Libya
- The government does not license any primary care provider who is not part of MoH services (through direct or contractual service) to ensure equity and maintain the quality, integrity, and comprehensiveness of the service
- The MoH explores incentives needed to attract high-calibre health professionals to primary care (through training in family medicine)
- The MoH invests in preparing the future leadership in primary care (through advanced training in leadership)

THE KEY CHALLENGES TO FAMILY PRACTICE

- The small number of family physicians graduating each year
- No dedicated fund for the implementation of family practice service delivery
- No approved professional career (cadres) for family physicians
- Family physicians are considered a threat to other specialties
- Lack of coordination between MoH and the Ministry of Health Education
- Little demand from the community for family physicians
- During the current crisis, family practice is not one of the top priorities of the MoH

THE ROLE OF THE PRIVATE HEALTH SECTOR IN EXPANDING UNIVERSAL HEALTH COVERAGE

The private sector plays a significant role in providing out-patient services. Currently, it is considered as the preferred place for seeking health care. The proportion of patients seeking health-care services outside public primary health-care facilities is estimated to be 40%. Family physicians are limited in number and their role in the private sector is not well-established. Public confidence in public health facilities is declining because they do not have adequate staffing, equipment, or medicines. In contrast, the private sector is expanding rapidly and is providing higher-quality services in most areas. The role of the private sector is crucial for expanding universal health coverage, especially when the country is facing an emergency.

PROVIDING PHC SERVICES FOR MIGRANTS

Libya continues to have one of the most complex mixed migration situations in the world. According to the Displaced Tracking Matrix, November 2017, there are 192,762 internally displaced persons (IDPs) and 43,5574 migrants in Libya. However, the number of migrants is estimated to be over 700,000 across the country. Out of the reported number, approximately 20,000 migrants are placed in 32 detention centres under the control of the Department of Combating Illegal Migration (DCIM, under MOI) and militias.

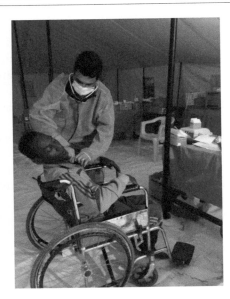

WHO-run the PHC centre in Tawerga IDP camp

Provisions for the deprivation of liberty of non-citizens for immigration-related violations are contained in two laws: Law No. 6 (1987) Regulating Entry, Residence and Exit of Foreign Nationals to/from Libya as amended by Law No. 2 (2004) and Law No. 19 (2010) on Combating Irregular Migration. Under both laws, violations of migration provisions are criminalized and sanctioned with fines and imprisonment. According to observers, the 2010 Law on Combating Irregular Migration (Law No. 19) allows for the indefinite detention, followed by deportation, of those considered to be irregular migrants.

Fragmented government, widespread insecurity, a collapsed economy, long porous borders, and disrupted social services are the main contributors to migration challenges in Libya. Health is a major concern in addressing the issues of migrants in Libya. The journey to or through Libya is both difficult and dangerous, and it exposes migrants to many health risks as they move towards their destination or are detained. Some die tragically during the journey. Poor living conditions, inappropriate nutrition, and barriers to access to preventive and curative health services may put migrants at risk of serious health problems. For those living in detention centres, this risk is compounded by extremely poor living conditions; even for migrants who reside within Libyan communities, the conditions are precarious as they have limited access to health and other essential services, or chances to earn a livelihood.

The availability of health services to migrants is erratic. The International Organization for Migration (IOM) is leading efforts to ensure that PHC services are available to the migrants in detention centres and supporting referral to public and private sector hospitals. In most cases, it pays for hospital services needed by migrants in detention centres. UNHCR is also providing psycho-social support as well as some lifesaving medicines to hospitals catering for the migrants. WHO, working closely with IOM and MoH, established a disease early warning system (EWARS) in the detention centres which IOM is now managing. For migrants outside the detention centres (who run into the hundreds of thousands), WHO is providing life-saving medicines and supplies to hospitals and PHC centres in areas hosting most of the migrants. IOM also provides medicines/supplies to some of these health facilities.

According to IOM's Displacement Tracking Matrix (DTM), November 2017, there are 192,762 IDPs and 435,574 migrants in Libya. The health system of Libya has been severely affected by the crisis and the additional population requiring health care further strains its capacity. In 2017, the Libyan MoH and WHO conducted SARA, which showed that the system was having the greatest difficulties coping with the health needs of the population in areas affected by conflict or with large populations of migrants or displaced persons. The assessment showed an imbalance of health workers and shortages of medicines, equipment, and diagnostic materials. These findings support investing in strengthening the health system to be able to respond to the needs of migrant and refugees.

IOM has conducted a Public Health Risk Assessment in a Detention Centre, and WHO expanded the Early Warning and Response Network (EWARN) of communicable diseases in Libya and supported IOM technically for selected detention centres to be covered by EWARN.

In collaboration with local NGOs and the MoH, WHO provides medical supplies and mobile medical teams as part of the emergency response for IDPs in schools and camps. This started in 2016 and continues. In collaboration with the United Nations International Children's Emergency Fund (UNICEF) and the National Center of Disease Control, WHO was able to vaccinate IDPs and migrants during polio and measles national immunization campaigns in 2017.

REFERENCES

1. WHO. The Service Availability and Readiness Assessment survey in Libya. 2017 (SARA). Available from: http://www.who.int/hac/crises/lby/en/ [Accessed 20 April 2018].
2. WHO Eastern Mediterranean Region Office. Eastern Mediterranean Region Framework for health information systems and core indicators for monitoring health situation and health system performance 2016. 2016. Available from: http://applications.emro.who.int/dsaf/EMROPUB_2016_EN_19169.pdf?ua=1&ua=1 [Accessed 20 April 2018].
3. WHO. The service availability and readiness assessment survey in Libya. 2012. Available from: http://www.who.int/hac/crises/lby/en/ [Accessed 20 April 2018].
4. 2017 Review of Health Sector in Libya. https://reliefweb.int/report/libya/2017-review-health-sector-libya
5. Sullivan R, McQuinn B, Purushotham A. How are we going to rebuild public health in Libya? *Journal of the Royal Society of Medicine*, 2011; 104(12): 490–492. doi:10.1258/jrsm.2011.110230. Available from: https://www.ncbi.nlm.nih.gov/pmc/articles/PMC3241510/table/JRSM-11-0230TB1/.
6. WHO. Humanitarian crisis in Libya; Public health risk assessment and interventions. 2015. Available from: http://www.who.int/hac/crises/lby/libya__phra_may2015.pdf [Accessed 20 April 2018].

CHAPTER 23

Morocco

Amina Sahel and Hachri Hafid

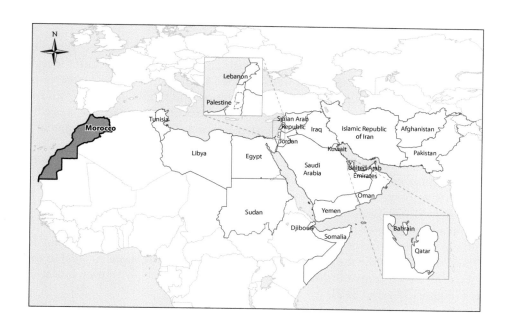

Total number of PHC facilities	2759 (760 managed by nurses in rural areas)[1]
Number of general practitioners working in public PHC facilities	3100
Number of certified family physicians working in PHC facilities	45
Average number of family physician graduates/year	40
Number of medical schools	5 public, 2 private
Number of family medicine departments	1

INTRODUCTION

An analysis of the current health situation in Morocco shows significant achievements in terms of reduced incidence of communicable diseases and maternal and child mortality ratios. However, although the burden of communicable diseases has diminished considerably, the country is currently facing an increase in non-communicable diseases (NCDs) and accidents. In 2011, 18.2% of Moroccans were suffering from a chronic disease, compared with 13.8% in 2004. The prevalence of diabetes among persons aged 20 and above accounted for around 6.6% of the population (i.e., 1.5 million people), while high blood pressure accounted for a further 33.6% (6 million). The provision of care for these diseases is decentralized and has been integrated at the primary health-care level.

As a signatory of the Alma-Ata Declaration, Morocco has included its PHC strategy in its priorities for governmental action for health. Morocco's first five-year plan for PHC spanned the period 1981–1985. Several sectoral projects targeting PHC development were launched with the support of technical and financial partners.

These projects made significant contributions to the improvement of health coverage in urban and rural environments, to the standardization of the approach to coverage and the restructuring of health programmes. These efforts were reflected in the performance levels recorded for prevention programme activities – notably immunization and family planning – and endemic disease control. This progress enabled the country to control and eliminate diseases which, just 40 years ago, were a considerable morbidity burden: poliomyelitis, diphtheria, neonatal tetanus, measles, pertussis, malaria, schistosomiasis, trachoma, leprosy, and others.

The coverage made available to the population by the primary health-care facilities (PHCFs) has improved significantly. The number of PHCFs rose from 1653 in 1990 to 2689 in 2014,[2] and to 2759 in 2015, a growth of 72% in 25 years.[3] Overall service was improved by 19%, with the ratio of facilities to inhabitants increasing from 1:14,600 in 1990, to 1:11,600 in 2015 (with figures ranging from a maximum of 1:4400 to a minimum of 1:19,750).

The ratio of nurses to the population changed little between 2007 and 2011 (from 1:3267 in 2009 to 1:3327 in 2011), while the coverage provided by general practitioners (GPs) in the public sector in the PHCFs fell from 1.01:10,000 to 0.94:10,000 inhabitants, with even less coverage in rural areas (Figures 23.1 and 23.2).

Despite the efforts made by the Ministry of Health (MoH) in terms of building PHCFs, the percentage of the population living more than six kilometres from any such facility remained high at 43%, and mobile coverage remains a valuable alternative.

PRIMARY HEALTH-CARE FACILITIES INFRASTRUCTURE

The health services package is defined at the national level and by type of PHCF: rural dispensary and Level 1 or 2 health centre. PHCF activities are set out in the health coverage extension plan,

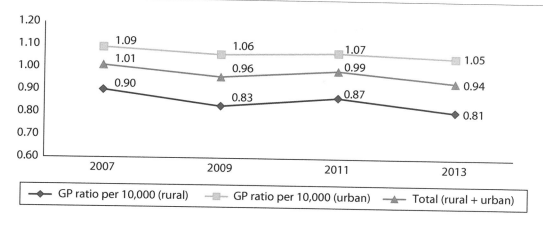

FIGURE 23.1 Evolution of the ratio of public sector GPs per 10,000 (national, urban, and rural areas) inhabitants

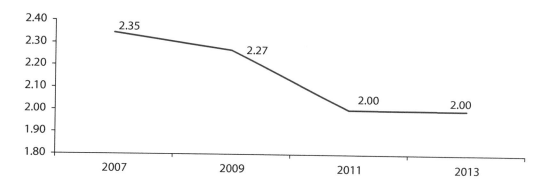

FIGURE 23.2 Evolution of the ratio of GPs per 10,000 (public and private sectors) inhabitants

an official scoping document published by the MoH.[4] In view of the ongoing epidemiological and demographic transition in Morocco, this health services package has been remodelled and the technical platform reinforced to address NCDs. The current health services package includes coverage for chronic diseases, notably cardiovascular diseases and diabetes, as well as screening for breast and cervical cancer. At the same time, some PHCFs have recently been provided with obstetric echography, equipment for providing care for local emergencies, and automated devices for biological investigations for pregnant women and diabetic patients. Recently, the health services package has been reviewed and redefined as part of a project to reinforce the health-care system with support from the Global Fund.

The first list of essential medicines was produced in the 2000s. It addressed the programme needs via care protocols.

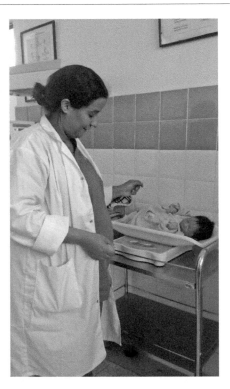

Baby care in a PHC facility

The list is regularly reviewed at the request of the programme providers or managers as new protocols are issued. It identifies the list of medicines and medical equipment in the PHCFs and hospitals at each care level (rural dispensary, Level 1 or 2 health-care centre). Medicines are ordered by the team at the health centre in line with the available budget, while medicine purchasing is centralized.

The contents of the PHCF technical platform were defined in 1999, then again in 2010. This has been subsequently reinforced in accordance with the epidemiological context and depending on the relevance of introducing new technology. Most medicalized PHCFs have the equipment to offer the updated health services package (e.g., obstetric echography, electrocardiography, otoscopes, glucometers). Because of the inadequacy of the operating resources, maintenance, trained human resources, and reagents, this technical platform is under-used in some cases.

The health system in Morocco is a four-tier organization:

- The first-line health service (PHC)
- Level 1 reference facility (local hospital and provincial hospital)
- Level 2 reference facility (regional hospital)
- Level 3 reference facility (university hospital)

With the exception of emergencies, the transfer from one level to another is through the referral system. Since the introduction of the health insurance system for those in need (RAMED), the national authorities have made referrals via the associated health centre a mandatory process for accessing free care in hospitals.

The referral system is one way only, from the health centre to the hospital, and the connection is via the referral form. Counter-referrals are limited, despite the existence of guidelines, procedures, and coordination protocols. Each facility has its own mission, attributions, and responsibilities, operating as a self-enclosed entity relative to the rest of the system.

Health services provided in PHCFS are currently being reorganized and redefined with a view to fulfilling a coordinating role between the primary care level and the hospital referral level.

The different programmes integrated into PHC are managed via guides and therapeutic protocols (guidelines for the management of sexually transmitted infections, integrated care for children, diabetes, high blood pressure, and others).

Physician with a patient in a PHC facility

The information system available at the PHCF level is fragmented, oriented towards vertical health programmes, and not focused on patients and their families. It has not yet been computerized, represents a workload for the service providers, and is rarely analysed on-site for decision making.

Regarding the quality of PHC, the MoH has introduced a range of quality measures to instil this culture in the PHCFs. The two most recent measures concern the certification of specialized maternity homes and the quality competition, which constitute a systematic approach to the continuous improvement of care management and quality. The MoH has launched a process for PHCF accreditation.

PATIENT SATISFACTION WITH QUALITY OF SERVICE DELIVERY

Several important shortcomings still characterize the current health situation, in terms of the medical services available; they are perceived as of debatable quality and insensitive to patient needs. They are delivered by GPs who focus on the diseases and not on individuals and their community. The lack of motivation of health professionals and the offer of a standardized package of services ill-suited to patient demand, notably for chronic diseases such as diabetes, cancer, and mental health, make this first-line health care unattractive to patients. The rate of medical consultation currently does not exceed 0.7 contacts per inhabitant per year, even though care at this level is free of charge.

KEY CHALLENGES TO ACCESSING QUALITY SERVICE DELIVERY IN PUBLIC PHCFs

There are many challenges facing access to high-quality PHC.

- There is a shortage of human resources, exacerbated by the inadequacy of the basic training received by GPs relative to first-line needs. Effectively, the training offered at the faculty of medicine is inadequate for fulfilling the expected role of family doctors. It focuses on a bio-medical, hospital, and clinical approach while neglecting the mission of the GP which is essentially about patient–doctor communication and a biopsychosocial approach centred on the individual. Faculties of Medicine do not use a job description for family doctors to define their training programme policy in terms of both training content and educational methods.
- Population dispersal is another challenge, and there is resistance from doctors and nurses to working in remote areas.
- The referral system is weak, with excessive demand for specialized consultations resulting in longer waits for appointments with specialists. Unnecessary referrals and the lack of care coordination between the first level and hospital services lead to tense relations between GPs and specialists; GPs feel undervalued and suffer from an identity crisis.
- The vertical programmes and the fragmented information system are a burden on information system management and prevent integrated patient care. All these aspects lead to dissatisfaction among the population and a negative perception of the quality of first-line care.

FAMILY PRACTICE

Political commitments to family practice

The political commitment of the MoH in favour of the promotion of family practice has been embodied in the national health strategy for 2012–2016 and the new sectoral plan for 2017–2021 which calls for the development of PHC and a revised role for GPs in the implementation of the family and community health training programme. At the same time, several important projects have also been launched, notably:

- The reorganization and standardization of care access paths
- A redefined minimum health-care and services package
- The standardization of basic equipment in health centres with a childbirth unit
- The introduction of a health information system, based on the family folder
- The development of guidelines for prevalent long-term diseases
- Greater availability of medicines

This political commitment should be strengthened by the commitment of other stakeholders involved in the development of family practice, such as faculties of medicine, the Medical Syndicate, and the Ministry of Finance.

Family practice and national public health initiatives

Currently, the development of PHC and family practice is supported by several cooperation partners via health projects and programmes, such as the health system strengthening programme with the Global Fund, and the project to reinforce PHC supported by the European

Union, World Health Organization (WHO), and Spanish cooperation. The main national public health initiatives linked to the development of family practice in Morocco are outlined below:

- The establishment, in 2015, of a training programme in family/community health (FH/CH) in the form of a two-year master's degree course at the National School of Public Health (NSPH). The decision to run this course initially at the NSPH instead of the faculties of medicine was due to the resistance by the deans to the creation of a diploma of this kind and also because it would have required four years of specialization. The aim of the new master's course is to complete the technical skill sets of GPs and foster a change in their attitude, encouraging them to broaden their perspectives. It is designed to produce an enhanced GP focused on patients and their families, with the skill sets required to redirect the role of the PHC teams towards the provision of holistic support for family health, while enabling them to explore and support community participation.

  This training is based on the principles of family medicine (FM) adopted by the World Organization of Family Doctors (WONCA) and are based on skill benchmarks organized around integrated and overall management of patients, taking into consideration the MoH's programmes and strategy. The course targets the specific level of skills required for a GP in a synergistic relationship with specialists, without creating a duality and leaving gaps in the range of skills offered. To date, 45 doctors specialized in family health have completed their training and have been recruited to work in PHCFs.

- Support for a faculty of medicine developing FM as a pilot scheme; the MoH is collaborating with the Faculty of Medicine in Marrakech to develop FM as a specialty. This work could provide a basis for the other faculties of medicine who will be required to set up a programme of FM by 2022. In Morocco, the Family Medicine specialty was for long considered by the faculties of medicine as worthless. Basic training for doctors lasts seven years. At the end of this period, students who have failed to graduate as specialists (medical or surgical) will become GPs with no further training. It is only since medical studies were reformed, introducing the need to create FM as a specialty by 2020, that the faculties have started to make preparations.

- The preparation of a continuous distance learning programme for GPs working in PHCFs and private practices. Given that the NSPH only has the capacity to train 50 family doctors per year, the decision was taken to switch to distance learning as a more expedient way to train more doctors. Currently, more than 8000 GPs across the public and private sectors have no training as family doctors. In this context, WHO supports Morocco's bridging programme initiative to strengthen the GPs' capacities in FM.

- The creation of a training programme in family/community health in 2016 for the benefit of nurses working as a team with the family doctors in the PHCFs. This programme has been set up in the nursing schools and aims to prepare nurses to work in accordance with the family health and community health philosophies.

- The MoH staff visits to countries with acknowledged experience in the field of FM (Quebec, Spain, Portugal) for the benefit of 150 GPs, nurses, and district managers. This enabled them to learn more about the practice of FM.

- In 2014, a minimum health services package was defined for each type of PHCF to be delivered to the population in accordance with the available resources and technology.

This package was defined in more detail in 2017; it also included the definition of additional services to be provided by the PHCF to make the care accessible, acceptable, integrated, and patient-centric (as required by the imperatives of FM and the service-based approach).

- The MoH is in the process of updating the list of standard equipment required for the practice of family medicine that must be available in all PHC facilities.
- The list of essential medicines for PHC is currently being revised. The list is issued to all health-care facilities, which use it as a basis for annual medicine procurement. In Morocco, the vaccination programme is free for the whole population, as are medicines for a range of priority health issues such as diabetes, tuberculosis, and human immunodeficiency virus (HIV). For other health issues, some care is offered free of charge, the outstanding prescription cost being borne by the patients.
- Introduction of a patient registration system enabling a given number of patients to register with each GP under the latter's responsibility; the feasibility of the system is currently being tested at health district level prior to full deployment.
- A computerized medical folder has been developed to enable integrated information management and continuous, integrated patient care. This computerized system is currently being tested at the health district level prior to general deployment.

Family practice contributions towards universal health coverage (UHC)

In Morocco, family practice is the entry point to the health system. It is free of charge at the national level, which enables equitable coverage for the population for prevention programmes (over 98% immunization coverage), antenatal and postnatal consultations, family planning, and so on.

The MoH has issued a draft decree for partnerships with private GPs, specialists, pharmacists, and dental surgeons. The decree allows contractual agreements with these professionals to work on a part-time basis in public health facilities, according to availability and required skills in each health territory. This public–private partnership has been expanded by the involvement of the private sector in the strategies and programmes to address a range of priority health issues.

The experience of tuberculosis (TB) and, more recently, HIV/acquired immunodeficiency syndrome (AIDS) control is an example of the partnership. It has resulted in signed agreements between the MoH, non-profit organizations, and national professional bodies for GPs and private sector specialists, in order to strengthen health action to counter these two destructive diseases.

Family practice teams

Since its first health coverage plan, Morocco has maintained standards for human resources per PHCF, associating programme functionality with population levels in the area served by the PHCFs. In 2008, these standards were revised, enabling the definition of needs for GPs, multi-skilled nurses, and midwives for each PHCF at the national level. Human resources are assigned based on these standards, with rural areas being prioritized.

The teams that work in the PHCF are made up of GPs, multi-skilled nurses, and midwives, notably in specialized maternity homes, and may include specialist doctors, especially in urban areas, and environmental hygiene technicians. Currently, the MoH has decided to include new job profiles, such as medical secretary and social worker. Health centres are managed by doctors and head nurses. The MoH plans to set up local management committees in the PHCFs as part of a project supported by the WHO.

Rural outreach

There are 2012 PHCFs in rural areas for a rural population of 13.4 million, that is one PHCF per 6700 inhabitants. These are the most decentralized facilities and, being the closest to the population, are best positioned to address their needs in preventive, promotional, and curative health. Yet, these health-care facilities are not all adequately medically equipped. There are in fact 958 GPs working in PHCFs, that is a ratio of 1:2330 inhabitants.

Family practice financing

An analysis of the data in the national health accounts for 2013 shows that the financial resources mobilized by the national health system in 2013 (52 billion Dirhams) were essentially channelled into private clinics and practices, accounting for 36.7% in 2013. The MoH, via its different structures, only receives 27.3% of national health system funding.

This MoH funding is apportioned as follows: 53.1% is assigned to the hospitals (21.3% to university hospitals and 31.8% to others), compared with 33% to the network of PHCFs. The institutes, centres, and national laboratories, which essentially provide support to programmes and training, only receive 3% of these allocations. Meanwhile, central and local administration absorbs up 10% of the MoH's expenditure. To accompany this reform process and progress towards universal health coverage, there is a need for strengthened PHC funding.

Family practice research

Several surveys and assessments have been carried out at PHCF level via the NSPH and other research and health governance institutions:

- A survey of "Disparities in Access to Primary Health Care in Morocco", carried out by the National Observatory of Human Development in 2011, showed a mismatch between the basic medical training received by GPs and the reality in the field as they address the first-line needs of the population. Continuous training was neither institutionalized nor mandatory. It also showed that general medicine was undervalued and viewed as a "profession for the failed specialists".
- Another area evaluated was the impact of free childbirth on the quality of care at both PHCF level, with specialized, maternity homes, and in hospitals.
- Surveys are regularly conducted to gauge the satisfaction levels of the population regarding the care offered in PHCs.

Key challenges in implementing family practice

The main challenges in the implementation of family practice are as follows:

- Weak political commitment, given that, to date, medical studies have not been reformed to introduce the FM specialty into the faculties of medicine. Moreover, the MoH has not officially announced its reform of PHC based on family practice.
- Lack of training of family doctors.
- Insufficient regulation and financial support to implement family practice.
- Absence of registration of the population with PHC doctors.
- Inadequate system of orientation and a lack of feedback mechanisms.
- Insufficient private sector commitment and involvement.
- Community dissatisfaction with public PHC services and low participation and involvement of the community.

Successful experiences in family practice

Some successful initiatives, achievements, and experiences are outlined below:

- The establishment of a national commission on PHC and family practice able to monitor the implementation of projects to reinforce care at this level.
- The creation and implementation of a national plan to develop PHC in the rural environment.
- The development of basic training in family and community health for nurses working in PHC.
- Free preventive, promotional, and curative care offered at PHCF level.
- The development of a health map to regulate the provision of equally distributed PHCFs and hospitals.
- Private sector doctors organizing to move into family medicine – a vital requirement if they are to raise the value of their general practice

Family medicine

As early as 2000, the Ministry of Health established the family medicine specialty as a core aspect of the reinforcement of primary health care. An initial project for the creation of a family health department at the Faculty of Medicine in Casablanca was drafted in 2004.[5] This project was aborted and was followed by conducting an assessment on how to strengthen the technical capacities of GPs in 2005.[6]

In 2009, the year after WHO published its report on "Primary Health Care: Now More than Ever", Morocco organized a national forum on PHC. The main recommendations of this forum included the development of FM as a new discipline aimed at improving the quality of care offered to the population in a local community setting. Thus, FM has acquired a pivotal role in health system reforms and initiatives. This role was strengthened at the second health conference organized in 2013 under the patronage of His Majesty King Mohamed VI. In 2015, an initial cohort of 50 GPs took the master's course in family and community health at the NSPH.

It should also be noted that in 1998–1999 the Faculty of Medicine in Rabat introduced an FM certificate for private sector doctors with the support of USAID/John Snow, Inc. (JSI). This experiment involved a number of doctors, but the certificate was of little value and was not repeated.

PRIVATE HEALTH SECTOR

With 5750 general practices, the private sector is strongly represented at the national level, accounting for 68% of first-line facilities. These practices deliver curative, preventive, and promotional care, without necessarily always being in line with the programme directives outlined by the MoH. The private sector is, however, clearly onboard regarding the promotion of family practice. The practice of family medicine in the private sector is an individual activity with group practice being a very rare exception.

The MoH has no information system capable of collecting reliable, valid data on the private sector. Information on the private sector has not been built into the national health information systems. Nonetheless, according to surveys carried out in Morocco, a relatively large part of the population turn to the private sector for curative care, even though the public sector is free of charge.

The private health sector is relatively developed in Morocco, but concentrated in the big cities. The partnership developed with this sector by the MoH has now given the population better access to technologies and certain specialties. The MoH has now developed a legal platform enabling private sector doctors to work in public health facilities, thereby making care and services more readily available, a step forward along the road to UHC. There is, however, a lack of vision and clear strategy defining the role to be played by the private sector along this road.

REFERENCES

1. Ministry of Health, Morocco. *Santé en chiffre 2014*. Available from: http://www.sante.gov.ma/Publications/Etudes_enquete/Pages/default.aspx.
2. Ministry of Health, Morocco. *Sectoral Strategy for Health 2012–2016*. Available from: https://www.mindbank.info/item/3714 [Accessed 22 September 2018].
3. Ministry of Health, Morocco. *Hospitals and Ambulatory Health Department Database*. 2017.
4. Ministry of Health, Morocco. *Health Coverage by the Basic Health Care Network. Methodological Guide for the Production of an Extension Plan*. 1990.
5. Project supported by Canadian Cooperation in 2004.
6. Consultation on the reinforcement of the general practitioner: 5-star doctor. MoH/WHO, Charles Boelen, WHO 2005.

CHAPTER 24

Oman

Said Al Lamki and Ahmed Salim Saif Al-Mandhari

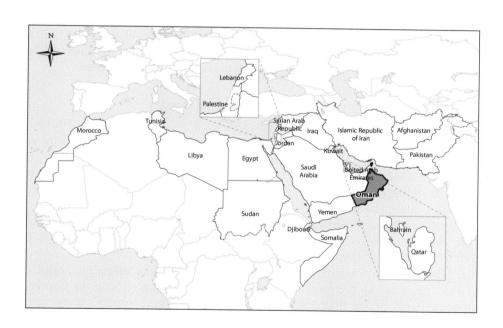

Total number of PHC facilities	235
Number of general practitioners working in public PHC facilities	3837
Number of certified family physicians working in PHC facilities	143
Average number of family physicians graduates/year	16–20
Number of medical schools	2
Number of family medicine departments	2

INTRODUCTION

Primary Health Care (PHC) is considered as the first point of contact between the individual and the health-care system in Oman; it serves as a liaison between the community and the specialized levels of health care.

During the past 40 years, a huge quantitative and qualitative development in health services and health institutions occurred in the Sultanate of Oman. In the late 1970s, the Sultanate had only a handful of health professionals. People had to travel up to four days just to reach a hospital, where hundreds of patients would already be waiting. All this changed in less than a generation. Oman has invested consistently in a national health service and sustained that investment over time. Its crude death rate, infant mortality rate, and fertility rate have all registered significant declines in recent decades, with life expectancy having risen to 76 years.

In just three decades, Oman has successfully controlled and eradicated major communicable diseases. It is now recognized as a country with successful health development. A health transition is evident as morbidity and mortality due to communicable diseases declines and death and disability from non-communicable diseases related to lifestyle and ageing rises.

CURRENT STATUS OF PRIMARY HEALTH CARE IN OMAN

Oman is divided into 11 governorates: Muscat, Dhofar, Musandam, Buraimi, North Batinah, South Batinah, Adh Dhahirah, Dakhliyah, North Sharqiyah, South Ash Sharqiyah, and Al Wusta. These governorates are further divided into a total of 61 Wilayats.

According to the most recent annual report of the Ministry of Health (MoH), there are 65 hospitals in Oman with total of 5977 beds and 1217 health centres/dispensaries/clinics. The majority of these facilities (49 hospitals and 182 health centres, including 24 extended health centres, 59 health centres with beds, and 99 health centres without beds) are under the umbrella of the MoH. These institutions receive 73% of all visits to the MoH facilities in Oman. The total number of visits to PHC facilities in 2012 reached 10.7 million (Figure 24.1).

As reflected by the above statistics, the MoH is facing a few challenges maintaining access to quality PHC services. An increase in population has been coupled with the unprecedented expansion of residential areas that need health-care facilities. Like other Gulf states, Oman is constrained by a shortage of skilled staff, and the competition between regional and international markets for skilled health-care professionals strains health-care budgets by increasing staff salaries. This is complicated by a dependence on expatriate medical personnel, with related challenges of differences in culture, medical practice, and patient care. In addition, there is a high turnover of expatriate staff, who view work in the Gulf countries as a learning experience providing international exposure, later moving back to their home countries or to developed markets for higher paid jobs.[2] Furthermore, increased prevalence of lifestyle-related diseases such as diabetes and hypertension puts pressure on PHC facilities, redirecting resources from

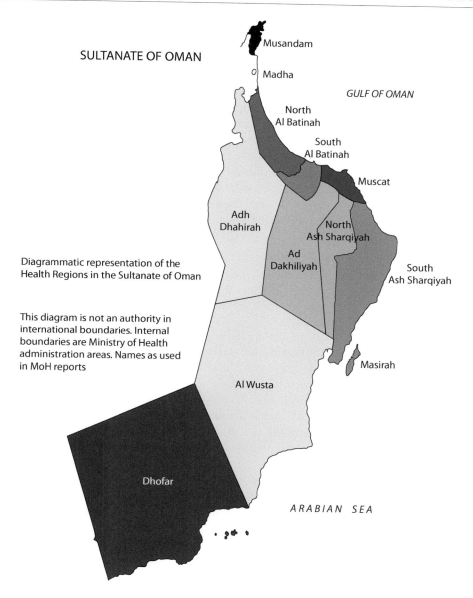

SULTANATE OF OMAN

Musandam

Madha

GULF OF OMAN

North
Al Batinah

South
Al Batinah

Muscat

Adh
Dhahirah

North
Ash Sharqiyah

Ad
Dakhiliyah

South
Ash Sharqiyah

Diagrammatic representation of the
Health Regions in the Sultanate of Oman

This diagram is not an authority in
international boundaries. Internal
boundaries are Ministry of Health
administration areas. Names as used
in MoH reports

Masirah

Al Wusta

Dhofar

ARABIAN SEA

FIGURE 24.1 Map of Oman governorates.

other programs to the management of these diseases. For example, a study showed that the age-adjusted prevalence of diabetes among Omanis aged 30–64 years reached 16.1 in 2000 compared with 12.2 in 1991.[3]

Notably, the International Diabetes Federation reveals that the prevalence of diabetes in Oman for the population aged 20–79 years is >9%.[4,5] Such high prevalence is compounded by the fact that the average cost of these lifestyle-related ailments is higher and extends over a longer term than other conditions, leading to higher health-care–related spending.[2] Furthermore, this was coupled with the increasing cost and government spending on health-care service. The effects of these have been reflected in the World Health Organization

(WHO) report that highlighted an increase in government spending from 56.4% in 2000 to 60.5% in 2008.[6,7]

In order to ensure the continuous and sustainable provision of high quality and safe PHC services to the public, the MoH made it a target to have a national accreditation system by the end of the ninth five-year strategic plan for the period 2016–2020. This would cover the continuum of care starting from the primary health care up to the tertiary level.

Stakeholders were invited into a national committee that is supervising this project and a group of 11 patient safety standards have been developed as an initial step toward creating standards for other areas/services. As one of the tools used to develop a quality system, satisfaction surveys are conducted by health-care facilities on a regular basis, with actions for development taken accordingly. Furthermore, in 2017, in order to standardize the process of assessing satisfaction and to ensure sustainability, a national patient satisfaction questionnaire was developed for patients visiting primary health-care facilities.

PHC FACILITIES INFRASTRUCTURE

The primary care service delivery system is well-established and is based on clear principles. The size and type of structures of PHC facilities depend on the population, distance from other referral centres/hospitals, and logistics. PHC services in Oman are provided through the facilities shown in the diagram (Figure 24.2).[8]

- *The health centre:* Typically serving a local population of about 10,000–15,000, the health centre has a team comprising doctors, nurses, and support staff, with on-site diagnostic facilities and pharmacy.
- *The health centre with beds:* This is a health centre with a small number of attached beds (2–4 beds), mainly for maternity care and observation; some may operate with less staffing and reduced facilities due to the size of the population in the catchment area. This makes health care more accessible to populations who would otherwise have to travel long distances to visit a health centre.
- *The polyclinic/extended health centre:* Extended health centres provide out-patient access to specialist clinics in a polyclinic setting with certain basic specialties (such as obstetrics and gynaecology; paediatrics, ophthalmology; ear, nose, and throat [ENT]; and family medicine), as an alternative to referral to hospital out-patient departments. Specialist, secondary, and tertiary care is accessed through referral from health centres. Health centres do not provide any in-patient care services.

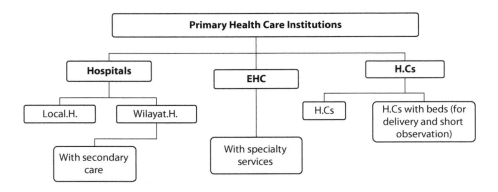

FIGURE 24.2 Primary health care institutions in Oman.

- *The local hospital:* Local hospitals, all with a small number of beds, provide PHC services to the people in the hospital catchment area and give basic in-patient care if necessary. Some of the local hospitals provide secondary care services, particularly those located far from the regional hospital.

Community health – home visit

The Omani health system uses the basic client-oriented (patient-centred) approach. The health centres work in close cooperation with community support groups actively involved in health care planning, monitoring, and implementation.

ESSENTIAL HEALTH SERVICES PACKAGE

PHC facilities are generally classified as health centres; extended health centres (with delivery facility); polyclinics, and local hospitals. They provide the following services:

- General clinics
- Diabetic clinic
- Hypertension clinic
- Asthma clinic
- Screening clinic
- Antenatal and postnatal care
- Infertility clinic
- Integrated Management of Childhood Illness (IMCI) clinic
- Expanded Programme on Immunization (EPI) clinic
- Elderly care clinic
- Pre-marital counselling clinic
- Congenital screening and counselling clinic
- Dental services
- Mental health care services
- Laboratory services
- Radiology (in some facilities)

- Health education
- Dietetic clinic

In addition to the above-mentioned services, polyclinics provide the following extra services:

- Specialty clinics
- Psychiatry
- General internal medicine
- Ophthalmology
- ENT

In addition to the PHC centre services, local hospitals provide the following services:

- In-patient services, including delivery

INTEGRATION OF CHRONIC DISEASE MANAGEMENT AT PRIMARY HEALTH CARE FACILITIES

In the past, communicable diseases caused substantial morbidity and mortality in Oman, but in recent years lifestyle-related or non-communicable diseases (NCDs) and the changing age structure of the population have begun to reveal morbidity patterns similar to those in high-income countries.[9] The results of the National Health Survey 2000, conducted by MoH in 1999–2000, portrayed a worrisome picture of the risk factors for NCDs. The morbidity statistics in 2011 for MoH health facilities show that about 49.9% of all out-patient visits and 37.6% of hospital admissions are for NCDs. This has led to an important transformation in the PHC programs, with a shift in focus towards NCDs and PHC services such as:

Health education in the PHC facility waiting area

1. *Mini-diabetes clinics*: For patients with diabetes mellitus (DM), a mini-diabetes clinic has been available in almost every health centre since 1996, with a comprehensive trained team including a family physician/trained general practitioner (GP), a nurse, a health educator, and a dietitian. This service provides the basic medications for diabetes management and arranges for referral and follow-up as needed.[10]

2. *Services for diabetic foot care*: Since 2008, there has been structured health education on diabetic foot care, with a guideline for diabetic foot assessment and management.[11]
3. *Services for hypertensive patients*: Since 1998, doctors and nurses in PHC settings have been trained to diagnose and treat patients with hypertension (HTN).
4. *Services for mental illness*: Oman started integrating mental health in its PHC programmes in 2010, with the goal of training all the PHC doctors and nurses by the year 2013. Integrating mental health services into primary care is the most viable way of ensuring that people have access to the mental health care they need. People can access mental health services closer to their homes, thus keeping their families together and maintaining their daily activities. In addition, they avoid indirect costs associated with seeking specialist care in distant locations.
5. *NCD screening programme*: This programme is directed towards screening of those 40 years and above for early detection and prevention of non-communicable diseases, mainly hypertension, diabetes, hyperlipidaemia, obesity, and renal disease.
6. *Elderly care*: PHC in Oman is the pioneer in introducing elderly care within its services. Since 2010, the programme has provided comprehensive assessment of elder patients and suitable interventions like clinical intervention, physiotherapy provided by mobile physiotherapy units, social interventions, referral services to secondary or tertiary care, and outreach services for the bedridden.

STAFF PATTERNS

The current density of family physicians in Oman is 0.3/10,000 population, which is lower than the rate recommended by the Ministry of Health (2/10 000 population, based recommendations of Gulf Cooperation Council Ministers Qarar, Kuwait 2007).[12] The density of nurses is below the European standard of 65/100,000 population (Table 24.1).[13]

PHC facilities are staffed with general practitioners, nurses, pharmacists, assistant pharmacists, dentists, dental assistant nurses, lab technicians, radiographers, health educators, dieticians, medical orderlies, medical record clerks, and drivers.

TRAINING PROGRAMS

- Continuing professional development (CPD)
- CPD activities are conducted at all levels of PHC and in every MoH facility. They include workshops, seminars, lectures, conferences, and training courses. The accreditation of most of these activities is done by the Oman Medical Specialty Board (OMSB)

TABLE 24.1 Rate of PHC facilities and PHC workforce, 2012

Indicators	Situation in 2012
Health centres/10,000 population	0.63
PHC doctors/10,000 population	5.09
Family physicians/10,000 population	0.30
PHC nurses/10,000 population	12.21
PHC dentists/10,000 population	0.52
PHC assistant pharmacist or pharmacist/10,000 population	2.43
PHC laboratory technicians/10,000 population	2.01
PHC radiographers/10,000 population	0.84
PHC dietitians/10,000 population	0.33
PHC health educators/10,000 population	0.40

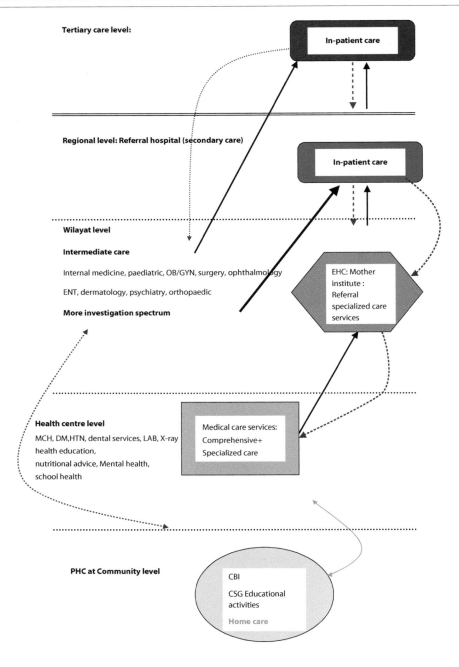

FIGURE 24.3 Current PHC model.

- Family physician training
- OMSB was first established by a royal decree in 2006. By the end of 2012, a total of 65 family physicians had been qualified and distributed among all PHC settings.
- In-service training for GPs.
- In order to improve the quality of services of general practitioners working in PHC, in-service training was established in 2009.

REFERRAL SYSTEM

Different levels of health services are provided through a network of health facilities. Every governorate is equipped with a network of health centres. The health centres are considered the first contact point for all citizens and residents. These centres are supported by Wilayat (governorate), local, and regional referral hospitals. From the primary health-care centre/facility, patients are referred to a higher level of care with more advanced services such as in-patient services, surgery, or intensive care. In general, patients are referred from a health centre to the local hospital or polyclinic. From local hospitals/polyclinics, patients will be referred to regional hospitals (secondary care level) and later, as needed, to tertiary care hospitals. All four tertiary care hospitals in Oman are located in the capital. A comprehensive manual was developed to govern and guide the process of referral and back referral (2004). Some of these manuals have not been updated since then (Figure 24.3).

KEY CHALLENGES

Despite the above-mentioned achievements, the following summarizes the main challenges facing PHC:

- Most PHC facilities have too little space, with inadequate consultation rooms and little emergency space and equipment.
- Inadequate support services including laboratory, imaging services, diagnostic services, and equipment.
- Shortage of skilled health-care workers such as family physicians.
- Increasing magnitude of chronic diseases.
- Newly emerging global public health threats.
- Inadequate resources/budget.

REFERENCES

1. Gulf Talent. *Employment and Salary Trends in the Gulf.* 2012. Available from: https://www.gulftalent.com/resources/market-research-reports/download-confirmation?reportid=33&from=registration&emailSubmit=Receive+By+Email [Accessed 16 April 18].
2. Alpen Capital. *GCC Healthcare Industry 2011.* Available from: http://itac.ca/wp-content/uploads/2013/03/Alpen-Capitals-GCC-Healthcare-report-2011.pdf [Accessed 16 April 2018].
3. Al-Lawati, JA, Al-Riyami, AM, Mohammed, AJ, Jousilahti, P. Increasing prevalence of diabetes mellitus in Oman. *Diabetic Medicine.* 2002, 19 (11): 954–957. Available from: https://doi.org/10.1046/j.1464-5491.2002.00818.x [Assessed 23 September 2018].
4. International Diabetes Federation IDF Diabetes Atlas–Eighth edition. 2017. Available from: http://www.diabetesatlas.org/[Accessed 17 April 2018].
5. Al-Lawati, JA, Al-Riyami, AM, Mohammed, AJ, Jousilahti, P. Increasing prevalence of diabetes mellitus in Oman. *Diabetic Medicine.* 2002, 19 (11): 954–957. Available from: https://doi.org/10.1046/j.1464-5491.2002.00818.x [Assessed 23 September 2018].
6. Alpen Capital. *GCC Healthcare Industry 2011.* Available from: http://itac.ca/wp-content/uploads/2013/03/Alpen-Capitals-GCC-Healthcare-report-2011.pdf [Assessed 23 September 2018].
7. Sultanate of Oman Cost Effectiveness Review of the Health Sector (Main report).
8. Primary health care vision 2050 documents presented in health care vision of Oman 2050 conference. May 2012.
9. WHO Regional Health Systems Observatory EMRO, 2006. *Health System Profile-Oman.* Available from: http://apps.who.int/medicinedocs/documents/s17304e/s17304e.pdf. [Accessed 17 April 2018].
10. International Diabetes Federation IDF Diabetes Atlas–Eighth edition. 2017. Available from: http://www.diabetesatlas.org/[Accessed 17 April 2018].

11. Al-Lawati, JA, Al-Riyami, AM, Mohammed, AJ, Jousilahti, P. Increasing prevalence of diabetes mellitus in Oman. *Diabetic Medicine*. 2002, 19 (11): 954–957. Available from: https://onlinelibrary.wiley.com/doi/pdf/10.1046/j.1464-5491.2002.00818.x [Accessed 17 April 2018].

12. MoH, Sultanate of Oman. 8th Five-Year Plan for Health Development, 2011–2015. Available from: http://www.nationalplanningcycles.org/sites/default/files/country_docs/Oman/five_year_plan_for_health_development_2011-2015.pdf [Accessed 17 April 2018].

13. MoH, Sultanate of Oman, 2016. Annual Health Report 2016.

CHAPTER 25

Pakistan

Waris Qidwai, Marie Andrades,
Zia UlHaq, and Kashmira Nanji

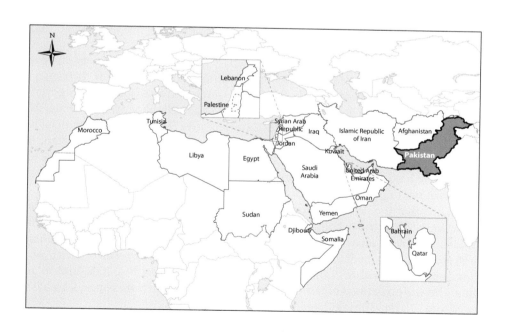

Total number of PHC facilities	11,530
Number of general practitioners working in public PHC facilities	Data is not available
Number of certified family physicians working in PHC facilities	18
Average number of family physician graduates/year	Data is not available
Number of medical schools*	107
Number of family medicine departments	7

*41 Public and 66 private.

INTRODUCTION

The health system in Pakistan comprises a mix of an extensive public sector of primary, secondary, and tertiary care, and quaternary teaching hospitals. In addition, the private medical sector also caters to the health-care needs of the country. There is also an "alternative and complementary" system of health care is also in Pakistan.

Primary health-care (PHC) services are both community and facility-based. Community health workers include lady health workers (LHWs), community midwives (CMWs), vaccinators, and sanitary inspectors.[1] Approximately 92,900 LHWs (density 0.43 per 1000 population) provide PHC services at the community level. Facility-based services are offered via a network of civil dispensaries (CDs), basic health units (BHUs), and rural health centres (RHCs).[2] The temporal aspects of service delivery may differ from facility to facility, for example, some BHUs provide a 24-hour service, while others do not. The same is the case with RHCs, but recently in some provinces, they have upgraded to a 24-hour service and linked to a network of remote diagnostic services.[3] These health facilities are linked at the district level with secondary healthcare facilities: Tehsil/Taluka, civil, and district headquarter (DHQ) hospitals. In addition, there are tuberculosis (TB) and maternal and child health (MCH) centres.

The PHC services at the district level is managed by the district government and each province is now responsible for developing and implementing health policies for their own regions. In the recent past PHC services, mainly the BHUs were contracted out to non-governmental organizations (NGOs), which brought many positive changes.[3] Public–private partnerships were governed through the People Primary Health-Care Initiative (PPHI) at the provincial level.[4]

There is a nominal fee for emergency services in the PHC facilities in Pakistan, however, the majority of Pakistanis spend out-of-pocket for health care.[2,5] As a path to achieve universal health care, the federal and provincial governments in Pakistan have launched social health protection initiatives to provide financial protection for its populations.

It is estimated that the private sector provides 70–80% of out-patient services.[5] The private health sector in Pakistan today comprises general medical practitioners (GPs), specialist medical practitioners, nurses, pharmacists, traditional and alternative medical practitioners, allied health professionals, paramedics, and a diverse group of informally trained health workers. It ranges from numerous private clinics to dispensaries, to teaching hospitals, and to academic institutions. There is no defined organizational structure for the private sector, which is not well documented and is largely unregulated.

INTEGRATION OF ESSENTIAL HEALTH SERVICES PACKAGE

The 63rd session of the Eastern Mediterranean Regional Committee (EMRO) endorsed a resolution in which it urged Member States to incorporate the Family Practice (FP) approach into PHC services as an overarching strategy towards Universal Health Coverage; strengthen the capacity of Family Medicine (FM) departments and also establish bridging programmes for GPs to reach three FPs per 10,000 by 2030; strengthen public–private partnerships in service delivery;

ensure availability of sustainable funding for programmes; strengthen and cost Essential Health Services Packages (EHSPs) and adopt the World Health Organization (WHO) framework for quality improvements at the PHC facilities.[6,7]

The PHC facilities focus on the prevention and management of all forms of malnutrition. Diseases like cholera, typhoid, and hepatitis are the leading causes of under-5 mortality in developing countries, including Pakistan. As per WHO estimates, by adopting proper hand washing and sanitation, 94% of these hygiene-related deaths could be prevented.

A home visit for vaccination

Basic Emergency Obstetrics and Neonatal Care (EmoNC) services are targeted to be provided in every BHU and comprehensive EmoNC services at the RHC level, as well as a need to strengthen the routine lab test and blood transfusion services.[8] The community-based action includes four postpartum visits of LWH/CMW. Integrated management of childhood illness (IMNCI) services are attempted to be provided at all levels of PHC facilities.[8]

Provision of family planning services is attempted at the PHC facility and community level including counselling on birth spacing, adopting modern techniques, and empowering women to adopt family planning. Routine immunization, public health emergency and disaster preparedness, disability, mental health, and oral health are the essential components of PHC services.[9]

PATIENT SATISFACTION

Limited studies have been conducted to assess the satisfaction of quality of service delivery from PHC.[10,11] The available literature shows that patients are more satisfied with private hospitals than the public sector.[11] The rates of dissatisfaction with the public sector are as high as 80%.[10]

KEY CHALLENGES TO ACCESSING QUALITY SERVICE DELIVERY IN PUBLIC PRIMARY CARE FACILITIES

The total number of PHC facilities in Pakistan is 11,530, which are managed by GPs. However, only 18 facilities are run by a certified FP. Out of 107 medical schools there are only four FM departments in Pakistan.[12] Availability of EHSPs varies from province to province depending on its location, which creates inequity in access to the services. Shortage of staff in public health care facilities, particularly in the remote areas, hinders delivery of comprehensive quality care services. Currently, there is no well organized GP system in Pakistan. However, the Ministry of Health (MoH), in collaboration with the Institute of Public Health & Social Sciences, Khyber Medical University Peshawar, the Family Medicine Department of Aga Khan University, and WHO have developed a strategy for introducing the family Medicine system in Pakistan. Two districts in each province are selected as pilot districts for the implementation of the Family Medicine System.

There is very little coordination or systematic referrals from primary to secondary level care. There is no systematic recording of patient consultations, and if available, this is mostly in the form of handwritten notes, which produces a huge volume of physical documents, thus creating a storage and retrieval nightmare. Independent studies suggest a referral rate of 2% to 28% by physicians and a 55% rate by LHWs.[13]

Due to the non-availability of patients' records in an electronic form, HCPs are usually unaware of the past medical history of the patients, resulting in wastage of time for re-diagnosing and even incorrect diagnosis in some cases.[13] Thus, the government cannot plan immediate strategies if an epidemic occurs, such as the current dengue virus outbreak in Peshawar.

POLITICAL COMMITMENTS TO FAMILY PRACTICE

Pakistan is a country beset with a high burden of disease. Its public health system is fragmented and of low quality. The populations' trust in the public health system is low, thus resulting in out-of-pocket expenditure on private services. In 2012, the government's total health expenditure accounted for only 2.7% of the country's gross domestic product (GDP), half the average of 4.5% for other lower to middle-income countries.[14]

Family Medicine plays a critical role in improving health indicators for any country.[15] The government of Pakistan has not previously shown the will to make it an integral part of the health system.[16]

The National Health Vision 2016–2020 for Pakistan has articulated eight thematic pillars for the health system. These include health financing, health service delivery, human resources, health information systems, governance, essential medicines and technology, cross-sectoral linkages, and global health responsibilities. Preventive and promotive health services will be ensured by introducing family medicine clinics. This vision has also been rearticulated in the provincial health visions.[17]

Elements of Family Practice are visible in different provinces. The Punjab government has laid out an Essential Package of Health Services (EPHS) in an integrated form at the primary care level. The focus of this package is on MNCH and does not include non-communicable diseases (NCDs).[8,18]

The Sindh Health Sector 2012–2020 clearly lays out the need to develop an Integrated Family Health Practice Model of a "One Stop Shop for Health and Population".[14]

Postnatal follow-up at a PHC facility

The Khyber Pukhtunkhwa health vision states that at least 70% of the population will have access to the Minimum Health Service Package (part of family practice).[4]

In order for family practice to succeed in terms of affordability, access, and quality of care, reaching out to the community through home health-care services and a strong link with secondary and tertiary care centres for a functioning referral system are essential. There is a need to link primary care family practice centres with the other NGOs already working in Pakistan, in order to fill in the gaps in services where required. Linkages with private quality maternity homes would help in providing obstetric care where quality care is not available. An innovative way of using e.g. specialist help would be through telemedicine. The government can sign a contract with universities to provide specialist services through telemedicine, thus enhancing access to specialized care without a major increase in cost. In addition, government health insurance schemes need to be linked with the practice to make the services affordable for the population.

CONTRIBUTIONS OF FAMILY PRACTICE TO UNIVERSAL HEALTH COVERAGE

Pakistan is ranked as a lower to middle-income country with expectations for improved health indicators. The government has documented universal health coverage (UHC) as its prime agenda for the health sector. Attempts have been made by introducing EHSPs at the provincial level, public–private partnerships for enhancing the quality and extent of services while reducing the financial load on the government and social protection for the underprivileged through government insurance schemes like the Employee Social Security Institute.[7,15]

FAMILY PRACTICE IN RURAL AREAS

There is no comprehensive package of primary health services in the rural areas of Pakistan. LHWs provide MNCH services and are effective in improving the care-seeking behaviour of families and encouraging greater utilization of skilled care providers. In the private sector in rural areas (e.g. Aga Khan Health Services Pakistan), nurses use e-Health to provide care to the population. Low-cost and simple e-Health solutions have been beneficial for communities living in the remote mountainous regions of Pakistan. The Provincial Rural Support Programme in Punjab has outsourced its rural BHUs to an NGO for providing care to the rural population.[8]

FAMILY PRACTICE FINANCING

There are various models of family practice financing globally. The EHSP introduced in Punjab is financed with assistance from the World Bank. The Prime Minister's National Health Programme (PMNHP) Pakistan is to be implemented nationally by 2022 and aims to provide social health protection (health insurance) against all sorts of health epidemics to all families living below the poverty line of US$2 per day. As yet, family practice services are not in the forefront of this package.[18]

FAMILY PRACTICE RESEARCH

There is a dearth of data on actual family practice in Pakistan. However, individual elements of family practice have been studied.[19] An analytical look at the Pakistan health-care system using the WHO health-care system framework concludes that to achieve access, coverage, and quality, safety, monitoring and evaluation play an important role in improving health outcomes and efficiency in the health-care system of Pakistan.[19]

A system analysis of patient referral conducted in Punjab showed that first level care facility utilization was 0.6 patient visits/person/year.[13] Only 15% of the patients were referred with the prescribed referral form. None of the higher-level facilities provided feedback to the first level facility.[13]

Detailed cost analysis of out-patient visits to BHUs in Pakistan showed the average recurring cost was PKR.245 (US$4.1) per visit to a BHU.[5] Staff salaries constituted 90% of the recurrent cost. The estimated recurrent cost was six times higher than the average consultation charge with a private GP (PKR 50/GP consultation).[5] The performance of the majority of the BHUs was far below the performance target (50 patients per day).[5]

KEY CHALLENGES TO IMPLEMENTING FAMILY PRACTICE

- *Political*: The foremost challenge in implementing family practice in Pakistan is political. Pakistan is a complex county with multiple ethnic and regional groups. The political agenda of the policy makers, the health-care providers, and the people all have an influence on the health system. Until a few years ago, health had not been a priority of the political hierarchy. However, the increasing deterioration of health indicators and its visibility internationally has forced the political forces to realign their priorities to health and education. This is particularly apparent in the National Health Vision 2020.[17]
- *Health system*: The health system infrastructure is not consistent with family practice requirements. Currently, prevention is not the primary focus, leading to its lack of integration into the health system. NCDs, geriatric, and mental health issues have not been made a part of the health services package. The health information and surveillance system needs strengthening as most information received is inaccurate, incomplete, and unused.
- *Human resource deficit*: The need for trained FPs and other health of professionals to run efficient and quality family practices is immense. Pakistan has over 168,000 registered MBBS doctors. Presuming even half are practicing as GPs, this is a huge number and they need to be trained to enhance their competencies as FPs.[20] A short diploma programme of one year, similar to that offered by the American University in Beirut, can be implemented. In addition, family medicine as already mandated by the Pakistan Medical and Dental Council (PMDC) should be taught as a subject in the final year of the undergraduate medical curriculum.[21] Currently, any physician who has passed the MBBS and is been licensed with the PMDC can start practicing as a general physician. This needs to change as family practice requires special competencies.
- *Recognition by other specialties*: Other challenges include the perceived threat by specialists who consider the frontline family health-care model to be a threat to their practice. This is a misconception as trained FPs in a well-run family practice would not only reduce the disease burden but also send appropriate referrals to the specialist, therefore shifting their workload from an unnecessary or inappropriate patient load to patient volumes more reflective of their competency.
- *Using the private sector resources*: Public–private partnerships have been tried for implementing a new model of health service in family practice.[16] These have not been very successful as there is a lack of clarity concerning the mechanism for contracting with the private sector and a lack of clearly outlined indicators of performance and outcomes.
- *Lack of awareness*: The concept of a holistic comprehensive family service catering to all primary care issues in the population is non-existent. In fact, most of the population has no expectations of the government with regard quality of care. Mass education to raise awareness of the need for family practice should be carried out using academia,

and electronic, print, and social media. Public demand would automatically reorient the political leaderships' agenda towards this focus of health.

THE ROLE OF THE PRIVATE HEALTH SECTOR IN EXPANDING UNIVERSAL HEALTH COVERAGE

The Pakistan government spends a very small portion of its budget on health, thereby limiting its ability to provide UHC to its entire population.[22] Therefore, it is necessary to involve the private sector to help deliver basic health-care facilities to the entire population. This will require training FPs in the delivery of UHC as well as the availability of the necessary resources to run the required facilities.

The private sector is already heavily involved in providing health-care services, but this can result in financial hardship for those utilizing them. Moreover, the quality and effectiveness of such services require better monitoring and regulation.[23] A public–private partnership will be required to ensure high-quality universal health services are provided to the entire population at an affordable cost. The private sector should be encouraged to invest with a reasonable return on investment, but with government monitoring of efficiency and quality.

FAMILY MEDICINE IN PAKISTAN

- *Training in FM:* Pakistan not only faces a scarcity of FPs but also faces a lack of training and competence of FPs who are already practicing.[22] Gaps in the knowledge of FPs in Pakistan have already been highlighted in the medical the literature.[23]

  Most development in the discipline of Family Medicine has happened in the private health sector of Pakistan. The first organized efforts came in 1973 with the establishment of the College of Family Medicine Pakistan (CFMP) in Karachi.[24] The college provided a platform for the academic and professional activities of FPs including providing CME programs and preparatory sessions for postgraduate examinations in Family Medicine.

- *Undergraduate studies in FM:* In November 2015, the PMDC notified all medical colleges that they should establish FM departments and announced the introduction of FM as a mandatory subject in final year MBBS studies.[12,25] The implementation of this notification is still pending, as has the curriculum has not been finalized and faculty recruitment rules have not been designed for Family Medicine.[21] The Aga Khan University Karachi introduced a six-week compulsory rotation in FM in 1986 which later evolved into a complete three-month rotation in the final year of MBBS. Ziauddin University since its establishment in 1997 has also included FM in its MBBS curriculum.[12] Shifa College of Medicine Islamabad introduced a two-week rotation in FM in 2008. Shifa College's experience with FM highlighted that if students are exposed to FM in undergraduate studies they are more inclined to choose Family Medicine as a career in the future.[26]

- *Postgraduate education in FM:* The College of Physicians and Surgeons, Pakistan (CPSP) designed and approved a Diploma in Family Medicine (DFM) programme in June 1988, now renamed as Membership of the College of Physicians and Surgeons Pakistan (MCPS).[27,28] Currently, Dow University Karachi, Indus Hospital Karachi, Liaquat National Hospital Karachi, FMH College of Medicine and Dentistry Lahore, Ayub Medical College Abbottabad, PGMI Lady Reading Hospital Peshawar, PGMI Hayatabad Medical Complex, and Khyber Medical College Peshawar are recognized for MCPS in Family Medicine, but only Indus Hospital and FMH College have residents enrolled in their MCPS programs.[28] The MCPS programme allows practicing doctors with five or more years' experience in Family Practice to sit for the MCPS examination. This has recently attracted more interest and over 400 doctors registered for the MCPS examination in 2017 alone.[28,29]

After a poor start in 1989, the Department of Community Health Sciences, Aga Khan University, Karachi, finally launched the first ever Family Medicine Residency in Pakistan in 1991 which was approved by CPSP for Fellowship in 1992.[28] This Family Medicine Residency at Aga Khan University Karachi is the leading Family Medicine programme in the country and has produced more than 90 Fellows so far. Ziauddin University Karachi in 1999, FMH College of Medicine and Dentistry Lahore in 2013, Indus Hospital Karachi in 2014, and Liaquat National Hospital and Medical College Karachi in 2017 also were recognized for FCPS in Family Medicine.[28]

Apart from the Fellowship programmes, Dow University of Medical Sciences Karachi runs a two-year Diploma in Family Medicine and a five-year Masters in Family Medicine. Ziauddin University Karachi also offers a two-year modular Diploma in Family Medicine.[27,28]

- *Faculty development:* Lack of faculty has been one of the most significant impediments to the development of Family Medicine in Pakistan.[12] This situation is fuelled by PMDC's failure to incorporate FM into the undergraduate curriculum and the absence of a budget for faculty positions for Family Medicine.[21] As a result, newly qualified Fellows do not find opportunities in Pakistan and migrate to either Middle Eastern countries or countries like Canada and Australia. To break this vicious cycle, there is a need to produce a cohort of master trainers in FM so that at least training programmes can be initiated in various institutes.[29]

- *Continuing medical education:* Continuing medical education (CME) has been present in an erratic way in the form of guest lectures, seminars, conferences, and pharmaceutical company-driven update sessions for decades. The first organized attempts for planned and well-organized CME in FM were made in 1990 for candidates of MCPS Family Medicine in Karachi. In 2005, similar planned CME sessions were initiated in the College of Family Medicine in Karachi with the support of the faculty of Family Medicine, Aga Khan University, but this time in preparation for the MRCGP [INT] South Asia examination. Very similar CME related to MRCGP [INT] was initiated in 2006 by FMH College of Medicine and Dentistry Lahore in collaboration with the Pakistan Society of Family Physician and the Pakistan Academy of Family Physicians. It is worth mentioning that the CME of FMH is sustained without pharmaceutical sponsorship by charging a fee from participants. The speakers in CME of FMH are all faculty members of Family Medicine in different institutes of Pakistan. Currently, there are four Family Medicine organizations in Lahore which are providing regular CME sessions once or twice a week on common topics. All four Family Medicine organizations (Pakistan Society of Family Physicians, Pakistan Academy of Family Physicians, Association of Family Physicians of Pakistan, and the Family Medicine Education Centre) also organize annual conferences and hands-on workshops on ultrasound, communications skills, minor surgical skills, and use of clinical equipment.[12]

REFERENCES

1. Sixth Five-Year Plan 1978–1983, Chapter 19: Towards a Comprehensive National Coverage. Planning Commission, Government of Pakistan. Available from: http://www.pakistan.gov.pk/ministries/planninganddevelopment-ministry/index.htm [Accessed 20 December 2017].

2. Hafeez A, Mohamud BK, Shiekh MR, Shah SAI, Jooma R. Lady health workers programme in Pakistan: challenges, achievements and the way forward. *JPMA*, 2011; 61(3): 210.

3. Shaikh B, Rabbani F, Safi N, Dawar Z. Contracting of primary health care services in Pakistan: is up-scaling a pragmatic thinking? *JPMA*, 2010; 60(5): 387.

4. Imtiaz A, Farooq G, Haq ZU, Ahmed A, Anwer S. Public private partnership and utilization of maternal and child health services in district Abbottabad, Pakistan. *Journal of Ayub Medical College Abbottabad*, 2017; 29(2): 275–279.

5. Malik MA, Gul W, Iqbal SP, Abrejo F. Cost of primary health care in Pakistan. *Journal of Ayub Medical College Abbottabad*, 2015; 27(1): 88–92.

6. World Health Organization. Integrated vector management: strategic framework for the Eastern Mediterranean Region 2016–2020. 2017.

7. Strengthening health systems for universal health coverage. World Health Organization. Available from: http://www.emro.who.int/annual-report/2014/strengthening-health-systems.html [Accessed 10 December 2017].

8. Majrooh MA, Hasnain S, Akram J, Siddiqui A, Memon ZA. Coverage and quality of antenatal care provided at primary health care facilities in the Punjab province of Pakistan. *PloS One*, 2014; 9(11): e113390. [Accessed 22 September 2018].

9. Qidwai W. Primary care: A mandatory requirement for effective health care. *Journal of the College of Physicians and Surgeons Pakistan*, 2008; 18(4): 199–200. Available from: http://ecommons.aku.edu/pakistan_fhs_mc_fam_med/60 [Accessed 22 September 2018].

10. Qamar FM, Baloch QB. Job satisfaction and performance: A comparative study of private and public sector hospitals. *Abasyn Journal of Social Sciences*, 2011; 4(1): 56–69.

11. Raheem AR, Nawaz A, Fouzia N, Imamuddin K. Patients satisfaction and quality health services: an investigation from private hospitals of Karachi, Pakistan. *Research Journal of Recent Sciences*, 2014; 2277: 2502.

12. Sabzwari SR. The case for family medicine in Pakistan. *JPMA*, 2015; 65(6): 660–664.

13. Siddiqi S, Kielmann AA, Khan MS, Ali N, Ghaffar A, Sheikh U, et al. The effectiveness of patient referral in Pakistan. *Health Policy and Planning*, 2001; 16(2): 193–198.

14. Zaidi S. Sindh health sector strategy 2012–2020. *Government of Sindh*, 1–124. [serial on the Internet]. 2012; 1: Available from: http://ecommons.aku.edu/pakistan_fhs_mc_chs_chs/213 [Accessed 22 September 2018].

15. Haq CL, De Maeseneer J, Markuns J, Montenegro H, Qidwai W, Švab I, et al. In Kidd M.R. (editor). The contribution of family medicine to improving health systems: a guidebook from the World Organization of Family Doctors. *Radcliffe*. 2013.

16. Dar SB, Khan HS. Family medicine: a missing link in health system of Pakistan. *Biomedica*, 2014; 30(4): 301–306.

17. National Health Vision Pakistan 2016–2025. Government of Pakistan. Available from: http://www.nationalplanningcycles.org/sites/default/files/planning_cycle_repository/pakistan/national_health_vision_2016-25_30-08-2016.pdf [Accessed 8 December 2017].

18. Mazhar MA, Shaikh BT. Constitutional reforms in Pakistan: turning around the picture of health sector in Punjab Province. *Journal of Ayub Medical College Abbottabad*, 2016; 28(2): 386–391.

19. Beasley JW, Dovey S, Geffen LN, Gómez-Clavelina FJ, Haq CL, Inem V, et al. The contribution of family doctors to primary care research: a global perspective from the International Federation of Primary Care Research Networks (IFPCRN). *Primary Health Care Research & Development*, 2004; 5(4): 307–316.

20. Biggs JS. Postgraduate medical training in Pakistan: observations and recommendations. *Journal of the College of Physicians and Surgeons Pakistan*, 2008; 18(1): 58–63.

21. Iqbal SP. Family medicine in undergraduate medical curriculum: a cost-effective approach to health care in Pakistan. *Journal of Ayub Medical College*, 2010; 22(4): 207–209.

22. Qidwai W, Beasley JW, Gomez-Clavelina FJ. The present status and future role of family doctors: a perspective from the International Federation of Primary Care Research Networks. *Primary Health Care Research & Development*, 2008; 9(3): 172–182.

23. Khan AS. Paradox in family medicine: where we need more, we have less! *JPMA*, 2013; 63(3): 413.

24. College of Family Physician Pakistan—History. Available from: http://cfmp.org.pk/history/ [Accessed 15 December 2017].

25. Qidwai W. Family medicine made compulsory subject in MBBS program: implications for health care in Pakistan and the region. *Annals of Abbasi Shaheed Hospital & Karachi Medical & Dental College*, 2015; 20(1): 85–86.

26. Meraj L, Gul N, Zubaidazain IA, Iram F, Khan AS. Perceptions and attitudes towards research amongst medical students at Shifa College of Medicine. *JPMA*, 2016; 66: 1657–1689.

27. Zuberi RW, Jafarey NA, Elahi F, Qureshi AF. The diploma in family medicine examination; a scientific exercise. *JPMA*, 1993; 43(10): 217.

28. College of Physicians and Surgeons Pakistan. Accredited Institutes. [Available from: http://cpsp.edu.pk/accredited-institutes.php?ref=MCPS [Accessed 15 December 2017].

29. Zuberi RW, Jafarey NA, Elahi F, Qureshi AF. The diploma in family medicine examination; a scientific exercise. *JPMA*, 1993; 43(10): 217.

CHAPTER 26

Palestine

Rand Salman, Gerald Rockenschaub, and Asa'd Ramlawi

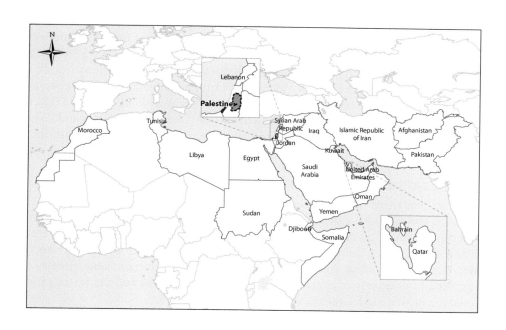

Indicator	Region		
	West Bank	Gaza Strip	Total
PHC facilities (MoH, UNRWA, NGOs, and military services)	587	152	739
General practitioners	4671	1745	6416
General practitioners working in PHC public facilities of MoH	400	153	553
Certified family physicians working in PHC facilities	25 within MoH PHC	21 in MoH PHC, 15 in UNRWA	61
Family physician graduates/year (average)	3–5 per year	Not reported	
Medical schools	2 (An-Najah and Al-Quds University)	2 (Islamic University and a branch of Al-Quds University)	4
Family medicine departments	1 (An-Najah University)	1 (Al-Azhar University)	2
MoH family medicine training centres	3	3	6

INTRODUCTION

Primary health-care (PHC) services in Palestine are provided by the Ministry of Health (MoH), non-governmental organizations (NGOs), the United Nations Relief and Works Agency (UNRWA), military medical services, and the private sector. There are 587 PHC centres in the West Bank and 152 centres in Gaza reported in 2016.[1] Out of the total of 739 PHC centres, 466 (63.1%) are managed by the Palestinian MoH, and 189 PHCs are managed by NGOs, which constitutes 25.6%. UNRWA operates 64 centres, which accounts for 8.7%, while the Military Medical Services run 20 centres, which accounts for 2.7% of the total. Out of the total number of PHC centres managed by the MoH, 71 (15.2%) are Level 1 centres, 245 (52.6%) are Level 2, 121 (26%) are Level 3, and 24 (5.1%) are Level 4. In addition, five of the MoH centres are mobile clinics covering remote areas in Jericho, the Jordan Valley, Jerusalem, Bethlehem, and Yatta governorates.[2]

There are 4671 general practitioners (GPs) working in the West Bank and 1745 GPs working in the Gaza Strip; 400 GPs work in PHC clinics of the MoH in the West Bank and 153 in MoH clinics in Gaza. The PHC system in Palestine suffers from overall staffing constraints with a shortage of trained and specialized family physicians.

CHALLENGES FACING PRIMARY HEALTH-CARE SERVICES

Despite the fact that there is good coverage of PHC centres across the governorates, there are challenges with the equitable distribution of those centres across the West Bank; in addition, there are severe access restrictions, especially in "Area C" and the areas affected by the separation wall and settlements.* The current primary health-care structure is characterized by multiple providers, and its focus on maternal and child health and communicable diseases services. This is evident and positively reflected in high immunization rates and the broad provision of both antenatal and postnatal care.

Effective management and control of chronic diseases require a more comprehensive and continuous approach to service provision, which has been partly implemented through the roll out of the package of essential non-communicable disease (NCD) interventions for primary health care which is a part of the essential health services package.

---

* **Area C** is an administrative division of the West Bank, set out in the Oslo II Accord. Area C constitutes about 61% of the West Bank territory. The Jewish population in Area C is administered by the Judea and Samaria Area administration, whereas the Palestinian population is directly administered by the Coordinator of Government Activities in the Territories and indirectly by the Palestinian National Authority in Ramallah.

ESSENTIAL HEALTH SERVICES PACKAGE

The essential health services package (EHSP) included in the basic services package covers services for reproductive health, newborn and child health, an expanded programme of immunization, communicable diseases, non-communicable diseases, general clinic services, mental health, behavioural change communication, first aid, dental health, nutrition, laboratory services, and pharmaceutical services. Some or all of these services are available at PHC centres. Each PHC centre offers the following basic services: general curative care, antenatal care, post-natal care, immunization, and non-communicable disease management.

QUALITY OF PHC SERVICES

The PHC services provided by the MoH do not always cover all of the services included in an adequately defined EHSP. Shortages of essential medicines and the limited accessibility resulting from restricted working hours remain of concern. The essential drugs list, which was developed in year 2000, includes some 500 essential pharmaceuticals, including 210 items for PHC services. There are constant supply challenges related to essential medicines, and there is limited monitoring to ensure the prescribed medications are aligned with the established treatment protocols. Enhanced coordination is needed to improve the continuity of care between primary health care and referral services. This will improve and progress through the introduction of a comprehensive patient records system.

FAMILY PRACTICE IN PALESTINE

Family practice services are provided by family doctors, supported by a multidisciplinary team. The family practice approach is characterized by comprehensive, continuous, integrated, coordinated, collaborative, personal, family, and community-oriented services. It provides comprehensive medical and psychosocial care with an emphasis on integrated person care within the family as a unit. The goal of the family practice model is to ensure high-quality primary care. Any adjustments introduced are therefore directed towards creating the conditions for improving the quality of care.

ACHIEVEMENTS IN PROVIDING FAMILY PRACTICE SERVICES

The Palestinian Ministry of Health is fully committed to re-orienting the existing PHC system towards Family Practice (FP). This political step has translated into the establishment of the first Family Medicine postgraduate course in 2010 in the West Bank and in 1990 in Gaza.

Vaccination in a PHC facility

The World Health Organization (WHO) has worked closely with the MoH and partners in promoting the transformation to a family practice-oriented PHC system. In 2017, WHO provided technical support through a team of consultants who developed a strategic outline to implement the family practice approach at the national level.[3] The MoH has established three training centres in the West Bank districts of Tulkarem, BirNabala (Jerusalem), and Al-Daheriah (South Hebron). These training centres provide clinical and educational supervision for the FM residents. The MoH has agreed with An-Najah University to ensure the supervisory presence of a university tutor in each of the three training centres. With the support of Medical Aid for Palestinians, consultants from the Royal College in the United Kingdom have also been continuously engaged in providing supervision and technical support to the residents in the training sites. Similarly, three MoH training centres were established in Gaza in Al-Rimal, Sabha al-Harazeen, and Aldraj health centres to provide training for family medicine specialty doctors. The Ministry of Health, is committed to implementing the family practice model including the following seven pillars:[3]

- **Pillar 1**
  Responsible FP teams: professionals linked to stable teams with greater continuity and less rotation.
  A specified number of patients will be registered to assigned clinics according to functions and staff capacity.
- **Pillar 2**
  Registration of patients with a specific FP team: patients subscribe to their personal GP/FP team.
  Clients will be able to confirm registration with the FP team and accept to be registered with the responsible GP/FP practitioner. The core of the family practice team is the physician and the nurse, with expanded teams including a midwife or female doctor, supported by pharmacists and laboratory technicians.
- **Pillar 3**
  There is a single electronic patient record using a national identification number.
  With technical support from the Palestinian National Institute of Public Health and funding from the World Bank, the MoH in the West Bank is in the process of establishing an electronic family practice file for each patient under the patient's unique ID number. The patient record will be web-based and accessible at any place with the authentication of the FP team provider. In Gaza, an electronic family medicine record has been established in three training centres. A number of quality, process, and outcome indicators will be included for monitoring purposes and to support better utilization of data. The MoH has agreed to use and integrate the WHO PHC quality indicators into the existing health information system.
- **Pillar 4**
  Introduction of a tailored appointment system to reduce waiting time and increase contact time.
  Based on agreed guidelines, nurses are responsible for scheduling appointments and for responding to routine queries. This will further improve the efficiency of PHC

clinics by reducing the number of walk-in visits, which will in turn allow for the FP practitioner to dedicate more time to scheduled patients.

The MoH has started with the implementation of an appointment system for Non-Communicable Diseases (NCDs) and Maternal and Child Health (MCH) services.

- **Pillar 5**

  Repeat prescriptions, rational drug use, and optimizing NCD/chronic disease management.

  The predictable availability of drugs and an efficient information communication technology (ICT) system are prerequisites for repeat prescriptions to manage chronic illnesses such as hypertension, diabetes, etc. The FP teams should prescribe essential drugs, determine the duration of their use, and consult with the pharmacist.

- **Pillar 6**

  Gatekeeping: FP physicians provide quality comprehensive care, thereby reducing referrals.

  Gatekeeping is an important challenge for FP teams. It requires competent staff, cordial and trusted relationships with patients, and well-organized clinics. Referrals should always take place based on written referral documents to the specialist.

- **Pillar 7**

  Integrated care: FP teams are community-oriented.

  FP teams develop their services based on the needs of their target population. Involvement of the community in the work of the clinics should be stimulated, as well as home visits and visits to remote areas.

LINKS BETWEEN FAMILY PRACTICE AND NATIONAL PUBLIC HEALTH INITIATIVES

The Palestinian National Health Strategy 2017–2022 comprises two main national policy priorities: comprehensive health services for all and improving public health and well-being. The full adoption of family practice will be critical for achieving the policy objectives. The first goal of the Palestinian National Health Strategy is "the provision of comprehensive health services for all citizens and the localization of health services in Palestine". The strategy reflects the plan for universal health coverage (UHC) to be achieved by 2022 through a number of strategic interventions, including the introduction of family practice in all health directorates. The National Health Strategy's goal of universal health coverage will be promoted by reorienting PHC services towards family practice.[4]

Several indicators will allow the tracking of progress towards universal health coverage. First, 12.9% of the Palestinian population suffers from deep poverty, according to figures published by the Palestinian Central Bureau of Statistics (PCBS) in 2011.[5] Also, out-of-pocket expenditure is high, representing 45.5% of total health expenditure in 2015, according to the PCBS.[6]

The Palestinian health system will require consolidated multisectoral action to progress towards universal health coverage and to address the complex political and social challenges. The epidemiological and demographic transition in Palestine, with non-communicable diseases becoming more common than communicable diseases, in an ageing Palestinian population with a high percentage of youth, is further compounding the challenges ahead.[2]

Pharmacy in a PHC facility

CHALLENGES FOR FAMILY PRACTICE IMPLEMENTATION

Although adaptations have been introduced to improve the PHC system, there are persistent challenges to continuously enhance service quality through family practice. Gaps remain in dedicated family practice services for rural outreach or to support the health needs of marginalized groups in rural or vulnerable areas. Community participation needs further strengthening, but there are a few initiatives in which "Friends of the Clinic" work hand-in-hand with the village health council through the donation of available land to build a clinic or through the donation of equipment. Family practice research initiatives were not conducted in Palestine previously and, therefore, more research and case studies are needed to better monitor and evaluate the family practice services.

To implement the family practice model, adjustments in three main areas are under consideration:[3]

- To improve the image and quality of PHC services and strengthen patient–provider relationships
- To provide more client-friendly organization of services
- To expand the model and quality of services

These factors are linked to the following specific challenges in the implementation of family practice:

- Lack of a fully adopted appointment system results in overcrowding during early operating hours and inefficient utilization during the remaining hours
- Limited opening hours of many PHC facilities from 8:00 am to 3:00 pm
- Lack of a comprehensive patient records system
- Inadequate emphasis on the gatekeeping role, which impacts service utilization, health outcomes, health-care costs, and patient satisfaction
- Challenges with national health workforce planning and a severe shortage of family physicians
- The ongoing occupation of the West Bank and the closure of Gaza hinder the provision of supplies, causing chronic shortages of drugs and equipment, and restricted access to services, and complicate referrals to outside hospitals

TRAINING OF FAMILY PRACTICE PRACTITIONERS

The West Bank currently has 25 graduated family doctors and has 21 residents in training. The MoH provided the resources for 15 residents in 2017, and there is a commitment to support three to five residents each year. In Gaza, 36 GPs graduated as family medicine physicians with certificates from the Palestinian Medical Council. The four-year residency programme is supported by the PHC department in Gaza.

The following training options are available or are being introduced to prepare FP practitioners in the West Bank and Gaza Strip:

- **Short orientation courses for staff at all clinics to introduce family practice**

    The United Nations Relief and Works Agency for Palestine Refugees in the Near East (UNWRA) organized orientation workshops for their staff in a consolidated effort to roll out the family health team approach. The MoH organized three-day orientation courses for all PHC staff with support from the Italian Agency for Development Cooperation. Recently, three day on-line training, with a face-to-face interaction module, has been conducted targeting health care providers. The aim of the training is to provide an overall understanding of the concept of family practice and its implications in primary health care settings.

- **A one-year programme for GPs and staff to obtain a diploma (or equivalent) in FP**

    The MoH supports curriculum development efforts for a multidisciplinary training programme. In close collaboration with An-Najah National University (ANNU) and the MoH, International Development of Family Medicine in Palestine (IDFMP) is designing a curriculum with online learning modules similar to transitional courses used by UNRWA in Jordan. A diploma training for GPs will cover district clinics in selected pilot areas.[3]

    In Gaza, trials to establish family practice training programmes commenced in 1990, enrolling 40 GPs. The course was initially designed as one-day of training per week for two years but terminated before its completion. Al-Azhar University in Gaza established a one-year Family Medicine Diploma course in collaboration with Middlesex University London at the request of UNRWA. As a result, 15 doctors with a family medicine diploma graduated and are working at UNRWA PHC centres, with another 18 GPs engaged in ongoing training. Al-Azhar University is working on official accreditation of the diploma by the Ministry of Education and Higher Education.

- **Four-year residency Family Medicine Specialist (FMS)**

    An-Najah National University (ANNU) runs a Family Medicine residency programme that started in 2010. There are currently 25 certified FM graduates working in the MoH and private PHC centres and a further 21 residents are in training. The four-year training programme has been designed to comply with the requirements for specialist training in FM as specified by the Palestine Medical Council and the Arab Medical Board.[5] In a memorandum of understanding, the MoH agreed to ensure the presence of a university tutor in each of the three training centres in Tulkarem, BirNabala (Jerusalem), and Al-Daheriah (South Hebron). These training centres provide clinical and educational supervision for the FM residents, primarily in the third and fourth years of the programme, in addition to collaborating with IDFMP/Medical Aid for Palestinians. These centres could also play a role in continuous medical education.

    In 2003, the Egyptian Fellowship Program accepted the family practice training centre in Gaza. As a result, three GPs passed exams and became certified family medicine doctors. In 2005, the Palestinian Medical Council started the programme of Family Medicine specialty, in which 18 candidates graduated and received their board certificates. The Ministry of Health has established new regulations restricting the ability of MoH General Practitioners above 32 years of age from obtaining specialty board certification.

THE ROLE OF THE PRIVATE HEALTH SECTOR IN FAMILY PRACTICE

There are a number of private providers who offer out-patient clinic services ranging from solo practices to sophisticated clinics. The professionals involved also often work in public or NGO clinics. The proportion of private sector out-patient services used by the population is 50% at the lowest estimate. There is no defined system or strategy to address enrolment of the private sector in the delivery of family practice services. A strategy should provide details about the relationship between the public and private sectors. There is insufficient information on the financial burden incurred by users of these services.[7]

SUCCESSFUL EXPERIENCE IN FAMILY PRACTICE IN PALESTINE

The implementation of family practice in Palestine has evolved in several phases. Initially, the MoH established a task force to support the implementation of family practice. With the technical and logistic support of WHO, it introduced family practice in 31 health centres located in the Tubas and Salfeet districts in the West Bank, covering a catchment area of 139,133 of the Palestinian population, complemented by training and capacity building efforts. In the Gaza Strip, family practice was introduced in three clinics with the integration of mental health. The intervention has not been evaluated to measure the impact of the family practice approach on improving the quality of care. A family medicine residency programme was established at An-Najah University to meet the need for adequately qualified health professionals to deliver family practice. The MoH further organized training programmes and introductory courses for health centre staff on family practice principles.[3]

In addition, the Palestinian National Institute of Public Health, one of the WHO projects in Palestine, has signed an agreement with the Palestinian MoH to implement the family practice model in three to four districts in the West Bank and five to seven clinics in the Gaza Strip. The agreement is in cooperation with the World Bank as part of the "Health System Resiliency Strengthening" project. The project includes the development of an electronic medical record system, procurement of equipment, management structure reform of human resources, and strengthening the technical capacity of health-care providers. The electronic system will be able to generate quality-related performance indicators for monitoring and better utilization of information.

CONCLUSION

In conclusion, ensuring access to quality health care in Palestine is an ongoing struggle. The prevailing political context and unpredictable financial situation challenge rational planning and service delivery. Shortages of medicines and other products are a recurring problem that has a negative impact on the quality of care and patient satisfaction. In spite of these difficulties, Palestine has a well-developed PHC system with excellent geographical coverage, a defined package of PHC services, and a clear organizational structure. Implementation of the family practice model is therefore consolidating the strong foundations, while necessary adjustments are made to orient the PHC system to fully meet the evolving challenges.[3]

REFERENCES

1. Palestinian Ministry of Health. Annual report of the Ministry of Health 2016. 2017. Gaza Strip. p. 68.
2. Palestinian Ministry of Health. Annual report of the general administration of primary health care for 2016. 2017. Palestinian Ministry of Health, Palestine. p. 281.
3. World Health Organization Towards family practice (FP) in Palestine (WHO recommendations for developing a Family Practice Strategy). 2017. Palestine. p. 41.
4. Palestinian Ministry of Health. National Health Strategy 2017–2022. 2016. Palestine. p. 148.
5. Palestinian Central Bureau of Statistics. Palestine in Figures 2016. 2017. Palestine.
6. Palestinian Central Bureau of Statistics. Palestinian Health Accounts 2015. 2017. Palestine. p. 80.
7. World Health Organization. WHO – World Bank mission on improving health system financing and service provision for universal health coverage in Palestine – addressing the challenges for a sustainable and equitable health system development. 2016. Palestine. p. 38.

CHAPTER 27

Qatar

*Mariam Ali Abdulmalik, Zelaikha Mohsin Al-Wahedi,
and Muna Taher Aseel*

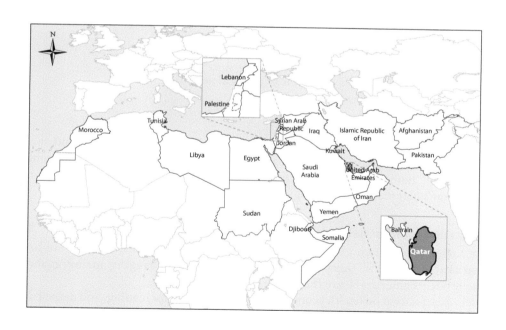

Total number of PHCC facilities	26
Number of general practitioners working in public PHCC facilities	220
Number of certified family physicians working in PHCC facilities	321
Average number of family physician graduates/year	8
Number of medical schools	2
Number of family medicine departments	1

PRIMARY HEALTH CARE IN THE STATE OF QATAR

Introduction

In Qatar, both public and private facilities provide nationals and residents with primary health-care services. The Primary Health Care Corporation (PHCC) is the main and largest public-sector provider of primary care services.

The Qatar Red Crescent Society, a charitable organization, is contracted by the Ministry of Public Health to provide primary care services to single male individuals and workers across the state, and there are a significant number of private primary care facilities available to patients through self-funding or private health insurance.

Previously under the auspices of Hamad Medical Corporation (HMC), PHCC became a stand-alone entity in 2012 and currently operates 23 health centres, including three state-of-the-art health and wellness facilities with additional new and replacement health centres to be built over the coming years to serve the growing population. This huge expansion plan is an essential component of the State Vision 2030.

There are a number of challenges currently facing the health of Qatar's population:[1]

- 69% of mortalities in new mothers are because of chronic conditions
- 70.1% of Qatari adults are overweight
- 43.9% of Qatari adults have low levels of physical activity
- 88% of Qatari children have dental caries
- 23% of mortalities are due to injury

In the past, the health system in Qatar was focused heavily on secondary and specialized care; however, the importance of primary care as the first and continuous point of contact and the primary care "home" for patients is recognized, and this shift in health-care planning is evident in Qatar's national health strategies.

Integration of essential health services package (EHSP)

There are 1.65 million patients registered for PHCC services, of which 1.24 million have been confirmed as active patients. This population base is constantly changing, mainly as short-term expatriate residents enter and leave the country.[2]

New services, focused on health promotion, prevention, early screening, and disease and continuous care management, will become more centred on groups of patients defined as "Priority Populations" with the greatest need focused on children and adolescents, women, the ageing population and healthy elderlies, employees, mental health patients, people with chronic disease, and people with special needs.

The following is the range of services provided by PHCC:

- General practice
- SMART health check
- NCDs
- Wellness
- Mental health services/psychological service
- Home health care
- Maternal and newborn
- Well-baby
- CSSD
- Travel clinics
- Postnatal
- Adolescent service
- Cancer screenings
- Oral health – beautiful smile
- Dental
- Ophthalmology
- Optometry
- Ear, nose, and throat
- Pre-marital service
- Minor injuries service
- Laboratory
- Radiology and ultrasound
- School health
- Emergency services
- Physiotherapy
- Dermatology
- Dietetics

The PHCC is introducing a family medicine model of care, which is changing the way in which PHCC delivers consultant-led care. Patients will be assigned to a family medicine doctor who will supervise the care delivered through their multidisciplinary clinical team. The doctor will be a continuing point of care for the patient and his/her family, and responsible for developing a personalized system of care.

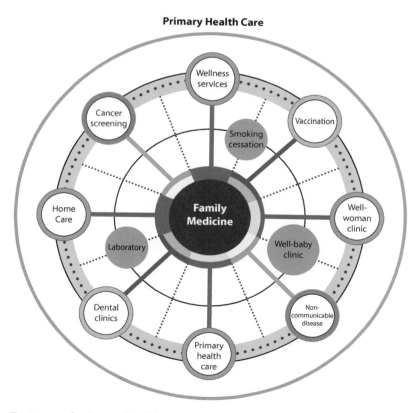

Features of primary health care in Qatar

Primary health care facilities infrastructure

The National Primary Health Care Strategy recommended the building of 20 new health centres, to provide additional capacity and replace some of the old existing facilities. Of the 23 existing health centres, six have become operational since June 2015 including new and replacement health centres. Three of these are state-of-the-art health and wellness centres providing pool, gym, and massage therapy services.

In 2018, PHCC plans to open a further four health centres including two health and wellness centres, with the remaining 10 centres planned to be delivered prior to 2022.

Essential health services package (EHSP)

New health centres will be mobilized with an EHSP. Several health centres will be established as Regional Specialist Centres (RSC) to provide best practice ultrasound, ophthalmology, cancer screening, mental health, and laboratory services. The service configuration for each health centre will include the services listed above or a referral pathway to RSCs or health centres where the service is available.

Essential drug list (EDL)

The National Health System (2011–2016) identified the need to establish a Qatar National Formulary (QNF). The Supreme Council for Health (SCH) (now known as Ministry of Public Health) developed the QNF, which provides a comprehensive reference tool, to manage the increasing range of medicines available in Qatar, as part of the overall economic and social expansion of the country. This comprehensive reference is to be used by all health-care professionals in the country.

Family physician with patient in PHCC facility

PHCC has had a drug formulary since April 2014; the responsibility for creating and updating the formulary rests with the Pharmacy and Therapeutics Committee (PTC), which is comprised of family physicians, general physicians, nurses, and pharmacists. The current formulary consists of a list of medications (medication name, strength, and formulation) based on current existing services and their scope of practice taking into account clinical guidelines and best practice. The EDL and the PHCCs complete formulary are reviewed and updated annually.

Health teams

PHCC has a highly skilled and motivated primary care workforce, working in teams and centred on patient and family care. Recruitment challenges are faced across the whole health sector, and across the Gulf Cooperation Council (GCC) countries alike. However, all 23 Primary Care Centres are run by family medicine specialists supported by multidisciplinary teams.

The PHCC Medium Term Workforce Plan (MTWP) challenges staff to think differently about how the teams work and how services are delivered in the future. Greater emphasis on increasing national workforce capacity through initiatives such as the Qatari Senior Leadership Programme ensures the supply of health professionals and the workforce skill mix in primary care and keeps pace with the demand for primary care services and innovation.

Standard set of medical equipment and furniture

Biomedical engineering plays a pivotal role in monitoring and aiding in the technology upgrade of medical equipment. Global health-care quality standards and specifications as published by the World Health Organization (WHO), the United States Food and Drug Administration (FDA), European Union "Conformité Européenne" (CE) mark, and International Electrotechnical Commission (IEC) serve to enhance clinical diagnostic capability and improved workflows which impact on patients' safety and the performance of clinical staff.

The biomedical engineering department at the PHCC ensures the provision of upgraded technology to all the equipment in all health centres, while considering connectivity and integration with the electronic system to avoid human error and provide a faster and more intelligent service among all the health centres in the country.

Clinical guidelines

In order to realize Qatar's National Health Strategy goal of embedding evidence-based clinical practice, a clinical guidelines adoption programme was initiated in PHCC with the formation of a Guideline Review Committee to ensure appropriate governance of the development of clinical guidelines. The Clinical Affairs Directorate has successfully led this activity over the past three years and facilitated the adoption of 58 evidence-based clinical practice guidelines for use within PHCC, as a means to influence clinical practice. Examples of the approved clinical guidelines including different clinical conditions in areas such as maternal and newborn health, non-communicable diseases, and urgent care. Below is an illustration of the published clinical practice guidelines by models of care from 2012 to 2017:

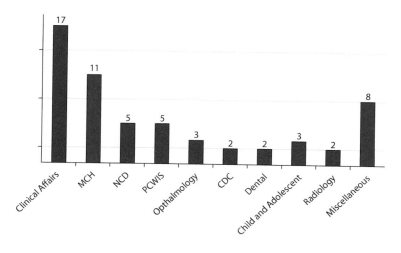

- *PCWIS*: Primary care walk-in services
- *MCH*: Maternal and child health
- *NCD*: Non-communicable diseases
- *CDC*: Communicable disease centre

Information system

The PHCC has laid a new foundation of interconnected infrastructure to support its mission for comprehensive, integrated, person-centred, and affordable health care with the introduction of electronic medical records using the Clinical Information Systems (CIS) solution from early 2015.

The benefits of CIS have been revolutionary for primary care in Qatar by improving the safety and quality of data capture and retention and enabling easy access to patient information including diagnostics and prescribing across all PHCC health centres, as well as external secondary and tertiary heath care facilities.

As more information is captured, reporting will increase in sophistication and population data will be made available to track national patterns of health conditions in Qatar. This information is invaluable to inform national public health projections, and to improve planning for local services. The modernization of PHCC extends far beyond electronic health records including the following initiatives:

- The introduction of Q-matic, an integrated electronic patient queuing system
- The implementation of electronic customer feedback systems
- The implementation of a radiology information system (RIS), picture archiving system, and communication system (PACS)
- The introduction of SMS appointment notifications to improve non-attendance rates
- Future implementation of website and mobile phone app patient education systems

Referral systems

The implementation of an information system was pivotal to ensuring a more streamlined approach to internal and external referrals. Steady progress is being made to implement electronic referrals to external providers, and PHCC has established joint-working protocols with the public secondary and tertiary providers, HMC and Sidra Medicine, to enhance patient pathways between primary, secondary, and specialist care.

As of October 2017, electronic referrals are in place between all PHCC health centres and HMC sites at Al Wakra Hospital, Heart Hospital, Cuban Hospital, Qatar Rehabilitation Institute (QRI), and Communicable Diseases Centre (CDC) with the view to scaling up across all HMC sites including an e-triage pathway. The necessary referral guidelines and discharge pathways will be defined to ensure a best practice and quality referrals service is in place.

Quality and accreditation programme

In 2017, PHCC completed its second accreditation survey facilitated by Accreditation Canada International (ACI). The Quality and Performance Management Department successfully led the organization to achieving the highest accreditation status and was awarded Diamond Level status by ACI.

Patient satisfaction with quality of service delivery

Integration of services across the health economy has streamlined the journey for patients, improved continuity of care, and improved health outcomes. PHCC's core belief is "patient-centredness" and it has created purpose-built solutions to improve patient experience and realize better health outcomes for the population. This has been achieved through the modernization of clinical and health information systems and the built environment and through the provision of services such as family medicine, population-based call and recall cancer screening, proactive wellness and mental health assessment, and referral and discharge management.

PHCC customer services were initiated in mid-2013 with customer service staff placed in all health centres and patient feedback collected and reported monthly. The information gathered is used to assess existing services and support the planning of improvements.

Although Qatar has made significant advancement in recent years, there are still many challenges faced by the health system. A number of challenges were addressed in health strategies as well as PHCC's own Corporate Strategic Plan 2018–2022; they are as follows:[1,3]

- Population changes and complex demographics
- Influencing change in a culture based on treating illness
- Establishing leadership in prevention, education, and self-care
- Effective and sustainable funding and regulation
- Local and global staffing constraints
- Pace and scale of transformation in the health system
- Rapid changes from medical advances, technology, and innovation
- Resistance to change and ever-increasing patient expectations
- Strengthening collaboration and integration across the health system

FAMILY PRACTICE

Political commitments to family practice

In Qatar, there is a clear determination to shift the balance from secondary to primary care, and this national commitment is both demonstrated in the establishment of PHCC and supported by the goals spelt out in the National Health Strategy 2011–2016. The NHS provides an overarching strategic vision and direction for health-care delivery with a clear shift from treatment of illness to prevention and health promotion. This is further strengthened in the NHS 2018–2022 with clear initiatives dedicated to the delivery of a family medicine model in primary care.

Family physicians celebrating World Family Doctor Day (19 May)

The implementation of a family medicine model across all PHCC facilities is a clear directive of the Mid-Term Review of the National Primary Health Care Strategy 2013–2018 and PHCC has committed to mobilizing new health centres with the family practice model and transitioning all existing health centres starting in 2018.

Link between family practice and national public health initiatives

Qatar's National Public Health Strategy was recently launched for consultation and proposes a robust framework to improve the public health of the nation.[1] It addresses 16 public health domains including healthy lifestyles, diabetes, mental health, road safety, tobacco control, and communicable diseases. Four strategic enablers have also been identified to drive the implementation of the strategy. These are community engagement and empowerment, data-driven intelligence, workforce and system capability, and leadership, regulation, and accountability.

PHCC is at the forefront of implementing the public health strategy. Often, primary care is the first and continuous point of contact for the majority of people, which places primary care in an ideal position to promote health, wellbeing, and deliver preventative and curative health-care services. PHCC's comprehensive range of services addresses the majority of the public health domains identified in the strategy.

Link between family practice and other health initiatives (e.g. hospitals, specialists, home care)

Primary care family medicine practice offers treatment but also preventive health services. The patient's family physician will refer them to internal specialist primary care services such as home care services, dermatology, ENT, ophthalmology, and dental, as well as secondary and tertiary care services as needed.

A SMART health checks service was introduced in 2016, which screens patients for health risks and signs of disease, aims to act as a gateway into the full range of primary health care services on offer at PHCC and supports the population of Qatar to take steps to maintain or improve their health.

Contributions of family practice to universal health coverage (UHC)

The NHS 2018–2022 has been developed using the triple aim approach of "better health, better care, better value". A key component of delivering "better care" is to ensure that primary care is at the centre of a system-wide model of care. A family medicine integrated model of care is the key to increasing coordination and continuity and improving value.

The successful piloting, evaluation, and implementation of a family practice model at PHCC will set the precedent for standardizing primary care services across the health sector. Implementation of a standardized family practice approach to primary care services should be mandated across all public and private sector facilities with performance and quality monitored at a ministerial level.

All Qatari national and residents can obtain a health card, which entitles nationals to free health care and expatriate residents to heavily subsidized services at the public providers.

Family practice teams (links with nurses, community health workers, midwives, and others)

The family practice health centre involves an interdisciplinary team of health professionals managing the care of their registered health centre population. The family physicians are the primary provider of services within the health centre leading the team.

With the rise in Qatar's population, the increasing disease burden, and high prevalence of risk factors, it is unsustainable for physicians to continue to work in isolation as the patient provider. Evolution to panels of patients and an interdisciplinary team and an inter-professional collaboration approach will enable the health centre and its providers to meet patient need in a more effective and efficient way. Offering continuity of care enhances patient satisfaction and provides a positive experience for the clinical team allowing the doctor–patient relationship to grow.

In PHCC's pilot health centre, there are two interdisciplinary teams in place comprising physicians and nurses. All physicians have a panel and are working to their maximum scope of practice. Allied health professionals are currently working as shared health centre resources due to the small numbers of these staff. The vision for the future is that they will be allocated to the teams.

Family practice role in social accountability (supporting vulnerable or marginalized groups of people)

NHS 2018–2022 focuses on seven priority population groups, which reflects an investment in Qatar's most vulnerable groups such as children, mothers, older people, those with mental health concerns, and those with special needs. At the centre of patient pathways, serving these vulnerable populations will be a team of multidisciplinary family practice professionals, ensuring that all necessary aspects of their care are provided in a holistic way.

PHCC has established SMART Accountable Care clinics, which identify at-risk patients and proactively contact them and invite them in for an assessment. The focus of these clinics has been primarily diabetes patients.

Under the Better Together programme and in collaboration with HMC, the Home Health Care service provides care for Qatari and GCC nationals over the age of 60 in their homes. Their care is provided by a multidisciplinary team consisting of family physicians, nurses, physiotherapists, dieticians, and pharmacists.

Family practice financing in the country

There is growing pressure on health budgets globally. The government has stated its continued commitment to investing in the health and education of its citizens.

It is important that patients have a wider choice of providers, and that additional capacity is made in crucial areas such as primary care. It is expected that when the new health insurance system is launched, it will enable many more people to access the private sector directly through their benefit plans.

PHCC is also looking at the possibility of opening some of the new health centres with private sector operators. Other areas where PHCC has collaborated with external providers includes the transfer of two health centres to Qatar Red Crescent, and the introduction of new services, such as cancer screening in collaboration with private sector partners.

Public–private partnerships and developments using private finance are being considered and are expected to become more significant over time.

Family practice research

At PHCC, the Research Section, in collaboration with the Department of Workforce Development and Training, established an accredited staff research, training, and capacity building programme in 2015 to boost research capability among family physicians and other frontline staff. A new research module, embedded in the Family Medicine Residency training programme, further emphasizes the priority attached to research. Postgraduate residents work closely with faculty mentors to design relevant research projects, which they undertake as part of their training.

The introduction of an annual Primary Care Research Conference since 2015 has also provided an outlet for research dissemination among family physicians. This has resulted in a year-on-year increase in the number of abstracts received from family physicians encompassing areas of family practice such as pedagogical issues, quality improvement, patient satisfaction, and clinical and epidemiological research. There has also been a year-on-year increase in research publications in international peer-reviewed journals among PHCC family practitioners. (PHCC staff publications in Appendix 1 for.)

Current research topics include:

- Assessing knowledge, attitudes, and practices regarding cervical cancer screening among female physicians in primary health care in Qatar
- Implementing professional development for family medicine residents in Qatar
- Introducing reflective practice into a family medicine residency programme in Qatar
- Prevalence and determinants of burnout among primary health-care physicians in Qatar
- Examining implications and perceptions of introducing reflective practice to health-care practitioners in PHCC, Qatar
- Assessing learning styles among family medicine residents in Qatar
- Quality of Continuity Care Clinics (CCCs) in a family medicine residency programme in Qatar

Key challenges in implementing family practice in the country[4]

A formal evaluation of the family practice pilot is underway at the time of writing this chapter.

Throughout the implementation of the family practice pilot in 2017, several challenges arose, the most significant of these included:

- Cultural acceptance of key aspects of scheduled care such as making appointments, timeliness of attendance, and the unique provision of primary care from 7:00 am to 11:00 pm. Priority consideration is given for Qatari nationals to be seen at any health centre, which supports access but challenges the principle of family practice, encouraging patients to see their assigned physician and build continuity of care. The benefits of family practice are not as evident for the transient population; however, the local Qatari population has much to gain from having an assigned family physician promoting the benefits of continuity of care.
- Collaboration with partners and continuing care/integrated services support from the wider health system is needed to embed the principles across the health economy and support the enhancement of clinical roles such as nursing and allied health professionals. This would engender a change in clinical and community culture regarding provision of and access to primary health care. Appropriate funding to support primary care as the first and continuous point of contact.

Qatar's successful experience in implementing family practice

All families in the catchment area of the pilot health centre are assigned to a family physician. The health-care team are trained to discuss the benefits of the new model when patients visit for any services (planned or triage visits). A growing number of patients are being seen by appointment and there are more and more repeat visits linking patients with their assigned physicians and care teams. All services are being provided by the assigned family physician, moving away from a model where there were separate clinics on different days by different physicians.

Family practice offers holistic preventive and curative treatment services to the community by teams of highly skilled staff working to international best practice and evidence-based models. This is improving health literacy and community health outcomes. Access to data has increased capacity to support population health management and the delivery of locally relevant services.

FAMILY MEDICINE

Family practice development in the country

In 2015, a committee was formed and published a "Vision for Family Practice" in PHCC health centres in Qatar. Throughout 2015 and 2016, a team was assigned to plan for the implementation of the new family practice model. From the end of 2016, the pilot site changed to the new model. Throughout the year, several additions/modifications/upgrades were made including CIS optimization, SMART screening, and nursing service expansion.

Starting in 2018, all new health centres will be mobilized with the new family practice model and all existing health centres will begin the transition.

Family medicine education (medical student education, postgraduate or residency training in family medicine, continuing education in family medicine)

The family medicine residency is a four-year programme. The first 36 months of training are structured to help residents obtain the knowledge, experience, and skills required for attaining the ACGME-I (Accreditation Council for Graduate Medical Education) requirements in six competencies including patient care, medical knowledge, practice-based learning and improvement, systems-based practice, professionalism, and interpersonal skills and communication. The additional 12 months are designed to meet Arab Board of Medical Specialization in Family Medicine requirements by applying their medical knowledge while acquiring the necessary clinical skills in primary health-care settings. Family medicine currently does not have a fellowship programme, but it is highly likely to happen in the future. Family medicine follows the graduate medical education policies in every aspect of its educational operation.

During the four-year training period, family medicine resident physicians must perform a rigorous mixture of patient care activities, attend clinical rounds and seminars, show timely completion of medical records, and assume other responsibilities as required by the different departments they rotate through. Residents are also required to deliver case presentations, attend continuity care clinics, and update their medical knowledge with the latest medical guidelines.[5]

The medical department rotations in hospital are divided into two categories: mandatory and elective. The mandatory rotations (that also include sub-specialties) are allocated to the three postgraduate-year (PGY) residencies as follows:

- *PGY1 Level*: Paediatrics (4 months), community medicine (1 month), adult medicine (5 months), human behaviour and mental behaviour health (1 month)
- *PGY2 Level*: Adult medicine (2 months), general surgery (2.5 months), urology (2 weeks), human behaviour and mental health (1 month), orthopaedics (1 month), sport medicine (1 month), maternity care/obstetrics (2 months), gynaecology (1 month), laboratory (2 weeks), and radiology (2 weeks)

- *PGY3 Level*: Accident and emergency medicine (2 months), dermatology (2 months), ENT (1.5 months), oral health (2 weeks), ophthalmology (1.5 months), human and behavioural medicine (2 weeks), adult medicine (1 month), and 3 months of elective rotations

In addition to the hospital rotations, residents are required to attend continuity of care clinics (CCC) during the first three years of their residency. During these clinics, the resident will be trained to implement different consultation models to patients of all ages and both genders with a wide range of diverse presentations. Upon completion of three months, each resident is required to submit a practice management report bundle comprising:

- A practice management report template
- A chart audit (10 patients in quarter)
- Patient satisfaction forms (three forms quarterly, in Arabic and English)
- Patient visit lists

In CCCs, there is a minimum number of patients to be seen by each resident in each PGY level as follows: PGY1 residents to see at least 60 patients quarterly; PGY2 residents to see at least 168 patients quarterly; and PGY3 residents to see at least 324 patients quarterly. By the end of the third year of residency, each resident is required to accumulate a total number of 1650 patient visits. This is a mandatory component in ACGME-I requirements.

Furthermore, didactic teaching requires residents to attend one whole-day academic activity weekly that covers all medical subjects. At least one journal club is also required from residents in a month. During the didactic activity, residents are actively involved in education, as they have to prepare presentations and lead discussions under the supervision of the family medicine faculty and guest lecturers.

By conforming to the ACGME-I standards in six core competencies, obvious improvement in residents' performance has been noticed. Residents are also trained to practice safely and are properly supervised to reach standardized patient load according to each residency training level. They have also become more aware of implementing a holistic approach in patient care, addressing health-care needs of patients, as well as practicing safely in family and community context. All of these have, in turn, been reflected in greater patient satisfaction toward the health-care service in Qatar.

The Family Medicine Residency Programme is a core foundation to the standards required which are critical to developing physicians for the family medicine model adopted by the PHCC. Once the four-year training is complete, PHCC ensures the ongoing development of physicians, in line with organizational commitment to the strategic goal for "Excellence in Workforce and Organizational Learning", by providing physicians with the appropriate competency-based programmes, orientation, and professional development aligned to professional standards and practice.

As the family medicine model evolves, health-care professional learning and development is being redefined as informed by best practice and research highlighted by J S Carroll et al to develop plans that reflect the importance of an effective skilled, competent, and motivated multi-disciplinary team, supported by the shared vision and purpose of PHC in preventative care, management of NCDs, specialist care, and wellness.

Professional development embeds lifelong reflective practice and nurtured learning focused on strong foundations to improve patient outcomes and experience. PHCC maintains the importance of a professional learning culture between clinicians, non-clinician peers, and leadership.

Development plans embed best practice learning in PHC that support professional development through effective professional orientation, career framework and employability, mentorship and coaching, inter-professional education, e-learning, peer-to-peer review, and competency assessment.

PRIVATE HEALTH SECTOR

Private health sector's role in the delivery of out-patient clinic services

The private providers in Qatar include hospitals, clinics and polyclinics, providers of ancillary services, pharmacies, and others. In 2014, there were four private hospitals, over 250 medical and dental clinics and polyclinics, 32 diagnostic centres, and over 300 pharmacies and medicine stores.[6]

The private hospitals deliver specialist out-patient services, in addition to their in-patient services, and the many clinics and polyclinics deliver both primary care services, and non-primary ambulatory care services.

In 2013, the government established the National Health Insurance Company (NHIC) which trialled a social health insurance programme "Seha". Qatari nationals were able to access approved private sector providers for their health care. This scheme undoubtedly provided a boost to the development of the private health sector in 2014 and 2015, and Seha was intended to be extended to the expatriate population in a later phase. However, Seha services were terminated at the end of 2015, and a new insurance system is being developed, which will build on the Seha experience.

Services in the private sector are, therefore, funded through private health insurance plans, or by direct and co-payments from individuals.

As far as primary health care is concerned, there are around 600 general practitioners (GPs) in the private sector, although only around 2% are family medicine specialists. This compares with around 700 GPs in the public sector (including Qatar Red Crescent), over 50% of whom are family medicine specialists, mainly in the PHCC. The balance between GPs and family medicine specialists and the impact on the model of care in the country is considered further below. The private clinics and polyclinics perform an important role in extending access for patients who need primary or urgent care for minor ailments, or non-primary ambulatory care based in the community.

The National Health Strategy 2018–2022 highlights the importance of developing the private health sector and sets a national target to expand the private sector's role. This should be facilitated by the future insurance-based funding initiative.

Family physician's role in the private health sector

There are over 120 private medical clinics in Qatar, providing both primary and other ambulatory services. Table 27.1 shows the distribution of GPs in Qatar (June 2017).

Definitions:

- *General practitioner*: A medical graduate
- *General practitioner – limited*: A medical graduate without further specialist qualification but with a minimum of 3 years' experience in a specialty and some limited privileges
- *Family medicine specialists*: A medical graduate with a specialist qualification in family medicine/general practice

TABLE 27.1 Distribution of GPs in Qatar (June 2017)

Scope of work	Private sector	Public sector			Total
		PHCC	Qatar Red Crescent	HMC	
General practitioner	254	147	106	–	507
General practitioner – limited	330	73	–	–	403
Family medicine specialist	14	321	–	59	394
Total	598	541	106	59	1304
Percentage	46%	41%	8%	5%	100%

The table shows that whilst 46% of practitioners are working in the private sector, only 3.5% of family physicians are currently employed in the private sector. It is expected that this percentage will increase over time with the launch of the new National Health Strategy 2018–2022, and its focus on a family medicine model of care.

Patients seeking health services outside public PHC facilities

The number of patients seeking health services in the private sector can only be estimated from the relative proportion of relevant physicians. Around 46% of GPs and family physicians are employed in the private sector, and it is reasonable to assume that a similar proportion of the activity is serviced there. Over 96% of the physicians have limited qualifications and scopes of practice; they are likely to be dealing with more minor ailments, and referring patients to specialist departments in the polyclinics, as required. Patients can access the specialist departments and medical clinics directly. The separate classifications of out-patient services, between primary and specialist services, are not currently quantified at that level of detail.

There are over 250 private health centres, clinics, polyclinics, and dental clinics. Around half of them are dental clinics or include dental services. This provides patients with improved access, and extends their choice; however, services in the private sector are chargeable to patients or their insurers, which currently restricts their use. The government is supporting plans to extend the role of the private sector in the provision of health-care services.

Private health sector's role in expanding universal health coverage

The State of Qatar is committed to providing a system of universal health coverage for its citizens and residents. Currently, that is provided through the public health system. Each resident can obtain a Health Card, which entitles them to a broad range of services, through Hamad Medical Corporation, Primary Health Care Corporation, and the Qatar Red Crescent Society. The services, including medications are either free, or heavily subsidized. Emergency services are free.

As an illustration, the Qatar National Health Accounts for 2014 estimated that the current health expenditure was a total of QAR18.2 billion. Almost 87% was financed by the government, 6% by private health insurance, and 7% by other domestic revenues, mainly out-of-pocket household expenditure. This provides an indication that the total value of the private health-care sector was around 13%, and the primary care element around 1% to 2%.

One of the main objectives of the Seha social health insurance initiative was to expand the private sector's role, and we can expect that the planned future health insurance system will also expand the role of the private sector in providing universal health coverage.

REFERENCES

1. Ministry of Public Health, Qatar. *National Health Strategy 2018-2022*. 2018. Available from: https://www.moph.gov.qa/HSF/Pages/NHS-18-22.aspx [Accessed 29 March 2018].
2. Health Information Management Department - PHCC Qatar. *December Report, HIM Statistical Monthly Report*. 2017.
3. *National Health Strategy 2018–2022*.
4. Primary Health Care Corporation, Family Medicine Project Team, 2017.
5. Carroll JS, Edmondson AC. Leading organisational learning in health care. *BMJ Quality & Safety*. 2002;11:51–56. Available from: http://dx.doi.org/10.1136/qhc.11.1.51 [Accessed 22 September 2018].
6. Health Activities Policy Planning Unit, Ministry of Public Health, Qatar. *August Report, Health Facilities Review 2017–2022*. 2017.

CHAPTER 28

Saudi Arabia

Noha Dashash, Lubna A. Al-Ansary,
and Ibrahim El-Ziq

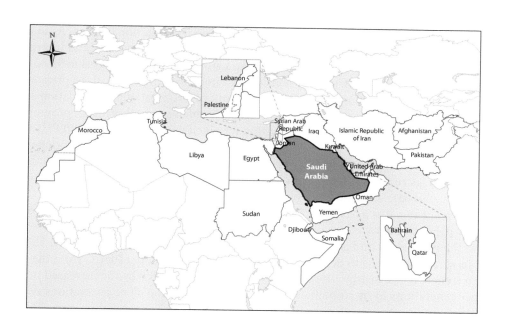

Total number of PHC facilities[1]	2400
Number of general practitioners working in public PHC facilities[2]	6107
Number of certified family physicians[3] working in PHC facilities[2]	636
Average number of family physicians (Board and Diploma) graduates/year[2]	100–120
Total family medicine residents enrolled in 2015[2]	226
Number of governmental medical schools	25
Number of private medical schools[4]	6
Number of family medicine departments in medical colleges[2]	25
Number of family medicine programmes within medical colleges or joint postgraduate programmes[2]	18

INTRODUCTION

The total population of the Kingdom of Saudi Arabia (KSA) according to a 2017 survey is 32.5 million, of whom 20.1 million are Saudis. Males compose 50.94% of Saudis; 30% of the population is under 15 years of age and 4.2% is above 65 years.[1] Life expectancy is 74.4 years, and by 2030 it is expected to rise to 80 years.[2]

PRIMARY HEALTH CARE (PHC)

In November 1983, the Saudi Ministry of Health (MoH) took the decision to establish the Primary Health-Care Sector as "the basic [provider of] health services for all members of the community, [representing] the first level of community contact with the health services". The implementation of PHC involved extensive training of health-care providers at all levels of care and passed through several phases. By 1985, PHC began to function in Saudi Arabia by laying the foundations, providing extensive training, implementing expansion and improvement in the provision of services, and producing vital indicators. Subsequent phases focused on total quality management and supportive supervision and implementing specialized programmes.

The Primary Health Care Centres (PHCCs) network covers most of the population and provides comprehensive care for acute and chronic health problems as well as health promotion services such as health education and immunization for all citizens.[3] There are 2400 PHCCs, 60% of which are in rural areas all over KSA. Service is covered by 6107 general practitioners (GPs) and 636 family physicians. Most family physicians are based in cities who run less than 10% of all PHCCs, whereas rural PHCCs are run by GPs. Other physician specialties include dentists, paediatricians, obstetricians, and a few others.

Rural coverage remains a challenge in Saudi Arabia. The MoH has specific criteria for establishing new PHCs to ensure coverage of health-care needs in remote rural areas. These include the size of the population and geographic distance to existing health-care facilities. The nature of tribes in rural areas leads to demands on tribal leaders to request a PHCC from the government even if there is one nearby. The challenge is further aggravated by the increased migration of younger generations to metropolitan and large cities while the older generations remain in their villages, leading to a smaller population within the PHCC's catchment area. This eventually leads to under-utilization of physicians and other health-care providers. The MoH has developed several solutions to address these situations and continues to ensure nationwide health-care coverage. PHCCs covering areas where populations have decreased have full-time nurses year-round but share a physician with another PHCC. This way utilization of physicians improves. Moreover, the MoH has recently launched free virtual consultation services and is working with telecom companies to establish Internet services in all PHCCs. Once this is established in rural PHCCs, tele-consultations with hospital consultants will take place.

PHCC buildings are either government owned and built, or rented. Rented buildings pose a challenge to the MoH as they are usually not designed for the purpose of being used as a health-care facility. In the past years, the MoH has worked hard to substitute these buildings with government-owned PHCC buildings. These were designed to accommodate the main primary health-care functions. They include triage areas, physician clinics, emergency/dressing clinics, well-baby clinics, immunization clinics, antenatal clinics, health education clinics, social worker rooms, and separate waiting areas for men and women. Many PHCCs have dental clinics and some have a dental hygienist clinic. In main cities, large PHCCs provide mental health services by trained family physicians and psychologists.

Recently, the MoH has launched an extensive renovation project to renew all governmental PHCC buildings thereby transforming them into modern attractive facilities. This project aims at attracting the population to utilize primary health-care services appropriately, correcting the current under usage of these facilities. A total of five PHCCs have been renovated to the *new identity* of PHCCs. They are fully functional. The aim is to renovate 200 PHCCs per year. In addition to the structural reform (building and furniture), the *new identity* will also include the transformation to a paperless full Health Information System (HIS) and Electronic Medical Records (EMR). The total number of visits to PHCCs in 2016 was 49,817,811 visits.

Radiological services are present in 35% of PHCCs. 61% have laboratories.[2] However, in order to improve the efficiency of laboratory services, the MoH is currently centralizing this service in cities (urban areas) where a central lab will be responsible for running all lab tests while phlebotomy remains in the PHCCs. Small rural PHCCs (category A) will continue to have laboratories.

Essential drugs are available in most of PHCCs. The number of drugs included has doubled over the past few years to include more than 350 items. This change reflects the advances in health-care services provided by PHCCs and increasing use of clinical practice guidelines. Another reason for the expansion of the basic drug list is to enable proper care for the increasing numbers of patients with chronic diseases. In the past few years, the main care for chronic disease patients has been assigned by the MoH to the PHC sector. The increasing number of family physicians practising in PHCCs has also enabled the provision of care for mild to moderate mental health problems to be conducted by these family physicians.

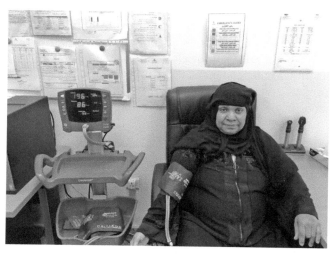

Patient having a periodic checkup

Clinical practice guidelines are available in PHCCs. Most have guidelines on diabetes mellitus, hypertension, asthma, geriatric care, sexually transmitted infections, and tuberculosis (TB), but guidelines on other important conditions are few.[2]

Referral between PHCCs and hospitals is generally below the desired standard.[2] Feedback from hospitals to primary care remains deficient.[4]

Patient satisfaction studies with PHCCs have had conflicting results. A study in Riyadh[5] showed that about 30% of the participants perceive PHCC services as weak or ineffective. With regard to the likelihood of choosing PHCCs as the first choice of health-care service, 75% of the participants admitted that PHCCs are not their first choice. Some of the reasons for this were that PHCCs are not comprehensive and the scope of service does not cover all specialties (33%), mistrusting staff (28%), inappropriate working hours (24%), distance (2%), and having health-care insurance (13%).

However, another study in Majmaah demonstrated satisfaction with PHCCs to be 82%. Reasons for satisfaction were attributed to provision of suitable buildings (30%), adequate number of staff (22%), dental services (19.3%), public health education (11.4%), and advanced equipment and an increased number of physicians (7%).[5]

The benefits of PHC are clear from a study which showed that the pooled results for all-cause mortality suggest that an increase of one primary care physician per 10,000 population is associated with an average mortality reduction of 5.3% or 49:100,000.[6]

In order to improve the quality of care provided in PHCCs, the MoH has set an extensive quality control and accreditation programme for all PHCCs in the kingdom. The Central Board for Accreditation of Health-Care Institutions (CBAHI) is the local health-care accreditation body responsible for implementation. By the end of this project, it is expected that all MoH PHCCs will have acquired the CBAHI accreditation. The first edition of primary care standards was approved in 2011.[7] The target for 2016/2017 was to accredit 93 PHCCs. The results were that 55 out of 93 PHCCs received accreditation (59%), 20 received conditional accreditation (22%), and the remainder were denied accreditation.[8]

HEALTH CARE REFORM

Saudi Arabia is currently undergoing a huge reform for the whole country. The aim of the reform is reaching the 2030 vision set by the Crown Prince. The health-care sector is one of several sectors in the country undergoing overall reform, due in 2020. The Ministry of Health (MoH) is on a path to implement a significant transformation of the health-care system. The reform will result in separating health-care provision from the regulator, through bold steps towards achieving the Vision 2030 commitment for efficient and high-quality health care. Health-care institutes will operate under independent health-care companies and the MoH will become the regulatory body. Figure 28.1 presents the themes of the health-care reform.

The reform focuses on current health-care system challenges in Saudi Arabia, which include:[9]

- Limited focus on health wellness and citizen activation
- Rising overall health-care costs
- Uncoordinated and inefficiently run network of health-care service providers
- Governance structures that prevent effectively tracking performance
- Lack of digital solutions to drive patient self-service, prevention, and connected care
- Increasing reliance on foreign professionals

Health-care reform will result in a sustainable health-care system that focuses on the health and wellbeing of people; it comprises seven main themes (Figure 28.1):[8]

FIGURE 28.1 Themes of Saudi health-care reform.

1. Model of care
2. Health-care financing
3. Corporatization
4. Private sector participation
5. Governance
6. e-Health
7. Workforce

The core of health-care reform is the model of care. The model of care includes six areas. These focus on people in the community where they are screened and receive health promotion. A great deal of the models of care will be carried out by family physicians within the PHCCs (Figure 28.2). In fact, the Saudi Arabian health-care leadership recognizes that the most efficient way to provide high-quality, efficient health care is through effective PHC run by family physicians. This has encouraged the political leadership to support and commit to plans that aim at increasing the numbers of qualified family physicians.

Saudi Arabia has one of the highest prevalence rates of diabetes mellitus in the world, and with expected increased longevity, the burden of chronic diseases is expected to rise.

Primary health care is considered a main crosscutting solution that will be enhanced and supported during the health-care reform (Figure 28.3). The pilot phase implementation of the models of care is currently being launched in four regions of the Kingdom. The model of care adopts an integrated, patient-centred, health-care delivery system. Although it aims at reducing morbidity and mortality as well as health-care expenditure, it focuses on the patient experience and satisfaction. A great emphasis is placed on health promotion, screening, and virtual care. The initial outcomes of the models of care pilots are very promising.

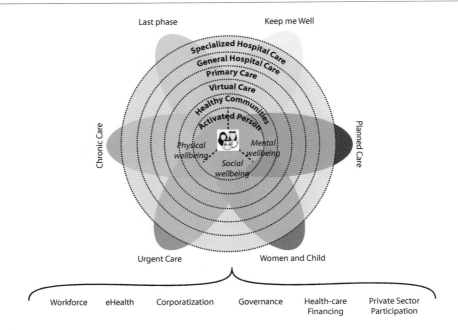

FIGURE 28.2 Shift of care to community and PHC.

PHC CLINICAL PRACTICE GUIDELINES (CPGs)

CPGs are defined as "systematically developed statements/recommendations to assist practitioner and patient decisions about appropriate health care for specific clinical circumstances thereby distilling a large body of medical knowledge into a convenient, readily usable format". CPGs are based on good research evidence of clinical effectiveness. They form the basis for the standards against which a comparative audit can be conducted. They are an important tool for evidence-based decision making. Research has shown that implementing CPGs improves the quality of patient care in clinical practice and identifies research gaps thus directing research to actual needs. Given the lack of local PHC CPGs, the need for developing ones was identified as urgent. A team put together a plan for developing National PHC CPGs. The options were to develop CPGs de novo, adopt international CPGs, or locally adapt high-quality international CPGs. Given the lack of required expertise and resources, developing CPGs locally was not a reasonable option. Adoption of international CPGs *as is* poses challenges in implementation as some aspects of these CPGs are not implementable in countries with different health-care systems. Therefore, the choice was to locally adapt international CPGs to fit local circumstances and constraints. This generated a sense of ownership and avoided duplication of efforts. In addition, several developed countries (e.g. New Zealand, Germany, and Iceland) encourage local adaptation of international high-quality guidelines.

The aim of this project was to improve the quality of care provided in PHC. Its objectives included:

- Improving the level of care provided to PHCC patients and the population (preventive, diagnostic, and curative) and improving health-care outcomes
- Providing a measuring tool that assists in medico-legal investigations
- Reducing inappropriate variations in clinical care practice provided by physicians and other health-care providers

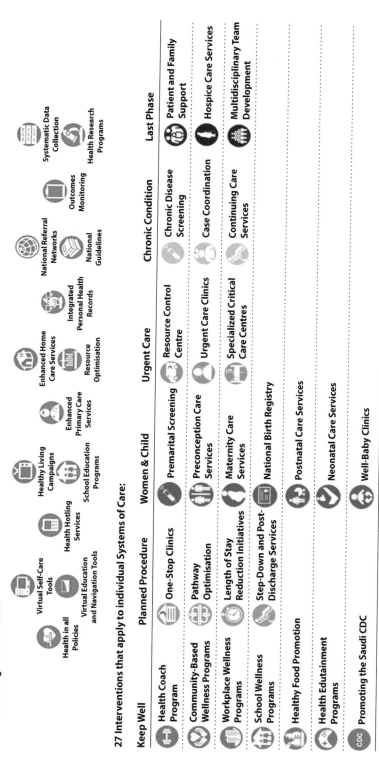

FIGURE 28.3 Six models of care, including 27 interventions and 15 cross-cutting interventions.

- Providing an evidence base for selecting the PHC basic list of medications and basic investigations
- Educating patients and professionals about current best practice
- Improving the cost-effectiveness of health services

The project proposal was detailed and approvals of the MoH leadership were obtained. The PHC CPG team set a plan for prioritizing GPGs to be included in the first phase of the project. This included high demand as ranked by PHC physicians and high volume based on PHC statistics. After setting a list of the most prevalent 10 conditions, the methodology was agreed. The New Zealand adaptation model was adopted. The AGREE instrument was used to appraise CPGs and high scoring CPGs were chosen. The SORT taxonomy was used to re-rank levels of evidence. A standardized final guideline format was developed, and implementation plans were designed. The final outcome of two years of work was a total of five PHC CPGs. The "Primary Care Type II Diabetes Clinical Practice Guideline" was reviewed by the WHO. These CPGs were updated three years later.

FAMILY PRACTICE

In Saudi Arabia there are 18 recognized family medicine residency programmes. In 1983, Saudi universities started the postgraduate family medicine programme. Most of them collaborated with the Family Medicine Arab Board Council and aligned training to fulfil its requirements, giving graduates the opportunity of getting an additional certification. This gave the opportunity of collaboration and standardization of family medicine residency training across Arab countries. In 1995, the Saudi Commission for Health Specialties was established, and the Saudi Family Medicine Board Programme started. The first batch of Family Medicine Saudi Board graduated in 1999.

One of the main challenges that Saudi Arabia faces in providing optimal primary health-care services, is the lack of certified family physicians. This shortage is not only a local shortage, it is a regional one. In other words, there is strong competition between the Gulf Cooperation Council (GCC) countries to attract family physicians from neighbouring countries to work in the Kingdom.

Family Medicine Residency Training

The number of family physicians working in the MoH in 2016 included 355 consultants and 911 registrars. On the other hand, other governmental sectors (the military, national guard, universities, etc.) had 433 consultants and 790 registrars.[10]

Family physicians constitute 3% of physicians in Saudi Arabia as compared to countries like Canada were family physicians constitute more than 50% of all physicians. While the standard is one family physician per 1000 to 2500 population, there is one family physician per 16,000 population. Moreover, current family medicine residency programmes accept only 8%–10% of medical graduates. Therefore, to reach the desired standard, Saudi Arabia needs 2000 family medicine graduates annually as opposed to the current 300–350 graduates (data from the Saudi Commission of Health Specialties). The Saudi Commission for Health Specialties (SCHS) provides two types of family medicine certification; the Saudi Board in Family Medicine (SBFM), a four-year residency programme; and the Saudi Diploma in Family Medicine (SDFM), a two-year residency programme. The existing family medicine residency programmes provide thorough good quality training. It would be challenging to find solutions to rapidly increase the numbers of qualified family physicians while maintaining high-quality training.

Recognizing the need to increase the number of family physicians, the SCHS and the MoH have worked together to come up with plans to combat the shortage. The numbers of residents accepted for enrolment in each postgraduate programme has been almost doubled. In addition, health-care institutions (both public and private) have been encouraged and supported to open new family medicine postgraduate programmes. Furthermore, the SCHS signed an agreement with the Irish College of General Practitioners to establish family medicine academies in two medical cities in Riyadh. The target is to increase the annual number of family medicine board graduates from 350 to 2000 family medicine certified physicians per year.[11] Results of these efforts are beginning to appear, as in 2017 the number of Family Medicine Board graduates was more than 300 family physicians.

RESEARCH INITIATIVE IN THE FAMILY MEDICINE BOARD PROGRAMME

This initiative involved a reform project of the research unit at the Joint Programme of Family Medicine in Jeddah. The goal of medical research is to improve health and the quality of life of individuals and communities. It produces the evidence that supports health-care decision making. In several developed countries, family medicine research has helped develop the health-care system.

In 1995, upon the establishment of SCHS, the Saudi Board in Family Medicine was developed. Since then, the Board required all residents to conduct research. Research has recently become a requirement for other residency programmes as well. This new requirement demands a support system that includes several requirements but mostly training and supervision. Research conduct should follow a structured process and must adhere to known research ethics. Although this is common sense and seems to be taken for granted, adhering to it is a problem in residency programmes. Communications with several programme directors and trainers in several regions of the kingdom led to a clearer view of this problem. Accordingly, a focus group of trainers and trainees discussed issues related to candidates, supervisors, training courses, and administration. Problems identified included: a lack of written rules/regulations, a lack of sufficient training on research ethics, and a lack of experienced supervisors especially statisticians. Solutions were proposed and discussed. Further detailed solutions were refined. The training course was reformed into a practical, hands-on course where each candidate finalizes a complete research proposal during the training course. It focused on teaching research ethics and designing tools that ensure reinforcing them. Accordingly, a handbook containing a detailed explanation of the process of conducting research, obligations of the candidate, and duties of the supervisors was developed. It also included specific forms on a research code of conduct, authorship code, supervision agreement and other forms that help support the process of conducting research.

This project was granted the Family Medicine Scientific Board Award in 2015. The true success in this project was the great transformation in types of studies conducted by family physicians. In previous years, almost all family medicine residents conducted cross-sectional studies. The transformation resulted in randomized controlled trials, non-randomized interventional studies, cohort (retrospective) studies, case-control studies, and quantitative research. This is extremely important, as it helps fill the scientific knowledge gap in PHC in Saudi Arabia. In addition, this new trend in types of research helped in identifying effective interventions for modifying behaviour and lifestyles contributing to chronic diseases. A significant increase in publishing family medicine research was also noted.

SUCCESS STORY: QUALITY ACCREDITATION OF PHCCs

Quality in primary care began as a very basic project. However, in 2006 some PHC administrations began communication with the Joint Commission International (JCI), to be enrolled in the pilot phase of the newly developed PHC standards. Later, a group of family physicians with special interest in quality were trained to receive a Diploma in Quality. These became the core group to establish local PHC quality standards. In 2011, four PHCCs were JCI accredited for the first time in Saudi Arabia. These were in the Makkah Region. Furthermore, CBAHI standards were developed for PHC and the MoH adapted a timeline to get PHCCs accredited.

PRIVATE SECTOR

The private sector has shown interest in providing family practice services in the past few years. Statistics of the MoH show that, in 2016, there were 47 family medicine consultants, 59 registrars, and 10 residents. Several private hospitals now have family medicine departments. This seems to have been motivated by insurance companies who recognize that family physicians provide a wide variety of health-care services at a lower cost than hospital specialists, while maintaining reasonable quality of care. Moreover, large companies who pay directly for private health-care services of their employees, such as Saudi ARAMCO, mandate that the private hospitals providing care for their employees have a family medicine system.

Private hospitals are currently moving towards providing family medicine services through small family medicine community-based clinics away from the main hospital. Examples are family medicine clinics in King Abdullah Economic City and in King Abdullah University for Science and Technology.

In addition, in the current health-care transformation project, the private sector is being invited to invest in PHC. This will lead to more involvement of the private sector in PHC and a positive shift in the private sector health-care provision where it shall begin to shift from secondary to primary care level.

REFERENCES

1. General Authority for Statistics. *Population Characteristics Surveys*. 2017. Available from: https://www.stats.gov.sa/.
2. Al-Khaldi YM, Al-Ghamdi EA, Al-Mogbil TI, Al-Khashan HI. Family medicine practice in Saudi Arabia: The current situation and proposed strategic directions plan 2020. *Journal of Family and Community Medicine*. 2017;24(3): 156–163. doi:10.4103/jfcm.JFCM_41_17.

3. Primary Healthcare Center Accreditation Program. https://portal.cbahi.gov.sa/english/accreditation-programs/primary-healthcare-center-accreditation-program.

4. Ministry of Education. Moe.gov.sa. 2018 Available from: https://www.moe.gov.sa/ (accessed 26 March 2018).

5. Mohamed EY, Sami W, Alotaibi A, Alfarag A, Almutairi A, Alanzi F. Patients' Satisfaction with Primary Health Care Centers' Services, Majmaah, Kingdom of Saudi Arabia. *International Journal of Health Sciences*. 2015;9(2): 163–170.

6. Birrer RB, Al-Enazy H, Sarru E. Family medicine in Saudi Arabia: Next steps. *Journal of Community Medicine and Health Education*. 2014;S2. doi:10.4172/2161-0711.S2-005.

7. https://portal.cbahi.gov.sa/english/accreditation-programs/primary-healthcare-center-accreditation-program.

8. Alsakkak MA, Alwahabi SA, Alsalhi HM, Shugdar MA. Outcome of the first Saudi Central Board for Accreditation of Healthcare Institutions (CBAHI) primary health care accreditation cycle in Saudi Arabia. *Saudi Medical Journal*. 2017;38(11): 1132–1136. Available from: doi:10.15537/smj.2017.11.20760.

9. Ministry of Health, Vision Realization Office. *Corporatization Guide*. Nov 2017.

10. Ministry of Health. *Statistical Year Book 2016*. Available from: https://www.moh.gov.sa/en/Ministry/Statistics/book/Pages/default.aspx.

11. Family Medicine Academy Agreement in the Kingdom. Makkah AlMukarramah. 2018 [cited 28 January 2018]. Available from: http://makkahnewspaper.com/article/684655/البلد/اتفاقية-إنشاء-أكاديمية-طب-الأسرة-بالمملكة.

CHAPTER 29

Somalia

*Mona Ahmed Almudhwahi and
Abdihamid Ibrahim*

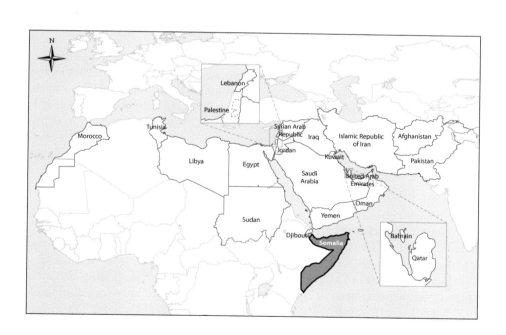

Total number of PHC facilities	457
Number of general practitioners working in public PHC facilities	1065 in hospitals only. No doctors working in PHC facilities
Number of certified family physicians working in PHC facilities	Data is not available
Average number of family physician graduates/year	0
Number of medical schools	6*
Number of family medicine departments	1 (Borama University)

* These are the recognized medical schools only.

INTRODUCTION

The Somali population has transitioned from decades of complex emergencies and civil unrest that inflicted significant damage to the health system, with substantive destruction of the services delivery network infrastructure. The country has experienced a prolonged conflict spanning over two decades since December 1990, with more than 40% of the population living on less than US$1 per day and 73% on less than US$2 per day.[1]

The country's health service delivery is provided through a two-pronged approach. The first is through the Somali Humanitarian Fund (SHF) formerly known as Common Humanitarian Fund (CHF) or the Humanitarian Response Plan, aimed to deliver relief operations. The 2018 humanitarian response plan targets a population of 4.3 million people including 2.1 million internally displaced persons (IDPs) for primary health-care services. Part of these interventions are also designed to deal with future crises, reduce vulnerability and lead to robust resilience-building activities, while disaster risk reduction and management will shape the longer-term perspective action agenda.[2]

The second approach is through a recently developed, piloted, and adopted package called the Essential Package of Health Services (EPHS). The framework was launched in 2014 by the Federal Government of Somalia and is aimed at improving equitable access to acceptable, affordable, and quality health services. This developmental health process envisages the scaling up of government leadership, management, and service delivery capacity, while sustaining health partners' support, thus averting the transitional funding gap, often encountered during the post-conflict period, when the health system is transiting to recovery, institutional building and development.

THE ESSENTIAL PACKAGE OF HEALTH SERVICES (EPHS)

The EPHS helps define health system standards for the government, United Nations (UN) and non-governmental organizations (NGOs), agencies, and private service providers. It's a prime mechanism for strategic service provision of the public sector health service. It constitutes a fundamental outline and framework for the organization of the Somali health-care delivery system. It is founded on a standardized package of health services, comprising six core and four additional programmes that need to be delivered in the four health-care provision levels.

The health workers, the essential drugs and technologies necessary for implementing the EPHS programmatic interventions were also standardized. Although the long-term vision of EPHS is to provide universal health care (UHC) to the entire population, its current performance capacity is limited to a number of regions in each zone. The accelerated control of vaccine-preventable diseases; the control of major communicable diseases focused on the fight against acquired immune deficiency syndrome (AIDS), tuberculosis (TB), and malaria; and the primary prevention and management of non-communicable diseases, particularly mental health disorders, are integral components of the EPHS programme.

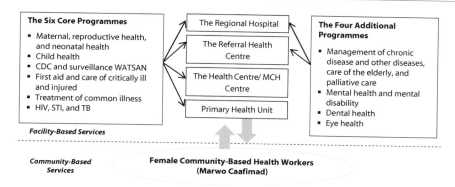

FIGURE 29.1 EPHS programmes.

The provision of effective service delivery is facing many challenges such as inadequate access and underutilization of available services. Contributing factors include poor regional and district leadership skills and managerial capacities; insufficient capacities and resources for supervision, monitoring, and evaluation; fragmented multi-stakeholder service delivery with weak mechanisms for coordination; and the lack of linkages between the private health sector performance and the public sector EPHS. Moreover, the local communities are not sufficiently empowered to make healthy decisions and actively participate in improving their health status, while cultural and economic factors also contribute to decreased utilization of available health services.[3] Figure 29.1 illustrates the ten EPHS programmes implemented at the four health-care provision levels and the recently introduced community-based level of care.

THE EPHS COMPOSITION

The EPHS consists of the following:

1. Four levels of service provision:
    The essential package is implemented across four levels of service provision, each with a standardized service profile and each supported by a standardized set of management and support components:
    - Primary health unit (PHU)
    - Health centre (HC)
    - Referral health centre (RHC)
    - Hospital

2. Ten health programmes:
    There are six core programmes which are found at all four levels and four additional programmes that are found only at the referral levels. The six core programmes are:
    - Maternal, reproductive, and neonatal health
    - Child health
    - Communicable disease surveillance and control, including WATSAN promotion
    - First aid and care of critically ill and injured
    - Treatment of common illness
    - HIV, STIs, and TB

3. The four additional programmes are:
    - Management of chronic disease and other diseases, care of the elderly, and palliative care

- Mental health and mental disability
- Dental health
- Eye health

4. Six management components which include:
   - Finance
   - Human resource management and development
   - EPHS coordination, development, and supervision
   - Community participation
   - Health systems support components
   - Health management information system

EPHS CURRENT SITUATION AND IMPLEMENTATION

Health service delivery is structured around the framework of the EPHS, developed in 2009.[4] However, it is not being implemented uniformly across the country and covers only nine of the 18 regions, due to factors such as limited resources and security challenges. In the remaining nine regions, health service delivery is inconsistent and dependent on the presence of humanitarian organizations. In 2015, the maternal mortality ratio was estimated at 732 per 100,000 live births, an improvement since 1990, when the figure was 1210 per 100,000 live births, but still poor compared to Kenya (510) or Ethiopia (353) in 2015. The under-five mortality rate was 137 per 1000 live births in 2015, compared to Kenya (49) and Ethiopia (59).[5]

At 42%, Somalia has one of the lowest diphtheria-tetanus-pertussis (DTP3) coverage rates in the world.[6] In terms of joint reporting framework data, Penta I coverage was estimated at 50%, Penta III at 46%, and measles at 43%.[7] The burden of disease is dominated by communicable diseases, reproductive health challenges, and under-nutrition, although non-communicable diseases (NCDs) and mental disorders are also on the rise. Routine immunization coverage remains very low. Malaria and TB are highly prevalent, with malaria endemic in some parts of the country.[8]

Community outreach

The human immunodeficiency virus (HIV) epidemic is growing at a rate of about 1%, with higher prevalence among high-risk groups. Diarrheal diseases account for the majority of deaths among children, along with respiratory infections. The epidemiological profile is characterized by high maternal, neonatal, and child mortalities, prevalent communicable diseases, high rates of under-nutrition, and a range of other public health problems, while the non-communicable diseases are gaining momentum, although not captured by the current health information system. Figure 29.2 presents a distribution of health facility visits due to specific diseases.

Table 29.1 provides a summary account of the health management information system (HMIS) data collection and analysis. The health system is also faced with a high burden of TB and malaria, with imminent risk of an explosive HIV/AIDS epidemic.

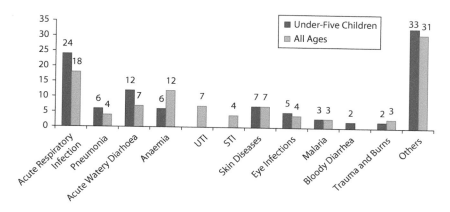

FIGURE 29.2 Distribution of health facility visits due to specific diseases in the National Health Management Information System, 2011 report.

TABLE 29.1   Indicators reflecting the poor coverage of reproductive health services

Indicators	North West	North East	Central South	Source
Total fertility rate (TFR)	5.9	6.2	7.1	MICS (2006) and WHOSIS (2008)
Modern contraceptive prevalence rate (%)	4.6	0.1	0.3	MICS (2006)
Maternal mortality ratio	1044–1400	1044–1400	1044–1400	MICS (2006), MDGs' reports
Antenatal care (ANC) coverage				
ANC: at least one visit (%)	32	26	24	HMIS report: UNICEF (2011)
ANC: at least four visits (%)	10.3	5.8	5.2	
Births in a health facility (%)	21	8	6	HMIS report: UNICEF (2011)
Births attended by skilled health personnel (%)	21	7	6	HMIS report: UNICEF (2011)
Basic emergency obstetric care (BemOC) facilities per 500,000 population	1.1	0.1	1.3	MICS (2006)
Comprehensive emergency obstetric care (CemOC) facilities per 500,000 population	1.7	2.2	1.7	HMIS report: UNICEF (2011)
Low birth weight prevalence	6	11	21	UNICEF (2008)
Reported prevalence of FGM	94	98	99	MICS (2006)
Under-five mortality rate per 1000 live births	116	135	200	MICS (2006) & (2011): MDG zonal reports
Infant mortality rate per 1000 live births	73	86	119	MICS (2006) & (2011): MDG zonal reports
Moderate malnutrition rate	10	15	28	MDG reports

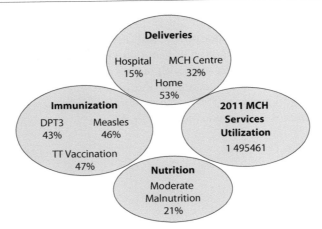

FIGURE 29.3 Health service utilization and paucity of service delivery. (*Source*: 2011 National Health Management Information System, Updated Report, 2012.)

Figure 29.3 indicates limited access and utilization of essential reproductive health services, low vaccination coverage against vaccine-preventable diseases, and high rates of undernutrition. This corroborates the gravity of the above indicated underprivileged outcomes of the health system.

EPHS IMPLEMENTATION CHALLENGES

- **Financing of EPHS**: The country's health sector programmes are donor dependent and the government's contribution is less than 2%. A joint health and nutrition programme, a multi-donor pool funded, multi-year project which was financing the roll out of EPHS in nine regions across the country came to an end last year and over 50/90 districts are facing disruption of basic health-care services.[9]
- **Human resources for health**: The health workforce is the backbone of the health system and often constitutes the most significant element in the provision of essential and lifesaving health services to the population. During the first decade of the civil conflict, almost all public sector higher medical education and mid-level training institutions were destroyed, creating a colossal and acute shortage of qualified health workforce.
- **Insecurity and access issues**: Anti-government elements control some regions in the south and central states of Somalia. This limited the ability of health sector partners and authorities to scale up health services and ensure equitable health service distribution.
- **Institutional and governance capacities**: Prolonged conflict has led to total health system collapse and poor institutional capacity to oversee, manage and provide leadership for the country's health sector programmes. NGOs, both international and national, with financial support from UN/donors provide delivery of basic health services in the country.
- **Regulatory framework for the health sector**: Weak regulatory frameworks and limited capacity of law enforcement contributed to the poor quality of health services. Counterfeit drugs imported from abroad are sold freely in the markets. Health-care institutions and professionals are not fully licensed and accredited.

RECOMMENDATIONS FOR EPHS IMPLEMENTATION[10,11]

- **Predictable and sustainable financing for the EPHS**: The government needs to increase budgetary allocation for EPHS implementation. Financing for continued roll out of EPHS and scaling it up to uncovered areas is a major challenge for the country's health authorities. The current external financing is not only insufficient, but also not sustainable; thus the government needs to provide budgetary allocation to ensure basic health services are delivered to its citizens across all regions of Somalia.

- **Enhanced production of qualified and competent mid-level health workforce**: The availability of qualified, competent staff with the right skill mix is at the heart of a revived Somalia health sector. Because of the limited number of public universities, the government needs to partner with private medical institutions and enhance production of the health workforce through developed and agreed regulatory and partnership frameworks.
- **Strengthened institutional capacity for health authorities at all levels to support government ownership and leadership**: International development partners supporting the country's sector need to invest in building national capacities at federal, state, and regional levels to ensure government ownership, leadership, and sustainability of health sector programmes. Particularly, recently formed states in the south and central parts of the country need to be supported to ensure decentralized health systems governance and services delivery.
- **Scale up and ensuring of equitable access to basic health services and moving towards UHC**: For the country to move towards achievement of UHC and to ensure equity of basic health service delivery, EPHS need to be scaled up to nomadic and rural districts of the country.
- **Continuing re-building and improving regulatory framework to improve quality of health-care services and infrastructure**: Since public institutions and universities are weak or non-existent due to prolonged conflict and social unrest, the country needs to work closely with the private sector so that basic services are delivered to its citizens. A holistic public–private partnership approach with a well-defined regulatory framework is required to be put in place for achievement of UHC in Somalia.

THE SOMALI PRIVATE HEALTH SECTOR

The Somali private health sector is a fast-growing sector that is dominating health service provision. The private sector is not well regulated and there is no reliable data about the size, distribution, quality, and type of services provided. However, the Somali health authorities recognize the private sector, whether the health-care delivery part or the teaching institutions, as major stakeholders that are strongly supporting the health sector and contributing to the expansion of services and an increase in the health workforce.

DEFINITION OF THE PRIVATE HEALTH SECTOR

When it comes to defining the private sector, there is no clear definition to date. However, DFID produced a report[12] defining the private sector based on the results of discussions with local private sector health-care service providers, other health-care actors and the government in Hargeisa. This definition was subsequently validated in Hargeisa, Garowe, Mogadishu, and Nairobi. DFID found that there are two forms of private health providers: informal (traditional) and formal (which is, however, only loosely regulated and controlled). The private sector does have a profit-seeking motivation but may also have social objectives. "Public" relates to government ownership and control. The more of this there is, the closer to a public sector service it becomes. The private sector does not include NGOs, which are classified as charitable organizations that sit between the public and private (stakeholder definition).[13]

TYPES OF SERVICE PROVIDERS

The private sector consists of several facilities that provide health services, which include:

- **Pharmacies**: The total number of pharmacies in Somalia is not known but they are widely spread all over the country and most of them are just drug sellers.[14] They still lack quality control and regulations. It is estimated that the private sector provides around 60%–80% of the country's medicines through importation and distribution via private retail outlets and pharmacies.[8] There is no domestic production of pharmaceutical products or medical supplies and equipment.
- **Health facilities (mainly hospitals and clinics)**: Private hospitals are rapidly increasing in major cities. Clinics on the other hand are small facilities in which there are out-patients; they are found in the main cities, and mostly run by doctors. They lack other qualified personnel and are not suitable for hosting in-patients.

UTILIZATION OF THE PRIVATE SECTOR

Evidence shows that the majority of patients seek help from the private sector which indicates poor access to public health facilities, particularly for rural and nomadic populations. The study done by the United Nations International Children's Emergency Fund (UNICEF) in Somalia found that the private sector is the dominant choice for those seeking health care for children, especially pharmacies.[15] There is no information regarding privacy, respect, and patient safety in the private sector.

Dual practice is common across the country and the private sector offers additional job opportunities for public sector health workers, especially for physicians, most of whom engage in private practice during office hours, resulting in a high level of absenteeism in their official posts.

ROLE OF THE PRIVATE SECTOR IN TRAINING AND EDUCATION[16]

There is a notable rise in the number of private medical colleges and health professional training institutions and programmes. However, despite these programmes, several serious challenges were encountered which can be summarized as follows:[17]

- Lack of regulation
- Lack of focus on mid-level professionals
- Shortage of faculty development opportunities
- Disparity between production and demand

In total, it is estimated that around 3647 health workers graduate annually from these private institutes. This includes doctors, nurses, midwives, and pharmacists among others. The World Health Organization (WHO) involves health workers from the private sector in a number of training activities. Some examples include:

- Training pharmacists on the WHO Somalia Standard Treatment Guidelines and Training Manual on Rational Management and Use of Medicines at the Primary Health-Care Level[18]
- Malaria Control Programme, which trained a total of 120 health-care providers in the private sector on case management and microscopy in 2017

The training of the staff working in private and public facilities is based on the WHO recommended training modules and is usually conducted by national trainers supported by WHO. This model is being strengthened so as to enable the programme to reach the patients who may have no access to National TB Programme (NTP) facilities. Another new strategy that the programme is engaging in this year is to integrate the TB programme into the primary health programme.

QUALITY CONTROL OF THE PRIVATE HEALTH SECTOR

The absence of quality control mechanisms undoubtedly allows for negative practices that lead to the sale of sub-standard products such as expired medicines. There have been some efforts to establish national health medical councils (NHMC). So far only Somaliland has managed to establish the National Health Professions Commission while others are still under development.

PUBLIC–PRIVATE PARTNERSHIP

The TB programme has been engaging the private sector and other public health sector institutions such as prisons since 2011 as part of its programme on public–private mix (PPM). This is a strategy developed by WHO as a means of involving the public and private sector in TB management. These sectors are usually involved in either:

- Identification of presumptive TB cases and referring them to TB centres for confirmation and treatment
- Diagnosis of patients and referring them to TB centres for treatment
- Diagnosis and treatment of TB cases in which case the private or public clinic becomes a TB centre whereby in addition to treatment of cases, it also has a TB treatment and laboratory register
- Treating TB patients who have started treatment in a TB centre, usually during the continuation phase of the treatment

Since the start of the collaboration between the TB programme and private centres in 2011 up to 2016, these institutions have been identifying presumptive TB cases and referring them to the TB centres in all the three zones of Somalia. However, in 2017, one private clinic in Mogadishu, called Guled Clinic, has earned the designation of being a TB centre. This centre diagnoses patients and treats them in the clinic which means they have the lab and TB treatment registers. Every quarter they report their cases to the national TB programme manager. In 2017 alone, the clinic diagnosed and treated 368 TB cases. Similarly, one public institution, Mogadishu Central Prison, has also been designated a TB centre and in 2017, it diagnosed and treated 20 TB patients.

Usually, before engaging any private or public health institution in the TB programme, the programme identifies the institution concerned and discusses the role it can play. Once this is done, a plan for capacity building is made, based on the roles assigned to the institution, and then WHO trains the staff. For those facilities that only identify presumptive cases or diagnose and refer the cases, they are provided with presumptive TB case registers to report their cases to the NTP; while those facilities that engage in treatment are provided with a lab, TB treatment registers and TB medicines.

CHALLENGES

Summarizing the above description of the Somali private sector, concrete challenges prevail as follows:

- Lack of data and information
- Limited information about the quality of health-care services provided
- Weak regulatory framework and lack of clear policies
- Difficulty in involving private health-care workers in training because employers object to their absence for full working days

CONCLUSION AND RECOMMENDATIONS[19]

- There is a need to further understand the current role of the private sector in health service delivery, its costs, and its relationship to EPHS service resources and delivery.
- There is a need for mapping and developing a database of the private sector facilities.
- Studies on consumer satisfaction need to be conducted.
- There is a need for improved regulation and enforcement.
- There is a need to strengthen the private sector including its partnership with the public sector.

REFERENCES

1. WHO. *Health System Profile Somalia 2006.* Available from: http://apps.who.int/medicinedocs/documents/s17309e/s17309e.pdf.
2. Ministry of Health and Human Services, Federal Government of Somalia. *Prioritization of Health Policy Actions in the Somali Health Sector.* September 2014.
3. *Somalia Health Sector Strategic Plan 2016–2020.*
4. Pearson N, Muschell J. *Essential Package of Health Services Somaliland 2009.* UNICEF. Available from: https://www.unicef.org/somalia/SOM_EssentialSomalilandReport_3_WEB.pdf.
5. United Nations. Levels and Trends in Child Mortality. 2015. Available from: https://www.unicef.org/publications/files/Child_Mortality_Report_2015_Web_9_Sept_15.pdf.
6. Global Alliance for Vaccines and Immunization- health system strengthening support for Somalis, 2016.
7. The Somali Human Resources for Health Development Policy, 2009.
8. Somalia National Health Management Information System. 2015.
9. Modol X. *Somalia Health Public Expenditure Review: An Unfinished Exercise.* January 2015.

10. WHO. *Strategic review of the Somali Health Sector: Challenges and Prioritized Actions. Report of the WHO mission to Somalia.* September 2015.

11. MOH HMIS 2012/13/14.

12. World Bank report 2011.

13. *Health sector strategic plan 2012–2016.*

14. WHO Somalia emergency response plan, 2017.

15. UNICEF: *Health care seeking behaviour in Somalia: a literature review.* Available from: https://www.unicef.org/somalia/SOM_HealthcareseekingbehaviourReport_10-WEB.pdf.

16. HEART (Health & Education Advice & Resource Team), DFID, UK.

17. *The Somali Human Resources for Health Development Policy 2016–2021.*

18. WHO. *Somalia Standard Treatment Guidelines and Training Manual on Rational Management and Use of Medicines at the Primary Health Care.* 2007. Available from: http://www.who.int/selection_medicines/country_lists/som_stg_2007.pdf.

19. Buckley J, O'Neill E, Aden AM. *Assignment Report: Assessment of the private health sector in Somaliland, Puntland and South Central.* Health and Education Advice and Resource Team (HEART): Oxford, UK (2015).

CHAPTER 30

Sudan

Abdalla Sid Ahmed Osman, Eiman Hag,
Hind Amin Merghani, and Naeema Al Gasseer

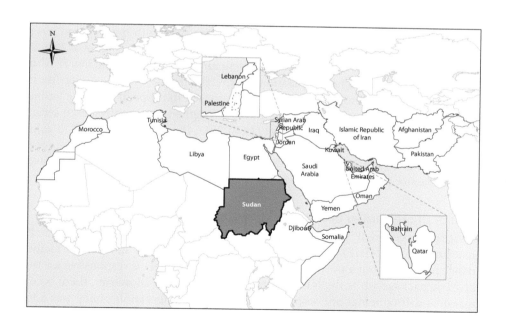

Total number of PHC facilities	6220
Number of general practitioners working in public PHC facilities	NA
Number of certified family physicians working in PHC facilities	46
Average number of family physician graduates/year	40 MD, 300 MSc
Number of medical schools	37
Number of family medicine departments	5

PRIMARY HEALTH CARE

The current status of primary health care in the country

Primary health care (PHC) is high on the agenda of the ongoing health system reform. The health system in Sudan is decentralized with three levels of governance: federal, state, and locality. The interim Constitution of Sudan ensures the promotion of public health and guarantees equal access and free primary health care to all its citizens. Primary care services are provided through Family Health Centres (FHCs) and Family Health Units (FHUs), in addition to the first referral level – the rural hospitals. The government of Sudan is highly committed to achieving universal health coverage (UHC) by the year 2020.[1] The National Health Policy (NHP 2012–2016) set out three key strategic directions: strengthening PHC services, improving and strengthening referral systems, and enhancing social protection and reducing reliance on out-of-pocket spending. The government commitment to achieving UHC is also evident in the implementation of three projects: the National Project for Expansion of PHC services, the National Project for Human Resources for Health Redistribution and Retention, and the National Project for the Expansion of Specialized Health Care Services to states.[1]

Currently, PHC coverage is reported to be 95%. However, the health map showed less progress in the coverage of functioning FHCs and FHUs; by mid-2017 the coverage was 88% and 77% respectively. With increased government commitment and sustainable financing, PHC coverage is expanding to reach the unreached population groups. The free care for the under-five initiative increases opportunities to improve the utilization of services. Its scope of coverage has now been expanded to include some chronic conditions and to strengthen community-based services.

According to the Joint Assessment Report (JAR) 2017, three states reported to achieve full functionality of FHUs namely: Gadarif, Sinnar, and River Nile; while two states reported less than 50% functional FHCs namely: Red Sea and South Kordofan; and another two states, namely: North Darfur and Central Darfur have less than 50% of functional FHCs.[2]

Integration of the essential health services package

Health service packages are fragmented and not unified across providers including the National Health Insurance Fund (NHIF), the Ministry of Health (MoH), and state health facilities. The health finance policy sets out a provider/purchaser split.[3] The MoH is responsible for the provision of the basic package while the NHIF is the purchasing body. Moreover, there is continued verticalization and fragmentation, despite the fact that the integration policy was adopted as part of the 2012-2016 strategy. The vertical programmes continue to implement their interventions with a silo mentality.[1]

Infrastructure

Primary health-care infrastructure has received great attention from the MoH in recent years. An expansion project started in 2012 and focuses mainly on infrastructure and Human Resources for Health (HRH) training; a large share of the project budget is devoted to it. The

TABLE 30.1 PHC expansion project targets and achievements (infrastructure)

Activity	Project target	Achievements till September 2017	Achievements (%)
Build FH Centres	355	174 built 181 under construction	100
Build FH Units	763	441 built 196 tender opened	83

Source: PHC Expansion Project, Annual Report 2017.

project target was to build 763 FHUs and 355 FHCs in addition to the provision of the required equipment and medicines (Table 30.1).[4] In 2015, a midterm evaluation of the expansion project was conducted and found that targets of construction of health facilities were well identified and building standards were also well developed. In addition, an implementation plan of construction activities was clearly explained; a standard list of equipment for each health facility was also developed; and targets were identified for each facility level. Moreover, procurement arrangements and handover Standard Operating Procedures (SOPs) were well described. However, an equipment management system was not mentioned (PHI, 2015).[6]

Essential health service package

The content of the essential health service package (EHSP) provided at PHC level which is based on the burden of diseases includes the promotion of child health (immunization against vaccine-preventable diseases, nutrition counselling, and growth-monitoring, and implementation of the Integrated Management of Childhood Illness package); the promotion of school health; the promotion of reproductive health (safe motherhood, including safe pregnancy and family planning); the control of endemic diseases (malaria, tuberculosis, HIV/AIDS, schistosomiasis, etc.); the protection and promotion of environmental health and sanitation; and the treatment of simple diseases and injuries and mental health. The EHSP is available in 46% of PHC facilities at national level.[5]

PHC physician with a patient

The finance policy ensures that the NHIF provides the EHSP and the comprehensive package for all the insured population in addition to the poor.[3] The essential package as mentioned above includes PHC services, maternal health services, and emergency services, while the

TABLE 30.2 PHC coverage indicators

Indicator	Strategic target (2016)	Achievement
% population covered by functioning health service delivery points providing services according to the standards	All states meet the minimum national target of PHC facility ratio 1:5500 pop.	92
% of PHC facilities providing all five elements of the integrated PHC package (by state)	90	77
Annual number of out-patient department visits, per capita/10,000 population	NA	2991
% of PHC facilities providing the essential package for NCDs	25	No data available

Source: Joint Assessment Report, 2017.

comprehensive package includes the current package of service purchased by NHIF. The number of health facilities providing complete PHC minimum package increased from 24% to 62% between 2011 and 2016. This improvement in access to services is attributable to the implementation of the PHC services expansion project which was adopted in 2012.[2] Table 30.2 presents PHC coverage indicators.

Essential drug list (EDL)

One of the PHC expansion project objectives is to provide free medicines at the PHC level especially for women and children under five, in addition to treatment for malaria, tuberculosis (TB) and human immunodeficiency virus (HIV). About 85% of the malaria drugs, 92% of TB drugs, and 97% of HIV/acquired immunodeficiency syndrome (AIDS) drugs are covered by the Global Fund. The target of the expansion project is to increase the supply chain to cover 5986 health facilities. The achievement till November 2017 is 88% of the target. It is also reported that only 69% of mother and child health (MCH) and 77% of pregnancy essential medicines are provided to PHC facilities. In addition, 82% of the under-five drugs are available at PHC level. The expansion evaluation in 2015 found that only 50% of EDL is available in PHC facilities. Distribution of medicines and equipment was recentralized as a mechanism.[5] A recent study showed that the availability of essential medicines at public and private health facilities reached 73% and 90%, respectively.[1] The monitoring system for availability and quality of medicines at health facilities is ineffective.

Staff pattern

The target of the national PHC expansion project is to train 1000 family physicians, integrated in-service training of 2665 medical assistants and 3654 vaccinators and nutritional assistants by the year 2020. Due to the human resources deficiency especially in rural and remote areas, innovative approaches such as task-shifting strategies were developed and adopted, in addition to increasing skill mix production focusing on PHC with more emphasis on family health physicians, community health workers, social workers, and other related disciplines.[5]

STANDARD SET OF MEDICAL EQUIPMENT AND FURNITURE

The regulation of the pharmaceutical sector has been established at different levels (federal and state) with a well-developed drug registration system; however, there are challenges facing all aspects of its management especially at sub-national level. A supreme council for the coordination of pharmaceutical services was formulated and the governance framework was developed to improve regulation, coordination, and transparency in the sector.[1]

The procurement of medical devices in the public sector takes place through the National Medical Supply Fund (NMSF). Management of health technologies is poor, resulting in more than 50% of health facilities having less than the minimally required equipment with lack of maintenance systems. There is no health technology assessment system in place (Table 30.3).

Training programmes

The PHC expansion project trains a large number of human resources for health. There are two types of training programmes for FHC staff; general training for all staff and specific training for each staff category. The project target is to train 13,902 community midwives, 5110 medical assistants, 6574 community health workers (including 1414 nomadic health workers); and integrated in-service training for 2665 medical assistants and 3654 vaccinators and nutritional assistants.[5] Table 30.4 shows trained staff since the project started till November 2017.

Treatment protocols

Several treatment protocols and guidelines are developed by the MoH. However, they are neither unified nor implemented at different levels. Furthermore, there is no supervision, monitoring or evaluation of the adherence of the care providers to the protocols. Accreditation of PHC is one way to strengthen adherence to national protocols and guidelines.[5]

TABLE 30.3 Performance of medicine and technology indicators

Indicator	Target by 2016 (%)	Achievement (%)
Availability of affordable basic technologies and essential medicines, including generics, required to treat major NCDs in both public and private facilities	NA	77
% public health facilities equipped with the appropriate drugs and technology services (TS) for the level	92 for drugs 50 for TS	66.3 for drugs No data for TS
% of health facilities that have stock of essential medicines during the past three months (by state, level of facility)	80	NA
Availability of free malaria medicines	80	71.1
Availability of free TB medicines	80	83.4
Availability of free HIV medicines	80	86.7
Availability of free medicines for children under 5 years	80	68.5
Availability of free pregnancy-related medicines	80	13.8

Source: Joint Assessment Report, 2017.

TABLE 30.4 PHC expansion project targets and achievements (human resources for health)

Activity	Project target	Achievements till September 2017	Achievements (%)
Basic training for midwives	13,522	12,571	93
Basic training for community health workers	5160	4222	82
In-service training for medical assistants	5110	2144	42

Source: PHC Expansion Project, Annual Report 2017.

The referral system

One of the priority areas of the National Health Strategic Plan service delivery was strengthening efficient ambulatory systems and emergency medical care through the development and implementation of referral systems and guidelines as well as strengthening emergency care and triage systems. There have been a number of efforts undertaken to strengthen the referral system. Of the 600 ambulances needed throughout the country, there are now about 110 functioning. For instance, Gedaref State reported that there is no ambulance to transfer patients for tertiary care to Khartoum. In North Kordofan, however, a central management for ambulances based in the general state hospital at Obeid was established.[5]

El Margei Family Health Centre

Information system

Reform in health information is underway to promote more integration and to improve reporting and quality of information at different levels of the health system including the PHC level. However, health information is primarily based on health facility reporting supplemented by surveys. Moreover, data quality assurance is limited and systems for data management and analysis are largely manual.[1] The system focuses on the public sector, while data from the private sector is rarely gathered or included. The main challenges in the health-care information system (HIS) include fragmentation, low reporting rates especially at PHC facilities (reporting rate is 85% from hospitals and 30% from PHC facilities). In order to address challenges of fragmentation and verticality, Sudan adopted the District Health Information System (DHIS) software to digitalize the integrated information system with the aim of reducing fragmentation, enhancing data quality, and strengthening decentralization.[1]

Quality and accreditation programme

Another priority area in the previous National Health Strategic Plan is strengthening the quality, safety, and efficiency of health services in the country. An accreditation council was established to govern the quality at federal levels. It is planned that the accreditation of PHC facilities will come second to the secondary hospitals. A manual for the standards in infrastructure, equipment, and human resources at the PHC level was developed and endorsed in 2017.[1]

Meeting PHC standards as stipulated in the guideline remains an issue, which affects the quality of care provided by the public health facilities. This is further compromised by a deficient referral system. The service providers in NHIF facilities are not assuring the quality.[2]

Patient satisfaction with quality of service delivery

Patient satisfaction is an area that is not well addressed as studies focus more on the satisfaction of care providers rather than patients. However, community involvement was implemented during the process of updating the National Health Policy (NHP) by conducting large-scale community consultation meetings at different levels and among different groups of the population. The purpose was to have a better understanding of the needs and perceptions of the community around health issues and services and to incorporate them in the new NHP. Consultations were conducted with women, youth, HIV and TB patients, and communities from poor and rich neighbourhoods.

Key challenges to ensuring quality service delivery in public primary care facilities

Although one of the three main objectives targeted by the PHC expansion project is to ensure quality and sustainability of PHC services, there is no well-functioning quality assurance system in place; there is a lack of clinical protocols, guidelines, quality standards, and indicators. On the other hand, some strategies and activities were put in place to improve the quality of PHC services such as standards for building and rehabilitating the infrastructure and equipment of health facilities, as well as the recruitment and training of family physicians and the family health team.[5]

FAMILY PRACTICE

The implementation of the family health approach started in five states with the deployment of 40 family physicians holding an MD and 300 family physicians with master's degrees. There is an effort to develop one package for the community health training programmes. There is also innovative financing for service delivery in some states through the private sector.[6]

Political commitments to family practice

Political commitment at the national level to family practice has increased during recent years. The higher authority in Sudan is the National Health Coordination Council (NHCC) chaired by the president of Sudan. This council is committed to universal health coverage (UHC) and endorses the family health policy. The MoH is working towards UHC and implementing the family health approach through PHC expansion and training of doctors in family medicine in addition to other health staff. At the level of states, the commitment is also noticeable as they nominate their trainees for family medicine and they manage the training and PHC facilities.[4,6]

The family health policy has three main objectives: to strengthen the PHC service delivery system in order to enable the provision of efficient and equitable quality health services, which are responsive to the population's expectations; to improve the recognition of the specialty of family medicine (FM), and increase the attraction, recruitment and retention of family physicians; and to ensure the production of competent family physicians and allied health workers to provide integrated, people-centred health services at PHC level.[7]

How family practice links with national public health initiatives

Strengthening PHC through the family health approach is integrated into the National Health Policy. It focuses on family practice by providing family health services and ensuring availability and accessibility to the whole population across the country. The family health policy focuses on family health services as the entry point to the health system for citizens. The policy suggests that this can be implemented in a gradual manner before adopting the gatekeeping policy.

Together, the implementation of the family health approach and the PHC expansion programme are seen as tools to speed up the movement towards UHC. The other initiative that incorporates family health is the Health Finance Policy. This can be clear from the vision of the policy which states that "all Sudanese are covered by prepayment arrangements for an essential health-care package and are financially protected".[1]

The contribution of family practice to UHC

The vision of the family health policy is "a nation of healthy individuals, families and communities where UHC is achieved for all". This policy was developed with the primary intention to strengthen PHC, which is high on the political and national health agenda. According to the policy, family health is seen as a people-centred holistic health-care approach with the aim of improving the health of the population and thereby achieving UHC.[7]

Family practice teams

The aim of the family health approach is to strengthen the PHC system by setting up family health teams with a holistic patient-centred approach at PHC centres. Three categories of health providers will practice the family health approach; family physicians, medical assistants, and community health workers according to the availability depending on the geographic area.

Family practice rural outreach

The policy recommends that the population living in urban areas be offered services by family physicians; those in rural areas are to be served by family physicians, medical assistants (MAs), and community health workers (CHWs); and those living in remote rural areas are to be offered services by MAs where available or CHWs (in areas lacking health facilities) who are supervised and report directly to family physicians (Figure 30.1).

Family practice financing

The priority of the NHIF in the coming years is to enrol all the poor through governmental subsidies. The government increased coverage of the poor from 500,000 to 750,000 to 1 million families during the last three years. Moreover, as an implementation strengthening mechanism, the purchasing guidelines were developed. Additionally, the PHC expansion project is high on the government agenda and is funded by the Ministry of Finance. The PHC directorates, which receive the funds to facilitate the implementation of the PHC expansion, finance family health practice teams including the family medicine training programme in nine states

FIGURE 30.1 Different categories of health-care providers.

in Sudan in addition to the in-service training of MAs and CHWs.[1] They also finance the PHC facilities' infrastructure. However, the service package has not been included in the fund neither has it been costed yet. The health finance policy recommends the service package be funded through the NHIF pooled funds. Despite the finance policy being in place, there are still some challenges to be addressed such as provider payment mechanisms and efficiency of purchasing. No interventions to improve provider payment and efficiency of purchasing have been considered.[1]

Family practice research

A number of studies were conducted in the area of family medicine and practice. A comprehensive situational analysis was conducted in 2014 as an assessment, prior to the family health policy development. It targeted family medicine trainees and physicians in two states (these are the only two states that have institutions offering a family medicine programme). In addition, policy makers' interviews were conducted using a tool adapted from the WHO for assessment of service provision of family practice. Midterm evaluation of the expansion project was also conducted in 2015. Prior to the policy implementation a baseline assessment for PHC readiness to implement a family health approach was conducted in 2017.

Key challenges in implementing family practice in the country

Family health policy implementation started in 2017 under the leadership of the UHC Committee and the Operational Committee (OC). The OC, joint between the PHI and PHC Directorates, is responsible for closely monitoring the implementation of the family health operational plan and reports to the UHC Committee. With regard to family medicine training, the specialty is still considered in its infancy and it requires a great deal of effort and attention to grow and flourish. One of the biggest challenges is the fact that the majority of university graduates migrate to the Gulf and elsewhere leaving an exceptionally small number of physicians in the country to lead this profession.[1] The PHC expansion project started in 2012 as part of the government commitment to achieve UHC. It is considered as a big milestone and a success story for Sudan efforts to achieve UHC. The project goals were to focus on expanding the PHC services to rural and remote areas to reduce inequalities between states and localities in addition to improving current services at all levels. The project has six components including:

- UHC project (started in October 2012)
- Free PHC services project (started in July 2013)
- Rural hospitals development project (started in January 2014)
- Specialists transfer to states project (started in January 2014)
- Sub-specialties transfer to states project (started in January 2014)
- Referral system expansion project (started in April 2015)

The project objectives were to:

- Increase the population coverage by PHC services from 86% to 100%
- Increase the service package delivered at PHC units from 24% to 100%
- Improve the quality of PHC services and ensure sustainability
- Insurance coverage or financial protection especially to cover all the poor population

The PHC expansion project was evaluated in 2015 as a midterm evaluation and found to be on the right track to achieve its objectives by the end of the project.

Another successful story in the family health model is the Shambat Centre. The centre implemented a model of family health in Khartoum State that provides integrated service in the field of family health practice through the provision of diagnostics and treatment, raising the level of health awareness, building partnerships with relevant bodies and training students and cadres with a commitment to the values of ensuring high-quality, continuous, and comprehensive health care. The family health team led by the family physician conducted the first survey for registration of catchment area population, collected the required health data, performed the first medical checkup of all family members, and developed the family file.

There are about 4070 families receiving the service in the Shambat Health Centre. Most of them have been given a family card bearing the name of the head of the household, address, and number of the health file. A clear patient flow and roadmap are followed in the Shambat Health Centre starting from reception where registration takes place, the sorting office where a well-trained nurse is available for sorting, the file office, until lastly the patient is directed to one of the four clinics:

- Acute cases clinic
- Chronic disease clinic
- Antenatal care and women's health clinic
- Well-baby clinic

Shambat Health Centre has a facility that has an essential health services package, essential drug list, and is supplied with a suitable set of medical equipment and furniture. Staff receive regular on the job training and follow the available treatment protocols and are participating in developing treatment protocols and local treatment guidelines. One of the reasons for building trust between the population of Shambat and the health centre is the efficiency of the referral system.

Family medicine education

There are five institutes that offer family medicine programmes in Sudan. Four are located in Khartoum State and one in Gezira State. Nine states have trainees enrolled in the PHI Masters programme as part of the PHC expansion project, managed by Federal Ministry of Health (FMoH) and funded by Federal Ministry of Finance (FMoF) and donors. The PHI together with the Sudan Medical Specialization Board (SMSB) offers training in Khartoum State and also offers a partly distance learning course in several states outside Khartoum (Kassala, Gadarif, Red Sea, White Nile, North Kordofan, River Nile, Sinnar, and Gezira) as a decentralization and retention strategy. Trainees from the eight states attend the theoretical lectures and examinations at PHI while all the clinical part of training is conducted in their states.[4]

THE PRIVATE HEALTH SECTOR'S ROLE IN THE DELIVERY OF OUT-PATIENT CLINIC SERVICES

The majority of family physicians provide care in public facilities with only a few practising in the private sector. However, private medical education in Sudan has a good example of family medicine training producing competent diploma and master holders.[4]

The private sector in Sudan has little role in offering the family health approach although it is rapidly expanding and owns a big share of health services with a focus on specialized tertiary care. However, it can be used especially in remote areas where there are no public facilities; accreditation of these facilities is a prerequisite. According to the JAR, River Nile State is a successful example of public–private partnership (PPP); it started to mobilize the private sector to assist its effort in expanding PHC services as part of meeting its social responsibility. It is reported that this additional financing is "unconditional" and covers the priorities and the plan of the State Ministry of Health (SMoH) – fully aligned to the SMoH's one plan. So far, private actors engaged in mining and cement industries contributed to this initiative. This is one form of innovative financing for health, by mobilizing the private sector.[2]

REFERENCES

1. Federal Ministry of Health, Public Health Institute. *The National Health Policy 2017–2030.*
2. Federal Ministry of Health. *Joint Assessment Report, Sudan.* 2017.
3. Federal Ministry of Health, Public Health Institute. *Health Finance Policy.* 2015.
4. Federal Ministry of Health, Primary Health Care General Directorate, Expansion Project. *Annual Report 2017.*
5. Federal Ministry of Health, Directorate of Planning, Research and International Health. *Sudan Health System Performance Assessment 2014.*
6. Federal Ministry of Health, Public Health Institute. *Family Medicine in Sudan: A Situation Analysis Report.* 2015.
7. Federal Ministry of Health. *Strengthening Primary Health Care in Sudan through a Family Health Approach: Policy Options.* 2016.

Syria

Majid Bitar and Arwa Eissa

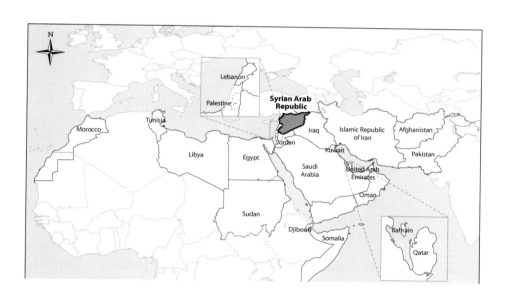

Total number of primary health-care facilities	1826
Number of general practitioners (GPs) working in public primary health-care facilities	850
The number of specialist family physicians working in primary health-care facilities	100
Average number of family physician graduates/year	8
Number of medical universities or colleges	8
Number of family medicine divisions or departments	2

PRIMARY HEALTH CARE

Current state

There is no doubt that the crisis that Syria has undergone for the past seven years, has affected all sectors. The health sector has borne a large proportion of these negative impacts the most significant of which are:

- **Impact on infrastructure**: The crisis, especially in the governorates that have suffered the most, left a clear impact on the health sector in its entirety. Many hospitals and health centres have suffered structural damage in whole or in part. Some of them have gone out of service; others had services reduced or were forced to use neighbouring buildings to provide services. Additionally, public electricity and water supply was disrupted, which often was almost permanent.

    Many of the Ministry of Health (MoH)'s vehicles, especially ambulances, were rendered non-operational, because of direct or indirect targeting. The fact that many national drug factories – unfortunately many of them were in high-risk governorates – have been rendered non-operational, in addition to the unjust blockade that prevented the supply of basic materials and medical equipment, and coupled with security risks concerning the delivery of medicine, vaccines, and health supplies to these governorates, has left a very serious impact on the population.

    Moreover, "terrorist groups" occupied some of these health centres to use them for their own benefit or to deny the population access to services, especially vaccines for children under the pretext that they do not trust the effectiveness of these medicines because they are supplied by the central government. Table 31.1 shows the status of primary health care (PHC) centres at the end of the first quarter of 2017 according to the statistics by the Health Centres Department at the Primary Health Care Directorate.[1]
- **Human resources**: The number of health professionals has shrunk dramatically, especially among physicians, specialists in particular, as a result of the migration of many of them abroad. Moreover, health human resources were disproportionately deployed. For instance, there were many health workers (especially nurses) in relatively stable regions, unlike other dangerous areas, which are suffering from a severe shortage of medical staff of various categories. At the end of the third quarter of 2016, there were 850 general practitioners, 1290 specialist physicians, 53 resident physicians, 2044 dentists, 11,502 nurses, 1219 laboratory technicians, 2329 midwives, and 946 pharmacists.[2]
- **Environment and war risks**: The difficulty of gaining access to clean water; the damage sewage networks have suffered; overcrowding, especially in shelters, resulting from the arrival of displaced population from unsafe places; food insecurity in varying degrees and increasing pressure on many functioning health centres.
- **Other issues include**: Low-coverage rates of vaccination and reproductive health services for target groups, especially children and mothers; accumulation of waste as a

TABLE 31.1   Primary health-care facilities at the end of the first quarter of 2017

	Governorate	In-service + partially in-service	Out of service	Total
1	Damascus	43	9	52
2	Damascus countryside	27 + 98	54	179
3	Hama	154	23	177
4	Homs	178	43	221
5	Idlib	97	12	109
6	Tartus	154	0	154
7	Latakia	106	9	115
8	Aleppo	111 + 21	117	249
9	Quneitra	33	30	63
10	As-Suwayda	89	2	91
11	Al-Hasakah	51	22	73
12	Deir ez-Zor	50	18	68
13	Daraa	70	28	98
14	Raqqa	20	36	56
	Total	1303	403	1706

result of limited municipal services; the emergence of morbidities introduced by foreign fighters and their families in some specific regions (index cases); extreme poverty among those affected by the war; rising numbers of war-wounded and related disabilities; high rates of child labour; child marriage and abuse, and high mortality rates due to chronic diseases.

Additionally, the number of those suffering from psychological distress, depression, addiction, and serious mental illness as well as suicide cases has doubled. This has seriously worsened the health situation in the country. Vaccination coverage rates have dwindled; multiple cases of malnutrition have been recorded; and polio, measles, and other diseases, especially communicable diseases, have emerged.[3]

The Ministry of Health continued its work and adjusted its priorities to cope with the crisis. In cooperation with organizations operating in the country, especially the World Health Organization (WHO), the MoH worked hard to make use of available resources and capabilities, albeit scarce, to address the needs. As a response to surveillance of many pathological cases, the MoH has continued to carry out national immunization campaigns against poliomyelitis, measles, and other diseases.[4] Now, with the gradual improvement in security and with the help of NGOs and civil associations, many of the affected health centres are being rehabilitated and restored according to situational priorities. These centres are being supplied with trained personnel and necessary medical equipment. Further steps carried out by the MoH in the primary health care domain are as follows:

- The MoH has continued to provide basic primary health care services even to places that are difficult to reach and out of control, with the cooperation of organizations such as the Red Crescent and others.
- Further, it has carried out and continues to implement vigorous national vaccination campaigns, especially against polio.

Mobile clinic

- From the beginning, the MoH was alert to the danger of malnutrition, especially among children and pregnant women. It conducted several studies and surveys to identify the problem and address it. In response, many health centres and hospitals have been rehabilitated and assigned to treat moderate and severe malnutrition.[5] With the help of the WHO, many food supplements (such as preventive and therapeutic peanut butter) have been procured and distributed to a wide range of target populations with special attention to areas with a high percentage of children, even in locations that were difficult to access. The MoH advised that all private associations, organizations, and charitable centres that provide health services, are to be carefully monitored in order to preserve their credibility.
- The MoH has provided shelters, across all governorates and regions, with the necessary medical staff, medicines, and the possibility of referral of critical cases through health districts or health centres. These cases and other health issues are followed up and monitored through weekly reports that are integrated with early warning and rapid response reports.
- One of the outcomes and repercussions of the crisis, according to evidence and evidence-based studies, is the doubling of mental illness rates such as depression, psychological distress, suicide, and substance abuse.[6] As a result, the MoH has developed, since the beginning of the crisis, a strategic plan to provide mental health services and primary psychological care through selected primary health care centres. In the same context, adolescent health and school health programs have been supported by training health staff in selected centres to provide their own services. Within the same framework, as part of a high-level partnership between the Ministry of Health and various NGOs, volunteers have been trained to perform various tasks such as health awareness dissemination and surveys in some affected areas and villages. Work has been ongoing, and the number of health volunteers is on the rise in all governorates.

- Shortly after the onset of the crisis, in September 2012, the Early Warning Alert and Response System (EWARS) was activated as a health priority to reduce the incidence of epidemics, especially communicable diseases and those covered by vaccination, and to supplement the routine surveillance system. The program has achieved good results (according to experts from the WHO Regional Office 2017). The utilization of this program and its affiliated reporting centres has been increasing, especially with the return of security to many places. Targeted diseases are reported, and cases are addressed, monitored, and documented through rapid response teams deployed on the health district level in all governorates. The program has delivered remarkable results, not only by reporting suspected cases of targeted diseases, but also in helping to integrate efforts with all sectors, including the private sector, and activating coordination and feedback between all health care levels. This is very important under a referral system, which, unfortunately, is currently inactive.

- To assess the current situation and to update the data on the assessment and readiness of health services provided in all health centres, the Service Availability and Readiness Assessment (SARA) survey is being conducted in collaboration with the WHO. This survey comes at the right time, especially after the devastating years of the war, as its results will give decision makers evidence-based conclusions on urgent needs, prioritized according to the available resources on all levels. The survey assesses the extent of damage to the facilities and delivers a full assessment of infrastructure, human resources, basic health services, and essential medicines regulations in terms of availability and readiness. Researchers have been identified and data is being collected, revised and corrected through the SPSS software. Currently, key indicators are available including; the number of active centres; the availability of the basic services; their affiliation and classification; the number, distribution, and sufficiency of human cadres; the availability essential medicines lists in each centre, among other services. The results will be useful for building a good database to address challenges during the reconstruction phase. The survey will be conducted periodically to monitor progress on achievements.

- Work has been underway for more than two years on the rehabilitation and restoration of health centres. The directorates of health in all governorates, especially those severely affected and that have come again under government control, sent reports regarding the scale of damage, personnel, and equipment. The MoH, with the support of some governmental organizations and non-governmental actors, selected the centres for restoration or reconstruction according to priorities, available resources, and well-considered criteria.

- The Ministry of Health has given considerable attention to the issue of infection control through coordination and cooperation with concerned authorities and ministries such as municipalities and education directorates. This has been specifically undertaken in shelters, overcrowded places and other areas where water networks have been damaged. To address this situation, the MoH provided clean drinking water, water chlorination, and safe food, as well as raised awareness and education about infectious diseases such as tuberculosis and hepatitis. It has also supplied health centres with personal protective equipment and vaccines for the prevention of hepatitis B and influenza. It also has paid attention to the issue of the safe disposal of hazardous medical waste through the training of health personnel and provision of necessary equipment such as incinerators.

- For the past year, the MoH has been reviewing and updating the regulatory decision governing the primary health care sector.[7] The project has been completed, deployed, and distributed to all primary health-care facilities. The project resulted in the reclassification of health centres according to WHO recommendations, in which each centre serves up to 5000 people.

- A new mobile clinic program has recently been introduced to reach difficult-to-access areas. In this context, the MoH has provided training to health staff, mobile teams, and volunteers, drawn up criteria and indicators and supplied them with vehicles as well.

Basic health service package, essential drug list, and treatment protocols

The basic health services package is nationally recognized and implemented in a comprehensive approach in all health centres. The package includes health education services, child and maternal care, immunization against infectious diseases, treatment of widespread diseases and injuries, provision of essential medicines, infectious diseases control, and provision of safe drinking water, food, and food supplements. It also includes the provision of services on a large scale, such as school health, adolescents, the elderly, and oral and dental health services. The provided health services vary according to the classification of the centres (the classification of the primary health care centres has recently been updated to: (A) classified centres serving fewer than 5000 people; (B) classified centres serving from 5000 to 15,000 people; and (C) classified centres serving more than 15,000 people). Also, medical points have been abolished and declared A-classified health centres. Comprehensive medical clinics have also been abolished and declared specialized health centres). These services are reviewed periodically (mostly annually) and are now being reviewed through the Service Availability and Readiness Assessment survey.

Nowa el Awal Family Health Centre, Deraa

The essential drug list is available in primary health care facilities and is regularly updated and reviewed (regulations, classifications, and updates were reviewed in 2017). Health facilities are supplied with medicines on a quarterly basis (four times a year) and when necessary.

Treatment protocols are not universally available in health centres. Treatment protocols for diarrhea, dehydration, typhoid fever, brucellosis, tuberculosis, and food poisoning are available in 10%–20% of PHC facilities. Some of these protocols have been developed by experts and specialists from the Ministry of Health and based on WHO guidance. It is worth noting the urgent need to develop and disseminate treatment protocols for common communicable and chronic diseases to all PHC centres.

Integration of basic health services package

The provision of integrated health services in the context of a protracted crisis has a major impact on the health sector, especially on PHC facilities. The priority has been, and remains, to restore basic services, rehabilitate and renovate affected centres, provide human cadres, reassign them, and restore all programs' coverage rates to what they had been before the crisis. However, there are some ongoing efforts and attempts, notably:

- Integration of early childhood with PHC services through a cooperation project between the Ministry of Health and the Aga Khan Development Network. The project is being piloted in selected centres according to particular criteria and in four governorates only.
- Integration of nutritional surveillance services for children and pregnant women. It was agreed to conduct a nutritional survey of random samples of pregnant women and their children on a large scale. The survey is still in progress.
- Integration of school health services with health care services at a comprehensive level in accordance with a memorandum of understanding signed a year ago.
- Integration of adolescent health services with mental health services in selected centres and in most governorates.

Referral and information systems

The referral system is currently inactive, therefore it is not possible to estimate the proportion of patients who need to be referred to hospitals. However, the system was completed, automated, supplied with logistics and had its staff trained to work at a universal level and in all governorates in 2006.

The primary health care information system is the routine health information system, which is based on health centres' monthly statistical reports, which are collected every month by the Primary Health Care Directorate and according to a specific administrative structure. There is no electronic information system at the level of health centres in general, and there are no family medical records in most centres except for 30 centres that provide family medicine services.

Quality and accreditation of service delivery

The quality of the services provided in PHC facilities is monitored and evaluated through supervisory visits carried out by the relevant programs. Quality and infection control committees have been trained at the health-centre level. National standards have been established by the MoH for the accreditation of health care centres, establishment of new centres, and measurement of the quality of services.

There is no system or mechanism for the accreditation of primary health centres. In this context, the MoH has started to set up and define quality committees at a central level for quality management at affiliated directorates (including the Primary Health Care Directorate) in order to fulfil the ISO 9001/2015 requirements. Work is ongoing, and we hope that this step serves as a starting point for the accreditation of health centres.

Patient satisfaction with service quality

It is not possible to statistically measure patient satisfaction with the quality of services provided due to the crisis. However, there is a good level of satisfaction with the services provided through some large-scale programs, such as the vaccination and child nutrition surveillance services, which are considered health priorities in the crisis.

Main challenges facing access to quality services

Access to quality services is facing with the following significant challenges:

- Many health centres have been rendered completely out of service, and many others have also been partially affected, with an urgent need to rehabilitate them.
- Poor distribution of human resources in health centres and severe lack of some specialties in different categories.
- Poor capabilities and resources and the consequent impact on centres' readiness and services' quality.
- The number of visitors to some centres has doubled as a result of the population's relocation to safer places, which in turn has made it difficult to provide fair, quality services to all patients.
- The severe shortage of physicians in health centres, especially family physicians, as many of them have left the country due to the crisis. There is an urgent need to encourage those physicians to return.
- Poor geographical distribution of many health centres and the failure to adopt criteria for the establishment of health centres in this regard.
- The absence or training of substitutes for those who perform particular services in some health centres.
- The urgent need to involve local communities in the development of service plans and the urgent need to further educate them on the importance of primary health care services.
- Lack of partnership and integration with other activities such as school health, water, electricity, and sanitation bodies and municipalities.

FAMILY PRACTICE

Policy commitments towards family medicine

Despite positive encouragement, a fairly good start, and promises to support this specialty since its inception in the mid-1990s, and despite the graduation of many family physicians at the time (approximately 50 doctors annually), the experience was not sustainable. Encouragement and commitment started to decline and the number of graduates as family doctors decreased over time. In addition, many of them have left to work abroad.

The decline in support and commitment to this program coupled with the seven-year crisis led the Ministry of Health to de-prioritize the program. Additionally, NGOs did not prioritize this program in its annual support plans. In early 2018, with the rapid restoration of stability, senior decision makers took serious actions toward restoration of the family practice programme.

The contributions of family practice towards comprehensive health coverage

A report was submitted at the "Regional Consultation on Strengthening Service Provision Through the Family Practice Approach: Towards Universal Health Coverage in EMR", which was held in Cairo, Egypt, from 18–20 November 2014, by the WHO Regional Office in collaboration with the World Organization of Family Doctors (WONCA). The recommendations will be adopted in the future, especially as stability and reconstruction are taking place rapidly.

Family practice teams (nursing staff, community health workers, midwives, and others)

Health personnel working in family practice clinics are trained in the health centres that carry out the program, including nurses or administrators through on-the-job training by family doctors working in these clinics. Meanwhile, there is no program for the training of health personnel working independently. There is training for community health workers through some programs such as the Healthy Villages Program and the Adolescent Health Program. There is no coordination between these programs and the cadres implementing the family medicine program. The same can be said of midwives who are trained through reproductive health programs, but there is no connection with family medicine clinic services in these centres.

Research and studies on family practice

There is no research worthy of mention because of the limited adoption of the family practice program by decision makers and because of a lack of the capability needed to conduct research. However, there are some studies conducted by the graduates of the Centre for Strategic Health Studies in Damascus, such as a survey on the satisfaction of patients and beneficiaries of centres providing family medicine services. The survey showed greater satisfaction rates in these centres compared with lower satisfaction rates in centres that do not provide a family practice program.

FAMILY MEDICINE

Family medicine began as a medical specialty in Syria in the mid-1990s. The pace of registration and graduation was limited (40–50 family physicians per year). Graduates are working in less that 5% of the total PHC centres. Family files were introduced at the time and families were registered. It was estimated that Syria needed 7000 family physicians (one family physician for 1500–2500 individuals) to deploy the program nationwide. Work strategies have been developed regarding cost-effectiveness and efficiency, standardization of information sources, results-based management, referral system, and gradual project expansion.

At the beginning of 2006, and to improve their quality, a plan was developed to implement family practice on a phased basis. It was agreed to choose Daraa, Latakia, Idlib, Hama, and As-Suwayda, in addition to the Rif Dimashq Governorate. Gradual expansion was planned to take place over the next five years. The crisis has adversely affected the process of advancing the family practice program since 2011.

Main challenges in family medicine in Syria

- The lack of a supportive political decision. Family practice was adopted as a new specialty but the interest and desire clearly diminished on the part of relevant decision makers, in addition to the fact that instability imposed new priorities on the ground.

- The Ministry of Health's financial and moral neglect of family medicine specialists, and the failure to issue a decision enabling doctors to work on a full-time basis.
- Misunderstanding and failure to recognize the importance of this specialty by universities, other specialist doctors, and the community as a whole.
- Problems with how to deal with the resident family doctor, the lack of clear reference or study curricula, and the lack or failure to adopt sub-specialties for family physicians (such as geriatrics, sports medicine, nutrition).
- Lack of adequate motivation for skilled family doctors, and the need to work in private clinics as well as in health care facilities.
- Lack of public or private initiatives to empower or encourage family medicine (such as prioritizing the employment of family doctors with health insurance companies.
- As a result of the above, specialist family physicians prefer job opportunities abroad that provide them with satisfaction at all levels.
- The difficult security conditions in the previous seven years led to the emigration of many specialist doctors, including a large proportion of family physicians.
- All the above has led to a severe shortage of family physicians working in primary health care facilities and has led resident physicians to become unwilling to experience the same unpleasant experience their fellow colleagues had undergone.

PRIVATE HEALTH SECTOR

The private health sector (private hospitals or private health centres or private clinics) plays an important role in providing quality health services to a segment of the population who can afford such services. This sector is supervised by the Ministry of Health represented by the health directorates, the directorate of hospitals and professional medical associations.

The private sector's role in the provision of out-patient services is increasing, particularly following the adoption of the health insurance system for large segments of the population and employees. Out-patient clinic services, in hospitals or private medical centres or in specialist doctors' clinics, are characterized by the variety of available medical advice, often good quality, speedy response to patients and their specified pricing. The private sector serves as a substitute and supplements public health centres, especially in the provision of medical services that might not be available in public centres in a sustainable manner.

Also noteworthy is the cooperation and coordination between the private and public sectors in the reporting of some communicable diseases, as well as the provision of vaccination and reproductive health services. Additionally, both sectors pay special attention to some of the country's health priorities through participation in seminars, workshops, and medical courses.

The family doctor should play a key role in the private health sector, but unfortunately many factors have significantly contributed to minimizing this role for the following reasons:

- The shortage of family doctors.
- Lack of community awareness of this specialty.
- Failure to endorse family doctors' employment with private health insurance providers.

It is not possible here to provide statistics on a precise proportion of patients seeking services beyond PHC facilities (public and specialized health centres). This proportion differs from one region to another and depends on the classification of health centres and the quality of their services in these regions. They also differ in terms of the socioeconomic status of patients and the extent to which they can afford such services, not to mention the absence of statistical studies in this regard.

It should be noted that, as a result of the crisis, the deteriorating financial status of a large proportion of the population, the fact that many health facilities have gone out of service and the lack of support (especially medicines), the number of patients coming to clinics run by civil societies, relief centres, Red Crescent seeking free medical services, including medicine, has increased.

Progressing towards the provision of comprehensive, adequate, and affordable primary health care coverage for the entire target population is critical and requires concerted efforts, not only between the public and private sectors, but also between all stakeholders in the health domain.

The private health sector should be presented in remote areas in rural regions and villages with low population density (fewer than 5000 inhabitants) not serviced by public health centres in order to provide services to the local population. Regarding the cost of services provided by the private health sector, the Ministry of Health and other relevant bodies have worked to specify the pricing of diagnosis and other medical services in a manner that suits the average income of citizens. Additionally, the MoH and other concerned bodies have been encouraging the private health sector to enter into contracts with health insurance companies.

ANNEX 1: HUMAN RESOURCES STANDARDS

A: Classified Health Centre[8]

Classification of the Centre	Service Type	General Medicine, General Health, Family Medicine – Dentistry	Nursing — Midwife	Nursing — Nurse	Assistant Technician — Lab Technician	Assistant Technician — General Health	Assistant Technician — Pharmacist	Assistant Technician — Health Educator	Other — Administrative Employee	Other — Support Worker	Other — Supply and Storage Officer
Health Centre A: Fewer than 5000 people	Family and Dental Health	1–2	1	2–3	–	–	–	–	–	–	–
	Vaccination	–	–	1–2	–	–	–	–	–	–	–
	Oral Health	–	–	0–1	–	–	–	–	–	–	–
	Lab Technician	–	–	–	0–1	–	–	–	–	–	–
	Archive and Administration	–	–	–	–	–	–	–	1	1	–
	Reception	–	–	–	–	–	–	–	1–2	–	–
	Health Advice	–	–	–	–	–	–	1	–	–	–
	Pharmacy	–	–	–	–	–	1	–	–	–	–
	Supply Warehouse	–	–	–	–	–	–	–	–	–	1
	Community Health Services	0–1	–	–	–	1	–	–	–	–	–
Total		1–3	1	3–6	0–1	1	1	1	2–3	1	1

B: Classified Health Centre

| | | Human Resources | | | | | | | | | | | |
| | | Physician | | Nursing | | Assistant Technician | | | | | Other | | |
Classification of the Centre	Service Type	General Medicine, General Health Family	Dentistry	Midwife	Nurse	Lab Technician	General Health	Counselling Psychologist	Pharmacist	Health Educator	Administrative Employee	Support Worker	Supply and Storage Officer Storage
Health Centre B: 5000–15,000 people	Family Health	1–4	–	2	3–5	–	–	–	–	–	–	2–3	–
	Vaccination	–	–	–	3	–	–	–	–	–	–	–	–
	Oral Health	–	2–3	–	1–2	–	–	–	–	–	–	–	–
	Lab Technician	–	–	–	–	1–2	–	–	–	–	–	–	–
	Archive and Administration	–	–	–	–	–	–	–	–	–	2–3	–	–
	Reception	–	–	–	–	–	–	–	–	–	2–4	–	–
	Health Advice	–	–	–	–	–	–	1	–	–	–	–	–
	Pharmacy	–	–	–	–	–	–	–	2–3	–	–	–	–
	Community Health Services	1	–	–	–	–	1	–	–	1	–	–	–
	Supply Warehouse	–	–	–	–	–	–	–	–	–	–	–	1
Total		2–5	2–3	2	7–11	1–2	1	1	2–3	1	4–7	2–3	1

C: Classified Health Centre

Level	Service Type	Physician General Medicine, General Health, Family	Physician Dentistry	Nursing Midwife	Nursing Nurse	Assistant Technician Lab Technician	Assistant Technician General Health	Assistant Technician Pharmacist	Assistant Technician Educator Counselling Psychologist	Other Administrative Employee	Other Support Worker	Other Supply and Storage Officer
Health Centre C:1 5,000+ people	Family Health	2–5	–	2–3	3–5	–	–	–	–	–	–	–
	Specialists	4–11	–	–	4–5	–	–	–	–	–	–	–
	Vaccination	–	–	–	3	–	–	–	–	–	–	–
	Oral Health	–	3–4	–	2	–	–	–	–	–	–	–
	Lab Technician	–	–	–	–	3–4	–	–	–	–	–	–
	Administration	–	–	–	–	–	–	–	–	2	2–3	–
	Reception	–	–	–	–	–	–	–	–	3–5	–	–
	General Health	1–2	–	–	–	–	1–2	–	2	–	–	–
	Pharmacy	–	–	–	–	–	–	3–4	–	–	–	–
	Supply Warehouse	–	–	–	–	–	–	–	–	–	–	1
Total		7–18	3–4	2–3	12–15	3–4	1–2	3–4	2	5–7	2–3	1

REFERENCES

1. Annual Statistical Report (2017), Health Centers Department of the PHC in Syrian MoH.
2. Statistical Memorandum of the Directorate of Planning and International Cooperation (2017). Available from: http://www.moh.gov.sy/.
3. Epidemiological Bulletins of the WHO for Early Warning Alert and Response System (EWARS), for the 2017 year. Available from: http://www.emro.who.int/syr/ewars-workshops/ewars-bulletins-2017.html.
4. Annual Plan of the Child Department in the PHC Directorate of the Syrian MoH, about the Syrian National Immunization Program (2016).
5. Quarterly Statistical Report (4:2017), of the Nutrition Department in the PHC Directorate of the Syrian MoH.
6. Research. Available from: http://reliefweb.int/report/syrian-arab-republic/invisible-wounds-inpact-six-years-war-mental-health-syria-s-children/.
7. Regulatory Decision No T/8 (Oct 2017), Integrated Health Centers (Health Centers-Specialized Health Centers), Published in the *Official Gazette* in December 2017.
8. Regulatory Decision No T/8 (Oct 2017), Integrated Health Centers (Health Centers-Specialized Health Centers), [supplement No 1: Human Resources].

CHAPTER 32

Tunisia

Ali Mtiraoui and Belgacem Sabri

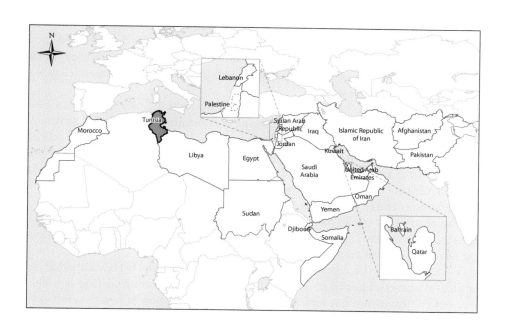

Total number of PHC facilities	2091
Number of general practitioners working in public PHC facilities	5000
Number of certified family physicians working in PHC facilities	150
Average number of family physician graduates/year	80
Number of medical schools	4
Number of FM departments	4

INTRODUCTION

The model of medical practice in Tunisia is strongly influenced by the history of its national health system and by reforms that have been implemented since the Alma-Ata Declaration on Primary Health Care (PHC) and the global goal of health for all by the year 2000.

After the country's independence in 1956, Tunisia had a limited number of doctors, most of whom were trained in the old metropolis and were mainly based in the country's major cities and coastal areas.

The establishment of the first medical school in 1964, with World Health Organization (WHO) technical cooperation, enabled the country to start local training of its medical staff, which began to take over from French and other international partners, and to gradually settle in the inner regions of the country. The national basic health-care programme, which was established in the early 1980s, made good progress and had significant positive health outcomes.

The medical training drive has been strengthened by the establishment of three other medical faculties in Sousse, Sfax, and Monastir. However, the role of general practitioners (GPs) who were the pioneers of the country's health development was gradually downgraded in favour of specialization and hospital-university careers and due to the lack of attractiveness of careers in general practice. Some people considered academic training for GPs to be insufficient for proper management of the population served.

Reforms in medical education have been directed towards the production of GPs adapted to the expectations of the population and having a community and public health vocation. This dynamic at the Faculty of Medicine in Sousse (a community-based faculty), echoed by the Departments of Preventive and Social Medicine, has led to a renewed interest in the practice of general medicine with a community-based approach. This latter is directed towards addressing the social determinants of health and towards greater involvement in the public health action research programmes and in the management of national health promotion and prevention programmes. The promotion of the community general practitioner model by some faculties has been supported by cooperation with countries, particularly Canada, which have adopted this model and have made significant advances in family medicine (FM).

Tunisia's adherence to the reforms proposed and promoted by WHO, aimed at achieving health for all and universal health coverage (UHC) through community-based services centred on the needs of communities, has renewed interest in the adoption of health services based on health and FM. A programme to reform FM training has been adopted by Tunisia and its implementation has begun in all medical schools since 2017.

BACKGROUND

Tunisia has a health-care system based on an extensive network of facilities, notably for first-line health care, offering full territorial coverage and care for the whole of the Tunisian population. Nearly half of Tunisian doctors (public and private sectors) work in first-line facilities such as basic health-care centres, local hospitals, or general practice. For health authorities, the need to improve the quality and performance of the health-care services provided in these facilities is a priority.

Underlying this priority is an undertaking to adapt the health-care system to the needs of the population, in response to the major changes that have affected the national environment in recent years. Several determinants have clearly influenced the evolution of the health-care services, notably: demographic and epidemiologic profile, lifestyle, technological progress, health resource management, and globalization of the services market.

Effectively, improved living conditions, socio-demographic conditions (demographic and epidemiological transition with the corollary change in the morbidity profile), the rapid change in social values, and the remarkable progress accomplished in medical science have had a deep impact on the health-care services expected and delivered in Tunisia. The increase in life expectancy (75.4 years at birth, 73.8 for men and 78.5 for women) and changes in habits have revealed more complex health situations: often individuals suffer from multiple, chronic pathologies (diabetes, high blood pressure, cardiovascular diseases, etc.). This trend has also been influenced by high levels of salt consumption and increased smoking (50% among men and 10% of women). In the 35–70 age group, 27% of individuals suffer from obesity, 63% are overweight, and 13% suffer from hypercholesterolemia. Diabetes affects 19% of the population, high blood pressure 32%, and both figures are expected to rise[22]. Most of these patients require complex care involving examinations that can be sophisticated, as well as long-term monitoring. Moreover, the population, often relatively well-educated and informed, and has high expectations.

Tunisia consequently has a twofold challenge: the health-care issues characteristic of developing countries (emerging and re-emerging infectious diseases, for example) and those of developed countries (such as chronic diseases, sedentary lifestyles, and damaging habits). Many of these issues could be covered in an integrated manner by efficient, competent first-line health care.

The Tunisian health-care system, which has, to date, succeeded in achieving acceptable health indicators, is now at a crossroads and is under pressure to quickly address the multiplicity of demographic, epidemiological, and socioeconomic changes, as well as the new challenges of improving service quality and controlling costs.[1]

In its current form, the health-care system no longer has the capacities required to address the population's demands for better quality health care. The current situation has arisen in the international and domestic environments. To adapt, the system must face the internal complexity of the decision-making mechanisms within health-care organizations.[2–4] Because social determinants are increasingly important to health care and campaigns to reduce risk factors, there is a need for a stronger community-based approach better capable of addressing health care needs, especially at first line level.[5–7]

HEALTH-CARE PROFESSIONALS AND FACILITIES

The originality of general practice lies in both the broad scope of its action and the complex part it plays in the health-care system. The general basis of its activity has been defined since the early 1980s, when Tunisia adopted the Alma-Ata Declaration (Health for All) and organized its health-care system with the implementation of basic health care with the general practitioner as the keystone.[8–10]

Public sector health care in Tunisia is a three-tiered organization: the first tier is provided by the Basic Health Centre (BHC), focusing mainly on the problems of the population it serves, and the local hospital to which it belongs; the second tier is made up of the regional hospital and the specialized diagnostic and treatment centres; the third tier is represented by the university hospital and the hyper-specialized diagnostic and treatment centres that have a mission to provide care, education, and research.

Community health program

The Tunisian health-care system also has a number of specific characteristics. It is organized around the patient's free choice and offers a number of different entry points. In reality, it is made up of two sectors (sub-systems): a public sector and a private sector. Nearly half the clinicians in Tunisia are GPs (5651 out of 12,760 in 2014). General practice is split into almost equal halves: the private sector had 912 doctors and the public sector had 2739 doctors by October 2014. Private doctors work in medical practices that are in themselves small independent enterprises often in solo practice; civil servants work in basic health-care centres covering the whole domestic territory with a density of 1 per 4800 in 2014. In Tunisia the public first-line sector covers around 50% of all the nation's medical consultations and 10% of public sector hospital discharges.[11] In addition to these clinical activities, GPs play an important part in prevention and health promotion among the population under their responsibility.

Overall, the public sector provides 60% of ambulatory care and 75% of hospitalizations and remains the main health-care provider. It is based on three dovetailing levels of care:

- The first level is made up of 2091 basic health-care centres and 109 district hospitals (representing 15% of public beds in 2014).
- The second level is covered by 34 regional hospitals (35% of public beds in 2014); they are usually located in the principal town of each governorate.
- The third level is completed by the university hospitals, of which there are 23 (in 2014, 50% of public beds, with a total of 196 services with over 40 specialties).[11]

Alongside this public infrastructure, there is a semi-public infrastructure: six polyclinics run by the national social security organization (CNSS Caisse Nationale de Sécurité Sociale), which deliver generic ambulatory care, specialized care, and diagnostic services to social affiliates.

The private sector health-care infrastructure is made up of a network delivering ambulatory general practice or specialized infrastructure, paramedical care, and hospital facilities. This infrastructure is made up of:

- 80 private hospitals offering multiple disciplines or a single discipline (15% of all hospital beds and 70% of all the nation's heavy equipment)
- 3293 private medical clinics, 50.9% of which are specialist
- 940 dental surgeries and 1392 pharmacies (1259 daytime and 133 nighttime)
- Other facilities such as haemodialysis centres (99), paramedical private sector clinics (567), private radiologists (107), and medical analysis laboratories (149 medical pathology laboratories)[11]

Lastly, it is worth noting that health risk coverage is under the auspices of the National Health Insurance Fund, which offers social security beneficiaries a choice between three options for care coverage:

1. Public sector coverage, under which affiliates and related beneficiaries have access to all health-care services (such as consultations or hospitalizations) provided by all public health facilities, against the payment of the standard minimum fee
2. Family physician track where a GP operates as the gatekeeper for insured patients and their dependents
3. Refund system whereby social security beneficiaries are entitled to receive care from all public or private sector health-care providers, supporting the costs themselves and subsequently seeking refund from the national health insurance scheme, Caisse Nationale d'Assurance Maladie (CNAM) services with a predefined rate and an annual cap

HISTORY OF THE DEVELOPMENT OF FIRST-LINE HEALTH-CARE SERVICES

We shall attempt to quickly summarize the evolution of the concept of first-line health care (first contact with patients) and consequently of general practice, via an analysis of the following periods:

- The immediate post-independence years: introduction of a national health system based on public health
- The 1980s and the reform of basic health care
- The loss of momentum of basic health care in the last years of the twentieth century and the advent of the revolution

As soon as the country gained its independence, the Tunisian government made extensive efforts to develop a network of public health services, with the dispensary as its core facility. This was designed to cover the whole country, giving access to health-care services even in the remotest parts of the country. The Tunisian people recognized that the two state networks that provided the most comprehensive territorial coverage were schools and dispensaries. This reflected the commitment of the authorities to human development through free education and health care. One of the key aspects of the development of general medical practice was political support for strengthening social solidarity to counter disease by offering the whole population access to health care. The result was the setup of the national public health system, with GPs referred to as public health doctors and given a role in improving both individual health care (to restore health) and collective health care (protection and promotion of health at community level). Though this created some semantic confusion between the health system and public health personnel (public health: specialized in prevention), it did enable all doctors to develop health protection and promotion activities by leading multidisciplinary teams around priority health-care issues.

Given the significant shortage of doctors in Tunisia, in the early post-independence years, the preventive activities undertaken by the Ministry of Health (MoH) were essentially performed by nurses and assistant nurses, who were sometimes trained in the field.

This period, characterized by preventive programme action and campaigns on major social issues (such as trachoma, malaria, tuberculosis, and food-borne diseases) was the benchmark in terms of efficiency and, above all, impact. The first major achievement was a reduction in disease and a stronger grip on the main public health issues. The second was the development of a health care model that enabled the whole population to have access to a doctor, using the dispensary as the entry point to the system.[4,12]

This brought the GP to the front of the stage and rekindled interest. This interest was clearly perceived by decision makers who noted that the most efficient health-care systems are those that make general practice a compulsory gateway to health care.

Overall, the health-care system achieved good results in terms of controlling demographic growth, improving health indicators, and delivering health care; however, it did not achieve the levels of efficiency and service quality required. Performance was reflected notably in controlled demographic growth and a global improvement in the state of health, reflected by the elimination or significant reduction of infectious diseases that had been targeted by the national health programmes. This improved indicators on life expectancy at birth, child mortality, and maternal mortality; Tunisia compared well countries with comparable income and health care expenditure.[1,13]

Many factors generated a renewed interest for general practice among young Tunisian medical graduates, including: the control of "major social problems" via programme action; the search for an alternative to a hospital-centric model; and the wealth of ideas emerging in the international arena exploring new health-care models such as community medicine, integrated medicine, community health, global medicine, and PHC.

A MILESTONE: THE 1978 ALMA-ATA DECLARATION

Since the 1950s, the WHO had been emphasizing the need to develop basic health services in developing countries, in a concerted effort to eradicate infectious diseases. On several occasions, it prompted member countries to stimulate the participation of their populations in the implementation of public health programmes in order to promote responsible individual and collective attitudes to health. It was through projects funded by WHO that developing countries like India, and those in South-East Asia and Central America developed basic health services that directly involved communities in solving their health problems. In 1978 these efforts resulted in the adoption of the Alma-Ata Declaration, which stipulated that PHC was the only strategy capable of providing a framework for the "Health for All by the Year 2000" movement. The initiative gave considerable momentum to this alternative approach based on the integral nature of health care and the need for the population to take health care into its own hands.[8,9,14,15]

Tunisia was receptive to the changes instigated by WHO in the realm of health-care services. On the eve of the 1980s, and in the wake of the pilot experiments conducted in several regions (such as integrated medicine in Mjez Elbab and Nabeul, community medicine in Sousse, and the Hope project in Jemmal), the PHC concept, known as "basic health care" in Tunisia, was adopted and the health system reorganized accordingly. Two levels of action were planned: (1) a conceptual level in the principal town (*chef-lieu*) of each health region referred to as "regional basic health-care services", and (2) a basic operational level organized at local (*circonscription*:

district health system) level that included the health centres designed to be the entry point to the system.[1,12]

The basic health-care project was built on four approaches:

- The functional integration of preventive, curative, and promotional activities
- Programme action targeting priority health issues
- Teamwork harnessing different skill sets
- The introduction of the concept of community involvement

The combination of these four approaches led to basic health care being defined as "an approach to the provision of health care with the goal of improving the state of health of population via preventive, curative, and promotional activities, supported by other measures of a social, economic, and political nature, delivered by a multidisciplinary team and broadly seeking the participation of the community".[8,9]

First-line care, (the first patient contact with the system) normally took place in the BHCs, which offered PHC (preventive and curative) services practically free of charge. There were four categories of BHC depending on equipment and personnel: some were associated with maternity wards, others were, for example, centres for the diagnosis or monitoring of tuberculosis.

Moreover, patients also often went directly to local hospitals, where the presence of qualified personnel and equipment led to intensive ambulatory care. They almost always had a maternity ward and a round-the-clock emergency ward. These two activities were a substantial part of the first-line health care. Given that the BHCs were only open in the mornings, many consultations often took place in the emergency wards during the afternoon. Lastly, some patients went directly to the regional hospitals or even tertiary hospitals even though these were theoretically accessed by referrals only. Specialists were often only available at that level and were sometimes consulted directly.

By contrast, local hospitals had no surgical activity and rarely admitted patients for hospitalization apart from normal deliveries. They essentially fulfilled an ambulatory role. Many emergency services were in fact ambulatory consultations that took place outside normal working hours. The number of childbirths remained relatively low as women, even with no particular risk, preferred to give birth in a regional hospital with an attendant gynaecologist and an operating theatre.

Screening for diabetes and hypertension

Yet while the function of the general practitioner clearly existed in the public sector, its range of action in the BHC centres was limited, and the career of "public health doctor" (the title given to doctors in basic health centres) became increasingly unappealing to ambitious medical students. The prevailing idea was in fact comparable to that which we discussed in relation to the ongoing practice in the immediate post-independence years: hospitals were considered to be the place for curative care, and BHCs the place for preventive and promotional medicine. We should, however, emphasize that the health authorities had a genuine intention to enlarge the functions of the BHCs and to improve their quality.[2,16]

The work of a public health doctor focused essentially on public health programmes (such as tuberculosis, diarrhea, mother and child protection, vaccinations) and generic curative consultations, broadly concerning only common ailments. The introduction of the care programme for chronic diseases (high blood pressure and diabetes) was appreciated by GPs, even though it required them to follow diagnostic and therapeutic procedures; it expanded their autonomy and improved their public image, breaking with the image of the doctor who only attended to bumps and bruises.

The frustration expressed by public health doctors was not brought on only by their working conditions, but also by the uninteresting nature of their work. They complained about the trivial nature of the problems they had to deal with in their consultations, and the lack of response from specialists for the "serious" referrals. Consultations were often overly busy.

With the biomedical level on which public health doctors found themselves operating in their clinical practice offering scant intellectual challenge, many sought a fresh identity via epidemiology and public health. This offered the doctors a good grounding to describe the local population in social or cultural terms. Consideration for the actual experience of the population – whether as individual patients or as a local community – was not deemed intellectually interesting – except in terms of obstacles that could be removed by appropriate health education.[16-18]

It is worth noting that during this period there were no initiatives in the field to develop FM. The term "FM" was used only by some doctors in the private sector, and in this case referred to "family doctors" providing care to the "urban bourgeoisie" in the French tradition of private sector medicine; the term was adopted by the CNAM during the 2007 reform of the health insurance system. There were, however, ongoing discussions involving both the health authorities and the universities to develop FM training for doctors and thus restore the intellectual value of general medicine, while improving its quality.[13,19]

CHALLENGES FACING PHC

A number of issues contribute to the difficulties of strengthening first-line health care: the recurrent difficulties encountered in the funding of health expenditure against a backdrop of severe economic constraints imposed by the programme of structural adjustment; the modest position of health education and prevention relative to curative care; the persistence of significant inequality in access to health; recurrent difficulties in the organization of the health system; and the insufficient means and other constraints limiting research.

It is important to note that in general, most partners share similar viewpoints as to the overall situation of the Tunisian health-care system, singling out in particular a relatively good general health coverage, but underlining the scale of fragmentation and the need to remedy this situation through better coordination, with a view to improving performance in the achievement of quality goals, equity, relevance, and cost-effective health services.[2,3,12] This is a reassuring assessment, given that the project to revive general medicine will require concerted action between the main stakeholders in the health system: political decision makers, health managers, health professionals, and academic and civil society institutions.

Moreover, the potential of general medicine to deliver quality first-line care, continuity of care, and a global approach to the coverage of health problems is unanimously acknowledged, with the provisos that GPs receive high-quality training and that basic health care is prioritized in the health system.[17,18,20]

Tunisia has been adhering to the principles and strategies of primary health care since the 1978 declaration of Alma-Ata. However, there is a growing impression that basic health care is no longer being prioritized within the health system as a whole. There are sometimes significant constraints creating obstacles to easily available access to first-line health care, with proven quality, and at an affordable cost for the majority of the population.

There are many reasons for this handicap, including the insufficient equipment of first-line health facilities, a lack of qualification of health-care personnel due to inappropriate training, discrimination between the public and private sectors, and the lack of a strong policy on accreditation that is based on ongoing assessment.[12,21]

Clearly this perception must be corrected if confidence is to be established in the project to develop general medicine, with stakeholders participating actively to bring success. An official, explicit declaration on the pre-eminence of basic health care would help to bring greater coherence between the different health initiatives and create a propitious environment in which the positioning of general medicine can be improved.

The optimal, sustainable development of general medicine is dependent on a statement of intent by the political powers that PHC forms the basis on which the Tunisian health system can be built in a way that better addresses the priority health needs of the population.

Given the number of factors liable to influence the sustainable redevelopment of general medicine, there is a need for coordination between the partners of the health system (authorities, health managers, health professionals, academic institutions, and civil society). Coordination between the different parties appears to be limited to occasional problem-solving with arbitration essentially directed towards the satisfaction of sectoral requests from different parties. Thus, at the most basic level of collaboration that it would be reasonable to expect, between "trainers" and "users", the Ministry of Health and the faculties of medicine do not maintain a formal coordination mechanism ensuring that enough high-quality doctors will be trained to address the country's needs in coming decades.[22,23,20,10,19]

This situation is leading to a chronic mismatch between medical training and the specific national context of Tunisia. Today it is acknowledged that the project to redevelop general medicine can only succeed if there is a sustained and coordinated effort, such is its interdependence with the very nature of national health policy.

Observation shows that GPs, while being committed to progressing their cause, are disheartened by the constantly preferential image enjoyed by specialist doctors and by the lack of acknowledgement of their potential by both population and MoH.

Moreover, the voice of general practitioners does not receive sufficient attention and their representation within professional bodies does not carry enough political weight. Also, there is an observable discord between GPs in the private and public sectors: public sector doctors embrace a range of activities relative to individual care and public health programmes, while private sector doctors seem to focus their attention on curative activities.[4]

The public image of general practitioners, other health professions, and health authorities is in need of substantial improvement. While it is accepted that GPs are called on to play a pivotal role in the organization of first-line health care in a geographical area and for a given population and a coordinator of first-line care, there is a need for advocacy to encourage acknowledgement of their true value. These functions should lead to ways of practicing general medicine in multidisciplinary teams and to a level of responsibility deserving statutory acknowledgement and appropriate remuneration.

THE 2011 REVOLUTION: FAMILY MEDICINE

Over the last 30 years, general medicine has been the subject of a significant revival of interest, notably in developed countries. It is centre stage and the subject of intense debate. This revival of interest is particularly evident among decision makers who have realized that the most efficient health systems are those in which general medicine is a mandatory entry point for accessing health care. It has indeed become clear that, faced with the growing rise of costs, the only way to control rocketing health expenditure is to set up mechanisms to regulate consumption via reassessment of the way general medicine is practiced.[7,18,20,21]

Paradoxically, in the context of Tunisia, the positive perception of the role played by general medicine in other countries contrasts with the deterioration of the image of GPs within the population. General medicine is increasingly viewed as the profession of those who have failed to move on to specialist studies (accessed via a competitive residency) and as a second-class medicine capable only of addressing simple health demands. We are consequently witnessing an increasingly systematic recourse to specialists and to the excessive organization of sophisticated and costly additional examinations.

Today, undeniably, the exercise of general medicine raises questions. One of the main reasons why GPs are unable to optimally address the expectations of the population is inadequate preparation. Trained solely by specialists in a hospital environment, GPs only come face to face with the type of medicine they are expected to deliver when they enter professional life and find themselves alone facing situations never encountered during their training. It is a fact that general medicine differs from hospital medicine in a number of different aspects: it is holistic and not focused on organs, it requires the ability to listen, communicate and work in proximity, and, lastly to provide global care and support. These aspects cannot be mastered during internships in specialized hospital departments and, consequently, it is obvious that basic medical studies do not provide adequate grounding for the practice of general medicine.

It is to counter this situation that, since 2008, four medical universities in Tunisia and health system decision makers have been working together to design a development plan for FM in Tunisia. WHO has played an important role advocating the commitment to FM via its cooperation programme with Tunisia, organizing educational visits to deans and health professionals and facilitating partnerships with countries such as the United Kingdom and Canada that offer good FM programmes.[13,19]

THE DEVELOPMENT OF FAMILY MEDICINE IN TUNISIA

The main reference point is that the family doctor (FD) must address the whole human being: the individual dimension, changing over time, and the interactions between individual and social environment, starting with the smallest unit, namely the family. More specifically, the FD must be capable of addressing demands for care from all members of society, irrespective of age. The FD has the family's trust, and in this capacity is asked to provide not just care but also advice and assistance. Because, unlike specialists, the FD has insights into the dynamics of each family member and the interactions with the other members, located in a "personal path through life" on physical and emotional levels.[15,20,24,25]

The examples of European and North American countries show that basic medical studies no longer provide future GPs with the expected skill sets. Basic medical studies give the scientific and technical skills platform on which to train for a career as a practicing doctor, but do not directly provide that training. Some have opted to pursue postgraduate studies in general medicine in France, while others have organized specialist cycles in FM in the United States and Canada.[18,20,26]

Tunisia has no choice but to follow this international movement if it wishes to safeguard the quality of the GPs that it trains. In the short term, specific training in FM will be an obligatory part of the preparation for a career as a GP. This training will need to involve all stakeholders, educational institutions and care providers, but will be organized and directed by the universities of medicine. Practical training will be organized in the facilities in which FM is exercised and overseen by supervisors trained and prepared for the task.[4,19]

The preparation of young medical graduates for a career in FM would benefit from the following measures:

- Consolidation of the basic curriculum for medical studies by teaching adapted to FM
- Creation of a specific training cycle in FM, this postgraduate course enabling all would-be GPs to have better insights into the expectations of the population and to address these more adequately and appropriately
- A plan to provide FM training to all GPs already in activity

CONCLUSIONS

Basic health care forms the foundation of the health-care system in Tunisia. The first line is not only an entry point for users of the health-care system, but it also guarantees continuity of care across the system as a whole. Most definitions of first-line health care also include health promotion, disease prevention, and the need to attach greater importance to health determinants and strategies aimed at improving individual health and the health of the population. First-line health care provides short-term solutions to health issues and the management of most chronic diseases.

Tunisia can draw inspiration from its initiatives launched in the late 1970s and from many models and international examples. Many countries have achieved remarkable results by restructuring their PHC services. They have succeeded in improving their results for patients by emphasizing greater access to a broader range of services, providing complete disease management programmes, supporting the teams, measuring quality, and insisting on the continuous improvement of health-care services.

It is only common sense to set as the ultimate goal of revitalized basic health care the possibility for all Tunisians, irrespective of where they live, to have 24/7 access to the right health-care professional.

These then are the key goals:

- Increase the number of persons with access to primary health-care organizations responsible for the planned delivery of a defined set of comprehensive services to a predetermined population
- Focus on health promotion, disease prevention, and the management of chronic diseases
- Increase 24/7 access to essential services
- Train interdisciplinary teams of first-line health-care providers to ensure that the most appropriate care is delivered by the most appropriate professionals
- Facilitate coordination and integration with other health-care services

ANNEX

1. Demographic indicators

	2012	2013	2014
Population (in thousands)	10,777.6	10,887.8	11,007.3
Natural movements (in thousands)			
Births	207.9	223.0	225.9
Deaths	61.3	61.7	62.8
Stillbirths	2.6	2.5	2.4
Demographic indicators			
Natural growth rate	1.4	1.5	1.5
Total fertility rate	2.2	2.4	2.5
Life expectancy	73.8	76.2	76.1
Men	71.6	73.9	73.8
Women	76.6	78.5	78.5
Infant mortality rate	16.1	15.4	15.7

2. Health workforce, hospitals, and pharmacies

	2012	2013	2014
Medical personnel			
Doctors	–	12,107	12,770
Dentists	3627	3142	–
Pharmacists	4557	2583	
Paramedical personnel (MSP)	28,656	39,358	43,197
Senior technicians	9798	12,160	13,346
Nurses and medical auxiliaries	18,858	27,198	29,851
Hospitals			
General hospitals	11	12	14
Institutes and specialized centres	21	21	21
University hospitals, regional hospitals, and local hospitals	142	142	140
Basic Health Centre	2098	2104	2109
Number of active beds	19,750	20,154	20,207
Pharmacies	1935	1972	–

Source: Tunisian National Institute of Statistics; Bulletin, Tunisia in figures 2013–2014.

REFERENCES

1. Mtiraoui A, Gueddana N. The family and reproductive health program in underprivileged areas in Tunisia; *Actes CICRED Seminar on Reproductive Health, Unmet Needs and Poverty: Issues of Access and Quality of Services*, Bangkok 25–30 November 2002, pp 11.
2. Ayoub F. Profil de l'exercice actuel de la médecine générale dans le secteur public. *Actes du colloque Tuniso-Canadien de médecine familiale "mieux harmoniser la fonction formation & la fonction emploi*; Sousse: 17–19 June 2004.
3. Bchir A. Le rôle des départements de médecine communautaire dans la formation en médecine générale MSP/DSSP/Community Department, University Hospital of Monastir. Actes de la table ronde. La médecine générale en Tunisie: formation et exercice Xémes entretiens médicochirurgicaux de Monastir; 2 June 1995.

4. Mtiraoui A. La pratique médicale ambulatoire: quelle spécificité Conference proceedings: *Pratique Médicale Ambulatoire: spécificité, outils et méthodes*; Sousse, June 2003; pp 23–28.

5. Forum national sur la santé. Rapport de synthèse du groupe de travail sur les déterminants de la santé. 1997. Available from: http://www.hc-sc.gc.ca/hcs-sss/pubs/care-soins/1997-nfoh-fnss-v2/legacy_her itage4_f.html.

6. Ghannem H, Limam K, Ben Abdelaziz A, Mtiraoui A, Hadj Fredj A; Marzouki M. Risk factors in cardiovascular diseases in a semi-urban community of the Tunisian Sahel. *Revue d'épidémiologie et de santé publique*. 1992;40(2):108–112.

7. WONCA. Primary care/specialty care in the Era of multimorbidity. *19th WONCA World Conference of Family Doctors*. Cancun, Mexico; 19–23 May 2010.

8. WHO. Primary health care. *Report of the International Conference on Primary Health Care*. Available from: http://apps.who.int/iris/bitstream/10665/39228/1/9241800011.pdf [Accessed 17 March 2018].

9. WHO. *The World Health Report 2008. Primary health care. Now more than ever*. WHO, 2008. Available from: http://www.who.int/whr/2008/en/ [Accessed 17 August 2018].

10. WHO. *Declaration on strengthening District Health Systems based on Primary Health Care*. Harare, Zimbabwe. 7 August 1987.

11. INS. Tunisian National Institute of Statistics. *Bulletin, Tunisia in Figures 2013–2014*.

12. Mtiraoui A, MIllette B. Les fonctions du médecin généraliste. Evolution des concepts; *Actes du colloque Tuniso-Canadien de médecine familiale "mieux harmoniser la fonction formation & la fonction emploi*. Sousse: 17-19 June 2004.

13. World Health Organization (WHO/EMRO): *Cooperation Strategy for WHO and Morocco 2005–2009*, 80 p, EM/ARD/017/F/R.

14. WHO. *Preventing Chronic Diseases: A Vital Investment*, World Health Organization, 2005. Available from: http://www.who.int/chp/chronic_disease_report/en/ [Accessed 17 March 2018].

15. Van Dormael M. Le Centre de santé intégré et les maisons médicales. Jalons pour les soins de santé primaires. *Cahier du Germ*. 1981;152.

16. Zouari B. Quelle formation pour le médecin généraliste tunisien? *Actes du colloque Tuniso-Canadien de médecine familiale "mieux harmoniser la fonction formation & la fonction emploi"*; Sousse: 17–19 June 2004.

17. Martin D, Pollack K, Woollard RF: What would an Ian McWhinney health care system look like? *Canadian Family Physician*. 2014; 60(1): 30–32.

18. McWhinney IR. Being a general practitioner: What it means. *European Journal of General Practice*. 2000; 6(4): 135–139.

19. Groupe Inter-facultaire pour le développement de la médecine familiale en Tunisie (GIF-DMFT). *Cadre pour le développement de la médecine familiale en Tunisie*; mai 2008, 62 p.

20. Starfield B. The future of primary care: Refocusing the system. *New England Journal of Medicine*. 2009; 359(20): 2087–2091.

21. Walsh J, Warren K. Selective primary health care. An interim strategy for disease control in developing countries. *New England Journal of Medicine*. 1979; 301: 967–974.

22. Bourgueil Y, Marek A, Mousquès J. La participation des infirmières aux soins primaires dans 6 pays d'Europe, en Ontario et au Québec. IRDES. Available from: http://www.irdes.fr/Publications/Bulletins/ QuestEco/pdf/qesnum95.pdf.

23. Gataa R, Ajmi ThN, Bougmiza I, Mtiraoui A. Diagnosed morbidity in primary health care in the sanitary region of Sousse (Tunisia)]. *Revue médicale de Bruxelles*. 2008; 29(5): 471–480.

24. Primary Health Care Performance Initiative. 2015. Available from http://phcperformanceinitiativ e.org/sites/default/files/PHCPI%20Technical%20Definition%20of%20Primary%20Health%20Care.pdf [Accessed 17 March 2018].

25. WONCA EUROPE. *European definition of the characteristics of the discipline of general practice/family medicine, the role of the general practitioner, and a description of the core competencies of the general practitioner–family doctor*. WONCA EUROPE, 2002. Available from: http://citeseerx.ist.psu.edu/viewdo c/download?doi=10.1.1.379.9875&rep=rep1&type=pdf [Accessed 17 March 2018].

26. Heath I, Evans P, van Weel C. The specialist of the discipline of general practice. *British Medical Journal*. 2000; 320: 326–327.

CHAPTER 33

United Arab Emirates

Haifa Hamad Fares Al Ali and Wadeia Mohammed Al Sharief

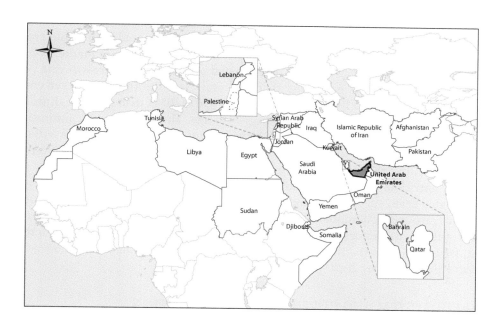

Total number of PHC facilities	131
Number of general practitioners working in public PHC facilities	968
Number of certified family physicians working in PHC facilities	382
Average number of family physician graduates/year	25
Number of medical schools	6
Number of family medicine departments	6

INTRODUCTION

The United Arab Emirates (UAE), the federation of seven emirates, has witnessed a dramatic expansion of its health-care industry over the past four decades. Indeed, at the time of the UAE founding in 1971, the country had just seven hospitals and 12 health centres. Today, it has well over 132 public and private hospitals throughout the seven emirates. In addition, there are 131 public centres focusing on primary health care (PHC) services, where 382 qualified family physicians (out of the 968 physicians in public PHC) are working. Good access to PHC has been achieved throughout the country; no more than 200 persons live in an area greater than 30 km away from health services without a PHC centre.[1]

The country has made remarkable progress in all maternal and child health indicators. However, UAE is experiencing strongly emerging health issues arising from non-communicable diseases (NCDs) such as diabetes and child obesity, and is beginning to vigorously address a number of these issues. The burden of disease attributable to communicable diseases in 2012 was 11.5%; for NCDs it was 65.2%, and for injuries, 23.2%.[2]

Population growth is one key driver of health-care expansion. The 2015 United Nations (UN) report predicted that the UAE's indigenous and expatriate population would grow from 9.16 million to 10.98 million by 2030. Accordingly, the UAE health-care market is expected to experience tremendous growth, with a forecasted annual average growth rate of 12.7% between 2015 and 2020: it is estimated that the total UAE health-care market will reach $19.5 billion by 2020.[3] With a life expectancy of 77.1 years (2015), demographic shifts are also occurring as the UAE's population slowly begins to age. The percentage of Emiratis above the age of 60 is set to double from around 5.2% at present to 11% by 2032.[4] This will increase demand for health care in general and NCDs and geriatric care in particular. Lifestyle habits are also propelling this growth; there is a high prevalence of chronic diseases induced by unhealthy nutrition, sedentary behaviour, and smoking. The World Health Survey 2010 Report estimated that 74% of adults are overweight and 37% of adults are clinically obese. At the same time, around 22% adults in the UAE are estimated to smoke tobacco. As a result of high levels of these risk factors, diabetes, cardiovascular diseases, and cancer are increasingly prevalent. Diabetes is a particular problem, with an estimated prevalence of 18.6% according to the World Health Survey 2010.[5]

UAE HEALTH SYSTEM AND GOVERNMENT COMMITMENTS

The UAE health-care sector is divided between public and private health-care providers. Public health-care services are managed and regulated by the Federal Ministry of Health and Prevention (MoHAP) and local government entities such as the Department of Health Abu Dhabi, the Abu Dhabi Health Services Company (SEHA), and Dubai Health Authority (DHA). Private health-care service providers provide specialty and full-spectrum care for the UAE population. As the nation strives to realize its health-care goals under the direction of MoHAP, it is important to note that the evolution of health-care services is a top priority in all seven emirates. In fact, health-care development and spending are emphasized as key pursuits in the UAE's federal diversification plan.

The UAE federal government – which oversees the country's health care sector and funds almost all non-private health care in the Northern Emirates – has developed strategic plans to respond to the growing demand for health care, meet the associated challenges and meet its commitment to reach the health targets of the sustainable developmental goals (SDGs). The SDG health target aims to ensure healthy lives and promote wellbeing for all at all ages. This can be achieved by universal health coverage (UHC), reducing maternal and under-five mortality, and reducing the prevalence of NCDs and related risk factors.

The UAE Vision 2021, which is well aligned with SDG targets, states that "the UAE [will] … invest continually to build world-class health-care infrastructure, expertise and services in order to fulfil citizens' growing needs and expectations".[6] This vision aims to increase the standard of health care through the accreditation of all health facilities by 2021. It also aims to reduce non-communicable diseases and increase healthy lifestyles in the community. To reach this vision, a national agenda was developed by the government with measurable indicators. It emphasizes the importance of prevention to reduce lifestyle-related diseases such as diabetes, cardiovascular diseases, and cancer, in order to ensure a longer, healthier life for citizens. In addition, the agenda aims to reduce the prevalence of smoking and increase the health-care system's readiness to deal with epidemics and health risks. Accordingly, to ensure universal and quality-based health services to their populations, different national multi-sectorial plans were developed in 2017, including the National Non-Communicable Disease (NCD) plan, National Nutrition plan, National Maternal and Child Health (MCH) plan, and Childhood Obesity Framework.[6]

PRIMARY HEALTH CARE AND FAMILY PRACTICE

All of these efforts have had a positive effect on the growth of PHC facilities in UAE; these grew by 30% from 2008 to 2012.[2] At present, there are 131 governmental PHC facilities. PHC focuses on family medicine as a medical specialty that provides continuous, integrated, and comprehensive health care for individuals and families. Primary care practices provide patients with ready access to their own personal physician or to an established backup physician when the assigned physician is not available. Primary care services across the country provide essential health service packages and the essential medicine list. The scope of service in the primary care sector is increasing and more effort is devoted to integrating services in primary care.

In UAE, PHC, with its main focus on aligning with national targets, provides an integrated programme with services such as school health, adolescent health, maternal and child health, screening programmes, NCD management and control, mental health, community dental services, and geriatric services. Federal and local governmental providers have established a standard that defines the requirements for PHC services to provide patient-centred, comprehensive, coordinated, and accessible care.[7,8]

IMPACT OF PRIMARY CARE ON THE IMPROVEMENT OF QUALITY OF THE SERVICES DELIVERY IN UAE

Maternal and child health services

In UAE, health-care services are provided throughout life. PHC programmes and services for pregnant women, infant and children are available in primary care facilities throughout the country. All pregnant women and children under five years of age have access to comprehensive, evidence-based insured health care through antenatal and well-baby clinics that are found in PHCs. Mothers and children also receive supportive services in term of breast feeding and nutrition counselling.

Furthermore, screening services for breast and cervical cancer are offered to women attending primary care and national awareness campaigns targeting women are conducted regularly. These services have significantly reduced the risks of illnesses and health complications for both the mother and the child. As a result, the country has made remarkable progress in all maternal and child health indicators: it has an under-five mortality rate of 7 per 1000 live births and an infant mortality rate at 6 deaths per 1000 live births; the maternal mortality rate is at six deaths per 100 000 live births; and there is a high vaccination coverage.[9,10]

One of the most successful programmes in maternal and child health is the UAE National Breastfeeding Programme. This programme was launched in 1992 to: encourage health facilities (hospitals, PHCs) to be baby-friendly facilities and train health workers in the skills necessary to promote and protect breastfeeding by providing a 20-hour course to health professionals and a 90-hour course for lactation consultants.

To date, 16 public hospitals and 19 public PHCs throughout the country have met the international criteria and have been designated as baby-friendly facilities. Those PHCs provide lactation counselling and support to all women attending antenatal and postnatal clinics. The number of registered locations around the country has reached 380.

Screening and awareness

The expanded programme of immunization is another successful programme in PHC. The programme was initiated in 1975 when the UAE adopted the WHO and United Nations International Children's Emergency Fund (UNICEF) resolutions pertaining to the immunization of children against childhood diseases. The program succeeded because of the free vaccines and the encouragement of physicians in the private sector as well as those in the public sector to contribute their services to immunize children. The implementation of the programme has resulted in the immunization of more than 90% of children under two years of age.

Non-communicable disease (NCD) management and control

To ensure comprehensive services provided to patients with NCDs, primary care centres started to integrate NCD management and control in their services. This service is provided through

NCD clinics that are run by a multidisciplinary team of a family physician, a trained nurse, a dietitian, and a health educator with supportive secondary services. The model of an NCD clinic within PHC provides integrated preventive, treatment, and control care to patients with diabetes, hypertension, dyslipidaemia, chronic pulmonary diseases, and mental illnesses. It also delivers supportive care to individuals with a high risk of developing NCDs. The model is based on a patient-centred approach where individual patient preferences, needs, and values are ensured to guide individuals' decisions about their health. In order to improve self-management in diabetic patients, doctors, nurses, and dieticians are using the Diabetes Conversation Map, which is an educational tool used to educate the patients and their families on self-management steps. Those clinics are also supported with specialized services, include podiatry clinics recently introduced to primary care.

Although this integration is in its initial stage, a significant improvement in patient care has been noticed; targeted blood pressures were achieved in 82% of the patients attending NCD clinics, compared to only 75% of those attending general clinics. Furthermore, 41% of diabetic patients followed in NCD clinics have achieved a targeted HbA1c of less than seven.[11]

School health services

The school health programme is one of the pioneer PHC programmes that deliver preventive, promotive, and curative services through well-qualified nurses and general practitioners. All public and private schools provide evidence-based vaccination services to their students, with an average annual coverage of around 93%.[12] A screening programme in schools is also provided according to standard guidelines, with an average coverage of 98% of targeted groups. In 2015, an interactive health education guide for school nurses was introduced; it aims to equip the nurses with a standardized guide to help students choose healthy lifestyles in an interactive and interesting way.

A collaboration with the Ministry of Education continues with efforts to reduce childhood obesity by managing school canteens and increasing physical activity. In addition, a national school programme to enhance mental health has been launched with trainer training. A national adolescent health strategic plan of action is under development. School health services and programmes are also planned and expanded depending on the need to overcome health challenges among students. Health indicators are measured every five years using the Global School Health Survey, which UAE had been conducting since 2005.

Smoking cessation counselling services

Smoking cessation counselling services in primary care motivate and support smokers to quit smoking, which in turn will reduce the risk of occurrence of cardiovascular disease and cancer. It provides counselling and medications through a smoking cessation package to help all referred smokers to quit smoking. There are several smoking cessation clinics distributed in public primary care facilities throughout the country.

UAE WORKFORCE

In UAE, the health workforce is expanding: there are 22.3 physicians and 50.4 nursing personnel per 10,000 population.[13] The workforce in the primary care field is also growing. At present there are 382 certified family physicians working in the public sector. The "Professional Qualification Requirements PQR", a standardized reference for regulating the health-care workforce (including general practitioners), has been developed at national level. The challenges in terms of the workforce are mainly due to the shortage of skilled local health professionals, especially nurses: just 3% of the 23,000–25,000 nurses in the country are Emirati.[1] The government is exerting great effort to overcome these challenges; in 2015, MoHAP introduced an initiative to enhance the attractiveness of the nursing profession among Emiratis. The initiative provides scholarships for the local population, to encourage and qualify them for the employment.

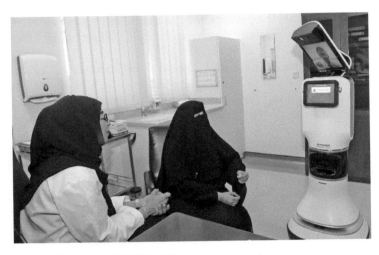

Telemedicine in a PHC facility

Professional development of health professionals in primary care is a great priority. In primary care facilities across the country, all newly recruited health-care workers undergo a competency-based programme. Continuous training is done based on any new services or programmes implemented in primary care. In addition, regular short-term courses or diplomas, on topics such as diabetes and mental health, are provided as needed. In collaboration with the WHO, MoHAP has introduced a capacity building programme where blended short-term on-the-job training courses will be provided to general practitioners working in primary care who did not receive any vocational training in family medicine.

ELECTRONIC MEDICAL RECORDS/INFORMATION SYSTEM

The medical information system is a major priority for UAE. There are two key elements that health authorities in UAE are working to achieve by 2021. The unified electronic medical record, where one medical record is available for each individual and is directly linked with his/her national ID card, is one of them. Today, around 85% of primary care centres are using electronic health records. In addition, the government introduced a patient smart portal application through which users can have access to their records. It offers secure management of users' health information, appointments, and communication with health facilities. In the last few years, several electronic health applications were introduced by primary care to facilitate patient engagement in their health care. For example, the Hayati application, launched by the Dubai Health Authority, is a personal diabetes guide to keep the patient informed, on track, and in control. Another example is the Tateem application where individuals will be informed about vaccination recommendations and how to manage their appointment with the health centre.

QUALITY AND PATIENT SATISFACTION

A continuous monitoring process has been established to ensure that the provision of PHC services meets both customer expectations and professional standards. In accordance with UAE Vision 2021, health authorities in the country have started to increase facilities' safety and quality of care by getting international accreditation for their facilities from bodies such as the Joint Commission International Accreditation (JCIA), International Organization for Standardization (ISO), and Accreditation Canada International (ACI). Today, 60% of public primary care centres are accredited by JCIA; the target is to reach 100% by 2021. Moreover, as an empowering and supervising entity, the Prime Minister's Office conducts an annual survey that measures user satisfaction with all services including PHC. In addition, health authorities are conducting continuous external auditing to measure the quality of the services and patient satisfaction. In 2016 the patient satisfaction survey, conducted among MoHAP primary care service clients, showed 77% client stratification with the services compared to 55% in 2015.[14]

The patient satisfaction survey conducted by the Abu Dhabi Health Authority in 2015 found a higher level of satisfaction among Abu Dhabi's residents. More than 38,000 people in Abu Dhabi were interviewed for the survey. The results showed that overall, patient satisfaction in Abu Dhabi stands at 8.57 out of 10, with an out-patient satisfaction of 86%, which comes in higher than other countries.[15]

COMMUNITY PARTICIPATION WITHIN PRIMARY CARE

As UAE Vision 2021 concentrates on reducing the prevalence of lifestyle-related diseases, health authorities act to intervene within the community to reach the targeted goals. They have started to invest in community health-promoting activities; annual awareness campaigns focusing on cardiovascular risk factors and cancers are conducted across the country by primary health care professionals. These campaigns are supported by non-government organizations (NGOs) and stakeholders from the community. For example, Pink Caravan, which is a Pan UAE breast cancer initiative, encourages breast cancer-related NGOs to join and unify their efforts for breast cancer early detection screening. In 2017, the Pink Caravan campaign broke its previous records, offering free screenings, mammograms, and expert medical advice to 7108 people.[16]

FAMILY MEDICINE TRAINING

The family medicine residency training programme established in Dubai in 1993 was followed by the establishment of similar programmes in Al Ain, Abu Dhabi Emirates, and the Ministry of Health and Prevention. All four programmes are well structured and recognized by the Arab Board of Health Specializations Council with four-year curricula with competency-based systems. In addition, the Al Ain and Abu Dhabi programmes are accredited by the Accreditation Council for Graduate Medical Education (ACGME). Furthermore, since 2006 there has been a collaboration between Dubai and the Royal College of General Practitioners in the United Kingdom to conduct the Membership of the Royal College of General Practitioners (MRCGP - International/Dubai). The exam is conducted twice yearly to the meet the national demand for specialized family physicians. Six examiner training courses were conducted for Membership of the Royal College of General Practitioners (MRCGP–International/Dubai) resulting in certifying 86 examiners out of 94 applicants, and currently 67 examiners are active members. All active examiners are reaccredited every three years to maintain high standards. The total number of graduates since establishment of the MRCGP–International/Dubai exam centre is 425.

On average, 25 UAE family physicians graduate each year; this is not enough to meet the demand generated by the expected growth of PHC in the coming years. Therefore, there is an urgent need to expand the number of UAE qualified family physicians and maximize the size of the workforce needed to cover the ongoing growth of society.

Today, all six undergraduate medical colleges in UAE have family community medicine departments with a structured undergraduate curriculum. To meet the demand of family physicians, it is crucial to develop and expand those family medicine academic departments to run residency programmes accredited by an international accreditation body. The other challenge is to allocate protected time for faculty, supervisors, and trainers in primary care centres with a proper balance between clinical work and academic responsibilities. Other steps that will improve family medicine training include: implementing a workplace-based assessment method for evaluating residents; adopting postgraduate enhanced skills and fellowships in high-demand family medicine subspecialties; and creating an interactive learning interface for knowledge sharing and case discussions.

CHALLENGES AND OPPORTUNITIES

In UAE, health care in general and primary care in particular face many challenges that need to be addressed, these include:

1. *Workforce development* is an area that will require significant and sustainable growth especially in specialties like family medicine, community nursing, health education, and public health. Medical schools in the country should work to invest in the postgraduate programme of family and community medicine. Today, the UAE is working to establish the Emirate Board of Medical Specialization that will help confront the challenges of developing a sufficient medical workforce.
2. *The demographic shift* which will double the percentage of Emiratis above 60 years of age by 2032 is posing a big challenge to improving geriatric care in the country. In the UAE, geriatric care is a relatively new branch of medicine. Therefore, increasing the workforce related to geriatrics is essential. Although there have been some local efforts made in this respect, there is a greater need for national home-based elderly care where a team from primary and community health care provide well-structured services to elders in need.
3. *High prevalence of cardiovascular disease, obesity, and diabetes* increases the burden on health care. Although these problems are well recognized by the government and well-structured actions are implemented within the national agenda, reaching and sustaining the national targets is a big challenge to health authorities in the country. In October 2016, the Prime Minister's Office issued a decree to establish the "Government Accelerators", a new initiative that seeks to accelerate the progress on the objectives of the National Agenda of the UAE Vision 2021 including the health indicators. "Government Accelerators" form a platform for teams from various UAE government departments to work together, address challenges and it is based on the 100-Day Challenge. The MoHAP led the government accelerator for breast cancer screening. This was to overcome the challenges of low uptake in the screening in certain areas. The PHC team led the initiative and established teams from various departments including volunteers from the community. They worked together to develop indices, programmes, and activities to reach the target of screening 2000 females in the Emirate of Fujairah in 100 days. By the end of the targeted period,

2201 women had been screened for breast cancer in the Emirate of Fujairah in 100 days compared to 1200 in the full preceding year.[17]

4. *Activity around medical research*, including primary care–related research, is limited in the UAE. Investment in this area by public and private organizations is needed. The National Strategy for Innovation, launched in 2014, is one opportunity to strengthen medical research in the UAE. Health is one of the seven sectors targeted by the strategy for stimulation of innovation. The strategy aims to promote advanced technologies in health care services, stimulate the growth of the biotechnology and pharmaceutical industries and work with strategic partners to support medical research.

5. *Access for all to the right level of care at the right time* is one of the major challenges for UAE health care. Currently, with the tremendous development in the private health care sector, there is overutilization of certain types of services, this increases costs and reduces efficiency. The UAE government is currently working to develop the Unified Medical Record, established for each individual and accessed using his national ID; this promises to help overcome current inefficiencies.

SUCCESS STORIES IN PRIMARY CARE

Clinical transformational project: A model for world-class primary care

The Primary Care Medical Home (PCMH) or Baytona Al Tebbi is a system improvement project adapted by ambulatory health services in the Abu Dhabi Health Services Company (SEHA); it is a model of care based on family medicine principles. The model is based on enhanced access, personal providers and patient engagement and self-management. The patient registered to any primary care centre will consider the centre his or her medical home. The primary care physician, as the primary care provider (PCP), will be accountable for meeting that patient's current and future needs. The PCP will be working in "Shared Care Model" where the PCP is a member of a multidisciplinary team caring for the patient as part of the doctor panel or a population along the life course. This enhances care coordination and integration. It also provides care that is organized across all elements of the broader health-care system, including specialty care, hospitals, long-term and home health care, and broader community services. PCMH transformation is enabling the system to give better performance by default. Since the adoption of this project, an improvement has been noted in clinical and operational performance indicators of chronic patients attending PHC.[18]

Mobile health-care services

Government efforts are continuing to meet the health needs of all segments of society, significantly enhancing access to comprehensive health services. In 2010 SEHA mobile clinic was introduced and has been deployed to serve remote areas of Abu Dhabi Emirate that have difficulty in accessing health-care facilities, and to bring health-care services to users at public events, work sites, and schools.[19] In 2016, the MoHAP also introduced the mobile health clinic. It is a community mobile clinic equipped with the latest medical equipment, designed to reach citizens in their places of residence and provide medical, preventive, and specialized services that they need. This service targets people living in rural areas of Fujairah and Ras Al Khaimah emirates, where certain factors may affect access to health services. The services provided in the mobile clinic are dental preventive services, school screening services, periodic health and cancer screening, dietitian, and laboratory services.

Elderly care unit in Dubai

An elderly care unit, which was established in the Dubai Health Authority in 2006, consists of a multidisciplinary team with a geriatrician, family medicine physician, community medicine physician, physiatrist, physiotherapist, nurses, social worker, and dietitian. The continuum of care in the unit is provided to the elderly through the acute, sub-acute, and long-term care with the aim to improve the function of elderly and their quality of life to the optimum. To enhance the role of primary care in serving the elderly, in 2016 a survey was conducted to evaluate the fitness of services provided in health centres to meet the needs of the senior population. The project has two phases; the first phase is a quantitative assessment of infrastructure characteristics, and the second, based on focus group discussions, is a qualitative assessment of services. During the first (quantitative assessment) phase, 12 primary care centres were targeted with visits to check properties of the infrastructure which are relevant to the use of elderly people attending the out-patient clinic. These properties are matched with the WHO's recommendations in the "Age-Friendly Primary Health Care Centres Toolkit".

Two health centres hosted the assessment visit every week, starting from 19 September 2016. During each visit the properties of the infrastructure were inspected and checked against the WHO's standards in the toolkit's infrastructure and signage checklist. Also, the availability of a group of medical services relevant to the elderly in primary care was checked in each health centre.

In the second (qualitative phase) of the project, three focus groups were conducted in November 2016, which included the elderly, their caregivers, and health-care professionals in the health centres. The focus groups discussed services provided to the elderly in the health centres.

The detailed survey of the 12 health centres in Dubai showed that their structure closely matches the WHO recommendations, as there was 81.6% matching between the current structure properties, and the WHO's recommendations posted in their "Age-Friendly Primary Health Care Centres Toolkit". Furthermore, this is not just a high degree of matching, but it's also the highest reported in socially and culturally similar health-care systems. The detailed results of these surveys were published in a peer-reviewed journal in October 2017.[20]

PHC centres in Dubai have also started to provide specialized services for the elderly, including geriatric clinics, memory and dementia clinic, osteoporosis clinic, and rehabilitation and fall clinics. In 2017, the total number of patient visits to the specialized clinic for elderly in PHC was 7688 visits, including 5308 and 1972 visits to geriatrics and osteoporosis clinics, respectively.

REFERENCES

1. U.S.–U.A.E. Business Council. *The U.A.E. Healthcare Sector.* Available from: http://www.uaeinteract.com/society/health.asp [Accessed 10 December 2017].
2. WHO. *United Arab Emirates: WHO Statistical Profile 2012.* Available from: http://www.who.int/gho/countries/are.pdf?ua=1 [Accessed 7 December 2017].
3. U.S.-U.A.E. Business Council. *The U.A.E. Healthcare Sector: An Update.* September 2016. Available from: http://usuaebusiness.org/wp-content/uploads/2016/09/Health care-Report-Final.pdf.
4. World Population Prospects. *Global Demographic Estimates and Projections by the United Nations: United Arab Emirates Population.* Available from: http://worldpopulationreview.com/countries/united-arab-emirates-population/ [Accessed 10 December 2017].
5. WHO. *World Health Survey UAE 2010.* Available from: http://apps.who.int/fctc/implementation/database/sites/implementation/files/documents/reports/uae_annex1_whs_2010_presentation.pdf [Accessed 11 December 2017].
6. *UAE Vision 2021, National Agenda.* Available from: https://www.vision2021.ae/en/national-priority-areas [Accessed 11 December 2017].

7. Dubai Health Authority. *Scope of Practice and Clinical Responsibilities, General Practitioner, 2016.* https://www.dha.gov.ae/Documents/HRD/Healthcare%20professionals/Scope%20Of%20Practice/General%20Practitioner.pdf [Accessed 11 December 2017].
8. HAAD. *Standard for Primary Health Care in the Emirate of Abu Dhabi*, 2016. Available from: https://www.haad.ae/HAAD/LinkClick.aspx?fileticket=-XhrrLg5CwM%3d&tabid=819 [Accessed 07 December 2017].
9. United Arab Emirates Demographics Profile 2017. Available from: http://www.indexmundi.com/united_arab_emirates/demographics_profile.html [Accessed 11 December 2017].
10. WHO. *WHO Vaccine-Preventable Diseases: Monitoring System. 2017 Global Summary.* Available from: http://apps.who.int/immunization_monitoring/globalsummary/countries?countrycriteria%5Bcountry%5D%5B%5D=ARE&commit=OK [Accessed 12 December 2017].
11. MoHAP. *Hypertension Audit – NCD Clinic – 2016–2017.*
12. MoHAP. *School Health Immunization Coverage Report for Academic Year 2016–2017.*
13. WHO. Eastern Mediterranean Region Framework for Health Information Systems and Core Indicators for Monitoring Health Situation and Health System Performance. 2017. Available from: http://applications.emro.who.int/dsaf/EMROPUB_2016_EN_19169.pdf?ua=1&ua=1 [Accessed 12 December 2017].
14. MoHAP. Executive Report of the 2016 Patient Satisfaction Study.
15. HAAD Media Center. *Patient Satisfaction Levels Improve in Abu Dhabi.* Available from: https://www.haad.ae/haad/tabid/58/ctl/Details/Mid/417/ItemID/491/Default.aspx [Accessed 26 March 2018].
16. HAAD. *Patient Satisfaction Levels Improve in Abu Dhabi.* Media centre. Available from: https://www.haad.ae/haad/tabid/58/ctl/Details/Mid/417/ItemID/491/Default.aspx [Accessed 26 March 2018)].
17. UAE Cabinet. *Government Accelerators.* Available from: https://uaecabinet.ae/en/details/prime-ministers-initiatives/government-accelerators [Accessed 26 March 2018].
18. Raglow GJ. *Enabling Healthcare in Out-Patient Settings and the Patient Centered Medical Home of the Future.* Group Health Informatics Officer Abu Dhabi Health Services—SEHA. Available from: http://docplayer.net/18848009-Enabling-healthcare-in-out-patient-settings-and-the-patient-centered-medical-home-of-the-future.html [Accessed 19 March 2018].
19. *Annual report 2010.* Abu Dhabi Health Services Co. (SEHA). Available from: https://www.seha.ae/English/aboutus/annualreport/Pages/AR%202010/review_achieve_08.html [Accessed 28 March 2018].
20. Dubai Primary Health Care Centers Conformation to WHO Age-Friendly Primary Healthcare Recommendations. *Advances in Aging Research*, 2017, 6, 83–92. Available from: http://www.scirp.org/journal/aar/ [Accessed 25 March 2018].

CHAPTER 34

Yemen

Ali Al-Mudhwahi

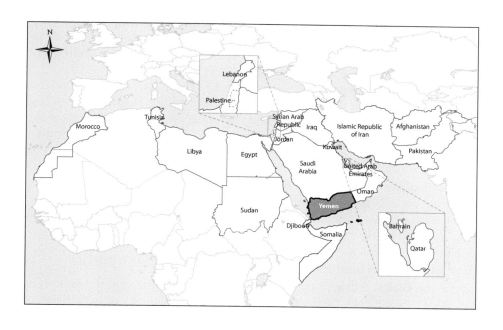

Total number of PHC facilities	Total HFs: 4602 Hospitals: 255 HCs: 1055 HUs: 3289 Others: 3
Number of general practitioners working in public PHC facilities	2389
Number of certified family physicians working in PHC facilities	3
Average number of family physician graduates/year	6
Number of medical schools	9
Number of family medicine departments	3

HF, health facility; HC, health centre; HU, health unit.

PRIMARY HEALTH CARE

The current status of primary health care (PHC) in the country

Ongoing war in Yemen has left 18.8 million people in need of humanitarian assistance and placed an overwhelming strain on the country's health system at a time when it is needed most. Approximately 7 million people are in dire need of food and levels of malnutrition are on the rise, leaving the country on the brink of famine. Almost 462,000 children suffer from severe acute malnutrition with a risk of life-threatening complications.

In many governorates in the country, vulnerability to disease outbreaks has become very high. Almost 14.5 million people, including 3 million internally displaced persons (IDPs), lack access to clean water, sanitation and hygiene services, increasing the risk of infectious diseases such as acute watery diarrhea, malaria, and scabies with an increased need of basic health care.[1]

A second wave of cholera outbreak was announced in April 2017; it has affected most of the country. As of 4 January 2018, there had been more than 1 million suspected cases and around 2237 deaths, with a case fatality rate of 0.22%.[2] As of January 6, 2018, a diphtheria outbreak had affected 19 of the country's 23 governorates, resulting in 514 cumulative cases and 48 deaths, with a case fatality rate of 9%.[3] Most of the deaths (90%) occurred among children below the age of 15.

Less than 45% of health facilities are fully functioning: at least 274 of them have been damaged or destroyed during the current conflict, which started in March 2015.[4] Health-care workers have been forced to relocate and the ones still working have not received their salaries regularly for around a year and a half.

Integration of essential health services package

Supported by the Global Alliance for Vaccines (GAVI), the Ministry of Public Health and Population (MoPHP) initiated the integrated approach in its delivery of basic health services, using fixed facilities and outreach sessions. The district health system represented the basis on which the model of integration was developed.

The importance of preventive and promotive health care is underemphasized. Although the number of PHC units and centres has grown, the present network still suffers from regional maldistribution and deficiencies in the services that are provided. Two of the factors that have led to this situation are the rugged terrain and geographic dispersion of the population. Administrative and management weaknesses, together with the strong urban bias of government employees working in the health sector, are further challenges for the health system. Additionally, insufficient community participation and inadequate supplies of medicines and equipment have deprived remote areas and hard-to-reach populations of essential health and nutrition services. Therefore, access to public health facilities remains limited. Access is better in urban areas than in rural areas. Averages mask even larger regional variations within a population that is widely scattered in some 133,000 towns, villages, and population sites.

Immunization campaign

Recently, the MoPHP, with the support of the World Health Organization (WHO), has started to implement the Minimum Service Package (MSP). The MSP includes:

- Supporting and ensuring the availability of the health workforce
- Emergency and essential surgical care (surgical services + ICUs + oxygen supply or oxygen stations)
- Trauma and acute care
- Mother and child health
- Nutrition, including therapeutic feeding centres (TFCs)
- Patient safety and infection prevention and control, including case management and water, sanitation, and hygiene (WASH)
- Surveillance and information
- Blood safety
- Non-communicable diseases (NCDs)
- Mental health
- Civil society and community engagement
- Health education and communication (HEC)

PHC infrastructure, essential drugs, staff patterns, equipment, and training programme

Health services in Yemen face many shortfalls at all levels of the national health system. The possibilities of achieving universal health coverage (UHC) are limited by the inaccessibility of health care and financial barriers, and complicated by the inequitable distribution of health services. Even before the current emergency, only 60% of the total population of Yemen was covered by facility-based health services. Rural communities are the most affected by the current conflict, with almost 77% of the Yemeni population living in rural areas.[5]

Despite extensive support from the WHO and Health Cluster members, medicines and medical supplies are in increased demand and there is a severe and chronic shortage of supplies. This situation further complicates the delivery of lifesaving health care in the country. Stocks of essential drugs are insufficient at all levels of health care. This has reduced the utilization of health services, including preventive interventions. The essential drug list was last updated in 2014 and contains 437 items. Although Yemen has 10 certified local pharmaceutical manufacturers, most drugs are imported.

The Supreme Board for Drugs and Medical Appliances has responsibility for drug registration: 13,000 products were registered in 2014. The authority performs centrally managed tasks including the inspection of public and private facilities, licensing of pharmaceutical products, and quality assurance and control.

The national health policy aiming at improving accessibility to basic health services is faced with many challenges as the armed conflict increases needs for curative care and trauma care services. There is an urgent need to establish technical standards for health professionals and facilities and coordinate environmental health programmes.

The 2015 Human Development Report points to provincial inequalities in the delivery of PHC services; Yemen was ranked as number 160 out of 188 countries in the Human Development Index. Yemen ranks lowest of the 155 countries listed in the Gender Inequality Index.

In spite of the current emergency, the MoPHP succeeded in leading training programmes for health staff with more focus on epidemiology training. In this respect, the Global Health Development (GHD) and the Eastern Mediterranean Public Health Network (EMPHNET) and the WHO supported the MoPHP in introducing the Public Health Empowerment Programme (PHEP). The PHEP capacity building programme has qualified 139 surveillance officers at governorate and district levels to better respond to outbreaks and to manage epidemiological activities in a more efficient way.

Patient satisfaction with quality of service delivery

Unfortunately, most basic health services are either unavailable or of unsatisfactory quality. The percentage of the population with access to health-care services is low; the percentage of actual utilization is even lower. The concepts of access and utilization imply that the facilities exist, people know how to properly use them, patients can reach them, the facilities have adequate supplies and equipment, and are able to provide services in an acceptable manner to the local population. Moreover, qualified health personnel in rural areas-are inadequate and the war has forced many of them to flee their homes. More specifically, in many districts there are few qualified female nurses and midwives due to security concerns and economic constraints.

The lack of staff and life-saving medicines in many war-affected areas has given rise to dissatisfaction among those who seek curative services. It has also limited the utilization of preventive care, including immunization, in many districts. This situation has further deteriorated with the emergence of outbreaks including vaccine-preventable diseases such as diphtheria and measles. Polio-free since 2006, Yemen now faces the risk of re-importation of the wild poliovirus.

Key challenges to access quality services delivery in public primary care facilities

Despite efforts to reduce high maternal and under-five mortality rates, malnutrition continues to be a major health problem. High levels of stunting, underweight, and wasting were already documented before the war in the Family Health Survey of 2003.[6]

El Gadad PHC Centre

A significant improvement in the health of mothers and children under five has been made over the past 15 years. The under-five mortality rate dropped by nearly 50%, from 102 in 2003 to 51 in 2013; the maternal mortality ratio dropped from 365 to 148 during the same period.[7] Although Yemen has made great strides in reducing the maternal mortality rate, it still remains high and translates to around six women dying every day due to pregnancy and birth-related complications. With the ongoing emergency, this ratio is expected to increase as the capacity to provide women with antenatal services declines. Most mothers still deliver at home with little or no support. Although Yemen's maternal health policy refers to skilled attendants such as doctors, nurses, and midwives, nearly 21% of births are attended by traditional birth attendants and only 36% of births are attended by skilled health staff.[8] Again, health policies are fully dependent on donors' support in almost all related activities, especially with the ongoing crisis.

According to the WHO's 2013 Statistical Profile for Yemen, the most common causes of death were lower respiratory infection (28%), ischemic heart disease (9.5%), stroke (6.8%), and preterm birth complications (6.6%). Road injury (3.8%) ranked as the fifth cause of mortality.[9]

According to a World Bank report, "the ongoing conflict has caused a dramatic deterioration in the country's economic and social situation".[10] In 2015, the gross domestic product (GDP) contracted by 28% and inflation rose 40%. Tax revenues amounted to 10% of the GDP, not enough to cover even the public wage bill (11% of GDP). Public investment has stopped, and development partners have moved to emergency and relief operations. The government also estimates that real GDP per capita has fallen from US$518 in 2014 to US$290 in 2016, and that more than half of the country's businesses have laid off employees and/or cut their salaries.[1,11] Even prior to the escalation of the crisis in 2012, more than half of the population lived below the poverty line and almost 10 million people suffered multi-dimensional poverty.[12]

FAMILY HEALTH PRACTICE

Political commitments to family practice

Responding to the increased demand for patient-centred services, a structural reform of the MoPHP took place in 2004. As part of strengthening the national health system, MoPHP adopted a family-centred care approach. It established a family health general directorate, led by a Deputy Minister, which works towards an integrated approach to health-care decision making within the PHC sector. However, reproductive health services have been vertically provisioned since then through a general directorate under the population sector. As an approach towards universal health coverage, family practice, and patient-centred care has been recognized within the health system strengthening programme responsible for the integrated health, which mainly serves women of reproductive age and children under five. Yemen's health-care system, at central and governorate levels, has introduced family health practice as an integral initiative to patient health, client satisfaction, and improved quality of care.

How family practice links with national public health initiatives and other health initiatives

The family health department of the MoPHP has been successful in leading integrated primary health-care interventions through PHC facilities and outreach activities. The focus on core public health programmes was well demonstrated at the local level through capacity building programmes that enhanced the provision of basic health services. These include maternal and child health, nutrition, immunization, disease surveillance, and health education. Community-based initiatives, on the other hand, have been effectively implemented despite the verticality of the corresponding public health programmes. For instance, community-based nutrition was a well-established programme; the family health department followed its model to integrate the community component through trained volunteers that serve populations in need, including internally displaced persons and the communities most vulnerable to conflict or disease outbreaks.

This family practice commentary draws on the preventive and clinical experience of the MoPHP reaching hard-to-reach populations over the past 14 years. The integrated approach of primary health-care services resulted in significant improvement in mother and child health. This improvement has been set back since the start of the war in March 2015.

Family practice financing in the country

The National Health Accounts of 2007 estimated drug expenditures at 40% of the Total Health Expenditure (THE), at a per capita cost of US$24. Government health expenditure has dropped as a percentage of the Total Health Expenditure (THE), from 54% in 2000 to 23% in 2014; out-of-pocket (OOP) expenditure had increased to 76% in 2014, making Yemen the country with the highest OOP share in the region.[13]

Due to the war and blockade, resulting in a chronic economic crisis, development partners have become the main source for covering the expenses of health and nutrition activities.

Family practice research

Between 2006 and 2010, the MoPHP developed training manuals, guidelines and policy on integrated services. These documents have been adopted for implementation by health partners, even during the current emergency, to qualify volunteers and community health workers to respond to the health priorities targeted towards the neediest populations.

There are few research studies on family practice and there is little documentation of field experience or review of integrated services as part of the health systems strengthening programme.

Details of key challenges in implementing family practice in the country

Considering the overwhelming challenges faced in the country, family practice is currently at a crossroads in terms of its implementation. Neither the government nor development partners have determined the family-centredness of services provided. Since March 2015, security challenges and growing demands for trauma care have weakened the ability of family practice to deliver on its promises. Health-care providers, on the other hand, are unable to optimally perform duties due to the ongoing political and economic crises.

To implement the family practice approach in Yemen during this emergency requires provision of integrated primary health-care services including maternal and child health and immunization. Furthermore, it is extremely important to deploy local female health workers to priority health facilities to increase utilization of services. In addition, local communities demand that health facilities in conflict-affected areas have enough drugs, vaccines, medical supplies, trauma kits, and surgical supplies. Development partners are expected to facilitate the importation of essential and life-saving drugs and essential laboratory, diagnostic, and dialysis equipment. They are also expected to secure the operation of health facilities through provision of fuel and water supplies.

Country's successful experience in family practice

Yemen has adopted the PHC approach since the early 1970s. Well-established programmes such as the Expanded Programme for Immunization (EPI), malaria, mother and child health (MCH), and disease surveillance and control have been successful, even during emergencies. The health system's failures, in relation to primary care activities, are predictable, considering the security situation and economic crisis. Yet, family health programmes are still able to perform basic services and because of that, the delivery of the minimum service package is possible.

FAMILY MEDICINE

The story of family medicine development in the country

In 2007, Yemen hosted the Family Medicine Conference for Eastern Mediterranean countries which generated the Sana'a Declaration. The Human Resources Department, Family Health Department, MoPHP, and the Yemeni Council for Medical Specialties established a family medicine programme with the participation of academic institutes.

Family medicine education

Since 2011, efforts to launch family medicine practice in Yemen have been hampered by the continuous unrest in the country. Family medicine has only been taught in Hadhramout, one of the nine medical schools in Yemen. Since 2012, Hadhramout University has graduated 28 family physicians. Other qualified physicians who studied abroad never returned after being recruited by medical institutions in neighbouring countries. With the exception of the University of Hadhramout, family medicine practice has not yet been instituted in the country.

PRIVATE HEALTH-CARE SYSTEM

Delivery of primary care at private facilities in Yemen is limited. The private sector provides mainly curative services to limited populations, on a fee-for-service basis. According to the last (2007) National Health Accounts (NHA), around 67% of the health expenditure was OOP; 30% of all expenses were incurred at hospital level (13% in private hospitals and 16% in public facilities). Additionally, 30% of medicines were purchased in private pharmacies.[14] If drug-dispensing facilities, private clinics, and laboratories are taken into account, the total number of private health facilities exceeds those in the public sector. The modern for-profit private sector is concentrated in Sana'a City, the capital of Yemen, and a few other cities. Almost all doctors working in the public sector are engaged in private practice to supplement their meagre government salaries.

Expansion of regulated private health practice in Yemen is essential to improve both preventive and curative care, and respond to the double burden of disease faced in Yemen. It is estimated that the total Health Expenditure (THE) is US$80 per capita and drug expenditure is estimated at around US$250–300 million per year.[15] According to the 2007 National Health Accounts, drug expenditure represented 40% of THE at a per capita cost of US$24. Three-quarters of the drug expenditure was incurred by households through direct purchases at retail pharmacies. At a per capita cost of US$18, private drug purchases made up 47% of OOP expenditure. Average prices paid to suppliers are competitive when compared with international figures.

The private sector's role in primary health care is not sufficiently addressed. MoPHP views the private sector as a potential partner for development, which can be contracted to provide coverage in the areas the public sector cannot, especially for immunization and reproductive health services. Few initiatives for introducing public–private partnership in the field of primary health care have been documented, especially in the area of maternal and newborn health. The voucher project is an example of a successful partnership in selected governorates of Yemen supported by interested donors.

A partnership between MoPHP, the Social Fund for Development, the World Bank, and other international NGOs has improved maternal indicators in a few districts of Sana's city where the safe motherhood project was implemented between 2008 and 2013.

Due to economic constraints and cultural norms, traditional medicine is still practiced in many areas in the country. Some of these techniques include cupping to draw off blood, cautery, and bone setting. Also, local birth attendants help with delivery and offer postnatal care, which negatively affects maternal health and increases morbidity and mortality among women during pregnancy and delivery.

The interaction between the private and public sectors needs to be institutionalized within the national health system. Encouragement of the private sector to invest in health care should be reflected in the enactment of laws, bylaws, and national health policies regulating private health institutions. The private sector needs to be engaged in planning and implementing primary care activities and practicing preventive measures according to the public health law. Higher medical education at private institutions should be mainstreamed with government human resource policies and mapping resources. In this respect, licensing of private health facilities must be reorganized according to national health strategies and policies, including components of health sector reform components. Monitoring and evaluation of the performance of the private sector, which needs to be executed based on a set of criteria and legal justifications, is a shared responsibility of MoPHP and local authorities.

REFERENCES

1. WHO EMRO. *The Daily Epidemiological Update, Electronic Disease Early Warning System (eDEWS),* Yemen, November 2017.
2. MoPHP. *Yemen Weekly Epidemiological Bulletin,* week 52, 29 December 2017–4 January 2018.
3. MoPHP, Yemen, *Daily Summary of Diphtheria Outbreak, Early Disease Warning System,* 6 January 2018.
4. WHO, *Health Resources Availability Mapping System* (HeRAMS), Yemen, 2017.
5. MoPHP. Yemen. *National Health Strategy 2010–2025.* 2010. Available from: http://www.nationalplanningcycles.org/sites/default/files/planning_cycle_repository/yemen/nat_health_strategy_-_yemen_eng.pdf [Accessed 24 April 2018].
6. MoPHP, Yemen. *Family Health Survey, Yemen, 2003.*
7. MoPHP, Yemen. *Yemen National Health and Demographic Survey,* 2013. Available from: https://dhsprogram.com/pubs/pdf/SR220/SR220English.pdf [Accessed 24 April 2018].
8. World Health Organization. *World Health Statistics,* 2012. Available from: http://www.who.int/gho/publications/world_health_statistics/2012/en/ [Accessed 24 April 2018].

9. *The Health Cluster Response Strategy to Yemen's Crisis for 2015–2016*, Yemen, October 2015.

10. World Bank. *Yemen's Economic Outlook, 2016.* Available from: http://pubdocs.worldbank.org/en/652 161460138333795/MEM-Yemen.pdf [Accessed 24 April 2018].

11. Ministry of Planning & International Cooperation. *Yemen Socio-Economic Update.* November 2016.

12. UNDP. *Human Development Report 2015.* Available from: http://fscluster.org/yemen/document/yemen-socio-economic-update-issue-20 [Accessed 24 April 2018].

13. WHO. *Feasibility Analysis of the Delivery of the Minimum Service Package, a Simplified Health System Review*, Yemen, 2017.

14. MoPHP. *Yemen National Health Accounts*, 2007.

15. Alshakka M, Al-Mansoub MA, Babakri M et al. Current Pharmaceutical Situation (Services) in Yemen and Future Challenges. *Indian Journal of Pharmaceutical and Biological Research*. 2014;2(4):77–83.

Index